# THE LEGAL RESEARCHER'S DESK REFERENCE 2012-13

Compiled and Edited
by Arlene L. Eis

INFOSOURCES
PUBLISHING

# THE LEGAL RESEARCHER'S DESK REFERENCE 2012-13

While every effort has been made to ensure that the information in this directory is accurate, Infosources Publishing and Arlene Eis do not assume, and hereby disclaim any liability for any errors or omissions herein. Please inform the Publisher of any errors or omissions.

Printed in the United States of America.

ISBN 978-0-9842214-8-6
ISSN 1050-3056

Price $109.

Order from:
Infosources Publishing
140 Norma Road
Teaneck, New Jersey 07666
Phone: (201) 836-7072
http://www.infosourcespub.com
Email:arlene.eis@infosourcespub.com

# TABLE OF CONTENTS

Check out our

# LEGAL RESEARCHERS' ZONE

to view
## THE LEGAL RESEARCHER'S DESK REFERENCE 2012-13
on the Web

*Where to find it -*

Go to our website www.infosourcespub.com

click on LEGAL RESEARCHERS' ZONE in the left frame

then choose *The Legal Researcher's Desk Reference*

your password is **rvx44**

**All the links in the book, plus more, are live**

# INTRODUCTION

**THE LEGAL RESEARCHER'S DESK REFERENCE** is designed to provide the legal researcher with a sourcebook of useful information in a handy one-volume format. Previous editions have been great successes, both in popular demand and in critical acclaim. The reviewer in Law Library Journal wrote: "If you do not have it, order it." The 2012-13 edition is revised, expanded and improved thanks to the input we received from you, the user. We considered all of your suggestions, advice, criticism, and comments, and this book is the net result.

Subscribers now have full access to the book on the Web, with hyperlinks. This benefit is FOR SUBSCRIBERS ONLY, and is available at a password-protected area of our website **http://www.infosourcespub.com** Click on the LEGAL RESEARCHERS' ZONE link on the left frame. The password is **rvx44** (lower case letters).

We are continuing to use our tabbing system. Turn to the Table of Contents and you will see black edge tabs at each section. Bend the book back and the black edge tabs throughout the book will be visible. These tabs should help you find the section you want.

The book is divided into the following major categories:

| | |
|---|---|
| Federal Government | Associations and Organizations |
| Legislative Information | Law Librarianship |
| State Information | Law Schools in the U.S. and Canada |
| International Information | Bar Admissions |
| Law Library Suppliers Directory | Legal Periodicals |

Financial and Economic Information

In most sections, there are directory-type listings with full addresses, telephone numbers, FAX numbers and email addresses and URLs. In addition, there are lists, tables, charts and maps with other types of information. It is advisable to study the detailed Table of Contents and to peruse the book carefully to be fully aware of what is contained herein.

Some of the information presented in this volume is reprinted from respected current published sources. Most of the data, which is not offered anywhere else as we wished to offer it, was compiled by us. In either case, the information is current and reliable as of Fall 2011. The information we included in this volume was chosen because of its value in everyday use to the legal researcher. If you feel that there are other subjects which should be covered, please write to us with your suggestions.

It is hoped that **THE LEGAL RESEARCHER'S DESK REFERENCE** will provide you with the answers to many thousands of reference questions and will serve you in many ways in the course of your work. This reference book is published biennially, with interim supplements as needed.

December, 2011                                                                                     Arlene L. Eis

# FEDERAL GOVERNMENT

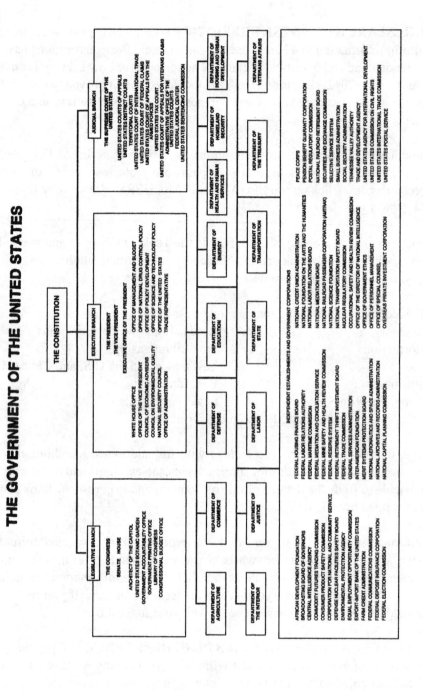

THE GOVERNMENT OF THE UNITED STATES

# THE DECLARATION OF INDEPENDENCE

IN CONGRESS, JULY 4, 1776.

**THE UNANIMOUS DECLARATION of the thirteen united STATES OF AMERICA,**

WHEN in the Course of human events, it becomes necessary for one people to dissolve the political bands which have connected them with another, and to assume among the powers of the earth, the separate and equal station to which the Laws of Nature and of Nature's God entitle them, a decent respect to the opinions of mankind requires that they should declare the causes which impel them to the separation.—We hold these truths to be self-evident, that all men are created equal, that they are endowed by their Creator with certain unalienable Rights, that among these are Life, Liberty and the pursuit of Happiness.—That to secure these rights, Governments are instituted among Men, deriving their just powers from the consent of the governed,—That whenever any Form of Government becomes destructive of these ends, it is the Right of the People to alter or to abolish it, and to institute new Government, laying its foundation on such principles and organizing its powers in such form, as to them shall seem most likely to effect their Safety and Happiness. Prudence, indeed, will dictate that Governments long established should not be changed for light and transient causes; and accordingly all experience hath shown, that mankind are more disposed to suffer, while evils are sufferable, than to right themselves by abolishing the forms to which they are accustomed. But when a long train of abuses and usurpations, pursuing invariably the same Object evinces a design to reduce them under absolute Despotism, it is their right, it is their duty, to throw off such Government, and to provide new Guards for their future security.— Such has been the patient sufferance of these Colonies; and such is now the necessity which constrains them to alter their former Systems of Government. The history of the present King of Great Britain is a history of repeated injuries and usurpations, all having in direct object the establishment of an absolute Tyranny over these States. To prove this, let Facts be submitted to a candid world.—He has refused his Assent to Laws, the most wholesome and necessary for the public good.—He has forbidden his Governors to pass Laws of immediate and pressing importance, unless suspended in their operation till his Assent should be obtained; and when so suspended, he has utterly neglected to attend to them.—He has refused to pass other Laws for the accommodation of large districts of people, unless those people would relinquish the right of Representation in the Legislature, a right inestimable to them and formidable to tyrants only.—He has called together legislative bodies at places unusual, uncomfortable, and distant from the depository of their public Records, for the sole purpose of fatiguing them into compliance with his measures.—He has dissolved Representative Houses repeatedly, for opposing with manly firmness his invasions on the rights of the people.—He has refused for a long time, after such dissolutions, to cause others to be elected; whereby the Legislative powers, incapable of Annihilation, have returned to the People at large for their exercise; the State remaining in the mean time exposed to all the dangers of invasion from without, and convulsions within.—He has endeavored to prevent the population of these States; for that purpose obstructing the Laws for Naturalization of Foreigners; refusing to pass others to encourage their migration hither, and raising the conditions of new Appropriations of Lands.—He has obstructed the Administration of Justice, by refusing his Assent to Laws for establishing Judiciary powers.—He has made Judges dependent on his Will alone, for the tenure of their offices, and the amount and payment of their salaries.—He has erected a multitude of New Offices, and sent hither swarms of Officers to harrass our people, and eat out their substance.—He has kept among us, in times of peace, Standing Armies, without the Consent of our legislatures.—He has affected to render the Military independent of and superior to the Civil power.—He has combined with others to subject us to a jurisdiction foreign to our constitution, and unacknowledged by our laws; giving his Assent to their Acts of pretended Legislation:—For quartering large bodies of armed troops among us:—For protecting them, by a mock Trial, from punishment for any Murders which they should commit on the Inhabitants of these States:—For cutting off our Trade with all parts of the world:—For imposing Taxes on us without our Consent:—For depriving us in many cases, of the benefits of Trial by Jury:—For transporting us beyond Seas to be tried for pretended offences:—For abolishing the free System of English Laws in a neighbouring Province, establishing therein an Arbitrary government, and enlarging its Boundaries so as to render it at once an example and fit instrument for introducing the same absolute rule into these Colonies:—For taking away our Charters, abolishing our most valuable Laws, and altering fundamentally the Forms of our Governments:—For suspending our own Legislatures, and declaring themselves invested with power to legislate for us in all cases whatsoever.—He has abdicated Government here, by declaring us out of his Protection and waging War against us.—He has plundered our seas, ravaged our Coasts, burnt our towns, and destroyed the lives of our people.—He is at this time transporting large Armies of foreign Mercenaries to compleat the works of death, desolation and tyranny, already begun with circumstances of Cruelty & perfidy scarcely paralleled in the most barbarous ages, and totally unworthy the Head of a civilized nation.—He has constrained our fellow Citizens taken Captive on the high Seas to bear Arms against their Country, to become the executioners of their friends and Brethren, or to fall themselves by their Hands.—He has excited domestic insurrections amongst us, and has endeavoured to bring on the inhabitants of our frontiers, the merciless Indian Savages, whose known rule of warfare, is an undistinguished destruction of all ages, sexes and conditions. In every stage of these Oppressions We have Petitioned for Redress in the most humble terms: Our repeated Petitions have been answered only by repeated injury. A Prince, whose character is thus marked by every act which may define a Tyrant, is unfit to be the ruler of a free people. Nor have We been wanting in attentions to our Brittish brethren. We have warned them from time to time of attempts by their legislature to extend an unwarrantable jurisdiction over us. We have reminded them of the circumstances of our emigration and settlement here. We have appealed to their native justice and magnanimity, and we have conjured them by the ties of our common kindred to disavow these usurpations, which, would inevitably interrupt our connections and correspondence. They too have been deaf to the voice of justice and of consanguinity. We must, therefore, acquiesce in the necessity, which denounces our Separation, and hold them, as we hold the rest of mankind, Enemies in War, in Peace Friends.—

WE, THEREFORE, the Representatives of the UNITED STATES OF AMERICA, in General Congress, Assembled, appealing to the Supreme Judge of the world for the rectitude of our intentions, do, in the Name, and by Authority of the good People of these Colonies, solemnly publish and declare, That these United Colonies are, and of Right ought to be FREE AND INDEPENDENT STATES; that they are Absolved from all Allegiance to the British Crown, and that all political connection between them and the State of Great Britain, is and ought to be totally disolved; and that as Free and

# THE DECLARATION OF INDEPENDENCE

Independent States, they have full Power to levy War, conclude Peace, contract Alliances, establish Commerce, and to do all other Acts and Things which Independent States may of right do.—And for the support of this Declaration, with a firm reliance on the protection of Divine Providence, we mutually pledge to each other our Lives, our Fortunes and our sacred Honor.

John Hancock
Button Gwinnett
Lyman Hall
Geo. Walton
Wm. Hooper
Joseph Hewes
John Penn
Edward Rutledge
Thos. Heyward, Jr.
Thomas Lynch, Jr.
Arthur Middleton
Samuel Chase
Wm. Paca
Thos. Stone
Charles Carroll of
   Carrollton
George Wythe
Richard Henry Lee
Th. Jefferson

Benj. Harrison
Thos. Nelson, Jr.
Francis Lightfoot Lee
Carter Braxton
Robt. Morris
Benjamin Rush
Benj. Franklin
John Morton
Geo. Clymer
Jas. Smith
Geo. Taylor
James Wilson
Geo. Ross
Caesar Rodney
Geo. Read
Tho. M: Kean
Wm. Floyd
Phil. Livingston
Frans. Lewis

Lewis Morris
Richd. Stockton
Jno. Witherspoon
Fras. Hopkinson
John Hart
Abra. Clark
Josiah Bartlett
Wm. Whipple
Saml. Adams
John Adams
Robt. Treat Paine
Elbridge Gerry
Step. Hopkins
William Ellery
Roger Sherman
Sam. Huntington
Wm. Williams
Oliver Wolcott
Matthew Thornton

# THE CONSTITUTION OF THE UNITED STATES

WE THE PEOPLE of the United States, in Order to form a more perfect Union, establish Justice, insure domestic Tranquility, provide for the common defence, promote the general Welfare, and secure the Blessings of Liberty to ourselves and our Posterity, do ordain and establish this Constitution for the United States of America.

## Article I

*Section 1.* All legislative Powers herein granted shall be vested in a Congress of the United States, which shall consist of a Senate and House of Representatives.

*Section 2.* The House of Representatives shall be composed of Members chosen every second Year by the People of the several States, and the Electors in each State shall have the Qualifications requisite for Electors of the most numerous Branch of the State Legislature.

No Person shall be a Representative who shall not have attained to the Age of twenty five Years, and been seven Years a Citizen of the United States, and who shall not, when elected, be an Inhabitant of that State in which he shall be chosen.

Representatives and direct Taxes shall be apportioned among the several States which may be included within this Union, according to their respective Numbers, which shall be determined by adding to the whole Number of free Persons, including those bound to Service for a Term of Years, and excluding Indians not taxed, three fifths of all other Persons. The actual Enumeration shall be made within three Years after the first Meeting of the Congress of the United States, and within every subsequent Term of ten Years, in such Manner as they shall by Law direct. The Number of Representatives shall not exceed one for every thirty Thousand, but each State shall have at Least one Representative; and until such enumerations shall be made, the State of New Hampshire shall be entitled to chuse three, Massachusetts eight, Rhode-Island and Providence Plantations one, Connecticut five, New-York six, New Jersey four, Pennsylvania eight, Delaware one, Maryland six, Virginia ten, North Carolina five, South Carolina five, and Georgia three.

When vacancies happen in the Representation from any State, the Executive Authority thereof shall issue Writs of Election to fill such Vacancies.

The House of Representatives shall chuse their speaker and other Officers; and shall have the sole Power of Impeachment.

*Section 3.* The Senate of the United States shall be composed of two Senators from each State, chosen by the Legislature thereof, for six Years; and each Senator shall have one Vote.

Immediately after they shall be assembled in Consequence of the first Election, they shall be divided as equally as may be into three Classes. The Seats of the

Senators of the first Class shall be vacated at the Expiration of the second Year, of the second Class at the Expiration of the fourth Year, and of the third Class at the Expiration of the sixth Year, so that one third may be chosen every second Year; and if Vacancies happen by Resignation, or otherwise, during the Recess of the Legislature of any State, the Executive thereof may make temporary Appointments until the next Meeting of the Legislature, which shall then fill such Vacancies.

No Person shall be a Senator who shall not have attained to the Age of thirty Years, and been nine Years a Citizen of the United States, and who shall not, when elected, be an Inhabitant of that State for which he shall be chosen.

The Vice President of the United States shall be President of the Senate, but shall have no Vote, unless they be equally divided.

The Senate shall chuse their other Officers, and also a President pro tempore, in the Absence of the Vice President, or when he shall exercise the Office of President of the United States.

The Senate shall have the sole Power to try all Impeachments. When sitting for that Purpose, they shall be on Oath or Affirmation. When the President of the United States is tried, the Chief Justice shall preside: And no Person shall be convicted without the concurrence of two thirds of the Members present. Judgment in Cases of Impeachment shall not extend further than to removal from Office, and disqualification to hold and enjoy any Office of honor, Trust or Profit under the United States: but the Party convicted shall nevertheless be liable and subject to Indictment, Trial, Judgment and Punishment, according to law.

*Section 4.* The Times, Places and Manner of holding Elections for Senators and Representatives, shall be prescribed in each State by the Legislature thereof; but the Congress may at any time by Law make or alter such Regulations, except as to the Places of chusing Senators.

The Congress shall assemble at least once in every Year, and such Meeting shall be on the first Monday in December, unless they shall by Law appoint a different Day.

*Section 5.* Each House shall be the Judge of the Elections, Returns and Qualifications of its own Members, and a Majority of each shall constitute a Quorum to do business; but a smaller Number may adjourn from day to day, and may be authorized to compel the Attendance of absent Members, in such Manner, and under such Penalties as each House may provide.

Each House may determine the Rules of its Proceedings, punish its Members for disorderly Behaviour, and, with the Concurrence of two thirds, expel a Member.

Each House shall keep a Journal of its Proceedings, and from time to time publish the same, excepting such Parts as may in their Judgment require Secrecy; and the yeas and Nays of the Members of either House on any question shall, at the Desire of one fifth of those Present, be entered on the Journal.

Neither House, during the Session of Congress, shall, without the Consent of the other, adjourn for more than three days, nor to any other place than that in which the two Houses shall be sitting.

*Section 6.* The Senators and Representatives shall receive a Compensation for their Services, to be ascertained by Law, and paid out of the Treasury of the United States. They shall in all Cases, except Treason, Felony and Breach of the Peace, be privileged from Arrest during their Attendance at the Session of their respective Houses, and in going to and returning from the same; and for any Speech or Debate in either House, they shall not be questioned in any other Place.

No Senator or Representative shall, during the Time for which he was elected, be appointed to any civil Office under the Authority of the United States, which shall have been created, or the Emoluments whereof shall have been encreased during such time; and no Person holding any Office under the United States, shall be a Member of either House during his Continuance in Office.

*Section 7.* All Bills for raising Revenue shall originate in the House of Representatives; but the Senate may propose or concur with Amendments as on other Bills.

Every Bill which shall have passed the House of Representatives and the Senate, shall, before it become a Law, be presented to the President of the United States; If he approve he shall sign it, but if not he shall return it, with his Objections to that House in which it shall have originated, who shall enter the Objections at large on their Journal, and proceed to reconsider it. If after such Reconsideration two thirds of that House shall agree to pass the Bill, it shall be sent, together with the Objections, to the other House, by which it shall likewise be reconsidered, and if approved by two thirds of that House, it shall become a Law. But in all such Cases the Votes of both Houses shall be determined by yeas and Nays, and the Names of the Persons voting for and against the Bill shall be entered on the Journal of each House respectively. If any Bill shall not be returned by the President within ten Days (Sundays excepted) after it shall have been presented to him, the Same shall be a Law, in like Manner as if he had signed it, unless the Congress by their Adjournment prevent its Return, in which Case it shall not be a Law.

Every Order, Resolution, or Vote to which the Concurrence of the Senate and House of Representatives may be necessary (except on a question of Adjournment) shall be presented to the President of the United States; and before the Same shall take Effect, shall be approved by him, or being disapproved by him, shall be repassed by two thirds of the Senate and House of Representatives, according to the Rules and Limitations prescribed in the Case of a Bill.

*Section 8.* The Congress shall have Power To lay and collect Taxes, Duties, Imposts and Excises, to pay the Debts and provide for the common Defence and general Welfare of the United States; but all duties, Imposts and Excises shall be uniform throughout the United States;

To borrow Money on the Credit of the United States;

To regulate Commerce with foreign Nations, and among the several States, and with the Indian Tribes;

To establish an uniform Rule of Naturalization, and uniform Laws on the subject of Bankruptcies throughout the United States;

To coin Money, regulate the Value thereof, and of foreign Coin, and fix the Standard of Weights and Measures;

To provide for the Punishment of counterfeiting the Securities and current Coin of the United States;

To establish Post Offices and post Roads;

To promote the Progress of Science and useful Arts, by securing for limited Times to Authors and Inventors exclusive Right to their respective Writings and Discoveries;

To constitute Tribunals inferior to the supreme Court;

To define and punish Piracies and Felonies committed on the high Seas, and Offences against the Law of Nations;

To declare War, grant Letters of Marque and Reprisal, and make rules concerning Captures on Land and Water;

To raise and support Armies, but no Appropriation of Money to that Use shall be for a longer Term than two Years;

To provide and maintain a Navy;

To make rules for the Government and Regulation of the land and naval Forces;

# THE CONSTITUTION

To provide for calling forth the Militia to execute the Laws of the Union, suppress Insurrections and repel Invasions;

To provide for organizing, arming, and disciplining, the Militia, and for governing such Part of them as may be employed in the Service of the United States, reserving to the States respectively, the Appointment of the Officers, and the Authority of training the Militia according to the discipline prescribed by Congress;

To exercise exclusive Legislation in all Cases whatsoever, over such District (not exceeding ten Miles square), as may, by Cession of particular States, and the Acceptance of Congress, become the Seat of the Government of the United States, and to exercise like Authority over all Places purchased by the Consent of the Legislature of the State in which the Same shall be for the Erection of Forts, Magazines, Arsenals, dock-Yards, and other needful Buildings;—And

To make all Laws which shall be necessary and proper for carrying into Execution the foregoing Powers, and all other Powers vested by this Constitution in the Government of the United States, or in any Department or Officer thereof.

*Section 9.* The Migration or Importation of such Persons as any of the States now existing shall think proper to admit, shall not be prohibited by the Congress prior to the Year one thousand eight hundred and eight, but a Tax or duty may be imposed on such Importation, not exceeding ten dollars for each Person.

The Privilege of the Writ of Habeas Corpus shall not be suspended, unless when in Cases of Rebellion or Invasion the public Safety may require it.

No Bill of Attainder or ex post facto Law shall be passed.

No Capitation, or other direct, Tax shall be laid, unless in Proportion to the Census or Enumeration herein before directed to be taken.

No Tax or Duty shall be laid on Articles exported from any State.

No Preference shall be given by any Regulation of Commerce or Revenue to the Ports of one State over those of another: nor shall Vessels bound to, or from, one State, be obliged to enter, clear, or pay Duties in another.

No money shall be drawn from the Treasury, but in Consequence of Appropriations made by Law; and a regular Statement and Account of the Receipts and Expenditures of all public Money shall be published from time to time.

No Title of Nobility shall be granted by the United States: And no Person holding any Office of Profit or Trust under them, shall, without the Consent of the Congress, accept of any present, Emolument, Office, or Title, of any kind whatever, from any King, Prince, or foreign State.

*Section 10.* No State shall enter into any Treaty, Alliance, or Confederation; grant Letters of Marque and Reprisal; coin Money; emit Bills of Credit; make any Thing but gold and silver Coin a Tender in Payment of Debts; pass any Bill of Attainder, ex post facto Law, or Law impairing the Obligation of Contracts, or grant any Title of Nobility.

No State shall, without the Consent of the Congress, lay any Imposts or Duties on Imports or Exports, except what may be absolutely necessary for executing it's inspection Laws: and the net Produce of all Duties and Imposts, laid by any State on Imports or Exports, shall be for the Use of the Treasury of the United States; and all such Laws shall be subject to the Revision and Controul of the Congress.

No State shall, without the Consent of Congress, lay any Duty of Tonnage, keep Troops, or Ships of War in time of Peace, enter into any Agreement or Compact with another State, or with a foreign Power, or engage in War, unless actually invaded, or in such imminent Danger as will not admit of delay.

# THE CONSTITUTION

## Article II

*Section 1.* The executive Power shall be vested in a President of the United States of America. He shall hold his Office during the Term of four Years, and, together with the Vice President, chosen for the same term, be elected, as follows

Each State shall appoint, in such Manner as the Legislature thereof may direct, a Number of Electors, equal to the whole Number of Senators and Representatives to which the State may be entitled in the Congress: but no Senator or Representative, or Person holding an Office of Trust or Profit under the United States, shall be appointed an Elector.

The Electors shall meet in their respective States, and vote by Ballot for two Persons, of whom one at least shall not be an Inhabitant of the same State with themselves. And they shall make a List of all the Persons voted for, and of the Number of Votes for each; which List they shall sign and certify, and transmit sealed to the Seat of the Government of the United States, directed to the President of the Senate. The President of the Senate shall, in the Presence of the Senate and House of Representatives, open all the Certificates, and the Votes shall then be counted. The Person having the greatest Number of Votes shall be the President, if such Number be a Majority of the whole Number of Electors appointed; and if there be more than one who have such Majority, and have an equal Number of Votes, then the House of Representatives shall immediately chuse by Ballot one of them for President: and if no Person have a Majority, then from the five highest on the List the said House shall in like Manner chuse the President. But in chusing the President, the Votes shall be taken by States, the Representation from each State having one Vote; A quorum for this Purpose shall consist of a Member or Members from two thirds of the States, and a Majority of all the States shall be necessary to a Choice. In every Case, after the Choice of the President, the Person having the greatest Number of Votes of the Electors shall be the Vice President. But if there should remain two or more who have equal Votes, the Senate shall chuse from them by Ballot the Vice President.

The Congress may determine the Time of chusing the Electors, and the Day on which they shall give their Votes; which Day shall be the same throughout the United States.

No Person except a natural born Citizen, or a Citizen of the United States, at the time of the Adoption of this Constitution, shall be eligible to the Office of President; neither shall any Person be eligible to that Office who shall not have attained to the Age of thirty five Years, and been fourteen Years a Resident within the United States.

In Case of the Removal of the President from Office, or of his Death, Resignation, or Inability to discharge the Powers and Duties of the said Office, the Same shall devolve on the Vice President, and the Congress may by Law provide for the Case of Removal, Death, Resignation or Inability, both of the President and Vice President declaring what Officer shall then act as President, and such Officer shall act accordingly, until the Disability be removed, or a President shall be elected.

The President shall, at stated Times, receive for his Services, a Compensation, which shall neither be encreased nor diminished during the Period for which he shal have been elected, and he shall not receive within that Period any other Emolument from the United States, or any of them.

Before he enter on the Execution of his Office, he shall take the following Oath or Affirmation:—"I do solemnly swear (or affirm) that I will faithfully execute the Office of President of the United States, and will to the best of my Ability, preserve, protect and defend the Constitution of the United States."

*Section 2.* The President shall be Commander in Chief of the Army and Navy of the United States, and of the Militia of the several States, when called into the actual

Service of the United States; he may require the Opinion, in writing, of the principal Officer in each of the executive Departments, upon any Subject relating to the Duties of their respective Offices, and he shall have Power to grant Reprieves and Pardons for Offences against the United States, except in Cases of Impeachment.

He shall have Power, by and with the Advice and Consent of the Senate, to make Treaties, provided two thirds of the Senators present concur; and he shall nominate, and by and with the Advice and Consent of the Senate, shall appoint Ambassadors, other public Ministers and Consuls, Judges of the supreme Court, and all other Officers of the United States, whose Appointments are not herein otherwise provided for, and which shall be established by Law: but the Congress may by Law vest the Appointment of such inferior Officers, as they think proper, in the President alone, in the Courts of Law, or in the Heads of Departments.

The President shall have Power to fill up all Vacancies that may happen during the Recess of the Senate, by granting Commissions which shall expire at the End of their next Session.

*Section 3.* He shall from time to time give to the Congress Information of the State of the Union, and recommend to their Consideration such Measures as he shall judge necessary and expedient; he may, on extraordinary Occasions, convene both Houses, or either of them, and in Case of Disagreement between them, with Respect to the Time of Adjournment, he may adjourn them to such Time as he shall think proper; he shall receive Ambassadors and other public Ministers; he shall take Care that the Laws be faithfully executed, and shall Commission all the Officers of the United States.

*Section 4.* The President, Vice President and all civil Officers of the United States, shall be removed from Office on Impeachment for, and Conviction of, Treason, Bribery, or other High Crimes and Misdemeanors.


## Article III

*Section 1.* The judicial Power of the United States, shall be vested in one supreme Court, and in such inferior Courts as the Congress may from time to time ordain and establish. The Judges, both of the supreme and inferior Courts, shall hold their Offices during good Behaviour, and shall, at stated Times, receive for their Services, a Compensation, which shall not be diminished during their Continuance in Office.

*Section 2.* The judicial Power shall extend to all Cases, in Law and Equity, arising under this Constitution, the Laws of the United States, and Treaties made, or which shall be made, under their Authority;—to all Cases affecting Ambassadors, other public Ministers and Consuls;—to all Cases of admiralty and maritime Jurisdiction;—to Controversies to which the United States shall be a Party;—to Controversies between two or more States; between a State and Citizens of another State;—between Citizens of different States;—between Citizens of the same State claiming Lands under Grants of different States, and between a State, or the Citizens thereof, and foreign States, Citizens or Subjects.

In all Cases affecting Ambassadors, other public Ministers and Consuls, and those in which a State shall be Party, the supreme Court shall have original Jurisdiction. In all the other Cases before mentioned, the supreme Court shall have appellate Jurisdiction, both as to Law and Fact, with such Exceptions, and under such Regulations as the Congress shall make.

The Trial of all Crimes, except in Cases of Impeachment, shall be by Jury; and such Trial shall be held in the State where the said Crimes shall have been committed; but when not committed within any State, the Trial shall be at such Place or Places as the Congress may by Law have directed.

*Section 3.* Treason against the United States, shall consist only in levying War against them, or in adhering to their Enemies, giving them Aid and Comfort. No Person shall be convicted of Treason unless on the Testimony of two Witnesses to the same overt Act, or on Confession in open Court.

The Congress shall have Power to declare the Punishment of Treason, but no Attainder of Treason shall work Corruption of Blood, or Forfeiture except during the Life of the Person attainted.

## Article IV

*Section 1.* Full Faith and Credit shall be given in each State to the public Acts, Records, and judicial Proceedings of every other State. And the Congress may by general Laws prescribe the Manner in which such Acts, Records and Proceedings shall be proved, and the Effect thereof.

*Section 2.* The Citizens of each State shall be entitled to all Privileges and Immunities of Citizens in the several States.

A Person charged in any State with Treason, Felony, or other Crime, who shall flee from Justice, and be found in another State, shall on Demand of the executive Authority of the State from which he fled, be delivered up, to be removed to the State having Jurisdiction of the Crime.

No person held to Service or Labour in one State, under the Laws thereof, escaping into another, shall, in Consequence of any Law or Regulation therein, be discharged from such Service or Labour, but shall be delivered up on Claim of the Party to whom such Service or Labour may be due.

*Section 3.* New States may be admitted by the Congress into this Union; but no new State shall be formed or erected within the Jurisdiction of any other State; nor any State be formed by the Junction of two or more States, or Parts of States, without the Consent of the Legislatures of the States concerned as well as of the Congress.

The Congress shall have Power to dispose of and make all needful Rules and Regulations respecting the Territory or other Property belonging to the United States; and nothing in this Constitution shall be so construed as to Prejudice any Claims of the United States, or of any particular State.

*Section 4.* The United States shall guarantee to every State in this Union a Republican Form of Government, and shall protect each of them against Invasion; and on Application of the Legislature, or of the Executive (when the Legislature cannot be convened) against domestic Violence.

## Article V

The Congress, whenever two thirds of both Houses shall deem it necessary, shall propose Amendments to this Constitution, or, on the Application of the Legislatures of two thirds of the several States, shall call a Convention for proposing Amendments, which, in either Case, shall be valid to all Intents and Purposes, as Part of this Constitution, when ratified by the Legislatures of three fourths of the several States, or by Conventions in three fourths thereof, as the one or the other Mode of Ratification may be proposed by the Congress; Provided that no Amendment which may be made prior to the Year One thousand eight hundred and eight shall in any Manner affect the first and fourth Clauses in the Ninth Section of the first Article; and that no State,without its Consent, shall be deprived of its equal Suffrage in the Senate.

## Article VI

All Debts contracted and Engagements entered into, before the Adoption of this Constitution, shall be as valid against the United States under this Constitution, as under the Confederation.

This Constitution, and the Laws of the United States which shall be made in Pursuance thereof; and all Treaties made, or which shall be made, under the Authority of the United States, shall be the supreme Law of the Land; and the Judges in every State shall be bound thereby, any Thing in the Constitution or Laws of any State to the Contrary notwithstanding.

The Senators and Representatives before mentioned, and the Members of the several State Legislatures, and all executive and judicial Officers, both of the United States and of the several States, shall be bound by Oath or Affirmation, to support this Constitution; but no religious Test shall ever be required as a Qualification to any Office or public Trust under the United States.

## Article VII

The Ratification of the Conventions of nine States, shall be sufficient for the Establishment of this Constitution between the States so ratifying the Same.

*done* in Convention by the Unanimous Consent of the States present the Seventeenth Day of September in the Year of our Lord one thousand seven hundred and Eighty seven and of the Independence of the United States of America the Twelfth *In witness whereof We have hereunto subscribed our Names,*

G° Washington—Presid<sup>t</sup>
and deputy from Virginia

| | |
|---|---|
| New Hampshire | John Langdon |
| | Nicholas Gilman |
| Massachusetts | Nathaniel Gorham |
| | Rufus King |
| Connecticut | Wᵐ Sam! Johnson |
| | Roger Sherman |
| New York | Alexander Hamilton |
| New Jersey | Wil: Livingston |
| | David Brearley. |
| | Wᵐ Paterson. |
| | Jona: Dayton |
| Pennsylvania | B Franklin |
| | Thomas Mifflin |
| | Robᵗ Morris |
| | Geo. Clymer |
| | Thoˢ FitzSimons |
| | Jared Ingersoll |

# THE CONSTITUTION

|            |                                  |
|------------|----------------------------------|
| Delaware   | James Wilson                     |
|            | Gouv Morris                      |
|            | Geo: Read                        |
|            | Gunning Bedford jun              |
|            | John Dickinson                   |
|            | Richard Bassett                  |
|            | Jaco: Broom                      |
| Maryland   | James McHenry                    |
|            | Dan of St Thos Jenifer           |
|            | Danl Carroll                     |
| Virginia   | John Blair—                      |
|            | James Madison Jr.                |
| North Carolina | Wm Blount                    |
|            | Richd Dobbs Spaight.             |
|            | Hu Williamson                    |
| South Carolina | J. Rutledge                  |
|            | Charles Cotesworth Pinckney      |
|            | Charles Pinckney                 |
|            | Pierce Butler.                   |
| Georgia    | William Few                      |
|            | Abr Baldwin                      |

## Amendments

*(The first 10 Amendments were ratified December 15, 1791, and form what is known as the Bill of Rights)*

## Amendment 1

Congress shall make no law respecting an establishment of religion, or prohibiting the free exercise thereof; or abridging the freedom of speech, or of the press; or the right of the people peaceably to assemble, and to petition the Government for a redress of grievances.

## Amendment 2

A well regulated Militia, being necessary to the security of a free State, the right of the people to keep and bear Arms, shall not be infringed.

# THE CONSTITUTION

## Amendment 3

No Soldier shall, in time of peace be quartered in any house, without the consent of the Owner, nor in time of war, but in a manner to be prescribed by law.

## Amendment 4

The right of the people to be secure in their persons, houses, papers, and effects, against unreasonable searches and seizures, shall not be violated, and no Warrants shall issue, but upon probable cause, supported by Oath or affirmation, and particularly describing the place to be searched, and the persons or things to be seized.

## Amendment 5

No person shall be held to answer for a capital, or otherwise infamous crime, unless on a presentment or indictment of a Grand Jury, except in cases arising in the land or naval forces, or in the Militia, when in actual service in time of War or public danger; nor shall any person be subject for the same offence to be twice put in jeopardy of life or limb; nor shall be compelled in any criminal case to be a witness against himself, nor be deprived of life, liberty, or property, without due process of law; nor shall private property be taken for public use, without just compensation.

## Amendment 6

In all criminal prosecutions, the accused shall enjoy the right to a speedy and public trial, by an impartial jury of the State and district wherein the crime shall have been committed, which district shall have been previously ascertained by law, and to be informed of the nature and cause of the accusation; to be confronted with the witnesses against him; to have compulsory process for obtaining witnesses in his favor, and to have the Assistance of Counsel for his defence.

## Amendment 7

In Suits at common law, where the value in controversy shall exceed twenty dollars, the right of trial by jury shall be preserved, and no fact tried by a jury, shall be otherwise re-examined in any Court of the United States, than according to the rules of the common law.

## Amendment 8

Excessive bail shall not be required, nor excessive fines imposed, nor cruel and unusual punishments inflicted.

# THE CONSTITUTION

## Amendment 9

The enumeration in the Constitution, of certain rights, shall not be construed to deny or disparage others retained by the people.

## Amendment 10

The powers not delegated to the United States by the Constitution, nor prohibited by it to the States, are reserved to the States respectively, or to the people.

## Amendment 11

*(Ratified February 7, 1795)*

The Judicial power of the United States shall not be construed to extend to any suit in law or equity, commenced or prosecuted against one of the United States by Citizens of another State, or by Citizens or Subjects of any Foreign State.

## Amendment 12

*(Ratified July 27, 1804)*

The Electors shall meet in their respective states, and vote by ballot for President and Vice-President, one of whom, at least, shall not be an inhabitant of the same state with themselves; they shall name in their ballots the person voted for as President, and in distinct ballots the person voted for as Vice-President, and they shall make distinct lists of all persons voted for as President, and of all persons voted for as Vice-President, and of the number of votes for each, which lists they shall sign and certify, and transmit sealed to the seat of the government of the United States, directed to the President of the Senate;—The President of the Senate shall, in the presence of the Senate and House of Representatives, open all the certificates and the votes shall then be counted;—The person having the greatest number of votes for President, shall be the President, if such number be a majority of the whole number of Electors appointed; and if no person have such majority, then from the persons having the highest numbers not exceeding three on the list of those voted for as President, the House of Representatives shall choose immediately, by ballot, the President. But in choosing the President, the votes shall be taken by states, the representation from each state having one vote; a quorum for this purpose shall consist of a member or members from two-thirds of the states, and a majority of all the states shall be necessary to a choice. And if the House of Representatives shall not choose a President whenever the right of choice shall devolve upon them, before the fourth day of March next following, then the Vice-President shall act as President, as in the case of the death or other constitutional disability of the President.—The person having the greatest number of votes as Vice-President, shall be the Vice-President, if such number be a majority of the whole number of Electors appointed, and if no person have a majority, then from the two highest numbers on the list, the Senate shall choose the Vice-President; a quorum for the purpose shall consist of two-thirds of the whole number of Senators, and a majority of the whole number shall be necessary to a choice. But no person constitutionally ineligible to the office of President shall be eligible to that of Vice-President of the United States.

## Amendment 13

*(Ratified December 6, 1865)*

*Section 1.* Neither slavery nor involuntary servitude, except as a punishment for crime whereof the party shall have been duly convicted, shall exist within the United States, or any place subject to their jurisdiction.

*Section 2.* Congress shall have power to enforce this article by appropriate legislation.

## Amendment 14

*(Ratified July 9, 1868)*

*Section 1.* All persons born or naturalized in the United States, and subject to the jurisdiction thereof, are citizens of the United States and of the State wherein they reside. No State shall make or enforce any law which shall abridge the privileges or immunities of citizens of the United States; nor shall any State deprive any person of life, liberty, or property, without due process of law; nor deny to any person within its jurisdiction the equal protection of the laws.

*Section 2.* Representatives shall be apportioned among the several States according to their respective numbers, counting the whole number of persons in each State, excluding Indians not taxed. But when the right to vote at any election for the choice of electors for President and Vice President of the United States, Representatives in Congress, the Executive and Judicial officers of a State, or the members of the Legislature thereof, is denied to any of the male inhabitants of such State, being twenty-one years of age, and citizens of the United States, or in any way abridged, except for participation in rebellion, or other crime, the basis of representation therein shall be reduced in the proportion which the number of such male citizens shall bear to the whole number of male citizens twenty-one years of age in such State.

*Section 3.* No person shall be a Senator or Representative in Congress, or elector of President and Vice President, or hold any office, civil or military, under the United States, or under any State, who, having previously taken an oath, as a member of Congress, or as an officer of the United States, or as a member of any State legislature, or as an executive or judicial officer of any State, to support the Constitution of the United States, shall have engaged in insurrection or rebellion against the same, or given aid or comfort to the enemies thereof. But Congress may by a vote of two-thirds of each House, remove such disability.

*Section 4.* The validity of the public debt of the United States, authorized by law, including debts incurred for payment of pensions and bounties for services in suppressing insurrection or rebellion, shall not be questioned. But neither the United States nor any State shall assume or pay any debt or obligation incurred in aid of insurrection or rebellion against the United States, or any claim for the loss or emancipation of any slave; but all such debts, obligations and claims shall be held illegal and void.

*Section 5.* The Congress shall have power to enforce, by appropriate legislation, the provisions of this article.

# THE CONSTITUTION

## Amendment 15

*(Ratified February 3, 1870)*

*Section 1.* The right of citizens of the United States to vote shall not be denied or abridged by the United States or by any State on account of race, color, or previous condition of servitude.

*Section 2.* The Congress shall have power to enforce this article by appropriate legislation.

## Amendment 16

*(Ratified February 3, 1913)*

The Congress shall have power to lay and collect taxes on incomes, from whatever source derived, without apportionment among the several States, and without regard to any census or enumeration.

## Amendment 17

*(Ratified April 8, 1913)*

The Senate of the United States shall be composed of two Senators from each State, elected by the people thereof for six years; and each Senator shall have one vote. The electors in each State shall have the qualifications requisite for electors of the most numerous branch of the State legislatures.

When vacancies happen in the representation of any State in the Senate, the executive authority of such State shall issue writs of election to fill such vacancies: *Provided,* That the legislature of any State may empower the executive thereof to make temporary appointments until the people fill the vacancies by election as the legislature may direct.

This amendment shall not be so construed as to affect the election or term of any Senator chosen before it becomes valid as part of the Constitution.

## Amendment 18

*(Ratified January 16, 1919. Repealed December 5, 1933 by Amendment 21)*

*Section 1.* After one year from the ratification of this article the manufacture, sale, or transportation of intoxicating liquors within, the importation thereof into, or the exportation thereof from the United States and all territory subject to the jurisdiction thereof for beverage purposes is hereby prohibited.

*Section 2.* The Congress and the several States shall have concurrent power to enforce this article by appropriate legislation.

*Section 3.* This article shall be inoperative unless it shall have been ratified as an amendment to the Constitution by the legislatures of the several States as provided in the Constitution, within seven years from the date of the submission hereof to the States by the Congress.

## Amendment 19

*(Ratified August 18, 1920)*

The right of citizens of the United States to vote shall not be denied or abridged by the United States or by any State on account of sex.

Congress shall have power to enforce this article by appropriate legislation.

## Amendment 20

*(Ratified January 23, 1933)*

*Section 1.* The terms of the President and Vice President shall end at noon on the 20th day of January, and the terms of Senators and Representatives at noon on the 3d day of January, of the years in which such terms would have ended if this article had not been ratified; and the terms of their successors shall then begin.

*Section 2.* The Congress shall assemble at least once in every year, and such meeting shall begin at noon on the 3d day of January, unless they shall by law appoint a different day.

*Section 3.* If, at the time fixed for the beginning of the term of the President, the President elect shall have died, the Vice President elect shall become President. If a President shall not have been chosen before the time fixed for the beginning of his term, or if the President elect shall have failed to qualify, then the Vice President elect shall act as President until a President shall have qualified; and the Congress may by law provide for the case wherein neither a President elect nor a Vice President elect shall have qualified, declaring who shall then act as President, or the manner in which one who is to act shall be selected, and such person shall act accordingly until a President or Vice President shall have qualified.

*Section 4.* The Congress may by law provide for the case of the death of any of the persons from whom the House of Representatives may choose a President whenever the right of choice shall have devolved upon them, and for the case of the death of any of the persons from whom the Senate may choose a Vice President whenever the right of choice shall have devolved upon them.

*Section 5.* Sections 1 and 2 shall take effect on the 15th day of October following the ratification of this article.

*Section 6.* This article shall be inoperative unless it shall have been ratified as an amendment to the Constitution by the legislatures of three-fourths of the several States within seven years from the date of its submission.

## Amendment 21

*(Ratified December 5, 1933)*

*Section 1.* The eighteenth article of amendment to the Constitution of the United States is hereby repealed.

*Section 2.* The transportation or importation into any State, Territory, or possession of the United States for delivery or use therein of intoxicating liquors, in violation of the laws thereof, is hereby prohibited.

*Section 3.* This article shall be inoperative unless it shall have been ratified as an amendment to the Constitution by conventions in the several States, as provided in the Constitution, within seven years from the date of the submission hereof to the States by the Congress.

## Amendment 22

*(Ratified February 27, 1951)*

*Section 1.* No person shall be elected to the office of the President more than twice, and no person who has held the office of President, or acted as President, for more than two years of a term to which some other person was elected President shall be elected to the office of the President more than once. But this Article shall not apply to any person holding the office of President when this Article was proposed by the Congress, and shall not prevent any person who may be holding the office of President, or acting as President, during the term within which this Article becomes operative from holding the office of President or acting as President during the remainder of such term.

*Section 2.* This article shall be inoperative unless it shall have been ratified as an amendment to the Constitution by the legislatures of three-fourths of the several States within seven years from the date of its submission to the States by the Congress.

## Amendment 23

*(Ratified March 29, 1961)*

*Section 1.* The District constituting the seat of Government of the United States shall appoint in such manner as the Congress may direct:

A number of electors of President and Vice President equal to the whole number of Senators and Representatives in Congress to which the District would be entitled if it were a State, but in no event more than the least populous State; they shall be in addition to those appointed by the States, but they shall be considered, for the purposes of the election of President and Vice President, to be electors appointed by a State; and they shall meet in the District and perform such duties as provided by the twelfth article of amendment.

*Section 2.* The Congress shall have power to enforce this article by appropriate legislation.

## Amendment 24

*(Ratified January 23, 1964)*

*Section 1.* The right of citizens of the United States to vote in any primary or other election for President or Vice President, for electors for President or Vice President, or for Senator or Representative in Congress, shall not be denied or abridged by the United States or any State by reason of failure to pay any poll tax or other tax.

*Section 2.* The Congress shall have power to enforce this article by appropriate legislation.

# THE CONSTITUTION

## Amendment 25

*(Ratified February 10, 1967)*

*Section 1.* In case of the removal of the President from office or of his death or resignation, the Vice President shall become President.

*Section 2.* Whenever there is a vacancy in the office of the Vice President, the President shall nominate a Vice President who shall take office upon confirmation by a majority vote of both Houses of Congress.

*Section 3.* Whenever the President transmits to the President pro tempore of the Senate and the Speaker of the House of Representatives his written declaration that he is unable to discharge the powers and duties of his office, and until he transmits to them a written declaration to the contrary, such powers and duties shall be discharged by the Vice President as Acting President.

*Section 4.* Whenever the Vice President and a majority of either the principal officers of the executive departments or of such other body as Congress may by law provide, transmit to the President pro tempore of the Senate and the Speaker of the House of Representatives their written declaration that the President is unable to discharge the powers and duties of his office, the Vice President shall immediately assume the powers and duties of the office as Acting President.

Thereafter, when the President transmits to the President pro tempore of the Senate and the Speaker of the House of Representatives his written declaration that no inability exists, he shall resume the powers and duties of his office unless the Vice President and a majority of either the principal officers of the executive department or of such other body as Congress may by law provide, transmit within four days to the President pro tempore of the Senate and the Speaker of the House of Representatives their written declaration that the President is unable to discharge the powers and duties of his office. Thereupon Congress shall decide the issue, assembling within forty-eight hours for that purpose if not in session. If the Congress, within twenty-one days after receipt of the latter written declaration, or, if Congress is not in session, within twenty-one days after Congress is required to assemble, determines by two-thirds vote of both Houses that the President is unable to discharge the powers and duties of his office, the Vice President shall continue to discharge the same as Acting President; otherwise, the President shall resume the powers and duties of his office.

## Amendment 26

*(Ratified July 1, 1971)*

*Section 1.* The right of citizens of the United States, who are eighteen years of age or older, to vote shall not be denied or abridged by the United States or by any State on account of age.

*Section 2.* The Congress shall have the power to enforce this article by appropriate legislation.

## Amendment 27

*(Ratified May 7, 1992)*

No law, varying the compensation for the services of the Senators and Representatives, shall take effect, until an election of Representatives shall have intervened.

# THE EXECUTIVE BRANCH

## The President

Barack H. Obama  www.whitehouse.gov  202-456-1414

## The Vice-President

Joseph R. Biden  202-456-7549

## Cabinet Members

| | | | |
|---|---|---|---|
| Secretary of State | Hillary R.Clinton | 202-647-5291 | www.state.gov |
| Secretary of the Treasury | Timothy F. Geithner | 202-622-1100 | www.treasury.gov |
| Secretary of Defense | Leon E. Panetta | 703-692-7100 | www.defenselink.mil |
| Attorney General | Eric H. Holder, Jr. | 202-514-2001 | www.usdoj.gov |
| Secretary of the Interior | Kenneth L. Salazar | 202-208-7351 | www.doi.gov |
| Secretary of Agriculture | Thomas J. Vilsack | 202-720-3631 | www.usda.gov |
| Secretary of Commerce | Acting Secy. Rebecca M. Blank | 202-482-2112 | www.commerce.gov |
| Secretary of Labor | Hilda L. Solis | 202-693-6000 | www.dol.gov |
| Secretary of Education | Arne Duncan | 202-401-3000 | www.ed.gov |
| Secretary of Health and Human Services | Kathleen Sebelius | 202-690-7000 | www.hhs.gov |
| Secretary of Housing and Urban Development | Shaun L.S. Donovan | 202-708-0417 | www.hud.gov |
| Secretary of Transportation | Raymond L. LaHood | 202-366-1111 | www.dot.gov |
| Secretary of Energy | Steven Chu | 202-586-6210 | www.energy.gov |
| Secretary of Veterans' Affairs | Eric K. Shinseki | 202-273-4800 | www.va.gov |
| Secretary of Homeland Security | Janet A. Napolitano | 202-282-8000 | www.dhs.gov |

## Cabinet Rank Positions:

| | | |
|---|---|---|
| Council of Economic Advisers | VACANT | www.whitehouse.gov/administration/eop/cea/ |
| Environmental Protection Agency | Lisa P. Jackson | www.epa.gov |
| Office of Management & Budget | Jacob J. Lew | www.whitehouse.gov/omb |
| U.S. Trade Representative | Ronald Kirk | www.ustr.gov |
| U.S. Ambassador to the UN | Susan Rice | www.usunnewyork.usmission.gov/ |
| White House Chief of Staff | Bill Daley | |

# EXECUTIVE BRANCH

## EXECUTIVE OFFICE OF THE PRESIDENT

### The White House Office
1600 Pennsylvania Ave., NW
Washington, DC 20500
(202) 456-1414
Library (202) 395-7000
FAX (202) 456-2461
Law Library (202) 395-3397
president@whitehouse.gov
www.whitehouse.gov/

### Office of Management and Budget
725 17th St., NW
Washington, DC 20503
(202) 395-3080
Library (202) 395-3654
www.whitehouse.gov/omb/

### Office of Administration
725 17th St., NW
Washington, DC 20503
(202) 456-2861
www.whitehouse.gov/administration/
eop/oa/

### Office of National Drug Control Policy
750 17th St., NW
Washington, DC 20500
(202) 395-6700
www.whitehousedrugpolicy.gov/

### Domestic Policy Council
Executive Office of the President
Washington, DC 20500
(202) 456-5594
www.whitehouse.gov/administration/
eop/dpc/

### National Economic Council
Executive Office of the President
Washington, DC 20502
(202) 456-2800
www.whitehouse.gov/administration/
eop/nec/

### National Security Council
Eisenhower Executive Office Building
Washington, DC 20504
(202) 456-9271
www.whitehouse.gov/administration/
eop/nsc/

### Council of Economic Advisers
725 17th St., NW
Washington, DC 20502

(202) 395-5042
www.whitehouse.gov/administration/
eop/cea/

### Council on Environmental Quality
722 Jackson Place, NW
Washington, DC 20503
(202) 395-5750
www.whitehouse.gov/administration/
eop/ceq/

### Office of the U.S. Trade Representative
600 17th St., NW
Washington, DC 20508
(202) 395-3230
www.ustr.gov

### Office of Science and Technology Policy
725 17th St., NW, Suite 5228
Washington, DC 20502
(202) 456-7116
www.whitehouse.gov/administration/
eop/ostp/

### Office of Faith-Based and Community Initiatives
708 Jackson Place, NW
Washington, DC 20503
(202) 456-4708
www.whitehouse.gov/
our_government/fbci/

### President's Intelligence Advisory Board
725 17th St., NW, Room 5020
Washington, DC 20502
(202) 456-2352
www.whitehouse.gov/administration/
eop/piab/

### Office of National AIDS Policy
736 Jackson Place, NW
Washington, DC 20502
(202) 456-4533
FAX (202) 456-7315
www.whitehouse.gov/administration/
eop/onap/

### Corporation for National and Community Service
1201 New York Ave., NW
Washington, DC 20525
(202) 606-5000
www.serve.gov

### White House Military Office

www.whitehouse.gov/administration/
eop/whmo/

### Office of the Vice-President
Eisenhower Executive Office Building
Washington, DC 20501
(202) 456-7549
vice_president@whitehouse.gov
www.whitehouse.gov/administration/
vice-president-biden/

### THE DEPARTMENTS
Note: Those sub-departments which do not have addresses listed are located at the main department address.

### Department of Agriculture
1400 Independence Ave., SW
Washington, DC 20250
(202) 720-4623
Library (202) 720-3434
Law Library (202) 720-7751
NAL (301) 504-5755
www.usda.gov

### Department of Commerce
1401 Constitution Ave., NW
Washington, DC 20230
(202) 482-2000; (800) 872-8723
Library (202) 482-5511
Law Library (202) 482-1154
www.doc.gov

Bureau of the Census
Suitland, MD 20746
(301) 763-4748
Library (301) 763-2511
www.census.gov

Bureau of Economic Analysis
1441 L St., NW
Washington, DC 20230
(202) 606-9900
www.bea.gov

Bureau of Industry and Security
(202) 482-4811
www.bis.doc.gov

Economic Development
Administration
(202) 482-4085
www.eda.gov

Economics and Statistics
Administration
(202) 482-6607
www.esa.doc.gov/

# THE DEPARTMENTS

International Trade Administration
(202) 482-3809
trade.gov

Minority Business Development
  Agency
(202) 482-2332; (888) 324-1551
www.mbda.gov/

National Institute of Standards and
  Technology
100 Bureau Drive
Gaithersburg, MD 20899
(301) 975-6478
Library (301) 975-3053
www.nist.gov

National Oceanic and Atmospheric
  Administration
(202) 482-6090
Library (301) 713-2600 x157
www.noaa.gov

National Technical Information
  Service
5285 Port Royal Road
Springfield, VA 22161
(703) 605-6000; (800) 553-6847
www.ntis.gov

National Telecommunications and
  Information Administration
(202) 482-2000
www.ntia.doc.gov

Patent and Trademark Office
600 Dulany St.
Alexandria, VA  22314
(571) 272-1000; (800) 786-9199
Library (571) 272-3547
www.uspto.gov

**Department of Defense**
The Pentagon
Washington, DC 20301
(703) 692-7100
www.defense.gov

Department of the Air Force
The Pentagon
Washington, DC 20330
(703) 697-6061
Law Library (703) 614-4958
www.af.mil

Department of the Army
The Pentagon
Washington, DC 20310
(703) 695-1717

Pentagon Library/Law Library
(703) 695-1997

www.army.mil

Department of the Navy
The Pentagon, Rm. 4B463
Washington, DC 20350
(703) 697-7491
Law Library (202) 543-0247
www.navy.mil

National Security Agency
9800 Savage Road
Fort Meade, MD 20755
(301) 688-6524
www.nsa.gov

Defense Intelligence Agency
(703) 695-0071
www.dia.mil

**Department of Education**
400 Maryland Ave., SW
Washington, DC 20202-0498
(202) 401-2000; (800) USA-LEARN
Library  (202) 205-5015
www.ed.gov

**Department of Energy**
1000 Independence Ave., SW
Washington, DC 20585
(202) 586-5000; (800) DIAL-DOE
Library  (202) 586-3112
Law Library  (202) 586-4848
www.energy.gov

Energy Information Administration
(202) 586-8800 (Natl. Energy Info.
  Center)
www.eia.doe.gov/

Federal Energy Regulatory
  Commission
888 First St., NE
Washington, DC 20426-4205
(202) 502-8371
www.ferc.gov

**Department of Health & Human
  Services**
200 Independence Ave., SW
Washington, DC 20201
(202) 690-7850
Law Library (202) 619-0190
www.dhhs.gov

National Institutes of Health
9000 Rockville Pike
Bethesda, MD 20892
(301) 496-4000
www.nih.gov

Food & Drug Administration
10903 New Hampshire Ave.

Silver Spring, MD 20993-0002
(301)796-5000; (888) 463-6332
Library  (301) 827-1175
www.fda.gov

Centers for Medicare and Medicaid
  Services
7500 Security Blvd.
Baltimore, MD 21244
(410) 786-3000
cms.hhs.gov

**Department of Homeland Security**
Washington, DC 20528
(202) 282-8000
www.dhs.gov

U.S. Citizenship and Immigration
  Services
111 Massachusetts Ave. NW
Washington, DC 20529-2260
(202) 272-1200; (800) 375-5283
www.uscis.gov

U.S. Coast Guard
2100 Second St., SW
Washington, DC 20593-0001
(202) 372-4620
Law Library (202) 372-3825
www.uscg.mil/

U.S. Customs & Border Protection
1300 Pennsylvania Ave., NW
Washington, DC 20229
(202) 344-1770
Library  (202) 572-0600
www.cbp.gov/

U.S. Secret Service
245 Murray Lane, SW, Bldg. T5
Washington, DC 20223
(202) 406-5708
www.secretservice.gov

Transportation Security Administration
601 S. 12 St.
Arlington, VA 22202
(571) 227-2829
www.tsa.gov

Federal Law Enforcement Training
 Center
1131 Chapel Crossing Rd.
Glynco, GA 31524
(912) 267-2447
www.fletc.gov

U.S. Immigration and Customs
  Enforcement
(202) 732-4242
www.ice.gov

# THE DEPARTMENTS

**Department of Housing and
Urban Development**
451 Seventh St., SW
Washington, DC 20410
(202) 708-1455
Library (202) 708-2370
www.hud.gov

**Department of the Interior**
1849 C St., NW
Washington, DC 20240
(202) 208-3100
Library (202) 208-5815
www.doi.gov

U.S. Geological Survey
12201 Sunrise Valley Drive
Reston, VA 20192
(703) 648-5953
Library (703) 648-4486
www.usgs.gov

Bureau of Reclamation
(202) 513-0575
www.usbr.gov

National Park Service
(202) 208-6843
www.nps.gov

Bureau of Indian Affairs
(202) 208-3710
www.doi.gov/
  bureau-indian-affairs.html

Bureau of Land Management
(202) 208-3801
www.blm.gov

Bureau of Ocean, Energy
Management, Regulation and
Enforcement
(202) 208-3985
www.boemre.gov

U.S. Fish and Wildlife Service
4401 N. Fairfax Drive
Arlington, VA 22203
(202) 358-2240; (800) 344-WILD
www.fws.gov

**Department of Justice**
950 Pennsylvania Ave., NW,
  Rm. 7238
Washington, DC 20530-0001
(202) 514-2000
Library (202) 514-3775
www.justice.gov

Bureau of Alcohol, Tobacco,
  Firearms, and Explosives
99 New York Ave., NE, MS 5S144

Washington, DC 20226
(202) 648-8500
www.atf.gov/

Federal Bureau of Investigation
935 Pennsylvania Ave., NW
Washington, DC 20535
(202) 324-3000
www.fbi.gov/

Antitrust Division
(202) 514-2401
Library (202) 514-5870
www.justice.gov/atr/

U.S. Marshals Service
(202) 307-9100
www.usmarshals.gov

Drug Enforcement Administration
8701 Morrissette Drive
Springfield, VA 22152
(202) 307-1000
Library (202) 307-8932
www.dea.gov

Criminal Division
(202) 514-2601
Library (202) 616-8942
www.justice.gov/criminal/

Federal Bureau of Prisons
320 First St., NW
Washington, DC 20534-0002
(202) 307-3198
www.bop.gov

INTERPOL
Washington, DC 20530
(202) 616-9000
www.justice.gov/usncb

Tax Division
(202) 514-2901
Library (202) 616-5564
www.justice.gov/tax

Civil Division
(202) 514-3301
Library (202) 616-8942
www.justice.gov/civil/

Civil Rights Division
(202) 514-4609
Library (202) 616-8942
www.justice.gov/crt

Environment and Natural
  Resources Division
(202) 514-2701
Library (202) 616-5564
www.justice.gov/enrd/

Justice Management Division
(202) 514-1843
Library (202) 514-3775
www.justice.gov/jmd/

Executive Office of U.S. Attorneys
(202) 252-6246
www.justice.gov/usao/eousa/

**Department of Labor**
200 Constitution Ave., NW
Washington, DC 20210
(202) 693-4676
Library (202) 693-6600
Law Library (202) 693-6615
www.dol.gov

Bureau of Labor Statistics
2 Massachusetts Ave., NE, Rm. 2860
Washington, DC 20212-4225
(202) 691-5200
www.bls.gov

Mine Safety and Health
  Administration
1100 Wilson Blvd., 21st fl.
Arlington, VA 22209
(202) 693-9400
www.msha.gov

Occupational Safety and Health
  Administration
(202) 693-2000
www.osha.gov

**Department of State**
2201 C St., NW
Washington, DC 20520-0001
(202) 647-4000
Library (202) 647-1099
www.state.gov

**Department of Transportation**
1200 New Jersey Ave., SE
Washington, DC 20590
(202) 366-4000
Library (202) 366-0746
www.dot.gov

Federal Aviation Administration
800 Independence Ave., SW
Washington, DC 20591-0002
(202) 267-3111
Law Library (202) 267-3174
www.faa.gov

Federal Railroad Administration
1200 New Jersey Ave., SE, MS 25
Washington, DC 20590
(202) 493-6024
www.fra.dot.gov

# THE DEPARTMENTS

Federal Highway Administration
(202) 366-4000
www.fwha.dot.gov/

Maritime Administration
1200 New Jersey Ave., SE
Washington, DC 20590
(202) 366-5807
www.marad.dot.gov

National Highway Traffic Safety
Administration
(202) 366-9550; (888) 327-4236
www.nhtsa.dot.gov

Federal Transit Administration
(202) 366-4043
www.fta.dot.gov

Research and Innovative Technology
Administration
(202) 366-3492
www.rita.dot.gov

St. Lawrence Seaway Development
Corp.
(202) 366-0091
www.seaway..dot.gov

**Department of the Treasury**
1500 Pennsylvania Ave., NW
Washington, DC 20220
(202) 622-2000
Library (202) 622-0990
www.treasury.gov

Alcohol and Tobacco Tax and Trade
Bureau
1310 G Street, NW, Suite 300
Washington, DC 20220
(202) 453-2000
www.ttb.gov

U.S. Mint
801 Ninth St., NW
Washington, DC 20220
(202) 756-6468
www.usmint.gov

Comptroller of the Currency
250 E St., SW
Washington, DC 20219-3202
(202) 874-5000
Library (202) 874-4720
www.occ.gov

Bureau of Engraving & Printing
14th and C Streets, SW
Washington, DC 20228
(202) 874-8888
www.bep.treas.gov/

Bureau of the Public Debt
799 9th St., NW
Washington, DC 20239
(202) 504-3502
www.publicdebt.treas.gov/

Internal Revenue Service
1111 Constitution Ave., NW
Washington, DC 20224-0002
(800) 829-1040
FOIA Reading Rm. (202) 622-5164
Law Library (202) 622-8050
www.irs.gov

Consumer Financial Protection Bureau
www.cfpb.gov

**Department of Veterans Affairs**
810 Vermont Ave., NW
Washington, DC 20420-0001
(202) 273-5400
Library (202) 461-7580
Law Library (202) 273-6558
www.va.gov

Veterans Benefits Administration
(800) 827-1000
www.vba.va.gov/

## INDEPENDENT
## GOVERNMENTAL AGENCIES

**Access Board**
1331 F St., NW, Suite 1000
Washington, DC 20004-1111
(202) 272-0080; (800) 872-2253
www.access-board.gov/

**Advisory Council on Historic
Preservation**
1100 Pennsylvania Ave., NW
Suite 803
Washington, DC 20004-2501
(202) 606-8503
www.achp.gov

**African Development Foundation**
1400 I St., NW, Suite 1000
Washington, DC 20005-2248
(202) 673-3916
www.adf.gov

**American Battle Monuments
Commission**
Courthouse Plaza II, Suite 500
2300 Clarendon Blvd.
Arlington, VA 22201
(703) 696-6900
www.abmc.gov/

**Appalachian Regional Commission**
1666 Connecticut Ave., NW,
Suite 700
Washington, DC 20009-1068
(202) 884-7700
www.arc.gov

**Central Intelligence Agency**
Washington, DC 20505
(703) 482-0623
Law Library (703) 874-3187
www.cia.gov/

**Chemical Safety Board**
2175 K St., NW, Suite 400
Washington, DC 20037-1809
(202) 261-7600
www.csb.gov

**Commission of Fine Arts**
401 F St., NW, Suite 312
Washington, DC 20001-2728
(202) 504-2200
www.cfa.gov

**Commission on Civil Rights**
624 9th St., NW
Washington, DC 20425-0001
(202) 376-7700
Library (202) 376-8110
www.usccr.gov

**Commodity Futures Trading
Commission**
1155 21st St., NW
Washington, DC 20581
(202) 418-5000
Library (202) 418-5255
www.cftc.gov

**Consumer Product Safety
Commission**
4330 East West Hwy.
Bethesda, MD 20814
(301) 504-7923
Library (301) 504-7622
www.cpsc.gov

**Corporation for National and
Community Service**
1201 New York Ave., NW
Washington, DC 20525-0001
(202) 606-5000
www.nationalservice.gov

**Defense Nuclear Facilities Safety
Board**
625 Indiana Ave., NW, Suite 700
Washington, DC 20004
(202) 694-7000; (800) 788-4016
www.dnfsb.gov

# INDEPENDENT GOVERNMENTAL AGENCIES

**Delaware River Basin Commission**
P.O. Box 7360
W. Trenton, NJ 08628-0360
(609) 883-9500
www.state.nj.us/drbc/drbc.htm

**Environmental Protection Agency**
1200 Pennsylvania Ave., NW
Washington, DC 20460-0001
(202) 272-0167
Library (202) 566-0556
Law Library (202) 564-3971
Legislative Library (202) 564-2782
www.epa.gov

**Equal Employment Opportunity Commission**
131 M Street NE
Washington, DC 20507
(202) 663-4900
Library (202) 663-4630
www.eeoc.gov

**Export-Import Bank of the U.S.**
811 Vermont Ave., NW
Washington, DC 20571-0001
(202) 565-3946; (800) 565-3946
Library (202) 565-3980
www.exim.gov

**Farm Credit Administration**
1501 Farm Credit Drive
McLean, VA 22102-5090
(703) 883-4056
www.fca.gov

**Federal Communications Commission**
445 12th St., SW
Washington, DC 20554
(888) 225-5322
Library (202) 418-0450
www.fcc.gov

**Federal Deposit Insurance Corporation**
550 Seventeenth St., NW
Washington, DC 20429-0001
(202) 898-7192; (877) 275-3342
Library (202) 898-3631
www.fdic.gov

**Federal Election Commission**
999 E St., NW
Washington, DC 20463-0001
(202) 694-1000; (800) 424-9530
Law Library (202) 694-1600
www.fec.gov

**Federal Emergency Management Agency**
500 C St., SW
Washington, DC 20472
(202) 646-2500
www.fema.gov

**Federal Home Loan Mortgage Corp.**
8200 Jones Branch Drive
McLean, VA 22102-3110
(703) 903-2000
Library (703) 903-2773
www.freddiemac.com

**Federal Housing Finance Agency**
1700 G St., NW
Washington, DC 20552
(202) 414-3800
www.fhfa.gov/

**Federal Labor Relations Authority**
1400 K St. NW, Suite 200
Washington, DC 20424
(202) 218-7770
Library (202) 218-7798
www.flra.gov/

**Federal Laboratory Consortium for Technology Transfer**
950 N. Kings Highway, Suite 208
Cherry Hill, NJ 08034
(856) 667-7727; (888) 388-5227
www.federallabs.org/

**Federal Maritime Commission**
800 N. Capitol St., NW
Washington, DC 20573
(202) 523-5800
Library (202) 523-5762
www.fmc.gov/

**Federal Mediation & Conciliation Service**
2100 K St., NW
Washington, DC 20427-0001
(202) 606-8100
www.fmcs.gov/

**Federal Mine Safety and Health Review Commission**
601 New Jersey Ave., NW, Suite 9500
Washington, DC 20001
(202) 434-9935
Law Library (202) 434-9986
www.fmshrc.gov/

**Federal Reserve System**
20th & Constitution Ave., NW
Washington, DC 20551
(202) 452-3000
Library (202) 452-3332
Law Library (202) 452-3283
www.federalreserve.gov/

**Federal Retirement Thrift Investment Board**
1250 H St., NW
Washington, DC 20005-3952
(202) 942-1600
Library (202) 942-1695
www.frtib.gov

**Federal Trade Commission**
600 Pennsylvania Ave., NW
Washington, DC 20580
(202) 326-2222
Library (202) 326-2395
www.ftc.gov/

**General Services Administration**
1275 First St., NE
Washington, DC 20417
(202) 501-0800
www.gsa.gov

**Inter-American Foundation**
901 N. Stuart St., 10th fl.
Arlington, Virginia 22203
(703) 306-4301
www.iaf.gov/index/index_en.asp

**International Broadcasting Bureau**
330 Independence Ave., SW
Washington, DC 20237
(202) 203-4400
www.ibb.gov/

**International Trade Commission**
500 E St., SW
Washington, DC 20436-2760
(202) 205-2000; (800) 343-9822
Library (202) 205-2630
Law Library (202) 205-3287
www.usitc.gov/

**Legal Services Corporation**
3333 K St., NW, 3rd fl.
Washington, DC 20007-3522
(202) 295-1500
www.lsc.gov

**Marine Mammal Commission**
4340 East West Highway, Suite 700
Bethesda, MD 20814
(301) 504-0087
www.mmc.gov

**Medicare Payment Advisory Commission**
601 New Jersey Ave., NW, Suite 9000
Washington, DC 20001
(202) 220-3700
www.medpac.gov/

# INDEPENDENT GOVERNMENTAL AGENCIES

**Merit Systems Protection Board**
1615 M St., NW
Washington, DC 20419
(202) 653-7200; (800) 209-8960
Law Library (202) 653-6772
www.mspb.gov

**National Aeronautics and Space
   Administration**
300 E St., SW
Washington, DC 20546-0001
(202) 358-0001; (800) 424-9183
Library (202) 358-2078
www.nasa.gov/

**National Archives & Records
   Administration**
8601 Adelphi Road
College Park, MD 20740-6001
(301) 837-1600; (866) 272-6272
Library (301) 837-3415
www.archives.gov/

   Office of the Federal Register
   800 N. Capitol St., NW, Suite 700
   Washington, DC 20001
   (202) 741-6000
   www.archives.gov/federal_register/
      index.html

   Office of Presidential Libraries
   8601 Adelphi Road, Rm. 2200
   College Park, MD 20740-6001
   (301) 837-3250
   www.archives.gov/presidential-
      libraries/contact

   Herbert Hoover Library
   210 Parkside Drive
   West Branch, IA 52358
   (319) 643-5301
   www.hoover.archives.gov/

   Franklin D. Roosevelt Library
   4079 Albany Post Road
   Hyde Park, NY 12538
   (845) 486-7770; (800) FDR-VISIT
   www.fdrlibrary.marist.edu/

   Harry S. Truman Library
   500 W. U.S. Highway 24
   Independence, MO 64050
   (816) 268-8200; (800) 833-1225
   www.trumanlibrary.org/

   Dwight D. Eisenhower Library
   200 SE Fourth St.
   Abilene, KS 67410
   (785) 263-6700; (877) RING-IKE
   www.eisenhower.utexas.edu

   John F. Kennedy Library

   Columbia Point
   Boston, MA 02125
   (617) 514-1600; (866) JFK-1960
   www.jfklibrary.org/

   Lyndon B. Johnson Library
   2313 Red River St.
   Austin, TX 78705
   (512) 721-0200
   www.lbjlibrary.org

   Nixon Presidential Library
   8601 Adelphi Road, Rm. 1320
   College Park, MD 20740-6001
   (301) 837-3290
   www.nixonlibrary.gov

   Gerald R. Ford Library
   1000 Beal Ave.
   Ann Arbor, MI 48109
   (734) 205-0555
   www.ford.utexas.gov

   Jimmy Carter Library
   441 Freedom Pkwy.
   Atlanta, GA 30307-1498
   (404) 865-7100
   www.jimmycarterlibrary.org/

   Ronald Reagan Library
   40 Presidential Drive
   Simi Valley, CA 93065
   (800) 410-8354; (805) 577-4000
   www.reagan.utexas.edu/

   Bush Presidential Library
   1000 George Bush Dr. West
   College Station, TX 77845
   (979) 691-4000
   bushlibrary.tamu.edu

   William J. Clinton Presidential
      Library and Museum
   1200 President Clinton Ave.
   Little Rock, AR 72201
   (501) 374-4242
   www.clintonlibrary.gov/

   George W. Bush Presidential
   Library
   1725 Lakeside Drive
   Lewisville, TX 75057
   (972) 353-0545
   www.georgewbushlibrary.gov

**National Capital Planning
   Commission**
401 9th St., NW, North Lobby,
   Suite 500
Washington, DC 20004
(202) 482-7200
www.ncpc.gov/

**National Council on Disability**
1331 F St., NW, Suite 850
Washington, DC 20004-1107
(202) 272-2004
www.ncd.gov/

**National Credit Union
   Administration**
1775 Duke St.
Alexandria, VA 22314-3428
(703) 518-6300
Law Library (703) 518-6546
www.ncua.gov/

**National Foundation on the Arts
   and the Humanities**
National Endowment for the Arts
1100 Pennsylvania Ave., NW
Washington, DC 20506
(202) 682-5400
arts.endow.gov

National Endowment for the
   Humanities
(202) 606-8400
Library (202) 606-8244
www.neh.gov

Institute of Museum and Library
   Services
1800 M Street NW, 9th fl.
Washington, DC 20036
(202) 653-4757
www.imls.gov

**National Indian Gaming
   Commission**
1441 L St., NW, Suite 9100
Washington, DC 20005
(202) 632-7003
www.nigc.gov

**National Labor Relations Board**
1099 14th St., NW, Suite 5530
Washington, DC 20570-0001
(202) 273-1991
Library (202) 273-3720
www.nlrb.gov/

**National Mediation Board**
1301 K St., NW, Suite 250 East
Washington, DC 20005-7011
(202) 692-5050
www.nmb.gov

**National Science Foundation**
4201 Wilson Blvd.
Arlington, VA 22230-0001
(703) 292-5111
Library (703) 292-7830
www.nsf.gov/

# INDEPENDENT GOVERNMENTAL AGENCIES

**National Transportation Safety
  Board**
490 L'Enfant Plaza, SW
Washington, DC 20594
(202) 314-6100
www.ntsb.gov

**Nuclear Regulatory Commission**
One White Flint North
11555 Rockville Pike
Rockville, MD 20852-2738
(301) 415-7000
Library (301) 415-4737
Law Library (301) 415-1526
www.nrc.gov/

**Occupational Safety and Health
  Review Commission**
1120 20th St., NW, 9th fl.
Washington, DC 20036-3419
(202) 606-5400
Library (202) 606-5729
www.oshrc.gov/

**Office of Compliance**
110 2nd St., SE, Rm. LA200
Washington, DC 20540-1999
(202) 724-9250
www.compliance.gov

**Office of Government Ethics**
1201 New York Ave., NW, Suite 500
Washington, DC 20005-3917
(202) 482-9300
www.usoge.gov/

**Office of Personnel Management**
1900 E St., NW
Washington, DC 20415
(202) 606-1800
Library (202) 606-1432
www.opm.gov/

**Office of Special Counsel**
1730 M St., NW, Suite 218
Washington, DC 20036-4505
(202) 254-3670; (800) 872-9855
www.osc.gov

**Office of the Director of National
  Intelligence**
Washington, DC 20511
(703) 733-8600
www.dni.gov

**Office of the National
  Counterintelligence Executive**
CS5, Rm. 300
Washington, DC 20505
(703) 682-4500
www.ncix.gov

**Overseas Private Investment Corp.**
1100 New York Ave., NW
Washington, DC 20527
(202) 336-8488
www.opic.gov

**Peace Corps**
1111 20th St., NW
Washington, DC 20526-0001
(202) 692-2000; (800) 424-8580
Library (202) 692-2640
www.peacecorps.gov/

**Pension Benefit Guaranty
  Corporation**
1200 K Street NW, Suite 12531
Washington, DC 20005
(202) 326-4000; (800) 400-7242
www.pbgc.gov/

**Postal Rate Commission**
901 New York Ave., NW, Suite 200
Washington, DC 20268-0001
(202) 789-6800
Library (202) 789-6877
www.prc.gov/

**Railroad Retirement Board**
844 North Rush St.
Chicago, IL 60611-2092
(312) 751-4300
Law Library (312) 751-4926
www.rrb.gov/

**Securities and Exchange
  Commission**
100 F Street NE
Washington, DC 20549
(202) 942-8088
Library (202) 551-5458
www.sec.gov/

**Selective Service System**
1515 Wilson Blvd.
Arlington, VA 22209-2425
(703) 605-4100
www.sss.gov/

**Small Business Administration**
409 Third St., SW
Washington, DC 20416
(202) 205-6605; (800) 827-5722
Law Library (202) 205-6849
www.sbaonline.sba.gov/

**Smithsonian Institution**
1000 Jefferson Drive, SW, Rm. 153
Washington, DC 20013
(202) 633-1000
Library (202) 633-1700
www.si.edu/

**Social Security Administration**
6401 Security Blvd.
Baltimore, MD 21235-6401
(410) 965-3120; (800) 772-1213
Library (410) 965-6107
www.ssa.gov/

**Susquehanna River Basin
  Commission**
1721 N. Front St
Harrisburg, PA 17102
(717) 238-0423
www.srbc.net/

**Tennessee Valley Authority**
400 W. Summit Hill Drive
Knoxville, TN 37902-1499
(865) 632-2101; (800) 323-3835
Library (865) 632-3464
www.tva.gov/

**U.S. Agency for International
  Development**
1300 Pennsylvania Ave., NW
Washington, DC 20523-1000
(202) 712-4320
www.usaid.gov

**U.S. Holocaust Memorial Museum**
100 Raoul Wallenberg Place, SW
Washington, DC 20024-2126
(202) 488-0400
www.ushmm.gov

**U.S. Postal Service**
475 L'Enfant Plaza, SW
Washington, DC 20260-1000
(202) 268-4800
Library (202) 268-2900
www.usps.com/

**U.S. Trade and Development Agency**
1000 Wilson Blvd., Suite 1600
Arlington, VA 22209-3901
(703) 875-4357
www.ustda.gov/

# LEGISLATIVE BRANCH
# CONGRESSIONAL AGENCIES

Congressional Budget Office
Ford House Office Bldg.
Second & D Streets, SW
Washington, DC 20515
(202) 226-2602
Library (202) 226-2635
www.cbo.gov

Government Accountability Office
441 G Street, NW
Washington, DC 20548-0001
(202) 512-4800
Law Library (202) 512-2585
www.gao.gov

Government Printing Office
North Capitol & H Streets, NW
Washington, DC 20401
(202) 512-0000
To Order (866) 512-1800
www.gpo.gov

Library of Congress
101 Independence Avenue, SE
Washington, DC 20540-1000
(202) 707-5000
Ref. Online www.loc.gov/rr/askalib/
www.loc.gov

Copyright Application Forms
(202) 707-3000
www.copyright.gov/forms

Congressional Research Service
(202) 707-5775
lcweb.loc.gov/crsinfo

CRS Library
(202) 707-8500

Digital Preservation
(202) 707-3300
www.digitalpreservation.gov

Law Library
(202) 707-5079

Cataloging Division
(202) 707-8040

Federal Research Division
(202) 707-3900

Register of Copyrights
(202) 707-8350

National Library Service for the
 Blind & Physically Handicapped
1291 Taylor St. NW
Washington, DC 20011
(202) 707-5100
nls@loc.gov
www.loc.gov/nls/

# SENATE OFFICERS AND LEADERSHIP, 112th CONGRESS

## Senate Leadership

| | | |
|---|---|---|
| Majority Leader | Harry Reid | 202-224-3542 |
| Majority Whip | Richard Durbin | 202-224-2152 |
| Senate Republican Leader | Mitch McConnell | 202-224-2541 |
| Republican Whip | John Kyl | 202-224-4521 |

## Officers of the Senate

| | | |
|---|---|---|
| President | Joseph R. Biden | 202-224-2424 |
| President Pro Tempore | Daniel K. Inouye | 202-224-3934 |
| Secretary of the Senate | Nancy Erickson | 202-224-3622 |
| Sergeant at Arms | Terrance W. Gainer | 202-224-2341 |
| Secretary for the Majority (Democ.) | Gary Myrick | 202-224-3735 |
| Secretary for the Minority (Repub.) | David Schiappa | 202-224-3835 |
| Parliamentarian | Alan Frumin | 202-224-6128 |
| Chaplain | Barry C. Black | 202-224-2510 |

# SENATORS

SR—Russell Building
SD—Dirksen Building
SH—Hart Building

All telephone numbers
preceded by 22 prefix

## 112th CONGRESS
## SUITE and TELEPHONE LIST

Copies available in Sergeant at Arms/IT Support Services, SD–180

INFORMATION
From Outside Dial:
Senate—224–3121
House—225–3121
From Inside Dial:
0 for Capitol Operator
Assistance
9 for an Outside Line

| Senator | | Suite | Phone | Senator | | Suite | Phone |
|---|---|---|---|---|---|---|---|
| **Vice President** | | | | KIRK, Mark | (R-IL) | SH-524 | 4-2854 |
| BIDEN, Jr., Joseph R. | | | 4-2424 | KLOBUCHAR, Amy | (D-MN) | SH-302 | 4-3244 |
| AKAKA, Daniel K. | (D-HI) | SH-141 | 4-6361 | KOHL, Herb | (D-WI) | SH-330 | 4-5653 |
| ALEXANDER, Lamar | (R-TN) | SD-455 | 4-4944 | KYL, Jon | (R-AZ) | SH-730 | 4-4521 |
| AYOTTE, Kelly | (R-NH) | SR-144 | 4-3324 | LANDRIEU, Mary L. | (D-LA) | SD-431 | 4-5824 |
| BARRASSO, John | (R-WY) | SD-307 | 4-6441 | LAUTENBERG, Frank R. | (D-NJ) | SH-324 | 4-3224 |
| BAUCUS, Max | (D-MT) | SH-511 | 4-2651 | LEAHY, Patrick J. | (D-VT) | SR-437 | 4-4242 |
| BEGICH, Mark | (D-AK) | SR-111 | 4-3004 | LEE, Mike | (R-UT) | SH-316 | 4-5444 |
| BENNET, Michael F. | (D-CO) | SR-458 | 4-5852 | LEVIN, Carl | (D-MI) | SR-269 | 4-6221 |
| BINGAMAN, Jeff | (D-NM) | SH-703 | 4-5521 | LIEBERMAN, Joseph I. | (ID-CT) | SH-706 | 4-4041 |
| BLUMENTHAL, Richard | (D-CT) | SH-702 | 4-2823 | LUGAR, Richard G. | (R-IN) | SH-306 | 4-4814 |
| BLUNT, Roy | (R-MO) | SR-260 | 4-5721 | MANCHIN III, Joe | (D-WV) | SH-303 | 4-3954 |
| BOOZMAN, John | (R-AR) | SH-320 | 4-4843 | McCAIN, John | (R-AZ) | SR-241 | 4-2235 |
| BOXER, Barbara | (D-CA) | SH-112 | 4-3553 | McCASKILL, Claire | (D-MO) | SH-506 | 4-6154 |
| BROWN, Scott P. | (R-MA) | SD-359 | 4-4543 | McCONNELL, Mitch | (R-KY) | SR-317 | 4-2541 |
| BROWN, Sherrod | (D-OH) | SH-713 | 4-2315 | MENENDEZ, Robert | (D-NJ) | SH-528 | 4-4744 |
| BURR, Richard | (R-NC) | SR-217 | 4-3154 | MERKLEY, Jeff | (D-OR) | SH-313 | 4-3753 |
| CANTWELL, Maria | (D-WA) | SH-311 | 4-3441 | MIKULSKI, Barbara A. | (D-MD) | SH-503 | 4-4654 |
| CARDIN, Benjamin L. | (D-MD) | SH-509 | 4-4524 | MORAN, Jerry | (R-KS) | SR-354 | 4-6521 |
| CARPER, Thomas R. | (D-DE) | SH-513 | 4-2441 | MURKOWSKI, Lisa | (R-AK) | SH-709 | 4-6665 |
| CASEY, Jr., Robert P. | (D-PA) | SR-393 | 4-6324 | MURRAY, Patty | (D-WA) | SR-448 | 4-2621 |
| CHAMBLISS, Saxby | (R-GA) | SR-416 | 4-3521 | NELSON, Ben | (D-NE) | SH-720 | 4-6551 |
| COATS, Daniel | (R-IN) | SR-493 | 4-5623 | NELSON, Bill | (D-FL) | SH-716 | 4-5274 |
| COBURN, Tom | (R-OK) | SR-172 | 4-5754 | PAUL, Rand | (R-KY) | SR-208 | 4-4343 |
| COCHRAN, Thad | (R-MS) | SD-113 | 4-5054 | PORTMAN, Rob | (R-OH) | SR-338 | 4-3353 |
| COLLINS, Susan M. | (R-ME) | SD-413 | 4-2523 | PRYOR, Mark L. | (D-AR) | SD-255 | 4-2353 |
| CONRAD, Kent | (D-ND) | SH-530 | 4-2043 | REED, Jack | (D-RI) | SH-728 | 4-4642 |
| COONS, Christopher A. | (D-DE) | SR-127A | 4-5042 | REID, Harry | (D-NV) | SH-522 | 4-3542 |
| CORKER, Bob | (R-TN) | SD-185 | 4-3344 | RISCH, James E. | (R-ID) | SR-483 | 4-2752 |
| CORNYN, John | (R-TX) | SH-517 | 4-2934 | ROBERTS, Pat | (R-KS) | SH-109 | 4-4774 |
| CRAPO, Mike | (R-ID) | SD-239 | 4-6142 | ROCKEFELLER IV, John D. | (D-WV) | SH-531 | 4-6472 |
| DeMINT, Jim | (R-SC) | SR-167 | 4-6121 | RUBIO, Marco | (R-FL) | SH-317 | 4-3041 |
| DURBIN, Richard J. | (D-IL) | SH-711 | 4-2152 | SANDERS, Bernard | (I-VT) | SD-332 | 4-5141 |
| ENZI, Michael B. | (R-WY) | SR-379A | 4-3424 | SCHUMER, Charles E. | (D-NY) | SH-322 | 4-6542 |
| FEINSTEIN, Dianne | (D-CA) | SH-331 | 4-3841 | SESSIONS, Jeff | (R-AL) | SR-326 | 4-4124 |
| FRANKEN, Al | (D-MN) | SH-309 | 4-5641 | SHAHEEN, Jeanne | (D-NH) | SH-520 | 4-2841 |
| GILLIBRAND, Kirsten E. | (D-NY) | SR-478 | 4-4451 | SHELBY, Richard C. | (R-AL) | SR-304 | 4-5744 |
| GRAHAM, Lindsey | (R-SC) | SR-290 | 4-5972 | SNOWE, Olympia J. | (R-ME) | SR-154 | 4-5344 |
| GRASSLEY, Chuck | (R-IA) | SH-135 | 4-3744 | STABENOW, Debbie | (D-MI) | SH-133 | 4-4822 |
| HAGAN, Kay R. | (D-NC) | SD-521 | 4-6342 | TESTER, Jon | (D-MT) | SH-724 | 4-2644 |
| HARKIN, Tom | (D-IA) | SH-731 | 4-3254 | THUNE, John | (R-SD) | SD-511 | 4-2321 |
| HATCH, Orrin G. | (R-UT) | SH-104 | 4-5251 | TOOMEY, Patrick J. | (R-PA) | SH-502 | 4-4254 |
| HELLER, Dean | (R-NV) | SR-361A | 4-6244 | UDALL, Mark | (D-CO) | SH-328 | 4-5941 |
| HOEVEN, John | (R-ND) | SR-120 | 4-2551 | UDALL, Tom | (D-NM) | SH-110 | 4-6621 |
| HUTCHISON, Kay Bailey | (R-TX) | SR-284 | 4-5922 | VITTER, David | (R-LA) | SH-516 | 4-4623 |
| INHOFE, James M. | (R-OK) | SR-205 | 4-4721 | WARNER, Mark R. | (D-VA) | SR-475 | 4-2023 |
| INOUYE, Daniel K. | (D-HI) | SH-722 | 4-3934 | WEBB, Jim | (D-VA) | SR-248 | 4-4024 |
| ISAKSON, Johnny | (R-GA) | SR-131 | 4-3643 | WHITEHOUSE, Sheldon | (D-RI) | SH-717 | 4-2921 |
| JOHANNS, Mike | (R-NE) | SR-404 | 4-4224 | WICKER, Roger F. | (R-MS) | SD-555 | 4-6253 |
| JOHNSON, Ron | (R-WI) | SR-386 | 4-5323 | WYDEN, Ron | (D-OR) | SD-223 | 4-5244 |
| JOHNSON, Tim | (D-SD) | SH-136 | 4-5842 | | | | |
| KERRY, John F. | (D-MA) | SR-218 | 4-2742 | | | | |

Published by the Senate Sergeant at Arms/IT Support Services
September 1, 2011

# SENATORS' WEB AND EMAIL ADDRESSES

URL and Email

| | |
|---|---|
| Akaka, Daniel K. (HI) | akaka.senate.gov/ |
| Alexander, Lamar (TN) | alexander.senate.gov/ |
| Ayotte, Kelly (NH) | ayotte.senate.gov/ |
| Barrasso, John (WY) | barrasso.senate.gov/ |
| Baucus, Max (MT) | baucus.senate.gov/ |
| Begich, Mark (AK) | begich.senate.gov/ |
| Bennet, Michael F. (CO) | bennet.senate.gov/ |
| Bingaman, Jeff (NM) | bingaman.senate.gov/ |
| Blumenthal, Richard (CT) | blumenthal.senate.gov/ |
| Blunt, Roy (MO) | blunt.senate.gov/ |
| Boozman, John (AR) | boozman.senate.gov/ |
| Boxer, Barbara (CA) | boxer.senate.gov/ |
| Brown, Scott, P. (MA) | scottbrown.senate.gov/ |
| Brown, Sherrod (OH) | brown.senate.gov/ |
| Burr, Richard (NC) | burr.senate.gov/ |
| Cantwell, Maria (WA) | cantwell.senate.gov/ |
| Cardin, Benjamin (MD) | cardin.senate.gov/ |
| Carper, Thomas (DE) | carper.senate.gov/ |
| Casey, Robert P., Jr. (PA) | casey.senate.gov/ |
| Chambliss, Saxby (GA) | chambliss.senate.gov/ |
| Coats, Daniel (IN) | coats.senate.gov/ |
| Coburn, Tom (OK) | coburn.senate.gov/ |
| Cochran, Thad (MS) | cochran.senate.gov/ |
| Collins, Susan M. (ME) | collins.senate.gov/ |
| Conrad, Kent (ND) | conrad.senate.gov/ |
| Coons, Christopher A. (DE) | coons.senate.gov/ |
| Corker, Bob (TN) | corker.senate.gov/ |
| Cornyn, John (TX) | cornyn.senate.gov/ |
| Crapo, Michael (ID) | crapo.senate.gov/ |
| DeMint, Jim (SC) | demint.senate.gov/ |
| Durbin, Richard J. (IL) | durbin.senate.gov/ |
| Enzi, Michael B. (WY) | enzi.senate.gov/ |
| Feinstein, Dianne (CA) | feinstein.senate.gov/ |
| Franken, Al (MN) | franken.senate.gov |
| Gillibrand, Kirsten (NY) | gillibrand.senate.gov/ |
| Graham, Lindsey (SC) | lgraham.senate.gov/ |
| Grassley, Charles E. (IA) | grassley.senate.gov/ |
| Hagan, Kay R. (NC) | hagan.senate.gov/ |
| Harkin, Thomas (IA) | harkin.senate.gov/ |
| Hatch, Orrin G. (UT) | hatch.senate.gov/ |
| Heller, Dean (NV) | heller.senate.gov/ |
| Hoeven. John (ND) | hoeven.senate.gov/ |
| Hutchison, Kay Bailey (TX) | hutchison.senate.gov/ |
| Inhofe, James M. (OK) | inhofe.senate.gov/ |
| Inouye, Daniel K. (HI) | inouye.senate.gov/ |
| Isakson, Johnny (GA) | isakson.senate.gov/ |
| Johanns, Mike (NE) | johanns.senate.gov/ |
| Johnson, Ron (WI) | ronjohnson.senate.gov/ |
| Johnson, Tim (SD) | johnson.senate.gov/ |

# SENATORS' WEB AND EMAIL ADDRESSES

URLand Email

| | |
|---|---|
| Kerry, John F. (MA) | kerry.senate.gov/ |
| Kirk, Mark (IL) | kirk.senate.gov/ |
| Klobuchar, Amy (MN) | klobuchar.senate.gov/ |
| Kohl, Herbert H. (WI) | kohl.senate.gov/ |
| Kyl, Jon (AZ) | kyl.senate.gov/ |
| Landrieu, Mary L. (LA) | landrieu.senate.gov/ |
| Lautenberg, Frank (NJ) | lautenberg.senate.gov/ |
| Leahy, Patrick J. (VT) | leahy.senate.gov/ |
| Lee, Mike (UT) | lee.senate.gov/ |
| Levin, Carl (MI) | levin.senate.gov/ |
| Lieberman, Joseph I. (CT) | lieberman.senate.gov/ |
| Lugar, Richard G. (IN) | lugar.senate.gov/ |
| Manchin, Joe, III (WV) | manchin.senate.gov/ |
| McCain, John (AZ) | mccain.senate.gov/ |
| McCaskill, Claire (MO) | mccaskill.senate.gov/ |
| McConnell, Mitch (KY) | mcconell.senate.gov/ |
| Menendez, Robert (NJ) | menendez.senate.gov/ |
| Merkley, Jeff (OR) | merkley.senate.gov/ |
| Mikulski, Barbara A. (MD) | mikulski.senate.gov/ |
| Moran, Jerry (KS) | moran.senate.gov/ |
| Murkowski, Lisa (AK) | murkowski.senate.gov/ |
| Murray, Patty (WA) | murray.senate.gov/ |
| Nelson, Ben (NE) | bennelson.senate.gov |
| Nelson, Bill (FL) | billnelson.senate.gov/ |
| Paul, Rand (KY) | paul.senate.gov/ |
| Portman, Rob (OH) | portman.senate.gov/ |
| Pryor, Mark (AR) | pryor.senate.gov/ |
| Reed, Jack (RI) | reed.senate.gov/ |
| Reid, Harry (NV) | reid.senate.gov/ |
| Risch, James E. (ID) | risch.senate.gov/ |
| Roberts, Pat (KS) | roberts.senate.gov/ |
| Rockefeller, John D., IV (WV) | rockefeller.senate.gov/ |
| Rubio, Marco (FL) | rubio.senate.gov/ |
| Sanders, Bernard (VT) | sanders.senate.gov/ |
| Schumer, Charles (NY) | schumer.senate.gov/ |
| Sessions, Jeff (AL) | sessions.senate.gov/ |
| Shaheen, Jeanne (NH) | shaheen.senate.gov/ |
| Shelby, Richard C. (AL) | shelby.senate.gov/ |
| Snowe, Olympia J. (ME) | snowe.senate.gov/ |
| Stabenow, Debbie (MI) | stabenow.senate.gov/ |
| Tester, Jon (MT) | tester.senate.gov/ |
| Thune, John (SD) | thune.senate.gov/ |
| Toomey, Patrick J. (PA) | toomey.senate.gov/ |
| Udall, Mark (CO) | markudall.senate.gov/ |
| Udall, Tom (NM) | tomudall.senate.gov/ |
| Vitter, David (LA) | vitter.senate.gov/ |
| Warner, John W. (VA) | warner.senate.gov/ |
| Webb, Jim (VA) | webb.senate.gov/ |
| Whitehouse, Sheldon (RI) | whitehouse.senate.gov/ |
| Wicker, Roger F. (MS) | wicker.senate.gov/ |
| Wyden, Ron (OR) | wyden.senate.gov/ |

# SENATE COMMITTEES

Room numbers beginning with SR are in the Russell Senate Office Building, room numbers beginning with SD are in the Dirksen Senate Office Building, and room numbers beginning with SH are in the Hart Senate Office Building.

## STANDING COMMITTEES

| | Phone | Room |
|---|---|---|
| Agriculture, Nutrition, and Forestry | 42035 | SR-328A |
| Appropriations | 47363 | S-128 |
| Armed Services | 43871 | SR-228 |
| Banking, Housing, and Urban Affairs | 47391 | SD-534 |
| Budget | 40642 | SD-624 |
| Commerce, Science, and Transportation | 40411 | SR-254 |
| Energy and Natural Resources | 44971 | SD-304 |
| Environment and Public Works | 48832 | SD-410 |
| Finance | 44515 | SD-219 |
| Foreign Relations | 44651 | SD-444 |
| Health, Education, Labor, and Pensions | 45375 | SD-428 |
| Homeland Security and Governmental Affairs | 42627 | SD-340 |
| Indian Affairs | 42251 | SH-838 |
| Judiciary | 47703 | SD-224 |
| Rules and Administration | 46352 | SR-305 |
| Small Business and Entrepreneurship | 45175 | SR-428A |
| Veterans' Affairs | 49126 | SR-412 |

## SPECIAL AND SELECT COMMITTEES

| | Phone | Room |
|---|---|---|
| Aging | 45364 | SD-G31 |
| Ethics | 42981 | SH-220 |
| Intelligence | 41700 | SH-211 |

## JOINT COMMITTEES

| | Phone | Room |
|---|---|---|
| Economic | 45171 | SD-G01 |
| Library | 46352 | SR-305 |
| Printing | 58281 | 1309 |
| Taxation | | |
| LHOB | 53621 | 1625 |
| DSOB | 45561 | SD-G18 |

# SENATE ORGANIZATION CHART

## Constitutionally Mandated Officers

- Vice President
- President Pro Tempore

## Political Party Leaders

- Majority Leader
- Majority Whip
- Democratic Conference
- Dem. Conference Cmte. Vice Chair & Policy Cmte. Chair
- Democratic Conference Secretary
- Minority Leader
- Minority Whip
- Republican Conference Chair
- Republican Conference Vice Chair
- Republican Policy Committee Chair

## Committee Chairmen and Ranking Members

### Standing Committees

- Agriculture, Nutrition, and Forestry
- Appropriations
- Armed Services
- Banking, Housing, and Urban Affairs
- Budget
- Commerce, Science, and Transportation
- Energy and Natural Resources
- Environment and Public Works
- Finance
- Foreign Relations
- Health, Education, Labor, and Pensions
- Homeland Security and Governmental Affairs
- Judiciary
- Rules and Administration
- Small Business
- Veterans' Affairs

### Special, Select, and Other Committees

- Select Committee on Ethics
- Select Committee on Intelligence
- Committee on Indian Affairs
- Special Committee on Aging

### Joint Committees

- Joint Economic Committee
- Joint Committee on Printing
- Joint Committee on Taxation
- Joint Committee on the Library
- Joint Select Committee on Deficit Reduction

## Senate-Elected Officers & Officials

- Secretary
- Sergeant at Arms
- Parliamentarian
- Secretary for the Majority
- Secretary for the Minority
- Chaplain

# COMPARISON OF SENATE LEGISLATIVE ACTIVITY

## 20-YEAR COMPARISON OF SENATE LEGISLATIVE ACTIVITY

| | 1991 | 1992 | 1993 | 1994 | 1995 | 1996 | 1997 | 1998 | 1999 | 2000 | 2001 | 2002 | 2003 | 2004 | 2005 | 2006 | 2007 | 2008 | 2009 | 2010 |
|---|---|---|---|---|---|---|---|---|---|---|---|---|---|---|---|---|---|---|---|---|
| Senate Convened | 1/3 | 1/3 | 1/5 | 1/25 | 1/4 | 1/3 | 1/3 | 1/27 | 1/6 | 1/24 | 1/3 | 1/23 | 1/7 | 1/20 | 1/4 | 1/3 | 1/4 | 1/3 | 1/6 | 1/5 |
| Senate Adjourned | 1/3/92 | 10/9 | 11/26 | 12/01 | 1/3/96 | 10/4 | 11/13 | 10/21 | 11/19 | 12/15 | 12/20 | 11/20 | 12/9 | 12/8 | 12/22 | 12/9 | 12/31 | 1/2 | 12/24 | 12/22 |
| Days in Session | 158 | 129 | 153 | 138 | 211 | 132 | 153 | 143 | 162 | 141 | 173 | 149 | 167 | 133 | 159 | 138 | 189 | 184 | 191 | 158 |
| Hours in Session | 1,200'44 | 1,091'09 | 1,269'41 | 1,243'33 | 1,839'10 | 1,036'45 | 1,093'07 | 1,095'05 | 1,183'57 | 1,017'51 | 1,236'15 | 1,043'23 | 1,454'05 | 1,031'31 | 1,222'26 | 1,027'48 | 1,375'54 | 988'31 | 1,420'39 | 1,074'40 |
| Average Hours per Day | 7.6 | 8.5 | 8.3 | 9.0 | 8.7 | 7.8 | 7.1 | 7.7 | 7.3 | 7.2 | 7.1 | 7.0 | 8.7 | 7.7 | 7.7 | 7.4 | 7.2 | 5.37 | 7.44 | 6.8 |
| Total Measures Passed | 626 | 651 | 473 | 465 | 346 | 476 | 386 | 506 | 549 | 696 | 425 | 523 | 590 | 663 | 624 | 635 | 621 | 589 | 478 | 569 |
| Roll Call Votes | 280 | 270 | 395 | 329 | 613 | 306 | 298 | 314 | 374 | 298 | 380 | 253 | 459 | 216 | 366 | 279 | 442 | 215 | 397 | 299 |
| Quorum Calls | 3 | 5 | 2 | 6 | 3 | 2 | 6 | 4 | 7 | 6 | 3 | 2 | 3 | 1 | 3 | 1 | 6 | 3 | 3 | 8 |
| Public Laws | 243 | 347 | 210 | 255 | 88 | 245 | 153 | 241 | 170 | 410 | 136 | 241 | 198 | 300 | 169 | 313 | 180 | 280 | 125 | 258 |
| Treaties Ratified | 15 | 32 | 20 | 8 | 10 | 28 | 15 | 53 | 13 | 39 | 3 | 17 | 11 | 15 | 6 | 14 | 8 | 30 | 1 | 6 |
| Nominations Confirmed | 45,369 | 30,619 | 38,676 | 37,446 | 40,535 | 33,176 | 25,576 | 20,302 | 22,468 | 22,512 | 25,091 | 23,633 | 21,580 | 24,420 | 25,942 | 29,603 | 22,892 | 21,785 | 23,051 | 23,327 |
| Average Voting Attendance | 97.16 | 95.4 | 97.6 | 97.02 | 98.07 | 98.22 | 98.68 | 97.47 | 98.02 | 96.99 | 98.29 | 96.36 | 96.07 | 95.54 | 97.41 | 97.13 | 94.99 | 94.36 | 96.99 | 95.88 |
| Sessions Convened Before 12 Noon | 126 | 112 | 128 | 120 | 184 | 113 | 115 | 109 | 118 | 107 | 140 | 119 | 133 | 104 | 121 | 110 | 156 | 147 | 148 | 116 |
| Sessions Convened at 12 Noon | 9 | 6 | 6 | 9 | 2 | 15 | 12 | 31 | 17 | 25 | 10 | 12 | 4 | 9 | 1 | 4 | 4 | 4 | 2 | 6 |
| Sessions Convened after 12 Noon | 23 | 10 | 15 | 17 | 12 | 7 | 7 | 2 | 19 | 24 | 21 | 23 | 23 | 21 | 36 | 24 | 32 | 33 | 41 | 36 |
| Sessions Continued after 6 p.m. | 102 | 91 | 100 | 100 | 158 | 88 | 96 | 93 | 113 | 94 | 108 | 103 | 134 | 129 | 120 | 129 | 144 | 110 | 152 | 116 |
| Sessions Continued after 12 Midnight | 4 | 9 | 7 | 3 | 1 | 0 | 0 | 0 | 0 | 2 | 3 | 8 | 2 | 3 | 3 | 4 | 4 | 2 | 2 | 1 |
| Saturday Sessions | 2 | 2 | 2 | 3 | 5 | 1 | 1 | 1 | 3 | 1 | 3 | 0 | 1 | 2 | 2 | 2 | 1 | 3 | 5 | 2 |
| Sunday Sessions | 0 | 0 | 0 | 0 | 3 | 0 | 1 | 0 | 0 | 1 | 0 | 0 | 1 | 1 | 2 | 0 | 1 | 1 | 4 | 1 |

Prepared by the Senate Daily Digest--Office of the Secretary--01/05/11

# U.S. HOUSE OF REPRESENTATIVES

## House Leadership

| | | | |
|---|---|---|---|
| Speaker | John Boehner | 202-225-0600 | www.speaker.gov |
| Majority Leader | Eric Cantor | 202-225-4000 | majorityleader.gov |
| Majority Whip | Kevin McCarthy | 202-226-2915 | republicanwhip.house.gov |
| Senior Chief Deputy Majority Whip | Peter Roskam | 202-226-4561 | roskam.house.gov |
| Minority Leader | Nancy Pelosi | 202-225-0100 | democraticleader.gov |
| Minority Whip | Steny Hoyer | 202-225-3130 | democraticwhip.gov |
| Chief Deputy Democratic Whip | Janice Schakowsky | 202-225-2111 | |

## Officers of the House

| | | | |
|---|---|---|---|
| Clerk of the House | Karen L. Haas | 202-225-7000 | H154 Capitol |
| Sergeant at Arms | Wilson Livingood | 202-225-2456 | H124 Capitol |
| Chief Administrative Officer | Dan Strodel | 202-225-6969 | HB28 Capitol |
| Chaplain | Rev. Patrick J. Conroy | 202-225-2509 | HB25 Capitol |

## Capitol Officials

| | | | |
|---|---|---|---|
| Architect of the Capitol | Stephen T. Ayers | 202-228-1793 | SB15 Capitol |
| Attending Physician | Dr. Brian Monahan | 202-225-5421 | H166 Capitol |

# REPRESENTATIVES

Republicans in roman; Democrats in *italic*; Resident Commissioner and Delegates in **boldface**.
The names of Members who have died or resigned appear in bold brackets [ ].
Three-digit room numbers are in the Cannon House Office Building, four-digit room numbers beginning with 1 are in the Longworth House Office Building, and four-digit numbers beginning with 2 are in the Rayburn House Office Building.
Calls from outside the Capitol complex can be made by dialing (202) 22 plus the five-digit number listed in this directory.

Washington, DC 20515

Compiled by KAREN L. HAAS, Clerk of the House
http://clerk.house.gov

| Name | Phone | Room | Name | Phone | Room |
|---|---|---|---|---|---|
| *Ackerman, Gary L.*, 5th NY | 52601 | 2111 | **Bordallo, Madeleine Z.** (Delegate), GU | 51188 | 2441 |
| Adams, Sandy, 24th FL | 52706 | 216 | *Boren, Dan*, 2d OK | 52701 | 2447 |
| Aderholt, Robert B., 4th AL | 54876 | 2264 | *Boswell, Leonard L.*, 3d IA | 53806 | 1026 |
| Akin, W. Todd, 2d MO | 52561 | 117 | Boustany, Charles W., Jr., 7th LA | 52031 | 1431 |
| Alexander, Rodney, 5th LA | 58490 | 316 | Brady, Kevin, 8th TX | 54901 | 301 |
| *Altmire, Jason*, 4th PA | 52565 | 332 | *Brady, Robert A.*, 1st PA | 54731 | 102 |
| Amash, Justin, 3d MI | 53831 | 114 | *Braley, Bruce L.*, 1st IA | 52911 | 1727 |
| *Andrews, Robert E.*, 1st NJ | 56501 | 2265 | Brooks, Mo, 5th AL | 54801 | 1641 |
| Austria, Steve, 7th OH | 54324 | 439 | Broun, Paul C., 10th GA | 54101 | 325 |
| *Baca, Joe*, 43d CA | 56161 | 2366 | *Brown, Corrine*, 3d FL | 50123 | 2336 |
| Bachmann, Michele, 6th MN | 52331 | 103 | Buchanan, Vern, 13th FL | 55015 | 221 |
| Bachus, Spencer, 6th AL | 54921 | 2246 | Bucshon, Larry, 8th IN | 54636 | 1123 |
| *Baldwin, Tammy*, 2d WI | 52906 | 2446 | Buerkle, Ann Marie, 25th NY | 53701 | 1630 |
| Barletta, Lou, 11th PA | 56511 | 510 | Burgess, Michael C., 26th TX | 57772 | 2241 |
| *Barrow, John*, 12th GA | 52823 | 2202 | Burton, Dan, 5th IN | 52276 | 2308 |
| Bartlett, Roscoe G., 6th MD | 52721 | 2412 | *Butterfield, G. K.*, 1st NC | 53101 | 2305 |
| Barton, Joe, 6th TX | 52002 | 2109 | Calvert, Ken, 44th CA | 51986 | 2269 |
| Bass, Charles F., 2d NH | 55206 | 2350 | Camp, Dave, 4th MI | 53561 | 341 |
| *Bass, Karen*, 33d CA | 57084 | 408 | Campbell, John, 48th CA | 55611 | 1507 |
| *Becerra, Xavier*, 31st CA | 56235 | 1226 | Canseco, Francisco "Quico", 23d TX | 54511 | 1339 |
| Benishek, Dan, 1st MI | 54735 | 514 | Cantor, Eric, 7th VA | 52815 | 303 |
| Berg, Rick, At Large, ND | 52611 | 323 | Capito, Shelley Moore, 2d WV | 52711 | 2443 |
| *Berkley, Shelley*, 1st NV | 55965 | 405 | *Capps, Lois*, 23d CA | 53601 | 2231 |
| *Berman, Howard L.*, 28th CA | 54695 | 2221 | *Capuano, Michael E.*, 8th MA | 55111 | 1414 |
| Biggert, Judy, 13th IL | 53515 | 2113 | *Cardoza, Dennis A.*, 18th CA | 56131 | 2437 |
| Bilbray, Brian P., 50th CA | 50508 | 2410 | *Carnahan, Russ*, 3d MO | 52671 | 1710 |
| Bilirakis, Gus M., 9th FL | 55755 | 407 | *Carney, John C., Jr.*, At Large, DE | 54165 | 1429 |
| Bishop, Rob, 1st UT | 50453 | 123 | *Carson, André*, 7th IN | 54011 | 425 |
| *Bishop, Sanford D., Jr.*, 2d GA | 53631 | 2429 | Carter, John R., 31st TX | 53864 | 409 |
| *Bishop, Timothy H.*, 1st NY | 53826 | 306 | Cassidy, Bill, 6th LA | 53901 | 1535 |
| Black, Diane, 6th TN | 54231 | 1531 | *Castor, Kathy*, 11th FL | 53376 | 137 |
| Blackburn, Marsha, 7th TN | 52811 | 217 | Chabot, Steve, 1st OH | 52216 | 2351 |
| *Blumenauer, Earl*, 3d OR | 54811 | 1502 | Chaffetz, Jason, 3d UT | 57751 | 1032 |
| Boehner, John A., 8th OH | 56205 | 1011 | *Chandler, Ben*, 6th KY | 54706 | 1504 |
| Bonner, Jo, 1st AL | 54931 | 2236 | **Christensen, Donna M.** (Delegate), VI | 51790 | 1510 |
| Bono Mack, Mary, 45th CA | 55330 | 104 | *Chu, Judy*, 32d CA | 55464 | 1520 |

# REPRESENTATIVES

| Name | Phone | Room |
|------|-------|------|
| *Cicilline, David N.*, 1st RI | 54911 | 128 |
| *Clarke, Hansen*, 13th MI | 52261 | 1319 |
| *Clarke, Yvette D.*, 11th NY | 56231 | 1029 |
| *Clay, Wm. Lacy*, 1st MO | 52406 | 2418 |
| *Cleaver, Emanuel*, 5th MO | 54535 | 1433 |
| *Clyburn, James E.*, 6th SC | 53315 | 2135 |
| Coble, Howard, 6th NC | 53065 | 2188 |
| Coffman, Mike, 6th CO | 57882 | 1222 |
| *Cohen, Steve*, 9th TN | 53265 | 1005 |
| Cole, Tom, 4th OK | 56165 | 2458 |
| Conaway, K. Michael, 11th TX | 53605 | 2430 |
| *Connolly, Gerald E.*, 11th VA | 51492 | 424 |
| *Conyers, John, Jr.*, 14th MI | 55126 | 2426 |
| *Cooper, Jim*, 5th TN | 54311 | 1536 |
| *Costa, Jim*, 20th CA | 53341 | 1314 |
| *Costello, Jerry F.*, 12th IL | 55661 | 2408 |
| *Courtney, Joe*, 2d CT | 52076 | 215 |
| *Cravaack, Chip*, 8th MN | 56211 | 508 |
| Crawford, Eric A. "Rick", 1st AR | 54076 | 1408 |
| Crenshaw, Ander, 4th FL | 52501 | 440 |
| *Critz, Mark S.*, 12th PA | 52065 | 1022 |
| *Crowley, Joseph*, 7th NY | 53965 | 2404 |
| *Cuellar, Henry*, 28th TX | 51640 | 2463 |
| Culberson, John Abney, 7th TX | 52571 | 2352 |
| *Cummings, Elijah E.*, 7th MD | 54741 | 2235 |
| *Davis, Danny K.*, 7th IL | 55006 | 2159 |
| Davis, Geoff, 4th KY | 53465 | 1119 |
| *Davis, Susan A.*, 53d CA | 52040 | 1526 |
| *DeFazio, Peter A.*, 4th OR | 56416 | 2134 |
| *DeGette, Diana*, 1st CO | 54431 | 2335 |
| *DeLauro, Rosa L.*, 3d CT | 53661 | 2413 |
| Denham, Jeff, 19th CA | 54540 | 1605 |
| Dent, Charles W., 15th PA | 56411 | 1009 |
| DesJarlais, Scott, 4th TN | 56831 | 413 |
| *Deutch, Theodore E.*, 19th FL | 53001 | 1024 |
| Diaz-Balart, Mario, 21st FL | 54211 | 436 |
| *Dicks, Norman D.*, 6th WA | 55916 | 2467 |
| *Dingell, John D.*, 15th MI | 54071 | 2328 |
| *Doggett, Lloyd*, 25th TX | 54865 | 201 |
| Dold, Robert J., 10th IL | 54835 | 212 |
| *Donnelly, Joe*, 2d IN | 53915 | 1530 |
| *Doyle, Michael F.*, 14th PA | 52135 | 401 |
| Dreier, David, 26th CA | 52305 | 233 |
| Duffy, Sean P., 7th WI | 53365 | 1208 |
| Duncan, Jeff, 3d SC | 55301 | 116 |
| Duncan, John J., Jr., 2d TN | 55435 | 2207 |
| *Edwards, Donna F.*, 4th MD | 58699 | 318 |
| *Ellison, Keith*, 5th MN | 54755 | 1027 |
| Ellmers, Renee L., 2d NC | 54531 | 1533 |
| Emerson, Jo Ann, 8th MO | 54404 | 2230 |
| *Engel, Eliot L.*, 17th NY | 52464 | 2161 |
| *Eshoo, Anna G.*, 14th CA | 58104 | 205 |
| ***Faleomavaega, Eni F. H.*** (Delegate), AS | 58577 | 2422 |
| Farenthold, Blake, 27th TX | 57742 | 2110 |
| *Farr, Sam*, 17th CA | 52861 | 1126 |
| *Fattah, Chaka*, 2d PA | 54001 | 2301 |
| *Filner, Bob*, 51st CA | 58045 | 2428 |
| Fincher, Stephen Lee, 8th TN | 54714 | 1118 |
| Fitzpatrick, Michael G., 8th PA | 54276 | 1224 |
| Flake, Jeff, 6th AZ | 52635 | 240 |
| Fleischmann, Charles J. "Chuck", 3d TN | 53271 | 511 |
| Fleming, John, 4th LA | 52777 | 416 |
| Flores, Bill, 17th TX | 56105 | 1505 |
| Forbes, J. Randy, 4th VA | 56365 | 2438 |
| Fortenberry, Jeff, 1st NE | 54806 | 1514 |
| Foxx, Virginia, 5th NC | 52071 | 1230 |
| *Frank, Barney*, 4th MA | 55931 | 2252 |
| Franks, Trent, 2d AZ | 54576 | 2435 |
| Frelinghuysen, Rodney P., 11th NJ | 55034 | 2369 |
| *Fudge, Marcia L.*, 11th OH | 57032 | 1019 |
| Gallegly, Elton, 24th CA | 55811 | 2309 |
| *Garamendi, John*, 10th CA | 51880 | 228 |
| Gardner, Cory, 4th CO | 54676 | 213 |
| Garrett, Scott, 5th NJ | 54465 | 2244 |
| Gerlach, Jim, 6th PA | 54315 | 2442 |
| Gibbs, Bob, 18th OH | 56265 | 329 |
| Gibson, Christopher P., 20th NY | 55614 | 502 |
| *Giffords, Gabrielle*, 8th AZ | 52542 | 1030 |
| Gingrey, Phil, 11th GA | 52931 | 442 |
| Gohmert, Louie, 1st TX | 53035 | 2440 |
| *Gonzalez, Charles A.*, 20th TX | 53236 | 1436 |
| Goodlatte, Bob, 6th VA | 55431 | 2240 |
| Gosar, Paul A., 1st AZ | 52315 | 504 |
| Gowdy, Trey, 4th SC | 56030 | 1237 |
| Granger, Kay, 12th TX | 55071 | 320 |
| Graves, Sam, 6th MO | 57041 | 1415 |
| Graves, Tom, 9th GA | 55211 | 1113 |
| *Green, Al*, 9th TX | 57508 | 2201 |
| *Green, Gene*, 29th TX | 51688 | 2470 |
| Griffin, Tim, 2d AR | 52506 | 1232 |
| Griffith, H. Morgan, 9th VA | 53861 | 1108 |
| *Grijalva, Raúl M.*, 7th AZ | 52435 | 1511 |
| Grimm, Michael G., 13th NY | 53371 | 512 |
| Guinta, Frank C., 1st NH | 55456 | 1223 |
| Guthrie, Brett, 2d KY | 53501 | 308 |
| *Gutierrez, Luis V.*, 4th IL | 58203 | 2266 |
| *Hahn, Janice*, 36th CA | 58220 | 2400 |
| Hall, Ralph M., 4th TX | 56673 | 2405 |
| *Hanabusa, Colleen W.*, 1st HI | 52726 | 238 |
| Hanna, Richard L., 24th NY | 53665 | 319 |

# REPRESENTATIVES

| Name | Phone | Room | Name | Phone | Room |
|---|---|---|---|---|---|
| Harper, Gregg, 3d MS | 55031 | 307 | Kline, John, 2d MN | 52271 | 2439 |
| Harris, Andy, 1st MD | 55311 | 506 | Kucinich, Dennis J., 10th OH | 55871 | 2445 |
| Hartzler, Vicky, 4th MO | 52876 | 1023 | Labrador, Raúl R., 1st ID | 56611 | 1523 |
| Hastings, Alcee L., 23d FL | 51313 | 2353 | Lamborn, Doug, 5th CO | 54422 | 437 |
| Hastings, Doc, 4th WA | 55816 | 1203 | Lance, Leonard, 7th NJ | 55361 | 426 |
| Hayworth, Nan A. S., 19th NY | 55441 | 1440 | Landry, Jeffrey M., 3d LA | 54031 | 206 |
| Heck, Joseph J., 3d NV | 53252 | 132 | Langevin, James R., 2d RI | 52735 | 109 |
| Heinrich, Martin, 1st NM | 56316 | 336 | Lankford, James, 5th OK | 52132 | 509 |
| [Heller, Dean], 2d NV | 56155 | 125 | Larsen, Rick, 2d WA | 52605 | 108 |
| Hensarling, Jeb, 5th TX | 53484 | 129 | Larson, John B., 1st CT | 52265 | 1501 |
| Herger, Wally, 2d CA | 53076 | 242 | Latham, Tom, 4th IA | 55476 | 2217 |
| Herrera Beutler, Jaime, 3d WA | 53536 | 1130 | LaTourette, Steven C., 14th OH | 55731 | 2371 |
| Higgins, Brian, 27th NY | 53306 | 2459 | Latta, Robert E., 5th OH | 56405 | 1323 |
| Himes, James A., 4th CT | 55541 | 119 | Lee, Barbara, 9th CA | 52661 | 2267 |
| Hinchey, Maurice D., 22d NY | 56335 | 2431 | Levin, Sander M., 12th MI | 54961 | 1236 |
| Hinojosa, Rubén, 15th TX | 52531 | 2262 | Lewis, Jerry, 41st CA | 55861 | 2112 |
| Hirono, Mazie K., 2d HI | 54906 | 1410 | Lewis, John, 5th GA | 53801 | 343 |
| Hochul, Kathleen C., 26th NY | 55265 | 1711 | Lipinski, Daniel, 3d IL | 55701 | 1717 |
| Holden, Tim, 17th PA | 55546 | 2417 | LoBiondo, Frank A., 2d NJ | 56572 | 2427 |
| Holt, Rush D., 12th NJ | 55801 | 1214 | Loebsack, David, 2d IA | 56576 | 1527 |
| Honda, Michael M., 15th CA | 52631 | 1713 | Lofgren, Zoe, 16th CA | 53072 | 1401 |
| Hoyer, Steny H., 5th MD | 54131 | 1705 | Long, Billy, 7th MO | 56536 | 1541 |
| Huelskamp, Tim, 1st KS | 52715 | 126 | Lowey, Nita M., 18th NY | 56506 | 2365 |
| Huizenga, Bill, 2d MI | 54401 | 1217 | Lucas, Frank D., 3d OK | 55565 | 2311 |
| Hultgren, Randy, 14th IL | 52976 | 427 | Luetkemeyer, Blaine, 9th MO | 52956 | 1740 |
| Hunter, Duncan, 52d CA | 55672 | 223 | Luján, Ben Ray, 3d NM | 56190 | 330 |
| Hurt, Robert, 5th VA | 54711 | 1516 | Lummis, Cynthia M., At Large, WY | 52311 | 113 |
| Inslee, Jay, 1st WA | 56311 | 2329 | Lungren, Daniel E., 3d CA | 55716 | 2313 |
| Israel, Steve, 2d NY | 53335 | 2457 | Lynch, Stephen F., 9th MA | 58273 | 2348 |
| Issa, Darrell E., 49th CA | 53906 | 2347 | Mack, Connie, 14th FL | 52536 | 115 |
| Jackson, Jesse L., Jr., 2d IL | 50773 | 2419 | Maloney, Carolyn B., 14th NY | 57944 | 2332 |
| Jackson Lee, Sheila, 18th TX | 53816 | 2160 | Manzullo, Donald A., 16th IL | 55676 | 2228 |
| Jenkins, Lynn, 2d KS | 56601 | 1122 | Marchant, Kenny, 24th TX | 56605 | 1110 |
| Johnson, Bill, 6th OH | 55705 | 317 | Marino, Tom, 10th PA | 53731 | 410 |
| Johnson, Eddie Bernice, 30th TX | 58885 | 2468 | Markey, Edward J., 7th MA | 52836 | 2108 |
| Johnson, Henry C. "Hank", Jr., 4th GA | 51605 | 1427 | Matheson, Jim, 2d UT | 53011 | 2434 |
| Johnson, Sam, 3d TX | 54201 | 1211 | Matsui, Doris O., 5th CA | 57163 | 222 |
| Johnson, Timothy V., 15th IL | 52371 | 1207 | McCarthy, Carolyn, 4th NY | 55516 | 2346 |
| Jones, Walter B., 3d NC | 53415 | 2333 | McCarthy, Kevin, 22d CA | 52915 | 326 |
| Jordan, Jim, 4th OH | 52676 | 1524 | McCaul, Michael T., 10th TX | 52401 | 131 |
| Kaptur, Marcy, 9th OH | 54146 | 2186 | McClintock, Tom, 4th CA | 52511 | 428 |
| Keating, William R., 10th MA | 53111 | 315 | McCollum, Betty, 4th MN | 56631 | 1714 |
| Kelly, Mike, 3d PA | 55406 | 515 | McCotter, Thaddeus G., 11th MI | 58171 | 2243 |
| Kildee, Dale E., 5th MI | 53611 | 2107 | McDermott, Jim, 7th WA | 53106 | 1035 |
| Kind, Ron, 3d WI | 55506 | 1406 | McGovern, James P., 3d MA | 56101 | 438 |
| King, Peter T., 3d NY | 57896 | 339 | McHenry, Patrick T., 10th NC | 52576 | 224 |
| King, Steve, 5th IA | 54426 | 1131 | McIntyre, Mike, 7th NC | 52731 | 2133 |
| Kingston, Jack, 1st GA | 55831 | 2372 | McKeon, Howard P. "Buck", 25th CA | 51956 | 2184 |
| Kinzinger, Adam, 11th IL | 53635 | 1218 | McKinley, David B., 1st WV | 54172 | 313 |
| Kissell, Larry, 8th NC | 53715 | 1632 | McMorris Rodgers, Cathy, 5th WA | 52006 | 2421 |

# REPRESENTATIVES

| Name | Phone | Room | Name | Phone | Room |
|---|---|---|---|---|---|
| *McNerney, Jerry*, 11th CA | 51947 | 1210 | Posey, Bill, 15th FL | 53671 | 120 |
| Meehan, Patrick, 7th PA | 52011 | 513 | *Price, David E.*, 4th NC | 51784 | 2162 |
| *Meeks, Gregory W.*, 6th NY | 53461 | 2234 | Price, Tom, 6th GA | 54501 | 403 |
| Mica, John L., 7th FL | 54035 | 2187 | Quayle, Benjamin, 3d AZ | 53361 | 1419 |
| *Michaud, Michael H.*, 2d ME | 56306 | 1724 | *Quigley, Mike*, 5th IL | 54061 | 1124 |
| *Miller, Brad*, 13th NC | 53032 | 1127 | *Rahall, Nick J., II*, 3d WV | 53452 | 2307 |
| Miller, Candice S., 10th MI | 52106 | 1034 | *Rangel, Charles B.*, 15th NY | 54365 | 2354 |
| Miller, Gary G., 42d CA | 53201 | 2349 | Reed, Tom, 29th NY | 53161 | 1037 |
| *Miller, George*, 7th CA | 52095 | 2205 | Rehberg, Denny, At Large, MT | 53211 | 2448 |
| Miller, Jeff, 1st FL | 54136 | 2416 | Reichert, David G., 8th WA | 57761 | 1730 |
| *Moore, Gwen*, 4th WI | 54572 | 2245 | Renacci, James B., 16th OH | 53876 | 130 |
| *Moran, James P.*, 8th VA | 54376 | 2239 | *Reyes, Silvestre*, 16th TX | 54831 | 2210 |
| Mulvaney, Mick, 5th SC | 55501 | 1004 | Ribble, Reid J., 8th WI | 55665 | 1513 |
| *Murphy, Christopher S.*, 5th CT | 54476 | 412 | *Richardson, Laura*, 37th CA | 57924 | 1330 |
| Murphy, Tim, 18th PA | 52301 | 322 | *Richmond, Cedric L.*, 2d LA | 56636 | 415 |
| Myrick, Sue Wilkins, 9th NC | 51976 | 230 | *Rigell, E. Scott*, 2d VA | 54215 | 327 |
| *Nadler, Jerrold*, 8th NY | 55635 | 2334 | *Rivera, David*, 25th FL | 52778 | 417 |
| *Napolitano, Grace F.*, 38th CA | 55256 | 1610 | *Roby, Martha*, 2d AL | 52901 | 414 |
| Neal, Richard E., 2d MA | 55601 | 2208 | *Roe, David P.*, 1st TN | 56356 | 419 |
| Neugebauer, Randy, 19th TX | 54005 | 1424 | Rogers, Harold, 5th KY | 54601 | 2406 |
| Noem, Kristi L., At Large, SD | 52801 | 226 | Rogers, Mike, 3d AL | 53261 | 324 |
| ***Norton, Eleanor Holmes*** (Delegate), DC ... | 58050 | 2136 | Rogers, Mike, 8th MI | 54872 | 133 |
| Nugent, Richard B., 5th FL | 51002 | 1517 | Rohrabacher, Dana, 46th CA | 52415 | 2300 |
| Nunes, Devin, 21st CA | 52523 | 1013 | Rokita, Todd, 4th IN | 55037 | 236 |
| Nunnelee, Alan, 1st MS | 54306 | 1432 | Rooney, Thomas J., 16th FL | 55792 | 1529 |
| Olson, Pete, 22d TX | 55951 | 312 | Roskam, Peter J., 6th IL | 54561 | 227 |
| *Olver, John W.*, 1st MA | 55335 | 1111 | Ros-Lehtinen, Ileana, 18th FL | 53931 | 2206 |
| *Owens, William L.*, 23d NY | 54611 | 431 | Ross, Dennis A., 12th FL | 51252 | 404 |
| Palazzo, Steven M., 4th MS | 55772 | 331 | *Ross, Mike*, 4th AR | 53772 | 2436 |
| *Pallone, Frank, Jr.*, 6th NJ | 54671 | 237 | *Rothman, Steven R.*, 9th NJ | 55061 | 2303 |
| *Pascrell, Bill, Jr.*, 8th NJ | 55751 | 2370 | *Roybal-Allard, Lucille*, 34th CA | 51766 | 2330 |
| *Pastor, Ed*, 4th AZ | 54065 | 2465 | Royce, Edward R., 40th CA | 54111 | 2185 |
| Paul, Ron, 14th TX | 52831 | 203 | Runyan, Jon, 3d NJ | 54765 | 1239 |
| Paulsen, Erik, 3d MN | 52871 | 127 | *Ruppersberger, C. A. Dutch*, 2d MD | 53061 | 2453 |
| *Payne, Donald M.*, 10th NJ | 53436 | 2310 | *Rush, Bobby L.*, 1st IL | 54372 | 2268 |
| Pearce, Stevan, 2d NM | 52365 | 2432 | Ryan, Paul, 1st WI | 53031 | 1233 |
| *Pelosi, Nancy*, 8th CA | 54965 | 235 | *Ryan, Tim*, 17th OH | 55261 | 1421 |
| Pence, Mike, 6th IN | 53021 | 100 | ***Sablan, Gregorio Kilili Camacho*** | | |
| *Perlmutter, Ed*, 7th CO | 52645 | 1221 | (Delegate), MP | 52646 | 423 |
| Peters, Gary C., 9th MI | 55802 | 1609 | *Sánchez, Linda T.*, 39th CA | 56676 | 2423 |
| *Peterson, Collin C.*, 7th MN | 52165 | 2211 | *Sanchez, Loretta*, 47th CA | 52965 | 1114 |
| Petri, Thomas E., 6th WI | 52476 | 2462 | *Sarbanes, John P.*, 3d MD | 54016 | 2444 |
| ***Pierluisi, Pedro R.*** (Resident Commissioner), PR | 52615 | 1213 | Scalise, Steve, 1st LA | 53015 | 429 |
| *Pingree, Chellie*, 1st ME | 56116 | 1318 | *Schakowsky, Janice D.*, 9th IL | 52111 | 2367 |
| Pitts, Joseph R., 16th PA | 52411 | 420 | *Schiff, Adam B.*, 29th CA | 54176 | 2411 |
| Platts, Todd Russell, 19th PA | 55836 | 2455 | Schilling, Robert T., 17th IL | 55905 | 507 |
| Poe, Ted, 2d TX | 56565 | 430 | Schmidt, Jean, 2d OH | 53164 | 2464 |
| *Polis, Jared*, 2d CO | 52161 | 501 | Schock, Aaron, 18th IL | 56201 | 328 |
| Pompeo, Mike, 4th KS | 56216 | 107 | *Schrader, Kurt*, 5th OR | 55711 | 314 |
| | | | *Schwartz, Allyson Y.*, 13th PA | 56111 | 1227 |

# REPRESENTATIVES

| Name | Phone | Room | Name | Phone | Room |
|------|-------|------|------|-------|------|
| Schweikert, David, 5th AZ | 52190 | 1205 | *Tonko, Paul*, 21st NY | 55076 | 422 |
| Scott, Austin, 8th GA | 56531 | 516 | *Towns, Edolphus*, 10th NY | 55936 | 2232 |
| *Scott, David*, 13th GA | 52939 | 225 | *Tsongas, Niki*, 5th MA | 53411 | 1607 |
| *Scott, Robert C. "Bobby"*, 3d VA | 58351 | 1201 | Turner, Michael R., 3d OH | 56465 | 2454 |
| Scott, Tim, 1st SC | 53176 | 1117 | Upton, Fred, 6th MI | 53761 | 2183 |
| Sensenbrenner, F. James, Jr., 5th WI | 55101 | 2449 | *Van Hollen, Chris*, 8th MD | 55341 | 1707 |
| *Serrano, José E.*, 16th NY | 54361 | 2227 | *Velázquez, Nydia M.*, 12th NY | 52361 | 2302 |
| Sessions, Pete, 32d TX | 52231 | 2233 | *Visclosky, Peter J.*, 1st IN | 52461 | 2256 |
| *Sewell, Terri A.*, 7th AL | 52665 | 1133 | Walberg, Tim, 7th MI | 56276 | 418 |
| *Sherman, Brad*, 27th CA | 55911 | 2242 | Walden, Greg, 2d OR | 56730 | 2182 |
| Shimkus, John, 19th IL | 55271 | 2452 | Walsh, Joe, 8th IL | 53711 | 432 |
| *Shuler, Heath*, 11th NC | 56401 | 229 | *Walz, Timothy J.*, 1st MN | 52472 | 1722 |
| Shuster, Bill, 9th PA | 52431 | 204 | *Wasserman Schultz, Debbie*, 20th FL | 57931 | 118 |
| Simpson, Michael K., 2d ID | 55531 | 2312 | *Waters, Maxine*, 35th CA | 52201 | 2344 |
| *Sires, Albio*, 13th NJ | 57919 | 2342 | *Watt, Melvin L.*, 12th NC | 51510 | 2304 |
| *Slaughter, Louise McIntosh*, 28th NY | 53615 | 2469 | *Waxman, Henry A.*, 30th CA | 53976 | 2204 |
| *Smith, Adam*, 9th WA | 58901 | 2402 | Webster, Daniel, 8th FL | 52176 | 1039 |
| Smith, Adrian, 3d NE | 56435 | 503 | [*Weiner, Anthony D.*], 9th NY | 56616 | 2104 |
| Smith, Christopher H., 4th NJ | 53765 | 2373 | *Welch, Peter*, At Large, VT | 54115 | 1404 |
| Smith, Lamar, 21st TX | 54236 | 2409 | West, Allen B., 22d FL | 53026 | 1708 |
| Southerland, Steve, II, 2d FL | 55235 | 1229 | Westmoreland, Lynn A., 3d GA | 55901 | 2433 |
| *Speier, Jackie*, 12th CA | 53531 | 211 | Whitfield, Ed, 1st KY | 53115 | 2368 |
| *Stark, Fortney Pete*, 13th CA | 55065 | 239 | *Wilson, Frederica S.*, 17th FL | 54506 | 208 |
| Stearns, Cliff, 6th FL | 55744 | 2306 | Wilson, Joe, 2d SC | 52452 | 2229 |
| Stivers, Steve, 15th OH | 52015 | 1007 | Wittman, Robert J., 1st VA | 54261 | 1317 |
| Stutzman, Marlin A., 3d IN | 54436 | 1728 | Wolf, Frank R., 10th VA | 55136 | 241 |
| Sullivan, John, 1st OK | 52211 | 434 | Womack, Steve, 3d AR | 54301 | 1508 |
| *Sutton, Betty*, 13th OH | 53401 | 1519 | Woodall, Rob, 7th GA | 54272 | 1725 |
| Terry, Lee, 2d NE | 54155 | 2331 | *Woolsey, Lynn C.*, 6th CA | 55161 | 2263 |
| *Thompson, Bennie G.*, 2d MS | 55876 | 2466 | [*Wu, David*], 1st OR | 50855 | 2338 |
| Thompson, Glenn, 5th PA | 55121 | 124 | *Yarmuth, John A.*, 3d KY | 55401 | 435 |
| *Thompson, Mike*, 1st CA | 53311 | 231 | Yoder, Kevin, 3d KS | 52865 | 214 |
| Thornberry, Mac, 13th TX | 53706 | 2209 | Young, C. W. Bill, 10th FL | 55961 | 2407 |
| Tiberi, Patrick J., 12th OH | 55355 | 106 | Young, Don, At Large, AK | 55765 | 2314 |
| *Tierney, John F.*, 6th MA | 58020 | 2238 | Young, Todd C., 9th IN | 55315 | 1721 |
| Tipton, Scott R., 3d CO | 54761 | 218 | | | |

# REPRESENTATIVES' WEB ADDRESSES
### (in state order)

All representatives can be reached by email at www.house.gov/writerep

| | URL |
|---|---|
| AK Young, Don | donyoung.house.gov/ |
| AL Bonner, Jo | bonner.house.gov/ |
| AL Roby, Martha | roby.house.gov/ |
| AL Rogers, Michael | mike-rogers.house.gov/ |
| AL Aderholt, Robert | aderholt.house.gov/ |
| AL Brooks, Mo | brooks.house.gov/ |
| AL Bachus, Spencer | bachus.house.gov/ |
| AL Sewell, Terri A. | sewell.house.gov/ |
| AR Crawford, Rick | crawford.house.gov/ |
| AR Griffin, Tim | griffin.house.gov/ |
| AR Womack, Steve | womack.house.gov/ |
| AR Ross, Mike | ross.house.gov/ |
| AS Faleomavaega, Eni F.H. | www.house.gov/faleomavaega/ |
| AZ Flake, Jeff | flake.house.gov/ |
| AZ Pastor, Ed | www.pastor.house.gov/ |
| AZ Gosar, Paul R. | gosar.house.gov/ |
| AZ Quayle, Ben | quayle.house.gov/ |
| AZ Franks, Trent | www.franks.house.gov/ |
| AZ Grijalva, Raul | grijalva.house.gov/ |
| AZ Giffords, Gabrielle | giffords.house.gov/ |
| AZ Schweikert, David | schweikert.house.gov/ |
| CA Thompson, Mike | mikethompson.house.gov |
| CA Herger, Walter W. | herger.house.gov/ |
| CA Costa, Jim | costa.house.gov/ |
| CA McClintock, Tom | mcclintock.house.gov/ |
| CA Matsui, Doris O. | matsui.house.gov/ |
| CA Woolsey, Lynn | woolsey.house.gov/ |
| CA Miller, George | georgemiller.house.gov/ |
| CA Pelosi, Nancy | pelosi.house.gov/ |
| CA Lee, Barbara | lee.house.gov/ |
| CA Garamendi, John | garamendi.house.gov/ |
| CA Speier, Jackie | speier.house.gov/ |
| CA Stark, Fortney Pete | www.stark.house.gov/ |
| CA Eshoo, Anna G. | eshoo.house.gov/ |
| CA Honda, Michael | honda.house.gov/ |
| CA Lofgren, Zoe | lofgren.house.gov/ |
| CA Farr, Sam | www.farr.house.gov/ |
| CA Cardoza, Dennis | cardoza.house.gov/ |
| CA Denham, Jeff | denham.house.gov/ |
| CA Lungren, Daniel E. | lungren.house.gov/ |
| CA Nunes, Devin | nunes.house.gov/ |
| CA Capps, Lois | capps.house.gov/ |
| CA Gallegly, Elton | www.house.gov/gallegly/ |
| CA Sherman, Brad | bradsherman.house.gov/ |
| CA McKeon, Howard P. "Buck" | mckeon.house.gov/ |
| CA Berman, Howard L. | www.house.gov/berman/ |
| CA Schiff, Adam | schiff.house.gov/ |
| CA Dreier, David | dreier.house.gov/ |
| CA Waxman, Henry A. | www.henrywaxman.house.gov/ |
| CA Becerra, Xavier | becerra.house.gov/ |
| CA VACANCY | |
| CA Chu, Judy | chu.house.gov/ |
| CA Roybal-Allard, Lucille | roybal-allard.house.gov/ |

# REPRESENTATIVES' WEB ADDRESSES

URL

| | |
|---|---|
| CA Napolitano, Grace | napolitano.house.gov/ |
| CA Waters, Maxine | waters.house.gov/ |
| CA Bass, Karen | karenbass.house.gov/ |
| CA Richardson, Laura | richardson.house.gov/ |
| CA Sanchez, Linda | lindasanchez.house.gov/ |
| CA Royce, Ed | www.royce.house.gov/ |
| CA Lewis, Jerry | jerrylewis.house.gov/ |
| CA Miller, Gary | garymiller.house.gov/ |
| CA Baca, Joe | baca.house.gov/ |
| CA Calvert, Ken | calvert.house.gov/ |
| CA Bono, Mary | bono.house.gov/ |
| CA Rohrabacher, Dana | rohrabacher.house.gov/ |
| CA Sanchez, Loretta | lorettasanchez.house.gov/ |
| CA Issa, Darrell | issa.house.gov/ |
| CA Davis, Susan | www.house.gov/susandavis/ |
| CA Filner, Bob | filner.house.gov/ |
| CA Hunter, Duncan D. | hunter.house.gov/ |
| CA Bilbray, Brian P. | bilbray.house.gov/ |
| CA Campbell, John | www.campbell.house.gov/ |
| CA McCarthy, Kevin | kevinmccarthy.house.gov/ |
| CA McNerney, Jerry | mcnerney.house.gov/ |
| CO DeGette, Diana | degette.house.gov/ |
| CO Tipton, Scott | tipton.house.gov/ |
| CO Gardner, Cory | gardner.house.gov/ |
| CO Polis, Jared | polis.house.gov/ |
| CO Coffman, Mike | coffman.house.gov/ |
| CO Lamborn, Doug | lamborn.house.gov/ |
| CO Perlmutter, Ed | perlmutter.house.gov/ |
| CT Larson, John | www.larson.house.gov/ |
| CT DeLauro, Rosa L. | delauro.house.gov/ |
| CT Himes, Jim | himes.house.gov/ |
| CT Courtney, Joe | courtney.house.gov/ |
| CT Murphy, Christopher S. | chrismurphy.house.gov/ |
| DC Norton, Eleanor Homes | www.norton.house.gov/ |
| DE Carney, John | johncarney.house.gov/ |
| FL Southerland, Steve | southerland.house.gov/ |
| FL Brown, Corrine | corrinebrown.house.gov/ |
| FL Crenshaw, Ander | crenshaw.house.gov/ |
| FL Miller, Jeff | jeffmiller.house.gov/ |
| FL Nugent, Richard | nugent.house.gov/ |
| FL Stearns, Clifford B. | stearns.house.gov/ |
| FL Mica, John L. | mica.house.gov/ |
| FL Webster, Daniel | webster.house.gov/ |
| FL Ross, Dennis | dennisross.house.gov/ |
| FL Young, C.W. | www.house.gov/young/ |
| FL Wilson, Frederica | wilson.house.gov/ |
| FL Mack, Connie | mack.house.gov/ |
| FL Posey, Bill | posey.house.gov/ |
| FL Deutch, Ted | teddeutch.house.gov/ |
| FL Ros-Lehtinen, Ileana | ros-lehtinen.house.gov/ |
| FL West, Allen | west.house.gov/ |
| FL Wasserman Schultz, Debbie | wassermanschultz.house.gov/ |
| FL Adams, Sandy | adams.house.gov/ |
| FL Hastings, Alcee L. | www.alceehastings.house.gov/ |
| FL Rooney, Tom | rooney.house.gov/ |
| FL Diaz-Balart, Mario | mariodiazbalart.house.gov/ |
| FL Bilirakis, Gus M. | bilirakis.house.gov/ |
| FL Buchanan, Vern | buchanan.house.gov/ |
| FL Castor, Kathy | castor.house.gov/ |
| FL Rivera, David | rivera.house.gov/ |

# REPRESENTATIVES' WEB ADDRESSES

URL

| | |
|---|---|
| GA Kingston, Jack | kingston.house.gov/ |
| GA Bishop, Jr., Sanford D. | bishop.house.gov/ |
| GA Barrow, John | barrow.house.gov/ |
| GA Woodall, Robert | woodall.house.gov/ |
| GA Lewis, John | johnlewis.house.gov/ |
| GA Price, Tom | tomprice.house.gov/ |
| GA Gingrey, Phil | gingrey.house.gov/ |
| GA Westmoreland, Lynn A. | westmoreland.house.gov/ |
| GA Scott, David | davidscott.house.gov/ |
| GA Scott, Austin | austinscott.house.gov/ |
| GA Broun, Paul C. | broun.house.gov/ |
| GA Graves, Tom | tomgraves.house.gov/ |
| GA Johnson, Jr., Henry C. "Hank" | hankjohnson.house.gov/ |
| GU Bordallo, Madeleine | www.house.gov/bordallo/ |
| HI Hanabusa, Colleen | hanabusa.house.gov/ |
| HI Hirono, Mazie, K. | hirono.house.gov/ |
| IA Boswell, Leonard | boswell.house.gov/ |
| IA King, Steve | steveking.house.gov/ |
| IA Latham, Tom | www.tomlatham.house.gov/ |
| IA Braley, Bruce L. | braley.house.gov/ |
| IA Loebsack, David | loebsack.house.gov/ |
| ID Simpson, Mike | simpson.house.gov/ |
| ID Labrador, Raul R. | labrador.house.gov/ |
| IL Rush, Bobby L. | rush.house.gov/ |
| IL Jackson, Jr., Jesse | jackson.house.gov/ |
| IL Lipinski, Daniel | www.lipinski.house.gov/ |
| IL Gutierrez, Luis V. | luisgutierrez.house.gov/ |
| IL Walsh, Joe | walsh.house.gov/ |
| IL Dold, Robert | dold.house.gov/ |
| IL Davis, Danny K. | davis.house.gov/ |
| IL Kinzinger, Adam | kinzinger.house.gov/ |
| IL Schakowsky, Jan | schakowsky.house.gov/ |
| IL Hultgren, Randy | hultgren.house.gov/ |
| IL Quigley, Mike | quigley.house.gov/ |
| IL Costello, Jerry F. | www.costello.house.gov/ |
| IL Biggert, Judy | biggert.house.gov/ |
| IL Schock, Aaron | schock.house.gov/ |
| IL Johnson, Timothy V. | timjohnson.house.gov/ |
| IL Manzullo, Donald | manzullo.house.gov/ |
| IL Shimkus, John | shimkus.house.gov/ |
| IL Schilling, Bobby | schilling.house.gov/ |
| IL Roskam, Peter J. | roskam.house.gov/ |
| IN Visclosky, Peter J. | visclosky.house.gov/ |
| IN Pence, Mike | mikepence.house.gov/ |
| IN Stutzman, Marlin | stutzman.house.gov/ |
| IN Rokita, Todd | rokita.house.gov/ |
| IN Burton, Daniel | burton.house.gov/ |
| IN Carson, Andre | carson.house.gov/ |
| IN Donnelly, Joe | donnelly.house.gov/ |
| IN Bucshon, Larry | bucshon.house.gov/ |
| IN Young, Todd | toddyoung.house.gov/ |
| KS Huelskamp, Tim | huelskamp.house.gov/ |
| KS Yoder, Kevin | yoder.house.gov/ |
| KS Pompeo, Mike | pompeo.house.gov/ |
| KS Jenkins, Lynn | lynnjenkins.house.gov/ |

# REPRESENTATIVES' WEB ADDRESSES

URL

| | |
|---|---|
| KY Whitfield, Edward | whitfield.house.gov/ |
| KY Guthrie, S. Brett | guthrie.house.gov/ |
| KY Chandler, Ben | chandler.house.gov/ |
| KY Rogers, Harold | halrogers.house.gov/ |
| KY Davis, Geoff | geoffdavis.house.gov/ |
| KY Yarmuth, John A. | yarmuth.house.gov/ |
| LA Boustany, Jr., Charles W. | boustany.house.gov/ |
| LA Richmond, Cedric | richmond.house.gov/ |
| LA Cassidy, William | cassidy.house.gov/ |
| LA Fleming, John | fleming.house.gov/ |
| LA Alexander, Rodney | alexander.house.gov/ |
| LA Scalise, Steve | www.scalise.house.gov/ |
| LA Landry, Jeffrey | landry.house.gov/ |
| MA Olver, John W. | olver.house.gov/ |
| MA Neal, Richard E. | neal.house.gov/ |
| MA McGovern, James | mcgovern.house.gov/ |
| MA Frank, Barney | www.house.gov/frank/ |
| MA Tierney, John | tierney.house.gov/ |
| MA Markey, Edward J. | markey.house.gov/ |
| MA Capuano, Michael E. | www.house.gov/capuano/ |
| MA Keating, William | keating.house.gov/ |
| MA Lynch, Stephen F. | lynch.house.gov/ |
| MA Tsongas, Niki | tsongas.house.gov |
| MD Edwards, Donna F. | donnaedwards.house.gov/ |
| MD Ruppersberger, Dutch | dutch.house.gov/ |
| MD Harris, Andy | harris.house.gov/ |
| MD Hoyer, Steny H. | hoyer.house.gov/ |
| MD Bartlett, Roscoe G. | bartlett.house.gov/ |
| MD Cummings, Elijah | cummings.house.gov/ |
| MD Van Hollen, Christopher | vanhollen.house.gov/ |
| MD Sarbanes, John P. | sarbanes.house.gov/ |
| ME Pingree, Chellie | pingree.house.gov/ |
| ME Michaud, Michael | michaud.house.gov/ |
| MI Benishek, Dan | benishek.house.gov/ |
| MI Huizenga, Bill | huizenga.house.gov/ |
| MI Amash, Justin | amash.house.gov/ |
| MI Camp, David Lee | camp.house.gov/ |
| MI Upton, Frederick S. | upton.house.gov/ |
| MI Rogers, Mike | mikerogers.house.gov/ |
| MI Kildee, Dale E. | kildee.house.gov/ |
| MI Miller, Candice | candicemiller.house.gov/ |
| MI Peters, Gary | peters.house.gov/ |
| MI Levin, Sander M. | levin.house.gov/ |
| MI McCotter, Thaddeus | mccotter.house.gov/ |
| MI Conyers, Jr., John | conyers.house.gov/ |
| MI Walberg, Tim | walberg.house.gov/ |
| MI Dingell, John D. | dingell.house.gov/ |
| MI Clark, Hansen | hansenclark.house.gov/ |
| MN Paulsen, Erik | paulsen.house.gov/ |
| MN McCollum, Betty | www.mccollum.house.gov/ |
| MN Kline, John | kline.house.gov/ |
| MN Peterson, Collin C. | collinpeterson.house.gov/ |
| MN Cravaack, Chip | cravaack.house.gov/ |
| MN Bachmann, Michele | bachmann.house.gov/ |
| MN Ellison, Keith | ellison.house.gov/ |
| MN Walz, Timothy J. | walz.house.gov/ |
| MO Clay, Jr. William "Lacy" | lacyclay.house.gov/ |
| MO Akin, Todd | akin.house.gov/ |
| MO Carnahan, Russ | carnahan.house.gov/ |
| MO Hartzler, Vicky | hartzler.house.gov/ |

# REPRESENTATIVES' WEB ADDRESSES

URL

| | |
|---|---|
| MO Cleaver, Emanuel | www.house.gov/cleaver/ |
| MO Graves, Sam | www.house.gov/graves/ |
| MO Long, Billy | long.house.gov/ |
| MO Emerson, Jo Ann | emerson.house.gov/ |
| MO Luetkemeyer, Blaine | luetkemeyer.house.gov/ |
| MS Nunnelee, Alan | nunnelee.house.gov/ |
| MS Thompson, Bennie G. | benniethompson.house.gov/ |
| MS Harper, Gregg | harper.house.gov/ |
| MS Palazzo, Steven | palazzo.house.gov/ |
| MT Rehberg, Dennis | rehberg.house.gov/ |
| NC Butterfield, G.K. | butterfield.house.gov/ |
| NC Ellmers, Renee | ellmers.house.gov/ |
| NC Jones, Walter B. | jones.house.gov/ |
| NC Price, David | price.house.gov/ |
| NC Foxx, Virginia | foxx.house.gov/ |
| NC Coble, Howard | coble.house.gov/ |
| NC McIntyre, Mike | mcintyre.house.gov/ |
| NC Kissel, Larry | kissel.house.gov/ |
| NC Myrick, Sue | myrick.house.gov/ |
| NC McHenry, Patrick T. | mchenry.house.gov/ |
| NC Watt, Melvin | watt.house.gov/ |
| NC Miller, Brad | bradmiller.house.gov/ |
| NC Shuler, Heath | shuler.house.gov/ |
| ND Berg, Rick | berg.house.gov/ |
| NE Fortenberry, Jeff | fortenberry.house.gov/ |
| NE Terry, Lee | leeterry.house.gov/ |
| NE Smith, Adrian | www.adriansmith.house.gov/ |
| NH Guinta, Frank | guinta.house.gov/ |
| NH Bass, Charles | bass.house.gov/ |
| NJ Andrews, Robert E. | www.house.gov/andrews/ |
| NJ LoBiondo, Frank | www.house.gov/lobiondo/ |
| NJ Runyon, Jon | runyon.house.gov/ |
| NJ Smith, Christopher | chrissmith.house.gov/ |
| NJ Garrett, Scott | garrett.house gov/ |
| NJ Pallone, Jr., Frank | www.house.gov/pallone/ |
| NJ Lance, Leonard | lance.house.gov/ |
| NJ Pascrell, Jr., William | pascrell.house.gov/ |
| NJ Rothman, Steven | rothman.house.gov/ |
| NJ Payne, Donald M. | payne.house.gov/ |
| NJ Frelinghuysen, Rodney | frelinghuysen.house.gov/ |
| NJ Holt, Rush | holt.house.gov/ |
| NJ Sires, Albio | sires.house.gov/ |
| NM Heinrich, Martin T. | heinrich.house.gov/ |
| NM Lujan, Ben R. | lujan.house.gov/ |
| NM Pearce, Steve | pearce.house.gov/ |
| NV Berkley, Shelley | berkley.house.gov/ |
| NV Heck, Joe | heck.house.gov/ |
| NV VACANCY | |
| NY Bishop, Tim | timbishop.house.gov/ |
| NY Israel, Steve | israel.house.gov/ |
| NY King, Peter T. | peteking.house.gov/ |
| NY McCarthy, Carolyn | carolynmccarthy.house.gov/ |
| NY Ackerman, Gary L. | ackerman.house.gov/ |
| NY Meeks, Gregory | www.house.gov/meeks/ |
| NY Crowley, Joseph | crowley.house.gov/ |
| NY Nadler, Jerrold | nadler.house.gov/ |
| NY VACANCY | |
| NY Towns, Edolphus | towns.house.gov/ |
| NY Velazquez, Nydia M. | velazquez.house.gov/ |
| NY Grimm, Michael | grimm.house.gov/ |

# REPRESENTATIVES' WEB ADDRESSES

URL

| | |
|---|---|
| NY Maloney, Carolyn B. | maloney.house.gov/ |
| NY Rangel, Charles B. | rangel.house.gov/ |
| NY Serrano, Jose E. | serrano.house.gov/ |
| NY Engel, Eliot L. | engel.house.gov/ |
| NY Lowey, Nita M. | lowey.house.gov/ |
| NY Hayworth, Nan | hayworth.house.gov/ |
| NY Gibson, Chris | gibson.house.gov/ |
| NY Owens, Bill | owens.house.gov/ |
| NY Hanna, Richard | hanna.house.gov/ |
| NY Hinchey, Maurice D. | hinchey.house.gov/ |
| NY Buerkle, Ann Marie | buerkle.house.gov/ |
| NY Slaughter, Louise M. | www.louise.house.gov/ |
| NY Higgins, Brian | higgins.house.gov/ |
| NY Tonko, Paul D. | tonko.house.gov/ |
| NY Hochul, Kathy | hochul.house.gov/ |
| NY Clarke, Yvette D. | clarke.house.gov/ |
| NY Reed, Tom | reed.house.gov/ |
| OH Austria, Steve | austria.house.gov/ |
| OH Turner, Mike | turner.house.gov/ |
| OH Chabot, Steve | chabot.house.gov/ |
| OH Boehner, John Andrew | johnboehner.house.gov/ |
| OH Kaptur, Marcy | kaptur.house.gov/ |
| OH Kucinich, Dennis J. | kucinich.house.gov/ |
| OH Tiberi, Patrick | tiberi.house.gov/ |
| OH Johnson, Bill | billjohnson.house.gov/ |
| OH Fudge, Marcia L. | fudge.house.gov/ |
| OH Ryan, Tim | timryan.house.gov/ |
| OH LaTourette, Steven C. | latourette.house.gov/ |
| OH Jordan, Jim | jordan.house.gov/ |
| OH Stivers, Steve | stivers.house.gov/ |
| OH Sutton, Betty | sutton.house.gov/ |
| OH Renacci, Jim | renacci.house.gov/ |
| OH Schmidt, Jean | www.house.gov/schmidt/ |
| OH Latta, Robert E. | latta.house.gov/ |
| OH Gibbs, Bob | gibbs.house.gov/ |
| OK Sullivan, John | sullivan.house.gov/ |
| OK Boren, Dan | boren.house.gov/ |
| OK Cole, Ton | cole.house.gov/ |
| OK Lucas, Frank | www.house.gov/lucas/ |
| OK Lankford, James | landford.house.gov/ |
| OR Wu, David | www.house.gov/wu/ |
| OR Walden, Gregory | walden.house.gov/ |
| OR Blumenauer, Earl | blumenauer.house.gov/ |
| OR DeFazio, Peter A. | www.defazio.house.gov/ |
| OR Schrader, Kurt | schrader.house.gov/ |
| PA Brady, Robert | www.brady.house.gov/ |
| PA Fattah, Chaka | fattah.house.gov/ |
| PA Gerlach, Jim | gerlach.house.gov/ |
| PA Kelly, Mike | kelly.house.gov/ |
| PA Holden, Tim | www.holden.house.gov/ |
| PA Dent, Charles W. | dent.house.gov/ |
| PA Shuster, Bill | shuster.house.gov/ |
| PA Meehan, Pat | meehan.house.gov/ |
| PA Fitzpatrick, Michael G. | fitzpatrick.house.gov/ |
| PA Murphy, Tim | murphy.house.gov/ |
| PA Schwartz, Allyson L. | schwartz.house.gov/ |
| PA Pitts, Joseph R. | www.house.gov/pitts/ |
| PA Doyle, Mike | doyle.house.gov/ |
| PA Platts, Todd | www.house.gov/platts/ |
| PA Thompson, Glenn W. | thompson.house.gov/ |

# REPRESENTATIVES' WEB ADDRESSES

URL

| | |
|---|---|
| PA Altmire, Jason | almire.house.gov/ |
| PA Marino, Tom | marino.house.gov/ |
| PA Barletta, Lou | barletta.house.gov/ |
| PA Critz, Mark | critz.house.gov/ |
| PR Pierluisi, Pedro | pierluisi.house.gov/ |
| RI Cicilline, David | cicilline.house.gov/ |
| RI Langevin, James | langevin.house.gov/ |
| SC Scott, Tim | timscott.house.gov/ |
| SC Wilson, Joe | joewilson.house.gov/ |
| SC Duncan, Jeff | jeffduncan.house.gov/ |
| SC Gowdy, Trey | gowdy.house.gov/ |
| SC Mulvaney, Mick | mulvaney.house.gov/ |
| SC Clyburn, James E. | clyburn.house.gov/ |
| SD Noem, Kristi | noem.house.gov/ |
| TN Duncan, Jr., John J. | duncan.house.gov/ |
| TN Fleischmann, Chuck | fleischmann.house.gov/ |
| TN DesJarlais, Scott | desjarlais.house.gov/ |
| TN Cooper, Jim | cooper.house.gov/ |
| TN Black, Diane | black.house.gov/ |
| TN Blackburn, Marsha | blackburn.house.gov/ |
| TN Fincher, Stephen | fincher.house.gov/ |
| TN Cohen, Steve | cohen.house.gov/ |
| TN Roe, Phil | roe.house.gov/ |
| TX Conaway, K. Michael | conaway.house.gov/ |
| TX Cuellar, Henry | cuellar.house.gov/ |
| TX Johnson, Sam | www.samjohnson.house.gov/ |
| TX Hall, Ralph M. | ralphhall.house.gov/ |
| TX Sessions, Pete | sessions.house.gov/ |
| TX Barton, Joseph | joebarton.house.gov/ |
| TX Culberson, John | culberson.house.gov/ |
| TX Brady, Kevin | www.house.gov/brady/ |
| TX Gohmert, Louie | gohmert.house.gov/ |
| TX Doggett, Lloyd | doggett.house.gov/ |
| TX Flores, Bill | flores.house.gov/ |
| TX Granger, Kay | kaygranger.house.gov/ |
| TX Thornberry, William "Mac" | thornberry.house.gov/ |
| TX Paul, Ron | paul.house.gov/ |
| TX Hinojosa, Ruben | hinojosa.house.gov/ |
| TX Reyes, Silvestre | reyes.house.gov/ |
| TX Green, Al | www.house.gov/algreen/ |
| TX Jackson-Lee, Sheila | jacksonlee.house.gov/ |
| TX Hensarling, Jeb | hensarling.house.gov/ |
| TX Gonzalez, Charlie A. | gonzalez.house.gov/ |
| TX Smith, Lamar S. | lamarsmith.house.gov/ |
| TX Marchant, Kenny | marchant.house.gov/ |
| TX Neugebauer, Randy | randy.house.gov/ |
| TX McCaul, Michael T. | mccaul.house.gov/ |
| TX Burgess, Michael | burgess.house.gov/ |
| TX Carter, John | carter.house.gov/ |
| TX Canseco, Francisco | canseco.house.gov/ |
| TX Poe, Ted | poe.house.gov/ |
| TX Green, Gene | green.house.gov/ |
| TX Johnson, Eddie Bernice | ebjohnson.house.gov/ |
| TX Olson, Pete | olson.house.gov/ |
| TX Farenthold, Blake | farenthold.house.gov/ |
| UT Bishop, Rob | robbishop.house.gov/ |
| UT Matheson, Jim | matheson.house.gov/ |
| UT Chaffetz, Jason | chaffetz.house.gov/ |
| VA Wittman, Robert J. | wittman.house.gov/ |
| VA Rigell, Scott | rigell.house.gov/ |

# REPRESENTATIVES' WEB ADDRESSES

URL

| | |
|---|---|
| VA Scott, Robert C. | www.bobbyscott.house.gov/ |
| VA Forbes, J. Randy | forbes.house.gov/ |
| VA Connolly, Gerald E. | connolly.house.gov/ |
| VA Goodlatte, Robert W. | goodlatte.house.gov/ |
| VA Cantor, Eric | cantor.house.gov/ |
| VA Moran, James P. | moran.house.gov/ |
| VA Hurt, Robert | hurt.house.gov/ |
| VA Wolf, Frank R. | wolf.house.gov/ |
| VA Griffin, Morgan | morgangriffin.house.gov/ |
| VI Christensen, Donna M. | donnachristensen.house.gov/ |
| VT Welch, Peter | www.welch.house.gov/ |
| WA Inslee, Jay | www.house.gov/inslee/ |
| WA Larsen, Rick | larsen.house.gov/ |
| WA Herrera Beutler, Jaime | herrerabeutler.house.gov/ |
| WA Hastings, Doc | hastings.house.gov/ |
| WA McMorris Rogers, Cathy | mcmorris.house.gov/ |
| WA Dicks, Norman D. | www.house.gov/dicks/ |
| WA McDermott, James A. | mcdermott.house.gov/ |
| WA Reichert, David G. | reichert.house.gov/ |
| WA Smith, Adam | adamsmith.house.gov/ |
| WI Ryan, Paul | paulryan.house.gov/ |
| WI Baldwin, Tammy | tammybaldwin.house.gov/ |
| WI Kind, Ron | kind.house.gov/ |
| WI Moore, Gwen | gwenmoore.house.gov/ |
| WI Petri, Thomas E. | petri.house.gov/ |
| WI Duffy, Sean P. | duffy.house.gov/ |
| WI Sensenbrenner, F. James | sensenbrenner.house.gov/ |
| WI Ribble, Reid | ribble.house.gov/ |
| WV McKinley, David | mckinley.house.gov/ |
| WV Capito, Shelley Moore | capito.house.gov/ |
| WV Rahall, Nick | www.rahall.house.gov/ |
| WY Lummis, Cynthia M. | lummis.house.gov/ |

# HOUSE COMMITTEES

Three-digit room numbers are in the Cannon House Office Building, four-digit room numbers beginning with 1 are in the Longworth House Office Building, and four-digit room numbers beginning with 2 are in the Rayburn House Office Building. Room numbers beginning with H2 are in the Ford House Office Building, and room numbers beginning with CVC, HVC, or SVC are in the Capitol Visitor Center. Calls made from outside the Capitol complex can be made by dialing (202) 22 plus the five-digit number listed in this directory.

## STANDING COMMITTEES

|  | Phone | Room |
|---|---|---|
| **Agriculture** | 52171 | 1301 |
| Conservation, Energy, and Forestry | 52171 | 1301 |
| Department Operations, Oversight, and Credit | 52171 | 1301 |
| General Farm Commodities and Risk Management | 52171 | 1301 |
| Livestock, Dairy, and Poultry | 52171 | 1301 |
| Nutrition and Horticulture | 52171 | 1301 |
| Rural Development, Research, Biotechnology, and Foreign Agriculture | 52171 | 1301 |
| **Appropriations** | 52771 | H307 |
| Agriculture, Rural Development, Food and Drug Administration, and Related Agencies. | 52638 | 2362A |
| Commerce, Justice, Science, and Related Agencies | 53351 | H309 |
| Defense | 52847 | H405 |
| Energy and Water Development, and Related Agencies | 53421 | 2362B |
| Financial Services and General Government (RHOB) | 57245 | B300 |
| Homeland Security (RHOB) | 55834 | B307 |
| Interior, Environment, and Related Agencies (RHOB) | 53081 | B308 |
| Labor, Health and Human Services, Education, and Related Agencies | 53508 | 2358B |
| Legislative Branch | 67252 | HT2 |
| Military Construction, Veterans Affairs, and Related Agencies | 53047 | HVC227 |
| State, Foreign Operations, and Related Programs | 52041 | HT2 |
| Transportation, and Housing and Urban Development, and Related Agencies | 52141 | 2358A |
| **Armed Services** | 54151 | 2120 |
| Emerging Threats and Capabilities | 62843 | 2340 |
| Military Personnel | 57560 | 2340 |
| Oversight and Investigations | 65048 | 2117 |
| Readiness | 68979 | 2340 |
| Seapower and Projection Forces | 62211 | 2340 |
| Strategic Forces | 51967 | 2216 |
| Tactical Air and Land Forces | 54440 | 2340 |
| **Budget** | 67270 | 207 |
| **Education and the Workforce** | 54527 | 2181 |
| Early Childhood, Elementary, and Secondary Education | 54527 | 2181 |
| Health, Employment, Labor, and Pensions | 54527 | 2181 |
| Higher Education and Workforce Training | 54527 | 2181 |
| Workforce Protections | 54527 | 2181 |
| **Energy and Commerce** | 52927 | 2125 |
| Commerce, Manufacturing, and Trade | 52927 | 2125 |
| Communications and Technology | 52927 | 2125 |
| Energy and Power | 52927 | 2125 |
| Environment and the Economy | 52927 | 2125 |
| Health | 52927 | 2125 |
| Oversight and Investigations | 52927 | 2125 |

# HOUSE COMMITTEES

|  | Phone | Room |
|---|---|---|
| **Ethics** | 57103 | 1015 |
| **Financial Services** | 57502 | 2129 |
| Capital Markets and Government Sponsored Enterprises | 57502 | 2129 |
| Domestic Monetary Policy and Technology | 57502 | 2129 |
| Financial Institutions and Consumer Credit | 57502 | 2129 |
| Insurance, Housing and Community Opportunity | 57502 | 2129 |
| International Monetary Policy and Trade | 57502 | 2129 |
| Oversight and Investigations | 57502 | 2129 |
| **Foreign Affairs** | 55021 | 2170 |
| Africa, Global Health, and Human Rights | 67812 | H2-259A |
| Asia and the Pacific | 67825 | H2-255 |
| Europe and Eurasia | 66434 | H2-256 |
| Oversight and Investigations | 65045 | 2401A |
| Terrorism, Nonproliferation, and Trade | 61500 | H2-340 |
| The Middle East and South Asia (RHOB) | 53345 | B358 |
| The Western Hemisphere | 69980 | H2-257 |
| **Homeland Security** | 68417 | H2-176 |
| Border and Maritime Security | 68417 | H2-176 |
| Counterterrorism and Intelligence | 68417 | H2-176 |
| Cybersecurity, Infrastructure Protection, and Security Technologies | 68417 | H2-176 |
| Emergency Preparedness, Response and Communications | 68417 | H2-176 |
| Oversight, Investigations, and Management | 68417 | H2-176 |
| Transportation Security | 68417 | H2-176 |
| **House Administration** | 58281 | 1309 |
| Elections | 58281 | 1309 |
| Oversight | 58281 | 1309 |
| Commission on Congressional Mailing Standards: |  |  |
| Majority | 60647 | 1313 |
| Minority | 52061 | 1316 |
| **Judiciary** | 53951 | 2138 |
| Courts, Commercial and Administrative Law | 67680 | 517 |
| Crime, Terrorism, and Homeland Security (RHOB) | 55727 | B370 |
| Immigration Policy and Enforcement (RHOB) | 53926 | B353 |
| Intellectual Property, Competition, and the Internet (RHOB) | 55741 | B352 |
| The Constitution | 52825 | H2-362 |
| Publications (CHOB) | 50408 | B29 |
| **Natural Resources** | 52761 | 1324 |
| Energy and Mineral Resources | 59297 | 1333 |
| Fisheries, Wildlife, Oceans and Insular Affairs | 60200 | 140 |
| Indian and Alaska Native Affairs | 69725 | 1337 |
| National Parks, Forests and Public Lands | 67736 | 1017 |
| Water and Power | 58331 | 1522 |
| **Oversight and Government Reform** | 55074 | 2157 |
| Federal Workforce, U.S. Postal Service and Labor Policy | 55074 | 2157 |
| Government Organization, Efficiency and Financial Management | 55074 | 2157 |
| Health Care, District of Columbia, Census and the National Archives | 55074 | 2157 |
| National Security, Homeland Defense and Foreign Operations | 55074 | 2157 |
| Regulatory Affairs, Stimulus Oversight and Government Spending | 55074 | 2157 |
| TARP, Financial Services and Bailouts of Public and Private Programs | 55074 | 2157 |
| Technology, Information Policy, Intergovernmental Relations and Procurement Reform. | 55074 | 2157 |
| **Rules** | 59191 | H312 |
| Legislative and Budget Process | 52231 | 2233 |
| Rules and Organization of the House | 51002 | 1517 |

# HOUSE COMMITTEES

| | Phone | Room |
|---|---|---|
| Minority | 59091 | 1627 |
| **Science, Space, and Technology** | 56371 | 2321 |
| Energy and Environment | 58844 | 2319 |
| Investigations and Oversight (RHOB) | 58772 | B374 |
| Research and Science Education (RHOB) | 59644 | B374 |
| Space and Aeronautics (RHOB) | 57858 | B374 |
| Technology and Innovation | 59662 | 2321 |
| **Small Business** | 55821 | 2361 |
| Agriculture, Energy and Trade | 55821 | 2361 |
| Contracting and Workforce | 55821 | 2361 |
| Economic Growth, Tax and Capital Access | 55821 | 2361 |
| Healthcare and Technology | 55821 | 2361 |
| Investigations, Oversight and Regulations | 55821 | 2361 |
| **Transportation and Infrastructure** | 59446 | 2165 |
| Aviation | 63220 | 2251 |
| Coast Guard and Maritime Transportation | 63552 | H2-507 |
| Economic Development, Public Buildings, and Emergency Management | 53014 | H2-585 |
| Highways and Transit (RHOB) | 56715 | B376 |
| Railroads, Pipelines, and Hazardous Materials (RHOB) | 60727 | B376 |
| Water Resources and Environment (RHOB) | 54360 | B370A |
| **Veterans' Affairs** | 53527 | 335 |
| Disability Assistance and Memorial Affairs | 59164 | 337 |
| Economic Opportunity | 65491 | 335 |
| Health | 59154 | 338 |
| Oversight and Investigations | 53569 | 337A |
| **Ways and Means** | 53625 | 1102 |
| Health | 53943 | 1135 |
| Human Resources | 51025 | 1129 |
| Oversight | 55522 | 1136 |
| Select Revenue Measures | 55522 | 1136 |
| Social Security (RHOB) | 59263 | B317 |
| Trade | 56649 | 1104 |

## SELECT COMMITTEE

| | Phone | Room |
|---|---|---|
| **Permanent Select Committee on Intelligence** | 54121 | HVC304 |
| Oversight and Investigations | 54121 | HVC304 |
| Technical and Tactical Intelligence | 54121 | HVC304 |
| Terrorism, Human Intelligence, Analysis, and Counterintelligence | 54121 | HVC304 |

# TERMS OF SERVICE OF SENATORS

## CLASS III.—SENATORS WHOSE TERMS OF SERVICE EXPIRE IN 2011

[34 Senators in this group: Democrats, 16; Republicans, 18]

| Name | Party | Residence |
|---|---|---|
| Bayh, Evan | D. | Indianapolis, IN. |
| Bennet, Michael F.[1] | D. | Denver, CO. |
| Bennett, Robert F. | R. | Salt Lake City, UT. |
| Bond, Christopher S. | R. | Mexico, MO. |
| Boxer, Barbara | D. | Palm Springs, CA. |
| Brownback, Sam[2] | R. | Topeka, KS. |
| Bunning, Jim | R. | Southgate, KY. |
| Burr, Richard | R. | Winston-Salem, NC. |
| Burris, Roland W.[3] | D. | Chatham, IL. |
| Coburn, Tom | R. | Muskogee, OK. |
| Crapo, Mike | R. | Idaho Falls, ID. |
| DeMint, Jim | R. | Greenville, SC. |
| Dodd, Christopher J. | D. | East Haddam, CT. |
| Dorgan, Byron L.[4] | D. | Bismarck, ND. |
| Feingold, Russell D. | D. | Middleton, WI. |
| Grassley, Chuck | R. | Cedar Falls, IA. |
| Gregg, Judd | R. | Greenfield, NH. |
| Inouye, Daniel K. | D. | Honolulu, HI. |
| Isakson, Johnny | R. | Marietta, GA. |
| Leahy, Patrick J. | D. | Middlesex, VT. |
| LeMieux, George S.[5] | R. | Tallahassee, FL. |
| Lincoln, Blanche L. | D. | Helena, AR. |
| McCain, John | R. | Phoenix, AZ. |
| Mikulski, Barbara A. | D. | Baltimore, MD. |
| Murkowski, Lisa[6] | R. | Anchorage, AK. |
| Murray, Patty | D. | Seattle, WA. |
| Reid, Harry | D. | Searchlight, NV. |
| Schumer, Charles E. | D. | Brooklyn, NY. |
| Shelby, Richard C.[7] | R. | Tuscaloosa, AL. |
| Specter, Arlen[8] | D. | Philadelphia, PA. |
| Thune, John | R. | Sioux Falls, SD. |
| Vitter, David | R | Metairie, LA. |
| Voinovich, George V. | R. | Cleveland, OH. |
| Wyden, Ron[9] | D. | Portland, OR. |

[1] Senator Bennet was appointed on January 21, 2009, to fill the vacancy caused by the resignation of Kenneth L. Salazar. He took the oath of office on January 22, 2009.
[2] Senator Brownback was elected on November 5, 1996, to fill the remainder of the term of Senator Bob Dole. He took the oath of office on November 27, 1996; his seat was retroactive to November 7, 1996, when his Senate service began. He won the seat from Senator Sheila Frahm, who was appointed on June 11, 1996.
[3] Senator Burris was appointed on December 31, 2008, to fill the vacancy caused by the resignation of Barack H. Obama, his credentials were found in order on January 12, 2009, and he took the oath of office on January 15, 2009.
[4] Senator Dorgan was elected to a 6-year term on November 3, 1992, and subsequently was appointed December 14, 1992 to fill the vacancy caused by the resignation of Senator Kent Conrad.
[5] Senator LeMieux was appointed on September 9, 2009, to fill the vacancy caused by the resignation of Mel Martinez. He took the oath of office on September 10, 2009.
[6] Senator Murkowski was appointed on December 20, 2002, to fill the vacancy caused by the resignation of her father, Senator Frank Murkowski. She was elected to a full term in 2004.
[7] Senator Shelby changed parties on November 5, 1994.
[8] Changed party affiliation from Republican to Democrat on April 30, 2009.
[9] Senator Wyden won a special election on January 30, 1996, to fill the vacancy caused by the resignation of Senator Bob Packwood. He was reelected to a full term in 1998.

## CLASS I.—SENATORS WHOSE TERMS OF SERVICE EXPIRE IN 2013

[33 Senators in this group: Democrats, 22; Republicans, 9; Independent, 1; Independent Democrat, 1]

| Name | Party | Residence |
|---|---|---|
| Akaka, Daniel K.[1] | D. | Honolulu, HI. |
| Barrasso, John[2] | R. | Casper, WY. |
| Bingaman, Jeff | D. | Santa Fe, NM. |
| Brown, Sherrod | D. | Avon, OH. |
| Byrd, Robert C. | D. | Sophia, WV. |
| Cantwell, Maria | D. | Edmonds, WA. |
| Cardin, Benjamin L. | D. | Baltimore, MD. |
| Carper, Thomas R. | D. | Wilmington, DE. |
| Casey, Robert P., Jr. | D. | Scranton, PA. |
| Conrad, Kent[3] | D. | Bismarck, ND. |
| Corker, Bob | R. | Chattanooga, TN. |
| Ensign, John | R. | Las Vegas, NV. |
| Feinstein, Dianne[4] | D. | San Francisco, CA. |
| Gillibrand, Kirsten E.[5] | D. | Hudson, NY. |
| Hatch, Orrin G. | R. | Salt Lake City, UT. |
| Hutchison, Kay Bailey[6] | R. | Dallas, TX. |
| Kirk, Paul G., Jr.[7] | D. | Marstons Mills, MA. |
| Klobuchar, Amy | D. | Minneapolis, MN. |
| Kohl, Herb | D. | Milwaukee, WI. |
| Kyl, Jon | R. | Phoenix, AZ. |
| Lieberman, Joseph I. | I.D. | New Haven, CT. |
| Lugar, Richard G. | R. | Indianapolis, IN. |
| McCaskill, Claire | D. | Kirkwood, MO. |
| Menendez, Robert[8] | D. | Hoboken, NJ. |
| Nelson, Ben | D. | Omaha, NE. |
| Nelson, Bill | D. | Orlando, FL. |
| Sanders, Bernard | I | Burlington, VT. |
| Snowe, Olympia J. | R. | Auburn, ME. |
| Stabenow, Debbie | D. | Lansing, MI. |
| Tester, Jon | D. | Big Sandy, MT. |
| Webb, Jim | D. | Arlington, VA. |
| Whitehouse, Sheldon | D. | Providence, RI. |
| Wicker, Roger F.[9] | R. | Tupelo, MS. |

[1] Senator Akaka was appointed April 28, 1990, to fill the vacancy caused by the death of Senator Spark M. Matsunaga, and took the oath of office on May 16, 1990; subsequently elected in a special election on November 6, 1990, for the remainder of the term; subsequently elected to a full term in 1994.
[2] Senator Barrasso was appointed on June 22, 2007, to fill the vacancy caused by the death of Senator Craig Thomas, and took the oath of office on June 25, 2007.
[3] Senator Conrad resigned his term from Class III after winning a special election on December 4, 1992, to fill the vacancy caused by the death of Senator Quentin Burdick. Senator Conrad's seniority in the Senate continues without a break in service. He took the oath of office on December 15, 1992.
[4] Senator Feinstein won the special election held on November 3, 1992, to fill the vacancy caused by the resignation of Senator Pete Wilson. She took the oath of office on November 10, 1992. She won the seat from Senator John Seymour who had been appointed on January 7, 1991. She was elected to a full term in 1994.
[5] Senator Gillibrand was appointed on January 23, 2009, to fill the vacancy caused by the resignation of Hillary Rodham Clinton. She took the oath of office on January 27, 2009.
[6] Senator Hutchison won the special election held on June 5, 1993, to fill remainder of the term of Senator Lloyd Bentsen. She took the seat on June 14, 1993. She won the seat from Senator Bob Krueger, who had been appointed on January 21, 1993. She was elected to a full term in 1994.
[7] Senator Kirk was appointed on September 24, 2009, to fill the vacancy caused by the death of Edward M. Kennedy. He took the oath of office on September 25, 2009.
[8] Senator Menendez was appointed on January 17, 2006, to fill the vacancy caused by the resignation of Senator Jon S. Corzine; subsequently elected to a full term in November 2006.
[9] Senator Wicker was appointed on December 31, 2007, to fill the vacancy caused by the seat left vacant by the resignation of Trett Lott. He took the oath of office on December 31, 2007; subsequently elected in a special election on November 2008.

## CLASS II.—SENATORS WHOSE TERMS OF SERVICE EXPIRE IN 2015

[33 Senators in this group: Democrats, 20; Republicans, 13]

| Name | Party | Residence |
|---|---|---|
| Alexander, Lamar | R. | Nashville, TN. |
| Baucus, Max | D. | Helena, MT. |
| Begich, Mark | D. | Anchorage, AK. |
| Chambliss, Saxby | R. | Moultrie, GA. |
| Cochran, Thad | R. | Jackson, MS. |
| Collins, Susan M. | R. | Bangor, ME. |
| Cornyn, John | R. | San Antonio, TX. |
| Durbin, Richard | D. | Springfield, IL. |
| Franken, Al[1] | D. | Minneapolis, MN. |
| Enzi, Michael B. | R. | Gillette, WY. |
| Graham, Lindsey | R. | Seneca, SC. |
| Hagan, Kay R. | D. | Greensboro, NC. |
| Harkin, Tom | D. | Cumming, IA. |
| Inhofe, James M.[2] | R. | Tulsa, OK. |
| Johanns, Mike | R. | Omaha, NE. |
| Johnson, Tim | D. | Vermillion, SD. |
| Kaufman, Edward E.[3] | D. | Greenville, DE. |
| Kerry, John F. | D. | Boston, MA. |
| Landrieu, Mary L. | D. | New Orleans, LA. |
| Lautenberg, Frank R.[4] | D. | Cliffside Park, NJ. |
| Levin, Carl | D. | Detroit, MI. |
| McConnell, Mitch | R. | Louisville, KY. |
| Merkley, Jeff | D. | Portland, OR. |
| Pryor, Mark L. | D. | Little Rock, AR. |
| Risch, James E. | R. | Boise, ID. |
| Reed, Jack | D. | Jamestown, RI. |
| Roberts, Pat | R. | Dodge City, KS. |
| Rockefeller, John D., IV | D. | Charleston, WV. |
| Shaheen, Jeanne | D. | Madbury, NH. |
| Sessions, Jeff | R. | Mobile, AL. |
| Udall, Mark | D. | Eldorado Springs, CO. |
| Udall, Tom | D. | Santa Fe, NM. |
| Warner, Mark R. | D. | Alexandria, VA. |

[1] Contested election resolved June 30, 2009; Franken was sworn into office on July 7, 2009.
[2] Senator Inhofe won the special election held on November 8, 1994, to fill the remainder of the term of Senator David Boren, and took the oath of office on November 17, 1994. He was elected to a full term in 1996.
[3] Senator Kaufman was appointed on January 15, 2009, to fill the vacancy caused by the resignation of Joseph R. Biden, Jr. and took the oath of office on January 16, 2009.
[4] Senator Lautenberg replaced Senator Robert Torricelli as the Democratic candidate for the U.S. Senate in October 2002.

Credit: 2009-10 Official Congressional Directory 111th Congress

# Geographic Boundaries
of United States Courts of Appeals and United States District Courts

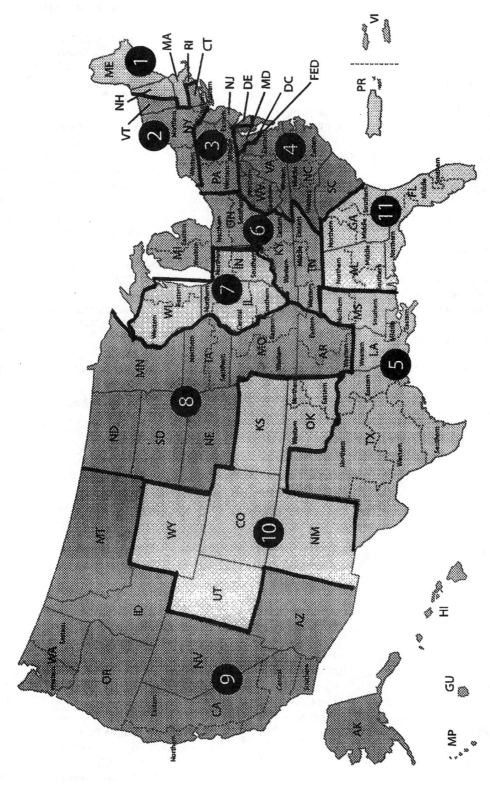

# JUDICIAL BRANCH
# FEDERAL JUDGES

**SUPREME COURT**
**One First Street, NE**
**Washington, DC 20543**
**(202) 479-3000**
**www.supremecourt.gov**

John G. Roberts, Chief Justice
Antonin Scalia
Anthony M. Kennedy
Clarence Thomas
Ruth Bader Ginsburg
Stephen G. Breyer
Samuel A. Alito, Jr.
Sonia Sotomayor
Elena Kagan

**U.S. COURT OF FEDERAL**
**CLAIMS**
**717 Madison Place, NW**
**Washington, DC 20005-1086**
**www.uscfc.uscourts.gov**

Emily C. Hewitt, Chief Judge
(202) 357-6564

Senior Judges

Thomas J. Lydon
(202) 357-6556

John Paul Wiese
(202) 357-6652

Robert J. Yock
(202) 357-6676

James F. Merow
(202) 357-6612

Reginald Gibson
(202) 357-6400

Lawrence S. Margolis
(202) 357-6604

Loren A. Smith
(202) 357-6636

Eric G. Bruggink
(202) 357-6524

Bohdan A. Futey
(202) 357-6548

Robert H. Hodges, Jr.
(202) 357-6572

Judges

Christine O.C. Miller
(202) 357-6620

Marian Blank Horn
(202) 357-6580

Francis M. Allegra
(202) 357-6492

Lawrence M. Baskir
(202) 357-6500

Lynn Jeanne Bush
(202) 357-6532

Nancy B. Firestone
(202) 357-6540

Edward J. Damich
(202) 357-6483

Lawrence J. Block
(202) 357-6508

Mary Ellen Coster Williams
(202) 357-6660

Charles F. Lettow
(202) 357-6588

Susan G. Braden
(202) 357-6516

Victor J. Wolski
(202) 357-6668

George W. Miller
(202) 357-6628

Margaret M. Sweeney
(202) 357-6644

Thomas C. Wheeler
(202) 357-6596

**FEDERAL CIRCUIT**
**www.cafc.uscourts.gov**

Senior Circuit Judges
Glenn L. Archer, Jr.
717 Madison Place, NW
Washington, DC 20439
(202) 275-8932

Daniel M. Friedman
(202) 275-8922

S. Jay Plager
(202) 275-8942

Raymond C. Clevenger, Jr.
(202) 275-8952

Alvin A. Schall
(202) 275-8962

Haldane Robert Mayer
(202) 275-8562

Arthur Gajarsa
(202) 275-8642

Circuit Judges

Randall R. Rader, C.J.
717 Madison Place, NW
Washington, DC 20439
(202) 275-8502

Pauline Newman
(202) 275-8542

Alan D. Lourie
(202) 275-8582

William C. Bryson
(202) 275-8620

Richard Linn
(202) 275-8662

Timothy B. Dyk
(202) 275-8682

Sharon Prost
(202) 275-8702

Kimberly Ann Moore
(202) 275-8722

# FEDERAL JUDGES

Jimmie V. Reyna
(202) 275-8000

Kathleen M. O'Malley
(202) 275-8000

## DISTRICT OF COLUMBIA CIRCUIT
www.cadc.uscourts.gov

Circuit Judges
David B. Sentelle, C.J.
U.S. Courthouse, Rm. 5400
333 Constitution Avenue, NW
Washington, DC 20001-2866
(202) 216-7330

Douglas Ginsburg
(202) 216-7190

Karen LeCraft Henderson
(202) 216-7370

Judith W. Rogers
(202) 216-7260

David S. Tatel
(202) 216-7160

Merrick B. Garland
(202) 216-7460

Thomas B. Griffith
(202) 216-7170

Janice R. Brown
(202) 216-7220

Brett Kavanaugh
(202) 216-7180

Senior Circuit Judges
Laurence H. Silberman
333 Constitution Ave., NW
Washington, DC 20001-2866
(202) 216-7353

Stephen F. Williams
(202) 216-7210

Harry T. Edwards
(202) 216-7380

A. Raymond Randolph
(202) 216-7425

District Judges

Royce C. Lamberth, C.J.
U.S. Courthouse, Rm. 4012
333 Constitution Avenue, NW
Washington, DC 20001
(202) 354-3380

John D. Bates
(202) 354-3430

Richard J. Leon
(202) 354-3580

Reggie B. Walton
(202) 354-3290

Rosemary M. Collyer
(202) 354-3560

Emmet G. Sullivan
(202) 354-3260

Colleen Kollar-Kotelly
(202) 354-3340

Henry H. Kennedy, Jr.
(202) 354-3350

Richard W. Roberts
(202) 354-3400

Ellen Segal Huvelle
(202) 354-3230

Beryl A. Howell
(202) 354-3450

Robert L. Wilkins
(202) 354-3480

James E. Boasberg
(202) 354-3300

Amy B. Jackson
(202) 354-3460

Senior District Judges
Gladys Kessler
U.S. Courthouse
333 Constitution Ave. NW, Rm.4006
Washington, DC 20001
(202) 354-3440

Louis F. Oberdorfer
(202) 354-3270

James Robertson
(202) 354-3460

Thomas F. Hogan
(202) 354-3420

Paul L. Friedman
(202) 354-3490

Ricardo M. Urbina
(202) 354-3390

## FIRST CIRCUIT
(Maine, Massachusetts, New Hampshire, Rhode Island, Puerto Rico)
www.ca1.uscourts.gov

Circuit Judges
Sandra L. Lynch, C.J.
8710 U.S. Courthouse
Boston, MA 02210
(617) 748-9014

Michael Boudin
7710 U.S. Courthouse
Boston, MA 02210
(617) 748-4431

Juan R. Torruella
300 Recinto Street, 4th fl.
San Juan, PR 00901
(787) 977-6146

Kermit V. Lipez
156 Federal St.
Portland, ME 04101
(207) 822-0455

Jeffrey R. Howard
55 Pleasant St.
Concord, NH 03301
(603) 225-1525

O. Rogeriee Thompson
1 Exchange Terrace
Providence, RI 02903
(401) 752-7155

Senior Circuit Judges
Norman H. Stahl
8730 U.S. Courthouse
Boston, MA 02210
(617) 748-4596

Levin H. Campbell
6720 U.S. Courthouse
Boston, MA 02210
(617) 748-9002

# FEDERAL JUDGES

Conrad K. Cyr
202 Harlow St., Rm. 214
Bangor, ME 04501-0635
(207) 941-8150

Bruce M. Selya
316 Federal Bldg.
Providence, RI 02903-1755
(401) 752-7140

District Judges

## Maine

John A. Woodcock, Jr., C.J.
P.O. Box 1007
Bangor, ME 04402
(207) 945-0549

George Z. Singal
156 Federal Street
Portland, ME 04101
(207) 780-3119

## Massachusetts

Mark L. Wolf, C.J.
U.S. Courthouse
One Courthouse Way
Boston, MA 02210
(617) 748-9272

William G. Young
U.S. Courthouse
Boston, MA 02210
(617) 748-4150

Joseph L. Tauro
7110 U.S. Courthouse
Boston, MA 02210
(617) 748-9288

Rya W. Zobel
U.S. Courthouse
Boston, MA 02210
(617) 748-9144

Douglas P. Woodlock
U.S. Courthouse
Boston, MA 02210
(617) 748-9293

Nathaniel M. Gorton
U.S. Courthouse
Boston, MA 02210
(617) 748-9248

Richard G. Stearns

U.S. Courthouse
Boston, MA 02210
(617) 748-9283

Patti B. Saris
U.S. Courthouse
Boston, MA 02210
(617) 748-4141

George A. O'Toole, Jr.
U.S. Courthouse
Boston, MA 02210
(617) 748-9618

F. Dennis Saylor IV
595 Main St., Rm. 502
Worcester, MA 01608-2076
(508) 929-9909

Denise J. Casper
U.S. Courthouse
Boston, MA 02210
(617) 748-9177

## New Hampshire

Steven J. McAuliffe, C.J.
55 Pleasant Street
Concord, NH 03301
(603) 226-7304

Paul J. Barbadoro
55 Pleasant Street
Concord, NH 03301
(603) 225-1423

Joseph N. Laplante
55 Pleasant Street
Concord, NH 03301
(603) 225-1423

## Rhode Island

Mary M. Lisi, C.J.
One Exchange Terrace, #310
Providence, RI 02903
(401) 752-7200

William E. Smith
One Exchange Terrace, #356
Providence, RI 02903
(401) 752-7200

John J. McConnell, Jr.
One Exchange Terrace
Providence, RI 02903
(401) 752-7200

## Puerto Rico

Aida Delgado-Colon, C.J.
150 Carlos Chardon Ave.
Hato Rey, PR 00918
(787) 772-3196

Jose Antonio Fuste
Room CH-133
150 Carlos Chardon Ave.
Hato Rey, PR 00918
(787) 772-3120

Carmen Consuelo Cerezo
Room CH-131
150 Carlos Chardon Ave.
Hato Rey, PR 00918
(787) 772-3110

Jay A. Garcia-Gregory
Federal Building, Rm. 151
150 Carlos-Chardon Ave.
Hato Rey, PR 00918
(787) 772-3171

Francisco Besosa
Room CH-119
150 Carlos Chardon Ave.
Hato Rey, PR 00918
(787) 772-3240

Gustavo Gelpi
150 Carlos Chardon Ave.
Hato Rey, PR 00918
(787) 772-3103

Senior District Judges

Gene Carter
156 Federal Street
Portland, ME 04101
(207) 780-3662

Edward F. Harrington
U.S. Courthouse
Boston, MA 02210
(617) 748-4131

Ronald R. Lagueux
One Exchange Terrace, #208
Providence, RI 02903
(401) 752-7200

Jaime Pieras, Jr.
353 U.S. Courthouse
300 Recinto Sur St.
San Juan, PR 00901
(787) 977-6050

# FEDERAL JUDGES

Morris E. Lasker
U.S. Courthouse
Boston, MA 02210
(617) 748-4134

Salvador E. Casellas
Room CH-111
150 Carlos Chardon Ave.
Hato Rey, PR 00918-1761
(787) 772-3150

Joseph A. DiClerico, Jr.
55 Pleasant Street
Concord, NH 03301
(603) 225-1423

Ernest C. Torres
One Exchange Terrace, #363
Providence, RI 02903
(401) 752-7200

Juan M. Perez-Gimenez
Room CH-125
150 Carlos Chardon Ave.
Hato Rey, PR 00918
(787) 772-3140

D. Brock Hornby
156 Federal Street
Portland, ME 04101
(207) 780-3280

Michael A. Ponsor
300 State St.
Springfield, MA 01105
(413) 785-6800

Daniel R. Dominguez
Room CH-129
150 Carlos Chardon Ave.
Hato Rey, PR 00918
(787) 772-3160

Nancy Gertner
U.S. Courthouse
Boston, MA 02210
(617) 748-4119

**SECOND CIRCUIT**
**(Connecticut, New York, Vermont)**
**www.ca2.uscourts.gov/**

Circuit Judges

Dennis G. Jacobs, C.J.
500 Pearl Street
New York, NY 10007

(212) 857-2150

Reena Raggi
500 Pearl Street
New York, NY 10007
(212) 857-8500

Jose A. Cabranes
U.S. Courthouse
141 Church Street
New Haven, CT 06510
(203) 773-2140

Rosemary S. Pooler
P.O. Box 7395
Syracuse, NY 13261-7395
(315) 448-0420

Robert A. Katzmann
500 Pearl Street
New York, NY 10007
(212) 857-2180

Richard C. Wesley
500 Pearl Street
New York, NY 10007
(212) 857-8500

Peter W. Hall
500 Pearl Street
New York, NY 10007
(212) 857-8662

Debra Ann Livingston
500 Pearl St.
New York, NY 10007
(212) 857-8500

Gerard E. Lynch
500 Pearl Street
New York, NY 10007
(212) 805-0427

Denny Chin
500 Pearl St.
New York, NY 10007
(212) 857-8500

Raymond J. Lohier, Jr.
500 Pearl St.
New York, NY 10007
(212) 857-8500

Susan L. Carney
500 Pearl St.
New York, NY 10007
(212) 857-8500

Senior Circuit Judges

Amalya Kearse
500 Pearl Street
New York, NY 10007
(212) 857-2250

Pierre N. Leval
500 Pearl Street
New York, NY 10007
(212) 857-2310

Wilfred Feinberg
500 Pearl Street
New York, NY 10007
(212) 857-8500

Chester J. Straub
500 Pearl Street
New York, NY 10007
(212) 857-8500

Roger J. Miner
445 Broadway, Suite 414
Albany, NY 12207
(518) 431-0401

Joseph M. McLaughlin
500 Pearl Street
New York, NY 10007
(212) 857-2200

Jon O. Newman
U.S. Courthouse
450 Main Street
Hartford, CT 06103
(860) 240-3260

Ralph K. Winter, Jr.
141 Church St.
New Haven, CT 06510
(203) 773-2140

John M. Walker, Jr.
157 Church St.
New Haven, CT 06510
(203) 773-2181

Robert D. Sack
500 Pearl Street
New York, NY 10007
(212) 857-2140

Guido Calabresi
157 Church Street
New Haven, CT 06510
(203) 773-2291

# FEDERAL JUDGES

Barrington D. Parker
500 Pearl Street
New York, NY 10007
(212) 857-2211

Richard Cardamone
500 Pearl St.
New York, NY 10007
(212) 857-8500

District Judges

## Connecticut

Alvin W. Thompson, C.J.
450 Main Street
Hartford, CT 06103
(860) 240-3224

Robert N. Chatigny
450 Main Street
Hartford, CT 06103
(860) 240-3659

Janet Bond Arterton
141 Church Street
New Haven, CT 06510
(203) 773-2456

Janet C. Hall
915 Lafayette Blvd.
Bridgeport, CT 06604
(203) 579-5554

Christopher F. Droney
450 Main St.
Hartford, CT 06103
(860) 240-2635

Stefan R. Underhill
915 Lafayette Boulevard
Bridgeport, CT 06604
(203) 579-5714

Mark R. Kravitz
141 Church Street
New Haven, CT 06510
(203) 773-2022

Vanessa Lynne Bryant
450 Main St.
Hartford, CT 06103
(860) 240-3123

## New York - Northern District

Norman A. Mordue, C.J.
P.O. Box 7336

Syracuse, NY 13261-7255
(315) 234-8570

David N. Hurd
10 Broad Street
Utica, NY 13501
(315) 793-9571

Gary L. Sharpe
445 Broadway
Albany, NY 12207
(518) 257-1874

Glenn T. Suddaby
100 S. Clinton St.
Syracuse, NY 13261
(315) 234-8580

Mae D'Agostino

## New York - Southern District

Loretta A. Preska, C.J.
500 Pearl Street
New York, NY 10007-1312
(212) 805-0240

Barbara S. Jones
500 Pearl Street
New York, NY 10007-1312
(212) 805-6185

Deborah A. Batts
500 Pearl Street
New York, NY 10007-1312
(212) 805-0186

William H. Pauley, III
500 Pearl Street
New York, NY 10007-1312
(212) 805-6387

John G. Koeltl
500 Pearl Street
New York, NY 10007-1312
(212) 805-0222

Denise Cote
500 Pearl Street
New York, NY 10007-1312
(212) 805-0202

Colleen McMahon
300 Quarropas Street
White Plains, NY 10601
(914) 390-4146

Naomi Reice Buchwald

500 Pearl Street
New York, NY 10007-1312
(212) 805-0194

George B. Daniels
500 Pearl St.
New York, NY 10007-1312
(212) 805-6735

Laura Taylor Swain
500 Pearl Street
New York, NY 10007-1312
(212) 805-0417

Richard J. Holwell
500 Pearl St.
New York, NY 10007-1312
(212) 805-0256

P. Kevin Castel
500 Pearl St.
New York, NY 10007-1312
(212) 805-0262

Vincent L. Briccetti
300 Quarropas St., Rm. 620
White Plains, NY 10601-4150
(914) 390-4166

Kenneth M. Karas
300 Quarropas St.
White Plains, NY 10601-4150
(914) 390-4145

Paul A. Crotty
500 Pearl Street
New York, NY 10007-1312
(212) 805-6309

Richard J. Sullivan
500 Pearl Street, Rm. 615
New York, NY 10007
(212) 805-0264

Cathy Seibel
300 Quarropas St.
White Plains, NY 10601-4150
(914) 390-4271

Paul G. Gardephe
500 Pearl St.
New York, NY 10007
(212) 805-0224

Paul A. Engelmayer

J. Paul Oetken

# FEDERAL JUDGES

**New York - Eastern District**

Carol Bagley Amon, C.J.
U.S. Courthouse
225 Cadman Plaza East
Brooklyn, NY 11201
(718) 613-2410

Joanna Seybert
100 Federal Plaza
Central Islip, NY 11722-4438
(631) 712-5610

John Gleeson
U.S. Courthouse
225 Cadman Plaza East
Brooklyn, NY 11201
(718) 613-2450

Nicholas G. Garaufis
U.S. Courthouse
225 Cadman Plaza East
Brooklyn, NY 11201
(718) 613-2540

Sandra J. Feuerstein
100 Federal Plaza
Central Islip, NY 11722
(631) 712-5630

Sandra L. Townes
225 Cadman Plaza East
Brooklyn, NY 11201
(718) 613-2160

Dora L. Irizarry
225 Cadman Plaza East
Brooklyn, NY 11201
(718) 613-2150

Joseph F. Bianco
U.S. Courthouse
100 Federal Plaza
Central Islip, NY 11722
(631) 712-5670

Brian M. Cogan
U.S. Courthouse
225 Cadman Plaza East
Brooklyn, NY 11201
(718) 613-2130

Eric N. Viliano
U.S. Courthouse
225 Cadman Plaza East
Brooklyn, NY 11201
(718) 613-2130

Roslynn R. Mauskopf
U.S. Courthouse
225 Cadman Plaza East
Brooklyn, NY 11201
(718) 613-2210

Kiyo A. Matsumoto
U.S. Courthouse
225 Cadman Plaza East
Brooklyn, NY 11201
(718) 613-2180

**New York - Western District**

William M. Skretny, C.J.
507 U.S. Courthouse
68 Court Street
Buffalo, NY 14202
(716) 332-1700

Richard J. Arcara
609 U.S. Courthouse
68 Court Street
Buffalo, NY 14202-3493
(716) 332-7810

Charles J. Siragusa
100 State Street, Rm. 1380
Rochester, NY 14614-1324
(716) 613-4050

**Vermont**

Christina Reiss, C.J.
P.O. Box 953
Burlington, VT 05402
(802) 951-6622

William K. Sessions, III
P.O. Box 928
Burlington, VT 05402
(802) 951-6350

Senior District Judges

Alfred V. Covello
450 Main Street
Hartford, CT 06103
(860) 240-3218

Sterling Johnson, Jr.
225 Cadman Plaza East
Brooklyn, NY 11201
(718) 613-2460

Lawrence McKenna
500 Pearl Street
New York, NY 10007-1312

(212) 805-0230

Thomas P. Griesa
500 Pearl St.
New York, NY 10007-1312
(212) 805-0210

Leonard B. Sand
500 Pearl Street
New York, NY 10007-1312
(212) 805-0244

Richard Owen
500 Pearl Street
New York, NY 10007-1312
(212) 805-6155

Michael A. Telesca
2720 U.S. Courthouse
100 State Street
Rochester, NY 14614-1323
(585) 613-4060

Charles S. Haight,, Jr.
500 Pearl Street
New York, NY 10007-1312
(212) 805-0214

John F. Keenan
500 Pearl Street
New York, NY 10007-1312
(212) 805-0220

Peter K. Leisure
500 Pearl Street
New York, NY 10007-1312
(212) 805-0226

Louis L. Stanton
500 Pearl Street
New York, NY 10007-1312
(212) 805-0252

Robert W. Sweet
500 Pearl Street
New York, NY 10007-1312
(212) 805-0254

Harold Baer, Jr.
500 Pearl Street
New York, NY 10007-1312
(212) 805-0184

John T. Curtin
624 U.S. Courthouse
68 Court Street
Buffalo, NY 14202-3496
(716) 332-7830

# FEDERAL JUDGES

John T. Elfvin
716 U.S. Courthouse
68 Court Street
Buffalo, NY 14202-3497
(716) 332-7840

Robert L. Carter
500 Pearl Street
New York, NY 10007-1312
(212) 805-0196

Ellen B. Burns
141 Church Street
New Haven, CT 06510
(203) 773-2105

Warren W. Eginton
915 Lafayette Boulevard
Bridgeport, CT 06604
(203) 579-5819

Neal P. McCurn
P.O. Box 7365
Syracuse, NY 13261-7365
(315) 234-8590

Jack B. Weinstein
U.S. Courthouse
225 Cadman Plaza East
Brooklyn, NY 11201
(718) 613-2520

I. Leo Glasser
225 Cadman Plaza East
Brooklyn, NY 11201
(718) 613-2440

Arthur D. Spatt
100 Federal Plaza
Central Islip, NY 11722-4438
(631) 712-5620

Denis R. Hurley
100 Federal Plaza
Central Islip, NY 11722-4438
(631) 712-5650

Leonard D. Wexler
100 Federal Plaza
Central Islip, NY 11722-4438
(631) 712-5640

Miriam G. Cedarbaum
500 Pearl Street
New York, NY 10007-1312
(212) 805-0198

Robert Patterson, Jr.

500 Pearl Street
New York, NY 10007-1312
(212) 805-0238

Peter C. Dorsey
141 Church Street
New Haven, CT 06510
(203) 773-2427

Thomas C. Platt
100 Federal Plaza
Central Islip, NY 11722-4438
(631) 712-5600

Thomas J. McAvoy
225 Federal Building
15 Henry St.
Binghamton, NY 13901
(607) 773-2892

Dominic J. Squatrito
450 Main Street
Hartford, CT 06103
(860) 240-3873

Frederick J. Scullin, Jr.
P.O. Box 7255
Syracuse, NY 13261-7255
(315) 234-8560

Edward R. Korman
U.S. Courthouse
225 Cadman Plaza East
Brooklyn, NY 11201
(718) 613-2470

Frederic Block
U.S. Courthouse
225 Cadman Plaza East
Brooklyn, NY 11201
(718) 613-2420

Lawrence E. Kahn
445 Broadway, Rm. 424
Albany, NY 12207
(518) 257-1830

Nina Gershon
U.S. Courthouse
225 Cadman Plaza East
Brooklyn, NY 11201
(718) 613-2650

David G. Larimer
2500 U.S. Courthouse
100 State Street
Rochester, NY 14614-1324
(716) 613-4040

Kimba Wood
500 Pearl Street
New York, NY 10007-1312
(212) 805-0258

J. Garvan Murtha
P.O. Box 760
Brattleboro, VT 05302-0760
(802) 258-4413

Jed S. Rakoff
500 Pearl Street
New York, NY 10007-1312
(212) 805-0401

Alvin K. Hellerstein
500 Pearl Street
New York, NY 10007-1312
(212) 805-0152

Lewis A. Kaplan
500 Pearl Street
New York, NY 10007-1312
(212) 805-0216

Sidney H. Stein
500 Pearl Street
New York, NY 10007-1312
(212) 805-0192

Victor Marrero
500 Pearl Street
New York, NY 10007-1312
(212) 805-6374

Shira Ann Scheindlin
500 Pearl Street
New York, NY 10007-1312
(212) 805-0246

Allyne R. Ross
U.S. Courthouse
225 Cadman Plaza East
Brooklyn, NY 11201
(718) 613-2380

Raymond J. Dearie
U.S. Courthouse
225 Cadman Plaza East
Brooklyn, NY 11201
(718) 613-2430

Richard M. Berman
500 Pearl Street
New York, NY 10007-1312
(212) 805-6715

# FEDERAL JUDGES

## THIRD CIRCUIT
**(Delaware, New Jersey, Pennsylvania, Virgin Islands)**
www.ca3.uscourts.gov

### Circuit Judges

Theodore A. McKee, C.J.
20614 U.S. Courthouse
601 Market Street
Philadelphia, PA 19106-1790
(215) 597-9601

Anthony J. Scirica
601 Market Street
Philadelphia, PA 19106-1790
(215) 597-2399

Dolores K. Sloviter
18614 U.S. Courthouse
601 Market Street
Philadelphia, PA 19106-1790
(215) 597-1588

D. Brooks Smith
1798 Old Rt. 220N, Suite 203
Johnstown, PA 16635
(814) 693-0570

Marjorie O. Rendell
21613 U.S. Courthouse
601 Market Street
Philadelphia, PA 19106-1790
(215) 597-3015

Thomas L. Ambro
844 King St., Lockbox 32
Wilmington, DE 19801
(302) 573-6500

Julio M. Fuentes
50 Walnut St.
Newark, NJ 07102
(973) 645-3831

D. Michael Fisher
700 Grant St., Suite 5360
Pittsburgh, PA 15219
(412) 208-7320

Thomas M. Hardiman
2270 U.S. Courthouse
700 Grant Street
Pittsburgh, PA 15219-1906
(412) 208-7440

Michael Chagares
50 Walnut Street

Newark, NJ 07102
(973) 368-6486

Kent A. Jordan
844 N. King St.
Wilmington, DE 19801
(302) 573-6001

Joseph A. Greenaway, Jr.
P.O. Box 999
Newark, NJ 07101-0999
(973) 622-4828

Thomas I. Vanaskie
235 N. Washington Ave.
Scranton, PA 18503
(570) 207-5720

### Senior Circuit Judges

Ruggero J. Aldisert
120 Cremona Drive, Suite D
Santa Barbara, CA 93117-5511
(805) 685-7466

Joseph F. Weis, Jr.
219 U.S. Post Office & Courthouse
7th & Grant Streets
Pittsburgh, PA 15219-1906
(412) 208-7310

Leonard I. Garth
50 Walnut Street, Rm. 5040
Newark, NJ 07102
(973) 645-6521

Robert E. Cowen
402 E. State St., Rm. 207
Trenton, NJ 08608
(609) 989-2188

Walter K. Stapleton
Lockbox 33
844 King Street
Wilmingon, DE 19801
(302) 573-6165

Morton I. Greenberg
402 E. State Street, Rm. 219
Trenton, NJ 08608
(609) 989-0436

Richard L. Nygaard
17 S. Park Row, Rm. B230
Erie, PA 16501
(814) 464-9640

Jane R. Roth

5100 Boggs Federal Bldg.
844 King Street
Wilmington, DE 19801
(302) 573-6104

Franklin S. Van Antwerpen
101 Larry Holmes Drive
Easton, PA 18042
(610) 252-6522

Edward Becker
601 Market Street
Philadelphia, PA 19106-1790
(215) 597-9642

Maryanne Trump Barry
333 U.S. Courthouse
P.O. Box 999
Newark, NJ 07101-0999
(973) 645-2133

### District Judges

**Delaware**

Gregory M. Sleet, C.J.
Lockbox 19
844 N. King Street, Rm. 4324
Wilmington, DE 19801-3570
(302) 573-6470

Sue L. Robinson
Lockbox 31
844 N. King Street, Rm. 6124
Wilmington, DE 19801
(302) 573-6310

Leonard P. Stark
Lockbox 26
844 N. King Street, Rm. 6100
Wilmington, DE 19801
(302) 573-4571

**New Jersey**

Garrett Brown, Jr.
402 E. State Street, #4050
Trenton, NJ 08608
(609) 989-2009

Dennis M. Cavanaugh
P.O. Box 999
Newark, NJ 07101-0999
(973) 645-3574

William J. Martini
50 Walnut St., Rm. 5076
Newark, NJ 07102

# FEDERAL JUDGES

(973) 654-6340

Jose L. Linares
50 Walnut St., Rm. 5054
Newark, NJ 07102
(973) 645-6042

Stanley R. Chesler
50 Walnut St.
Newark, NJ 07102
(973) 645-3136

Freda L. Wolfson
402 E. State Street
Trenton, NJ 08608
(609) 989-2182

Robert B. Kugler
400 Cooper St.
Camden, NJ 08101
(856) 757-5019

Jerome B. Simandle
P.O. Box 888
Camden, NJ 08101-0888
(856) 757-5167

Faith S. Hochberg
P.O. Box 999
Newark, NJ 07101-0999
(973) 297-4851

Joel A. Pisano
402 E. State St.
Trenton, NJ 08608
(609) 989-0502

Renee M. Bumb
400 Cooper St.
Camden, NJ 08101
(856) 757-5020

Noel L. Hillman
400 Cooper St.
Camden, NJ 08101
(856) 757-5027

Peter G. Sheridan
402 E. State Street
Trenton, NJ 08608
(609) 989-2065

Susan D. Wigenton
50 Walnut St.
Newark, NJ 07102
(973) 645-5903

Claire C. Cecchi

Esther Salas

**Pennsylvania - Eastern District**

J. Curtis Joyner, C.J.
17614 U.S. Courthouse
601 Market Street
Philadelphia, PA 19106
(215) 597-1537

Harvey Bartle, III
16614 U.S. Courthouse
601 Market Street
Philadelphia, PA 19106
(215) 597-2693

Cynthia M. Rufe
4000 U.S. Courthouse
601 Market St.
Philadelphia, PA 19106-1797
(267) 299-7490

Michael M. Baylson
3810 U.S. Courthouse
601 Market St.
Philadelphia, PA 19106-1797
(267) 299-7520

Timothy J. Savage
9614 U.S. Courthouse
601 Market St.
Philadelphia, PA 19106-1797
(267) 299-7480

James Knoll Gardner
504 W. Hamilton St., Suite 4701
Allentown, PA 18101
(610) 434-3457

Legrome D. Davis
6614 U.S. Courthouse
601 Market St.
Philadelphia, PA 19106-1797
(267) 299-7650

Stewart Dalzell
10613 U.S. Courthouse
601 Market Street
Philadelphia, PA 19106
(215) 597-9773

Eduardo C. Robreno
11614 U.S. Courthouse
601 Market Street
Philadelphia, PA 19106
(215) 597-4073

Mary A. McLaughlin

13614 U.S. Courthouse
601 Market Street
Philadelphia, PA 19106-1797
(267) 299-7600

Berle M. Schiller
13613 U.S. Courthouse
601 Market Street
Philadelphia, PA 19106-1797
(267) 299-7620

Petrese B. Tucker
9613 U.S. Courthouse
601 Market Street
Philadelphia, PA 19106-1797
(267) 299-7610

Gene E.K. Pratter
7614 U.S. Courthouse
601 Market Street
Philadelphia, PA 19106-1797
(267) 299-7350

Paul S. Diamond
6613 U.S. Courthouse
601 Market Street
Philadelphia, PA 19106-1797
(267) 299-7730

Lawrence F. Stengel
3809 U.S. Courthouse
601 Market Street
Philadelphia, PA 19106-1797
(267) 299-7760

Juan R. Sanchez
8613 U.S. Courthouse
601 Market Street
Philadelphia, PA 19106-1797
(267) 299-7780

Thomas M. Golden
400 Washington St., Suite 401
Reading, PA 19601
(610) 320-5097

Joel H. Slomsky
5614 U.S. Courthouse
601 Market Street
Philadelphia, PA 19106-1797
(267) 299-7340

C. Darnell Jones, II
5613 U.S. Courthouse
601 Market Street
Philadelphia, PA 19106-1797
(267) 299-7750

# FEDERAL JUDGES

Mitchell S. Goldberg
7614 U.S. Courthouse
601 Market Street
Philadelphia, PA 19106-1797
(267) 299-7500

## Pennsylvania - Middle District

Yvette Kane, C.J.
228 Walnut Street
Harrisburg, PA 17101
(717) 221-3990

James M. Munley
P.O. Box 1247
Scranton, PA 18501
(570) 207-5780

Christopher C. Conner
228 Walnut Street
Harrisburg, PA 17101
(717) 221-3945

James E. Jones, III
240 W. 3rd St.
Williamsport, PA 17701
(570) 601-1497

## Pennsylvania - Western District

Gary L. Lancaster, C.J.
700 Grant Street, Suite 3250
Pittsburgh, PA 15219
(412) 208-7400

Joy Flowers Conti
700 Grant Street, Suite 5250
Pittsburgh, PA 15219
(412) 208-7330

Sean J. McLaughlin
17 S. Park Row, Rm. A250
Erie, PA 16501
(814) 464-9610

Terrence F. McVerry
700 Grant St., Suite 6370
Pittsburgh, PA 15219
(412) 208-7495

David S. Cercone
700 Grant St., Suite 7270
Pittsburgh, PA 15219
(412) 208-7363

Arthur J. Schwab
700 Grant St., Suite 7280
Pittsburgh, PA 15219

(412) 208-7423

Kim R. Gibson
319 S. Washington St., Rm. 104
Johnstown, PA 15901
(814) 533-4514

Nora B. Fischer
700 Grant St., Suite 5260
Pittsburgh, PA 15219
(412) 208-7480

## Virgin Islands

Curtis V. Gomez, C.J.
5500 Veterans Drive, Suite 310
Charlotte Amalie, St. Thomas
 00802
(340) 774-0640

Wilma Antoinette Lewis
3013 Estate Golden Rock, Rm. 373
Christiansted, St. Croix 00820-4355
(340) 773-5021

## Senior District Judges

Joseph E. Irenas
P.O. Box 2097
Camden, NJ 08101-2097
(856) 757-5223

William L. Standish
700 Grant Street, Suite 6170
Pittsburgh, PA 15219
(412) 208-7430

Jan E. Dubois
12613 U.S. Courthouse
601 Market St.
Philadelphia, PA 19106
(215) 597-5579

Murray M. Schwartz
Lockbox 44
Federal Building
844 King Street
Wilmington, DE 19801
(302) 573-6355

Maurice B. Cohill, Jr.
700 Grant Street, Suite 8170
Pittsburgh, PA 15219
(412) 208-7380

Alan N. Bloch
700 Grant Street, Suite 8370

Pittsburgh, PA 15219
(412) 208-7360

Gustave Diamond
700 Grant Street, Suite 8270
Pittsburgh, PA 15219
(412) 208-7390

John P. Fullam
15614 U.S. Courthouse
601 Market Street
Philadelphia, PA 19106
(215) 597-0436

Edmund V. Ludwig
5118 U.S. Courthouse
601 Market Street
Philadelphia, PA 19106
(215) 580-2030

John R. Padova
17613 U.S. Courthouse
601 Market Street
Philadelphia, PA 19106
(215) 597-1178

Dickinson R. Debevoise
P.O. Box 999
Newark, NJ 07101-0999
(973) 645-6121

William J. Nealon, Jr.
P.O. Box 1146
Scranton, PA 18501-1148
(570) 207-5700

Malcolm Muir
240 W. 3rd St.
Williamsport, PA 17701
(570) 322-0287

Richard P. Conaboy
P.O. Box 189
Scranton, PA 18501-0189
(570) 207-5710

William W. Caldwell
228 Walnut St.
Harrisburg, PA 17101
(717) 221-3970

Donald W. Van Artsdalen
3040 U.S. Courthouse
601 Market Street
Philadelphia, PA 19106
(215) 597-9650

Edwin M. Kosik

# FEDERAL JUDGES

P.O. Box 856
Scranton, PA 18501-0856
(570) 207-5730

J. William Ditter, Jr.
3040 U.S. Courthouse
601 Market Street
Philadelphia, PA 19106
(215) 597-9640

Thomas N. O'Neill, Jr.
4007 U.S. Courthouse
601 Market Street
Philadelphia, PA 19106
(215) 597-2750

Louis H. Pollak
16613 U.S. Courthouse
601 Market Street
Philadelphia, PA 19106
(215) 597-9590

Joseph H. Rodriguez
P.O. Box 886
Camden, NJ 08101-0886
(856) 757-5002

Norma L. Shapiro
10614 U.S. Courthouse
601 Market Street
Philadelphia, PA 19106
(215) 597-9141

Lowell A. Reed, Jr.
4001 U.S. Courthouse
601 Market St.
Philadelphia, PA 19106
(215) 597-0022

Anne E. Thompson
U.S. Courthouse
402 E. State Street, #4000
Trenton, NJ 08608
(609) 989-2182

Sylvia H. Rambo
228 Walnut St.
Harrisburg, PA 17101
(717) 221-3960

Robert F. Kelly
11613 U.S. Courthouse
601 Market Street
Philadelphia, PA 19106
(215) 597-0736

William H. Walls
P.O. Box 999

Newark, NJ 07101-0999
(973) 645-2564

Ronald L. Buckwalter
14614 U.S. Courthouse
601 Market St.
Philadelphia, PA 19106
(215) 597-3084

William H. Yohn, Jr.
14613 U.S. Courthouse
601 Market Street
Philadelphia, PA 19106
(215) 597-4361

A. Richard Caputo
197 S. Main St.
Wilkes Barre, PA 18701
(570) 831-2556

Joseph J. Longobardi
844 King St.
Wilmington, DE 19801
(302) 573-6151

Anita A. Brody
7613 U.S. Courthouse
601 Market Street
Philadelphia, PA 19106
(215) 597-3978

Katharine S. Hayden
311 U.S. Courthouse
P.O. Box 999
Newark, NJ 07101-0999
(973) 645-4611

R. Barclay Surrick
8614 U.S. Courthouse
601 Market Street
Philadelphia, PA 19106-1797
(267) 299-7630

Donetta W. Ambrose
700 Grant Street, Suite 3280
Pittsburgh, PA 15219
(412) 208-7350

Mary L. Cooper
402 E. State Street, #5000
Trenton, NJ 08608
(609) 989-2105

Raymond L. Finch
3013 Estate Golden Rock, Rm. 373
Christiansted, St. Croix 00820-4355
(340) 773-5021

**FOURTH CIRCUIT**
**(Maryland, N. Carolina,**
**S. Carolina, Virginia,**
**West Virginia)**
**www.ca4.uscourts.gov**

Circuit Judges

William B. Traxler, Jr., C.J.
P.O. Box 10127
Greenville, SC 29603
(864) 241-2730

J. Harvie Wilkinson, III
255 West Main Street, Rm. 230
Charlottesville, VA 22902
(804) 296-7063

Dennis W. Shedd
1100 Laurel St.
Columbia, SC 29201
(803) 732-8250

Paul V. Niemeyer
101 W. Lombard St., Rm. 910
Baltimore, MD 21201
(410) 962-4210

Diane Gribbon Motz
101 W. Lombard Street, Rm. 920
Baltimore, MD 21201
(410) 962-3606

Robert B. King
300 Virginia Street E.
Charleston, WV 25301
(304) 347-3533

Roger L. Gregory
1000 East Main Street, Rm. 212
Richmond, VA 23219
(804) 916-2607

Allyson K. Duncan
4140 Parklake Ave., Suite 520
Raleigh, NC 27612
(919) 782-2554

G. Steven Agee
1100 E. Main St., Rm. 501
Richmond, VA 23219
(804) 916-2700

Andre M. Davis
101 W. Lombard St., Rm. 5B
Baltimore, MD 21201
(410) 962-0801

# FEDERAL JUDGES

Barbara M. Keenan
1100 E. Main St., Rm. 501
Richmond, VA 23219-3517
(703) 518-8180

James A. Wynn, Jr.
1100 E. Main St., Rm. 501
Richmond, VA 23219-3517
(804) 916-2700

Albert Diaz
1100 E. Main St., Rm. 501
Richmond, VA 23219-3517
(704) 444-7790

Senior Circuit Judges

Clyde H. Hamilton
1901 Main Street, Suite 1250
Columbia, SC 29201-2435
(803) 765-5461

District Judges

**Maryland**

Deborah K. Chasanow, C.J.
6500 Cherrywood Lane, Rm. 465A
Greenbelt, MD 20770
(301) 344-0634

Benson Everett Legg
101 W. Lombard Street, #7A
Baltimore, MD 21201
(410) 962-0723

James K. Bredar
101 W. Lombard St.
Baltimore, MD 21201
(410) 962-0950

Catherine C. Blake
101 W. Lombard St., #7D
Baltimore, MD 21201
(410) 962-3220

Alexander Williams, Jr.
6500 Cherrywood Lane, Rm. 445A
Greenbelt, MD 20770
(301) 344-0637

William D. Quarles, Jr.
101 W. Lombard St., #3A
Baltimore, MD 21201
(410) 962-0946

Richard D. Bennett
101 W. Lombard St., #5D

Baltimore, MD 21201
(410) 962-3190

Roger W. Titus
6500 Cherrywood Lane, Rm. 225A
Greenbelt, MD 20770
(301) 344-0052

Ellen Hollander
101 W. Lombard
Baltimore, MD 21201
(410) 962-0742

**North Carolina - Eastern District**

Louise Flanagan, C.J.
413-415 Middle St.
New Bern, NC 28560
(252) 638-3068

Terrence W. Boyle
P.O. Box 306
Elizabeth City, NC 27907-0306
(252) 338-4033

James C. Dever, III
310 New Bern Ave.
Raleigh, NC 27601
(919) 645-6570

**North Carolina - Middle District**

James A. Beaty, Jr., C.J.
251 N. Main Street, Rm. 248
Winston-Salem, NC 27101
(336) 734-2540

William L. Osteen, Jr.
P.O. Box 2708
Greensboro, NC 27402
(336) 332-6090

Thomas D. Schroeder
251 N. Main St.
Winston-Salem, NC 27101
(336) 734-2530

Catherine C. Eagles
324 W. Market, Rm. 401
Greensboro, NC 27401
(336) 332-6070

**North Carolina - Western District**

Robert J. Conrad, Jr., C.J.
401 West Trade St.
Charlotte, NC 28202
(704) 350-7400

Richard L. Voorhees
401 West Trade St., Rm. 250
Charlotte, NC 28202
(704) 350-7440

Frank DeArmon Whitney
401 West Trade St.
Charlotte, NC 28202
(704) 350-7480

Martin Karl Reidinger
110 U.S. Courthouse
100 Otis Street
Asheville, NC 28801-2611
(828) 771-7260

Max Cogburn
100 Otis St.
Asheville, NC 28801-2611
(828) 771-7250

**South Carolina**

David C. Norton, C.J.
P.O. Box 835
Charleston, SC 29402
(843) 579-1450

Joseph F. Anderson, Jr.
P.O. Box 447
Columbia, SC 29202-0447
(803) 765-5136

Cameron M. Currie
901 Richland St.
Columbia, SC 29201
(803) 253-3680

Terry L. Wooten
P.O. Box 2557
Florence, SC 29501-2557
(843) 676-3809

Margaret B. Seymour
901 Richland St.
Columbia, SC 29201
(803) 765-5590

Henry F. Floyd
201 Magnolia St.
Spartanburg, SC 29306
(864) 591-5303

Robert Bryan Harwell
P.O. Box 2317
Florence, SC 29503-2317
(843) 676-3800

# FEDERAL JUDGES

Richard M. Gergel
Broad & Meeting Streets
Charleston, SC 29401
(843) 579-2610

J. Michelle Childs
300 E. Washington St.
Greenville, SC 29601
(864) 241-2190

**Virginia - Eastern District**

James R. Spencer, C.J.
701 E. Broad St, Suite 3000
Richmond, VA 23219
(804) 916-2250

Henry E. Hudson
701 E. Broad St, Suite 3000
Richmond, VA 23219
(804) 916-2290

Rebecca B. Smith
358 U.S. Courthouse
600 Granby Street
Norfolk, VA 23510-1811
(757) 222-7001

Leonie M. Brinkema
401 Courthouse Square
Alexandria, VA 22314-5798
(703) 299-2116

Raymond Alvin Jackson
307 U.S. Courthouse
600 Granby Street
Norfolk, VA 23510-1811
(757) 222-7003

Gerald Bruce Lee
401 Courthouse Square
Alexandria, VA 22314-5798
(703) 299-2117

Mark S. Davis
600 Granby Street
Norfolk, VA 23510-1811
(757) 222-7014

Liam O'Grady
401 Courthouse Square
Alexandria, VA 22314-5798
(703) 299-2121

Anthony John Trenga
401 Courthouse Square
Alexandria, VA 22314-5798
(703) 299-2113

John A. Gibney, Jr.
701 E. Broad St.
Richmond, VA 23219-3528
(804) 916-2870

Arenda L. Wright Allen
600 Granby Street
Norfolk, VA 23510-1811
(757) 222-7013

**Virginia - Western District**

Glen E. Conrad, C.J.
210 Franklin Road, SW
Roanoke, VA 24011
(540) 857-5135

James P. Jones
P.O. Box 669
Abingdon, VA 24212-0669
(276) 628-4080

Samuel G. Wilson
242 Franklin Road SW
Roanoke, VA 24011-2220
(540) 857-5120

Michael Francis Urbanski
P.O. Box 38
Roanoke, VA 24002
(540) 857-5124

**West Virginia - Northern District**

John P. Bailey, C.J.
P.O. Box 551
Wheeling, VA 26003
(304) 233-1492

Irene M. Keeley
P.O. Box 2808
Clarksburg, VA 26302-2808
(304) 624-5850

**West Virginia - Southern District**

Joseph R. Goodwin, C.J.
P.O. Box 2546
Charleston, WV 25329
(304) 347-3192

John T. Copenhaver, Jr.
P.O. Box 2546
Charleston, WV 25329
(304) 347-3146

Robert C. Chambers
P.O. Box 1570

Huntington, WV 25716
(304) 528-7583

Thomas E. Johnston
P.O. Box 2546
Charleston, WV 25329
(304) 347-3217

Irene Cornelia Berger
P.O. Box 5009
Beckley, WV 25801
(304) 253-7481

Senior District Judges

William M. Nickerson
101 W. Lombard St., #3C
Baltimore, MD 21201
(410) 962-7810

James C. Turk
246 Franklin Road, SW, Rm. 220
Roanoke, VA 24011-2214
(540) 857-5122

Robert G. Doumar
183 U.S. Courthouse
600 Granby Street
Norfolk, VA 23510-1811
(757) 222-7006

Matthew J. Perry, Jr.
901 Richland Street
Columbia, SC 29201
(803) 765-5408

Solomon Blatt, Jr.
P.O. Box 835
Charleston, SC 29402
(843) 579-1470

Glen M. Williams
P.O. Box 339
Abingdon, VA 24212-0339
(276) 628-8147

Jackson L. Kiser
P.O. Box 3326
Danville, VA 24543-3326
(434) 799-8700

W. Earl Britt
P.O. Box 27504
Raleigh, NC 27611-7504
(919) 645-1745

James C. Cacheris
401 Courthouse Square

# FEDERAL JUDGES

Alexandria, VA 22314-5798
(703) 299-2110

James C. Fox
P.O. Box 2143
Wilmington, NC 28402-2143
(910) 815-4738

Marvin J. Garbis
101 W. Lombard St., #5C
Baltimore, MD 21201
(410) 962-7700

C. Weston Houck
P.O. Box 150
Charleston, SC 29402
(843) 579-1480

Henry C. Morgan, Jr.
U.S. Courthouse
600 Granby Street
Norfolk, VA 23510-1811
(757) 222-7002

Graham C. Mullen
401 West Trade St., Rm. 230
Charlotte, NC 28202
(704) 350-7450

Malcolm J. Howard
P.O. Box 5006
Greenville, NC 27835-5006
(252) 830-4976

Claude M. Hilton
401 Courthouse Square
Alexandria, VA 22314-5798
(703) 299-2112

Frederick P. Stamp, Jr.
P.O. Box 791
Wheeling, WV 26003
(304) 233-1120

T. S. Ellis, III
401 Courthouse Square
Alexandria, VA 22314-5798
(703) 299-2114

Robert E. Payne
U.S. Courthouse
701 E. Broad St.
Richmond, VA 23219-3528
(804) 916-2260

Peter J. Messitte
6500 Cherrywood Lane, Rm. 475A
Greenbelt, MD 20770

(301) 344-0632

N. Carlton Tilley, Jr.
P.O. Box 3443
Greensboro, NC 27402
(336) 332-6080

G. Ross Anderson, Jr.
P.O. Box 2147
Anderson, SC 29622-2147
(864) 226-9799

Frederick N. Smalkin
101 W. Lombard St., #3C
Baltimore, MD 21201
(410) 962-3840

David A. Faber
P.O. Box 2546
Charleston, WV 25329
(304) 347-3170

Henry M. Herlong, Jr.
P.O. Box 10469
Grenville, SC 29603
(864) 241-2720

Patrick Michael Duffy
P.O. Box 835
Charleston, SC 29402
(843) 579-1460

J. Frederick Motz
101 W. Lombard Street, #5A
Baltimore, MD 21201
(410) 962-0782

Jerome B. Friedman
600 Granby Street
Norfolk, VA 23510-1811
(757) 222-7004

Norman K. Moon
P.O. Box 657
Lynchburg, VA 24505
(434) 845-4891

## FIFTH CIRCUIT
**(Louisiana, Mississippi, Texas)**
**www.ca5.uscourts.gov**

Circuit Judges

Edith H. Jones, C.J.
12505 U.S. Courthouse
515 Rusk Avenue
Houston, TX 77002-2655

(713) 250-5484

Carolyn Dineen King
11020 U.S. Courthouse
515 Rusk Avenue
Houston, TX 77002
(713) 250-5750

E. Grady Jolly
245 E. Capitol St., Rm. 202
Jackson, MS 39201
(601) 965-4165

W. Eugene Davis
800 Lafayette St., Suite 5100
Lafayette, LA 70501-6883
(337) 593-5280

Jerry E. Smith
12621 U.S. Courthouse
515 Rusk Avenue
Houston, TX 77002
(713) 250-5101

James L. Dennis
600 Camp Street, Rm. 219
New Orleans, LA 70130-3425
(504) 310-8000

Emilio M. Garza
8200 IH-10 West, Suite 501
San Antonio, TX 78230-3878
(210) 525-2950

Fortunato P. Benavides
903 San Jacinto Blvd., Suite 450
Austin, TX 78701-2450
(512) 916-5796

Carl E. Stewart
U.S. Courthouse, Suite 2299
300 Fannin Street
Shreveport, LA 71101-3074
(318) 676-3765

Edith Brown Clement
600 Camp St., Rm. 220
New Orleans, LA 70130
(504) 310-8068

Edward C. Prado
755 E. Mulberry Ave., Suite 350
San Antonio, TX 78212
(210) 472-4060

Priscilla R. Owen
903 San Jacinto Blvd.
Austin, TX 78701-2450

# FEDERAL JUDGES

(512) 916-5167

Jennifer W. Elrod
515 Rusk Ave.
Houston, TX 77002-2603
(713) 257-7590

Leslie H. Southwick
245 E. Capitol St.
Jackson, MS 39201
(601) 965-4017

Catharina Haynes
1100 Commerce St., Rm. 1302
Dallas, TX 75242
(214) 753-2750

James E. Graves, Jr.
245 E. Capitol St.
Jackson, MS 39201
(601) 965-6083

Senior Circuit Judges

Will Garwood
903 San Jacinto Blvd., Suite 300
Austin, TX 78701-2450
(512) 916-5113

Thomas M. Reavley
11009 U.S. Courthouse
515 Rusk Avenue
Houston, TX 77002
(713) 250-5185

Patrick E. Higginbotham
903 San Jacinto Blvd., Suite 400
Austin, TX 78701-2450
(512) 916-5723

Harold R. DeMoss, Jr.
12015 U.S. Courthouse
515 Rusk Avenue
Houston, TX 77002
(713) 250-5462

Rhesa H. Barksdale
245 E. Capitol St., Rm. 200
Jackson, MS 39201-2414
(601) 965-5840

Jacques L. Wiener, Jr.
600 Camp Street, Rm. 244
New Orleans, LA 70130-3425
(504) 310-8098

District Judges

**Louisiana - Eastern District**

Sarah S. Vance, C.J.
U.S. Courthouse
500 Poydras Street, Rm. C-255
New Orleans, LA 70130
(504) 589-7595

Helen G. Berrigan
U.S. Courthouse
500 Poydras St., Rm. C-556
New Orleans, LA 70130-3353
(504) 589-7515

Jay C. Zainey
U.S. Courthouse
500 Poydras St., Rm. C-502
New Orleans, LA 70130
(504) 589-7590

Lance M. Africk
U.S. Courthouse
500 Poydras St., Rm .C-405
New Orleans, LA 70130
(504) 589-7605

Kurt D. Engelhardt
U.S. Courthouse
500 Poydras Street, Rm. C-317
New Orleans, LA 70130
(504) 589-7645

Eldon E. Fallon
U.S. Courthouse
500 Poydras Street, Rm. C-456
New Orleans, LA 70130
(504) 589-7545

Martin L. C. Feldman
U.S. Courthouse
500 Poydras Street, Rm. C-555
New Orleans, LA 70130-3318
(504) 589-7550

Stanwood R. Duval, Jr.
U.S. Courthouse
500 Poydras Street, Rm. C-368
New Orleans, LA 70130-3325
(504) 589-7540

Ivan L.R. Lemelle
500 Poydras Street, Rm. C-525
New Orleans, LA 70130
(504) 589-7555

Carl J. Barbier

500 Poydras Street, Rm. C-256
New Orleans, LA 70130
(504) 589-7525

**Louisiana - Middle District**

James J. Brady, C.J.
777 Florida Street, Rm. 369
Baton Rouge, LA 70801-1712
(225) 389-4030

Brian A. Jackson
777 Florida Street, Rm. 375
Baton Rouge, LA 70801-1712
(225) 389-3692

**Louisiana - Western District**

Robert G. James, C.J.
P.O. Drawer 3107
Monroe, LA 71210-3107
(318) 322-6230

Richard T. Haik
800 Lafayette Street, Room 4200
Lafayette, LA 70501
(337) 593-5100

Rebecca F. Doherty
800 Lafayette Street, Room 4900
Lafayette, LA 70501
(337) 593-5050

Dee D. Drell
P.O. Box 1071
Alexandria, LA 71309-1071
(318) 473-7420

Patricia Head Minaldi
611 Broad St., Suite 237
Lake Charles, LA 70601
(318) 437-3880

S. Maurice Hicks, Jr.
1167 U.S. Courthouse
300 Fannin St.
Shreveport, LA 71101
(318) 676-3055

Elizabeth Foote
300 Fannin St.
Shreveport, LA 71101
(318) 934-4780

**Mississippi - Northern District**

Michael P. Mills, C.J.
911 Jackson Ave.

# FEDERAL JUDGES

Oxford, MS 38655
(662) 234-1538

W. Allen Pepper, Jr.
205 Main Street
Greenville, MS 38701
(662) 335-4416

Sharion Aycock
301 W. Commerce St.
Aberdeen, MS 39730
(662) 369-2628

**Mississippi - Southern District**

Henry T. Wingate, C.J.
245 E. Capitol St., Suite 109
Jackson, MS 39201
(601) 965-4042

Louis Guirola, Jr.
2012 15th St., Suite 814
Gulfport, MS 39501
(228) 563-1767

Keith Starrett
701 N. Main Street, Suite 228
Hattiesburg, MS 39401
(601) 583-4422

Daniel P. Jordan, III
245 E. Capitol St., Suite 110
Jackson, MS 39201
(601) 965-4418

Halil Suleyman Ozerden
2012 15th St., Suite 714
Gulfport, MS 39501
(228) 679-1070

Carlton Reeves
245 E. Capitol St.
Jackson, MS 39201
(601) 965-6080

**Texas - Northern District**

A. Joe Fish, C.J.
U.S. Courthouse
1100 Commerce St., Rm. 1528
Dallas, TX 75242-1597
(214) 753-2310

Sidney A. Fitzwater
U.S. Courthouse
1100 Commerce St., Rm. 1520
Dallas, TX 75242
(214) 753-2333

Mary Lou Robinson
P.O. Box F13248
205 East Fifth Ave., #226
Amarillo, TX 79101
(806) 468-3822

Sam R. Cummings
C-210 U.S. Courthouse
1205 Texas Avenue
Lubbock, TX 79401
(806) 472-1922

John H. McBryde
401 U.S. Courthouse
501 W. 10th Street
Ft. Worth, TX 76102-3640
(817) 850-6650

Jorge A. Solis
U.S. Courthouse
1100 Commerce Street, Rm. 1654
Dallas, TX 75242
(214) 753-2342

Terry Means
201 U.S. Courthouse
501 W. 10th Street
Fort Worth, TX 76102
(817) 850-6670

David C. Godbey
U.S. Courthouse
1100 Commerce Street, Rm. 1358
Dallas, TX 75242
(214) 753-2700

James E. Kinkeade
1100 Commerce St., Rm. 1625
Dallas, TX 75242
(214) 753-2720

Sam A. Lindsay
1100 Commerce Street, Rm. 1312
Dallas, TX 75242-1003
(214) 753-2365

Barbara M.G. Lynn
1572 U.S. Courthouse
1100 Commerce Street
Dallas, TX 75242
(214) 753-2420

Jane J. Boyle
1100 Commerce St., Rm. 1376
Dallas, TX 75242-1003
(214) 753-2740

Reed Charles O'Connor

1100 Commerce St., Rm. 1359
Dallas, TX 75242-1003
(214) 753-2650

**Texas - Eastern District**

David Folsom, C.J.
500 State Line Avenue, Rm. 301
Texarkana, TX 75501
(903) 794-4067

Thad Heartfield
P.O. Box 949
Beaumont, TX 77004-0949
(409) 654-2860

Michael H. Schneider
100 U.S. Courthouse
221 West Ferguson Street
Tyler, TX 75702
(903) 590-1091

Richard A. Schell
200 N. Travis
Sherman, TX 75090
(903) 893-7667

Leonard E. Davis
211 W. Ferguson Street
Tyler, TX 75702
(903) 590-1084

Ronald H. Clark
300 Willow Street.
Beaumont, TX 77701
(409) 654-2800

Marcia A. Crone
P.O. Box 1470
Beaumont, TX 77704-1470
(409) 654-2880

**Texas - Southern District**

Ricardo H. Hinojosa, C.J.
1701 W. Business Hwy. 83
Suite 1028
McAllen, TX 78501
(956) 618-8100

Lynn N. Hughes
11122 Federal Building
515 Rusk Avenue
Houston, TX 77002
(713) 250-5900

Kenneth M. Hoyt
11144 Federal Building

# FEDERAL JUDGES

515 Rusk Avenue
Houston, TX 77002
(713) 250-5515

Sim Lake
9535 Federal Building
515 Rusk Avenue
Houston, TX 77002
(713) 250-5177

Melinda Harmon
9114 Federal Building
515 Rusk Avenue
Houston, TX 77002
(713) 250-5518

Nancy F. Atlas
9015 Federal Building
515 Rusk Avenue
Houston, TX 77002
(713) 250-5990

Lee H. Rosenthal
11535 Federal Building
515 Rusk Avenue
Houston, TX 77002
(713) 250-5517

Randy Crane
P.O. Box 5059
McAllen, TX 78502-5059
(956) 618-8063

Andrew S. Hanen
600 E. Harrison St.
Brownsville, TX 78520-7114
(956) 548-2591

Vanessa D. Gilmore
9513 Federal Building
515 Rusk Avenue
Houston, TX 77002
(713) 250-5512

Hilda G. Tagle
600 E. Harrison St., #306
Brownsville, TX 78520-7114
(956) 548-2510

Keith P. Ellison
8631 Federal Building
515 Rusk Avenue
Houston, TX 77208-1010
(713) 250-5806

Micaela Alvarez
P.O. Box 6065
Laredo, TX 78042

(956) 726-2242

Gray H. Miller
515 Rusk Avenue
Houston, TX 77002
(713) 250-5377

Diana Saldana
1300 Victoria St.
Laredo, TX 78040
(956) 790-1381

Nelva Gonzales Ramos
1133 N. Shoreline Blvd.
Corpus Christi, TX 78401
(361) 888-3142

## Texas - Western District

Samuel F. Biery, C.J.
U.S. Courthouse, 1st fl.
655 E. Durango Blvd.
San Antonio, TX 78206-1198
(210) 472-6505

Walter S. Smith, Jr.
800 Franklin Ave.
Waco, TX 76701
(254) 750-1519

Philip R. Martinez
U.S. Courthouse
511 E. San Antonio St.
El Paso, TX 79901-2401
(915) 534-6736

Sam Sparks
200 West Eighth Street, Suite 100
Austin, TX 78701
(512) 916-5230

Alia Moses Ludlum
111 E. Broadway
Del Rio, TX 78840-5573
(830) 703-2038

Robert A. Junell
200 E. Wall St.
Midland, TX 79701
(432) 686-4020

Orlando L. Garcia
U.S. Courthouse, 1st fl.
655 E. Durango Blvd.
San Antonio, TX 78206-1198
(210) 472-6565

Xavier Rodriguez

655 E. Durango Blvd.
San Antonio, TX 78206-1198
(210) 472-6575

Frank Montalvo
525 Magoffin Ave.
El Paso, TX 79901
(915) 534-6600

Kathleen Cardone
511 East San Antonio
El Paso, TX 79901-2401
(915) 534-6740

Earl L. Yeakel, III
200 W. Eighth St.
Austin, TX 78701
(512) 916-5756

Senior District Judges

James R. Nowlin
U.S. Courthouse
200 W. 8th Street
Austin, TX 78701
(512) 916-5675

James T. Trimble, Jr.
611 Broad Street, Suite 237
Lake Charles, LA 70601
(318) 437-3884

Donald E. Walter
300 Fannin Street, Suite 4200
Shreveport, LA 71101
(318) 676-3175

Charles Schwartz, Jr.
500 Poydras Street, Rm. C-317
New Orleans, LA 70130
(504) 589-7520

Frederick J. R. Heebe
U.S. Courthouse
500 Poydras Street
New Orleans, LA 70130
(504) 589-7520

Peter Beer
U.S. Courthouse
500 Poydras Street, Rm. C-117
New Orleans, LA 70130-3384
(504) 589-7510

Tom Stagg
300 Fannin Street, Suite 4100
Shreveport, LA 71101-3091
(318) 676-3260

# FEDERAL JUDGES

Dan M. Russell
2012 15th St., Suite 614
Gulfport, MS 39501
(228) 563-1744

John V. Parker
777 Florida Street, Room 355
Baton Rouge, LA 70801-1712
(225) 389-3568

A. J. McNamara
U.S. Courthouse
500 Poydras Street, Rm. C-107A
New Orleans, LA 70130-3342
(504) 589-7570

Neal B. Biggers, Jr.
P.O. Box 1238
Oxford, MS 38655-1238
(662) 234-3401

Harry Lee Hudspeth
903 San Jacinto, Suite 440
Austin, TX 78701
(512) 916-5837

David Hittner
8509 Federal Building
515 Rusk Avenue
Houston, TX 77002
(713) 250-5711

L.T. Senter, Jr.
2012 15th St., Suite 514
Gulfport, MS 39501
(228) 563-1755

Walter J. Gex, III
2012 15th St., Suite 714
Gulfport, MS 39501
(228) 563-1732

Ewing Werlein
9136 Federal Building
515 Rusk Avenue
Houston, TX 77002
(713) 250-5920

Frank J. Polozola
313 Federal Bldg.
777 Florida Street
Baton Rouge, LA 70801-1712
(225) 389-3576

Thomas S. Lee
245 E. Capitol St., Suite 110
Jackson, MS 39201
(601) 965-4963

William Henry Barbour, Jr.
245 E. Capitol Street, Suite 430
Jackson, MS 39201
(601) 965-4545

David Bramlette
P.O. Box 928
Natchez, MS 39121
(601) 442-3006

Glen H. Davidson
P.O. Box 767
Aberdeen, MS 39730-0767
(662) 369-6486

Tucker L. Melancon
800 Lafayette Street, Room 4700
Lafayette, LA 70501
(337) 593-5065

W. Royal Furgeson, Jr.
U.S. Courthouse
655 East Durango Blvd.
San Antonio, TX 78206
(210) 472-6570

David Briones
525 Magoffin Ave.
El Paso, TX 79901
(915) 534-6744

George P. Kazen
P.O. Box 1060
Laredo, TX 78042-1060
(956) 726-2237

Hayden W. Head, Jr.
1133 N. Shoreline Blvd., Rm. 308
Corpus Christi, TX 78401
(361) 888-3142

Mary Ann Vial Lemmon
U.S. Courthouse
500 Poydras Street, Rm. C-406
New Orleans, LA 70130
(504) 589-7565

John D. Rainey
312 S. Main, Rm. 406
Victoria, TX 77901
(361) 788-5030

Janis Graham Jack
1133 N. Shoreline Blvd., Rm. 321
Corpus Christi, TX 78401
(361) 888-3525

## SIXTH CIRCUIT
(Kentucky, Michigan, Ohio, Tennessee)
www.ca6.uscourts.gov

### Circuit Judges

Alice M. Batchelder, C.J.
143 West Liberty Street
Medina, OH 44256
(330) 764-6026

Danny J. Boggs
220 Gene Snyder U.S. Courthouse
601 West Broadway
Louisville, KY 40202
(502) 625-3900

Boyce F. Martin, Jr.
209 U.S. Courthouse
601 W. Broadway
Louisville, KY 40202
(502) 625-3800

Ransey Guy Cole, Jr.
127 U.S. Courthouse
85 Marconi Blvd.
Columbus, OH 43215
(614) 719-3350

Karen Nelson Moore
801 W. Superior Avenue
Cleveland, OH 44113-1830
(216) 357-7290

John M. Rogers
400 Community Trust Bldg.
100 E. Vine St.
Lexington, KY 40507
(859) 233-2680

Julia Smith Gibbons
481 N. Main St., Rm. 970
Memphis, TN 38103
(901) 495-1265

Eric L. Clay
481 U.S. Courthouse
231 W. Lafayette Blvd.
Detroit, MI 48226
(313) 234-5260

Deborah L. Cook
2 S. Main Street
Akron, OH 44308
(330) 252-6248

Jeffrey S. Sutton

# FEDERAL JUDGES

85 Marconi Blvd.
Columbus, OH 43215
(614) 849-0134

David W. McKeague
100 E. Fifth St.
Cincinnati, OH 45202
(513) 564-7448

Richard A. Griffin
13919 SW Bay Shore Drive
Traverse City, MI 49684
(231) 929-3190

Raymond M. Kethledge
100 E. Fifth St.
Cincinnati, OH 45202
(513) 564-7000

Helene N. White
100 E. Fifth St.
Cincinnati, OH 45202
(513) 564-7000

Jane B. Stranch
100 E. Fifth St.
Cincinnati, OH 45202
(513) 564-7000

Senior Circuit Judges

Damon J. Keith
240 U.S. Courthouse
231 W. Lafayette Blvd.
Detroit, MI 48226
(313) 234-5245

Eugene E. Siler, Jr.
310 S. Main St.
London, KY 40741
(606) 877-7930

Cornelia G. Kennedy
231 W. Lafayette Blvd.
744 U.S. Courthouse
Detroit, MI 48226
(313) 234-5240

Ralph B. Guy, Jr.
P.O. Box 7910
Ann Arbor, MI 48107
(734) 741-2300

Gilbert S. Merritt
303 Customs House
701 Broadway
Nashville, TN 37203
(615) 736-5957

Martha Craig Daughtrey
300 Customs House
701 Broadway
Nashville, TN 37203
(615) 736-7678

Ronald Lee Gilman
167 N. Main Street, Rm. 1176
Memphis, TN 38103
(901) 495-1575

Alan E. Norris
85 Marconi Blvd.
Columbus, OH 43215
(614) 719-3330

Richard F. Suhrheinrich
315 W. Allegan St., Suite 241
Lansing, MI 48933
(517) 377-1513

James L. Ryan
611 U.S. Courthouse
231 W. Lafayette Blvd.
Detroit, MI 48226
(313) 234-5250

District Judges

**Kentucky - Eastern District**

Jennifer B. Coffman, C.J.
P.O. Box 2228
Lexington, KY 40595-2228
(859) 233-2453

Karen K. Caldwell
330 W. Broadway
Frankfort, KY 40601
(606) 875-4777

Danny Reeves
310 S. Main St.
London, KY 40745
(606) 877-7960

David L. Bunning
P.O. Box 232
Covington, KY 41011
(859) 392-7907

Gregory F. Van Tatenhove
310 S. Main St.
London, KY 40745
(606) 877-7950

Amul R. Thapar
110 Main St.

Pikeville, KY 41501-1100
(606) 437-6160

**Kentucky - Western District**

Thomas B. Russell, C.J.
307 Federal Building
501 Broadway
Paducah, KY 42001
(270) 415-6430

John G. Heyburn, II
208 U.S. Courthouse
601 West Broadway
Louisville, KY 40202
(502) 625-3620

Charles R. Simpson, III
247 U.S. Courthouse
601 West Broadway
Louisville, KY 40202
(502) 625-3600

Joseph H. McKinley, Jr.
206 Federal Building
423 Frederica Street
Owensboro, KY 42301
(270) 684-4430

Jennifer B. Coffman
P.O. Box 2228
Lexington, KY 40588-2228
(859) 233-2453

**Michigan - Eastern District**

Gerald E. Rosen, C.J.
730 U.S. Courthouse
231 W. Lafayette Blvd.
Detroit, MI 48226
(313) 234-5135

Paul D. Borman
740 U.S. Courthouse
231 W. Lafayette Blvd.
Detroit, MI 48226
(313) 234-5120

Robert H. Cleland
707 U.S. Courthouse
231 W. Lafayette Blvd.
Detroit, MI 48226
(313) 234-5525

Nancy G. Edmunds
211 U.S. Courthouse
231 W. Lafayette Blvd.
Detroit, MI 48226

# FEDERAL JUDGES

(313) 234-5155

Denise Page Hood
251 U.S. Courthouse
231 W. Lafayette Blvd.
Detroit, MI 48226
(313) 234-5165

George Caram Steeh, III
238 U.S. Courthouse
231 W. Lafayette Boulevard
Detroit, MI 48226
(313) 234-5175

Victoria A. Roberts
123 U.S. Courthouse
231 W. Lafayette Blvd.
Detroit, MI 48226
(313) 234-5230

Marianne O. Battani
277 U.S. Courthouse
231 W. Lafayette Blvd.
Detroit, MI 48226
(313) 234-2625

David M. Lawson
P.O. Box 913
Bay City, MI 48707
(989) 894-8810

Sean F. Cox
235 U.S. Courthouse
231 W. Lafayette Blvd.
Detroit, MI 48226
(313) 234-2650

Thomas L. Ludington
1000 Washington Ave.
Bay City, MI 48707
(989) 894-8810

Stephen J. Murphy
231 W. Lafayette Blvd.
Detroit, MI 48226
(313) 234-2680

Mark A. Goldsmith
600 Church St., Rm. 132
Flint, MI 48502
(810) 341-7060

## Michigan - Western District

Paul L. Maloney, C.J.
410 W. Michigan Ave.
Kalamazoo, MI 49007
(269) 381-4741

Robert Holmes Bell
416 Federal Bldg.
110 Michigan St., NW
Grand Rapids, MI 49503-2363
(616) 456-2021

Robert James Jonker
110 Michigan St., NW
Grand Rapids, MI 49503-2363
(616) 456-2551

Janet T. Neff
110 Michigan St., NW
Grand Rapids, MI 49503-2363
(616) 456-6774

## Ohio - Northern District

Solomon Oliver, Jr., C.J.
U.S. Courthouse
801 W. Superior Ave.
Cleveland, OH 44113-1830
(216) 357-7171

Donald C. Nugent
U.S. Courthouse
801 W. Superior Ave.
Cleveland, OH 44113-1830
(216) 357-7160

Patricia A. Gaughan
U.S. Courthouse
801 W. Superior Ave.
Cleveland, OH 44113-1830
(216) 357-7210

James S. Gwin
U.S. Courthouse
2 S. Main Street
Akron, OH 44308
(330) 252-6050

John R. Adams
2 S. Main Street
Akron, OH 44308
(330) 252-6070

Dan A. Polster
801 W. Superior Ave.
Cleveland, OH 44113-1830
(216) 357-7190

Christopher A. Boyko
801 W. Superior Ave.
Cleveland, OH 44113-1830
(216) 357-7151

Sara Elizabeth Lioi

2 S. Main Street
Akron, OH 44308
(330) 252-6060

Jack Zouhary
1716 Spielbusch Ave.
Toledo, OH 43624
(419) 213-5675

Benita Y. Pearson
125 Market St., Rm. 313
Youngstown, OH 44503-1780
(330) 884-7435

## Ohio - Southern District

Susan J. Dlott, C.J.
227 U.S. Courthouse
100 E. Fifth Street
Cincinnati, OH 45202
(513) 564-7630

Edmund A. Sargus, Jr.
301 U.S. Courthouse
85 Marconi Blvd.
Columbus, OH 43215
(614) 719-3240

Algenon L. Marbley
319 U.S. Courthouse
85 Marconi Boulevard
Columbus, OH 43215
(614) 719-3260

Thomas M. Rose
200 W. 2nd Street
Dayton, OH 45402
(937) 512-1600

Gregory L. Frost
85 Marconi Blvd., Rm. 260
Columbus, OH 43215
(614) 719-3300

Michael H. Watson
322 U.S. Courthouse
85 Marconi Blvd.
Columbus, OH 45215
(614) 719-3280

Michael Ryan Barrett
815 U.S. Courthouse
100 E. Fifth St.
Cincinnati, OH 45202
(513) 564-7660

Timothy S. Black
100 E. Fifth St.

# FEDERAL JUDGES

Cincinnati, OH 45202
(513) 564-7640

**Tennessee - Middle District**

Todd J. Campbell, C.J.
A820 U.S. Courthouse
801 Broadway
Nashville, TN 37203-3869
(615) 736-5291

Aleta A. Trauger
825 U.S. Courthouse
801 Broadway
Nashville, TN 37203
(615) 736-7143

William Joseph Haynes, Jr.
A845 U.S. Courthouse
801 Broadway
Nashville, TN 37203-3869
(615) 736-7217

Kevin H. Sharp
A820 U.S. Courthouse
801 Broadway
Nashville, TN 37203-3869
(615) 736-2774

**Tennessee - Western District**

Jon Phipps McCalla, C.J.
907 Federal Bldg
167 North Main Street
Memphis, TN 38103
(901) 495-1291

Samuel H. Mays, Jr.
1111 Federal Building
167 North Main Street
Memphis, TN 38103
(901) 495-1283

Bernice B. Donald
951 Federal Building
167 North Main Street
Memphis, TN 38103
(901) 495-1299

J. Daniel Breen
167 North Main Street
Memphis, TN 38103
(901) 495-1312

S. Thomas Anderson
167 North Main Street
Memphis, TN 38103
(901) 495-1495

**Tennessee - Eastern District**

Curtis L. Collier, C.J.
P.O. Box 831
Chattanooga, TN 37401-0831
(423) 752-5287

Thomas A. Varlan
800 Market St., Suite 143
Knoxville, TN 37902
(865) 545-4762

Thomas W. Phillips
800 Market St., Suite 145
Knoxville, TN 37902
(865) 545-4255

J. Ronnie Greer
220 West Depot St., Suite 405
Greeneville, TN 37743
(423) 639-0063

Harry S. Mattice, Jr.
900 Georgia Ave.
Chattanooga, TN 37402
(423) 752-5184

Senior District Judges

Thomas A. Wiseman, Jr.
777 U.S. Courthouse
801 Broadway
Nashville, TN 37203-3869
(615) 736-7013

G. Wix Unthank
P.O. Box 5112
London, KY 40745-5112
(606) 864-0264

Edward H. Johnstone
219 Federal Bldg.
501 Broadway
Paducah, KY 42001
(270) 415-6450

Wendell A. Miles
236 Federal Bldg.
110 Michigan Street, NW
Grand Rapids, MI 49503-2363
(616) 456-2314

John Feikens
851 U.S. Courthouse
231 W. Lafayette Blvd.
Detroit, MI 48226
(313) 234-5125

Julian Abele Cook, Jr.
718 U.S. Courthouse
231 W. Lafayette Blvd.
Detroit, MI 48226
(313) 234-5100

S. Arthur Spiegel
838 U.S. Courthouse
100 E. Fifth Street
Cincinnati, OH 45202
(513) 564-7620

Anna Diggs Taylor
619 U.S. Courthouse
231 W. Lafayette Blvd.
Detroit, MI 48226
(313) 234-5105

John T. Nixon
745 U.S. Courthouse
801 Broadway
Nashville, TN 37203-3869
(615) 736-5778

R. Leon Jordan
800 Market Street, Rm. 141
Knoxville, TN 37901
(865) 545-4224

Herman J. Weber
801 U.S. Courthouse
100 E. Fifth Street
Cincinnati, OH 45202
(513) 564-7600

George C. Smith
101 U.S. Courthouse
85 Marconi Boulevard
Columbus, OH 43215
(614) 719-3220

Patrick J. Duggan
867 U.S. Courthouse
231 W. Lafayette Blvd.
Detroit, MI 48226
(313) 234-5145

Paul V. Gadola
600 Church Street, Rm. 140
Flint, MI 48502
(810) 341-7845

William O. Bertelsman
P.O. Box 1073
Covington, KY 41012-1073
(859) 392-7900

Avern Cohn

# FEDERAL JUDGES

219 U.S. Courthouse
231 W. Lafayette Blvd.
Detroit, MI 48226
(313) 234-5160

Henry R. Wilhoit, Jr.
320 Federal Bldg.
1405 Greenup Avenue
Ashland, KY 41101
(606) 329-2592

Karl S. Forester
P.O. Box 2165
Lexington, KY 40595-2165
(859) 233-2625

Walter H. Rice
909 Federal Bldg.
200 W. 2nd St.
Dayton, OH 45402
(937) 512-1500

James L. Graham
169 U.S. Courthouse
85 Marconi Boulevard
Columbus, OH 43215
(614) 719-3200

Richard A. Enslen
410 W. Michigan Ave.
Kalamazoo, MI 49007
(269) 343-7542

Gordon J. Quist
482 Federal Bldg.
110 Michigan St. NW
Grand Rapids, MI 49503-2363
(616) 456-2253

R. Allan Edgar
900 Georgia Ave.
Chattanooga, TN 37402
(423) 752-5220

Lawrence P. Zatkoff
526 Water St., 2nd fl.
Port Huron, MI 48060
(810) 984-3290

John Corbett O'Meara
200 E. Liberty St., Suite 400
Ann Arbor, MI 48103
(734) 741-2106

Joseph M. Hood
P.O. Box 2227
Lexington, KY 40595-2227
(859) 233-2415

Bernard A. Friedman
101 U.S. Courthouse
231 W. Lafayette Blvd.
Detroit, MI 48226
(313) 234-5170

Sandra S. Beckwith
810 U.S. Courthouse
100 E. Fifth Street
Cincinnati, Oh 45202
(513) 564-7610

James D. Todd
448 U.S. Courthouse
111 South Highland Avenue
Jackson, TN 38301
(731) 421-9222

Peter C. Economus
313 Federal Building
125 Market Street
Youngstown, OH 44503
(330) 884-7440

Arthur J. Tarnow
124 U.S. Courthouse
231 W. Lafayette Blvd.
Detroit, MI 48226
(313) 234-5180

James G. Carr
210 U.S. Courthouse
1716 Spielbusch Ave.
Toledo, OH 43624-1363
(419) 213-5555

David D. Dowd, Jr.
2 S. Main St.
Akron, OH 44308-1813
(330) 252-6034

David A. Katz
210 U.S. Courthouse
1716 Spielbusch Ave.
Toledo, OH 43624-1363
(419) 213-5710

Lesley B. Wells
201 East Superior Ave.
Cleveland, OH 44114-1201
(216) 615-4480

## SEVENTH CIRCUIT
**(Illinois, Indiana, Wisconsin)**
**www.ca7.uscourts.gov**

Circuit Judges

Frank H. Easterbrook, C.J.
U.S. Courthouse
219 South Dearborn Street, Rm. 2746
Chicago, IL 60604
(312) 435-5808

Joel M. Flaum
U.S. Courthouse
219 South Dearborn Street, Rm. 2702
Chicago, IL 60604
(312) 435-5626

Richard A. Posner
U.S. Courthouse
219 South Dearborn St., Rm. 2788-F
Chicago, IL 60604
(312) 435-5806

Diane P. Wood
U.S. Courthouse
219 South Dearborn Street, Rm. 2602
Chicago, IL 60604
(312) 435-5521

Terence T. Evans
517 E. Wisconsin Ave., Suite 721
Milwaukee, WI 53202
(414) 297-3222

Daniel A. Manion
301 Federal Building
204 S. Main Street
South Bend, IN 46601
(574) 246-8060

Michael S. Kanne
P.O. Box 1340
Lafayette, IN 47902-1340
(765) 420-6200

Ilana Diamond Rovner
U.S. Courthouse
219 South Dearborn Street, Rm. 2774
Chicago, IL 60604
(312) 435-5608

Ann Claire Williams
U.S. Courthouse
219 South Dearborn Street, Rm. 2612
Chicago, IL 60604
(312) 435-5532

Diane S. Sykes
517 E. Wisconsin Ave., Rm. 716
Milwaukee, WI 53202
(414) 727-6988

Richard D. Cudahy

# FEDERAL JUDGES

U.S. Courthouse
219 South Dearborn St., Rm. 2648
Chicago, IL 60604
(312) 435-5825

John L. Coffey
U.S. Courthouse
219 South Dearborn St., Rm. 2688A
Chicago, IL 60604
(312) 435-5850

William J. Bauer
U.S. Courthouse
219 South Dearborn St., Rm. 2754
Chicago, IL 60604
(312) 435-5810

John Daniel Tinder
46 E. Ohio St., Rm. 304
Indianapolis, IN 46204
(317) 229-3680

Kenneth F. Ripple
208 U.S. Courthouse
204 S. Main Street
South Bend, IN 46601
(574) 246-8150

David F. Hamilton
46 E. Ohio St., Rm. 304
Indianapolis, IN 46204
(317) 229-3640

District Judges

**Illinois - Northern District**

James F. Holderman, C.J.
2548 Dirksen Bldg.
219 South Dearborn Street
Chicago, IL 60604
(312) 435-5600

Joan B. Gottschall
2356 Dirksen Bldg.
219 South Dearborn Street
Chicago, IL 60604
(312) 435-5640

Charles R. Norgle, Sr.
2346 Dirksen Bldg.
219 South Dearborn Street
Chicago, IL 60604
(312) 435-5634

James B. Zagel
2188 Dirksen Bldg.
219 South Dearborn Street

Chicago, IL 60604
(312) 435-5713

Mark Filip
1978 Dirksen Bldg.
219 South Dearborn Street
Chicago, IL 60604
(312) 435-5667

Virginia M. Kendall
2378 Dirksen Bldg.
219 S. Dearborn St.
Chicago, IL 60604
(312) 435-5692

Ruben Castillo
2378 Dirksen Bldg.
219 South Dearborn Street
Chicago, IL 60604
(312) 435-5878

Rebecca R. Pallmeyer
2178 Dirksen Bldg.
219 South Dearborn Street
Chicago, IL 60604
(312) 435-5636

Matthew F. Kennelly
2188 Dirksen Bldg.
219 South Dearborn Street
Chicago, IL 60604
(312) 435-5670

William J. Hibbler
1262 Dirksen Bldg.
219 South Dearborn Street
Chicago, IL 60604
(312) 435-5670

Ronald A. Guzman
1278 Dirksen Bldg.
219 South Dearborn Street
Chicago, IL 60604
(312) 435-5363

John W. Darrah
1288 Dirksen Bldg.
219 South Dearborn Street
Chicago, IL 60604
(312) 435-5619

Joan Humphrey Lefkow
1956 Dirksen Bldg.
219 South Dearborn Street
Chicago, IL 60604
(312) 435-5832

Samuel Der-Yeghiayan

1988 Dirksen Bldg.
219 South Dearborn Street
Chicago, IL 60604
(312) 435-5675

Amy J. St. Eve
1260 Dirksen Bldg.
219 South Dearborn Street
Chicago, IL 60604
(312) 435-5686

Robert M. Dow
1773 Dirksen Bldg.
219 South Dearborn Street
Chicago, IL 60604
(312) 435-5665

Frederick J. Kapala
211 S. Court St.
Rockford, IL 61101
(815) 987-4354

Sharon J. Coleman
1460 Dirksen Bldg.
219 South Dearborn Street
Chicago, IL 60604
(312) 435-6885

Gary S. Feinerman
1078 Dirksen Bldg.
219 South Dearborn Street
Chicago, IL 60604
(312) 435-5627

Edmond E. Chang
1486 Dirksen Bldg.
219 South Dearborn Street
Chicago, IL 60604
(312) 435-5795

**Illinois - Southern District**

David R. Herndon, C.J.
750 Missouri Ave.
East St. Louis, IL 62201
(618) 482-9077

G. Patrick Murphy
750 Missouri Avenue
East St. Louis, IL 62201
(618) 482-9425

J. Phil Gilbert
U.S. Courthouse
301 West Main Street
Benton, IL 62812
(618) 439-7720

# FEDERAL JUDGES

Michael R. Reagan
750 Missouri Ave.
East St. Louis, IL 62201
(615) 482-9225

## Illinois - Central District

Michael P. McCuskey, C.J.
201 S. Vine Street, Rm. 318
Urbana, IL 61801
(217) 373-5837

Sue E. Myerscough
600 East Monroe St., Suite 319
Springfield, IL 62701
(217) 492-4000

James E. Shadid
204 Federal Building
100 NE Monroe Street
Peoria, IL 61602
(309) 671-4227

Sara Lynn Darrow
211 19th Street
Rock Island, IL 61201
(309) 793-5779

## Indiana - Northern District

Phillip Peter Simon, C.J.
5400 Federal Plaza, Suite 4200
Hammond, IN 46320
(219) 852-6740

Robert L. Miller, Jr.
325 Federal Bldg.
204 South Main Street
South Bend, IN 46601
(574) 246-8080

Joseph S. Van Bokkelen
5400 Federal Plaza, Suite 4200
Hammond, IN 46320
(219) 852-6720

Theresa Lazar Springmann
1300 S. Harrison St.
Fort Wayne, IN 46802
(260) 423-3050

Jon E. DeGuilio
204 South Main St., Rm. 124
South Bend, IN 46601
(574) 246-8170

## Indiana - Southern District

Richard L. Young, C.J.
353 U.S. Courthouse
46 East Ohio Street
Indianapolis, IN 46204
(317) 229-3692

Sarah Evans Barker
210 U.S. Courthouse
46 East Ohio Street
Indianapolis, IN 46204
(317) 229-3600

William T. Lawrence
U.S. Courthouse
46 East Ohio Street
Indianapolis, IN 46204
(317) 229-3610

Jane E. Magnus-Stinon
46 East Ohio St., Rm. 361
Indianapolis, IN 46204
(317) 229-3670

Tanya W. Pratt
46 East Ohio St., Rm. 459
Indianapolis, IN 46204
(317) 229-3981

## Wisconsin - Eastern District

Charles N. Clevert, C.J.
371 U.S. Courthouse
517 East Wisconsin Avenue
Milwaukee, WI 53202-5404
(414) 297-1585

Rudolph T. Randa
364 U.S. Courthouse
517 East Wisconsin Ave.
Milwaukee, WI 53202
(414) 297-3071

J.P. Stadtmueller
471 U.S. Courthouse
517 East Wisconsin Avenue
Milwaukee, WI 53202
(414) 297-1122

William C. Griesbach
P.O. Box 22370
Green Bay, WI 54305
(920) 884-7775

Lynn Adelman
364 U.S. Courthouse
517 East Wisconsin Ave.

Milwaukee, WI 53202
(414) 297-1285

## Wisconsin - Western District

William M. Conley, C.J.
P.O. Box 432
Madison, WI 53701
(608) 264-5156

### Senior District Judges

Marvin E. Aspen
2578 U.S. Courthouse
219 South Dearborn Street
Chicago, IL 60604
(312) 435-5600

William C. Lee
2100 Federal Building
1300 South Harrison Street
Fort Wayne, IN 46802
(260) 423-3030

Harry D. Lienenweber
1946 U.S. Courthouse
219 South Dearborn Street
Chicago, IL 60604
(312) 435-7612

William T. Hart
2246 U.S. Courthouse
219 South Dearborn Street
Chicago, IL 60604
(312) 435-5776

John F. Grady
2286 U.S. Courthouse
219 South Dearborn Street
Chicago, IL 60604
(312) 435-5848

Milton I. Shadur
2388 U.S. Courthouse
219 South Dearborn Street
Chicago, IL 60604
(312) 435-5766

John A. Nordberg
1886 U.S. Courthouse
219 South Dearborn Street
Chicago, IL 60604
(312) 435-5782

William D. Stiehl
750 Missouri Avenue
East St. Louis, IL 62201
(618) 482-9230

# FEDERAL JUDGES

Thomas J. Curran
250 U.S. Courthouse
517 East Wisconsin Avenue
Milwaukee, WI 53202-4504
(414) 297-4167

George M. Marovich
1900 U.S. Courthouse
219 South Dearborn Street
Chicago, IL 60604
(312) 435-5590

George W. Lindberg
1460 U.S. Courthouse
219 South Dearborn Street
Chicago, IL 60604
(312) 435-5356

James T. Moody
5400 Federal Plaza, Suite 4100
Hammond, IN 46320
(219) 852-3460

Suzanne B. Conlon
1746 Dirksen Bldg.
219 South Dearborn Street
Chicago, IL 60604
(312) 435-5595

Charles P. Kocoras
2548 Dirksen Bldg.
219 South Dearborn Street
Chicago, IL 60604
(312) 435-6872

Philip G. Reinhard
211 South Court Street
Rockford, IL 61101
(815) 987-4480

Harold A. Baker
201 S. Vine Street, Rm. 338
Urbana, IL 61801
(217) 373-5835

Richard Mills
600 East Monroe St., Suite 117
Springfield, IL 62701
(217) 492-4340

Rudy Lozano
5400 Federal Plaza, Suite 4300
Hammond, IN 46320
(219) 852-3600

Robert W. Gettleman
1788 Dirksen Bldg.
219 South Dearborn Street

Chicago, IL 60604
(312) 435-5543

John C. Shabaz
P.O. Box 432
Madison, WI 53701-0591
(608) 264-5156


Larry J. McKinney
204 U.S. Courthouse
46 East Ohio Street
Indianapolis, IN 46204
(317) 229-3650

Michael M. Mihm
204 Federal Building
100 NE Monroe Street
Peoria, IL 61602
(309) 671-7113

Blanche M. Manning
2156 Dirksen Bldg.
219 South Dearborn Street
Chicago, IL 60604
(312) 435-7608

Elaine E. Bucklo
1446 Dirksen Bldg.
219 South Dearborn Street
Chicago, IL 60604
(312) 435-7610

Joe Billy McDade
1227 Federal Building
100 NE Monroe Street
Peoria, IL 61602
(309) 671-7821

Barbara B. Crabb
P.O. Box 432
Madison, WI 53701
(608) 264-5156

## EIGHTH CIRCUIT
**(Arkansas, Iowa, Minnesota,
Missouri, Nebraska, North Dakota,
South Dakota)
www.ca8.uscourts.gov/**

Circuit Judges

William Jay Riley, C.J.
111 S. 18th Plaza, Suite 4303
Omaha, NE 68102-1322
(402) 661-7575

James B. Loken
U.S. Courthouse, Suite 11W
300 South 4th Street
Minneapolis, MN 55415
(612) 664-5810

Roger L. Wollman
315 Federal Bldg. & Courthouse
Sioux Falls, SD 57102
(605) 330-6680

Michael J. Melloy
625 1st St., Suite 200
Cedar Rapids, IA 52401
(319) 363-7580

Diana E. Murphy
300 South 4th Street, Suite 11E
Minneapolis, MN 55415
(612) 664-5820

Kermit Edward Bye
655 First Avenue N., Suite 330
Fargo, ND 58102-4952
(701) 297-7270

Lavenski R. Smith
425 W. Capitol Ave., Suite 3110
Little Rock, AR 72201
(501) 324-7310

Steven M. Colloton
110 E. Court Ave.
Des Moines, IA 50309
(515) 284-6356

Raymond W. Gruender
111 S. 10th Street
St. Louis, MO 63102
(314) 244-2820

William Duane Benton
400 East Ninth Street, Rm. 10-00
Kansas City, MO 64106-2605
(816) 512-5815

Bobby E. Shepherd
101 S. Jackson, Rm. 306
El Dorado, AR 71730
(870) 863-3173

Senior Circuit Judges

Myron H. Bright
655 First Avenue North, Rm. 340
Fargo, ND 58102-4952
(701) 297-7260

# FEDERAL JUDGES

C. Arlen Beam
435 Federal Bldg
Lincoln, NE 68508
(402) 437-1600

Pasco M. Bowman, II
400 East 9th Street, Rm. 10-50
Kansas City, MO 64106
(816) 512-5800

Morris S. Arnold
P.O. Box 2060
Little Rock, AR 72203-2060
(501) 324-6880

District Judges

## Arkansas - Eastern District

J. Leon Holmes, C.J.
500 W. Capitol Ave., Rm. D469
Little Rock, AR 72201-3325
(501) 604-5380

Susan Webber Wright
500 W. Capitol Ave., Rm. D157
Little Rock, AR 72201-3325
(501) 604-5100

Brian S. Miller
500 W. Capitol Ave., Rm. D258
Little Rock, AR 72201
(501) 604-5400

Denzil P. Marshall, Jr.
500 W. Capitol Ave.
Little Rock, AR 72201
(501) 604-5410

## Arkansas - Western District

Jimm L. Hendren, C.J.
35 E. Mountain St., Rm. 559
Fayetteville, AR 72701
(479) 444-7876

Paul K. Holmes, III
30 S. 6th St., Rm. 317
Fort Smith, AR 72901
(479) 783-1466

## Iowa - Northern District

Linda R. Reade, C.J.
4200 C St., SW
Cedar Rapids, IA 52401
(319) 286-2330

Mark W. Bennett
320 Sixth Street, Suite 313
Sioux City, IA 51101
(712) 233-3909

## Iowa - Southern District

Robert W. Pratt, C.J.
221 U.S. Courthouse
123 East Walnut Street
Des Moines, IA 50309
(515) 284-6254

James E. Gritzner
123 E. Walnut St.
Des Moines, IA 50309
(515) 284-6291

John A. Jarvey
131 E. 4th St.
Davenport, IA 52801
(563) 884-7607

## Minnesota

Michael J. Davis, C.J.
14E U.S. Courthouse
300 S. 4th Street
Minneapolis, MN 55415
(612) 664-5070

John R. Tunheim
13E U.S. Courthouse
300 S. 4th Street
Minneapolis, MN 55415
(612) 664-5080

Ann D. Montgomery
13W U.S. Courthouse
300 S. 4th Street
Minneapolis, MN 55415
(612) 664-5090

Joan Ericksen
700 Federal Bldg.
316 N. Robert St.
St. Paul, MN 55101
(651) 848-1230

Donovan W. Frank
738 Federal Bldg.
316 North Robert St.
St. Paul, MN 55101
(651) 848-1290

Patrick J. Schiltz
790 Federal Bldg.
316 N. Robert St.

St. Paul, MN 55101
(651) 848-1900

Susan R. Nelson
774 Federal Bldg.
316 N. Robert St.
St. Paul, MN 55101
(651) 848-1970

## Missouri - Eastern District

Catherine D. Perry, C.J.
U.S. Courthouse
111 S. 10th Street, 14th fl.
St. Louis, MO 63102
(314) 244-7520

Carol E. Jackson
U.S. Courthouse
111 S. 10th Street, 14th fl.
St. Louis, MO 63102
(314) 244-7540

Jean C. Hamilton
U.S. Courthouse
111 S. 10th Street, 16th fl.
St. Louis, MO 63102
(314) 244-7600

Henry E. Autrey
U.S. Courthouse
111 S. 10th St., 10th fl.
St. Louis, MO 63102
(314) 244-7450

Rodney W. Sippel
U.S. Courthouse
111 S. 10th Street, 10th fl.
St. Louis, MO 63102
(314) 244-7430

Stephen N. Limbaugh, Jr.
555 Independence St.
Cape Girardeau, MO 63701
(573) 331-8873

Audrey G. Fleissig
U.S. Courthouse
111 S. 10th Street
St. Louis, MO 63102
(314) 244-7420

## Missouri - Western District

Fernando J. Gaitan, Jr., C.J.
7952 U.S. Courthouse
400 East 9th Street
Kansas City, MO 64106

# FEDERAL JUDGES

(816) 512-5630

Gary A. Fenner
8452 U.S. Courthouse
400 East 9th Street
Kansas City, MO 64106
(816) 512-5660

Richard E. Dorr
222 N. John Q. Hammons Pkwy.
Springfield, MO 65806
(417) 865-3741

David Gregory Kays
400 E. Ninth St.
Kansas City, MO 64106
(816) 512-5600

**Nebraska**

Joseph F. Bataillon, C.J.
111 S. 18th Plaza, Suite 3259
Omaha, NE 68102-1322
(402) 661-7302

Laurie Smith Camp
111 S. 18th Plaza, Suite 3210
Omaha, NE 68102-1322
(402) 661-7302

**North Dakota**

Ralph R. Erickson, C.J.
655 1st Ave. N., Suite 410
Fargo, ND 58102
(701) 297-7080

Daniel L. Hovland
P.O. Box 670
Bismarck, ND 58502-0670
(701) 530-2320

**South Dakota**

Karen E. Schreier, C.J.
400 S. Phillips Ave.
Sioux Falls, SD 57704
(605) 330-6670

Jeffrey L. Viken
515 E. 9th Street
Rapid City, SD 57701
(605) 339-6020

Roberto A. Lange
225 S. Pierre St.
Pierre, SD 57501

(605) 945-4610

Senior District Judges

Garnett Thomas Eisele
500 W. Capitol Avenue, Rm. C244
Little Rock, AR 72201-3325
(501) 604-5160

Paul A. Magnuson
730 Federal Building
316 N. Robert Street
St. Paul, MN 55101
(651) 848-1150

Donald D. Alsop
754 Federal Building
316 N. Robert Street
St. Paul, MN 55101
(651) 848-1170

Lyle E. Strom
111 S. 18th Plaza, Suite 3190
Omaha, NE 68102-1322
(402) 661-7320

Edward L. Filippine
U.S. Court House
111 S. 10th Street, 10th fl.
St. Louis, MO 63102
(314) 244-7640

Howard F. Sachs
7462 U.S. Courthouse
400 East 9th Street
Kansas City, MO 64106
(816) 512-5715

Scott O. Wright
8662 U.S. Courthouse
400 East 9th Street
Kansas City, MO 64106
(816) 512-5700

John B. Jones
303 Federal Bldg. & U.S.
  Courthouse
400 S. Phillips Avenue
Sioux Falls, SD 57104-6851
(605) 330-6635

Edward J. McManus
4200 C St. SW
Cedar Rapids, IA 52401
(319) 286-2350

Donald E. O'Brien
P.O. Box 267

Sioux City, IA 51102-0267
(712) 233-3916

Warren K. Urbom
507 Federal Building
100 Centennial Mall North
Lincoln, NE 68508
(402) 437-1940

Harold D. Vietor
485 U.S. Courthouse
123 East Walnut St.
Des Moines, IA 50309-2038
(515) 284-6237

David S. Doty
14W U.S. Courthouse
300 S. 4th Street
Minneapolis, MN 55415
(612) 664-5060

Richard H. Battey
260 Federal Bldg. & U.S.
  Courthouse
515 9th Street
Rapid City, SD 57701
(605) 399-6040

Patrick A. Conmy
P.O. Box 1578
Bismarck, ND 58502-1578
(701) 530-2315

Charles R. Wolle
110 E. Court Ave.
Des Moines, IA 50309-2039
(515) 284-6289

Richard H. Kyle
764 Federal Building
316 N. Robert Street
St. Paul, MN 55101
(651) 848-1160

Ronald E. Longstaff
115 U.S. Courthouse
123 East Walnut Street
Des Moines, IA 50309-2036
(515) 284-6235

Donald J. Stohr
U.S. Courthouse
111 S. 10th Street, 16th fl.
St. Louis, MO 63102
(314) 244-7580

Dean Whipple
8652 U.S. Courthouse

# FEDERAL JUDGES

400 East 9th Street
Kansas City, MO 64106
(816) 512-5615

William R. Wilson
500 W. Capitol Ave., Rm. D444
Little Rock, AR 72201-3325
(501) 604-5140

James M. Moody
500 W. Capitol Ave., Rm. C446
Little Rock, AR 72201-3325
(501) 604-5150

Henry F. Barnes
P.O. Box 1735
El Dorado, AR 71731
(870) 862-1303

Charles Bruno Kornmann
225 S. Pierre St.
Pierre, SD 57501
(605) 945-4610

Robert T. Dawson
P.O. Box 1624
Fort Smith, AR 72902
(479) 783-2898

Lawrence L. Piersol
202 Federal Bldg. & U.S. Courthouse
400 S. Phillips Avenue
Sioux Falls, SD 57104-6851
(605) 330-6640

E. Richard Webber
U.S. Courthouse
111 S. 10th Street, 12th fl.
St. Louis, MO 63102
(314) 244-7460

Charles Shaw
U.S. Courthouse
111 S. 10th Street, 12th fl.
St. Louis, MO 63102
(314) 244-7480

Ortrie D. Smith
8552 U.S. Courthouse
400 East 9th Street
Kansas City, MO 64106
(816) 512-5645

Nanette K. Laughrey
131 W. High St., Rm. 307
Jefferson City, MO 65101
(573) 632-6623

Richard G. Kopf
586 Federal Bldg.
100 Centennial Mall North
Lincoln, NE 68508
(402) 437-1640

**NINTH CIRCUIT**
**(Arizona, California, Idaho,**
**Montana, Nevada, Oregon,**
**Washington, Alaska, Hawaii,**
**Guam, Northern Mariana Islands)**
**www.ca9.uscourts.gov**

Circuit Judges

Alex Kozinski, C.J.
125 South Grand Ave.
Pasadena, CA 91105
(626) 229-7140

Harry Pregerson
125 S. Grand Ave.
Pasadena, CA 91105
(818) 710-7791

Stephen Reinhardt
1747 U.S. Courthouse
312 North Spring Street
Los Angeles, CA 90012
(213) 894-3639

Diarmuid F. O'Scannlain
313 Pioneer Courthouse
700 SW 6th Ave.
Portland, OR 97204-1396
(503) 833-5380

Sidney R. Thomas
P.O. Box 31478
Billings, MT 59107-1478
(406) 657-5950

Pamela Ann Rymer
125 S. Grand Ave.
Pasadena, CA 91105
(626) 229-7210

Richard A. Clifton
1132 Bishop Street, Suite 601
Honolulu, HI 96813
(808) 522-7474

Barry G. Silverman
401 W. Washington St., Rm. 512
Phoenix, AZ 85003
(602) 322-7330

Susan P. Graber
Pioneer Courthouse
700 SW 6th Ave.
Portland, OR 97204
(503) 833-5360

M. Margaret McKeown
401 West A Street
San Diego, CA 92101
(619) 557-5300

Kim McLane Wardlaw
500 Court of Appeals Building
125 South Grand Avenue
Pasadena, CA 91105
(626) 229-7130

William A. Fletcher
95 Seventh St.
San Francisco, CA 94103
(415) 355-8000

Milan D. Smith, Jr.
222 N. Sepulveda Blvd., Suite 2325
El Segundo, CA 90245
(310) 607-4020

Raymond C. Fisher
125 S. Grand Avenue
Pasadena, CA 91105
(626) 229-7110

Ronald M. Gould
940 U.S. Courthouse
1010 Fifth Ave.
Seattle, WA 98104
(206) 224-2280

Richard A. Paez
125 S. Grand Avenue
Pasadena, CA 91105-1652
(626) 229-7180

Marsha S. Berzon
95 Seventh St.
San Francisco, CA 94103
(415) 355-8160

Richard C. Tallman
902 U.S. Courthouse
1010 Fifth Ave.
Seattle, WA 98104
(206) 224-2250

Johnnie B. Rawlinson
333 Las Vegas Boulevard #7072
Las Vegas, NV 89101
(702) 464-5670

# FEDERAL JUDGES

Carlos T. Bea
95 Seventh Street
San Francisco, CA 94103
(415) 355-8180

Jay S. Bybee
333 Las Vegas Blvd. #3099
Las Vegas, NV 89101
(702) 464-5650

Consuelo Maria Callahan
501 I Street
Sacramento, CA 95814
(916) 930-4160

Norman R. Smith
801 E. Sherman
Pocatello, ID 83201
(208) 478-4140

Sandra S. Ikuta
125 S. Grand Ave.
Pasadena, CA 91105
(626) 229-7339

Mary Helen Murguia
95 Seventh St.
San Francisco, CA 94103
(415) 355-8000

Senior Circuit Judges

Ferdinand F. Fernandez
125 S. Grand Ave.
Pasadena, CA 91105
(626) 229-7121

Procter Hug, Jr.
400 South Virginia Street, Suite 708
Reno, NV 89501
(775) 686-5949

Alfred T. Goodwin
125 S. Grand Avenue
Pasadena, CA 91105
(626) 229-7100

Otto R. Skopil, Jr.
827 U.S. Courthouse
1000 Southwest Third Avenue
Portland, OR 97204-2902
(503) 326-8390

Arthur L. Alarcon
1607 U.S. Courthouse
312 North Spring Street
Los Angeles, CA 90012
(213) 894-2693

Robert Boochever
125 S. Grand Ave.
Pasadena, CA 91105
(626) 229-7200

William C. Canby, Jr.
612 U.S. Courthouse
401 W. Washington St.
Phoenix, AZ 85003
(602) 322-7300

Jerome Farris
1030 U.S. Courthouse
1010 Fifth Avenue
Seattle, WA 98101
(206) 224-2260

Dorothy W. Nelson
125 S. Grand Ave.
Pasadena, CA 91105
(626) 229-7400

Robert R. Beezer
802 U.S. Courthouse
1010 Fifth Avenue
Seattle, WA 98104-1115
(206) 224-2270

Edward Leavy
226 Pioneer Courthouse
700 SW 6th Ave.
Portland OR 97204
(503) 833-5350

J. Clifford Wallace
4192 U.S. Courthouse
940 Front Street
San Diego, CA 92101-8918
(619) 557-6114

John T. Noonan, Jr.
95 Seventh St.
San Francisco, CA 94103
(415) 355-8130

Betty Binns Fletcher
1000 U.S. Courthouse
1010 Fifth Avenue
Seattle, WA 98104-1180
(206) 224-2240

James R. Browning
95 Seventh St.
San Francisco, CA 94103
(415) 355-8000

Thomas G. Nelson
P.O. Box 1339

Boise, ID 83701-1339
(208) 334-9744

A. Wallace Tashima
125 S. Grand Ave.
Pasadena, CA 91105
(626) 229-7373

Stephen S. Trott
550 W. Fort St., Rm. 667
Boise, ID 83724
(208) 334-1612

Andrew J. Kleinfeld
250 Cushman Street, Suite 3-A
Fairbanks, AK 99701-4665
(907) 456-0564

Michael Daly Hawkins
401 W. Washington St., Rm. 510
Phoenix, AZ 85003
(602) 322-7310

Mary M. Schroeder
610 U.S. Courthouse
401 W. Washington Street
Phoenix, AZ 8500325
(602) 322-7320

District Judges

**Alaska**

Ralph B. Beistline, C.J.
222 West 7th Avenue, #32
Anchorage, AK 99513
(907) 677-6257

Timothy M. Burgess
222 West 7th Avenue, #32
Anchorage, AK 99513
(907) 677-6203

**Arizona**

Roslyn O. Silver, C.J.
624 U.S. Courthouse
401 W. Washington St., SPC 59
Phoenix, AZ 85003
(602) 322-7520

James A. Teilborg
U.S. Courthouse
401 W. Washington St., SPC 51
Phoenix, AZ 85003
(602) 322-7560

Susan R. Bolton

# FEDERAL JUDGES

522 U.S. Courthouse
401 W. Washington St., SPC 50
Phoenix, AZ 85003
(602) 322-7570

Frederick J. Martone
526 U.S. Courthouse
401 W. Washington St., SPC 62
Phoenix, AZ 85003
(602) 322-7590

Cindy K. Jorgenson
405 W. Congress St., Rm. 5180
Tucson, AZ 85701-5010
(520) 205-4550

David C. Bury
405 W. Congress St., Rm. 6170
Tucson, AZ 85701-5010
(520) 205-4560

Raner Collins
405 W. Congress St., Rm. 5170
Tucson, AZ 85701
(520) 205-4540

David G. Campbell
623 U.S. Courthouse
401 W. Washington St., SPC 58
Phoenix, AZ 85003
(602) 322-7645

Neil Vincent Wake
524 U.S. Courthouse
401 W. Washington St., SPC 52
Phoenix, AZ 85003
(602) 322-7640

G. Murray Snow
401 W. Washington St., SPC1
Phoenix, AZ 85003
(602) 322-7650

## California - Northern District

James Ware, C.J.
U.S. Courthouse
280 South First Street
San Jose, CA 95113
(408) 535-5454

Susan Illston
P.O. Box 36060
450 Golden Gate Avenue
San Francisco, CA 94102-3489
(415) 522-2028

Saundra Brown Armstrong

1301 Clay Street, Suite 400S
Oakland, CA 94612-5212
(510) 637-3559

Claudia Wilken
1301 Clay Street, Suite 400S
Oakland, CA 94612-5212
(510) 637-3542

Charles R. Breyer
P.O. Box 36060
450 Golden Gate Avenue
San Francisco, CA 94102-3489
(415) 522-2062

Jeremy D. Fogel
2112 U.S. Courthouse
280 South First Street
San Jose, CA 95113
(408) 535-5166

William Alsup
P.O. Box 36060
450 Golden Gate Avenue
San Francisco, CA 94102-3489
(415) 522-2020

Phyllis Hamilton
P.O. Box 36060
450 Golden Gate Avenue
San Francisco, CA 94102-3489
(415) 522-4100

Jeffrey S. White
P.O. Box 36060
450 Golden Gate Avenue
San Francisco, CA 94102-3489
(415) 522-4173

Richard G. Seeborg
2112 U.S. Courthouse
280 South First Street
San Jose, CA 95113
(408) 535-5357

Lucy H. Koh
2112 U.S. Courthouse
280 South First Street
San Jose, CA 95113
(408) 535-5391

Edward J. Davila
2112 U.S. Courthouse
280 South First Street
San Jose, CA 95113
(408) 535-5418

Edward M. Chen

## California - Eastern District

Anthony W. Ishii, C.J.
U.S. Courthouse
2500 Tulare St.
Fresno, CA 93721
(559) 499-5660

Garland E. Burrell, Jr.
13-230 U.S. Courthouse
501 I Street
Sacramento, CA 95814-2322
(916) 930-4115

Morrison C. England, Jr.
15-220 U.S. Courthouse
501 I Street
Sacramento, CA 95814-2322
(916) 930-4205

Lawrence J. O'Neill
U.S. Courthouse
2500 Tulare St.
Fresno, CA 93721
(559) 499-5680

John A. Mendez
4-401 U.S. Courthouse
501 I St.
Sacramento, CA 95814
(916) 930-4250

Frank C. Damrell, Jr.
501 I Street, Suite 15-210
Sacramento, CA 95814-2322
(916) 930-4120

Kimberly J. Mueller
501 I Street, Suite 15-230
Sacramento, CA 95814-2322
(916) 930-4260

## California - Central District

Audrey B. Collins, C.J.
255 E. Temple Street
Los Angeles, CA 90012
(213) 894-3759

Manuel L. Real
U.S. Courthouse
312 N. Spring Street
Los Angeles, CA 90012
(213) 894-5696

Dean D. Pregerson
U.S. Courthouse
312 N. Spring Street

# FEDERAL JUDGES

Los Angeles, CA 90012
(213) 894-3913

John F. Walter
312 N. Spring St.
Los Angeles, CA 90012
(213) 894-5396

Percy Anderson
312 N. Spring St.
Los Angeles, CA 90012
(213) 894-1795

R. Gary Klausner
255 E. Temple Street
Los Angeles, CA 90012
(213) 894-2649

George H. King
255 E. Temple St., Suite 650
Los Angeles, CA 90012
(213) 894-6907

Stephen V. Wilson
U.S. Courthouse
312 N. Spring Street
Los Angeles, CA 90012
(213) 894-2881

Philip S. Gutierrez
255 E. Temple Street
Los Angeles, CA 90012
(213) 894-8899

Christina A. Snyder
U.S. Courthouse
312 North Spring Street
Los Angeles, CA 90012
(213) 894-3433

Margaret M. Morrow
255 East Temple Street
Los Angeles, CA 90012
(213) 894-7857

David O. Carter
411 W. 4th St.
Santa Ana, CA 92701
(714) 338-4543

Gary Feess
255 E. Temple Street
Los Angeles, CA 90012
(213) 894-3480

Virginia Anne Phillips
3470 12th St.
Riverside, CA 92501

(951) 328-4461

James V. Selna
U.S. Courthouse
411 West 4th Street, Rm. 1053
Santa Ana, CA 92701
(714) 338-2848

S. James Otero
U.S. Courthouse
312 N. Spring Street
Los Angeles, CA 90012
(213) 894-1796

Cormac J. Carney
U.S. Courthouse
411 West 4th Street, Rm. 1053
Santa Ana, CA 92701
(714) 338-2849

Dale S. Fischer
255 East Temple Street
Los Angeles, CA 90012
(213) 894-0435

Valerie L. Baker Fairbank
312 N. Spring St.
Los Angeles, CA 90012
(213) 894-0066

Andrew J. Guilford
411 West 4th Street
Santa Ana, CA 92701
(714) 338-4757

Otis D. Wright
312 N. Spring St.
Los Angeles, CA 90012
(213) 894-8266

George H. Wu
312 N. Spring St.
Los Angeles, CA 90012
(213) 894-0191

Jacqueline H. Nguyen
312 N. Spring St.
Los Angeles, CA 90012
(213) 894-2554

Dolly M. Gee
312 N. Spring St.
Los Angeles, CA 90012
(213) 894-5452

Josephine S. Tucker
411 West 4th Street
Santa Ana, CA 92701-4516

(714) 338-4750

John A. Kronstadt
255 East Temple Street
Los Angeles, CA 90012
(213) 894-2156

**California - Southern District**

Irma E. Gonzalez, C.J.
4194 U.S. Courthouse
940 Front Street
San Diego, CA 92101-8913
(619) 557-7107

Marilyn L. Huff
5135 U.S. Courthouse
940 Front Street
San Diego, CA 92101-8908
(619) 557-6016

Barry Ted Moskowitz
5160 U.S. Courthouse
940 Front Street
San Diego, CA 92101-8922
(619) 557-5583

Larry Alan Burns
2190 U.S. Courthouse
940 Front Street
San Diego, CA 92101
(619) 557-5874

John A. Houston
2140 U.S. Courthouse
940 Front Street
San Diego, CA 92101
(619) 557-5716

Dana Makato Sabraw
2160 U.S. Courthouse
940 Front Street
San Diego, CA 92101
(619) 557-6262

William Q. Hayes
4135 U.S. Courthouse
940 Front Street
San Diego, CA 92101
(619) 557-6420

Roger T. Benitez
4145 U.S. Courthouse
940 Front St.
San Diego, CA 92101
(619) 446-3589

Janis Lynn Sammartino

# FEDERAL JUDGES

940 Front St.
San Diego, CA 92101
(619) 557-5542

Michael M. Anello
940 Front St., Rm. 4290
San Diego, CA 92101
(619) 557-5960

Anthony J. Battaglia
940 Front St., Rm. 1145
San Diego, CA 92101
(619) 557-3446

## Hawaii

Susan Oki Mollway, C.J.
C-409 Federal Building
300 Ala Moana Blvd.
Honolulu, HI 96850-0435
(808) 541-1720

David A. Ezra
C-300 Federal Building
300 Ala Moana Blvd.
Honolulu, HI 96850-0400
(808) 541-1907

J. Michael Seabright
C-338 Federal Building
300 Ala Moana Blvd.
Honolulu, HI 96850-0435
(808) 541-1804

Leslie K. Kobayashi
C-353 U.S. Courthouse
300 Ala Moana Blvd.
Honolulu, HI 96850-0229
(808) 541-1331

## Idaho

B. Lynn Winmill, C.J.
U.S. Courthouse, MSC 040
550 West Fort Steet
Boise, ID 83724
(208) 334-9145

Edward J. Lodge
U.S. Courthouse, MSC 040
550 West Fort Street
Boise, ID 83724
(208) 334-9270

## Montana

Richard F. Cebull, C.J.
316 N. 26 St., Rm. 5428

Billings, MT 59101
(406) 247-4490

Sam E. Haddon
215 First Ave. N
Great Falls. MT 59401
(406) 727-8877

## Nevada

Robert Clive Jones, C.J.
400 S. Virginia St
Reno, NV 89501
(775) 686-5670

James C. Mahan
U.S. Courthouse
333 Las Vegas Blvd. S., #6085
Las Vegas, NV 89101
(702) 464-5520

Larry R. Hicks
U.S. Courthouse
400 S. Virginia St
Reno, NV 89501
(775) 686-5700

Kent J. Dawson
U.S. Courthouse
333 Las Vegas Blvd. S., #6006
Las Vegas, NV 89101
(702) 464-5560

Gloria M. Navarro
333 Las Vegas Blvd. S.
Las Vegas, NV 89101
(702) 464-5490

## Oregon

Ann L. Aiken, C.J.
1000 SW Third Ave.
Portland, OR 97204-2902
(503) 326-8250

Anna J. Brown
1407 U.S. Courthouse
1000 SW Third Avenue
Portland, OR 97204-2902
(503) 326-8350

Michael W. Mosman
1427 U.S. Courthouse
1000 SW Third Avenue
Portland, OR 97204-2902
(503) 326-8330

Marco A. Hernandez

1000 SW Third Ave.
Portland, OR 97204-2902
(503) 326-8210

Michael H. Simon
1000 SW Third Ave.
Portland, OR 97204-2902
(503) 326-8000

## Washington - Eastern District

Rosanna M. Peterson, C.J.
920 West Riverside Ave., Rm. 840
Spokane, WA 99201
(509) 458-3400

Lonny R. Suko
P.O. Box 2726
Yakima, WA 98907-2726
(509) 573-6650

Edward F. Shea
825 Jadwin Ave., Suite 190
Richland, WA 99352-1386
(509) 376-7261

## Washington - Western District

Robert S. Lasnik, C.J.
700 Stewart Street
Seattle, WA 98101
(206) 370-8800

Barbara Jacobs Rothstein
700 Stewart Street
Seattle, WA 98101
(206) 370-8840

Ronald B. Leighton
1717 Pacific Ave., Rm. 3100
Tacoma, WA 98402
(253) 882-3840

Marsha J. Pechman
700 Stewart Street
Seattle, WA 98101
(206) 370-8820

Ricardo S. Martinez
700 Stewart Street
Seattle, WA 98101
(206) 370-8880

James L. Robart
700 Stewart Street
Seattle, WA 98101
(206) 370-8920

# FEDERAL JUDGES

Benjamin H. Settle
1717 Pacific Ave., Rm. 3100
Tacoma, WA 98402
(253) 882-3850

Richard A. Jones
700 Stewart Street
Seattle, WA 98101
(206) 370-8870

**Guam**

Frances Marie Tydingco-Gatewood
520 W. Soledad Ave.
Hagatna, GU 96910
(671) 473-9200

**Northern Mariana Islands**

Ramona Villagomez Mangiona
P.O. Box 500687
Saipan, MP 96950
(670) 236-3902

Senior District Judges

Robert J. Kelleher
255 E. Temple Street
Los Angeles, CA 90012
(213) 894-5285

Gordon Thompson, Jr.
3195 U.S. Courthouse
940 Front Street
San Diego, CA 92101-8901
(619) 557-6480

Samuel Conti
P.O. Box 36060
450 Golden Gate Avenue
San Francisco, CA 94102-3489
(415) 522-2077

D. Lowell Jensen
1301 Clay Street, Suite 400S
Oakland, CA 94612-5212
(510) 637-3540

Earl H. Carroll
401 W. Washington St., SPC 48
Phoenix, AZ 85003
(602) 322-7530

Alfredo C. Marquez
405 W. Congress St.
Tucson, AZ 85701-5010
(520) 205-4500

Walter T. McGovern

700 Stewart St.
Seattle, WA 98101
(206) 370-8860

William W. Schwarzer
P.O. Box 36060
450 Golden Gate Avenue
San Francisco, CA 94102-3489
(415) 522-4660

Edward C. Reed, Jr.
U.S. Courthouse
400 S. Virginia St.
Reno, NV 89501
(775) 686-5919

Robert E. Coyle
U.S. Courthouse
2500 Tulare St.
Fresno, CA 93721
(559) 499-5640

Edward J. Garcia
13-200 U.S. Courthouse
501 I Street
Sacramento, CA 95814-2322
(916) 930-4225

Owen M. Panner
1207 U.S. Courthouse
1000 SW Third Avenue
Portland, OR 97204-2902
(503) 326-8290

James A. Redden
1527 U.S. Courthouse
1000 SW Third Avenue
Portland, OR 97204-2902
(503) 326-8370

James A. von der Heydt
222 W. 7th Avenue, #40
Anchorage, AK 99513
(907) 667-6254

Justin L. Quackenbush
P.O. Box 1432
Spokane, WA 99210-1432
(509) 458-5280

Thelton E. Henderson
P.O. Box 36060
450 Golden Gate Avenue
San Francisco, CA 94102-3489
(415) 522-2047

Mariana R. Pfaelzer
U.S. Courthouse

312 N. Spring Street
Los Angeles, CA 90012
(213) 894-5286

Rudi M. Brewster
4165 U.S. Courthouse
940 Front Street
San Diego, CA 92101-8902
(619) 557-6190

Lloyd D. George
6073 U.S. Courthouse
333 Las Vegas Blvd. South
Las Vegas, NV 89101
(702) 464-5500

Malcolm F. Marsh
1507 U.S. Courthouse
1000 SW Third Avenue
Portland, OR 97204-2902
(503) 326-8360

Carolyn R. Dimmick
700 Stewart St.
Seattle, WA 98101
(206) 370-8850

Robert C. Broomfield
401 W. Washington St., SPC 61
Phoenix, AZ 85003
(602) 322-7540

Robert E. Jones
1007 U.S. Courthouse
1000 SW Third Avenue
Portland, OR 97204-2902
(503) 326-8340

Charles C. Lovell
901 Front St.
Helena, MT 59626
(406) 441-1350

Alan C. Kay
C-415 Federal Building
300 Ala Moana Blvd.
Honolulu, HI 96850-0415
(808) 541-1904

H. Russel Holland
222 W. 7th Avenue, #54
Anchorage, AK 99513
(907) 677-6252

Jack D. Shanstrom
316 N. 26 St.
Billings, MT 59103-0985
(406) 247-7011

# FEDERAL JUDGES

Lawrence K. Karlton
15-200 U.S. Courthouse
501 I Street
Sacramento, CA 95814-2322
(916) 930-4130

William D. Keller
U.S. Courthouse
312 N. Spring Street
Los Angeles, CA 90012
(213) 894-5350

J. Spencer Letts
U.S. Courthouse
312 N. Spring Street
Los Angeles, CA 90012
(213) 894-0925

Robert J. Bryan
1717 Pacific Avenue, Rm. 4427
Tacoma, WA 98402
(253) 882-3870

Roger G. Strand
622 U.S. Courthouse
401 W. Washington St., SPC 57
Phoenix, AZ 85003
(602) 322-7550

Wm. Fremming Nielson
P.O. Box 2208
Spokane, WA 99210-2208
(509) 458-5290

Paul G. Rosenblatt
621 U.S. Courthouse
401 W. Washington St., SPC 56
Phoenix, AZ 85003
(602) 322-7510

Robert J. Timlin
312 N. Spring St.
Los Angeles, CA 90012
(213) 894-0593

Howard D. McKibben
U.S. Courthouse
400 S. Virginia St.
Reno, NV 89501
(775) 686-5880

James K. Singleton
222 West 7th Avenue, #41
Anchorage, AK 99513
(907) 677-6250

Thomas S. Zilly
700 Stewart Street

Seattle, WA 98101
(206) 370-8830

William B. Shubb
501 I St., Suite 14-210
Sacramento, CA 95814-2322
(916) 930-4230

William B. Enright
940 Front St.
San Diego, CA 92101-8905
(619) 557-5537

Terry J. Hatter, Jr.
U.S. Courthouse
312 N. Spring Street
Los Angeles, CA 90012
(213) 894-5276

Oliver W. Wanger
U.S. Courthouse
2500 Tulare St.
Fresno, CA 93721
(559) 499-5650

Consuelo B. Marshall
312 N. Spring Street
Los Angeles, CA 90012
(213) 894-5288

Ronald S. W. Lew
U.S. Courthouse
312 N. Spring Street
Los Angeles, CA 90012
(213) 894-2682

John C. Coughenour
700 Stewart Street
Seattle, WA 98101
(206) 370-8800

Stephen M. McNamee
U.S. Courthouse
401 W. Washington St., SPC 60
Phoenix, AZ 85003
(602) 322-7555

Ronald M. Whyte
U.S. Courthouse
280 South First Street
San Jose, CA 95113
(408) 535-5331

Alicemarie H. Stotler
1621 U.S. Courthouse
312 N. Spring St.
Los Angeles, CA 90012
(213) 894-2634

Garr M. King
907 U.S. Courthouse
1000 SW Third Avenue
Portland, OR 97204-2902
(503) 326-8230

Fred L. Van Sickle
P.O. Box 2209
Spokane, WA 99210-2209
(509) 458-5250

Maxine M. Chesney
P.O. Box 36060
450 Golden Gate Avenue
San Francisco, CA 94102-3489
(415) 522-2041

Helen Gillmor
C-400 Federal Building
300 Ala Moana Blvd.
Honolulu, HI 96850-0435
(808) 541-3502

Ancer L. Haggerty
1307 U.S. Courthouse
1000 SW Third Avenue
Portland, OR 97204-2902
(503) 326-8320

Robert H. Whaley
P.O. Box 283
Spokane, WA 99210-0283
(509) 458-5270

Marilyn Hall Patel
P.O. Box 36060
450 Golden Gate Avenue
San Francisco, CA 94102-3489
(415) 522-3140

M. James Lorenz
5145 U.S. Courthouse
940 Front Street
San Diego, CA 92101
(619) 557-7669

John W. Sedwick
222 West 7th Avenue, #32
Anchorage, AK 99513
(907) 677-6251

Frank R. Zapata
U.S. Courthouse
405 W. Congress St., Rm. 5160
Tucson, AZ 85701
(520) 205-4530

Jeffrey T. Miller

# FEDERAL JUDGES

3142 U.S. Courthouse
940 Front Street
San Diego, CA 92101-8906
(619) 557-6627

Thomas J. Whelan
3155 U.S. Courthouse
940 Front Street
San Diego, CA 92101
(619) 557-6625

Donald W. Molloy.
P.O. Box 7309
Missoula, MT 59807-7309
(406) 542-7286

A. Howard Matz
U.S. Courthouse
312 North Spring Street
Los Angeles, CA 90012
(213) 894-5283

Roger L. Hunt
U.S. Courthouse
333 Las Vegas Blvd. S., #6018
Las Vegas, NV 89101
(702) 464-5530

Michael R. Hogan
U.S. Courthouse
405 E. 8th Ave., Rm. 5700
Eugene, OR 97401
(541) 431-4150

Philip M. Pro
U.S. Courthouse
333 Las Vegas Blvd. S., #7015
Las Vegas, NV 89101
(702) 464-5510

**TENTH CIRCUIT**
**(Colorado, Kansas, New Mexico,**
**Oklahoma, Utah, Wyoming)**
**www.ca10.uscourts.gov/**

Circuit Judges

Mary Beck Briscoe, C.J.
645 Massachusetts Street, Rm. 400
Lawrence, KS 66044-2235
(785) 843-4067

Paul J. Kelly, Jr.
P.O. Box 10113
Santa Fe. NM 87504-6113
(505) 988-6541

Terrence L. O'Brien
2120 Capitol Ave.
Cheyenne, WY 82001-3631
(307) 433-2400

Timothy M. Tymkovich
1823 Stout Street
Denver, CO 80257
(303) 335-3300

Carlos F. Lucero
423 U.S. Courthouse
1823 Stout Street
Denver, CO 80257
(303) 844-2200

Michael R. Murphy
5438 Federal Building
125 South State Street
Salt Lake City, UT 84138-1181
(801) 524-5955

Harris L. Hartz
201 Third St. NW, Suite 1870
Albuquerque, NM 87102
(505) 843-6196

Jerome A. Holmes
215 Dean A. McGee, Rm. 315
Oklahoma City, OK 73102
(405) 609-5481

Neil M. Gorsuch
1823 Stout Street
Denver, CO 80257
(303) 335-2800

Scott M. Matheson, Jr.
125 South State Street
Salt Lake City, UT 84138-1181
(303) 844-3157

Senior Circuit Judges

William J. Holloway, Jr.
P.O. Box 1767
Oklahoma City, OK 73101-1767
(405) 609-5420

Robert H. McWilliams
U.S. Courthouse
1823 Stout Street
Denver, CO 80257
(303) 844-3430

Monroe G. McKay
6012 Federal Building
125 S. State Street

Salt Lake City, UT 84138-1181
(801) 524-5252

John C. Porfilio
217 U.S. Courthouse
1823 Stout Street
Denver, CO 80257
(970) 669-7696

Stephen H. Anderson
4201 Federal Building
125 South State Street
Salt Lake City, UT 84138-1102
(801) 524-6950

Bobby R. Baldock
P.O. Box 2388
Roswell, NM 88202-2388
(575) 625-2388

Wade Brorby
P.O. Box 1028
Cheyenne, WY 82003-1028
(307) 772-2885

Stephanie K. Seymour
4-562 U.S. Courthouse
333 W. 4th St.
Tulsa, OK 74103-3877
(918) 699-4745

David M. Ebel
109L U.S. Courthouse
1823 Stout Street
Denver, CO 80257
(303) 844-3800

Deanell Reece Tacha
643 Massachusetts St., Suite 301
Lawrence, KS 66044-2292
(785) 842-8556

James E. Barrett
1823 Stout Street
Denver, CO 80257
(303) 844-3157

District Judges

**Colorado**

Wiley Y. Daniel, C.J.
U.S. Courthouse
901-19th St., Rm. A1038
Denver, CO 80294-3589
(303) 844-2170

Marcia S. Krieger

# FEDERAL JUDGES

910-19th St., Rm. A941
Denver, CO 80294-3589
(303) 335-2289

Robert E. Blackburn
910-19th St., Rm. A741
Denver, CO 80294-3589
(303) 335-2350

Phillip A. Brimmer
910-19th St., Rm. A641
Denver, CO 80294-3589
(303) 335-2794

Christine M. Arguello
910-19th St., Rm. A638
Denver, CO 80294-3589
(303) 335-2174

Richard Brooke Jackson
910-19th St., Rm. A635
Denver, CO 80294-3589
(303) 335-2174

William J. Martinez
910-19th St., Rm. A641
Denver, CO 80294-3589
(303) 335-2805

## Kansas

Kathryn H. Vratil, C.J.
511 U.S. Courthouse
500 State Avenue
Kansas City, KS 66101
(913) 735-2300

John W. Lungstrum
517 U.S. Courthouse
500 State Avenue
Kansas City, KS 66101
(913) 735-2321

J. Thomas Marten
232 U.S. Courthouse
401 N. Market St.
Wichita, KS 67202
(316) 315-4300

Carlos Murguia
537 U.S. Courthouse
500 State Ave.
Kansas City, KS 66101
(913) 735-2340

Julia A. Robinson
405 U.S. Courthouse
444 SE Quincy

Topeka, KS 66683
(785) 338-5340

Eric F. Meigren
401 N. Market St.
Wichita, KS 67202
(316) 315-4320

John W. Lungstrum
517 U.S. Courthouse
500 State Ave.
Kansas City, KS 66101
(913) 735-2321

## New Mexico

Bruce D. Black, C.J.
106 S. Federal Place, 2nd fl.
Santa Fe, NM 87501
(505) 955-8850

Martha Vazquez
106 S. Federal Place, 2nd fl.
Santa Fe, NM 87501
(505) 988-6330

Christina M. Armijo
333 Lomas Blvd. NW, Suite 760
Albuquerque, NM 87102
(505) 348-2310

William Paul Johnson
333 Lomas Blvd. NW, Suite 640
Albuquerque, NM 87102
(505) 348-2330

James O. Browning
333 Lomas Blvd., NW, Suite 660
Albuquerque, NM 87102
(505) 348-2280

Robert C. Brack
100 Church St., Suite 280
Las Cruces, NM 88001
(505) 528-1450

Judith Herrera
333 Lomas Blvd., NW, Suite 710
Albuquerque, NM 87102
(505) 348-2390

## Oklahoma - Northern District

Claire V. Eagan, C.J.
333 W. 4th St.
Tulsa, OK 74103-3819
(918) 699-4795

James H. Payne
U.S. Courthouse
333 W. 4th Street
Tulsa, OK 74103-3819
(918) 699-4700

Gregory H. Frizzell
411 U.S. Courthouse
333 W. 4th St.
Tulsa, OK 74103-3819
(918) 699-4780

## Oklahoma - Western District

Vicki Miles-LaGrange, C.J.
3301 U.S. Courthouse
200 NW 4th Street
Oklahoma City, OK 73102
(405) 609-5400

Robin J. Cauthron
4001 U.S. Courthouse
200 NW 4th Street
Oklahoma City, OK 73102
(405) 609-5200

David L. Russell
3309 U.S. Courthouse
200 NW 4th Street
Oklahoma City, OK 73102
(405) 609-5100

Stephen P. Friot
3102 U.S. Courthouse
200 NW 4th Street
Oklahoma City, OK 73102
(405) 609-5500

Joe L. Heaton
3108 U.S. Courthouse
200 NW 4th Street
Oklahoma City, OK 73102
(405) 609-5600

Timothy D. DeGiusti
5012 U.S. Courthouse
200 NW 4th Street
Oklahoma City, OK 73102
(405) 609-5120

## Oklahoma - Eastern District

James H. Payne, C.J.
P.O. Box 2459
Muskogee, OK 74402-2459
(918) 684-7940

Ronald A. White

# FEDERAL JUDGES

101 N. 5th St.
Muskogee, OK 74401
(918) 684-7965

## Utah

Brian Ted Stewart, C.J.
148 U.S. Courthouse
350 S. Main Street
Salt Lake City, UT 84101-2180
(801) 524-6617

Dee V. Benson
253 U.S. Courthouse
350 South Main Street
Salt Lake City, UT 84101-2180
(801) 524-6160

Clark Waddoups
110 U.S. Courthouse
350 S. Main Street
Salt Lake City, UT 84101-2180
(801) 524-6600

## Wyoming

Nancy D. Freudenthal, C.J.
2120 Capitol Avenue
Cheyenne, WY 82001
(307) 433-2120

Alan B. Johnson
2241 Federal Building
2120 Capitol Avenue
Cheyenne, WY 82001
(307) 433-2170

Senior District Judges

C. Leroy Hansen
P.O. Box 669
Albuquerque, NM 87103-0669
(505) 348-2240

Richard P. Matsch
1823 Stout St.
Denver, CO 80294
(303) 844-4627

Lee R. West
3001 U.S. Courthouse
200 NW 4th St.
Oklahoma City, OK 73102
(405) 609-5140

Wesley E. Brown
414 U.S. Courthouse
401 North Market Street

Wichita, KS 67202
(316) 315-4280

Richard D. Rogers
410 Federal Building
444 SE Quincy Street
Topeka, KS 66683
(785) 338-5380

Sam A. Crow
430 Federal Building
444 SE Quincy Street
Topeka, KS 66683
(785) 338-5361

John L. Kane
U.S. Courthouse
901-19th St., Rm. A838
Denver, CO 80294-3589
(303) 844-6118

Bruce S. Jenkins
462 U.S. Courthouse
350 South Main Street
Salt Lake City, UT 84101-2180
(801) 524-5167

Zita Weinshienk
U.S. Courthouse
901-19th Street, Rm. A841
Denver, CO 80294-3589
(303) 844-2784

John E. Conway
740 U.S. Courthouse
333 Lomas Blvd., NW
Albuquerque, NM 87102
(505) 348-2200

David Sam
441 U.S. Courthouse
350 South Main Street
Salt Lake City, UT 84101-2180
(801) 524-6190

Frank H. Seay
P.O. Box 828
Muskogee, OK 74402-0828
(918) 684-7950

James A. Parker
P.O. Box 669
Albuquerque, NM 87103-0669
(505) 348-2220

Timothy Leonard
4301 U.S. Courthouse
200 NW 4th Street

Oklahoma City, OK 73102
(405) 609-5300

Clarence A. Brimmer
2120 Capitol Ave.
Cheyenne, WY 82001
(307) 433-2160

Lewis T. Babcock
U.S. Courthouse
901-19th St., Rm. A273
Denver, CO 80294-3589
(303) 844-2527

Walker D. Miller
U.S. Courthouse
901-19th St., Rm. A938
Denver, CO 80294-3589
(303) 844-2468

Monti L. Belot
111 U.S. Courthouse
401 N. Market Street
Wichita, KS 67202
(316) 315-4340

Dale A. Kimball
222 U.S. Courthouse
350 South Main Street
Salt Lake City, UT 84101-2180
(801) 524-6610

Tena Campbell
235 U.S. Courthouse
350 South Main Street
Salt Lake City, UT 84101-2180
(801) 524-6170

Terry L. Kern
333 W. 4th St.
Tulsa, OK 74103-3819
(918) 699-4770

## ELEVENTH CIRCUIT
(Alabama, Florida, Georgia)
www.ca11.uscourts.gov/

Circuit Judges

Joel F. Dubina, C.J.
One Church St.
Montgomery, AL 36104
(334) 954-3560

J. L. Edmondson
56 Forsyth St., NW
Atlanta, GA 30303-3147

# FEDERAL JUDGES

(404) 335-6230

Gerald Bard Tjoflat
300 N. Hogan
Jacksonville, FL 32202
(904) 301-6570

Stanley F. Birch, Jr.
56 Forsyth St., NW, #505
Atlanta, GA 30303-3147
(404) 335-6333

Ed Carnes
One Church St.
Montgomery, AL 36104
(334) 954-3580

Rosemary Barkett
99 NE Fourth Street, Rm. 1223
Miami, FL 33132
(305) 536-7335

Stanley Marcus
1262 Federal Justice Bldg.
99 NE Fourth Street
Miami, FL 33132
(305) 579-4420

Frank Mays Hull
238 U.S. Courthouse
56 Forsyth St., NW
Atlanta, GA 30303
(404) 335-6550

Charles R. Wilson
801 N. Florida Avenue, Rm. 16B
Tampa, FL 33602-3800
(813) 301-5650

William H. Pryor, Jr.
1729 Fifth Ave. North, Suite 900
Birmingham, AL 35203
(205) 278-2030

Beverly Martin
56 Forsyth St., NW
Atlanta, GA 30303-3147
(404) 335-6100

## Senior Circuit Judges

Phyllis A. Kravitch
56 Forsyth St., NW
Atlanta, GA 30303-3147
(404) 335-6300

R. Lanier Anderson, III
P.O. Box 977

Macon, GA 31202-0977
(478) 752-8101

James C. Hill
P.O. Box 52598
Jacksonville, FL 33201
(904) 301-6630

Peter T. Fay
99 NE Fourth Street, #1255
Miami, FL 33132
(305) 579-4390

Emmett Ripley Cox
113 St. Joseph Street, Rm. 433
Mobile, AL 36602
(251) 690-2055

Susan H. Black
300 N. Hogan, Suite 14-150
Jacksonville, FL 32202
(904) 301-6610

## District Judges

### Alabama - Northern District

Sharon Lovelace Blackburn, C.J.
730 U.S. Courthouse
1729 Fifth Ave. North
Birmingham, AL 35203
(205) 278-1810

Karon D. Bowdre
140 U.S. Courthouse
1729 Fifth Avenue North
Birmingham, AL 35203
(205) 278-1800

C. Lynwood Smith, Jr.
101 Holmes Ave. NE, Rm. 207
Huntsville, AL 35801
(256) 533-9490

Inge Prytz Johnson
U.S. Courthouse, 3rd fl.
1729 Fifth Avenue North
Birmingham, AL 35203
(205) 278-1970

R. David Proctor
1729 Fifth Avenue North
Birmingham, AL 35203
(205) 278-1980

L. Scott Coogler
1118 Greensboro Ave.
Tuscaloosa, AL 35401

(205) 561-1670

Virginia E. Hopkins
1729 Fifth Avenue North
Birmingham, AL 35203
(205) 278-1950

Abdul K. Kallon
1729 Fifth Avenue North
Birmingham, AL 35203
(205) 278-1700

### Alabama - Middle District

Mark E. Fuller, C.J.
One Church St., Rm. 300-A
Montgomery, AL 36104
(334) 954-3640

Myron H. Thompson
P.O. Box 235
Montgomery, AL 36101-0867
(334) 954-3650

W. Keith Watkins
One Church St.
Montgomery, AL 36104
(334) 954-3760

### Alabama - Southern District

William H. Steele, C.J.
113 St. Joseph Street
Mobile, AL 36602-3621
(251) 690-3239

Callie V.S. Granade
113 St. Joseph Street
Mobile, AL 36602-3621
(251) 690-3133

Kristi K. DuBose
113 St. Joseph Street
Mobile, AL 36602-3621
(251) 690-2020

### Florida - Southern District

Frederico A. Moreno, C.J.
400 N. Miami Ave., Rm. 13-3
Miami, FL 33128
(305) 523-5110

William J. Zloch
299 East Broward Blvd., Rm. 202B
Ft. Lauderdale, FL 33301
(954) 769-5480

# FEDERAL JUDGES

Kenneth A. Marra
701 Clematis St., Rm. 316
W. Palm Beach, FL 33401
(561) 514-3760

Jose E. Martinez
Federal Courthouse Sq.
400 N. Miami Ave., Rm. 10-2
Miami, FL 33128
(305) 523-5590

Cecilia Altonaga
Federal Courthouse Sq.
400 N. Miami Ave., Rm. 12-2
Miami, FL 33128-7788
(305) 528-5510

Donald L. Graham
400 N. Miami Ave., Rm. 13-4
Miami, FL 33128
(305) 523-5130

K. Michael Moore
400 N. Miami Ave., Rm. 13-1
Miami, FL 33128
(305) 523-5160

Ursula Ungaro
400 N. Miami Avenue, Rm. 12-4
Miami, FL 33128
(305) 523-5550

Joan A. Lenard
400 N. Miami Avenue, Rm. 12-1
Miami, FL 33128
(305) 523-5500

Donald M. Middlebrooks
701 Clematis St., Rm. 257
W. Palm Beach, FL 33401
(561) 514-3720

William P. Dimitrouleas
203F U.S. Courthouse
299 E. Broward Blvd.
Fort Lauderdale, FL 33301
(954) 769-5650

Patricia A. Seitz
Federal Courthouse Square
400 N. Miami Avenue, Rm. 11-4
Miami, FL 33128
(305) 523-5530

Adalberto Jordan
Federal Courthouse Square
400 N. Miami Avenue, Rm. 10-1
Miami, FL 33128-7788

(305) 523-5560

James I. Cohn
299 E. Broward Blvd., Rm. 203
Ft. Lauderdale, FL 33301
(954) 769-5490

Marcia G. Cooke
400 N. Miami Ave., Rm. 11-2
Miami, FL 33128
(305) 523-5150

Kathleen M. Williams
400 N. Miami Ave., Rm. 11-3
Miami, FL 33128
(305) 523-5540

**Florida - Middle District**

Anne C. Conway, C.J.
U.S. Courthouse
401 W. Central Blvd.
Orlando, FL 32801
(407) 835-4270

Mary S. Scriven
U.S. Courthouse
401 W. Central Blvd.
Orlando, FL 32801
(407) 835-3840

Elizabeth A. Kovachevich
U.S. Courthouse, Rm. 223
801 North Florida Avenue
Tampa, FL 33602-3800
(813) 301-5730

John E. Steele
2110 First St..
Ft. Myers, FL 33901
(239) 461-2140

James S. Moody, Jr.
801 N. Florida Ave., #13A
Tampa, FL 33602-3800
(813) 301-5680

Gregory A. Presnell
401 W. Central Blvd.
Orlando, FL 32801
(407) 835-4301

Timothy Currigan
300 N. Hogan St., #11-350
Jacksonville, FL 32202
(904) 549-1302

Steven D. Merryday

U.S. Courthouse
801 N. Florida Avenue, #223
Tampa, FL 33602-3800
(813) 301-5001

James D. Whittemore
U.S. Courthouse
801 N. Florida Avenue, #223
Tampa, FL 33602-3800
(813) 301-5880

John Antoon, II
U.S. Courthouse
401 W. Central Blvd.
Orlando, FL 32801
(407) 835-4334

Virginia M. Hernandez Covington
801 N. Florida Ave
Tampa, FL 33602
(813) 301-5340

Marcia M. Howard
300 N. Hogan St.
Jacksonville, FL 32202
(904) 301-6750

Charlene E. Honeywell
2110 First St.
Ft. Myers, FL 33901
(239) 461-2170

Roy B. Dalton

**Florida - Northern District**

Robert L. Hinkle
U.S. Courthouse
111 N. Adams Street
Tallahassee, FL 32301-7717
(850) 521-3601

Margaret C. Rodgers
1 N. Palafox St.
Pensacola, FL 32501-7717
(850) 435-8448

John R. Smoak, Jr.
30 W. Government St.
Panama City, FL 32401
(850) 785-9761

**Georgia - Northern District**

Julie E. Carnes, C.J.
2167 Russell Federal Bldg.
75 Spring Street, SW
Atlanta, GA 30303-3361

# FEDERAL JUDGES

(404) 215-1510

Harold L. Murphy
600 E. First St., Suite 311
Rome, GA 30161
(706) 378-4080

Thomas W. Thrash, Jr.
2188 Russell Federal Bldg.
75 Spring Street, SW
Atlanta, GA 30303-3361
(404) 215-1550

Richard W. Story
2121 Russell Federal Bldg.
75 Spring Street, SW
Atlanta, GA 30303-3361
(404) 215-1350

Charles A. Pannell, Jr.
2367 Russell Federal Bldg.
75 Spring Street, SW
Atlanta, GA 30303-3361
(404) 215-1580

William S. Duffey, Jr.
1721 Russell Federal Bldg.
75 Spring Street, SW
Atlanta, GA 30303-3361
(404) 215-1480

Timothy C. Batten, Sr.
2142 Russell Federal Bldg.
75 Spring Street, SW
Atlanta, GA 30303-3361
(404) 215-1420

Steve C. Jones
1909 Russell Federal Bldg.
75 Spring Street, SW
Atlanta, GA 30303-3361
(404) 215-1228

Amy Totenberg
2123 Russell Federal Bldg.
75 Spring Street, SW
Atlanta, GA 30303-3361
(404) 215-1438

## Georgia - Middle District

C. Ashley Royal, C.J.
P.O. Box 129
Macon, GA 31202
(478) 752-0739

W. Louis Sands
201 W. Broad St.

Albany, GA 31701
(229) 430-8553

Clay D. Land
P.O. Box 2017
Columbus, GA 31902
(706) 649-7812

Marc T. Treadwell
P.O. Box 65
Macon, GA 31202
(478) 752-0717

## Georgia - Southern District

Lisa Godbey Wood, C.J.
600 James Brown Blvd.
Augusta, GA 30901
(706) 849-4400

William T. Moore, Jr
P.O. Box 10245
Savannah, GA 31412
(912) 650-4173

James R. Hall
600 James Brown Blvd.
Augusta, GA 30901
(706) 849-6460

### Senior District Judges

Ira DeMent
P.O. Box 2149
Montgomery, AL 36102-1429
(334) 954-3680

Anthony A. Alaimo
801 Gloucester St.
Brunswick, GA 31521
(912) 280-1340

Truman M. Hobbs
One Church St., Rm. 300-D
Montgomery, AL 36104
(334) 954-3750

William H. Stafford, Jr.
U.S. Courthouse
111 N. Adams Street
Tallahassee, FL 32301-7717
(850) 521-3611

George C. Young
U.S. Courthouse
401 W. Central Blvd.
Orlando, FL 32801
(407) 835-4280

Howell W. Melton
300 N. Hogan St., #11-300
Jacksonville, FL 32202
(904) 549-1940

William J. Castagna
U.S. Courthouse
801 N. Florida Avenue
Tampa, FL 33602
(813) 301-5935

J. Foy Guin, Jr.
Federal Courthouse
1729 Fifth Avenue North
Birmingham, AL 35203
(205) 278-1830

Robert B. Propst
1729 Fifth Ave. North
Birmingham, AL 36202
(205) 278-1860

William M. Acker, Jr.
481 U.S. Courthouse
1729 Fifth Avenue North
Birmingham, AL 35203
(205) 278-1880

James Hughes Hancock
681 U.S. Courthouse
1729 Fifth Avenue North
Birmingham, AL 35203
(205) 278-1840

John H. Moore, II
300 N. Hogan St., #11-400
Jacksonville, FL 32202
(904) 594-1980

James Lawrence King
400 N. Miami Ave.
Miami, FL 33128
(305) 523-5000

William M. Hoeveler
Federal Courthouse Square
400 N. Miami Ave., 9th fl.
Miami, FL 33128
(305) 523-5570

Maurice M. Paul
Federal Building
401 SE First Ave.
Gainesville, FL 32601
(352) 380-2415

Marvin H. Shoob
1767 Russell Federal Bldg.
75 Spring Street, SW

# FEDERAL JUDGES

Atlanta, GA 30303-3361
(404) 215-1470

Robert L. Vining, Jr.
600 E. First St., Suite 345
Rome, GA 30161
(706) 378-4070

Jose A. Gonzalez, Jr.
205D U.S. Courthouse
299 E. Broward Blvd.
Ft. Lauderdale, FL 33301
(954) 769-5560

William Terrell Hodges
207 NW 2nd Street
Ocala, FL 34475
(352) 690-6907

Kenneth L. Ryskamp
701 Clematis Street, Rm. 416
West Palm Beach, FL 33401
(561) 803-3420

G. Kendall Sharp
U.S. Courthouse
401 W. Central Blvd.
Orlando, FL 32801
(407) 835-4260

G. Ernest Tidwell
1967 Russell Federal Bldg.
75 Spring Street, SW
Atlanta, GA 30303-3361
(404) 215-1460

Charles R. Butler, Jr.
113 St. Joseph Street
Mobile, AL 36602-3621
(334) 690-2175

C. Roger Vinson
U.S. Courthouse
1 N. Palafox Street
Pensacola, FL 32501
(850) 435-8444

Lacey A. Collier
U.S. Courthouse
1 N. Palafox Street
Pensacola, FL 32501
(850) 444-0174

J. Owen Forrester
1921 Russell Federal Bldg.
75 Spring Street, SW
Atlanta, GA 30303-3361
(404) 215-1310

W. Harold Albritton
P.O. Box 629
Montgomery, AL 36101-0629
(334) 954-3710

Willis B. Hunt, Jr.
1756 Russell Federal Bldg.
75 Spring Street, SW
Atlanta, GA 30303-3361
(404) 215-1450

Harvey E. Schlesinger
300 N. Hogan St., #11-150
Jacksonville, FL 32202
(904) 549-1990

Dudley H. Brown, Jr.
600 James Brown Blvd.
Augusta, GA 30901
(706) 849-4440

B. Avant Edenfield
P.O. Box 9865
Savannah, GA 31412
(912) 650-4080

William C. O'Kelley
1942 Russell Federal Bldg.
75 Spring Street, SW
Atlanta, GA 30303-3361
(404) 215-1530

Daniel T.K. Hurley
701 Clematis Street, Room 352
West Palm Beach, FL 33401
(561) 803-3450

Patricia C. Fawsett
U.S. Courthouse
401 W. Central Blvd.
Orlando, FL 32801
(407) 835-4250

Susan C. Bucklew
U.S. Courthouse
801 N. Florida Avenue, #223
Tampa, FL 33602-3800
(813) 301-5858

Orinda D. Evans
1988 Russell Federal Bldg.
75 Spring Street, SW
Atlanta, GA 30303-3361
(404) 215-1490

Clarence Cooper
1721 Russell Federal Bldg.
75 Spring Street, SW

Atlanta, GA 30303-3361
(404) 215-1390

Hugh Lawson
P.O. Box 838
Macon, GA 31202
(478) 752-3591

Alan S. Gold
400 North Miami Avenue, Rm. 11-1
Miami, FL 33128
(305) 523-5580

Paul C. Huck
400 N. Miami Avenue, Rm. 13-2
Miami, FL 33132
(305) 523-5520

Henry Lee Adams, Jr.
300 N. Hogan St., #11-200
Jacksonville, FL 32202
(904) 549-1930

Richard A. Lazzara
U.S. Courthouse
801 N. Florida Avenue, #223
Tampa, FL 33602-3800
(813) 301-5350

Shelby Highsmith
400 N. Miami Ave.
Miami, FL 33128
(305) 523-5170

Stephan P. Mickle
401 SE First Avenue
Gainesville, FL 32601
(352) 380-2742

**UNITED STATES TAX COURT**
**400 Second Street, NW**
**Washington, DC 20217-0002**
**www.ustaxcourt.gov**

John O. Colvin, Chief Judge
(202) 521-0777

Judges
Mary Ann Cohen
(202) 521-0655

Maurice B. Foley
(202) 521-0681

Joseph H. Gale
(202) 521-0688

# FEDERAL JUDGES

Joseph Robert Goeke
(202) 521-0690

David Gustafson
(202) 521-0850

James S. Halpern
(202) 521-0707

Mark Van dyke Holmes
(202) 521-0714

Diane L. Kroupa
(202) 521-0725

L. Paige Marvel
(202) 521-0740

Elizabeth Crewson Paris
(202) 521-0839

Michael B. Thornton
(202) 521-0766

Juan F. Vasquez
(202) 521-0778

Thomas B. Wells
(202) 521-0790

Robert Allen Wherry, Jr.
(202) 521-0800

Senior Judges
Renato Beghe
(202) 521-0638

Herbert L. Chabot
(202) 521-0644

Carolyn P. Chiechi
(202) 521-0650

Howard A. Dawson, Jr.
(202) 521-0670

Joel Gerber
(202) 521-0774

Harry A. Haines
(202) 521-0699

Julian I. Jacobs
(202) 521-0720

David Laro
(202) 521-0738

Arthur L. Nims, III
(202) 521-0750

Robert P. Ruwe
(202) 521-0751

Laurence J. Whalen
(202) 521-0792

Special Trial Judges

Peter J. Panuthos, Chief
(202) 521-4707

Robert N. Armen, Jr.
(202) 521-4711

Lewis R. Carluzzo
(202) 521-3339

John F. Dean
(202) 521-3366

Stanley J. Goldberg
(202) 521-3370

## U.S. COURT OF INTERNATIONAL TRADE
**One Federal Plaza**
**New York, NY 10278-0001**
**www.cit.uscourts.gov/**

Judges

Donald C. Pogue, C.J.
(212) 264-1628

Jane A. Restani
(212) 264-2018

Gregory W. Carman.
(212) 264-1625

Evan J. Wallach
(212) 264-1628

Delissa A. Ridgway
(212) 264-1615

Richard K. Eaton
(212) 264-1615

Timothy C. Stanceu
(212) 264-2923

Leo Gordon
(212) 264-2018

Senior Judges
Thomas J. Aquilino, Jr.
(212) 264-1625

Nicholas Tsoucalas
(212) 264-2923

R. Kenton Musgrave
(212) 264-1628

Richard W. Goldberg
(212) 264-1615

Judith M. Barzilay
(212) 264-2018

## FOREIGN INTELLIGENCE SURVEILLANCE COURT
333 Constitution Avenue, NW
Washington, DC 20001
(202) 357-6250

John Bates,
  Presiding Judge

## FOREIGN INTELLIGENCE SURVEILLANCE COURT OF REVIEW
**333 Constitution Avenue, NW**
**Washington, DC 20001**
(202) 357-6250

Bruce M. Selya,
  Presiding Judge

## JUDICIAL PANEL ON MULTIDISTRICT LITIGATION
**Thurgood Marshall Federal Judiciary Bldg.**
**One Columbus Circle, NE, Rm. G-255**
**Washington, DC 20002-8004**
**(202) 502-2800**
**www.jpml.uscourts.gov**
John G. Heyburn, II,
  Panel Chairman

Panel Judges
Barbara S. Jones
W. Royal Furgeson, Jr.
Kathryn H. Vratil
Marjorie O. Rendell
Frank C. Damrell, Jr.
Paul J. Barbadaro

# FEDERAL JUDGES

**U.S. SENTENCING
   COMMISSION**
**One Columbus Circle, NE**
**Suite 2-500, South Lobby**
**Washington, DC 20002-8002**
**(202) 502-4500**
**www.ussc.gov**

Office of the Chairman
(202) 502-4550

**U.S. COURT OF APPEALS FOR
   THE ARMED FORCES**
**450 E Street, NW**
**Washington, DC 20442-0001**
**(202) 761-1448**
**www.armfor.uscourts.gov/**

Andrew S. Effron, C.J.
James E. Baker
Charles E. Erdmann
Scott W. Stucky
Margaret A. Ryan

Senior Judges
Walter T. Cox, III
Eugene R. Sullivan
William H. Darden
Susan J. Crawford
H.F. "Sparky" Gierke

**U.S. COURT OF APPEALS FOR
   VETERANS CLAIMS**
**625 Indiana Avenue, NW**
**Suite 900**
**Washington, DC 20004-2950**
**(202) 501-5970**
**www.uscourts.cavc.gov**

Bruce E. Kasold
(202) 501-5890
William P. Greene, Jr.
Lawrence B. Hagel
William A. Moorman
Alan G. Lance
Robert N. Davis
Mary J. Schoelen

For more information regarding Federal
Courts and Judges contact:
**ADMINISTRATIVE OFFICE OF
   THE U.S. COURTS**
**Washington, DC 20544**
**(202) 502-3185**

# CLERKS OF THE COURTS

**Supreme Court of the United States**
www.supremecourt.gov
Decisions available at:
supct.law.cornell.edu/supct/
(1990-)
www.access.gpo.gov/su_docs/supcrt/
(1937-1975)
www.findlaw.com/casecode/
supreme.html (1893-)
William K. Suter
1 First Street, NE
Washington, DC 20543
(202) 479-3011

**Federal Circuit**
www.cafc.uscourts.gov
www.ll.georgetown.edu/
federal/judicial/cafed.cfm
Jan Horbaly
717 Madison Place, NW
Washington, DC 20439-0002
(202) 275-8000

**D.C. Circuit**
www.cadc.uscourts.gov
www.ll.georgetown.edu/
federal/judicial/cadc.cfm
www.findlaw.com/casecode/
courts/dc.html
Mark J. Langer
U.S. Courthouse
333 Constitution Ave., NW
Washington, DC 20001-2866
(202) 216-7300

**First Circuit**
www.ca1.uscourts.gov
www.law.emory.edu/1circuit/
www.findlaw.com/casecode/
courts/1st.html
Margaret Carter
1 Courthouse Way, Suite 2500
Boston, MA 02210-3002
(617) 748-9057

**Second Circuit**
www.ca2.uscourts.gov
library.law.pace.edu/
legal/us-legal/judiciary/
second-circuit.html
www.findlaw.com/casecode/
courts/2nd.html
Catherine O'Hagan Wolfe
U.S. Courthouse, Rm. 1702

500 Pearl Street
New York, NY 10007-1321
(212) 857-8500

**Third Circuit**
www.ca3.uscourts.gov
vls.law.vill.edu/locator/3/
ww.findlaw.com/casecode/
courts/3rd.html
Marcia M. Waldron
21400 U.S. Courthouse
601 Market Street
Philadelphia, PA 19106-1790
(215) 597-2995

**Fourth Circuit**
www.ca4.uscourts.gov
www.law.emory.edu/4circuit/
www.findlaw.com/casecode/
courts/4th.html
Patricia S. Connor
U.S. Courthouse
1100 East Main Street, Rm. 501
Richmond, VA 23219-3517
(804) 916-2700

**Fifth Circuit**
www.ca5.uscourts.gov
www.findlaw.com/casecode/
courts/5th.html
Charles R. Fulbruge III
600 S. Maestri Place
New Orleans, LA 70130
(504) 310-7700

**Sixth Circuit**
www.ca6.uscourts.gov
www.law.emory.edu/6circuit/
www.findlaw.com/casecode/
courts 6th.html
Leonard Green
540 Potter Stewart Courthouse Bldg.
Cincinnati, OH 45202-3988
(513) 564-7000

**Seventh Circuit**
www.ca7.uscourts.gov
www.findlaw.com/casecode/
courts/7th.html
Gino J. Agnello
Dirksen Building
219 South Dearborn Street
Chicago, IL 60604
(312) 435-5850

**Eighth Circuit**
www.ca8.courts.gov/
www.findlaw.com/casecode/
courts/8th.html
Michael E. Gans
111 S. 10th Street
St. Louis, MO 63102
(314) 244-2400

316 N. Robert Street
St. Paul, MN 55101-1423
(651) 848-1300

**Ninth Circuit**
www.ca9.uscourts.gov/
www.findlaw.com/casecode/
courts/9th.html
Molly C. Dwyer
951 7th St.
San Francisco, CA 94103
(415) 355-8000

125 S. Grand Ave.
Pasadena, CA 91105-1652
(626) 229-7250

1010 Fifth Avenue
Seattle, WA 98104
(206) 226-2200

700 SW 6th Ave., Rm. 126
Portland, OR 97204
(503) 833-5311

**Tenth Circuit**
www.ca10.uscourts.gov
www.law.emory.edu/10circuit/
www.kscourts.org/ca10/
www.findlaw.com/casecode/
courts/10th.html
Elisabeth A. Shumaker
U.S. Courthouse
1823 Stout Street
Denver, CO 80257
(303) 844-3157

**Eleventh Circuit**
www.ca11.uscourts.gov
www.law.emory.edu/11circuit/
www.findlaw.com/casecode/
courts/11th.html
John Ley
56 Forsyth St., NW
Atlanta, GA 30303
(404) 335-6100

# CLERKS OF THE COURTS

## U.S. Court of Appeals for the Armed Forces
www.armfor.uscourts.gov
William DeCicco
450 E Street, NW
Washington, DC 20442-0001
(202) 761-1448

## U.S. Court of Federal Claims
www.uscfc.uscourts.gov
Hazel Keahey
717 Madison Place, NW
Washington, DC 20005-1086
(202) 357-6411

## U.S. Court of International Trade
www.cit.uscourts.gov
Tina P. Kimble
1 Federal Plaza
New York NY 10278-0001
(212) 264-2814

## Judicial Panel on Multidistrict Litigation
www.jpml.uscourts.gov/
Jeffrey N. Luthi
1 Columbus Circle NE, Rm. G255N
Washington, DC 20002-8004
(202) 502-2800

## U.S. Tax Court
www.ustaxcourt.gov
Robert R. Di Trolio
400 Second Street, NW
Washington, DC 20217-0002
(202) 512-0700

## U.S. Court of Appeals for Veterans Claims
www.vetapp.gov/
Gregory O. Black
625 Indiana Ave., NW, Suite 900
Washington, DC 20004-2950
(202) 501-5970

## Foreign Intelligence Surveillance Court
LeeAnn Flynn Hall
333 Constitution Ave., NW
Washington, DC 20001
(202) 357-6250

## Foreign Intelligence Surveillance Court of Review
LeeAnn Flynn Hall
333 Constitution Ave., NW
Washington, DC 20001
(202) 357-6250

## DISTRICT COURT CLERKS

### Alabama - Northern District
www.alnd.uscourts.gov
Sharon Harris
1729 Fifth Ave. North
140 Federal Courthouse
Birmingham, AL 35203
(205) 278-1700

101 Holmes Ave. NE
Huntsville, AL 35801
(256) 534-6495

204 U.S. Courthouse
1129 Noble St.
Anniston, AL 36201
(256) 236-4170

400 Wells St.
Decatur, AL 35601
(256) 584-7900

210 N. Seminary St., Rm. 311
Florence, AL 35630
(256) 760-8415

206 Federal Bldg.
600 Broad St.
Gadsden, AL 35901
(256) 547-7301

304 Federal Building
Tuscaloosa, AL 35401
(205) 561-1670

### Alabama - Middle District
www.almd.uscourts.gov
Debra P. Hackett
U.S. Courthouse, P.O. Box 711
Montgomery, AL 36101-0711
(334) 954-3600

### Alabama - Southern District
www.alsd.uscourts.gov
Charles R. Diard, Jr.
113 St. Joseph Street
Mobile, AL 36602-3621
(251) 690-2371

### Alaska
www.akd.uscourts.gov
Marvel Hansbraugh
222 W. 7th Avenue, Rm. 229
Anchorage, AK 99513-7564
(907) 677-6100

332 Federal Bldg. & Courthouse
101 12th Avenue

Fairbanks, AK 99701-6283
(907) 451-5791

Box 020349
Juneau, AK 99802-0349
(907) 586-7458

648 Mission Street, Rm. 507
Ketchikan, AK 99901
(907) 247-7576

Box 130
Nome, AK 99762
(907) 443-5216

### Arizona
www.azd.uscourts.gov
Richard H. Weare
130 O'Connor U.S. Courthouse
Phoenix, AZ 85003-1228
(602) 322-7200

405 W. Congress St., Suite 1500
Tucson, AZ 85701-5010
(520) 205-4200

101 W. Goodwin Street, Rm. 203
Prescott, AZ 86303
(928) 445-6598

123 N. San Francisco Street
Flagstaff, AZ 86001
(928) 774-2566

325 W. 19th Street
Yuma, AZ 85364
(928) 329-4766

### Arkansas - Eastern District
www.are.uscourts.gov
James W. McCormack
600 W. Capitol Ave., Suite 402
Little Rock, AR 72201-3325
(501) 604-5351

312 Federal Building
Jonesboro, AR 72401
(870) 972-4610

100 E. 8th Ave., Rm. 3103
Pine Bluff, AR 71601
(870) 536-1190

### Arkansas - Western District
www.arwd.uscourts.gov
Christopher R. Johnson
P.O. Box 1547
Fort Smith, AR 72902-1547
(479) 783-6833

# CLERKS OF THE COURTS

500 N. State Line Ave., Rm. 302
Texarkana, AR 71854-5961
(870) 773-3381

100 Reserve St., Rm. 347
Hot Springs, AR 71901
(501) 623-6411

101 S. Jackson Ave., Rm. 205
El Dorado, AR 71731-1566
(870) 862-1202

35 E. Mountain St., Suite 510
Fayetteville, AR 72701
(479) 521-6980

**California - Northern District**
www.cand.uscourts.gov
Richard W. Wieking
P.O. Box 36060
San Francisco, CA 94102-3489
(415) 522-2000

1301 Clay St., Suite 400S
Oakland, CA 94612-5212
(510) 637-3530

2112 U.S. Courthouse
280 S. First Street
San Jose, CA 95113
(408) 535-5363

514 H Street
Eureka, CA 95501
(707) 445-3612

**California - Eastern District**
www.caed.uscourts.gov
Victoria C. Minor
501 I Street
Sacramento, CA 95814-2322
(916) 930-4000

2500 Tulare St., Rm. 1501
Fresno, CA 93721
(559) 499-5600

**California - Central District**
www.cacd.uscourts.gov
Terry Nafisi
U.S. Courthouse
312 N. Spring Street
Los Angeles, CA 90012
(213) 894-1565

225 E. Temple Street
Los Angeles, CA 90012
(213) 894-2215

3470 12th Street
Riverside, CA 92501
(951) 328-4450

411 W. Fourth Street
Santa Ana, CA 92701-4516
(714) 338-4750

**California - Southern District**
www.casd.uscourts.gov
W. Samuel Hamrick, Jr.
940 Front Street
San Diego, CA 92101-8900
(619) 557-5600

2003 W. Adams Ave., Suite 220
El Centro, CA 92243-2264
(760) 353-1271

**Colorado**
www.cod.uscourts.gov/
Gregory C. Langham
Rm. A105 U.S. Courthouse
901 19th Street, Rm. A105
Denver, CO 80294-3589
(303) 844-3433

**Connecticut**
www.ctd.uscourts.gov
Robin Tabora
141 Church Street
New Haven, CT 06510
(203) 773-2140

450 Main Street
Hartford, CT 06103
(860) 240-3200

915 Lafayette Blvd.
Bridgeport, CT 06604
(203) 579-5861

**Delaware**
www.ded.uscourts.gov
Peter T. Dalleo
Federal Bldg.
844 King Street, Rm. 4209
Wilmington, DE 19801-3570
(302) 573-6170

**District of Columbia**
www.dcd.uscourts.gov
Angela D. Caesar
U.S. Courthouse
333 Constitution Avenue NW
Washington, DC 20001-2802
(202) 354-3050

**Florida - Northern District**
www.flnd.uscourts.gov
Jessica J. Lyublanovits
111 N. Adams St.
Tallahassee, FL 32301-7717
(850) 521-3501

243 Federal Bldg.
Gainesville, FL 32601-6805
(352) 380-2400

U.S. Courthouse
1 N. Palafox St., Rm. 226
Pensacola, FL 32502
(850) 435-8440

30 W. Government Street
Panama City, FL 32401
(850) 769-4556

**Florida - Middle District**
www.flmd.uscourts.gov
Sheryl Loesch
401 W. Central Blvd., Suite 1200
Orlando, FL 32801
(407) 835-4200

300 N. Hogan St., Suite 9-150
Jacksonville, FL 32202
(904) 549-1900

223 U.S. Courthouse
Tampa, FL 33602
(813) 301-5400

2-194 U.S. Courthouse
2110 First St.
Ft. Myers, FL 33901
(239) 461-2000

207 NW Second Street
Ocala, FL 32678
(352) 369-4860

**Florida - Southern District**
www.flsd.uscourts.gov
Steven M. Larimore
Federal Courthouse Square
400 N. Miami Ave., 8th fl.
Miami, FL 33128-7788
(305) 523-5100

299 E. Broward Blvd.
Ft. Lauderdale, FL 33301
(954) 769-5400

300 S. Sixth St.
Fort Pierce, FL 34950
(772) 467-2300

Federal Building
701 Clematis Street
West Palm Beach, FL 33401
(561) 803-3400

301 Simonton Street, Rm. 130
Key West, FL 33040
(305) 295-8100

**Georgia - Northern District**
www.gand.uscourts.gov
James N. Hatten
2211 U.S. Courthouse
75 Spring Street, SW
Atlanta, GA 30303-3361
(404) 215-1660

Federal Building
600 E. First St., Rm. 304
Rome, GA 30161
(706) 378-4060

201 Federal Building
121 Spring Street, SE
Gainesville, GA 30501
(678) 450-2760

Federal Building
18 Greenville St., Rm 352
Newnan, GA 30264-0939
(678) 423-3060

**Georgia - Middle District**
www.gamd.uscourts.gov
Gregory J. Leonard
P.O. Box 128
Macon, GA 31202-0128
(478) 752-3497

201 W. Broad Ave.
Albany, GA 31701
(229) 430-8432

P.O. Box 124
Columbus, GA 31902-0124
(706) 649-7816

P.O. Box 68
Valdosta, GA 31601-0068
(229) 242-3616

P.O. Box 1106
Athens, GA 30603-1106
(706) 227-1094

**Georgia - Southern District**
www.gas.uscourts.gov
Scott L. Poff
P.O. Box 8286

Savannah, GA 31412-8286
(912) 650-4020

600 James Brown Blvd.
Augusta, GA 30901
(706) 849-4400

801 Gloucester St., Suite 220
Brunswick, GA 31520
(912) 280-1330

**Guam**
www.gud.uscourts.gov
Jeanne G. Quinata
520 W. Soledad Ave., 4th fl.
Hagatna, GU 96910
(671) 473-9100

**Hawaii**
www.hid.uscourts.gov
Sue Beitia
300 Ala Moana Blvd., Rm. C-338
Honolulu, HI 96850-0338
(808) 541-1300

**Idaho**
www.id.uscourts.gov
Elizabeth Smith
U.S. Courthouse
550 West Fort Street
Boise, ID 83724
(208) 334-1361

6450 N. Mineral Dr.
Coeur d'Alene, ID 83815
(208) 665-6850

Federal Bldg. #304
220 E. 5th Street
Moscow, ID 83843
(208) 882-7612

801 E. Sherman St.
Pocatello, ID 83201
(208) 478-4123

**Illinois - Northern District**
www.ilnd.uscourts.gov
Michael W. Dobbins
Dirksen Bldg.
219 South Dearborn Street
Chicago, IL 60604
(312) 435-5670

U.S. Courthouse
211 South Court Street, Rm. 252
Rockford, IL 61101
(815) 987-4354

**Illinois - Southern District**
www.ilsd.uscourts.gov
Nancy Rosenstengel
750 Missouri Ave.
East St. Louis, IL 62201
(618) 482-9371

U.S. Courthouse
301 W. Main St.
Benton, IL 62812-1362
(618) 439-7760

**Illinois - Central District**
www.ilcd.uscourts.gov
Pamela E. Robinson
600 E. Monroe St.
Springfield, IL 62701
(217) 492-4020

211 19th St.
Rock Island, IL 61201
(309) 793-5778

309 Federal Building
100 NE Monroe Street
Peoria, IL 61602
(309) 671-7117

201 S. Vine St.
Urbana, IL 61802
(217) 373-5830

**Indiana - Northern District**
www.innd.uscourts.gov
Stephen R. Ludwig
102 Federal Building
South Bend, IN 46601-2194
(574) 246-8000

1108 U.S. Courthouse
1300 S. Harrison Street
Fort Wayne, IN 46802
(260) 423-3000

Federal Building
P.O. Box 1498
Lafayette, IN 47902-1498
(765) 420-6250

5400 Federal Plaza
Suite 2300
Hammond, IN 46320
(219) 852-6500

**Indiana - Southern District**
www.insd.uscourts.gov
Laura A. Briggs
105 U.S. Courthouse
46 East Ohio Street

# CLERKS OF THE COURTS

Indianapolis, IN 46204
(317) 229-3700

304 Federal Building
Evansville, IN 47708
(812) 434-6410

121 W. Spring St.
New Albany, IN 47150
(812) 542-4510

921 Ohio St.
Terre Haute, IN 47808
(812) 234-9484

**Iowa - Northern District**
www.iand.uscourts.gov
Robert L. Phelps
4200 C Street SW
Cedar Rapids, IA 52401
(319) 286-2300

301 U.S. Courthouse
320 Sixth Street
Sioux City, IA 51101
(712) 233-3900

**Iowa - Southern District**
www.iasd.uscourts.gov
Marjorie E. Krahn
P.O. Box 9344
Des Moines, IA 50306-9344
(515) 284-6248

8 E. Sixth St., Rm. 313
Council Bluffs, IA 51502-0307
(712) 328-0283

131 E. 4th St., Rm. 150
Davenport, IA 52801
(563) 884-7607

**Kansas**
www.ksd.uscourts.gov
Timothy M. O'Brien
259 U.S. Courthouse
500 State Ave.
Kansas City, KS 66101-2430
(913) 735-2200

204 U.S. Courthouse
401 North Market Street
Wichita, KS 67202-2096
(316) 315-4200

Federal Building
444 SE Quincy
Topeka, KS 66683-3587
(785) 338-5400

**Kentucky - Eastern District**
www.kyed.uscourts.gov
Leslie G. Whitmer
P.O. Box 3074
Lexington, KY 40588-3074
(859) 233-2503

P.O. Box 1073
Covington, KY 41012
(859) 392-7925

310 S. Main St., Rm. 215
London, KY 40745-5121
(606) 877-7910

203 Federal Bldg.
Pikeville, KY 41501-1100
(606) 437-6160

313 Watts Federal Bldg.
Frankfort, KY 40601-1993
(502) 223-5225

1405 Greenup Ave.
Ashland, KY 41101-2187
(606) 329-8652

**Kentucky - Western District**
www.kywd.uscourts.gov
Jeffrey A. Apperson
106 U.S. Courthouse
Louisville, KY 40202
(502) 625-3500

322 Federal Building
Paducah, KY 42001-6801
(270) 415-6400

126 Federal Building
Owensboro, KY 42301-3013
(270) 689-4400

120 Federal Building
Bowling Green, KY 42101
(270) 393-2500

**Louisiana - Eastern District**
www.laed.uscourts.gov
Loretta G. Whyte
500 Poydras Street, C-151
New Orleans, LA 70130-3367
(504) 589-7650

**Louisiana - Middle District**
www.lamd.uscourts.gov
Nick Lorio
777 Florida St., Suite 139
Baton Rouge, LA 70801
(225) 389-3500

**Louisiana - Western District**
www.lawd.uscourts.gov
Tony Moore
300 Fannin Street, Suite 1167
Shreveport, LA 71101-3083
(318) 676-4273

800 Lafayette Street
Lafayette, LA 70501
(337) 593-5000

611 Broad St., Suite 188
Lake Charles, LA 70601
(337) 437-3870

515 Murray St.
Alexandria, LA 71301
(318) 473-7415

201 Jackson St.
Monroe, LA 71201
(318) 322-6740

**Maine**
www.med.uscourts.gov
Linda L. Jacobson
156 Federal Street
Portland, ME 04101
(207) 780-3356

P.O. Box 1007
Bangor, ME 04402-1007
(207) 945-0575

**Maryland**
www.mdd.uscourts.gov/
Felicia C. Cannon
101 W. Lombard Street
Baltimore, MD 21201-2691
(410) 962-2600

6500 Cherrywood Lane, 2nd fl.
Greenbelt, MD 20770
(301) 344-0660

**Massachusetts**
www.mad.uscourts.gov
Sarah Allison Thornton
1 Courthouse Way
Boston, MA 02210
(617) 748-9152

300 State Street
Springfield, MA 01105
(413) 785-6800

595 Main Street
Worcester, MA 01608-2076
(508) 929-9900

# CLERKS OF THE COURTS

**Michigan - Eastern District**
www.mied.uscourts.gov
David J. Weaver
231 W. Lafayette Blvd.
Detroit, MI 48226
(313) 234-5005

P.O. Box 8199
Ann Arbor, MI 48107-8199
(734) 741-2380

P.O. Box 913
Bay City, MI 48707
(989) 894-8800

140 Federal Building
600 Church Street
Flint, MI 48502
(810) 341-7840

**Michigan - Western District**
www.miwd.uscourts.gov
Tracy Cordes
452 Federal Bldg. & Courthouse
110 Michigan Street, NW
Grand Rapids, MI 49503
(616) 456-2381

P.O. Box 698
Marquette, MI 49855-0698
(906) 226-2021

B-35 U.S. Courthouse
410 W. Michigan Avenue
Kalamazoo, MI 49007
(269) 337-5706

315 W. Allegan Street
Lansing, MI 48933
(517) 377-1559

**Minnesota**
www.mnd.uscourts.gov
Richard D. Sletten
316 N. Robert Street
St. Paul, MN 55101
(651) 848-1100

417 U.S. Courthouse
Duluth, MN 55802
(218) 529-3500

202 U.S. Courthouse
300 S. 4th Street
Minneapolis, MN 55415
(612) 664-5000

118 S. Mill St.
Fergus Falls, MN 56537

(218) 739-5758

**Mississippi - Northern District**
www.msnd.uscourts.gov
David Crews
369 Federal Bldg.
Oxford, MS 38655-0727
(662) 234-1971

P.O. Box 704
Aberdeen, MS 39730-0704
(662) 369-4952

305 Main Street, Rm. 329
Greenville, MS 38701
(662) 335-1671

**Mississippi - Southern District**
www.mssd.uscourts.gov
J. T. Noblin
245 E. Capitol Street
Jackson, MS 39201
(601) 965-4440

2012 15th Street, Suite 403
Gulfport, MS 39501
(228) 563-1700

701 N. Main St., Suite 200
Hattiesburg, MS 39401
(601) 583-2433

**Missouri - Eastern District**
www.moed.uscourts.gov
James G. Woodward
U.S. Court & Custom House
111 S. 10th Street
St. Louis, MO 63102
(314) 244-7900

555 Independence St.
Cape Girardeau, MO 63703
(573) 331-8800

**Missouri - Western District**
www.mow.uscourts.gov
Patricia Brune
1510 U.S. Courthouse
400 E. Ninth St.
Kansas City, MO 64106
(816) 512-5000

310 U.S. Courthouse
131 West High Street
Jefferson City, MO 65101
(573) 636-4015

222 N. Hammons Pkwy.
Springfield, MO 65806

(417) 865-3869

**Montana**
www.mtd.uscourts.gov
Patrick Duffy
Federal Building, Rm. 5405
316 N. 26th Street
Billings, MT 59101
(406) 247-7000

P.O. Box 2186
Great Falls, MT 59403-2186
(406) 727-1922

400 N. Main Street, Rm. 303
Butte, MT 59701
(406) 782-0432

P.O. Box 8537
Missoula, MT 59807-8537
(406) 542-7260

901 Front St., Suite 2100
Helena, MT 59626
(406) 441-1355

**Nebraska**
www.ned.uscourts.gov
Denise M. Lucks
111 S. 18th Plaza, Suite 1152
Omaha, NE 68102-1322
(402) 661-7350

593 Federal Bldg.
100 Centennial Mall North
Lincoln, NE 68508-3468
(402) 437-1900

**Nevada**
www.nvd.uscourts.gov
Lance S. Wilson
333 Las Vegas Blvd. South
Las Vegas, NV 89101
(702) 464-5400

400 S. Virginia Street
Reno, NV 89501
(775) 686-5800

**New Hampshire**
www.nhd.uscourts.gov
James R. Starr
55 Pleasant St., Rm. 110
Concord, NH 03301-3941
(603) 225-1423

**New Jersey**
pacer.njd.uscourts.gov
William T. Walsh

# CLERKS OF THE COURTS

50 Walnut St., Rm 4015
Newark, NJ 07102
(973) 645-3730

402 E. State St.
Trenton, NJ 08608
(609) 989-2065

U.S. Courthouse
400 Cooper St., Rm. 1050
Camden, NJ 08101-2797
(856) 757-5021

**New Mexico**
www.nmcourt.fed.us/
Matthew J. Dykman
333 Lomas Blvd., NW, Suite 270
Albuquerque, NM 87102
(505) 348-2000

106 S. Federal Place
Santa Fe, NM 87504-2384
(505) 988-6481

100 N. Church St., Rm. 280
Las Cruces, NM 88001
(505) 528-1400

500 N. Richardson
Roswell, NM 88201
(575) 625-2388

**New York - Northern District**
www.nynd.uscourts.gov
Lawrence K. Baerman
P.O. Box 7367
Syracuse, NY 13261-7367
(315) 234-8500

445 Broadway
509 Courthouse Bldg.
Albany, NY 12207-2924
(518) 257-1800

A. Pirnie Federal Bldg.
10 Broad Street
Utica, NY 13501
(315) 793-8151

15 Henry Street
Binghamton, NY 13902
(607) 773-2893

157 Genessee St., 2nd fl.
Auburn, NY 13021
(313) 252-6555

14 Durkee St., Rm. 360
Plattsburgh, NY 12901

(518) 247-4501

Lewis Ave.
Fort Drum, NY 13602
(315) 234-8500

**New York - Southern District**
www.nysd.uscourts.gov
Ruby J. Krajick
Moynihan U.S. Courthouse
500 Pearl Street
New York, NY 10007-1312
(212) 805-0136

300 Quarropas St.
White Plains, NY 10601-4150
(914) 390-4100

**New York - Eastern District**
www.nyed.uscourts.gov
Robert C. Heinemann
225 Cadman Plaza East
Brooklyn, NY 11201
(718) 613-2600

100 Federal Plaza
Central Islip, NY 11722-4437
(631) 712-6000

**New York - Western District**
www.nywd.uscourts.gov
Michael Roemer
304 U.S. Courthouse
68 Court Street
Buffalo, NY 14202-3498
(716) 332-1700

100 State Street, Room 2120
Rochester, NY 14614-1368
(585) 613-4000

**North Carolina - Eastern District**
www.nced.uscourts.gov
Dennis P. Iavarone
P.O. Box 25670
Raleigh, NC 27611-5610
(919) 645-1700

201 South Evans Street, Rm. 209
Greenville, NC 27858
(252) 830-6009

2 Princess Street
Wilmington, NC 28401-0338
(910) 815-4663

413 Middle St.
New Bern, NC 28560
(252) 638-8534

**North Carolina - Middle District**
www.ncmd.uscourts.gov
John Brubaker
324 W. Market St., Rm 401
Greensboro, NC 27401
(336) 332-6000

**North Carolina - Western District**
www.ncwd.uscourts.gov
Frank G. Johns
210 Jonas Federal Building
401 W. Trade Street
Charlotte, NC 28202
(704) 350-7400

309 U.S. Courthouse
Asheville, NC 28801-2611
(828) 771-7200

P.O. Box 466
Statesville, NC 28687
(704) 883-1000

306 Main St.
Bryson City, NC 28713
(828) 488-3783

**North Dakota**
www.ndd.uscourts.gov
Robert Ansley
P.O. Box 1193
Bismarck, ND 58502-1193
(701) 530-2300

655 First Avenue North
Fargo, ND 58102-4932
(701) 297-7000

102 North 4th St.
Grand Forks, ND 58201
(701) 297-7000

100 1st St., SW
Minot, ND 58701
(701) 530-2300

**Northern Mariana Islands**
www.nmid.uscourts.gov
Galo L. Perez
P.O. Box 500687
Saipan, MP 96950-0687
(670) 236-2902

**Ohio - Northern District**
www.ohnd.uscourts.gov
Geri M. Smith
102 U.S. Courthouse
801 Superior Ave. West
Cleveland, OH 44113-1830

# CLERKS OF THE COURTS

(216) 357-7000

114 U.S. Courthouse
Toledo, OH 43624-1363
(419) 213-5500

337 U.S. Courthouse
125 Market Street
Youngstown, OH 44503-1780
(330) 884-7400

568 U.S. Courthouse
Akron, OH 44308-1813
(330) 252-6000

**Ohio - Southern District**
www.ohsd.uscourts.gov
James Bonini
260 U.S. Courthouse
85 Marconi Boulevard
Columbus, OH 43215
(614) 719-3000

103 U.S. Courthouse
100 East 5th Street
Cincinnati, OH 45202
(513) 564-7500

200 W. Second St., Rm. 712
Dayton, OH 45402-0970
(937) 512-1400

**Oklahoma - Northern District**
www.oknd.uscourts.gov
Philip B. Lombardi
411 U.S. Courthouse
Tulsa, OK 74103-3819
(918) 699-4700

**Oklahoma - Eastern District**
www.oked.uscourts.gov
William B. Guthrie
101 N. Fifth St., Rm. 208
Muskogee, OK 74401
(918) 684-7920

**Oklahoma - Western District**
www.okwd.uscourts.gov
Robert D. Dennis
1210 U.S. Courthouse
Oklahoma City, OK 73102-3092
(405) 609-5000

**Oregon**
Mary Moran
1000 SW Third Avenue
Portland, OR 97204-2902
(503) 326-8000

405 E. Eighth Ave., Rm. 2100
Eugene, OR 97401
(541) 431-4100

310 West Sixth Street
Medford, OR 97501
(541) 608-8777

**Pennsylvania - Eastern District**
www.paed.uscourts.gov/
Michael E. Kunz
2609 U.S. Courthouse
601 Market Street
Philadelphia, PA 19106-1797
(215) 597-7704

504 West Hamilton Street
Allentown, PA 18101-1500
(610) 434-3896

**Pennsylvania - Middle District**
www.pamd.uscourts.gov/
Mary E. D'Andrea
P.O. Box 1148
Scranton, PA 18501-1148
(570) 207-5680

P.O. Box 983
Harrisburg, PA 17108-0983
(717) 221-3920

240 W. Third Street
Williamsport, PA 17701-0608
(570) 323-6380

**Pennsylvania - Western District**
www.pawd.uscourts.gov
Robert V. Barth, Jr.
700 Grant St., Rm 311
Pittsburgh, PA 15230-1805
(412) 208-7500

P.O. Box 1820
Erie, PA 16501
(814) 464-9600

319 Washington Street, Rm. 208
Johnstown, PA 15901
(814) 533-4504

**Puerto Rico**
www.prd.uscourts.gov
Frances Rios de Moran
150 Carlos Chardon Ave., Rm. 150
Hato Rey, PR 00918-1767
(787) 772-3000

**Rhode Island**
www.rid.uscourts.gov

David DiMarzio
1 Exchange Terrace, #356
Providence, RI 02903-1720
(401) 752-7220

**South Carolina**
www.scd.uscourts.gov
Larry W. Propes
901 Richland Street
Columbia, SC 29201
(803) 765-5816

85 Broad St.
Charleston, SC 29401
(843) 579-1401

300 E. Washington St.
Greenville, SC 29601
(864) 241-2700

401 W. Evans St.
Florence, SC 29501
(843) 676-3820

223 Park Ave. SW
Aiken, SC 29801
(803) 648-6896

U.S. Courthouse
1501 Bay Street
Beaufort, SC 29902
(843) 521-2088

Russell Federal Bldg.
201 Magnolia Street
Spartanburg, SC 29306
(864) 241-2700

315 S. McDuffie St.
Anderson, SC 29624
(864) 241-2700

**South Dakota**
www.sdd.uscourts.gov
Joseph A. Haas
128 Federal Bldg. & Courthouse
400 South Phillips Avenue
Sioux Falls, SD 57104-6851
(605) 330-6600

U.S.P.O. & Courthouse, Rm. 405
Pierre, SD 57501
(605) 945-4600

Federal Bldg. & U.S. Courthouse
515 9th Street, Room 302
Rapid City, SD 57701
(605) 399-6000

# CLERKS OF THE COURTS

**Tennessee - Eastern District**
www.tned.uscourts.gov/
Patricia L. McNutt
800 Market Street
Knoxville, TN 37902
(865) 545-4228

200 S. Jefferson St.
Winchester, TN 37398
(931) 967-1444

900 Georgia Ave.
Chattanooga, TN 37402
(423) 752-5200

220 West Depot Street
Greeneville, TN 37743
(423) 639-3105

**Tennessee - Middle District**
www.tnmd.uscourts.gov/
Keith Throckmorton
800 U.S. Courthouse
Nashville, TN 37203-3869
(615) 736-2364

**Tennessee - Western District**
www.tnwd.uscourts.gov/
Thomas M. Gould
242 Federal Building
Memphis, TN 38103
(901) 495-1200

262 Federal Building
111 S. Highland Ave.
Jackson, TN 38301
(731) 421-9200

**Texas - Northern District**
www.txnd.uscourts.gov
Karen Mitchell
1100 Commerce Street, Rm. 1452
Dallas, TX 75242-1003
(214) 753-2200

341 Pine St.
Abilene, TX 79601
(325) 677-6311

205 E. Fifth St.
Amarillo, TX 79101
(806) 468-3800

310  U.S. Courthouse
Fort Worth, TX 76102-3673
(817) 850-6622

1205 Texas Avenue, Rm. 209
Lubbock, TX 79401-4091

(806) 472-1900

202 Federal Building
33 East Twohig St.
San Angelo, TX 76903
(325) 655-4506

1000 Lamar St., Rm. 203
Wichita Falls, TX 76307-3431
(940) 767-1902

**Texas - Eastern District**
www.txed.uscourts.gov
David J. Maland
211 W. Ferguson, Rm. 106
Tyler, TX 75702
(903) 590-1000

216 Federal Building
Sherman, TX 75090
(903) 892-2921

500 N. State Line Ave., Rm. 301
Texarkana, TX 75501
(903) 794-8561

300 Willow St., Rm. 320
Beaumont, TX 77701
(409) 654-7000

104 N. Third Street
Lufkin, TX 75901
(936) 632-2739

P.O. Box 1499
Marshall, TX 75672-1499
(903) 935-2912

**Texas - Southern District**
www.txs.uscourts.gov
David Bradley
P.O. Box 61010
Houston, TX 77208-1010
(713) 250-5500

600 E. Harrison Street, #101
Brownsville, TX 78520
(956) 548-2500

1133 N. Shoreline Blvd., Rm. 208
Corpus Christi, TX 78401
(361) 888-3142

P.O. Box 2300
Galveston, TX 77553-2300
(409) 766-3530

1300 Victoria St., Rm. 1131
Laredo, TX 78040

(956) 723-3542

P.O. Box 1638
Victoria, TX 77901-1638
(361) 788-5000

P.O. Box 5059
McAllen, TX 78502-5059
(956) 618-8065

**Texas - Western District**
www.txwd.uscourts.gov
William G. Putnicki
U.S. Courthouse
655 E. Durango Boulevard
San Antonio, TX 78206-1198
(210) 472-6550

200 W. 8th Street
Austin, TX 78701
(512) 916-5896

111 E. Broadway, Rm. L-100
Del Rio, TX 78840-5573
(830) 703-2054

U.S. Courthouse, Rm. 219
El Paso, TX 79901-2401
(915) 534-6725

800 Franklin Ave., Rm. 380
Waco, TX 76701
(254) 750-1501

200 E. Wall St., Rm. 222
Midland, TX 79701
(432) 686-4001

410 South Cedar St.
Pecos, TX 79772
(432) 445-4228

**Utah**
www.utd.uscourts.gov
D. Mark Jones
350 South Main Street, Rm. 150
Salt Lake City, UT 84101-2180
(801) 524-6100

**Vermont**
www.vtd.uscourts.gov
Jeffrey S. Eaton
P.O. Box 945
Burlington, VT 05402-0945
(802) 951-6301

P.O. Box 998
Brattleboro, VT 05302-0998
(802) 254-0250

# CLERKS OF THE COURTS

P.O. Box 607
Rutland, VT 05702-0607
(802) 773-0245

**Virgin Islands**
www.vid.uscourts.gov
Wilfred Morales
5500 Veterans Drive, Suite 310
Charlotte Amalie,
St. Thomas, VI 00802-6424
(340) 774-0640

3013 Estate Golden Rock, Rm. 219
Christiansted,
St. Croix, VI 00820-4366
(340) 773-1130

**Virginia - Eastern District**
www.vaed.uscourts.gov
Fernando Galindo
401 Courthouse Square
Alexandria, VA 22314-5798
(703) 299-2100

193 U.S. Courthouse
600 Granby Street
Norfolk, VA 23510-1811
(757) 222-7201

701 East Broad St., Rm. 3000
Richmond, VA 23219-3528
(804) 916-2200

2400 West Ave.
Newport News, VA 23607
(757) 247-0784

**Virginia - Western District**
www.vawd.uscourts.gov
Julia Dudley
P.O. Box 1234
Roanoke, VA 24011-1234
(540) 857-5108

180 W. Main St., Rm. 104
Abingdon, VA 24210
(276) 628-5116

P.O. Box 490
Big Stone Gap, VA 24219-0490
(276) 523-3557

255 W. Main Street, Rm. 304
Charlottesville, VA 22902
(434) 296-9284

700 Main St., Rm. 202
Danville, VA 24541
(434) 793-7147

116 N. Main Street
Harrisonburg, VA 22802
(540) 434-3181

1101 Court St.
Lynchburg, VA 24504
(434) 847-5722

**Washington - Eastern District**
www.waed.uscourts.gov
James R. Larsen
920 W. Riverside Ave.
Spokane, WA 99201
(509) 458-3500

25 S. Third St.
Yakima, WA 98907
(509) 573-6600

825 Jadwin Ave., Rm. 174
Richland, WA 99352-1386
(509) 376-7262

**Washington - Western District**
www.wawd.uscourts.gov
Bruce Rifkin
700 Stewart St., Lobby Level
Seattle, WA 98104-1125
(206) 370-8400

1717 Pacific Ave., Rm. 3100
Tacoma, WA 98402-3226
(253) 882-3800

**West Virginia - Northern District**
www.wvnd.uscourts.gov
Cheryl Dean Riley
P.O. Box 1518
Elkins, WV 26241-1518
(304) 636-1445

1125 Chapline St.
Wheeling, WV 26003
(304) 232-0011

500 W. Pike Street, Rm. 301
Clarksburg, WV 26301
(304) 622-8513

217 West King St., Rm. 102
Martinsburg, VA 25401
(304) 267-8225

**West Virginia - Southern District**
www.wvsd.uscourts.gov
Teresa L. Deppner
300 Virginia St. E., Rm. 2400
Charleston, WV 25301
(304) 347-3000

110 N. Heber St., Rm. 119
Beckley, WV 25801
(304) 253-7481

601 Federal St., Rm. 2303
Bluefield, WV 24701
(304) 327-9798

845 Fifth Ave., Rm. 101
Huntington, WV 25701
(304) 529-5588

425 Juliana St., Rm. 5102
Parkersburg, WV 26101
(304) 420-6490

**Wisconsin - Eastern District**
www.wied.uscourts.gov
Jon W. Sanfilippo
362 Federal Building
517 East Wisconsin Avenue
Milwaukee, WI 53202-4582
(414) 297-3372

125 S. Jefferson St.
Green Bay, WI 54301
(920) 884-3720

**Wisconsin - Western District**
www.wiw.uscourts.gov
Peter Oppeneer
P.O. Box 432
Madison, WI 53701-0432
(608) 264-5156

**Wyoming**
www.wyd.uscourts.gov
Stephan Harris
2120 Capitol Ave., Rm. 2141
Cheyenne, WY 82001-0727
(307) 433-2120

111 S. Wolcott Street
Casper, WY 82601
(307) 232-2620

105 Mammoth
Mammoth, WY 82190
(307) 344-2569

P.O. Box 4117
Jackson, WY 83001
(307) 773-4126

# FEDERAL BANKRUPTCY JUDGES

## DISTRICT OF COLUMBIA CIRCUIT
S. Martin Teel, Jr.
U.S. Courthouse
3rd & Constitution Ave., NW
Washington, DC 20001
(202) 354-3530

## FIRST CIRCUIT

### Maine
Louis H. Kornreich, C.J.
202 Harlow Street
Bangor, ME 04401
(207) 945-0550

James B. Haines, Jr.
537 Congress St., 2nd fl.
Portland, ME 04101-3318
(207) 780-3653

### Massachusetts
Frank J. Bailey, C.J.
5 P.O. Square, Rm.1150
Boston, MA 02109
(617) 748-5300

Joan N. Feeney
5 P.O. Square, Rm.1150
Boston, MA 02109
(617) 748-5300

William C. Hillman
5 P.O. Square, Rm.1150
Boston, MA 02109
(617) 748-5300

Henry J. Boroff
595 Main St.
Worcester, MA 01608-2076
(508) 770-8940

Melvin Hoffman
595 Main St.
Worcester, MA 01608-2076
(508) 770-8901

### New Hampshire
J. Michael Deasy
1000 Elm St., Suite 1001
Manchester, NH 03101
(603) 222-2640

### Rhode Island
Arthur N. Votolato, Jr.

Federal Center
380 Westminster Mall, 6th fl.
Providence, RI 02903
(401) 626-3060

### Puerto Rico
Brian K. Tester, C.J.
300 Recinto Sur, Suite 109
San Juan, PR 00901
(787) 977-6150

Enrique S. Lamoutte
300 Recinto Sur, Suite 109
San Juan, PR 00901
(787) 977-6030

Sara E. de Jesus
300 Recinto Sur, Suite 109
San Juan, PR 00901
(787) 977-6020

Mildred Caban Flores
93 Atocha St., 2nd fl.
Ponce, PR 00730
(787) 812-2215

## SECOND CIRCUIT

### Connecticut
Lorraine Murphy Weil, C.J.
157 Church Street, 17th fl.
New Haven, CT 06510
(203) 773-2425

Albert S. Dabrowski
450 Main St.
Hartford, CT 06103
(860) 240-3679

Alan H. W. Shiff
915 Lafayette Boulevard
Bridgeport, CT 06604
(203) 579-5806

### New York - Eastern District
Carla E. Craig, C.J.
271 Cadman Plaza East
Brooklyn, NY 11201
(347) 394-1840

Alan S. Trust
290 Federal Plaza, Rm. 960
Central Islip, NY 11722-4437
(631) 712-5680

Robert Grossman
290 Federal Plaza, Rm. 860
Central Islip, NY 11722-4437
(631) 712-5740

Jerome Feller
271 Cadman Plaza East
Brooklyn, NY 11201
(347) 394-1830

Dorothy Eisenberg (Recalled)
290 Federal Plaza, Rm. 760
Central Islip, NY 11722-4437
(631) 712-5690

Joel B. Rosenthal
271 Cadman Plaza East
Brooklyn, NY 11201
(347) 394-1850

Elizabeth S. Stong
271 Cadman Plaza East
Brooklyn, NY 11201-4201
(347) 394-1860

### New York - Northern District
Robert E. Littlefield, Jr., C.J.
445 Broadway
Albany, NY 12207
(518) 257-1661

Diane Davis
10 Broad St.
Utica, NY 13501
(315) 793-8111

Margaret M. Cangilos-Ruiz
100 S. Clinton St.
Syracuse, NY 13261
(315) 295-1682

### New York - Southern District
Arthur J. Gonzalez, C.J.
1 Bowling Green, 5th fl.
New York, NY 10004-1408
(212) 668-2894

Stuart M. Bernstein
1 Bowling Green, 6th fl.
New York, NY 10004-1408
(212) 668-2304

# FEDERAL BANKRUPTCY JUDGES

Cecelia G. Morris
355 Main Street
Poughkeepsie, NY 12601
(845) 452-4200

Robert E. Gerber
1 Bowling Green, 6th fl.
New York, NY 10004-1408
(212) 668-5660

Burton R. Lifland (Recalled)
1 Bowling Green, 6th fl.
New York, NY 10004-1408
(212) 668-5663

Martin Glenn
1 Bowling Green, 6th fl.
New York, NY 10004-1408
(212) 284-4551

James M. Peck
1 Bowling Green, 6th fl.
New York, NY 10004-1408
(212) 688-5632

Allan L. Gropper
1 Bowling Green, 6th fl.
New York, NY 10004-1408
(212) 668-5629

Robert D. Drain
1 Bowling Green, 6th fl.
New York, NY 10004-1408
(212) 668-2301

Shelley C. Chapman
1 Bowling Green, 6th fl.
New York, NY 10004-1408
(212) 668-2301

Sean Lane
1 Bowling Green, 6th fl.
New York, NY 10004-1408
(212) 668-5637

**New York - Western District**
Carl L. Bucki, C.J.
300 Pearl Street, Suite 350
Buffalo, NY 14202
(716) 362-3200

John Charles Ninfo II
1220 U.S. Courthouse
100 State Street
Rochester, NY 14614
(585) 613-4200

Michael J. Kaplan

300 Pearl Street, Suite 350
Buffalo, NY 14202
(716) 362-3200

**Vermont**
Colleen A. Brown
P.O. Box 6648
Rutland, VT 05702-6648
(802) 776-2030

## THIRD CIRCUIT

**Delaware**
Kevin J. Carey, C.J.
824 Market Street, 5th fl.
Wilmington, DE 19801-4937
(302) 252-2927

Mary F. Walrath
824 Market Street, 5th fl.
Wilmington, DE 19801-4937
(302) 252-2929

Peter J. Walsh
824 Market Street, 6th fl.
Wilmington, DE 19801-4937
(302) 252-2925

Kevin Gross
824 Market St., 6th fl.
Wilmington, DE 19801-4937
(302) 252-2913

Brendan L. Shannon
824 Market Street, 6th fl.
Wilmington, DE 19801-4937
(302) 252-2915

Christopher S. Sontchi
824 Market Street, 5th fl.
Wilmington, DE 19801-4937
(302) 252-2888

**New Jersey**
Judith H. Wizmur, C.J.
P. O. Box 2067
Camden, NJ 08101-2067
(856) 757-5366

Rosemary Gambardella
50 Walnut Street, 3rd floor
Newark, NJ 07102-3550
(973) 645-4763

Morris Stern
50 Walnut Street, 3rd fl.
Newark, NJ 07102-3550
(973) 368-1248

Kathryn C. Ferguson
402 East State Street, 4th fl.
Trenton, NJ 08608
(609) 989-2200

Gloria M. Burns
P. O. Box 2067
Camden, NJ 08101-2067
(856) 757-5375

Novalyn L. Winfield
50 Walnut Street, 3rd fl.
Newark, NJ 07102-3550
(973) 645-2187

Donald H. Steckroth
50 Walnut Street, 3rd fl.
Newark, NJ 07102-3550
(973) 645-4762

Raymond T. Lyons, Jr.
402 E. State Street
Trenton, NJ 08608
(609) 989-2200

Michael B. Kaplan
402 E. State Street
Trenton, NJ 08608
(609) 989-2002

**Pennsylvania - Eastern District**
Stephen Raslavich, C.J.
900 Market Street, Suite 204
Philadelphia, PA 19107-4295
(215) 408-2982

Bruce I. Fox
900 Market Street, Suite 202
Philadelphia, PA 19107-4297
(215) 408-2974

Eric L. Frank
201 Federal Bldg.
900 Market Street
Philadelphia, PA 19107-4298
(215) 408-2970

Richard Fehling
301 Madison Bldg.
400 Washington Street
Reading, PA 19601
(610) 208-5030

Jean FitzSimon
900 Market Street, Suite 214
Philadelphia, PA 19107-4295
(215) 408-2891

# FEDERAL BANKRUPTCY JUDGES

Magdeline D. Coleman
900 Market Street
Philadelphia, PA 19107-4298
(215) 408-2891

**Pennsylvania - Middle District**
Mary D. France, C.J.
228 Walnut Street
Harrisburg, PA 17108
(717) 901-2840

John J. Thomas
197 S. Main St.
Wilkes-Barre, PA 18701
(570) 831-2531

Richard N. Opel
197 S. Main St.
Wilkes-Barre, PA 18701
(570) 831-2536

**Pennsylvania - Western District**
Thomas P. Agresti, C.J.
17 South Park Row, Rm. A430
Erie, PA 16501
(814) 464-9760

Judith K. Fitzgerald
5490 USX Tower
600 Grant Street
Pittsburgh, PA 15219
(412) 644-3541

Jeffrey Deller
5436 USX Tower
600 Grant Street
Pittsburgh, PA 15219
(412) 644-4710

## FOURTH CIRCUIT

**Maryland**
Duncan W. Keir, C.J.
101 W. Lombard St.
Baltimore, MD 21201
(410) 962-3555

James F. Schneider
101 W. Lombard Street
Baltimore, MD 21201
(410) 962-2820

Paul Mannes
6500 Cherrywood Lane, #385A
Greenbelt, MD 20770
(301) 344-8040

E. Stephen Derby (Recalled)

101 W. Lombard Street
Baltimore, MD 21201
(410) 962-7801

Nancy V. Alquist
101 W. Lombard Street
Baltimore, MD 21201
(410) 962-7479

Thomas J. Catliota
6500 Cherrywood Lane
Greenbelt, MD 20770
(301) 344-3660

Robert A. Gordon
101 W. Lombard Street
Baltimore, MD 21201
(410) 962-4162

Wendelin I. Lipp
6500 Cherrywood Lane
Greenbelt, MD 20770
(301) 344-3377

David E. Rice
101 W. Lombard Street
Baltimore, MD 21201
(410) 962-4211

**North Carolina - Eastern District**
Randy D. Doub, C.J.
1760-A Parkwood Blvd.
Wilson, NC 27893
(252) 291-6413

J. Rich Leonard
P.O. Box 1441
Raleigh, NC 27607
(919) 856-4033

Stephani W. Humrickhouse
P.O. Drawer 2747
Raleigh, NC 27602
(919) 856-4194

**North Carolina - Middle District**
William L. Stocks, C.J.
P.O. Box 26100
Greensboro, NC 27402-6100
(336) 333-4080

Catherine R. Aron
P.O. Box 26100
Greensboro, NC 27402-6100
(336) 358-4150

Thomas W. Waldrep, Jr.
P.O. Box 26100

Greensboro, NC 27420-0543
(336) 358-4081

**North Carolina - Western District**
J. Craig Whitley, C.J.
401 W. Trade Street
Charlotte, NC 28202
(704) 350-7575

George R. Hodges
401 W. Trade Street
Charlotte, NC 28202
(704) 350-7575

**South Carolina**
John E. Waites, C.J.
1100 Laurel St.
Columbia, SC 29201
(803) 253-3030

David Robert Duncan
1100 Laurel St.
Columbia, SC 29201
(803) 765-5657

Helen Burris
P.O. Box 1985
Spartanburg, SC 29304
(864) 591-5315

**Virginia - Eastern District**
Dougles O. Tice, Jr., C.J.
701 E. Broad St., Suite 4000
Richmond, VA 23219
(804) 916-2460

Robert G. Mayer
200 S. Washington Street, #300
Alexandria, VA 22314-5405
(703) 258-1280

Stephen S. Mitchell
200 S. Washington Street, #206
Alexandria, VA 22314-5405
(703) 258-1240

Stephen C. St. John
600 Granby St.
Norfolk, VA 23510-1915
(757) 222-7480

Kevin R. Huennekens
701 E. Broad St., Suite 4000
Richmond, VA 23219
(804) 916-2455

Frank James Santoro
600 Granby St., Suite 400

# FEDERAL BANKRUPTCY JUDGES

Norfolk, VA 23510
(757) 222-7470

**Virginia - Western District**
Ross W. Krumm, C.J.
P.O. Box 191
Harrisonburg, VA 22803
(540) 434-6747

William E. Anderson
1101 Court St.
Lynchburg, VA 24504
(434) 846-3118

William F. Stone, Jr.
210 Church Ave. SW
Roanoke, VA 24010
(540) 857-2394

**West Virginia - Northern District**
Patrick M. Flatley, C.J.
P.O. Box 70
Wheeling, WV 26003
(304) 233-1655

**West Virginia - Southern District**
Ronald G. Pearson
300 Virginia St. East, Rm. 6408
Charleston, WV 25301
(304) 347-3238

**FIFTH CIRCUIT**

**Louisiana - Eastern District**
Jerry A. Brown, C.J.
601 Federal Bldg.
500 Poydras St.
New Orleans, LA 70130
(504) 589-7810

Elizabeth Manger
601 Federal Bldg.
500 Poydras St.
New Orleans, LA 70130
(504) 589-7800

**Louisiana - Middle District**
Douglas D. Dodd, C.J.
707 Florida Street, Rm. 236
Baton Rouge, LA 70801
(225) 346-3335

**Louisiana - Western District**
Robert Summerhays, C.J.
214 Jefferson St., Suite 100
Lafayette, LA 70501-7050
(337) 262-6383

Stephen V. Callaway
300 Fannin Street, Rm. 4400
Shreveport, LA 71101-3088
(318) 676-4269

Henley A. Hunter
P.O. Box 111
Alexandria, LA 71301
(318) 443-8083

**Mississippi - Northern District**
David W. Houston III
703 Hwy 145 North
Aberdeen, MS 39730-0867
(662) 369-2624

Neil P. Olack (Visiting Judge)
P.O. Box 2448
Jackson, MS 39225-2448
(601) 608-4690

**Mississippi - Southern District**
Edward Ellington, C.J.
P.O. Box 2448
Jackson, MS 39225-2448
(601) 608-4690

Katherine M. Samson
2012 - 15th St., Suite 814
Gulfport, MS 39501
(228) 563-1840

Neil P. Olack
P.O. Box 2448
Jackson, MS 39225-2448
(601) 608-4690

**Texas - Northern District**
Barbara J. Houser, C.J.
1100 Commerce St., Room 1254
Dallas, TX 75242-1496
(214) 758-2055

Stacey G.C. Jernigan
1100 Commerce Street, Rm. 1254
Dallas, TX 75242-1496
(214) 758-2040

Harlin D. Hale
1100 Commerce Street, Rm. 1254
Dallas, TX 75242-1496
(214) 753-2016

Russell F. Nelms
501 W. 10th St.
Fort Worth, TX 76102-3643
(817) 333-6025

Robert L. Jones
1205 Texas Avenue
Lubbock, TX 79401-4002
(806) 472-5020

D. Michael Lynn
U.S. Courthouse
501 W. 10th St.
Fort Worth, TX 76102-3643
(817) 333-6020

**Texas - Southern District**
Marvin P. Isgur, C.J.
515 Rusk Ave.
Houston, TX 77002
(713) 250-5421

Karen K. Brown
515 Rusk Ave., #10501
Houston, TX 77002
(713) 250-5250

Richard S. Schmidt
1133 N. Shoreline Blvd., Rm. 221
Corpus Christi, TX 78401
(361) 888-3207

Letitia Z. Paul
4019 U.S. Courthouse
515 Rusk Ave.
Houston, TX 77002
(713) 250-5410

Jeff E.T. Bohm
515 Rusk Ave.
Houston, TX 77002
(713) 250-5405

**Texas - Western District**
Ronald B. King, C.J.
P.O. Box 1439
San Antonio, TX 78295-1439
(210) 472-6609

Leif M. Clark
P.O. Box 1439
San Antonio, TX 78295-1439
(210) 472-5181

Craig A. Gargotta
903 San Jacinto Blvd., #326
Austin, TX 78701
(512) 916-5800

H. Christopher Mott
903 San Jacinto Blvd.
Austin, TX 78701
(512) 916-5800

# FEDERAL BANKRUPTCY JUDGES

**Texas - Eastern District**
Brenda T. Rhoades, C.J.
660 N. Central Expwy., Suite 300B
Plano, TX 75074
(972) 509-1250

Bill G. Parker
110 N. College Ave., 9th fl.
Tyler, TX 75702
(903) 590-3200

**SIXTH CIRCUIT**

**Kentucky - Eastern District**
Joseph M. Scott, C.J.
100 E. Vine St.
Lexington, KY 40507
(859) 233-2814

Tracey Wise
100 E. Vine St.
Lexington, KY 40507
(859) 233-2465

Joe Lee (Recalled)
P.O. Box 1111
Lexington, KY 40588-1111
(859) 233-2814

**Kentucky - Western District**
Joan Lloyd, C.J.
541 U.S. Courthouse
601 West Broadway
Louisville, KY 40202
(502) 627-5525

David T. Stosberg
601 W. Broadway, #533
Louisville, KY 40202
(502) 627-5575

Thomas H. Fulton
601 W. Broadway, #528
Louisville, KY 40202
(502) 627-5550

**Michigan - Eastern District**
Phillip J. Shefferly, C.J.
211 W. Fort St., Suite 1950
Detroit, MI 48226-3211
(313) 234-0040

Steven W. Rhodes
211 W. Fort St., Suite 1800
Detroit, MI 48226-3211
(313) 234-0020

Marci B. McIvor

211 W. Fort St., Suite 1850
Detroit, MI 48226-3211
(313) 234-0010

Thomas J. Tucker
211 W. Fort St., Suite 1900
Detroit, MI 48226-3211
(313) 234-0030

Walter Shapero
211 West Fort Street
Detroit, MI 48226
(810) 234-2640

Daniel Opperman
111 First Street
Bay City, MI 48707
(989) 894-8844

**Michigan - Western District**
James D. Gregg, C.J.
1 Division Ave. N., Rm. 200
Grand Rapids, MI 49503
(616) 456-2264

Scott W. Dales
1 Division Ave. N., Rm. 200
Grand Rapids, MI 49503
(616) 456-2949

Jeffrey R. Hughes
1 Division Ave. N., Rm. 200
Grand Rapids, MI 49503
(616) 456-2233

**Ohio - Northern District**
Marilyn Shea-Stonum, C.J.
240 Federal Building
2 South Main Street
Akron, OH 44308
(330) 252-6130

Randolph Baxter
201 Superior Ave.
Cleveland, OH 44114
(216) 615-4300

Richard L. Speer
113 U.S. Courthouse
Toledo, OH 43624
(419) 259-5631

Russ Kendig
401 McKinley Ave., SW
Canton, OH 44702
(330) 458-2120

Pat E. Morgenstern-Clarren

201 Superior Ave.
Cleveland, OH 44114
(216) 615-4422

Arthur I. Harris
201 Superior Ave.
Cleveland, OH 44114
(216) 615-4405

Mary Ann Whipple
1716 Spielbusch Avenue
Toldeo, OH 43624
(419) 213-5621

Kay Woods
10 E. Commerce St.
Youngstown, OH 44503
(330) 742-0900

**Ohio - Southern District**
Charles M. Caldwell, C.J.
170 N. High Street
Columbus, OH 43215
(614) 469-6638 x260

Guy R. Humphrey
120 W. Third Street
Dayton, OH 45402
(937) 225-2516 x338

C. Kathryn Preston
170 N. High Street
Columbus, OH 43215
(614) 469-6638 x250

Jeffery P. Hopkins
221 E. Fourth St., Suite 800
Cincinnati, OH 45202
(513) 684-2572 x146

Burton Perlman
221 E. Fourth St., Suite 800
Cincinnati, OH 45202
(513) 684-2572 x131

John E. Hoffman, Jr.
170 N. High St.
Columbus, OH 43215
(614) 469-6638 x282

Lawrence S. Walter
120 W. Third St., Rm. 109
Dayton, OH 45402
(937) 225-2516 x307

**Tennessee - Eastern District**
John C. Cook, C.J.
31 East 11th Street

# FEDERAL BANKRUPTCY JUDGES

Chattanooga, TN 37402-2722
(423) 752-5260

Richard S. Stair, Jr.
800 Market St., #330
Knoxville, TN 37902
(865) 545-4284

Marcia P. Parsons
220 W. Depot St.
Greeneville, TN 37743
(423) 638-2264

Shelley D. Rucker
31 East 11th Street
Chattanooga, TN 37402-2722
(423) 752-5104

**Tennessee - Middle District**
George C. Paine II, C.J.
Customs House
701 Broadway
Nashville, TN 37203-3976
(615) 736-5587

Keith M. Lundin
Customs House
701 Broadway
Nashville, TN 37203-3976
(615) 736-5586

Marian F. Harrison
701 Broadway
Nashville, TN 37203-3976
(615) 736-5589

**Tennessee - Western District**
David S. Kennedy, C.J.
200 Jefferson Ave., Suite 950
Memphis, TN 38103
(901) 328-3522

George Emerson, Jr.
200 Jefferson Ave.
Memphis, TN 38103
(901) 328-3614

G. Harvey Boswell
111 S. Highland Ave., 3rd fl.
Jackson, TN 38301
(731) 421-9372

Jennie D. Latta
200 Jefferson Ave., Suite 650
Memphis, TN 38103-2328
(901) 328-3542

Paulette J. Delk

200 Jefferson Ave.
Memphis, TN 38103
(901) 328-3534

**SEVENTH CIRCUIT**

**Illinois - Central District**
Thomas L. Perkins, C.J.
124 Federal Bldg.
100 NE Monroe St.
Peoria, IL 61602
(309) 671-7075

Gerald D. Fines
201 N. Vermilion Street, #127
Danville, IL 61832
(217) 431-4817

William V. Altenberger (Recalled)
Federal Building
100 NE Monroe Street
Peoria, IL 61602
(309) 671-7290

Mary Patricia Gorman
600 E. Monroe St., #226
Springfield, IL 62701
(217) 492-4566

**Illinois - Northern District**
Carol A. Doyle, C.J.
219 South Dearborn Street
Chicago, IL 60604
(312) 435-6010

Eugene R. Wedoff
219 South Dearborn Street
Chicago, IL 60604
(312 ) 435-5644

Susan Pierson Sonderby
219 South Dearborn Street
Chicago, IL 60604
(312) 435-5646

John D. Schwartz
219 South Dearborn Street
Chicago, IL 60604
(312) 435-5652

Manuel Barbosa
211 S. Court Street
Rockford, IL 61101
(815) 987-4366

Jack B. Schmetterer
219 South Dearborn Street
Chicago, IL 60604

(312) 435-5654

Bruce W. Black
219 South Dearborn Street
Chicago, IL 60604
(312) 435-6867

Jacqueline P.Cox
219 South Dearborn Street
Chicago, IL 60604
(312) 435-5679

John H. Squires
219 South Dearborn Street
Chicago, IL 60604
(312) 435-7580

A. Benjamin Goldgar
219 South Dearborn Street
Chicago, IL 60604
(312) 435-5642

Pamela S. Hollis
219 South Dearborn Street, #648
Chicago, IL 60604
(312) 435-5534

**Illinois - Southern District**
Laura K. Grandy, C.J.
750 Missouri Ave.
East St. Louis, IL 62201
(618) 482-9400

Kenneth J. Meyers
750 Missouri Ave.
East St. Louis, IL 62201
(618) 482-9307

**Indiana - Northern District**
Robert E. Grant, C.J.
2128 Federal Bldg.
1300 S. Harrison Street
Fort Wayne, IN 46802
(260) 426-2455

Harry C. Dees, Jr.
401 S. Michigan St.
South Bend, IN 46634
(574 ) 968-2280

Kent Lindquist (Recalled)
5400 Federal Plaza, Suite 3600
Hammond, IN 46320
(219) 852-3550

J. Phillip Klingeberger
5400 Federal Plaza
Suite 3800

# FEDERAL BANKRUPTCY JUDGES

Hammond, IN 46320
(219) 852-3575

**Indiana - Southern District**
Anthony John Metz III, C.J.
U.S. Courthouse
46 E. Ohio St.
Indianapolis, IN 46204
(317) 229-3880

Basil H. Lorch III
121 W. Spring Street
New Albany, IN 47150
(812) 542-4570

Frank J. Otte
335 U.S. Courthouse
46 E. Ohio St.
Indianapolis, IN 42604
(317) 229-3890

James K. Coachys
116 U.S. Courthouse
46 E. Ohio St.
Indianapolis, IN 46204
(317) 229-3870

**Wisconsin - Eastern District**
Pamela Pepper, C.J.
517 E. Wisconsin Avenue, #140
Milwaukee, WI 53202-4581
(414) 297-3291 x3211

Margaret Dee McGarity
517 E. Wisconsin Avenue, #162
Milwaukee, WI 53202-4581
(414) 297-3291 x3203

James E. Shapiro
140 U.S. Courthouse
517 E. Wisconsin Avenue
Milwaukee, WI 53202-4581
(414) 297-3291 x3201

Susan V. Kelley
517 E. Wisconsin Avenue, #162
Milwaukee, WI 53202-4581
(414) 297-3291 x3202

**Wisconsin - Western District**
Robert D. Martin, C.J. (Recalled)
P.O. Box 548
Madison, WI 53701
(608) 264-5188

Thomas S. Utschig
P.O. Box 5009
Eau Claire, WI 54702-5009

(715) 839-2985

## EIGHTH CIRCUIT

**Arkansas - Western & Eastern
  Districts**
Richard D. Taylor, C.J.
300 W. Second St.
Little Rock, AR 72203
(501) 918-5620

Audrey, R. Evans
300 W. Second St.
Little Rock, AR 72203
(501) 918-5660

James G. Mixon (Recalled)
300 W. Second St.
Little Rock, AR 72203
(501) 918-5647

Ben T. Barry
35 E. Mountain St.
Fayetteville, AR 72702
(479) 582-9809

**Iowa - Northern District**
Thad J. Collins, C.J.
P.O. Box 74890
Cedar Rapids, IA 52407
(319) 286-2230

Paul J. Kilburg
P.O. Box 74890
Cedar Rapids, IA 52407
(319) 286-2230

William L. Edmonds
U.S. Courthouse, 1st fl.
320 Sixth Street
Sioux City, IA 51101
(712) 233-3949

**Iowa - Southern District**
Lee M. Jackwig, C.J.
110 E. Court Avenue
Des Moines, IA 50309-2049
(515) 284-6231

Anita L. Shodeen
110 E. Court Avenue
Des Moines, IA 50309-2049
(515) 284-6118

**Minnesota**
Nancy C. Dreher, C.J.
7W U.S. Courthouse
300 S. Fourth St.

Minneapolis, MN 55415
(612) 664-5260

Gregory F. Kishel
316 N. Robert Street
St. Paul, MN 55101
(651) 848-1060

Dennis D. O'Brien
316 N. Robert Street
St. Paul, MN 55101
(651) 848-1050

Robert J. Kressel
8W U.S. Courthouse
300 S. Fourth St.
Minneapolis, MN 55415
(612) 664-5250

**Missouri - Eastern District**
Barry S. Schermer, C.J.
111 S. 10th Street
St. Louis, MO 63102
(314) 244-4531

Charles E. Rendlen III
111 S. 10th St.
St. Louis, MO 63102
(314) 244-4511

David P. McDonald
111 S. 10th Street
St. Louis, MO 63102
(314) 244-4521

Kathy A. Surratt-States
111 S. 10th Street
St. Louis, MO 63102
(314) 244-4541

**Missouri - Western District**
Dennis R. Dow, C.J.
400 E. Ninth St.
Kansas City, MO 64106
(816) 512-1880

Jerry W. Venters
400 E. Ninth St.
Kansas City, MO 64106
(816) 512-1895

Arthur B. Federman
400 E. Ninth St.
Kansas City, MO 64106
(816) 512-1910

**Nebraska**
Thomas L. Saladino, C.J.

# FEDERAL BANKRUPTCY JUDGES

463 U.S. Courthouse
100 Centennial Mall North
Lincoln, NE 68508
(402) 437-1620

Timothy J. Mahoney
111 S. 18th Plaza, Suite 1125
Omaha, NE 68102-1321
(402) 661-7480

**North Dakota**
William A. Hill
655 First Ave. N., #350
Fargo, ND 58102-4952
(701) 297-7140

**South Dakota**
Charles Nail, Jr.
211 Federal Bldg.
225 S. Pierre Street
Pierre, SD 57501-1115
(605) 945-4490

**NINTH CIRCUIT**

**Alaska**
Donald MacDonald IV, C.J.
605 W. 4th Ave., Suite 138
Anchorage, AK 99501-2296
(907) 271-2667

Herbert A. Ross (Recalled)
605 W. 4th Ave., Suite 138
Anchorage, AK 99501-2296
(907) 271-2655 x2630

**Arizona**
James M. Marlar, C.J.
38 S. Scott Ave.
Tucson, AZ 85701
(520) 682-4268

Redfield T. Baum
230 N. First Ave., Suite 101
Phoenix, AZ 85003
(602) 682-4184

Sarah S. Curley
230 N. First Ave., Suite 101
Phoenix, AZ 85003
(602) 682-4146

George B. Nielsen, Jr.
230 N. First Ave., Suite 101
Phoenix, AZ 85003
(602) 682-4164

Eileen W. Hollowell

38 S. Scott Ave.
Tucson, AZ 85701
(520) 682-4268

Charles G. Case II
230 N. First Ave., Suite 101
Phoenix, AZ 85003
(602) 682-4224

Randolph J. Haines
230 N. First Ave., Suite 101
Phoenix, AZ 85003
(602) 682-4244

**California - Central District**
Peter H. Carroll, C.J.
3420 12th Street
Riverside, CA 92501-3819
(951) 774-1031

Vincent P. Zurzolo
255 E. Temple Street, Suite 1360
Los Angeles, CA 90012
(213) 894-3755

Barry Russell
255 E. Temple Street, Suite 1660
Los Angeles, CA 90012
(213) 894-6092

Ellen Carroll
255 E. Temple Street, Suite 1634
Los Angeles, CA 90012
(213) 894-4033

Theodor Albert
411 W. Fourth St.
Santa Ana, CA 92701-4593
(714) 338-5430

Meredith Jury
3420 Twelfth St., Rm. 345
Riverside, CA 92501-3819
(951) 774-1043

Sheri Bluebond
255 E. Temple Street, Suite 1482
Los Angeles, CA 90012
(213) 894-8980

John E. Ryan
411 W. Fourth St., Rm. 5041
Santa Ana, CA 92701-4593
(714) 338-5450

Erithe A. Smith
411 W. Fourth St., Suite 5041
Santa Ana, CA 92701-4593

(714) 338-5440

Maureen A. Tighe
21041 Burbank Blvd., Suite 325
Woodland Hills, CA 91367
(818) 587-2806

Robin L. Riblet
1415 State Street
Santa Barbara, CA 93101-2511
(805) 884-4860

Alan M. Ahart
255 E. Temple Street, Suite 1382
Los Angeles, CA 90012
(213) 894-3745

Ernest Robles
255 E. Temple Street, Suite 1560
Los Angeles, CA 90012
(213) 894-1522

Thomas B. Donovan
255 E. Temple Street, Suite 1352
Los Angeles, CA 90012
(213) 894-3728

Richard Neiter
255 E. Temple Street, Suite 1652
Los Angeles, CA 90012
(213) 894-4080

Robert N. Kwan
411 W. Fourth St.
Santa Ana, CA 92701-4593
(714) 338-5450

Victoria Kaufman
255 E. Temple Street
Los Angeles, CA 90012
(213) 894-2552

Catherine E. Bauer
3420 Twelfth St.
Riverside, CA 92501-3819
(951) 774-1021

Deborah J. Saltzman
3420 Twelfth St.
Riverside, CA 92501-3819
(951) 774-1026

Scott C. Clarkson
411 W. Fourth St.
Santa Ana, CA 92701-4593
(714) 338-5460

Mark S. Wallace

# FEDERAL BANKRUPTCY JUDGES

411 W. Fourth St.
Santa Ana, CA 92701-4593
(714) 338-5470

Wayne E. Johnson
3420 Twelfth St.
Riverside, CA 92501-3819
(951) 774-1031

William Altenberger
255 E. Temple Street
Los Angeles, CA 90012
(213) 894-4065

Sandra R. Klein
255 E. Temple Street
Los Angeles, CA 90012
(213) 894-5856

**California - Eastern District**
Christopher M. Klein, C.J.
501 I Street, Rm. 3-200
Sacramento, CA 95814
(916) 930-4400

Michael McManus
501 I St., Rm. 3-200
Sacramento, CA 95814-2322
(916) 930-4400

David E. Russell (Recalled)
U.S. Courthouse
501 I Street, Rm. 3-200
Sacramento, CA 95814-2322
(916) 930-4400

Robert Bardwil
501 I Street, Rm. 3-200
Sacramento, CA 95814-2322
(916) 930-4400

Richard T. Ford (Recalled)
2500 Tulare Street
Fresno, CA 93721
(559) 499-5800

Ronald H. Sargis
2500 Tulare Street
Fresno, CA 93721
(559) 499-5800

W. Richard Lee
2500 Tulare Street
Fresno, CA 93721
(559) 499-5800

Whitney Rimel
2500 Tulare Street

Fresno, CA 93721
(559) 499-5800

Thomas C. Holman
501 I St., Rm. 3-200
Sacramento, CA 95814-2322
(916) 930-4400

Philip H. Brandt
501 I St., Rm. 3-200
Sacramento, CA 95814-2322
(916) 930-4400

**California - Northern District**
Alan Jaroslovsky, C.J.
99 South E Street
Santa Rosa, CA 95404
(707) 547-5900

Edward D. Jellen
P.O. Box 2070
Oakland, CA 94604
(510) 879-3525

Thomas E. Carlson
P.O. Box 7341
San Francisco, CA 94120-7341
(415) 268-2360

Charles Novack
3035 U.S. Courthouse
280 S. First Street
San Jose, CA 95113-3099
(408) 278-7538

William J. Lafferty III
P.O. Box 2070
Oakland, CA 94604-2070
(510) 879-3530

Roger Efremsky
3035 U.S. Courthouse
280 S. First Street
San Jose, CA 95113
(408) 879-3540

Arthur S. Weissbrodt
3035 U.S. Courthouse
280 S. First Street
San Jose, CA 95113-3099
(408) 278-7575

Denis Montali
P.O. Box 7341
San Francisco, CA 94120-7341
(415) 268-2320

Stephen L. Johnson

3035 U.S. Courthouse
280 S. First Street
San Jose, CA 95113-3099
(408) 278-7500

**California - Southern District**
Peter W. Bowie, C.J.
325 West F Street
San Diego, CA 92101-6989
(619) 557-5158

Laura S. Taylor
325 West F Street
San Diego, CA 92101-6989
(619) 557-6580

Louise D. Adler
325 West F Street
San Diego, CA 92101-6989
(619) 557-5661

James W. Meyers (Recalled)
325 West F Street
San Diego, CA 92101-6989
(619) 557-7642

Margaret M. Mann
325 West F Street
San Diego, CA 92101-6989
(619) 557-5848

**Hawaii**
Robert J. Faris, C.J.
1132 Bishop St., Suite 250-L
Honolulu, HI 96813
(808) 522-8111

Lloyd King (Recalled)
1132 Bishop Street, Suite 250L
Honolulu, HI 96813
(808) 522-8111

**Idaho**
Terry Myers, C.J.
550 West Fort Street, Box 042
Boise, ID 98724
(208) 334-9341

Jim D. Pappas
550 West Fort Street, Box 042
Boise, ID 83724
(208) 334-9369

**Montana**
John L. Peterson (Recalled)
400 N. Main St., Rm. 215
Butte, MT 59701
(406) 497-1240

# FEDERAL BANKRUPTCY JUDGES

Ralph B. Kirscher
400 N. Main St., Rm. 215
Butte, MT 59701
(406) 497-1240

**Nevada**
Mike Nakagawa, C.J.
300 Las Vegas Blvd., South
Las Vegas, NV 89101
(702) 527-7138

Gregg W. Zive
300 Booth Street
Reno, NV 89509
(775) 326-2107

Linda B. Riegle
300 Las Vegas Blvd., South
Las Vegas, NV 89101
(702) 527-7139

Bruce A. Markell
300 Las Vegas Blvd., South
Las Vegas, NV 89101
(702) 527-7030

Bruce T. Beesley
300 Las Vegas Blvd., South
Las Vegas, NV 89101
(702) 527-7140

**Oregon**
Frank R. Alley III, C.J.
405 E. 8th Ave.
Eugene, OR 97401-2649
(541) 431-4055

Elizabeth Perris
1001 SW 5th Ave., Rm. 700
Portland, OR 97204
(503) 326-1536

Trish M. Brown
1001 SW 5th Ave., Rm. 700
Portland, OR 97204
(503) 326-1592

Randall L. Dunn
1001 SW 5th Ave., Rm. 700
Portland, OR 97204
(503) 326-1538

**Washington - Eastern District**
Frank L. Kurtz, C.J.
402 E. Yakima Ave.
Yakima, WA 98907-2728
(509) 576-6124

John A. Rossmeissl (Recalled)
402 E. Yakima Ave., Suite 200
Yakima, WA 98907-2728
(509) 576-6122

Patricia C. Williams
P.O. Box 2164
Spokane, WA 99210
(509) 458-5340

**Washington - Western District**
Paul B. Snyder, C.J.
1717 Pacific Ave., Rm. 2100
Tacoma, WA 98402-3233
(253) 882-3950

Karen A. Overstreet
700 Stewart St.
Seattle, WA 98101-1271
(206) 370-5330

Philip H. Brandt
700 Stewart St., Rm. 6301
Seattle, WA 98101-1271
(206) 370-5320

Marc L. Barreca
700 Stewart St.
Seattle, WA 98101-1271
(206) 370-5310

Samuel J. Steiner (Recalled)
700 Stewart St.
Seattle, WA 98101-1271
(206) 370-5300

Brian D. Lynch
1717 Pacific Ave., Rm. 2100
Tacoma, WA 98402-3233
(253) 882-3960

Timothy W. Dore
700 Stewart St., Rm. 8131
Seattle, WA 98101-1271
(206) 370-5300

## TENTH CIRCUIT

**Colorado**
Howard R. Tallman, C.J.
721 19th Street
Denver, CO 80202-2508
(720) 904-7438

Sidney B. Brooks
721 19th Street
Denver, CO 80202-2508
(720) 904-7338

A. Bruce Campbell
721 19th Street
Denver, CO 80202-2508
(720) 904-7358

Elizabeth E. Brown
721 19th Street
Denver, CO 80202-2508
(720) 904-7346

Michael E. Romero
721 19th St.
Denver, CO 80202-2508
(720) 904-7413

**Kansas**
Robert E. Nugent, C.J.
167 Courthouse
401 North Market Street
Wichita, KS 67202
(316) 269-6404

Dale L. Somers
444 SE Quincy Street
Topeka, KS 66683
(785) 295-2786

Robert D. Berger
125 U.S. Courthouse
500 State Avenue
Kansas City, KS 66101-2417
(913) 551-6732

Janice Miller Karlin
225 Federal Building
444 SE Quincy Street
Topeka, KS 66683-3502
(785) 295-2646

**New Mexico**
James S. Starzynski, C.J.
P.O. Box 546
Albuquerque, NM 87103
(505) 348-2420

Robert H. Jacobvitz
P.O. Box 546
Albuquerque, NM 87103
(505) 348-2525

**Oklahoma - Eastern District**
Tom R. Cornish, C.J.
P.O. Box 1347
Okmulgee, OK 74447-1347
(918) 549-7200

**Oklahoma - Northern District**
Terrence L. Michael, C.J.

# FEDERAL BANKRUPTCY JUDGES

224 S. Boulder Ave
Tulsa, OK 74103-3015
(918) 699-4065

Dana L. Rasure
224 S. Boulder Ave.
Tulsa, OK 74103-3015
(918) 699-4085

**Oklahoma - Western District**
Niles L. Jackson, C.J.
215 Dean A. McGee Avenue
Oklahoma City, OK 73102
(405) 609-5678

Thomas M. Weaver
215 Dean A. McGee Avenue
Oklahoma City, OK 73102
(405) 609-5610

Sarah A. Hall
215 Dean A. McGee Avenue
Oklahoma City, OK 73102
(405) 609-5660

**Utah**
William T. Thurman, C.J.
358 U.S. Courthouse
350 South Main Street
Salt Lake City, UT 84101
(801) 524-6572

Russell Kimball Mosier
365 U.S. Courthouse
350 South Main Street
Salt Lake City, UT 84101
(801) 524-6549

Joel T. Marker
330 U.S. Courthouse
350 South Main Street
Salt Lake City, UT 84101
(801) 524-5749

**Wyoming**
Peter J. McNiff
P.O. Box 763
Cheyenne, WY 82003-0763
(307) 433-2250

**ELEVENTH CIRCUIT**

**Alabama - Middle District**
Dwight H. Williams, Jr., C.J.
P.O. Box 1248
Montgomery, AL 36102-1248
(334) 954-3890

William R. Sawyer
P.O. Box 1248
Montgomery, AL 36102-1248
(334) 954-3880

**Alabama - Northern District**
Thomas B. Bennett, C.J.
1800 Fifth Avenue North
Birmingham, AL 35203
(205) 714-3880

Benjamin Cohen
1800 5th Avenue North
Birmingham, AL 35203
(205) 714-3865

Tamara O. Mitchell
1800 5th Avenue North
Birmingham, AL 35203
(205) 714-3850

C. Michael Stilson
1118 Greensboro Ave., Rm. 209
Tuscaloosa, AL 35401
(205) 561-1623

John Andrew Caddell, Jr.
P.O. Box 1289
Decatur, AL 35602
(256) 584-7900

James J. Robinson
117 U.S. Courthouse
1129 Noble Street
Anniston, AL 36201
(256) 741-1529

**Alabama - Southern District**
Margaret A. Mahoney, C.J.
201 St. Louis Street
Mobile, AL 36602
(251) 441-5391

William S. Shulman
201 St. Louis Street
Mobile, AL 36602
(251) 441-5391

**Florida - Middle District**
Paul M. Glenn, C.J.
801 N. Florida Ave., Suite 8A
Tampa, FL 33602-3899
(813) 301-5100

Alexander L. Paskay (Recalled)
801 N. Florida Ave., Suite 932
Tampa, FL 33602-3899
(813) 301-5146

Catherine McEwen
801 N. Florida Ave.
Tampa, FL 33602-3899
(813) 301-5082

K. Rodney May
801 N. Florida Ave., Suite 9B
Tampa, FL 33602-3899
(813) 301-5200

Jerry A. Funk
300 N. Hogan St.
Jacksonville, FL 32201
(904) 301-6560

Karen S. Jennemann
135 W. Central Blvd.
Orlando, FL 32801
(407) 648-6832

Caryl E. Delano
801 N. Florida Ave.
Tampa, FL. 33602-3899
(813) 301-5190

Arthur B. Briskman
135 W. Central Blvd.
Orlando, FL 32801
(407) 648-6225

Michael G. Williamson
801 N. Florida, Suite 1054
Tampa, FL 33602-3899
(813) 301-5520

**Florida - Northern District**
Lewis M. Killian, Jr., C.J.
110 E. Park Ave., Suite 100
Tallahassee, FL 32301-1378
(850) 521-5031

William S. Shulman (Visiting)
201 St. Louis Street
Mobile, AL 36602
(251) 441-5391

Margaret A. Mahoney (Visiting)
201 St. Louis Street
Mobile, AL 36602
(251) 441-5391

**Florida - Southern District**
Paul G. Hyman. Jr., C.J.
1515 N. Flagler Dr., 8th fl.
West Palm Beach, FL 33401
(561) 514-4125

Robert A. Mark

# FEDERAL BANKRUPTCY JUDGES

51 SW First Ave., #1401
Miami, FL 33130
(305) 714-1760

A. Jay Cristol
51 SW First Ave., #1412
Miami, FL 33130
(305) 714-1770

Erik P. Kimball
1515 N. Flagler Dr., 8th fl.
West Palm Beach. FL 33401
(561) 514-4141

Raymond B. Ray
299 East Broward Blvd., #306
Ft. Lauderdale, FL 33301
(954) 769-5760

Laurel Isicoff
51 SW First Ave., #1411
Miami, FL 33130
(305) 714-1750

John K. Olson
299 E. Broward Blvd., Rm. 403
Ft. Lauderdale, FL 33301
(954) 769-5772

**Georgia - Middle District**
John T. Laney III, C.J.
901 Front Ave.
Columbus, GA 31902-1540
(706) 649-7840

Robert F. Hershner, Jr. (Recalled)
433 Cherry St.
Macon, GA 31201
(478) 752-3505

James D. Walker, Jr.
433 Cherry St.
Macon, GA 31201
(478) 752-3506

James P. Smith
433 Cherry St.
Macon, GA 31201
(478) 752-3506

**Georgia - Northern District**
Joyce Bihary, C.J.
75 Spring Street, SW, #1431
Atlanta, GA 30303-3367
(404) 215-1030

Mary Grace Diehl
1215 U.S. Courthouse

75 Spring Street, SW
Atlanta, GA 30303-3367
(404) 215-1202

Wendy L. Hagenau
1471 U.S. Courthouse
75 Spring Street, SW
Atlanta, GA 30303-3367
(404) 215-1190

C. Ray Mullins
75 Spring Street, SW, #1270
Atlanta, GA 30303-3367
(404) 215-1002

Margaret H. Murphy
75 Spring Street, SW, #1290
Atlanta, GA 30303-3367
(404) 215-1006

Robert E. Brizendine
75 Spring Street, SW, #1234
Atlanta, GA 30303-3367
(404) 215-1014

James E. Massey
75 Spring Street, SW, #1415
Atlanta, GA 30303-3367
(404) 215-1010

Paul W. Bonapfel
1492 Federal Building
75 Spring St. SW
Atlanta, GA 30303-3367
(404) 215-1018

W. Homer Drake, Jr.
P.O. Box 1408
Newnan, GA 30263
(678) 423-3000

James R. Sacca
1480 U.S. Courthouse
75 Spring Street, SW
Atlanta, GA 30303-3367
(404) 215-1790

**Georgia - Southern District**
Lamar W. Davis, Jr., C.J.
125 Bull St., 2nd fl.
Savannah, GA 31412
(912) 650-4100

Susan Barrett
600 James Brown Blvd.
Augusta, GA 30901
(706) 823-6000

John Dalis
801 Gloucester St., 3rd fl.
Brunswick, GA 31520
(912) 280-1376

# BANKRUPTCY COURT CLERKS

**Alabama - Northern District**
www.alnb.uscourts.gov
Scott W. Ford
1800 5th Ave. North, Rm. 120
Birmingham, AL 35203-2110
(205) 714-4000

117 U.S. Courthouse
Anniston, AL 36202
(256) 741-1500

P.O. Box 2775
Decatur, AL 35602-2775
(256) 584-7900

1118 Greensboro Ave., Rm 209
Tuscaloosa, AL 35401
(205) 561-1600

**Alabama - Middle District**
www.almb.uscourts.gov
Juan-Carlos Guerrero
1 Church St.
Montgomery AL 36104
(334) 954-3800

**Alabama - Southern District**
www.alsb.uscourts.gov
Leonard N. Maldonado
201 St. Louis St.
Mobile, AL 36602-2900
(251) 441-5391

**Alaska**
www.akb.uscourts.gov
Jan S. Ostrovsky
605 West Fourth Ave.
Anchorage, AK 99501-2296
(907) 271-2655

101-12th Ave., Rm. 370
Fairbanks, AK 99701
(907) 456-0349

709 W. 9th Ave., Rm. 979
Juneau, AK 99802
(907) 586-7458

648 Mission St., Rm. 507
Ketchikan, AK 99901
(907) 247-7576

P.O. Box 130
Nome, AK 99762
(907) 443-5216

**Arizona**
www.azb.uscourts.gov

Brian Karth
230 N. First Ave., Suite 101
Phoenix, AZ 85003
(602) 640-4000

38 S. Scott Ave.
Tucson, AZ 85701
(520) 202-7500

325 W. 19th St., Suite D
Yuma, AZ 85364
(928) 783-2288

101 W. Goodwin St.
Prescott, AZ 86303
(602) 682-4000

**Arkansas - Eastern & Western Districts**
www.arb.uscourts.gov
Jean Rolfs
P.O. Drawer 3777
Little Rock, AR 72203-3777
(501) 918-5500

P.O. Box 3097
Fayetteville, AR 72702-3097
(479) 582-9800

**California - Northern District**
www.canb.uscourts.gov
Gloria L. Franklin
P.O. Box 7341
San Francisco, CA 94120-7341
(415) 268-2300

99 South E St.
Santa Rosa, CA 95404
(707) 525-5900

P.O. Box 2070
Oakland, CA 94604-2070
(510) 879-3600

280 South First Street, Rm. 3035
San Jose, CA 95113-3099
(408) 278-7500

**California - Eastern District**
www.caeb.uscourts.gov
Wayne Blackwelder
501 I St., Suite 3-200
Sacramento, CA 95814
(916) 930-4400

1200 I Street, Suite 4
Modesto, CA 95354
(209) 521-5160

2500 Tulare St., Rm. 2501
Fresno, CA 93721
(559) 499-5600

**California - Central District**
www.cacb.uscourts.gov
Kathleen J. Campbell
225 East Temple St., Rm. 940
Los Angeles, CA 90012
(213) 894-3118

3420 Twelfth St., Rm. 125
Riverside, CA 92501-3819
(951) 774-1000

411 W. Fourth St.
Santa Ana, CA 92701
(714) 338-5300

21041 Burbank Blvd.
Woodland Hills, CA 91367
(818) 587-2900

1415 State St.
Santa Barbara, CA 93101
(805) 884-4800

**California - Southern District**
www.casb.uscourts.gov
Barry K. Lander
U.S. Courthouse
325 West F St.
San Diego, CA 92101-6991
(619) 557-6582

**Colorado**
www.cob.uscourts.gov/
Bradford L. Bolton
U.S. Custom House
721 19th St.
Denver, CO 80202-2508
(303) 904-7300

**Connecticut**
www.ctb.uscourts.gov
Deborah S. Hunt
450 Main St.
Hartford, CT 06103
(860) 240-3675

157 Church St., 18th fl.
New Haven, CT 06510
(203) 773-2009

U.S. Courthouse
915 Lafayette Blvd.
Bridgeport, CT 06604-4771
(203) 579-5808

# BANKRUPTCY COURT CLERKS

**Delaware**
www.deb.uscourts.gov
David D. Bird
824 Market St., 3rd Fl.
Wilmington, DE 19801
(302) 252-2900

**District of Columbia**
www.dcb.uscourts.gov
Angela D. Caesar
U.S. Courthouse
333 Constitution Ave., NW
Washington, DC 20001-2802
(202) 354-3280

**Florida - Middle District**
www.flmb.uscourts.gov
Lee Ann Bennett
801 N. Florida Ave.
Tampa, FL 33602-3899
(813) 301-5162

300 N. Hogan St.
Jacksonville, FL 32202
(904) 301-6490

135 W. Central Blvd., Suite 950
Orlando, FL 32801
(407) 648-6365

**Florida - Northern District**
www.flnb.uscourts.gov
William W. Blevins
110 E. Park Ave., Suite 100
Tallahassee, FL 32301-1378
(850) 521-5001

100 N. Palafox St.
Pensacola, FL 32502-5745
(866) 639-4615

**Florida - Southern District**
www.flsb.uscourts.gov
Katherine Gould Feldman
51 SW First Ave., Rm. 1510
Miami, FL 33130
(305) 714-1800

299 E. Broward Blvd., Rm. 112
Ft. Lauderdale, FL 33301
(954) 769-5700

1515 N. Flagler Drive, 8th fl.
West Palm Beach, FL 33401
(561) 514-4100

**Georgia - Northern District**
www.ganb.uscourts.gov
M. Regina Thomas
75 Spring St., SW, Rm. 1340

Atlanta, GA 30303-3367

(404) 215-1000

P.O. Box 2328
Newnan, GA 30264
(678) 423-3000

121 Spring St., SE
Gainesville, GA 30501
(678) 450-2700

600 E. First Ave.
Rome, GA 30161-3187
(706) 378-4000

**Georgia - Middle District**
www.gamb.uscourts.gov/
William E. Tanner
Post Office Box 1957
Macon, GA 31202-1957
(478) 752-3506

P.O. Box 2147
Columbus, GA 31902
(706) 649-7837

**Georgia - Southern District**
www.gas.uscourts.gov
Samuel L. Kay
P.O. Box 8347
Savannah, GA 31412-8347
(912) 650-4100

P.O. Box 1487
Augusta, GA 30903-1487
(706) 823-6000

801 Gloucester St.
Brunswick, GA 31520
(912) 280-1376

**Guam**
www.gud.uscourts.gov
Jeanne G. Quinata
520 W. Soledad Ave.
Hagatna, GU 96910
(671) 473-9200

**Hawaii**
www.hib.uscourts.gov
Michael Dowling
1132 Bishop St., Suite 250L
Honolulu, HI 96813-2830
(808) 522-8100

**Idaho**
www.id.uscourts.gov
Elizabeth Smith
550 West Fort St., MSC 042
Boise, ID 83724
(208) 334-1074

**Illinois - Northern District**

www.ilnb.uscourts.gov
Kenneth S. Gardner
Dirksen Bldg.
219 S. Dearborn St.
Chicago, IL 60604
(312) 435-5694

211 S. Court St.
Rockford, IL 61101
(815) 987-4350

**Illinois - Central District**
www.ilcb.uscourts.gov
Hardin W. Hawes
600 East Monroe St., Rm. 226
Springfield, IL 62701-1626
(217) 492-4551

201 North Vermilion St., Rm. 130
Danville, IL 61832
(217) 431-4820

100 NE Monroe, Rm. 131
Peoria, IL 61202
(309) 671-7035

**Illinois - Southern District**
www.ilsb.uscourts.gov
Donna Beyersdorfer
750 Missouri Ave.
East St. Louis, IL 62201
(618) 482-9400

301 W. Main St.
Benton, IL 62812-1362
(618) 435-2200

**Indiana - Northern District**
www.innb.uscourts.gov
Christopher M. DeToro
P.O. Box 7003
South Bend, IN 46634-7003
(574) 968-2100

5400 Federal Plaza
Hammond, IN 46320
(219) 852-3480

1300 S. Harrison St., Rm. 1188
Ft. Wayne, IN 46802
(260) 420-5100

230 N. 4th Street
Lafayette, IN 47901
(765) 420-6300

**Indiana - Southern District**
www.insb.uscourts.gov
Kevin P. Dempsey
116 U.S. Courthouse

46 East Ohio St.

# BANKRUPTCY COURT CLERKS

Indianapolis, IN 46204
(317) 229-3800

356 Federal Bldg.
Evansville, IN 47708
(812) 434-6470

121 W. Spring St., Rm. 110
New Albany, IN 47150
(812) 542-4540

921 Ohio St.
Terre Haute, IN 47807
(812) 231-1850

**Iowa - Northern District**
www.ianb.uscourts.gov
Sean P. McAvoy
P.O. Box 74890
Cedar Rapids, IA 52407-4890
(319) 286-2200

117 U.S. Courthouse
Sioux City, IA 51101
(712) 233-3939

**Iowa - Southern District**
www.iasb.uscourts.gov
Mary M. Weibel
P.O. Box 9264
Des Moines, IA 50306-9264
(515) 284-6230

**Kansas**
www.ksb.uscourts.gov
Fred W. Jamison
401 North Market St., Rm. 167
Wichita, KS 67202
(316) 315-4110

161 U.S. Courthouse
Kansas City, KS 66101-2417
(913) 551-6732

240 Federal Bldg.
444 SE Quincy
Topeka, KS 66683-3575
(785) 295-2750

**Kentucky - Eastern District**
www.kyeb.uscourts.gov
Jerry D. Truitt
100 E. Vine Street
Lexington, KY 40507
(859) 233-2608

**Kentucky - Western District**
www.kywb.uscourts.gov
Diane S. Robl
450 U.S. Courthouse
601 West Broadway
Louisville, KY 40202-2264

(502) 627-5700

**Louisiana - Eastern District**
www.laeb.uscourts.gov
R. Marla Hamilton
500 Poydras St., Rm. 601
New Orleans, LA 70130
(504) 589-7878

**Louisiana - Middle District**
www.lamb.uscourts.gov
Monica M. Menier
707 Florida St., Rm. 119
Baton Rouge, LA 70801
(225) 346-3333

**Louisiana - Western District**
www.lawb.uscourts.gov
J. Barry Dunford
300 Fannin St., Suite 2201
Shreveport, LA 71101-3089
(318) 676-4267

214 Jefferson St., Suite 100
Lafayette, LA 70501-7050
(337) 262-6800

300 Jackson Street
Alexandria, LA 71301
(318) 445-1890

**Maine**
www.meb.uscourts.gov
Alec Leddy
537 Congress St., 2nd fl.
Portland, ME 04101-3318
(207) 780-3482

311 U.S. Courthouse
202 Harlow St.
Bangor, ME 04401
(207) 945-0348

**Maryland**
www.mdb.uscourts.gov
Mark D. Sammons
U.S. Courthouse
101 West Lombard St.
Baltimore, MD 21201
(410) 962-2688

6500 Cherrywood Lane
Greenbelt, MD 20770
(301) 344-8018

**Massachusetts**
www.mab.uscourts.gov/mab/
James M. Lynch
5 P.O. Square, Rm. 1150
Boston, MA 02109
(617) 748-5300

595 Main St., Rm. 211
Worcester, MA 01608-2076
(508) 770-8900

300 State Street
Springfield, MA 01105
(413) 785-6900

**Michigan - Eastern District**
www.mieb.uscourts.gov
Kathleen B. Gullo
211 West Fort St., Suite 2100
Detroit, MI 48226-3211
(313) 234-0065

111 First St.
Bay City, MI 48707-0911
(989) 894-8840

226 West Second St.
Flint, MI 48502
(810) 235-4126

**Michigan - Western District**
www.miwb.uscourts.gov
Daniel M. LaVille
1 Division Ave., Rm. 200
Grand Rapids, MI 49503
(616) 456-2693

P.O. Box 909
Marquette, MI 49855-0909
(906) 226-2117

**Minnesota**
www.mnb.uscourts.gov
Lori Vosejpka
300 South Fourth St.
Minneapolis, MN 55415
(612) 664-5200

416 U.S. P.O. & Courthouse
Duluth, MN 55802
(218) 529-3600

118 S. Mill St.
Fergus Falls, MN 56537
(218) 739-4671

316 N. Robert St.
St. Paul, MN 55101
(651) 848-1000

**Mississippi - Northern District**
www.msnb.uscourts.gov
David J. Puddister
703 Hwy. 145 North
Aberdeen, MS 39730-0867
(662) 369-2596

**Mississippi - Southern District**
www.mssb.uscourts.gov

# BANKRUPTCY COURT CLERKS

Danny L. Miller
P.O. Drawer 2448
Jackson, MS 39225-2448
(601) 965-5301

2012 15th Street, Suite 244
Gulfport, MS 39501
(228) 563-1790

**Missouri - Eastern District**
www.moeb.uscourts.gov
Dana C. McWay
111 South 10th St.
St. Louis, MO 63102-2734
(314) 244-4500

**Missouri - Western District**
www.mow.uscourts.gov
Ann Thompson
2710 U.S. Courthouse
400 E. Ninth St.
Kansas City, MO 64106
(816) 512-1800

**Montana**
www.mtb.uscourts.gov
Bernard McCarthy
400 N. Main, Rm. 303
Butte, MT 59701
(406) 497-1240

**Nebraska**
www.neb.uscourts.gov
Diane L. Zech
111 S. 18th Plaza
Omaha, NE 68102-1321
(402) 661-7444

460 Federal Bldg.
100 Centennial Mall North
Lincoln, NE 68508
(402) 437-1625

**Nevada**
www.nvb.uscourts.gov
Mary A. Schott
300 Las Vegas Blvd. South
Las Vegas, NV 89101
(702) 527-7000

4005 Federal Bldg. and Courthouse
300 Booth St.
Reno, NV 89509
(775) 326-2100

**New Hampshire**
www.nhb.uscourts.gov
George A. Vannah
1000 Elm St., Suite 1001
Manchester, NH 03101-2411
(603) 222-2600

**New Jersey**
www.njb.uscourts.gov
James Waldron
50 Walnut St., 3rd floor
Newark, NJ 07102
(973) 645-4764

402 East State St.
Trenton, NJ 08608
(609) 989-2128

P.O. Box 2067
Camden, NJ 08101-2067
(856) 757-5485

**New Mexico**
www.nmcourt.fed.us/
Norman H. Meyer, Jr.
P.O. Box 546
Albuquerque, NM 87103-0546
(505) 348-2500

**New York - Northern District**
www.nynb.uscourts.gov
Kim F. Lefebvre
445 Broadway, Rm. 330
Albany, NY 12207-2965
(518) 257-1661

10 Broad St., Rm. 230
Utica, NY 13502
(315) 793-8101

**New York - Southern District**
www.nysb.uscourts.gov
Vito Genna
One Bowling Green, 6th Floor
New York, NY 10004-1408
(212) 668-2870

355 Main St.
Poughkeepsie, NY 12601
(845) 452-4200

300 Quarropas St.
White Plains, NY 10601-4150
(914) 390-4060

**New York - Eastern District**
www.nyeb.uscourts.gov
Robert A. Gavin, Jr.
271 Cadman Plaza East
Brooklyn, NY 11201-4201
(347) 394-1700

290 Federal Plaza
Central Islip, NY 11722
(631) 712-6200

**New York - Western District**
www.nywb.uscourts.gov
Paul R. Warren

300 Pearl St.
Buffalo, NY 14202-2501
(716) 362-3200

1220 New Federal Bldg
100 State St.
Rochester, NY 14614-1367
(585) 613-4200

**North Carolina - Eastern District**
www.nceb.uscourts.gov
Stephanie Edmondson
1760-A Parkwood Blvd.
Wilson, NC 27893-3564
(252) 237-0248

P.O. Box 1441
Raleigh, NC 27602-1441
(919) 856-4752

**North Carolina - Middle District**
www.ncmb.uscourts.gov
Reid Wilcox
P.O. Box 26100
Greensboro, NC 27402-6100
(336) 358-4000

226 South Liberty St.
Winston-Salem, NC 27101
(336) 397-7785

**North Carolina - Western District**
www.ncwb.uscourts.gov
Steven T. Salata
111 Jonas Federal Bldg.
401 West Trade St.
Charlotte, NC 28202
(704) 350-7500

100 Otis St.
Asheville, NC 28801
(828) 771-7300

**North Dakota**
www.ndb.uscourts.gov
Dianne G. Schmitz
655 First Ave. North
Fargo, ND 58102-4932
(701) 297-7100

**Ohio - Northern District**
www.ohnb.uscourts.gov
Kenneth J. Hirz
U.S. Court House
201 Superior Ave.
Cleveland, OH 44114
(216) 615-4300

455 U.S. Courthouse
2 South Main St.
Akron, OH 44308
(330) 252-6100

# BANKRUPTCY COURT CLERKS

401 McKinley Ave. SW
Canton, OH 44702
(330) 458-2120

411 U.S. Courthouse
1716 Spielbusch Ave.
Toledo, OH 43624
(419) 213-5600

10 East Commerce Street
Youngstown, OH 44503
(330) 742-0900

**Ohio - Southern District**
www.ohsb.uscourts.gov
Kenneth Jordan
120 West Third St.
Dayton, OH 45402
(937) 225-2516

170 N. High St.
Columbus, OH 43215-2403
(614) 469-6638

221 East Fourth St., Suite 800
Cincinnati, OH 45202
(513) 684-2572

**Oklahoma - Northern District**
www.oknb.uscourts.gov
Michael L. Williams
224 South Boulder Ave., Rm. 105
Tulsa, OK 74103-3015
(918) 699-4000

**Oklahoma - Eastern District**
www.okeb.uscourts.gov
Theresa Buthod
P.O. Box 1347
Okmulgee, OK 74447-1347
(918) 549-7221

**Oklahoma - Western District**
www.okwb.uscourts.gov
Grant E. Price
215 Dean A. McGee Ave.
Oklahoma City, OK 73102
(405) 609-5700

**Oregon**
www.orb.uscourts.gov
Charlene Hiss
1001 SW 5th Ave., Rm. 700
Portland, OR 97204
(503) 326-1500

405 E. 8th Ave., Suite 2600
Eugene, OR 97401
(541) 431-4000

**Pennsylvania - Eastern District**
www.paeb.uscourts.gov

Timothy B. McGrath
900 Market St., Rm. 400
Philadelphia, PA 19107-4299
(215) 408-2800

400 Washington St., Suite 300
Reading, PA 19601
(610) 208-5040

**Pennsylvania - Middle District**
www.pamb.uscourts.gov
Terrence S. Miller
197 South Main St.
Wilkes-Barre, PA 18701
(570) 831-2500

228 Walnut Street
Harrisburg, PA 17108-0908
(717) 901-2800

**Pennsylvania-Western District**
www.pawb.uscourts.gov
John J. Horner
600 Grant St.
Pittsburgh, PA 15219
(412) 644-2700

17 South Park Row, Rm. B160
Erie, PA 16501-1355
(814) 464-9740

Penn Traffic Bldg.
Johnstown, PA 15901
(814) 533-4240

**Puerto Rico**
www.prb.uscourts.gov
Celestino Matta-Mendez
300 Recinto Sur, Suite 109
San Juan, PR 00901
(787) 977-6000

**Rhode Island**
www.rib.uscourts.gov
Susan M. Thurston
380 Westminster Mall, Rm. 615
Providence, RI 02903
(401) 626-3100

**South Carolina**
www.scb.uscourts.gov
Tammi L. Hellwig
1100 Laurel St.
Columbia, SC 29201
(803) 765-5436

**South Dakota**
www.sdb.uscourts.gov
Frederick Entwistle
400 S. Phillips Ave., Rm. 104
Sioux Falls, SD 57104-6851
(605) 357-2400

225 S. Pierre St., Rm. 203
Pierre, SD 57501
(605) 945-4460

**Tennessee - Eastern District**
www.tneb.uscourts.gov
Danny Armstrong
31 E. 11th St.
Chattanooga, TN 37402-2722
(423) 752-5163

800 Market St.
Knoxville, TN 37902
(865) 545-4279

220 West Depot St.
Greeneville, TN 37743
(423) 787-0113

200 S. Jefferson St., Rm. 205
Winchester, TN 37398
(423) 752-5163

**Tennessee - Middle District**
www.tnmb.uscourts.gov
Matthew Loughney
701 Broadway, 22nd fl.
Nashville, TN 37203
(615) 736-5584

**Tennessee - Western District**
www.tnwb.uscourts.gov
Jed G. Weintraub
1 Memphis Place, Suite 413
Memphis, TN 38103-2328
(901) 328-3500

111 S. Highland Ave., Suite 107
Jackson, TN 38301
(731) 421-9300

**Texas - Northern District**
www.txnb.uscourts.gov
Tawana C. Marshall
1100 Commerce St., Rm. 1254
Dallas, TX 75242-1496
(214) 753-2000

147 U.S. Courthouse
Fort Worth, TX 76102-3643
(817) 333-6000

1205 Texas Ave., Rm. 306
Lubbock, TX 79401-4002
(806) 472-5000

624 Polk St., Suite 100
Amarillo, TX 79101
(806) 324-2302

**Texas - Southern District**
www.txs.uscourts.gov

# BANKRUPTCY COURT CLERKS

David Bradley
P.O. Box 61010
Houston, TX 77208-1010
(713) 250-5500

1133 N. Shoreline Blvd., Rm. 208
Corpus Christi, TX 78401
(361) 888-3142

**Texas - Eastern District**
www.txeb.uscourts.gov
Jeanne Henderson
110 N. College Ave, 9th Fl.
Tyler, TX 75702
(903) 590-3200

300 Willow St., Suite 100
Beaumont, TX 77701
(409) 839-2617

660 North Central Expwy., Suite 300B
Plano, TX 75074
(972) 509-1240

**Texas - Western District**
www.txwb.uscourts.gov
George D. Prentice II
P.O. Box 1439
San Antonio, TX 78295-1439
(210) 472-6720

903 San Jacinto Blvd.
Austin, TX 78701-2450
(512) 916-5237

8515 Lockheed Drive
El Paso, TX 79925
(915) 779-7362

U.S. Post Office Annex
100 East Wall St., Rm. P-613
Midland, TX 79701
(432) 683-1650

800 Franklin Ave.
Waco, TX 76701
(254) 750-1513

**Utah**
www.utb.uscourts.gov
David Sime
350 South Main St., Rm. 301
Salt Lake City, UT 84101-2106
(801) 524-6687

**Vermont**
www.vtb.uscourts.gov
Thomas J. Hart
P.O. Box 6648
Rutland, VT 05702-6648
(802) 776-2000

**Virgin Islands**
Wilfredo Morales
5500 Veterans Drive, Suite 310
Charlotte Amalie
St. Thomas, VI 00802-6424
(340) 774-8310

**Virginia - Eastern District**
www.vaeb.uscourts.gov
William Redden
701 E. Broad St.
Richmond, VA 23219
(804) 916-2400

200 S. Washington St., Suite 100
Alexandria, VA 22315-5405
(703) 258-1200

600 Granby St.
Norfolk, VA 23510
(757) 222-7500

2400 West Ave.
Newport News, VA 23607
(757) 247-0784

**Virginia - Western District**
www.vawb.uscourts.gov/
John W. L. Craig, II
210 Church Ave., Rm. 200
Roanoke, VA 24011
(540) 857-2391

116 N. Main St.
Harrisonburg, VA 22802
(540) 434-8327

1101 Court St., Rm. 166
Lynchburg, VA 24504
(434) 845-0317

**Washington - Eastern District**
www.waeb.uscourts.gov
Beverly A. Benka
P.O. Box 2164
Spokane, WA 99210-2164
(509) 458-5300

402 E. Yakima Ave., Suite 200
Yakima, WA 98901
(509) 576-6100

**Washington - Western District**
www.wawb.uscourts.gov
Mark L. Hatcher
700 Stewart St., Suite 6301
Seattle, WA 98101-1271
(206) 370-5200

1717 Pacific Ave., Rm. 2100
Tacoma, WA 98402-3233
(253) 882-3900

**West Virginia - Northern District**
www.wvnb.uscourts.gov
Michael D. Sturm
P.O. Box 70
Wheeling, WV 26003
(304) 233-1655

P.O. Box 2506
Clarksburg, WV 26301-2506
(304) 623-7866

**West Virginia - Southern District**
www.wvsd.uscourts.gov
Margaret Jo Proops
P.O. Box 2546
Charleston, WV 25329-2546
(304) 347-3003

110 N. Heber St.
Beckley, WV 25801
(304) 253-7402

601 Federal St.
Bluefield, WV 24701
(304) 327-9798

845 Fifth Ave.
Huntington, WV 25701
(304) 525-0375

425 Juliana St.
Parkersburg, WV 26101
(304) 420-6490

**Wisconsin - Eastern District**
www.wieb.uscourts.gov
Janet Medlock
517 East Wisconsin Ave, Rm. 126
Milwaukee, WI 53202-4581
(414) 297-3291

**Wisconsin - Western District**
www.wib.uscourts.gov
Marcia M. Anderson
P.O. Box 548
Madison, WI 53701-0548
(608) 264-5178

P.O. Box 5009
Eau Claire, WI 54702-5009
(715) 839-2980

**Wyoming**
www.wyb.uscourts.gov
Tim Ellis
2120 Capitol Ave., 6th fl.
Cheyenne, WY 82001
(307) 433-2200

111 South Wolcott
Casper, WY 82601
(307) 232-2650

# U.S. ATTORNEYS

| District | U.S. Attorneys | Address | Telephone |
|---|---|---|---|
| Alabama, Northern | Joyce White Vance | Birmingham 35203 | (205) 244-2001 |
| Alabama, Middle | George L. Beck | Montgomery 36104 | (334) 223-7280 |
| Alabama, Southern | Kenyen Ray Brown | Mobile 36602 | (251) 441-5845 |
| Alaska | Karen L. Loeffler | Anchorage 99513 | (907) 271-5071 |
| Arizona | Dennis K. Burke | Phoenix 85004 | (602) 514-7500 |
| Arkansas, Eastern | Christopher R. Thyer | Little Rock 72203 | (501) 340-2600 |
| Arkansas, Western | Conner Eldridge | Fort Smith 72901 | (479) 783-5125 |
| California, Northern | Melinda L. Haag | San Francisco 94102 | (415) 436-7200 |
| California, Eastern | Benjamin B. Wagner | Sacramento 95814 | (916) 554-2700 |
| California, Central | Andre Birotte, Jr. | Los Angeles 90012 | (213) 894-2434 |
| California, Southern | Laura E. Duffy | San Diego 92101 | (619) 557-5610 |
| Colorado | John F. Walsh | Denver 80202 | (303) 454-0100 |
| Connecticut | David B. Fein | New Haven 06510 | (203) 821-3700 |
| Delaware | Charles M. Oberly | Wilmington 19899 | (302) 573-6277 |
| District of Columbia | Ronald C. Machen | Washington 20530 | (202) 514-7566 |
| Florida, Northern | Pamela C. Marsh | Tallahassee 32301 | (850) 942-8430 |
| Florida, Middle | Robert E. O'Neill | Tampa 33602 | (813) 274-6000 |
| Florida, Southern | Wifredo A. Ferrer | Miami 33132 | (305) 961-9001 |
| Georgia, Northern | Sally Q. Yates | Atlanta 30303 | (404) 581-6000 |
| Georgia, Middle | Michael J. Moore | Macon 31202 | (478) 752-3511 |
| Georgia, Southern | Edward J. Tarver | Savannah 31412 | (912) 652-4422 |
| Guam | Alicia A.G. Limtiaco | Hagatna 96910 | (671) 472-7332 |
| Hawaii | Florence T. Nakakuni | Honolulu 96850 | (808) 541-2850 |
| Idaho | Wendy J. Olson | Boise 83712 | (208) 334-1211 |
| Illinois, Northern | Patrick Fitzgerald | Chicago 60604 | (312) 353-5300 |
| Illinois, Southern | Stephen R. Wigginton | Fairview Heights 62208 | (618) 628-3700 |
| Illinois, Central | James A. Lewis | Springfield 62701 | (217) 492-4450 |
| Indiana, Northern | David A. Capp | Hammond 46320 | (219) 937-5500 |
| Indiana, Southern | Joseph H. Hogsett | Indianapolis 46204 | (317) 226-6333 |
| Iowa, Northern | Stephanie M. Rose | Cedar Rapids 52401 | (319) 363-6333 |
| Iowa, Southern | Nicholas A. Klinefeldt | Des Moines 50309 | (515) 473-9300 |
| Kansas | Barry R. Grissom | Wichita 67202 | (316) 269-6481 |
| Kentucky, Eastern | Kerry B. Harvey | Lexington 40507 | (859) 233-2661 |
| Kentucky, Western | David J. Hale | Louisville 40202 | (502) 582-5911 |
| Louisiana, Eastern | James Letten | New Orleans 70130 | (504) 680-3000 |
| Louisiana, Middle | Donald J. Cazayoux, Jr. | Baton Rouge 70801 | (225) 389-0443 |
| Louisiana, Western | Stephanie A. Finley | Shreveport 71101 | (318) 676-3600 |
| Maine | Thomas E. Delahanty, II | Portland 04101 | (207) 780-3257 |
| Maryland | Rod J. Rosenstein | Baltimore 21201 | (410) 209-4800 |
| Massachusetts | Carmen M. Ortiz | Boston 02210 | (617) 748-3100 |
| Michigan, Eastern | Barbara L. McQuade | Detroit 48226 | (313) 226-9100 |
| Michigan, Western | Donald A. Davis | Grand Rapids 49501 | (616) 456-2404 |
| Minnesota | B. Todd Jones | Minneapolis 55415 | (612) 664-5600 |
| Mississippi, Northern | John Marshall Alexander | Oxford 38655 | (662) 234-3351 |
| Mississippi, Southern | John Dowdy | Jackson 39201 | (601) 965-4480 |
| Missouri, Eastern | Richard G. Callahan | St. Louis 63102 | (314) 539-2200 |
| Missouri, Western | Mary E. Phillips | Kansas City 64106 | (816) 426-3122 |
| Montana | Michael Cotter | Billings 59103 | (406) 657-6101 |
| Nebraska | Deborah K.R. Gilg | Omaha 68102 | (402) 661-3700 |
| Nevada | Daniel G. Bogden | Las Vegas 89101 | (702) 388-6336 |
| New Hampshire | John P. Kacavas | Concord 03301 | (603) 225-1552 |
| New Jersey | Paul J. Fishman | Newark 07102 | (973) 645-2700 |
| New Mexico | Kenneth J. Gonzales | Albuquerque 87103 | (505) 346-7274 |
| New York, Northern | Richard S. Hartunian | Syracuse 13261 | (315) 448-0672 |

# U.S. ATTORNEYS

| District | U.S. Attorneys | Address | Telephone |
|---|---|---|---|
| New York, Eastern | Loretta E. Lynch | Brooklyn 11201 | (718) 254-7000 |
| New York, Southern | Preet Bharara | New York 10007 | (212) 637-2200 |
| New York, Western | William J. Hochul, Jr. | Buffalo 14202 | (716) 843-5700 |
| North Carolina, Eastern | Thomas G. Walker | Raleigh 27601 | (919) 856-4530 |
| North Carolina, Middle | Ripley Rand | Greensboro 27402 | (336) 333-5351 |
| North Carolina, Western | Anne Tompkins | Charlotte 28202 | (704) 344-6222 |
| North Dakota | Timothy Q. Purdon | Fargo 58102 | (701) 297-7400 |
| Ohio, Northern | Steven M. Dettelbach | Cleveland 44113 | (216) 622-3600 |
| Ohio, Southern | Carter M. Stewart | Dayton 45402 | (937) 225-2910 |
| Oklahoma, Northern | Thomas S. Woodward | Tulsa 74119 | (918) 382-2700 |
| Oklahoma, Eastern | Mark F. Green | Muskogee 74401 | (918) 684-5100 |
| Oklahoma, Western | Sanford Coats | Oklahoma City 73102 | (405) 553-8700 |
| Oregon | Dwight C. Holton | Portland 97204 | (503) 727-1000 |
| Pennsylvania, Eastern | Zane D. Memeger | Philadelphia 19106 | (215) 861-8200 |
| Pennsylvania, Middle | Peter J. Smith | Scranton 18501 | (570) 348-2800 |
| Pennsylvania, Western | David J. Hickton | Pittsburgh 15219 | (412) 644-3500 |
| Puerto Rico | Rosa E. Rodriguez-Velez | San Juan 00918 | (787) 766-5656 |
| Rhode Island | Peter F. Neronha | Providence 02903 | (401) 709-5000 |
| South Carolina | William N. Nettles | Columbia 29201 | (803) 929-3000 |
| South Dakota | Brendan V. Johnson | Sioux Falls 57101 | (605) 330-4400 |
| Tennessee, Eastern | William C. Killian | Knoxville 37902 | (865) 545-4167 |
| Tennessee, Middle | Jerry E. Martin | Nashville 37203 | (615) 736-5151 |
| Tennessee, Western | Edward L. Stanton, III | Memphis 38103 | (901) 544-4231 |
| Texas, Northern | James T. Jacks | Dallas 75242 | (214) 659-8600 |
| Texas, Eastern | John Malcolm Bales | Beaumont 77701 | (409) 839-2538 |
| Texas, Western | John E. Murphy | San Antonio 78216 | (210) 384-7100 |
| Texas, Southern | Jose Angel Moreno | Houston 77208 | (713) 567-9000 |
| Utah | Carlie Christensen | Salt Lake City 84111 | (801) 524-5682 |
| Vermont | Tristam J. Coffin | Burlington 05402 | (802) 951-6725 |
| Virgin Islands | Ronald W. Sharpe | St. Thomas 00802 | (340) 774-5757 |
| Virginia, Eastern | Neil H. MacBride | Alexandria 22314 | (703) 299-3700 |
| Virginia, Western | Timothy J. Heaphy | Roanoke 24008 | (540) 857-2250 |
| Washington, Eastern | Michael Ormsby | Spokane 99210 | (509) 353-2767 |
| Washington, Western | Jenny A. Durkan | Seattle 98101 | (206) 553-7970 |
| West Virginia, Northern | William J. Ihlenfeld, III | Wheeling 26003 | (304) 234-0100 |
| West Virginia, Southern | R. Booth Goodwin, III | Charleston 25326 | (304) 345-2200 |
| Wisconsin, Eastern | James Santelle | Milwaukee 53202 | (414) 297-1700 |
| Wisconsin, Western | John W. Vaudreuil | Madison 53703 | (608) 264-5158 |
| Wyoming | Christopher A. Crofts | Cheyenne 82003 | (307) 772-2124 |

# ELECTRONIC PUBLIC ACCESS TO U.S. COURTS

## What is PACER?

Public Access to Court Electronic Records (PACER) is an electronic public access service that allows users to obtain case and docket information from Federal Appellate, District and Bankruptcy courts, and from the PACER Case Locator via the Internet. Links to all courts are provided from this web site.

Electronic access is available by registering with the PACER Service Center, the judiciary's centralized registration, billing, and technical support center.

Each court maintains its own databases with case information. Because PACER database systems are maintained within each court, each jurisdiction will have a different URL. Each court service is comparable to the others; however, the format and content of the information may differ slightly.

PACER is a service of the United States Judiciary. The PACER Service Center is operated by the Administrative Office of the United States Courts.

PACER provides access to federal case information nationwide. The PACER system offers quick, accurate information about current federal cases. You can obtain:

- A listing of all parties and participants including judges, attorneys and trustees
- A compilation of case related information such as cause of action, nature of suit and dollar demand
- A chronology of dates of case events entered in the case record
- A claims registry
- A listing of new cases each day in all courts
- Written judicial opinions
- Judgments or case status

---

## PACER Case Locator

The PACER Case Locator is a national locator index for PACER systems in the United States appellate, district and bankruptcy courts. Subsets of data are collected from each court and transferred to the PACER Service Center nightly. The PACER Case Locator allows searches by party name or social security number in the bankruptcy index, party name or nature of suit in the civil index, defendant name in the criminal index, and party name in the appellate index. The information provided by the search will include the party name, the court where the case is filed, the case number and the filing date.

To access PACER on the web, go to http://www.pacer.gov
Or, link to it from the web site of The Legal Researcher's Desk Reference 2012-13 at
http://www.infosourcespub.com/login/desk_ref/contents.cfm

# PRESIDENTS AND VICE-PRESIDENTS AND THE CONGRESSES COINCIDENT WITH THEIR TERMS

| President | Vice President | Service | Congresses |
|---|---|---|---|
| George Washington | John Adams | Apr. 30, 1789–Mar. 3, 1797 | 1, 2, 3, 4. |
| John Adams | Thomas Jefferson | Mar. 4, 1797–Mar. 3, 1801 | 5, 6. |
| Thomas Jefferson | Aaron Burr | Mar. 4, 1801–Mar 3, 1805 | 7, 8. |
| Do | George Clinton | Mar. 4, 1805–Mar. 3, 1809 | 9, 10. |
| James Madison | ....do.[2] | Mar. 4, 1809–Mar. 3, 1813 | 11, 12. |
| Do | Elbridge Gerry[3] | Mar. 4, 1813–Mar. 3, 1817 | 13, 14. |
| James Monroe | Daniel D. Tompkins | Mar. 4, 1817–Mar. 3, 1825 | 15, 16, 17, 18, 19 |
| John Quincy Adams | John C. Calhoun | Mar. 4, 1825–Mar. 3, 1829 | 19, 20. |
| Andrew Jackson | ....do.[4] | Mar. 4, 1829–Mar. 3, 1833 | 21, 22. |
| Do | Martin Van Buren | Mar. 4, 1833–Mar. 3, 1837 | 23, 24. |
| Martin Van Buren | Richard M. Johnson | Mar. 4, 1837–Mar. 3, 1841 | 25, 26. |
| William Henry Harrison[5] | John Tyler | Mar. 4, 1841–Apr. 4, 1841 | 27. |
| John Tyler | | Apr. 6, 1841–Mar. 3, 1845 | 27, 28. |
| James K. Polk | George M. Dallas | Mar. 4, 1845–Mar. 3, 1849 | 29, 30. |
| Zachary Taylor[5] | Millard Fillmore | Mar. 5, 1849–July 9, 1850 | 31. |
| Millard Fillmore | | July 10, 1850–Mar. 3, 1853 | 31, 32. |
| Franklin Pierce | William R. King[6] | Mar. 4, 1853–Mar. 3, 1857 | 33, 34. |
| James Buchanan | John C. Breckinridge | Mar. 4, 1857–Mar. 3, 1861 | 35, 36. |
| Abraham Lincoln | Hannibal Hamlin | Mar. 4, 1861–Mar. 3, 1865 | 37, 38. |
| Do.[5] | Andrew Johnson | Mar. 4, 1865–Apr. 15, 1865 | 39. |
| Andrew Johnson | | Apr. 15, 1865–Mar. 3, 1869 | 39, 40. |
| Ulysses S. Grant | Schuyler Colfax | Mar. 4, 1869–Mar. 3, 1873 | 41, 42. |
| Do | Henry Wilson[7] | Mar. 4, 1873–Mar. 3, 1877 | 43, 44. |
| Rutherford B. Hayes | William A. Wheeler | Mar. 4, 1877–Mar. 3, 1881 | 45, 46. |
| James A. Garfield[5] | Chester A. Arthur | Mar. 4, 1881–Sept. 19, 1881 | 47. |
| Chester A. Arthur | | Sept. 20, 1881–Mar. 3, 1885 | 47, 48. |
| Grover Cleveland | Thomas A. Hendricks[8] | Mar. 4, 1885–Mar. 3, 1889 | 49, 50. |
| Benjamin Harrison | Levi P. Morton | Mar. 4, 1889–Mar. 3, 1893 | 51, 52. |
| Grover Cleveland | Adlai E. Stevenson | Mar. 4, 1893–Mar. 3, 1897 | 53, 54. |
| William McKinley | Garret A. Hobart[9] | Mar. 4, 1897–Mar. 3, 1901 | 55, 56. |
| Do.[5] | Theodore Roosevelt | Mar. 4, 1901–Sept. 14, 1901 | 57. |
| Theodore Roosevelt | | Sept. 14, 1901–Mar. 3, 1905 | 57, 58. |
| Do | Charles W. Fairbanks | Mar. 4, 1905–Mar. 3, 1909 | 59, 60. |
| William H. Taft | James S. Sherman[10] | Mar. 4, 1909–Mar. 3, 1913 | 61, 62. |
| Woodrow Wilson | Thomas R. Marshall | Mar. 4, 1913–Mar. 3, 1921 | 63, 64, 65, 66, 67. |
| Warren G. Harding[5] | Calvin Coolidge | Mar. 4, 1921–Aug. 2, 1923 | 67. |
| Calvin Coolidge | | Aug. 3, 1923–Mar. 3, 1925 | 68. |
| Do | Charles G. Dawes | Mar. 4, 1925–Mar. 3, 1929 | 69, 70. |
| Herbert C. Hoover | Charles Curtis | Mar. 4, 1929–Mar. 3, 1933 | 71, 72. |
| Franklin D. Roosevelt | John N. Garner | Mar. 4, 1933–Jan. 20, 1941 | 73, 74, 75, 76, 77. |
| Do | Henry A. Wallace | Jan. 20, 1941–Jan. 20, 1945 | 77, 78, 79. |
| Do.[5] | Harry S. Truman | Jan. 20, 1945–Apr. 12, 1945 | 79. |
| Harry S. Truman | | Apr. 12, 1945–Jan. 20, 1949 | 79, 80, 81. |
| Do | Alben W. Barkley | Jan. 20, 1949–Jan. 20, 1953 | 81, 82, 83. |
| Dwight D. Eisenhower | Richard M. Nixon | Jan. 20, 1953–Jan. 20, 1961 | 83, 84, 85, 86, 87. |
| John F. Kennedy[5] | Lyndon B. Johnson | Jan. 20, 1961–Nov. 22, 1963 | 87, 88, 89. |
| Lyndon B. Johnson | | Nov. 22, 1963–Jan. 20, 1965 | 88, 89. |
| Do | Hubert H. Humphrey | Jan. 20, 1965–Jan. 20, 1969 | 89, 90, 91. |
| Richard M. Nixon | Spiro T. Agnew[11] | Jan. 20, 1969–Dec. 6, 1973 | 91, 92, 93. |
| Do.[13] | Gerald R. Ford[12] | Dec. 6, 1973–Aug. 9, 1974 | 93. |
| Gerald R. Ford | | Aug. 9, 1974–Dec. 19, 1974 | 93. |
| | Nelson A. Rockefeller[14] | Dec. 19, 1974–Jan. 20, 1977 | 93, 94, 95. |
| James Earl "Jimmy" Carter | Walter F. Mondale | Jan. 20, 1977–Jan. 20, 1981 | 95, 96, 97. |
| Ronald Reagan | George Bush | Jan. 20, 1981–Jan. 20, 1989 | 97, 98, 99, 100, 101. |
| George Bush | Dan Quayle | Jan. 20, 1989–Jan. 20, 1993 | 101, 102, 103. |
| William J. Clinton | Albert Gore | Jan. 20, 1993–Jan. 20, 2001 | 103, 104, 105, 106, 107. |
| George W. Bush | Richard B. Cheney | Jan. 20, 2001–Jan. 20, 2009 | 107, 108, 109, 110, 111. |
| Barack H. Obama | Joseph R. Biden, Jr. | Jan. 20, 2009– | 111. |

[1] From 1789 until 1933, the terms of the President and Vice President and the term of the Congress coincided, beginning on March 4 and ending on March 3. This changed when the 20th amendment to the Constitution was adopted in 1933. Beginning in 1934 the convening date for Congress became January 3, and beginning in 1937 the starting date for the Presidential term became January 20. Because of this change, the number of Congresses overlapping with a Presidential term increased from two to three, although the third only overlaps by a few weeks.

[2] Died Apr. 20, 1812.

[3] Died Nov. 23, 1814.

[4] Resigned Dec. 28, 1832, to become a United States Senator from South Carolina.

[5] Died in office.

[6] Died Apr. 18, 1853.

[7] Died Nov. 22, 1875.

[8] Died Nov. 25, 1885.

[9] Died Nov. 21, 1899.

[10] Died Oct. 30, 1912.

[11] Resigned Oct. 10, 1973.

[12] Nominated to be Vice President by President Richard M. Nixon on Oct. 12, 1973; confirmed by the Senate on Nov. 27, 1973; confirmed by the House of Representatives on Dec. 6, 1973; took the oath of office on Dec. 6, 1973 in the Hall of the House of Representatives This was the first time a Vice President was nominated by the President and confirmed by the Congress pursuant to the 25th amendment to the Constitution.

[13] Resigned from office.

[14] Nominated to be Vice President by President Gerald R. Ford on Aug. 20, 1974; confirmed by the Senate on Dec. 10, 1974; confirmed by the House of Representatives on Dec. 19, 1974; took the oath of office on Dec. 19, 1974, in the Senate Chamber.

# U.S. SUPREME COURT JUSTICES

**Chief Justices**

| | Term of Service |
|---|---|
| John Jay | Oct. 19, 1789 to June 29, 1795 |
| John Rutledge | Aug. 12, 1795 to Dec. 15, 1795 |
| Oliver Ellsworth | March 8, 1796 to Dec. 15, 1800 |
| John Marshall | Feb. 4, 1801 to July 6, 1835 |
| Roger Brooke Taney | March 28, 1836 to Oct. 12, 1864 |
| Salmon Portland Chase | Dec. 15, 1864 to May 7, 1873 |
| Morrison Remick Waite | Mar. 4, 1874 to Mar. 23, 1888 |
| Melville Weston Fuller | Oct. 8, 1888 to July 4, 1910 |
| Edward Douglas White | Dec. 19, 1910 to May 19. 1921 |
| William Howard Taft | July 11, 1921 to Feb. 3, 1930 |
| Charles Evans Hughes | Feb. 24, 1930 to June 30, 1941 |
| Harlan Fiske Stone | July 3, 1941 to April 22, 1946 |
| Frederick Moore Vinson | June 24, 1946 to Sept. 8, 1953 |
| Earl Warren | Oct. 5, 1953 to June 23, 1969 |
| Warren Earl Burger | June 23, 1969 to June 17, 1986 |
| William H. Rehnquist | Sept. 26, 1986 to Sept. 3, 2005 |
| John G. Roberts, Jr. | Sept. 29, 2005 to Present |

**Associate Justices**

| | |
|---|---|
| John Rutledge | Feb. 15, 1790 to Mar. 5, 1791 |
| William Cushing | Feb. 2, 1790 to Sept. 13, 1810 |
| James Wilson | Oct. 5, 1789 to Aug. 21, 1798 |
| John Blair | Feb. 2, 1790 to Jan. 27, 1796 |
| James Iredell | May 13, 1790 to Oct. 20, 1799 |
| Thomas Johnson | Aug. 6, 1792 to Feb. 1, 1793 |
| William Paterson | Mar. 11, 1793 to Sept. 9, 1806 |
| Samuel Chase | Feb. 4, 1796 to June 19, 1811 |
| Bushrod Washington | Feb. 4, 1799 to Nov. 26, 1829 |
| Alfred Moore | Aug. 9, 1800 to Jan. 26, 1804 |
| William Johnson | May 7, 1804 to Aug. 4, 1834 |
| Henry B. Livingston | Jan. 20, 1807 to Mar. 18, 1823 |
| Thomas Todd | May 4, 1807 to Feb. 7, 1826 |
| Gabriel Duvall | Nov. 23, 1811 to Jan. 14, 1835 |
| Joseph Story | Feb. 3, 1812 to Sept. 10, 1845 |
| Smith Thompson | Sept. 1, 1823 to Dec. 18, 1843 |
| Robert Trimble | June 16, 1826 to Aug. 25, 1828 |
| John McLean | Jan. 11, 1830 to Apr. 4, 1861 |
| Henry Baldwin | Jan. 18, 1830 to Apr. 21, 1844 |
| James Moore Wayne | Jan. 14, 1835 to July 5, 1867 |
| Philip Pendleton Barbour | May 12, 1836 to Feb. 25, 1841 |
| John Catron | May 1, 1837 to May 30, 1865 |
| John McKinley | Jan. 9, 1838 to July 19, 1852 |
| Peter Vivian Daniel | Jan. 10, 1842 to May 31, 1860 |
| Samuel Nelson | Feb. 27, 1845 to Nov. 28, 1872 |
| Levi Woodbury | Sept. 23, 1845 to Sept. 4, 1851 |
| Robert Cooper Grier | Aug. 10, 1846 to Jan. 31, 1870 |
| Benjamin Robbins Curtis | Oct. 10, 1851 to Sept. 30, 1857 |
| John Archibald Campbell | Apr. 11, 1853 to Apr. 30, 1861 |
| Nathan Clifford | Jan. 21. 1858 to July 25, 1881 |
| Noah Haynes Swayne | Jan. 27, 1862 to Jan. 24, 1881 |
| Samuel Freeman Miller | July 21, 1862 to Oct. 13, 1890 |
| David Davis | Dec. 10, 1862 to Mar. 4, 1877 |
| Stephen Johnson Field | May 20, 1863 to Dec. 1, 1897 |
| William Strong | Mar. 14, 1870 to Dec. 14, 1880 |
| Joseph P. Bradley | Mar. 23, 1870 to Jan. 22, 1892 |
| Ward Hunt | Jan. 9, 1873 to Jan. 27, 1882 |
| John Marshall Harlan | Dec. 10, 1877 to Oct. 14, 1911 |

# U.S. SUPREME COURT JUSTICES

| | |
|---|---|
| William Burnham Woods | Jan. 5, 1881 to May 14, 1887 |
| Stanley Matthews | May 17, 1881 to Mar. 22, 1889 |
| Horace Gray | Jan. 9, 1882 to Sept. 15, 1902 |
| Samuel Blatchford | Apr. 3, 1882 to July 7, 1893 |
| Lucius Quintus C. Lamar | Jan. 18, 1888 to Jan. 23, 1893 |
| Davis Josiah Brewer | Jan. 6, 1890 to Mar. 28, 1910 |
| Henry Billings Brown | Jan. 5, 1891 to May 28, 1906 |
| George Shiras, Jr. | Oct. 10, 1892 to Feb. 23, 1903 |
| Howell Edmunds Jackson | Mar. 4, 1893 to Aug. 8, 1895 |
| Edward Douglass White | Mar. 12, 1894 to Dec. 18, 1910 |
| Rufus Wheeler Peckham | Jan. 6, 1896 to Oct. 24, 1909 |
| Joseph McKenna | Jan. 26, 1898 to Jan. 5, 1925 |
| Oliver Wendell Holmes | Dec. 8, 1902 to Jan. 12, 1932 |
| William Rufus Day | Mar. 2, 1903 to Nov. 13, 1922 |
| William Henry Moody | Dec. 17, 1906 to Nov. 20, 1910 |
| Horace Harmon Lurton | Jan. 3, 1910 to July 12, 1914 |
| Charles Evans Hughes | Oct. 10, 1910 to June 10, 1916 |
| Willis Van Devanter | Jan. 3, 1911 to June 2, 1937 |
| Joseph Rucker Lamar | Jan. 3, 1911 to Jan. 2, 1916 |
| Mahlon Pitney | Mar. 18, 1912 to Dec. 31, 1922 |
| James Clark McReynolds | Oct. 12, 1914 to Jan. 31, 1941 |
| Louis Dembitz Brandeis | June 5, 1916 to Feb. 13, 1939 |
| John Hessin Clarke | Oct. 9, 1916 to Sept. 18, 1922 |
| George Sutherland | Oct. 2, 1922 to Jan. 17, 1938 |
| Pierce Butler | Jan. 2, 1923 to Nov. 16, 1939 |
| Edward Terry Sanford | Feb. 19, 1923 to Mar. 8, 1930 |
| Harlan Fiske Stone | Mar. 2, 1925 to July 2, 1941 |
| Owen Josephus Roberts | June 2, 1930 to July 31, 1945 |
| Benjamin Nathan Cardozo | Mar. 14, 1932 to July 9, 1938 |
| Hugo Lafayette Black | Aug. 19, 1937 to Sept. 17, 1971 |
| Stanley Forman Reed | Jan. 31, 1938 to Feb. 25, 1957 |
| Felix Frankfurter | Jan. 30, 1939 to Aug. 28, 1962 |
| William Orville Douglas | Apr. 17, 1939 to Nov. 12, 1975 |
| Frank Murphy | Feb. 5, 1940 to July 19, 1949 |
| James Francis Byrnes | July 8, 1941 to Oct. 3, 1942 |
| Robert H. Jackson | July 11, 1941 to Oct. 9, 1954 |
| Wiley Blount Rutledge | Feb. 15, 1943 to Sept. 10, 1949 |
| Harold Hitz Burton | Oct. 1, 1945 to Oct. 13, 1958 |
| Thomas Campbell Clark | Aug. 24, 1949 to June 12, 1967 |
| Sherman Minton | Oct. 12, 1949 to Oct. 15, 1956 |
| John Marshall Harlan | Mar. 28, 1955 to Sept. 23, 1971 |
| William J. Brennan, Jr. | Oct. 16, 1956 to July 20, 1990 |
| Charles Evans Whittaker | Mar. 25, 1957 to Mar. 31, 1962 |
| Potter Stewart | Oct. 14, 1958 to July 3, 1981 |
| Byron Raymond White | April 16, 1962 to June 28, 1993 |
| Arthur Joseph Goldberg | Oct. 1, 1962 to July 25, 1965 |
| Abe Fortas | Oct. 4, 1965 to May 14, 1969 |
| Thurgood Marshall | Oct. 2, 1967 to Oct. 1, 1991 |
| Harry A. Blackmun | June 9, 1970 to Aug. 3, 1994 |
| Lewis Franklin Powell, Jr. | Jan. 7, 1972 to June 26, 1987 |
| William H. Rehnquist | Jan. 7, 1972 to June 20, 1986 |
| John Paul Stevens | Dec. 19, 1975 to Present |
| Sandra Day O'Connor | Sept. 25, 1981 to Jan. 31, 2006 |
| Antonin Scalia | Sept. 26, 1986 to Present |
| Anthony M. Kennedy | Feb. 18, 1988 to Present |
| David H. Souter | Oct. 9, 1990 to June 29, 2009 |
| Clarence Thomas | Oct. 23, 1991 to Present |
| Ruth Bader Ginsburg | Aug. 10, 1993 to Present |
| Stephen G. Breyer | Aug. 3, 1994 to Present |
| Samuel A. Alito, Jr. | Jan. 31, 2006 to Present |
| Sonia Sotomayor | August 8, 2009 to Present |
| Elana Kagan | August 7, 2010 to Present |

# LEGISLATIVE INFORMATION

## U.S. CODE TITLES

1. General Provisions
2. The Congress
3. The President
4. Flag and Seal, Seat of Government and the States
5. Government Organization and Employees
6. Surety Bonds
7. Agriculture
8. Aliens and Nationality
9. Arbitration
10. Armed Forces
11. Bankruptcy
12. Banks and Banking
13. Census
14. Coast Guard
15. Commerce and Trade
16. Conservation
17. Copyrights
18. Crimes and Criminal Procedure
19. Customs Duties
20. Education
21. Food and Drugs
22. Foreign Relations and Intercourse
23. Highways
24. Hospitals and Asylums
25. Indians

26. Internal Revenue Code
27. Intoxicating Liquors
28. Judiciary and Judicial Procedure
29. Labor
30. Mineral Lands and Mining
31. Money and Finance
32. National Guard
33. Navigation and Navigable Waters
34. Navy (superseded by Title 10)
35. Patents
36. Patriotic Societies and Observances
37. Pay and Allowances of the Uniformed Services
38. Veterans' Benefits
39. Postal Service
40. Public Buildings, Property and Works
41. Public Contracts
42. The Public Health and Welfare
43. Public Lands
44. Public Printing and Documents
45. Railroads
46. Shipping
47. Telegraphs, Telephones, and Radio-telegraphs
48. Territories and Insular Possessions
49. Transportation
50. War and National Defense and Appendix

# CFR TITLES

| | | | | |
|---|---|---|---|---|
| 1. | General Provisions | 26. | Internal Revenue |
| 2. | Reserved | 27. | Alcohol, Tobacco Products and Firearms |
| 3. | The President | 28. | Judicial Administration |
| 4. | Accounts | 29. | Labor |
| 5. | Administrative Personnel | 30. | Mineral Resources |
| 6. | Economic Stabilization | 31. | Money and Finance |
| 7. | Agriculture | 32. | National Defense |
| 8. | Aliens and Nationality | 33. | Navigation and Navigable Waters |
| 9. | Animals and Animal Products | 34. | Education |
| 10. | Energy | 35. | Panama Canal |
| 11. | Federal Elections | 36. | Parks, Forests and Public Property |
| 12. | Banks and Banking | 37. | Patents, Trademarks and Copyrights |
| 13. | Business Credit and Assistance | 38. | Pensions, Bonuses, and Veterans' Relief |
| 14. | Aeronautics and Space | 39. | Postal Service |
| 15. | Commerce and Foreign Trade | 40. | Protection of Environment |
| 16. | Commercial Practices | 41. | Public Contracts and Property Management |
| 17. | Commodity and Securities Exchanges | 42. | Public Health |
| 18. | Conservation of Power and Water Resources | 43. | Public Lands: Interior |
| 19. | Customs Duties | 44. | Emergency Management and Assistance |
| 20. | Employees' Benefits | 45. | Public Welfare |
| 21. | Food and Drugs | 46. | Shipping |
| 22. | Foreign Relations | 47. | Telecommunication |
| 23. | Highways | 48. | Reserved |
| 24. | Housing and Urban Development | 49. | Transportation |
| 25. | Indians | 50. | Wildlife and Fisheries |

# ALPHABETICAL LIST OF AGENCIES APPEARING IN THE CFR

(Revised as of January 1, 2011)

| Agency | CFR Title, Subtitle or Chapter |
|---|---|
| Administrative Committee of the Federal Register | 1, I |
| Administrative Conference of the United States | 1, III |
| Advanced Research Projects Agency | 32, I |
| Advisory Council on Historic Preservation | 36, VIII |
| African Development Foundation | 22, XV |
|   Federal Acquisition Regulation | 48, 57 |
| Agency for International Development | 22, II |
|   Federal Acquisition Regulation | 48, 7 |
| Agricultural Marketing Service | 7, I, IX, X, XI |
| Agricultural Research Service | 7, V |
| Agriculture Department | 2, IV; 5, LXXIII |
|   Agricultural Marketing Service | 7, I, IX, X, XI |
|   Agricultural Research Service | 7, V |
|   Animal and Plant Health Inspection Service | 7, III; 9, I |
|   Chief Financial Officer, Office of | 7, XXX |
|   Commodity Credit Corporation | 7, XIV |
|   Economic Research Service | 7, XXXVII |
|   Energy Policy and New Uses, Office of | 2, IX; 7, XXIX |
|   Environmental Quality, Office of | 7, XXXI |
|   Farm Service Agency | 7, VII, XVIII |
|   Federal Acquisition Regulation | 48, 4 |
|   Federal Crop Insurance Corporation | 7, IV |
|   Food and Nutrition Service | 7, II |
|   Food Safety and Inspection Service | 9, III |
|   Foreign Agricultural Service | 7, XV |
|   Forest Service | 36, II |
|   Grain Inspection, Packers and Stockyards Administration | 7, VIII; 9, II |
|   Information Resources Management, Office of | 7, XXVII |
|   Inspector General, Office of | 7, XXVI |
|   National Agricultural Library | 7, XLI |
|   National Agricultural Statistics Service | 7, XXXVI |
|   National Institute of Food and Agriculture. | 7, XXXIV |
|   Natural Resources Conservation Service | 7, VI |
|   Operations, Office of | 7, XXVIII |
|   Procurement and Property Management, Office of | 7, XXXII |
|   Rural Business-Cooperative Service | 7, XVIII, XLII, L |
|   Rural Development Administration | 7, XLII |
|   Rural Housing Service | 7, XVIII, XXXV, L |
|   Rural Telephone Bank | 7, XVI |
|   Rural Utilities Service | 7, XVII, XVIII, XLII, L |
|   Secretary of Agriculture, Office of | 7, Subtitle A |
|   Transportation, Office of | 7, XXXIII |
|   World Agricultural Outlook Board | 7, XXXVIII |
| Air Force Department | 32, VII |
|   Federal Acquisition Regulation Supplement | 48, 53 |
| Air Transportation Stabilization Board | 14, VI |
| Alcohol and Tobacco Tax and Trade Bureau | 27, I |
| Alcohol, Tobacco, Firearms, and Explosives, Bureau of | 27, II |
| AMTRAK | 49, VII |
| American Battle Monuments Commission | 36, IV |
| American Indians, Office of the Special Trustee | 25, VII |
| Animal and Plant Health Inspection Service | 7, III; 9, I |
| Appalachian Regional Commission | 5, IX |
| Architectural and Transportation Barriers Compliance Board | 36, XI |
| Arctic Research Commission | 45, XXIII |
| Armed Forces Retirement Home | 5, XI |
| Army Department | 32, V |
|   Engineers, Corps of | 33, II; 36, III |
|   Federal Acquisition Regulation | 48, 51 |
| Bilingual Education and Minority Languages Affairs, Office of | 34, V |
| Blind or Severely Disabled, Committee for Purchase From People Who Are | 41, 51 |
| Broadcasting Board of Governors | 22, V |
|   Federal Acquisition Regulation | 48, 19 |
| Bureau of Ocean Energy Management, Regulation, and Enforcement | 30, II |
| Census Bureau | 15, I |
| Centers for Medicare & Medicaid Services | 42, IV |
| Central Intelligence Agency | 32, XIX |
| Chief Financial Officer, Office of | 7, XXX |
| Child Support Enforcement, Office of | 45, III |
| Children and Families, Administration for | 45, II, III, IV, X |
| Civil Rights, Commission on | 5, LXVIII; 45, VII |
| Civil Rights, Office for | 34, I |

# ALPHABETICAL LIST OF AGENCIES APPEARING IN THE CFR

| | |
|---|---|
| Coast Guard | 33, I; 46, I; 49, IV |
| Coast Guard (Great Lakes Pilotage) | 46, III |
| Commerce Department | 44, IV |
| Census Bureau | 15, I |
| Economic Affairs, Under Secretary | 37, V |
| Economic Analysis, Bureau of | 15, VIII |
| Economic Development Administration | 13, III |
| Emergency Management and Assistance | 44, IV |
| Federal Acquisition Regulation | 48, 13 |
| Foreign-Trade Zones Board | 15, IV |
| Industry and Security, Bureau of | 15, VII |
| International Trade Administration | 15, III; 19, III |
| National Institute of Standards and Technology | 15, II |
| National Marine Fisheries Service | 50, II, IV |
| National Oceanic and Atmospheric Administration | 15, IX; 50, II, III, IV, VI |
| National Telecommunications and Information Administration | 15, XXIII; 47, III, IV |
| National Weather Service | 15, IX |
| Patent and Trademark Office, United States | 37, I |
| Productivity, Technology and Innovation, Assistant Secretary for | 37, IV |
| Secretary of Commerce, Office of | 15, Subtitle A |
| Technology, Under Secretary for | 37, V |
| Technology Administration | 15, XI |
| Technology Policy, Assistant Secretary for | 37, IV |
| Commercial Space Transportation | 14, III |
| Commodity Credit Corporation | 7, XIV |
| Commodity Futures Trading Commission | 5, XLI; 17, I |
| Community Planning and Development, Office of Assistant Secretary for | 24, V, VI |
| Community Services, Office of | 45, X |
| Comptroller of the Currency | 12, I |
| Construction Industry Collective Bargaining Commission | 29, IX |
| Consumer Product Safety Commission | 5, LXXI; 16, II |
| Copyright Office | 37, II |
| Copyright Royalty Board | 37, III |
| Corporation for National and Community Service | 2, XXII; 45, XII, XXV |
| Cost Accounting Standards Board | 48, 99 |
| Council on Environmental Quality | 40, V |
| Court Services and Offender Supervision Agency for the District of Columbia | 28, VIII |
| Customs and Border Protection Bureau | 19, I |
| Defense Contract Audit Agency | 32, I |
| Defense Department | 5, XXVI; 32, Subtitle A; 40, VII |
| Advanced Research Projects Agency | 32, I |
| Air Force Department | 32, VII |
| Army Department | 32, V; 33, II; 36, III, 48, 51 |
| Defense Acquisition Regulations System | 48, 2 |
| Defense Intelligence Agency | 32, I |
| Defense Logistics Agency | 32, I, XII; 48, 54 |
| Engineers, Corps of | 33, II; 36, III |
| Human Resources Management and Labor Relations Systems | 5, XCIX |
| National Imagery and Mapping Agency | 32, I |
| Navy Department | 32, VI; 48, 52 |
| Secretary of Defense, Office of | 2, XI; 32, I |
| Defense Contract Audit Agency | 32, I |
| Defense Intelligence Agency | 32, I |
| Defense Logistics Agency | 32, XII; 48, 54 |
| Defense Nuclear Facilities Safety Board | 10, XVII |
| Delaware River Basin Commission | 18, III |
| District of Columbia, Court Services and Offender Supervision Agency for the | 28, VIII |
| Drug Enforcement Administration | 21, II |
| East-West Foreign Trade Board | 15, XIII |
| Economic Affairs, Under Secretary | 37, V |
| Economic Analysis, Bureau of | 15, VIII |
| Economic Development Administration | 13, III |
| Economic Research Service | 7, XXXVII |
| Education, Department of | 5, LIII |
| Bilingual Education and Minority Languages Affairs, Office of | 34, V |
| Civil Rights, Office for | 34, I |
| Educational Research and Improvement, Office of | 34, VII |
| Elementary and Secondary Education, Office of | 34, II |
| Federal Acquisition Regulation | 48, 34 |
| Postsecondary Education, Office of | 34, VI |
| Secretary of Education, Office of | 34, Subtitle A |
| Special Education and Rehabilitative Services, Office of | 34, III |
| Vocational and Adult Education, Office of | 34, IV |

# ALPHABETICAL LIST OF AGENCIES APPEARING IN THE CFR

# ALPHABETICAL LIST OF AGENCIES APPEARING IN THE CFR

| | |
|---|---|
| Federal Trade Commission | 5, XLVII; 16, I |
| Federal Transit Administration | 49, VI |
| Federal Travel Regulation System | 41, Subtitle F |
| Financial Crimes Enforcement Network | 31, X |
| Fine Arts, Commission on | 45, XXI |
| Fiscal Service | 31, II |
| Fish and Wildlife Service, United States | 50, I, IV |
| Food and Drug Administration | 21, I |
| Food and Nutrition Service | 7, II |
| Food Safety and Inspection Service | 9, III |
| Foreign Agricultural Service | 7, XV |
| Foreign Assets Control, Office of | 31, V |
| Foreign Claims Settlement Commission of the United States | 45, V |
| Foreign Service Grievance Board | 22, IX |
| Foreign Service Impasse Disputes Panel | 22, XIV |
| Foreign Service Labor Relations Board | 22, XIV |
| Foreign-Trade Zones Board | 15, IV |
| Forest Service | 36, II |
| General Services Administration | 5, LVII; 41, 105 |
| Contract Appeals, Board of | 48, 61 |
| Federal Acquisition Regulation | 48, 5 |
| Federal Management Regulation | 41, 102 |
| Federal Property Management Regulations | 41, 101 |
| Federal Travel Regulation System | 41, Subtitle F |
| General | 41, 300 |
| Payment From a Non-Federal Source for Travel Expenses | 41, 304 |
| Payment of Expenses Connected With the Death of Certain Employees | 41, 303 |
| Relocation Allowances | 41, 302 |
| Temporary Duty (TDY) Travel Allowances | 41, 301 |
| Geological Survey | 30, IV |
| Government Accountability Office | 4, I |
| Government Ethics, Office of | 5, XVI |
| Government National Mortgage Association | 24, III |
| Grain Inspection, Packers and Stockyards Administration | 7, VIII; 9, II |
| Harry S. Truman Scholarship Foundation | 45, XVIII |
| Health and Human Services, Department of | 2, III; 5, XLV; 45, Subtitle A, |
| Centers for Medicare & Medicaid Services | 42, IV |
| Child Support Enforcement, Office of | 45, III |
| Children and Families, Administration for | 45, II, III, IV, X |
| Community Services, Office of | 45, X |
| Family Assistance, Office of | 45, II |
| Federal Acquisition Regulation | 48, 3 |
| Food and Drug Administration | 21, I |
| Human Development Services, Office of | 45, XIII |
| Indian Health Service | 25, V |
| Inspector General (Health Care), Office of | 42, V |
| Public Health Service | 42, I |
| Refugee Resettlement, Office of | 45, IV |
| Homeland Security, Department of | 2, XXX; 6, I |
| Coast Guard | 33, I; 46, I; 49, IV |
| Coast Guard (Great Lakes Pilotage) | 46, III |
| Customs and Border Protection Bureau | 19, I |
| Federal Emergency Management Agency | 44, I |
| Human Resources Management and Labor Relations Systems | 5, XCVII |
| Immigration and Customs Enforcement Bureau | 19, IV |
| Immigration and Naturalization | 8, I |
| Transportation Security Administration | 49, XII |
| HOPE for Homeowners Program, Board of Directors of | 24, XXIV |
| Housing and Urban Development, Department of | 2, XXIV; 5, LXV; 24, Subtitle B |
| Community Planning and Development, Office of Assistant Secretary for | 24, V, VI |
| Equal Opportunity, Office of Assistant Secretary for | 24, I |
| Federal Acquisition Regulation | 48, 24 |
| Federal Housing Enterprise Oversight, Office of | 12, XVII |
| Government National Mortgage Association | 24, III |
| Housing—Federal Housing Commissioner, Office of Assistant Secretary for | 24, II, VIII, X, XX |
| Housing, Office of, and Multifamily Housing Assistance Restructuring, Office of | 24, IV |
| Inspector General, Office of | 24, XII |
| Public and Indian Housing, Office of Assistant Secretary for | 24, IX |
| Secretary, Office of | 24, Subtitle A, VII |

# ALPHABETICAL LIST OF AGENCIES APPEARING IN THE CFR

# ALPHABETICAL LIST OF AGENCIES APPEARING IN THE CFR

| Agency | CFR Title, Subtitle or Chapter |
|---|---|
| Federal Procurement Regulations System | 41, 50 |
| Labor-Management Standards, Office of | 29, II, IV |
| Mine Safety and Health Administration | 30, I |
| Occupational Safety and Health Administration | 29, XVII |
| Office of Workers' Compensation Programs | 20, VII |
| Public Contracts | 41, 50 |
| Secretary of Labor, Office of | 29, Subtitle A |
| Veterans' Employment and Training Service, Office of the Assistant Secretary for | 41, 61; 20, IX |
| Wage and Hour Division | 29, V |
| Workers' Compensation Programs, Office of | 20, I |
| Labor-Management Standards, Office of | 29, II, IV |
| Land Management, Bureau of | 43, II |
| Legal Services Corporation | 45, XVI |
| Library of Congress | 36, VII |
| Copyright Office | 37, II |
| Copyright Royalty Board | 37, III |
| Local Television Loan Guarantee Board | 7, XX |
| Management and Budget, Office of | 5, III, LXXVII; 14, VI; 48, 99 |
| Marine Mammal Commission | 50, V |
| Maritime Administration | 46, II |
| Merit Systems Protection Board | 5, II, LXIV |
| Micronesian Status Negotiations, Office for | 32, XXVII |
| Millenium Challenge Corporation | 22, XIII |
| Mine Safety and Health Administration | 30, I |
| Minority Business Development Agency | 15, XIV |
| Miscellaneous Agencies | 1, IV |
| Monetary Offices | 31, I |
| Morris K. Udall Scholarship and Excellence in National Environmental Policy Foundation | 36, XVI |
| Museum and Library Services, Institute of | 2, XXXI |
| National Aeronautics and Space Administration | 2, XVIII; 5, LIX; 14, V |
| Federal Acquisition Regulation | 48, 18 |
| National Agricultural Library | 7, XLI |
| National Agricultural Statistics Service | 7, XXXVI |
| National and Community Service, Corporation for | 45, XII, XXV |
| National Archives and Records Administration | 2, XXVI; 5, LXVI; 36, XII |
| Information Security Oversight Office | 32, XX |
| National Capital Planning Commission | 1, IV |
| National Commission for Employment Policy | 1, IV |
| National Commission on Libraries and Information Science | 45, XVII |
| National Council on Disability | 34, XII |
| National Counterintelligence Center | 32, XVIII |
| National Credit Union Administration | 12, VII |
| National Crime Prevention and Privacy Compact Council | 28, IX |
| National Drug Control Policy, Office of | 21, III |
| National Endowment for the Arts | 2, XXXII |
| National Endowment for the Humanities | 2, XXXIII |
| National Foundation on the Arts and the Humanities | 45, XI |
| National Highway Traffic Safety Administration | 23, II, III; 47, VI; 49, V |
| National Imagery and Mapping Agency | 32, I |
| National Indian Gaming Commission | 25, III |
| National Institute for Literacy | 34, XI |
| National Institute of Food and Agriculture. | 7, XXXIV |
| National Institute of Standards and Technology | 15, II |
| National Intelligence, Office of Director of | 32, XVII |
| National Labor Relations Board | 5, LXI; 29, I |
| National Marine Fisheries Service | 50, II, IV |
| National Mediation Board | 29, X |
| National Oceanic and Atmospheric Administration | 15, IX; 50, II, III, IV, VI |
| National Park Service | 36, I |
| National Railroad Adjustment Board | 29, III |
| National Railroad Passenger Corporation (AMTRAK) | 49, VII |
| National Science Foundation | 2, XXV; 5, XLIII; 45, VI |
| Federal Acquisition Regulation | 48, 25 |

# ALPHABETICAL LIST OF AGENCIES APPEARING IN THE CFR

# ALPHABETICAL LIST OF AGENCIES APPEARING IN THE CFR

| Agency | CFR Title, Subtitle or Chapter |
|---|---|
| Science and Technology Policy, Office of, and National Security Council | 47, II |
| Secret Service | 31, IV |
| Securities and Exchange Commission | 5, XXXIV; 17, II |
| Selective Service System | 32, XVI |
| Small Business Administration | 2, XXVII; 13, I |
| Smithsonian Institution | 36, V |
| Social Security Administration | 2, XXIII; 20, III; 48, 23 |
| Soldiers' and Airmen's Home, United States | 5, XI |
| Special Counsel, Office of | 5, VIII |
| Special Education and Rehabilitative Services, Office of | 34, III |
| Special Inspector General for Iraq Reconstruction | 5, LXXXVII |
| State Department | 2, VI; 22, I; 28, XI |
|   Federal Acquisition Regulation | 48, 6 |
| Surface Mining Reclamation and Enforcement, Office of | 30, VII |
| Surface Transportation Board | 49, X |
| Susquehanna River Basin Commission | 18, VIII |
| Technology Administration | 15, XI |
| Technology Policy, Assistant Secretary for | 37, IV |
| Technology, Under Secretary for | 37, V |
| Tennessee Valley Authority | 5, LXIX; 18, XIII |
| Thrift Supervision Office, Department of the Treasury | 12, V |
| Trade Representative, United States, Office of | 15, XX |
| Transportation, Department of | 2, XII; 5, L |
|   Commercial Space Transportation | 14, III |
|   Contract Appeals, Board of | 48, 63 |
|   Emergency Management and Assistance | 44, IV |
|   Federal Acquisition Regulation | 48, 12 |
|   Federal Aviation Administration | 14, I |
|   Federal Highway Administration | 23, I, II |
|   Federal Motor Carrier Safety Administration | 49, III |
|   Federal Railroad Administration | 49, II |
|   Federal Transit Administration | 49, VI |
|   Maritime Administration | 46, II |
|   National Highway Traffic Safety Administration | 23, II, III; 47, IV; 49, V |
|   Pipeline and Hazardous Materials Safety Administration | 49, I |
|   Saint Lawrence Seaway Development Corporation | 33, IV |
|   Secretary of Transportation, Office of | 14, II; 49, Subtitle A |
|   Surface Transportation Board | 49, X |
|   Transportation Statistics Bureau | 49, XI |
| Transportation, Office of | 7, XXXIII |
| Transportation Security Administration | 49, XII |
| Transportation Statistics Bureau | 49, XI |
| Travel Allowances, Temporary Duty (TDY) | 41, 301 |
| Treasury Department | 5, XXI; 12, XV; 17, IV; 31, IX |
|   Alcohol and Tobacco Tax and Trade Bureau | 27, I |
|   Community Development Financial Institutions Fund | 12, XVIII |
|   Comptroller of the Currency | 12, I |
|   Customs and Border Protection Bureau | 19, I |
|   Engraving and Printing, Bureau of | 31, VI |
|   Federal Acquisition Regulation | 48, 10 |
|   Federal Claims Collection Standards | 31, IX |
|   Federal Law Enforcement Training Center | 31, VII |
|   Financial Crimes Enforcement Network | 31, X |
|   Fiscal Service | 31, II |
|   Foreign Assets Control, Office of | 31, V |
|   Internal Revenue Service | 26, I |
|   Investment Security, Office of | 31, VIII |
|   Monetary Offices | 31, I |
|   Secret Service | 31, IV |
|   Secretary of the Treasury, Office of | 31, Subtitle A |
|   Thrift Supervision, Office of | 12, V |
| Truman, Harry S. Scholarship Foundation | 45, XVIII |
| United States and Canada, International Joint Commission | 22, IV |
| United States and Mexico, International Boundary and Water Commission, United States Section | 22, XI |
| Utah Reclamation Mitigation and Conservation Commission | 43, III |
| Veterans Affairs Department | 2, VIII; 38, I |
|   Federal Acquisition Regulation | 48, 8 |
| Veterans' Employment and Training Service, Office of the Assistant Secretary for | 41, 61; 20, IX |
| Vice President of the United States, Office of | 32, XXVIII |
| Vocational and Adult Education, Office of | 34, IV |
| Wage and Hour Division | 29, V |
| Water Resources Council | 18, VI |
| Workers' Compensation Programs, Office of | 20, I |
| World Agricultural Outlook Board | 7, XXXVIII |

# STATE INFORMATION

## STATE NAMES, ABBREVIATIONS, CAPITALS, CENTRAL SWITCHBOARDS AND POPULATIONS

| Official Names of State or Other Jurisdiction | Abbreviation | Capital | Central Switchboard | 2010 State Population (1,000) |
|---|---|---|---|---|
| Alabama, State of | AL | Montgomery | (334) 242-8000 | 4,779 |
| Alaska, State of | AK | Juneau | (907) 465-2111 | 710 |
| Arizona, State of | AZ | Phoenix | (602) 542-4900 | 6,392 |
| Arkansas, State of | AR | Little Rock | (501) 682-3000 | 2,915 |
| California, State of | CA | Sacramento | (916) 464-1580 | 37,253 |
| Colorado, State of | CO | Denver | (303) 866-5000 | 5,029 |
| Connecticut, State of | CT | Hartford | (860) 622-2200 | 3,574 |
| Delaware, State of | DE | Dover | (302) 739-4000 | 897 |
| Florida, State of | FL | Tallahassee | (850) 488-1234 | 18,801 |
| Georgia, State of | GA | Atlanta | (404) 656-2000 | 9,687 |
| Hawaii, State of | HI | Honolulu | (808) 586-2211 | 1,368 |
| Idaho, State of | ID | Boise | (208) 332-0102 | 1,567 |
| Illinois, State of | IL | Springfield | (217) 782-2000 | 12,830 |
| Indiana, State of | IN | Indianapolis | (317) 232-3140 | 6,483 |
| Iowa, State of | IA | Des Moines | (515) 281-5011 | 3,046 |
| Kansas, State of | KS | Topeka | (785) 296-0111 | 2,853 |
| Kentucky, Commonwealth of | KY | Frankfort | (502) 875-3733 | 4,339 |
| Louisiana, State of | LA | Baton Rouge | (225) 342-6600 | 4,533 |
| Maine, State of | ME | Augusta | (207) 624-9494 | 1,328 |
| Maryland, State of | MD | Annapolis | (877) 634-6361 | 5,773 |
| Massachusetts, Commonwealth of | MA | Boston | (617) 727-7030 | 6,547 |
| Michigan, State of | MI | Lansing | (517) 373-1837 | 9,883 |
| Minnesota, State of | MN | St. Paul | | 5,303 |
| Mississippi, State of | MS | Jackson | (601) 432-8168 | 2,967 |
| Missouri, State of | MO | Jefferson City | (573) 751-2000 | 5,988 |
| Montana, State of | MT | Helena | (406) 444-2511 | 989 |
| Nebraska, State of | NE | Lincoln | (402) 471-2311 | 1,826 |
| Nevada, State of | NV | Carson City | (775) 687-5000 | 2,700 |
| New Hampshire, State of | NH | Concord | (603) 271-1110 | 1,316 |
| New Jersey, State of | NJ | Trenton | (609) 292-2121 | 8,791 |
| New Mexico, State of | NM | Santa Fe | (800) 825-6639 | 2,059 |
| New York, State of | NY | Albany | (518) 474-2121 | 19,378 |
| North Carolina, State of | NC | Raleigh | (919) 733-1110 | 9,535 |
| North Dakota, State of | ND | Bismarck | (701) 328-2000 | 672 |
| Ohio, State of | OH | Columbus | (614) 466-2000 | 11,536 |
| Oklahoma, State of | OK | Oklahoma City | (405) 521-2011 | 3,751 |
| Oregon, State of | OR | Salem | (503) 986-1000 | 3,831 |
| Pennsylvania, Commonwealth of | PA | Harrisburg | (717) 787-2121 | 12,702 |
| Rhode Island and Providence Plantations, State of | RI | Providence | (401) 222-2000 | 1,052 |
| South Carolina, State of | SC | Columbia | (803) 896-0000 | 4,625 |
| South Dakota, State of | SD | Pierre | (605) 773-3011 | 814 |
| Tennessee, State of | TN | Nashville | (615) 355-8066 | 6,346 |
| Texas, State of | TX | Austin | (512) 463-4630 | 25,145 |
| Utah, State of | UT | Salt Lake City | (801) 538-3000 | 2,763 |
| Vermont, State of | VT | Montpelier | (802) 828-1110 | 625 |
| Virginia, Commonwealth of | VA | Richmond | (804) 786-0000 | 8,001 |
| Washington, State of | WA | Olympia | (360) 753-5000 | 6,724 |
| West Virginia, State of | WV | Charleston | (304) 558-3456 | 1,852 |
| Wisconsin, State of | WI | Madison | (608) 266-2211 | 5,686 |
| Wyoming, State of | WY | Cheyenne | (307) 777-7011 | 563 |
| District of Columbia | DC | Washington | (202) 727-1000 | 601 |

Source of population figures: U.S. Bureau of the Census

# STATE WEB ADDRESSES

| State | Website | Governor | Legislature |
|-------|---------|----------|-------------|
| Alabama | www.alabama.gov | www.governor.state.al.us | www.legislature.state.al.us |
| Alaska | www.alaska.gov | www.gov.state.ak.us/ | w3.legis.state.ak.us/ |
| Arizona | az.gov | www.governor.state.az.us/ | www.azleg.gov |
| Arkansas | portal.arkansas.gov | governor.arkansas.gov/ | www.arkleg.state.ar.us/ |
| California | www.ca.gov | gov.ca.gov/ | www.leginfo.ca.gov/ |
| Colorado | www.colorado.gov | www.colorado.gov/governor/ | www.leg.state.co.us/ |
| Connecticut | www.ct.gov/ | www.ct.gov/governorrell/ | www.cga.ct.gov |
| Delaware | delaware.gov | governor.delaware.gov | legis.delaware.gov/ |
| D.C. | dc.gov/DC/ | | www.dccouncil.washington.dc.us/ |
| Florida | www.myflorida.com | www.flgov.com | www.leg.state.fl.us/ |
| Georgia | www.georgia.gov | gov.georgia.gov/ | www.legis.ga.gov |
| Hawaii | portal.ehawaii.gov/ | www.hawaii.gov/gov | www.capitol.hawaii.gov/ |
| Idaho | www.state.id.us/ | gov.idaho.gov | www.legislature.idaho.gov |
| Illinois | www2.illinois.gov/ | www2.illinois.gov/gov/ | www.ilga.gov/ |
| Indiana | www.state.in.us/ | www.in.gov/gov/ | www.in.gov/legislative/ |
| Iowa | www.iowa.gov/ | www.governor.state.ia.us/ | www.legis.iowa.gov/ |
| Kansas | www.kansas.gov/ | governor.ks.gov | www.kslegislature.org |
| Kentucky | kentucky.gov | governor.ky.gov | www.lrc.state.ky.us/home.htm |
| Louisiana | www.state.la.us/ | gov.louisiana.gov | www.legis.state.la.us/ |
| Maine | www.maine.gov/ | www.maine.gov/governor/ | www.maine.gov/legis/ |
| Maryland | www.maryland.gov | www.gov.state.md.us | mlis.state.md.us/ |
| Massachusetts | www.mass.gov | www.mass.gov/ | www.malegislature.gov/ |
| Michigan | www.michigan.gov | www.michigan.gov/snyder | www.legislature.mi.gov |
| Minnesota | www.state.mn.us/ | mn.gov/governor/ | www.leg.state.mn.us/ |
| Mississippi | www.ms.gov | www.governorbarbour.com/ | billstatus.ls.state.ms.us/ |
| Missouri | www.mo.gov/ | governor.mo.gov/ | www.moga.mo.gov/ |
| Montana | www.mt.gov | governor.mt.gov/ | leg.mt.gov/css/default.asp |
| Nebraska | www.state.ne.us/ | governor.nebraska.gov/ | nebraskalegislature.gov/ |
| Nevada | www.nv.gov/ | nv.gov/govsandoval.aspx | www.leg.state.nv.us/ |
| New Hampshire | www.nh.gov/ | www.governor.nh.gov/ | www.gencourt.state.nh.us/ |
| New Jersey | www.state.nj.us/ | www.state.nj.us/governor/ | www.njleg.state.nj.us/ |
| New Mexico | www.newmexico.gov/ | www.governor.state.nm.us/ | www.nmlegis.gov/lcs/ |
| New York | www.ny.gov/ | www.governor.ny.gov/ | assembly.state.ny.us/ |
| North Carolina | www.ncgov.com | www.governor.state.nc.us/ | www.ncleg.net |
| North Dakota | www.nd.gov | www.governor.nd.gov/ | www.legis.nd.gov/ |
| Ohio | www.ohio.gov | governor.ohio.gov/ | www.legislature.state.oh.us/ |
| Oklahoma | www.ok.gov/ | www.ok.gov/governor/ | www.ok.gov/leg_info.html |
| Oregon | www.oregon.gov | governor.oregon.gov/ | www.leg.state.or.us/ |
| Pennsylvania | www.state.pa.us/ | www.governor.state.pa.us/ | www.legis.state.pa.us/ |
| Rhode Island | www.ri.gov/ | www.governor.ri.gov/ | www.rilin.state.ri.us |
| South Carolina | www.sc.gov/ | www.governor.sc.gov | www.scstatehouse.gov/ |
| South Dakota | www.sd.gov/ | sd.gov/governor/ | legis.state.sd.us/index.aspx |
| Tennessee | www.state.tn.us/ | www.tennessee.gov/governor/ | www.legislature.state.tn.us/ |
| Texas | www.texas.gov/ | www.governor.state.tx.us/ | www.capitol.state.tx.us/ |
| Utah | www.utah.gov | www.utah.gov/governor/ | le.utah.gov/ |
| Vermont | www.vermont.gov/ | governor.vermont.gov/ | www.leg.state.vt.us/ |
| Virginia | www.virginia.gov | www.governor.virginia.gov | legis.state.va.us |
| Washington | access.wa.gov/ | www.governor.wa.gov/ | www.leg.wa.gov/legislature |
| West Virginia | www.wv.gov/ | www.governor.wv.gov/ | www.legis.state.wv.us/ |
| Wisconsin | www.wisconsin.gov | www.wisgov.state.wi.us/ | legis.wisconsin.gov/ |
| Wyoming | www.wyoming.gov/ | governor.wy.gov | legisweb.state.wy.us/ |

# GOVERNORS AND THEIR OFFICE ADDRESSES

| State or jurisdiction | Governor | Phone | Office address |
|---|---|---|---|
| Alabama | *Robert Bentley (R)* | 334/ 242-7100 | State Capitol, 600 Dexter Ave., Montgomery, AL 36130-2751 |
| Alaska | *Sean Parnell (R)* | 907/ 465-3500 | P.O. Box 110001, Juneau, AK 99811-0001 |
| American Samoa | Togiola T.A. Tulafono (D) | 011/684/ 633-4116 | Executive Office Building, Third Floor, Utulei, Pago Pago, AS 96799 |
| Arizona | *Jan Brewer (R)* | 602/ 542-4331 | State Capitol, 1700 West Washington, Phoenix, AZ 85007 |
| Arkansas | Mike Beebe (D) | 501/ 682-2345 | State Capitol, Room 250, Little Rock, AR 72201 |
| California | Jerry Brown (D) | 916/ 445-2841 | Office of the Governor, State Capitol, Sacramento, CA 95814 |
| Colorado | John Hickenlooper (D) | 303/ 866-2471 | 136 State Capitol, Denver, CO 80203-1792 |
| Connecticut | Dan Malloy (D) | 800/ 406-1527 | 210 Capitol Avenue, Hartford, CT 06106 |
| Delaware | Jack Markell (D) | 302/ 744-4101 | Legislative Hall, Dover, DE 19902 |
| Florida | *Rick Scott (R)* | 850/ 488-7146 | PL 05 The Capitol, 400 South Monroe Street, Tallahassee, FL 32399-0001 |
| Georgia | *Nathan Deal (R)* | 404/ 656-1776 | 203 State Capitol, Atlanta, GA 30334 |
| Guam | *Eddie Calvo (R)* | 671/ 472-8931 | Executive Chamber, P.O. Box 2950, Agana, GU 96932 |
| Hawaii | Neil Abercrombie (D) | 808/ 586-0034 | Executive Chambers, State Capitol, Honolulu, HI 96813 |
| Idaho | *C.L. "Butch"Otter (R)* | 208/ 334-2100 | 700 West Jefferson, Second Floor, Boise, ID 83702 |
| Illinois | Pat Quinn (D) | 217/ 782-6830 | State Capitol, 207 Statehouse, Springfield, IL 62706 |
| Indiana | *Mitch Daniels (R)* | 317/ 232-4567 | State House, Room 206, Indianapolis, IN 46204-2797 |
| Iowa | *Terry Branstad (R)* | 515/ 281-5211 | State Capitol, Des Moines, IA 50319-0001 |
| Kansas | Sam Brownback (R) | 785/ 296-3232 | Capitol, 300 SW 10th Avenue, Suite 212S, Topeka, KS 66612-1590 |
| Kentucky | Steven L. Beshear (D) | 502/ 564-2611 | 700 Capitol Ave., Suite 100, Frankfort, KY 40601 |
| Louisiana | *Bobby Jindal (R)* | 225/ 342-7015 | P.O. Box 94004, Baton Rouge, LA 70804-9004 |
| Maine | *Paul LePage (R)* | 207/ 287-3531 | #1 State House Station, Augusta, ME 04333 |
| Maryland | Martin O'Malley (D) | 410/ 974-3901 | 100 State Circle, Annapolis, MD 21401 |
| Massachusetts | Deval Patrick (D) | 617/ 725-4000 | State House, Office of the Governor, Room 360, Boston, MA 02133 |
| Michigan | *Rick Snyder (R)* | 517/ 373-3400 | P.O. Box 30013, Lansing, MI 48909 |
| Minnesota | Mark Dayton (D) | 651/ 201-3400 | 130 State Capitol, 75 Rev. Dr. MLK Jr. Blvd., St. Paul, MN 55155 |
| Mississippi | *Phil Bryant (R)* | 601/ 359-3150 | P.O. Box 139, Jackson, MS 39205 |
| Missouri | Jay Nixon (D) | 573/ 751-3222 | Capitol Building, Room 218, P.O. Box 720, Jefferson City, MO 65102 |
| Montana | Brian Schweitzer (D) | 406/ 444-3111 | State Capitol, Helena, MT 59620 |
| Nebraska | *Dave Heineman (R)* | 402/ 471-2244 | P.O. Box 94848, Lincoln, NE 68509-4848 |
| Nevada | *Brian Sandoval (R)* | 775/ 684-5670 | Capitol Building, Carson City, NV 89701 |
| New Hampshire | John Lynch (D) | 603/ 271-2121 | Office of the Governor, 25 Capitol Street, Room 212, Concord, NH 03301 |
| New Jersey | *Chris Christie (R)* | 609/ 292-6000 | The State House, P.O. Box 001, Trenton, NJ 08625 |
| New Mexico | *Susana Martinez (R)* | 505/ 476-2200 | State Capitol, Fourth Floor, Santa Fe, NM 87300 |
| New York | Andrew Cuomo (D) | 518/ 474-7516 | State Capitol, Albany, NY 12224 |
| North Carolina | Beverly Perdue (D) | 919/ 733-4240 | Office of the Governor, 20301 Mail Service Center, Raleigh, NC 27699 |
| North Dakota | *Jack Dalrymple (R)* | 701/ 328-2200 | Dept. 101, 600 E. Boulevard Ave., Bismarck, ND 58505-0001 |
| Northern Mariana Is. | *Benigno Fitial (R)* | 670/ 664-2280 | Caller Box 10007, Saipan, MP 96950 |
| Ohio | *John Kasich (R)* | 614/ 466-3555 | 30th Floor, 77 South High Street, Columbus, OH 43215 |
| Oklahoma | *Mary Fallin (R)* | 405/ 521-2342 | Cap. Building, 2300 N. Lincoln Blvd., Rm. 212, Oklahoma City, OK 73105 |
| Oregon | John Kitzhaber (D) | 503/ 373-1027 | State Capitol, Room 160, 900 Court St. N., Salem, OR 97301 |
| Pennsylvania | *Tom Corbett (R)* | 717/ 787-2500 | Room 225, Main Capitol Building, Harrisburg, PA 17120 |
| Puerto Rico | *Luis G. Fortuño (R)* | 787/ 721-7000 | La Fortaleza, P.O. Box 9020082, San Juan, PR 00902-0082 |
| Rhode Island | Lincoln Chafee (Independent) | 401/ 222-2080 | State House, Providence, RI 02903 |
| South Carolina | *Nikki R. Haley (R)* | 803/ 734-2100 | 1205 Pendleton Street, Columbia, SC 29201 |
| South Dakota | *Dennis Daugaard (R)* | 605/ 773-3212 | 500 East Capitol Street, Pierre, SD 57501 |
| Tennessee | *Bill Haslam (R)* | 615/ 741-2001 | Tennessee State Capitol, Nashville, TN 37243-0001 |
| Texas | *Rick Perry (R)* | 512/ 463-2000 | P.O. Box 12428, Austin, TX 78711 |
| Utah | *Gary R. Herbert (R)* | 801/ 538-1000 | Utah State Capitol, Suite 200, Salt Lake City, UT 84114 |
| Vermont | Peter Shumlin (D) | 802/ 828-3333 | 109 State Street, Pavilion Office Building, Montpelier, VT 05609 |
| Virgin Islands | John deJongh, Jr. (D) | 340/ 774-0001 | Govt. House, 21-22 Kongens Gade, Charlotte Amalie, St. Thomas, VI 00802 |
| Virginia | *Bob McDonnell (R)* | 804/ 786-2211 | State Capitol, Third Floor, Richmond, VA 23219 |
| Washington | Chris Gregoire (D) | 360/ 902-4111 | Office of the Governor, P.O. Box 40002. Olympia, WA 98504-0002 |
| West Virginia | Earl Ray Tomblin (D) | 304/ 558-2000 | 1900 Kanawha Street, Charleston, WV 25305 |
| Wisconsin | *Scott Walker (R)* | 608/ 266-1212 | 115 East State Capitol, Madison, WI 53707 |
| Wyoming | *Matthew Mead (R)* | 307/ 777-7434 | State Capitol Building, Room 124, Cheyenne, WY 82002 |

Credit: National Governors' Association

# STATE ATTORNEYS GENERAL

**ALABAMA**
Honorable Luther Strange
Attorney General of Alabama
Office of the Attorney General
501 Washington Ave.
Montgomery, AL 36130
(334) 242-7300
www.ago.state.al.us/

**ALASKA**
Honorable John Burns
Acting Attorney General of Alaska
Office of the Attorney General
P.O. Box 110300
Juneau, AK 99811-0300
(907) 465-3600
www.law.state.ak.us/

**AMERICAN SAMOA**
Honorable Afa Ripley, Jr.
Attorney General of American Samoa
Office of the Attorney General
Executive Office Bldg., Utulei
Pago Pago, AS 96799
(684) 633-4163
americansamoa.gov/departments/depts/
  legal.htm

**ARIZONA**
Honorable Tom Horne
Attorney General of Arizona
Office of the Attorney General
1275 West Washington St.
Phoenix, AZ 85007
(602) 542-4266
www.azag.gov/

**ARKANSAS**
Honorable Dustin McDaniel
Attorney General of Arkansas
Office of the Attorney General
200 Tower Building, 323 Center St.
Little Rock, AR 72201-2610
(800) 482-8982
www.ag.arkansas.gov/

**CALIFORNIA**
Honorable Kamala Harris
Attorney General of California
Office of the Attorney General
1300 I Street, Suite 1740
Sacramento, CA 95814
(916) 445-9555
ag.ca.gov/

**COLORADO**
Honorable John W. Suthers
Attorney General of Colorado
Office of the Attorney General
Department of Law
1525 Sherman Street
Denver, CO 80203
(303) 866-4500
www.ago.state.co.us/index.cfm

**CONNECTICUT**
Honorable George Jensen
Attorney General of Connecticut
Office of the Attorney General
55 Elm Street
Hartford, CT 06141-0120
(860) 808-5318
www.ct.gov/ag/

**DELAWARE**
Honorable Joseph R. Biden, III
Attorney General of Delaware
Office of the Attorney General
820 North French Street
Wilmington, DE 19801
(302) 577-8338
attorneygeneral.delaware.gov/

**DISTRICT OF COLUMBIA**
Honorable Irvin Nathan
Attorney General of the District of
  Columbia
Office of the Corporation Counsel
John A. Wilson Bldg.
1350 Pennsylvania Ave. NW, Suite 409
Washington, DC 20009
(202) 727-3400
occ.dc.gov

**FLORIDA**
Honorable Pam Bondi
Attorney General of Florida
Office of the Attorney General
The Capitol, PL 01
Tallahassee, FL 32399-1050
(850) 414-3300
myfloridalegal.com/

**GEORGIA**
Honorable Sam Olens
Attorney General of Georgia
Office of the Attorney General
40 Capitol Square, SW
Atlanta, GA 30334-1300
(404) 656-3300

law.ga.gov/

**GUAM**
Honorable Lenny Rapadas
Attorney General of Guam
Office of the Attorney General
Judicial Center Building
287 West O'Brien Drive
Hagatna, GU 96910
(671) 475-3409
www.guamattorneygeneral.com

**HAWAII**
Honorable David Louie
Attorney General of Hawaii
Office of the Attorney General
425 Queen Street
Honolulu, HI 96813
(808) 586-1500
www.hawaii.gov/ag

**IDAHO**
Honorable Lawrence Wasden
Attorney General of Idaho
Office of the Attorney General
Statehouse
Boise, ID 83720-1000
(208) 334-2400
www2.state.id.us/ag/

**ILLINOIS**
Honorable Lisa Madigan
Attorney General of Illinois
Office of the Attorney General
100 West Randolph Street
Chicago, IL 60601
(312) 814-3000
illinoisattorneygeneral.gov

**INDIANA**
Honorable Greg Zoeller
Attorney General of Indiana
Office of the Attorney General
402 W. Washington St., 5th fl.
Indianapolis, IN 46204
(317) 232-6201
www.in.gov/attorneygeneral/

**IOWA**
Honorable Tom Miller
Attorney General of Iowa
Office of the Attorney General
1305 E. Walnut
Des Moines, IA 50319
(515) 281-5164

# STATE ATTORNEYS GENERAL

www.IowaAttorneyGeneral.org

**KANSAS**
Honorable Derek Schmidt
Attorney General of Kansas
Office of the Attorney General
120 SW 10th Ave., 2nd fl.
Topeka, KS 66612-1597
(785) 296-2215
www.ksag.org/home

**KENTUCKY**
Honorable Jack Conway
Attorney General of Kentucky
Office of the Attorney General
State Capitol, Rm. 118
Frankfort, KY 40601
(502) 696-5300
ag.ky.gov

**LOUISIANA**
Honorable James D. Caldwell
Attorney General of Louisiana
Office of the Attorney General
Department of Justice
P.O. Box 94095
Baton Rouge, LA 70804-4095
(225) 326-6000
www.ag.state.la.us/

**MAINE**
Honorable William J. Schneider
Attorney General of Maine
Office of the Attorney General
State House Station 6
Augusta, ME 04333
(207) 626-8800
www.maine.gov/ag/

**MARYLAND**
Honorable Douglas F. Gansler.
Attorney General of Maryland
Office of the Attorney General
200 Saint Paul Place
Baltimore, MD 21202-2202
(410) 576-6300
www.oag.state.md.us/

**MASSACHUSETTS**
Honorable Martha Coakley
Attorney General of Massachusetts
Office of the Attorney General
One Ashburton Place
Boston, MA 02108-1698
(617) 727-2200
www.mass.gov/ago/

**MICHIGAN**
Honorable Bill Schuette
Attorney General of Michigan
Office of the Attorney General

P.O. Box 30212
525 West Ottawa Street
Lansing, MI 48909-0212
(517) 373-1110
www.michigan.gov/ag

**MINNESOTA**
Honorable Lori Swanson
Attorney General of Minnesota
Office of the Attorney General
State Capitol, Suite 102
St. Paul, MN 55155
(651) 296-3353
www.ag.state.mn.us/

**MISSISSIPPI**
Honorable Jim Hood
Attorney General of Mississippi
Office of the Attorney General
Department of Justice
P.O. Box 220
Jackson, MS 39205-0220
(601) 359-3680
www.ago.state.ms.us/

**MISSOURI**
Honorable Chris Koster
Attorney General of Missouri
Office of the Attorney General
207 W. High St.
Jefferson City, MO 65101
(573) 751-3321
ago.mo.gov

**MONTANA**
Honorable Steve Bullock
Attorney General of Montana
Office of the Attorney General
Justice Building, 215 North Sanders
Helena, MT 59620-1401
(406) 444-2026
www.doj.mt.gov

**NEBRASKA**
Honorable Jon Bruning
Attorney General of Nebraska
Office of the Attorney General
State Capitol
P.O. Box 98920
Lincoln, NE 68509-8920
(402) 471-2682
www.ago.state.ne.us/

**NEVADA**
Honorable Catherine Cortez Masto
Attorney General of Nevada
Office of the Attorney General
Old Supreme Court Building
100 North Carson Street
Carson City, NV 89701
(775) 684-1100

ag.state.nv.us/

**NEW HAMPSHIRE**
Honorable Michael Delaney
Attorney General of New Hampshire
Office of the Attorney General
State House Annex, 33 Capitol Street
Concord, NH 03301-6397
(603) 271-3658
doj.nh.gov/

**NEW JERSEY**
Honorable Paula T. Dow
Attorney General of New Jersey
Office of the Attorney General
Richard J. Hughes Justice Complex
25 Market Street, CN 080
Trenton, NJ 08625
(609) 292-8740
www.state.nj.us/lps/

**NEW MEXICO**
Honorable Gary King
Attorney General of New Mexico
Office of the Attorney General
P.O. Drawer 1508
Santa Fe, NM 87504-1508
(505) 827-6000
www.nmag.gov/

**NEW YORK**
Honorable Eric Schneiderman
Attorney General of New York
Office of the Attorney General
Department of Law - The Capitol
2nd fl.
Albany, NY 12224
(518) 474-7330
www.ag.ny.gov/

**NORTH CAROLINA**
Honorable Roy Cooper
Attorney General of North Carolina
Office of the Attorney General
Department of Justice
P.O. Box 629
Raleigh, NC 27602-0629
(919) 716-6400
www.ncdoj.gov

**NORTH DAKOTA**
Honorable Wayne Stenehjem
Attorney General of North Dakota
Office of the Attorney General
State Capitol
600 East Boulevard Avenue
Bismarck, ND 58505-0040
(701) 328-2210
www.ag.state.nd.us/

# STATE ATTORNEYS GENERAL

**N. MARIANA ISLANDS**
Honorable Edward T. Buckingham
Acting Attorney General of N. Mariana
  Islands
Administration Bldg.
P.O. Box 10007, Capitol Hill
Saipan, MP 96950
(670) 664-2341
www.cnmiago.gov/mp/

**OHIO**
Honorable Mike Dewine
Attorney General of Ohio
Office of the Attorney General
30 East Broad Street
Columbus, OH 43266-0410
(614) 466-4320
www.ohioattorneygeneral.gov/

**OKLAHOMA**
Honorable Scott Pruitt
Attorney General of Oklahoma
Office of the Attorney General
State Capitol, Room 112
313 NE 21st St.
Oklahoma City, OK 73105
(405) 521-3921
www.oag.state.ok.us/

**OREGON**
Honorable John Kroger
Attorney General of Oregon
Office of the Attorney General
Justice Building
1162 Court St., NE
Salem, OR 97301
(503) 378-4732
www.doj.state.or.us/

**PENNSYLVANIA**
Honorable Linda J. Kelly
Attorney General of Pennsylvania
Office of the Attorney General
1600 Strawberry Square
Harrisburg, PA 17120
(717) 787-3391
www.attorneygeneral.gov/

**PUERTO RICO**
Honorable Guillermo Somoza-Colombani
Attorney General of Puerto Rico
Office of the Attorney General
GPO Box 9020192
San Juan, PR 00902-0192
(787) 721-2900
www.justicia.gobierno.pr

**RHODE ISLAND**
Honorable Peter Kilmartin
Attorney General of Rhode Island
Office of the Attorney General

150 South Main Street
Providence, RI 02903
(401) 274-4400
www.riag.state.ri.us/

**SOUTH CAROLINA**
Honorable Alan Wilson
Attorney General of South Carolina
Office of the Attorney General
P.O. Box 11549
Columbia, SC 29211-1549
(803) 734-3970
www.scattorneygeneral.org/

**SOUTH DAKOTA**
Honorable Marty J. Jackley
Attorney General of South Dakota
Office of the Attorney General
1302 East Highway 14, Suite 1
Pierre, SD 57501-8501
(605) 773-3215
atg.sd.gov/

**TENNESSEE**
Honorable Robert E. Cooper, Jr.
Attorney General of Tennessee
Office of the Attorney General
425 5th Ave. North
Nashville, TN 37243
(615) 741-3491
www.tn.gov/attorneygeneral

**TEXAS**
Honorable Greg Abbott
Attorney General of Texas
Office of the Attorney General
Capitol Station, P.O. Box 12548
Austin, TX 78711-2548
(512) 463-2100
www.oag.state.tx.us/

**UTAH**
Honorable Mark Shurtleff
Attorney General of Utah
Office of the Attorney General
State Capitol, Room 236
Salt Lake City, UT 84114-0810
(801) 538-9600
www.attorneygeneral.utah.gov

**VERMONT**
Honorable William H. Sorrell
Attorney General of Vermont
Office of the Attorney General
109 State Street
Montpelier, VT 05609-1001
(802) 828-3173
www.atg.state.vt.us/

**VIRGINIA**
Honorable Ken Cuccinelli

Attorney General of Virginia
Office of the Attorney General
900 East Main Street
Richmond, VA 23219
(804) 786-2071
www.oag.state.va.us/

**VIRGIN ISLANDS**
Honorable Vincent Frazer
Attorney General of the Virgin Islands
Office of the Attorney General
Department of Justice, G.E.R.S. Complex
48B-50C Kronprinsdens Gade
St. Thomas, VI 00802
(340) 774-5666

**WASHINGTON**
Honorable Rob McKenna
Attorney General of Washington
Office of the Attorney General
1125 Washington St. SE
Olympia, WA 98504-0100
(360) 753-6200
www.atg.wa.gov

**WEST VIRGINIA**
Honorable Darrell V. McGraw, Jr.
Attorney General of West Virginia
Office of the Attorney General
State Capitol
1900 Kanawha Boulevard, East
Charleston, WV 25305
(304) 558-2021
www.wvago.gov/

**WISCONSIN**
Honorable J.B. Van Hollen
Attorney General of Wisconsin
Office of the Attorney General
State Capitol, Suite 114E
P.O. Box 7857
Madison, WI 53707-7857
(608) 266-1221
www.doj.state.wi.us/

**WYOMING**
Honorable Greg Phillips
Attorney General of Wyoming
Office of the Attorney General
State Capitol Building
Cheyenne, WY 82002
(307) 777-7841
attorneygeneral.state.wy.us

# STATE BANKING AUTHORITIES

## Banking

Administers laws regulating the operation of banking institutions in the state.

**ALABAMA**
Mr. John D. Harrison
Superintendent
Banking Department
P.O. Box 4600
Montgomery, AL 36130
P: (334) 242-3452
F: (334) 242-3500
E: john.harrison
@banking.alabama.gov

**ALASKA**
Ms. Lori L. Hovanec
Director
Department of Commerce,
Community & Economic
Development
Division of Banking &
Securities
P.O. Box 110807
Juneau, AK 99811
P: (907) 465-2521
F: (907) 465-2549
E: lori.hovanec@alaska.gov

**AMERICAN SAMOA**
Mr. Lolo M. Moliga
President
Development Bank of American
Samoa
P.O. Box 9
Pago Pago, AS 96799
P: (684) 633-4565
F: (684) 633-1163

**ARIZONA**
Mr. Lauren W. Kingry
Superintendent
Department of Financial
Institutions
2910 North 44th Street, Suite
310
Phoenix, AZ 85018
P: (602) 771-2800
F: (602) 381-1225

**ARKANSAS**
Ms. Candace Franks
Commissioner
Securities Department
400 Hardin, Suite 100
Little Rock, AR 72211
P: (501) 324-9019
F: (501) 324-9028
E: cfranks
@banking.state.ar.us

**CALIFORNIA**
Mr. William S. Haraf
Commissioner
Department of Financial
Institutions
45 Fremont Street, Suite 1700
San Francisco, CA 94105
P: (415) 263-8507
F: (415) 288-8830
E: wharaf@dfi.ca.gov

**CONNECTICUT**
Mr. Howard F. Pitkin
Commissioner
Department of Banking
260 Constitution Plaza
Hartford, CT 06103
P: (860) 240-8100
F: (860) 240-8178
E: howard.pitkin@ct.gov

**DELAWARE**
Mr. Robert A. Glen
Commissioner
Office of State Bank
Commissioner
555 East Lockerman Street,
Suite 210
Dover, DE 19901
P: (302) 739-4235
F: (302) 739-3609

**DISTRICT OF COLUMBIA**
Mr. William P. White
Commissioner
Department of Insurance,
Securities & Banking
810 First Street, Northeast, Suite
70
Washington, DC 20002
P: (202) 727-8000
F: (202) 535-1196

**GEORGIA**
Mr. Rob Braswell
Commissioner
Department of Banking &
Finance
2990 Brandywine Road, Suite
200
Atlanta, GA 30341
P: (770) 986-1628
F: (770) 986-1654
E: robertb@dbf.state.ga.us

**GUAM**
Mr. John Camacho
Banking & Insurance
Commissioner
Department of Revenue &
Taxation
Regulatory Division
P.O. Box 23607 GMF
Barrigada, GU 96921
P: (671) 635-1817
F: (671) 633-2643

**HAWAII**
Ms. Iris Ikeda Catalani
Commissioner
Division of Financial
Institutions
King Kalakaua Building
335 Merchant Street, Room 221
Honolulu, HI 96813
P: (808) 586-2820
F: (808) 586-2818

**IDAHO**
Mr. Gavin M. Gee
Director
Department of Finance
800 Park Boulevard, Suite 200
Boise, ID 83712
P: (208) 332-8010
F: (208) 332-8097
E: ggee@finance.idaho.gov

**ILLINOIS**
Mr. Manuel Flores
Director
Division of Banking
122 South Michigan Avenue,
Suite 1900
Chicago, IL 60603
P: (312) 793-3000
F: (312) 793-0756

**INDIANA**
Mr. David Mills
Director
Department of Financial
Institutions
30 South Meridian Street, Suite
300
Indianapolis, IN 46204
P: (317) 233-9460
F: (317) 232-7655
E: DaMills@dfi.IN.gov

**IOWA**
Mr. James M. Schipper
Superintendent
Division of Banking
200 East Grand Avenue, Suite
300
Des Moines, IA 50309
P: (515) 281-4014
F: (515) 281-4862
E: jschipper
@idob.state.ia.us

**KANSAS**
Mr. Ed Splichal
Commissioner
Office of the State Banking
Commissioner
700 Jackson, Suite 300
Topeka, KS 66603
P: (785) 296-2266
F: (785) 296-0168

**KENTUCKY**
Mr. Charles A. Vice
Commissioner
Department of Financial
Institutions
1025 Capital Center Drive, Suite
200
Frankfort, KY 40601
P: (502) 573-3390
F: (502) 573-0086
E: charles.vice@ky.gov

**LOUISIANA**
Mr. John P. Ducrest
Commissioner
Office of Financial Institutions
8660 United Plaza Boulevard,
2nd Floor
P.O. Box 94095
Baton Rouge, LA 70804
P: (225) 925-4660
F: (225) 925-4548
E: jducrest@ofi.la.gov

**MAINE**
Mr. Lloyd P. LaFountain III
Superintendent
Bureau of Financial Institutions
Bureau of Financial Institutions
36 State House Station
Augusta, ME 04333
P: (207) 624-8570
F: (207) 624-8590
E: lloyd.p.lafountain.III
@maine.gov

**MARYLAND**
Mr. Mark Kaufman
Commissioner of Financial
Regulation
Department of Labor, Licensing
& Regulation
500 North Calvert Street, Room
402
Baltimore, MD 21202
P: (410) 230-6100
F: (410) 333-0475
E: mkaufman
@dllr.state.md.us

**MASSACHUSETTS**
Mr. David Cotney
Commissioner
Division of Banks
1000 Washington Street,
10th Floor
Boston, MA 02118
P: (617) 956-1500
F: (617) 956-1599

# STATE BANKING AUTHORITIES

**MICHIGAN**
Mr. R. Kevin Clinton
Commissioner
Office of Financial & Insurance
Regulation
P.O. Box 30220
Lansing, MI 48909
P: (517) 373-0220
F: (517) 373-4978

**MINNESOTA**
Mr. Mike Rothman
Commissioner of Commerce
Department of Commerce
85 7th Place East, Suite 500
St. Paul, MN 55101
P: (651) 296-6025
F: (651) 297-1959
E: commerce.commissioner
@state.mn.us

**MISSISSIPPI**
Mr. John S. Allison
Commissioner
Department of Banking &
Consumer Finance
501 North West Street
901 Woolfolk Building, Suite A
Jackson, MS 39202
P: (601) 359-1031
F: (601) 359-3557
E: john.allison@dbcf.ms.gov

**MISSOURI**
Mr. Richard J. Weaver
Commissioner
Division of Finance
Truman State Office Building,
Room 630
P.O. Box 716
Jefferson City, MO 65102
P: (573) 751-3242
F: (573) 751-9192
E: finance@dof.mo.gov

**MONTANA**
Ms. Melanie Griggs
Commissioner
Division of Banking &
Financial Institutions
301 South Park, Suite 316
P.O. Box 200546
Helena, MT 59620
P: (406) 841-2920
F: (406) 841-2930
E: mgriggs@mt.gov

**NEBRASKA**
Mr. John Munn
Director
Department of Banking &
Finance
P.O. Box 95006
Lincoln, NE 68509
P: (402) 471-2171
E: john.munn@nebraska.gov

**NEVADA**
Mr. Steven W. Kondrup
Administrator
Financial Institutions Division
Department of Business &
Industry
2785 East Desert Inn Road, Suite
180
Las Vegas, NV 89121
P: (702) 486-4120
F: (702) 486-4563
E: skondrup@fid.state.nv.us

**NEW HAMPSHIRE**
Mr. Ronald A. Wilbur
Commissioner
Banking Department
53 Regional Drive, Suite 200
Concord, NH 03301
P: (603) 271-3561
F: (603) 271-1090
E: Commissioner
@banking.state.nh.us

**NEW JERSEY**
Mr. Thomas B. Considine
Commissioner
Department of Banking &
Insurance
20 West State Street
P.O. Box 325
Trenton, NJ 08625
P: (609) 292-7272
F: (609) 663-3601
E: commissioner
@dobi.state.nj.us

**NORTH CAROLINA**
Mr. Joseph A. Smith Jr.
Commissioner of Banks
Banking Commission
316 West Edenton Street
4309 Mail Service Center
Raleigh, NC 27699
P: (919) 733-3016
F: (919) 733-6918
E: jsmith@nccob.org

**NORTH DAKOTA**
Mr. Robert J. Entringer
Commissioner
Department of Financial
Institutions
2000 Schafer Street, Suite G
Bismarck, ND 58501
P: (701) 328-9933
F: (701) 328-0290
E: rentring@nd.gov

**NORTHERN MARIANA
ISLANDS**
Mr. Sixto Igisomar
Acting Secretary
Department of Commerce
Caller Box 10007
Saipan, MP 96950
P: (670) 664-3064
F: (670) 664-3067

**OHIO**
Mr. Charles J. Dolezal
Superintendent
Division of Financial
Institutions
Department of Commerce
77 South High Street
Columbus, OH 43215
P: (614) 728-8400
F: (614) 728-0380

**OKLAHOMA**
Mr. Mick Thompson
Commissioner
State Banking Department
2900 North Lincoln Boulevard
Oklahoma City, OK 73105
P: (405) 521-2782
F: (405) 522-2993
E: rmt1@onenet.net

**OREGON**
Mr. David C. Tatman
Division Administrator
Division of Finance &
Corporate Securities
350 Winter Street, Northeast,
Room 410
Salem, OR 97301
P: (503) 378-4140
F: (503) 947-7862
E: dcbs.dfcsmail
@state.or.us

**PENNSYLVANIA**
Mr. Glenn E. Moyer
Secretary of Banking
Department of Banking
17 North 2nd Street, Suite 1300
Harrisburg, PA 17101
P: (717) 787-2665
F: (717) 787-8773
E: ra-pabanking@state.pa.us

**PUERTO RICO**
Mr. Alfredo Padilla
Commissioner of Financial
Institutions
Office of the Commissioner of
Financial Institutions
Commonwealth of Puerto Rico
P.O. Box 11855
San Juan, PR 00910
P: (787) 723-3131
F: (787) 723-4042
E: comisionado
@ocif.gobierno.pr

**SOUTH CAROLINA**
Ms. Paige H. Parsons
Senior Assistant State Treasurer,
Internal Auditor
Office of the State Treasurer
1200 Senate St., Wade Hampton
Bldg.
P.O. Box 11778
Columbia, SC 29211
P: (803) 734-9822
F: (803) 734-2690
E: paige.parsons@sto.sc.gov

**SOUTH DAKOTA**
Mr. Bret Afdahl
Director
Division of Banking
Department of Revenue &
Regulation
217 1/2 West Missouri Avenue
Pierre, SD 57501
P: (605) 773-3421
F: (866) 326-7504
E: drr.banking.info
@state.sd.us

**TENNESSEE**
Mr. Greg Gonzales
Commissioner
Department of Financial
Institutions
414 Union Street, Suite 1000
Nashville, TN 37219
P: (615) 741-2236
F: (615) 253-6306
E: Greg.Gonzales@tn.gov

**TEXAS**
Mr. Charles G. Cooper
Commissioner
Department of Banking
2601 North Lamar Boulevard
Austin, TX 78705
P: (512) 475-1323
F: (512) 475-1313
E: executive
@banking.state.tx.us

# STATE BANKING AUTHORITIES

**U.S. VIRGIN ISLANDS**
Mr. John McDonald
Director
Division of Banking &
Insurance
#18 Kongens Gade
St. Thomas, VI 00802
P: (340) 774-7166
F: (340) 774-9458

**UTAH**
Mr. G. Edward Leary
Commissioner
Department of Financial
Institutions
324 South State Street, Suite
201
P.O. Box 146800
Salt Lake City, UT 84114
P: (801) 538-8761
F: (801) 538-8894
E: ELEARY@utah.gov

**VERMONT**
Mr. Steve Kimbell
Commissioner
Department of Banking,
Insurance, Securities & Health
Care Administration
89 Main Street
Montpelier, VT 05620
P: (802) 828-3301
F: (802) 828-3306
E: steve.kimbell
    @state.vt.us

**VIRGINIA**
Mr. E. Joseph Face Jr.
Director
Bureau of Financial Institutions
1300 East Main Street, Suite
800
P.O. Box 640
Richmond, VA 23218
P: (804) 371-9657
F: (804) 371-9416
E: joe.face
    @scc.virginia.gov

**WASHINGTON**
Mr. Scott Jarvis
Director
Department of Financial
Institutions
P.O. Box 41200
Olympia, WA 98504
P: (360) 902-8700
F: (360) 586-5068
E: confsec@dfi.wa.gov

Ms. Gloria McVey
Acting Director of Banks
Division of Banks
Department of Financial
Institutions
P.O. Box 41200
Olympia, WA 98504
P: (360) 902-8704
F: (360) 753-6070
E: banks@dfi.wa.gov

**WEST VIRGINIA**
Ms. Sara M. Cline
Commissioner
Division of Banking
One Players Club Drive, Suite
300
Charleston, WV 25311
P: (304) 558-2294
F: (304) 558-0442
E: scline@wvdob.org

**WISCONSIN**
Mr. Michael Mach
Administrator
Division of Banking
345 West Washington Avenue
P.O. Box 7876
Madison, WI 53707
P: (608) 261-7578
F: (608) 267-6889
E: Mike.Mach
    @dfi.wisconsin.gov

**WYOMING**
Mr. Jeffrey C. Vogel
Commissioner
Division of Banking
Herschler Building, 3rd Floor,
East
122 West 25th Street
Cheyenne, WY 82002
P: (307) 777-7797
F: (307) 777-5341
E: jvogel
    @wyaudit.state.wy.us

# STATE INSURANCE REGULATORS

## Insurance

Licenses and regulates insurance agents and insurance and title companies in the state.

### ALABAMA
Mr. Jim L. Ridling
Commissioner
Department of Insurance
201 Monroe Street, Suite 1700
P.O. Box 303351
Montgomery, AL 36130
P: (334) 269-3550
F: (334) 241-4192

### ALASKA
Ms. Linda S. Hall
Director
Department of Commerce,
Community & Economic
Development
Division of Insurance
550 West 7th Avenue, Suite 1560
Anchorage, AK 99501
P: (907) 269-7900
F: (907) 269-7910
E: linda.hall@alaska.gov

### AMERICAN SAMOA
Mr. Aoomalo Manupo Turituri
Insurance Commissioner
Office of the Governor
American Samoa Government
Pago Pago, AS 96799
P: (684) 633-4116
F: (684) 633-2269

### ARIZONA
Ms. Christina Urias
Director
Department of Insurance
2910 North 44th Street, 2nd
Floor
Ste. 210
Phoenix, AZ 85018
P: (602) 364-3100

### ARKANSAS
Mr. Jay Bradford
Commissioner
Department of Insurance
1200 West Third Street
Little Rock, AR 72201
P: (501) 371-2600
F: (501) 371-2618

### CALIFORNIA
Mr. Dave Jones
Commissioner
Department of Insurance
300 Capitol Mall, 17th Floor
Sacramento, CA 95814
P: (916) 492-3500
F: (916) 445-5280

### COLORADO
Mr. John Postolowski
Interim Commissioner
Division of Insurance
Department of Regulatory
Agencies
1560 Broadway, Suite 850
Denver, CO 80202
P: (303) 894-7499
F: (303) 894-7455

### CONNECTICUT
Mr. Thomas B. Leonardi
Commissioner
Insurance Department
153 Market Street
P.O. Box 816
Hartford, CT 06142
P: (860) 297-3800
F: (860) 566-7410

### DELAWARE
Hon. Karen Weldin
    Stewart (D)
Commissioner
Insurance Department
841 Silver Lake Boulevard
Dover, DE 19904
P: (302) 674-7305
E: karen.stewart
    @state.de.us

### DISTRICT OF COLUMBIA
Mr. William P. White
Commissioner
Department of INsurance,
Securities & Banking
810 First Street, Northeast, Suite
70
Washington, DC 20002
P: (202) 727-8000
F: (202) 535-1196

### FLORIDA
Mr. Kevin M. McCarty
Commissioner
Office of Insurance Regulation
Department of Financial
Services
200 East Gaines Street
Tallahassee, FL 32399
P: (850) 413-3140
E: kevin.mccarty@fldfs.com

### GEORGIA
Hon. Ralph T. Hudgens (R)
Commissioner
Office of Insurance & Safety
Fire Commissioner
2 Martin Luther King Jr. Drive
West Tower, Suite 704
Atlanta, GA 30334
P: (404) 656-2070
F: (404) 657-8542

### GUAM
Mr. John Camacho
Banking & Insurance
Commissioner
Department of Revenue &
Taxation
Regulatory Division
P.O. Box 23607 GMF
Barrigada, GU 96921
P: (671) 635-1817
F: (671) 633-2643

### HAWAII
Mr. Gordon Ito
Commissioner
Division of Insurance
Commerce & Consumer Affairs
P.O. Box 3614
Honolulu, HI 96811
P: (808) 586-2799
F: (808) 586-2806
E: insurance
    @dcca.hawaii.gov

### IDAHO
Mr. Bill Deal
Director
Department of Insurance
700 West State Street
P.O. Box 83720
Boise, ID 83720
P: (208) 334-4250
F: (208) 334-4398

### ILLINOIS
Mr. Michael T. McRaith
Director
Department of Insurance
320 West Washington Street
Springfield, IL 62767
P: (217) 782-4515
F: (217) 782-5020
E: DOI.Director
    @illinois.gov

### INDIANA
Mr. Stephen W. Robertson
Commissioner
Department of Insurance
311 West Washington Street,
Suite 300
Indianapolis, IN 46204
P: (317) 232-3520
F: (317) 232-5251

### IOWA
Ms. Susan E. Voss
Commissioner
Insurance Division
330 Maple Street
Des Moines, IA 50319
P: (515) 281-5705
F: (515) 281-3059

### KANSAS
Hon. Sandy Praeger (R)
Commissioner of Insurance
Insurance Department
420 Southwest 9th Street
Topeka, KS 66612
P: (785) 296-3071
F: (785) 296-7805
E: commissioner
    @ksinsurance.org

### KENTUCKY
Ms. Sharon P. Clark
Commissioner
Department of Insurance
P.O. Box 517
Frankfort, KY 40602
P: (502) 564-3630
F: (502) 564-1453
E: Debbie.Stamper@ky.gov

### LOUISIANA
Hon. James J. Donelon (R)
Commissioner
Department of Insurance
P.O. Box 94214
Baton Rouge, LA 70804
P: (225) 342-5900
F: (225) 342-8622

### MAINE
Ms. Mila Kofman
Superintendent
Department of Professional &
Financial Regulation
Bureau of Insurance
34 State House Station
Augusta, ME 04333
P: (207) 624-8475
F: (207) 624-8599
E: Mila.Kofman@maine.gov

### MARYLAND
Ms. Beth Sammis
Acting Insurance Commissioner
Insurance Administration
200 Saint Paul Place, Suite 2700
Baltimore, MD 21202
P: (410) 468-2002
F: (410) 468-2020
E: bsammis
    @mdinsurance.state.md.us

### MASSACHUSETTS
Mr. Joseph Murphy
Commissioner
Division of Insurance
Consumer Affairs & Business
Regulation
One South Station, 5th Floor
Boston, MA 02110
P: (617) 521-7794

# STATE INSURANCE REGULATORS

**MICHIGAN**
Mr. R. Kevin Clinton
Commissioner
Office of Financial & Insurance
Regulation
P.O. Box 30220
Lansing, MI 48909
P: (517) 373-0220
F: (517) 373-4978

**MINNESOTA**
Mr. Mike Rothman
Commissioner of Commerce
Department of Commerce
85 7th Place East, Suite 500
St. Paul, MN 55101
P: (651) 296-6025
F: (651) 297-1959
E: commerce.commissioner
@state.mn.us

**MISSISSIPPI**
Hon. Mike Chaney (R)
Commissioner & State Fire
Marshal
Insurance Department
1001 Woolfolk State Office
Building
501 North West Street, P.O. Box
79
Jackson, MS 39205
P: (601) 359-3569
F: (601) 359-2543
E: mike.chaney
@mid.state.ms.us

**MISSOURI**
Mr. John Huff
Director
Department of Insurance,
Financial Institutions &
Professional Registration
301 West High Street, Room
530
P.O. Box 690
Jefferson City, MO 65102
P: (573) 751-1927

**MONTANA**
Hon. Monica J. Lindeen (D)
State Auditor
Office of the Auditor
840 Helena Avenue
Helena, MT 59601
P: (406) 444-2006
F: (406) 444-3497
E: monica@lindeen.net

**NEBRASKA**
Mr. Bruce Ramge
Director
Department of Insurance
941 O Street, Suite 400
Lincoln, NE 68508
P: (402) 471-2201
F: (402) 471-4610

**NEVADA**
Mr. Brett J. Barratt
Commissioner
Division of Insurance
Department of Buisness &
Industry
788 Fairview Drive, Suite 300
Carson City, NV 89701
P: (775) 687-0700
F: (775) 687-0787

**NEW HAMPSHIRE**
Mr. Roger A. Sevigny
Commissioner
Department of Insurance
21 South Fruit Street, Suite 14
Concord, NH 03301
P: (603) 271-7973
F: (603) 271-1406
E: roger.sevigny@ins.nh.gov

**NEW JERSEY**
Mr. Thomas B. Considine
Commissioner
Department of Banking &
Insurance
20 West State Street
P.O. Box 325
Trenton, NJ 08625
P: (609) 292-7272
F: (609) 663-3601
E: commissioner
@dobi.state.nj.us

**NEW MEXICO**
Mr. John G. Fanchini
Superintendent of Insurance
Insurance Division
Public Regulation Commission
P.O. Box 1269
Santa Fe, NM 87504
P: (505) 827-4601
F: (505) 827-4734

**NEW YORK**
Mr. James Wynn
Superintendent
Insurance Department
One Commerce Plaza
Albany, NY 12257
P: (518) 474-4567

**NORTH CAROLINA**
Hon. Wayne Goodwin (D)
Insurance Commissioner & State
Fire Marshal
Department of Insurance
430 North Salisbury Street
Raleigh, NC 27603
P: (919) 807-6750

**NORTH DAKOTA**
Hon. Adam Hamm (R)
Commissioner
Insurance Department
State Capitol, 5th Floor
600 East Boulevard Avenue
Bismarck, ND 58505
P: (701) 328-2440
F: (701) 328-4880
E: insurance@nd.gov

**NORTHERN MARIANA
ISLANDS**
Mr. Sixto Igisomar
Acting Secretary
Department of Commerce
Caller Box 10007
Saipan, MP 96950
P: (670) 664-3064
F: (670) 664-3067

**OHIO**
Hon. Mary Taylor (R)
Lieutenant Governor
Department of Insurance
77 South High Street, 30th Floor
Columbus, OH 43215
P: (614) 644-0935
F: (614) 466-9354

**OKLAHOMA**
Hon. John Doak
Insurance Commissioner
Insurance Department
3625 Northwest 56th, Suite 100
P.O. Box 53408
Oklahoma City, OK 73152
P: (405) 521-2828
F: (405) 521-6635

**OREGON**
Ms. Teresa Miller
Insurance Administrator
Insurance Division
P.O. Box 14480
350 Winter Street, Northeast
Salem, OR 97309
P: (503) 947-7980
F: (503) 378-4351
E: teresa.d.miller
@state.or.us

**PENNSYLVANIA**
Mr. Michael F. Consedine
Acting Insurance Commissioner
Insurance Department
13th Floor, Strawberry Square
Harrisburg, PA 17120
P: (717) 783-0442
F: (717) 772-1969

**PUERTO RICO**
Mr. Ramon Cruz-Colon
Commissioner
Office of the Insurance
Commissioner
B5 Tabonuco Street, Suite 216
PMB 356
Guaynabo, PR 00968
P: (787) 722-8686
F: (787) 273-6082

**RHODE ISLAND**
Mr. Joseph Torti III
Associate Director &
Superintendent
Department of Business
Regulation
Insurance Regulation Division
1511 Pontiac Avenue
Cranston, RI 02920
P: (401) 462-9520
F: (401) 462-9602
E: InsuranceInquiry
@dbr.state.ri.us

**SOUTH CAROLINA**
Mr. David Black
Director
Department of Insurance
1201 Main Street, Suite 1000
P.O. Box 100105
Columbia, SC 29202
P: (803) 737-6160
F: (803) 737-6205
E: info@doi.sc.gov

**SOUTH DAKOTA**
Mr. Merle Scheiber
Director
Division of Insurance
Department of Revenue &
Regulation
445 East Capitol Avenue
Pierre, SD 57501
P: (605) 773-3563
F: (605) 773-5369
E: insurance@state.sd.us

# STATE INSURANCE REGULATORS

**TENNESSEE**
Ms. Julie Mix McPeak
Commissioner
Department of Commerce &
Insurance
500 James Robertson Parkway
Davy Crockett Tower
Nashville, TN 37243
P: (615) 741-2176
F: (615) 532-6934
E: ask.tdci@tn.gov

**TEXAS**
Mr. Mike Geeslin
Commissioner of Insurance
Department of Insurance
333 Guadalupe
P.O. Box 149104
Austin, TX 78714
P: (512) 463-6468
F: (512) 475-2005

**U.S. VIRGIN ISLANDS**
Mr. John McDonald
Director
Division of Banking &
Insurance
#18 Kongens Gade
St. Thomas, VI 00802
P: (340) 774-7166
F: (340) 774-9458

**UTAH**
Mr. Neal Gooch
Commissioner
Department of Insurance
3110 State Office Building
Salt Lake City, UT 84114
P: (801) 538-3800
F: (801) 538-3829
E: ngooch@utah.gov

**VERMONT**
Mr. Steve Kimbell
Commissioner
Department of Banking,
Insurance, Securities & Health
Care Administration
89 Main Street
Montpelier, VT 05620
P: (802) 828-3301
F: (802) 828-3306
E: steve.kimbell
   @state.vt.us

**VIRGINIA**
Ms. Jacqueline K.
   Cunningham
Commissioner
Bureau of Insurance
State Corporation Commission
1300 East Main Street, P.O. Box
1157
Richmond, VA 23218
P: (804) 371-9741
F: (804) 371-9348

**WASHINGTON**
Hon. Mike Kreidler (D)
Commissioner
Office of the Insurance
Commissioner
302 Sid Snyder Avenue,
Southwest
Suite 200
Olympia, WA 98504
P: (360) 725-7000
E: askMike@oic.wa.gov

**WEST VIRGINIA**
Ms. Jane L. Cline
Commissioner
Insurance Commission
1124 Smith Street
Charleston, WV 25301
P: (304) 558-3029
F: (304) 558-0412
E: jane.cline
   @wvinsurance.gov

**WISCONSIN**
Mr. Ted Nickel
Commissioner
Office of the Commissioner of
Insurance
125 South Webster Street
Madison, WI 53703
P: (608) 266-3585
F: (608) 266-9935

**WYOMING**
Mr. Ken Vines
Commissioner of Insurance
Insurance Department
106 East 6th Avenue
Cheyenne, WY 82002
P: (307) 777-7401
F: (307) 777-2446

# SECRETARIES OF STATE

**ALABAMA**
Hon. Beth Chapman
Secretary of State
State House
P.O. Box 5616
Montgomery, AL 36103-5616
(334) 242-7200
FAX (334) 242-4993
www.sos.state.al.us/

**ALASKA**
Hon. Mead Treadwell
Lieutenant Governor
P.O. Box 110015
Juneau, AK 99811-0015
(907) 465-3520
FAX (907) 465-5400
ltgov.state.ak.us/

**AMERICAN SAMOA**
Hon. Faoa Sunia
Lieutenant Governor
Office of the Governor
Third Floor, Utulei
Pago Pago, AS 96799
(684) 633-4116
FAX (684) 633-2269
americansamoa.gov/

**ARIZONA**
Hon. Ken Bennett
Secretary of State
State Capitol, 7th fl.
1700 W. Washington
Phoenix, AZ 85007-2808
(602) 542-4285
FAX (602) 542-1575
www.azsos.gov/

**ARKANSAS**
Hon. Mark Martin
Secretary of State
256 State Capitol Building
Little Rock, AR 72201
(501) 682-1010
FAX (501) 682-3510
www.sos.arkansas.gov/

**CALIFORNIA**
Hon. Debra Bowen
Secretary of State
1500 11th Street
Sacramento, CA 95814
(916) 653-7244
FAX (916) 653-4795
www.sos.ca.gov/

**COLORADO**
Hon. Scott Gessler
Secretary of State
1700 Broadway, Suite 250
Denver, CO 80290
(303) 894-2200
FAX (303) 869-4860
www.sos.state.co.us/

**CONNECTICUT**
Hon. Denise Merrill
Secretary of State
State Capitol, Rm. 104
Hartford, CT 06105
(860) 509-6200
FAX (860) 509-6209
www.ct.gov/sots/

**DELAWARE**
Hon. Jeffrey Bullock
Secretary of State
Townsend Building
401 Federal St., Suite 3
Dover, DE 19901
(302) 739-4111
FAX (302) 739-3811
sos.delaware.gov/

**DISTRICT OF COLUMBIA**
Hon. Cynthia Brock-Smith
Secretary of the District
1350 Pennsylvania Ave. NW, Rm. 419
Washington, DC 20004
(202) 727-6306
FAX (202) 727-3582
os.dc.gov/

**FLORIDA**
Hon. Kurt Browning
Secretary of State
500 S. Bronough, Suite 100
Tallahassee, FL 32399
(850) 245-6500
FAX (850) 245-6125
www.dos.state.fl.us/

**GEORGIA**
Hon. Brian Kemp
Secretary of State
State Capitol, Rm. 214
Atlanta, GA 30334
(404) 656-2881
FAX (404) 656-0513
sos.georgia.gov/

**GUAM**
Hon. Ray Tenorio
Lieutenant Governor
P.O. Box 2950
Hagatna, GU 96932
(671) 474-9380 x9
FAX (671) 472-2007
www.guam.gov/

**HAWAII**
Hon. Brian Schatz
Lieutenant Governor
State Capitol, 5th fl.
Honolulu, HI 96813
(808) 586-0255
FAX (808) 586-0231
hawaii.gov/ltgov

**IDAHO**
Hon. Ben Ysursa
Secretary of State
State Capitol, Rm. 203
Boise, ID 83720
(208) 334-2300
FAX (208) 334-2282
www.sos.idaho.gov/

**ILLINOIS**
Hon. Jesse White
Secretary of State
213 State Capitol
Springfield, IL 62756
(217) 782-2201
FAX (217) 785-0358
www.cyberdriveillinois.com/

**INDIANA**
Hon. Charlie White
Secretary of State
201 State House
Indianapolis, IN 46204
(317) 232-6532
FAX (317) 233-3283
www.in.gov/sos/

**IOWA**
Hon. Matt Schultz
Secretary of State
State Capitol, Rm. 105
Des Moines, IA 50319
(515) 281-8993
FAX (515) 242-5952
www.sos.state.ia.us/

**KANSAS**
Hon. Kris Kobach

# SECRETARIES OF STATE

Secretary of State
120 SW 10th Ave.
Topeka, KS 66612
(785) 296-4575
FAX (785) 368-8033
www.kssos.org/main.html

## KENTUCKY
Hon. Elaine Walker
Secretary of State
700 Capital Ave., Rm. 152
Frankfort, KY 40601
(502) 564-3490
FAX (502) 564-5687
www.sos.ky.gov/

## LOUISIANA
Hon. Tom Schedler
Secretary of State
P.O. Box 94125
Baton Rouge, LA 70804
(225) 342-4479
FAX (225) 342-5577
www.sos.louisiana.gov/

## MAINE
Hon. Charles Summers
Secretary of State
148 State House Station
Augusta, ME 04333-0148
(207) 626-8400
FAX (207) 287-8598
www.state.me.us/sos/

## MARYLAND
Hon. John McDonough
Secretary of State
16 Francis Street
Annapolis, MD 21401
(410) 974-5521
FAX (410) 974-5527
www.sos.state.md.us/

## MASSACHUSETTS
Hon. William Galvin
Secretary of the Commonwealth
State House, Rm. 337
Boston, MA 02133
(617) 727-9180
FAX (617) 742-4722
www.sec.state.ma.us/sec/index.htm

## MICHIGAN
Hon. Ruth Johnson
Secretary of State
Treasury Building, 4th fl.
430 W. Allegan Street
Lansing, MI 48918
(517) 373-2510

FAX (517) 373-0727
www.michigan.gov/sos

## MINNESOTA
Hon. Mark Ritchie
Secretary of State
180 State Office Building
100 Rev. Dr. Martin Luther King
  Jr. Blvd.
St. Paul, MN 55155-1299
(651) 201-1328
FAX (651) 215-0682
www.sos.state.mn.us/

## MISSISSIPPI
Hon. C. Delbert Hosemann, Jr.
Secretary of State
P.O. Box 136
401 Mississippi St.
Jackson, MS 39205-0136
(601) 359-1350
FAX (601) 359-6700
www.sos.state.ms.gov/

## MISSOURI
Hon. Robin Carnahan
Secretary of State
State Capitol, Rm. 208
Jefferson City, MO 65101
(573) 751-4936
FAX (573) 552-3082
www.sos.mo.gov/

## MONTANA
Hon. Linda McCulloch
Secretary of State
P.O. Box 202801
Helena, MT 59620
(406) 444-2034
FAX (406) 444-4249
sos.mt.gov/

## NEBRASKA
Hon. John Gale
Secretary of State
State Capitol, Suite 2300
P.O. Box 94608
Lincoln, NE 68509-4608
(402) 471-2554
FAX (402) 471-3237
www.sos.state.ne.us/

## NEVADA
Hon. Ross Miller
Secretary of State
101 N. Carson St., Suite 3
Carson City, NV 89701
(775) 684-5708
FAX (775) 684-5724

nvsos.gov/

## NEW HAMPSHIRE
Hon. William Gardner
Secretary of State
State House, Rm. 204
Concord, NH 03301
(603) 271-3242
FAX (603) 271-6316
www.sos.nh.gov/index.html

## NEW JERSEY
Hon. Kim Guadagno
Lieutenant Governor
P.O. Box 300
Trenton, NJ 08625
(609) 777-2581
FAX (609) 777-1764
www.state.nj.us/state/index.html

## NEW MEXICO
Hon. Dianna Duran
Secretary of State
325 Don Gaspar, Suite 300
Santa Fe, NM 87503
(505) 827-3600
FAX (505) 827-3634
www.sos.state.nm.us/

## NEW YORK
Hon. Cesar Perales
Secretary of State
99 Washington Ave., Suite 1100
Albany, NY 12231
(518) 486-9844
FAX (518) 474-4765
www.dos.state.ny.us/

## NORTH CAROLINA
Hon. Elaine Marshall
Secretary of State
P.O. Box 29622
Raleigh, NC 27626-0622
(919) 807-2005
FAX (919) 807-2010
www.secstate.state.nc.us/

## NORTH DAKOTA
Hon. Alvin A. Jaeger
Secretary of State
600 East Boulevard, Dept. 108
Bismarck, ND 58505-0500
(701) 328-2900
FAX (701) 328-2992
www.nd.gov/sos

## OHIO
Hon. John Husted
Secretary of State

# SECRETARIES OF STATE

180 East Broad St.
Columbus, OH 43215
(614) 466-2655
FAX (614) 644-0649
ohio.gov/

## OKLAHOMA
Hon. Glenn Coffee
Secretary of State
State Capitol, Rm. 101
Oklahoma City, OK 73105
(405) 521-3912
FAX (405) 521-3771
www.sos.ok.gov/

## OREGON
Hon. Kate Brown
Secretary of State
136 State Capitol
Salem, OR 97301
(503) 986-1523
FAX (503) 986-1616
www.sos.state.or.us/

## PENNSYLVANIA
Hon. Carol Aichele
Acting Secretary of Commonwealth
302 North Capitol Building
Harrisburg, PA 17120
(717) 787-8727
FAX (717) 787-1734
www.dos.state.pa.us/

## PUERTO RICO
Hon. Kenneth McClintock
Secretary of State
Department of State
Box 9023271
San Juan, PR 00902-3271
(787) 722-4010
FAX (787) 722-2684
www.estado.gobierno.pr

## RHODE ISLAND
Hon. A. Ralph Mollis
Secretary of State
217 State House
Providence, RI 02903
(401) 222-1035
FAX (401) 222-1356
sos.ri.gov/

## SOUTH CAROLINA
Hon. Mark Hammond
Secretary of State
Edgar Brown Bldg., 5th fl.
P.O. Box 11350
Columbia, SC 29211
(803) 734-2170

FAX (803) 734-1661
www.scsos.com/

## SOUTH DAKOTA
Hon. Jason Gant
Secretary of State
500 E. Capitol Building, Suite 204
Pierre, SD 57501
(605) 773-3537
FAX (605) 773-6580
www.sdsos.gov/

## TENNESSEE
Hon. Tre Hargett
Secretary of State
First Floor, State Capitol
Nashville, TN 37243
(615) 741-2819
FAX (615) 741-5962
www.state.tn.us/sos/

## TEXAS
Hon. Esperanza "Hope" Andrade
Secretary of State
P.O. Box 12887
Austin, TX 78711-2887
(512) 463-5770
FAX (512) 475-2761
www.sos.state.tx.us/

## U.S. VIRGIN ISLANDS
Hon. Gregory R. Francis
Lieutenant Governor
18 Kongens Gade
St. Thomas, VI 00801
(340) 774-2991
FAX (340) 774-6953
ltg.gov.vi/

## UTAH
Hon. Greg Bell
Lieutenant Governor
220 State Capitol Building
Salt Lake City, UT 84114
(801) 538-1041
FAX (801) 538-1133
www.utah.gov/ltgovernor/

## VERMONT
Hon. Jim Condos
Secretary of State
128 State Street
Montpelier, VT 05633
(802) 828-2148
FAX (802) 828-2496
www.sec.state.vt.us/

## VIRGINIA
Hon. Janet Polarek

Secretary of Commonwealth
Capitol Square
P.O. Box 2454
Richmond, VA 23218
(804) 786-2441
FAX (804) 371-0017
www_commonwealth.virginia.gov/

## WASHINGTON
Hon. Sam Reed
Secretary of State
P.O. Box 40220
Olympia, WA 98504-0220
(360) 902-4151
FAX (360) 586-5629
www.sos.wa.gov/

## WEST VIRGINIA
Hon. Natalie Tennant
Secretary of State
Building 1, Suite 157K
1900 Kanawha Blvd., E.
Charleston, WV 25305
(304) 558-6000
FAX (304) 558-0900
www.sos.wv.gov/

## WISCONSIN
Hon. Douglas La Follette
Secretary of State
P.O. Box 7848
Madison, WI 53707
(608) 266-8888
FAX (608) 266-3159
www.sos.state.wi.us/

## WYOMING
Hon. Max Maxfield
Secretary of State
State Capitol Building
200 West 24th
Cheyenne, WY 82002
(307) 777-7378
FAX (307) 777-6217
soswy.state.wy.us/

# STATE CORPORATE RECORDS

# Corporate Records

**Maintains a variety of corporate filings, records and documents.**

## ALABAMA
Ms. Sharon Staton
Corporations Director
Corporations Division
RSA Union Building , Suite 770
100 North Union Street
Montgomery, AL 36103
P: (334) 242-5328
F: (334) 240-3138
E: Sharon.Staton
  @sos.alabama.gov

## ALASKA
Mr. Don Habeger
Director
Division of Corporations,
Business & Professional
Licensing
P.O. Box 110806
Juneau, AK 99811
P: (907) 465-2534
F: (907) 465-2974
E: don.habeger@alaska.gov

## AMERICAN SAMOA
Mr. Faleseu Eliu Paopao
Director
Department of Commerce
American Samoa Government
Executive Office Building,
Utulei
Pago Pago, AS 96799
P: (684) 633-5155
F: (684) 633-4195

## ARIZONA
Mr. Jeff Grant
Director
Corporations Division
Corporation Commission
1300 West Washington Street,
1st Floor
Phoenix, AZ 85007
P: (602) 542-3026
F: (602) 542-0900
E: director.corp@azcc.gov

## ARKANSAS
Hon. Mark Martin (R)
Secretary of State
Office of the Secretary of State
256 State Capitol Building
Little Rock, AR 72201
P: (501) 682-1010
F: (501) 682-3510
E: sos@sos.arkansas.gov

## CALIFORNIA
Ms. Betsy Bogart
Chief
Business Programs Division
1500 11th Street
Sacramento, CA 95814
P: (916) 653-6973

## COLORADO
Mr. Michael Hardin
Business Director
Department of State, Business
Division
1560 Broadway, Suite 200
Denver, CO 80202
P: (303) 894-2200
F: (303) 869-4864
E: michael.hardin
  @sos.state.co.us

## CONNECTICUT
Hon. Denise W. Merrill (D)
Secretary of State
Office of the Secretary of State
State Capitol, Room 104
Hartford, CT 06105
P: (860) 509-6200
F: (860) 509-6209
E: denise.merrill@ct.gov

## DELAWARE
Mr. Robert Mathers
Administrator
Division of Corporations
401 Federal Street, Suite 4
P.O. Box 898
Dover, DE 19903
P: (302) 857-3456
F: (302) 739-3812

## DISTRICT OF COLUMBIA
Mr. Nicholas A. Majett
Director
Department of Consumer &
Regulatory Affairs
1100 4th Street, Southwest
Washington, DC 20024
P: (202) 442-4400
F: (202) 442-9445
E: dcra@dc.gov

## FLORIDA
Mr. Jay Kassees
Director
Division of Corporations
Clifton Building
2661 Executive Center Circle
Tallahassee, FL 32301
P: (850) 245-6000
E: jkassees@dos.state.fl.us

## GEORGIA
Mr. Chauncey Newsome
Director
Corporations Division
2 Martin Luther King Jr. Drive
Southeast
Suite 315, Floyd West Tower ·
Atlanta, GA 30334
P: (404) 656-2817
F: (404) 657-2248

## GUAM
Mr. Juan Carlos
Administrator
Department of Revenue &
Taxation
Regulatory Division
P.O. Box 23607
GMF, GU 96921
P: (671) 635-1846
E: jqcarlos@revtax.gov.gu

## HAWAII
Ms. Keali'i S. Lopez
Director
Department of Commerce &
Consumer Affairs
King Kalakaua Building
335 Merchant Street
Honolulu, HI 96813
P: (808) 586-2850
F: (808) 586-2856
E: dcca@dcca.hawaii.gov

## IDAHO
Kim Hunter
Supervisor
Business Entity Division
450 North 4th Street
Boise, ID 83702
P: (208) 334-2301
F: (208) 334-2080
E: khunter@sos.idaho.gov

## ILLINOIS
Mr. Robert Durchholz
Administrator
Corporation Division
Howlett Building, Room 350
501 South 2nd Street
Springfield, IL 62756
P: (217) 782-4909

## INDIANA
Hon. Charlie White (R)
Secretary of State
Office of the Secretary of State
201 State House
Indianapolis, IN 46204
P: (317) 232-6532
F: (317) 233-3283
E: sos@sos.in.gov

## IOWA
Hon. Matt Schultz (R)
Secretary of State
Office of the Secretary of State
State Capitol, Room 105
1007 East Grand Avenue
Des Moines, IA 50319
P: (515) 281-8993
F: (515) 242-5952
E: sos@sos.state.ia.us

## KENTUCKY
Ms. Gail Hance
Assistant Director of
Corporations
Office of the Secretary of State
700 Capitol Avenue, Suite 152
Frankfort, KY 40601
P: (502) 564-3490
F: (502) 564-5687

## LOUISIANA
Hon. Tom Schedler (R)
Secretary of State
Office of Secretary of State
P.O. Box 94125
Baton Rouge, LA 70804
P: (225) 342-4479
F: (225) 342-5577

## MAINE
Ms. Julie L. Flynn
Deputy Secretary of State
Bureau of Corporation,
Elections & Commissions
101 State House Station
Augusta, ME 04333
P: (207) 624-7736
F: (207) 287-5874

## MARYLAND
Mr. C. John Sullivan Jr.
Director
Department of Assessments &
Taxation
300 West Preston Street, Room
605
Baltimore, MD 21201
P: (410) 767-1184
F: (410) 333-5873

## MASSACHUSETTS
Hon. William Francis
  Galvin (D)
Secretary of the Commonwealth
Office of the Secretary of the
Commonwealth
220 Morrissey Blvd.
Boston, MA 02125
P: (617) 727-2816
F: (617) 288-8429
E: cis@sec.state.ma.us

# STATE CORPORATE RECORDS

**MICHIGAN**
Mr. Steven Hilfinger
Director
Department of Licensing &
Regualtory Affairs
P.O. Box 30004
Lansing, MI 48909
P: (517) 373-1820
F: (517) 373-2129
E: bcslic@michigan.gov

**MINNESOTA**
Hon. Mark Ritchie (DFL)
Secretary of State
Office of the Secretary of State
180 State Office Building
100 Martin Luther King Jr.
Boulevard
St. Paul, MN 55155
P: (651) 201-1328
F: (651) 215-0682
E: secretary.state
   @state.mn.us

**MISSISSIPPI**
Mr. Thomas Riley
Assistant Secretary of State
Business Services Division
P.O. Box 136
Jackson, MS 39205
P: (601) 359-1350
F: (601) 359-1499

**MISSOURI**
Ms. Carol Fischer
Deputy Secretary of State for
Business Services
Business Services
Kirkpatrick State Information
Center
P.O. Box 778
Jefferson City, MO 65102
P: (573) 751-4153
F: (573) 526-3124
E: cfisher
   @mail.dor.state.mo.us

**MONTANA**
Hon. Linda McCulloch (D)
Secretary of State
Office of the Secretary of State
P.O. Box 202801
Helena, MT 59620
P: (406) 444-2034
F: (406) 444-4249
E: sos@mt.gov

**NEBRASKA**
Hon. John A. Gale (R)
Secretary of State
Office of the Secretary of State
P.O. Box 94608
Lincoln, NE 68509
P: (402) 471-2554
F: (402) 471-3237
E: secretaryofstate
   @nebraska.gov

**NEVADA**
Hon. Ross Miller (D)
Secretary of State
Office of the Secretary of State
101 North Carson Street, Suite 3
Carson City, NV 89701
P: (775) 684-5708
F: (775) 684-5724
E: sosmail@sos.nv.gov

**NEW HAMPSHIRE**
Hon. William M. Gardner (D)
Secretary of State
Office of the Secretary of State
State House, Room 204
Concord, NH 03301
P: (603) 271-3242
F: (603) 271-6316
E: kladd@sos.state.nh.us

**NEW JERSEY**
Mr. James J. Fruscione
Director
Division of Revenue
P.O. Box 628
Trenton, NJ 08646
P: (609) 984-3997

**NEW MEXICO**
Hon. Dianna J. Duran (R)
Secretary of State
Office of the Secretary of State
325 Don Gaspar, Suite 300
Capitol Annex
Santa Fe, NM 87503
P: (505) 827-3600
F: (505) 827-3634
E: diannaj.duran
   @state.nm.us

Ms. Ann Echols
Bureau Chief
Corporations Bureau
Public Regulation Commission
P.O. Box 1269
Santa Fe, NM 87504
P: (505) 827-4502
F: (505) 827-4387

**NEW YORK**
Ms. Sandra J. Tallman
Acting Director
Division of Corporations, State
Records & Uniform
Commercial Code
99 Washington Avenue, 6th
Floor
Albany, NY 12231
P: (518) 473-2281
F: (518) 474-1418

**NORTH CAROLINA**
Ms. Cheri Myers
Director
Department of the Secretary of
State
Corporations Division
2 South Salisbury Street
Raleigh, NC 27601
P: (919) 807-2225
F: (919) 807-2039
E: corpinfo@sosnc.com

**NORTH DAKOTA**
Ms. Clara Jenkins
Director, Central Indexing
Office of the Secretary of State
600 East Boulevard Avenue
Department 108, 1st Floor
Bismarck, ND 58505
P: (701) 328-3662
F: (701) 328-2992
E: cjenkins@nd.gov

**OHIO**
Hon. Jon Husted (R)
Secretary of State
Office of the Secretary of State
180 East Broad Street
Columbus, OH 43215
P: (614) 466-2655
F: (614) 644-0649
E: jhusted@sos.state.oh.us

**OREGON**
Mr. Peter Threlkel
Director
Secretary of State, Corporation
Division
Public Service Building
255 Capitol Street, Northeast,
Suite 151
Salem, OR 97310
P: (503) 986-2200
F: (503) 986-6355
E: peter.threlkel
   @state.or.us

**PENNSYLVANIA**
Mr. Richard K. House
Director
Corporation Bureau
401 North Street, Room 206
Harrisburg, PA 17120
P: (717) 787-1057
F: (717) 783-2244
E: RA-CORPS@state.pa.us

**RHODE ISLAND**
Hon. A. Ralph Mollis (D)
Secretary of State
Office of the Secretary of State
82 Smith Street
217 State House
Providence, RI 02903
P: (401) 222-1035
F: (401) 222-1356
E: armollis@sos.ri.gov

**SOUTH CAROLINA**
Hon. Mark Hammond (R)
Secretary of State
Office of the Secretary of State
P.O. Box 11350
Columbia, SC 29211
P: (803) 734-2170
F: (803) 734-1661
E: rdaggerhart@sos.sc.gov

**SOUTH DAKOTA**
Hon. Jason M. Gant (R)
Secretary of State
Office of the Secretary of State
500 East Capitol Avenue, Suite
204
Pierre, SD 57501
P: (605) 773-3537
F: (605) 773-6580
E: sdsos@state.sd.us

**TENNESSEE**
Mr. Nathan Burton
Director
Division of Business Services
312 Rosa L. Parks Avenue
Snodgrass Tower, 6th Floor
Nashville, TN 37243
P: (615) 741-2286
F: (615) 741-7310
E: business.services
   @state.tn.us

# STATE CORPORATE RECORDS

**TEXAS**
Ms. Lorna Wassdorf
Division Director
Business & Public Fillings
Division
Capitol Building, Rm. 1E.8
1100 Congress Avenue, P.O. Box
12697
Austin, TX 78711
P: (512) 463-5591
F: (512) 463-5709
E: lwassdorf
    @sos.state.tx.us

**U.S. VIRGIN ISLANDS**
Mr. John McDonald
Director
Division of Banking &
Insurance
#18 Kongens Gade
St. Thomas, VI 00802
P: (340) 774-7166
F: (340) 774-9458

**UTAH**
Ms. Kathy Berg
Director
Division of Corporations &
Commericial Code
160 East 300 South, 2nd Floor
Salt Lake City, UT 84111
P: (801) 530-6216
F: (801) 530-6438
E: kberg@utah.gov

**VERMONT**
Ms. Betty Poulin
Director
Corporations Division
Redstone Building
26 Terrace Street
Montpelier, VT 05609
P: (802) 828-2386
F: (802) 828-2853
E: bpoulin@sec.state.vt.us

**VIRGINIA**
Mr. Joel Peck
Clerk
State Corporation Commission
State Corporation Commission
Tyler Building, 1300 East Main
Street
Richmond, VA 23219
P: (804) 371-9733
F: (804) 371-9521
E: joel.peck
    @scc.virginia.gov

**WASHINGTON**
Hon. Sam Reed (R)
Secretary of State
Office of the Secretary of State
P.O. Box 40220
Olympia, WA 98504
P: (360) 902-4151
F: (360) 586-5629
E: sam.reed@sos.wa.gov

**WISCONSIN**
Ms. Jennifer Acker
Director
Corporations Bureau
P.O. Box 7846
Madison, WI 53707
P: (608) 261-7577
F: (608) 267-6813
E: Jennifer.Acker
    @dfi.wisconsin.gov

**WYOMING**
Hon. Max Maxfield (R)
Secretary of State
Office of the Secretary of State
State Capitol Building
200 West 24th
Cheyenne, WY 82002
P: (307) 777-7378
F: (307) 777-6217
E: Secofstate@state.wy.us

# STATE SECURITIES ADMINISTRATORS
## (including Canada and Mexico)

**ALABAMA**
Mr. Joseph P. Borg, Esq.
Director
Securities Commission
401 Adams Ave., 2nd fl.
Montgomery, AL 36130
(334) 242-2984; (800) 222-1253
www.asc.state.al.us/

**ALASKA**
Ms. Lorie Hovanec
Director
Department of Community and
　Economic Development
Division of Banking, Securities, &
　Corporations
150 Third Street, Room 217
P.O. Box 110807
Juneau, AK 99811-0807
(907) 465-2521
www.dced.state.ak.us/bsc/secur.htm

**ALBERTA**
Ms. Glenda Campbell
Vice-Chair
Securities Commission
Suite 600, 250 - 5th Street SW
Calgary, Alberta
T2P 0R4 Canada
(403) 297-6454
www.albertasecurities.com/

**ARIZONA**
Mr. Matthew J. Neubert
Director of Securities
Corporation Commission
Securities Division
1300 West Washington Street, 3rd fl.
Phoenix, AZ 85007
(602) 542-4242
www.ccsd.cc.state.az.us/

**ARKANSAS**
Mr. Heath Abshure
Securities Commissioner
201 E. Markham, Rm. 300
Little Rock, AR 72201-1692
(501) 324-9260
www.securities.arkansas.gov/

**BRITISH COLUMBIA**
Ms. Brenda Leong
Chair
Securities Commission
701 West Georgia Street
Vancouver, British Columbia
V7Y 1L2 Canada
(604) 899-6500
www.bcsc.bc.ca

**CALIFORNIA**
Mr. Preston DuFauchard
Corporations Commissioner
Department of Corporations
1515 K Street, Suite 200
Sacramento, CA 95814
(916) 445-7205
www.corp.ca.gov/

**COLORADO**
Mr. Fred J. Joseph
Securities Commissioner
Division of Securities
1560 Broadway Street, Suite 900
Denver, CO 80202
(303) 894-2320
www.dora.state.co.us/securities/

**CONNECTICUT**
Eric Wilder
Acting Director of Securities
Department of Banking
260 Constitution Plaza
Hartford, CT 06103-1800
(860) 240-8230
www.ct.gov/dob/

**DELAWARE**
Mr. Peter Jamison
Securities Commissioner
Department of Justice
Division of Securities
820 North French Street, 5th fl.
Wilmington, DE 19801
(302) 577-8424
www.state.de.us/securities/

**DISTRICT OF COLUMBIA**
Mr. Theodore A. Miles
Assoc. Commissioner, Securities
Department of Insurance and Securities
　Regulation
Securities Bureau
810 First Street NE., Suite 622
Washington, DC 20002
(202) 442-7800

www.disr.washingtondc.gov

**FLORIDA**
Mr. Franklin Widmann
Director, Div. of Securities
Office of Financial Regulation
200 East Gaines Street
Tallahassee, FL 32399-0372
(850) 410-9500
www.flofr.com/

**GEORGIA**
Mr. Vincent Russo
Interim Asst. Securities Commissioner
Office of the Secretary of State
Division of Business Services &
　Regulation
237 Coliseum Drive
Macon, GA 31217-3858
(404) 656-3920
sos.georgia.gov/securities/

**HAWAII**
Ms. Tung Chan
Commissioner of Securities
Department of Commerce & Consumer
　Affairs
Division of Business Registration
335 Merchant Street, Rm. 203
Honolulu, HI 96813
(808) 586-2744
hawaii.gov/dcca/sec

**IDAHO**
Ms. Marilyn T. Chastain
Securities Bureau Chief
Department of Finance
800 Park Blvd., Suite 200
Boise, ID 83712
(208) 332-8004
finance.idaho.gov/

**ILLINOIS**
Ms. Tanya Solov
Director of Securities
Office of the Secretary of State
Securities Department
69 West Washington Street, Suite 1220
Chicago, IL 60602
(312) 793-3384
www.cyberdriveillinois.com/
　departments/securities/

# STATE SECURITIES ADMINISTRATORS

**INDIANA**
Mr. Chris Naylor
Securities Commissioner
Office of the Secretary of State
Securities Division
302 West Washington, Rm. E-111
Indianapolis, IN 46204
(317) 232-6681
www.in.gov/sos/securities/

**IOWA**
Mr. Jim Mumford
Securities Administrator
Insurance Division
Securities Bureau
340 E. Maple Street
Des Moines, IA 50319-0066
(515) 281-4441
www.iid.state.ia.us/securities

**KANSAS**
Mr. Aaron Jack
Commissioner
Office of the Securities Commissioner
109 SW 9th St., Suite 600
Topeka, KS 66603-3804
(785) 296-3307
www.securities.state.ks.us

**KENTUCKY**
Ms. Shonita Bossier
Director, Div. of Securities
Department of Financial Institutions
1025 Capital Center Drive, Suite 200
Frankfort, KY 40601
(502) 573-3390; (800) 223-2579
www.kfi.ky.gov

**LOUISIANA**
Ms. Rhonda Reeves
Deputy Securities Commissioner
Securities Commission
Office of Financial Institutions
8660 United Plaza Blvd., 2nd fl.
Baton Rouge, LA 70809-7024
(225) 925-4512
www.ofi.louisiana.gov/

**MAINE**
Ms. Judith Shaw
Securities Administrator
Securities Division
State House Station 121
Augusta, ME 04333
(207) 624-8551
www.state.me.us/pfr/sec/
  sec_index.htm

**MANITOBA**
Mr. Donald G. Murray
Chairman
Securities Commission
500-400 St. Mary Ave.
Winnipeg, Manitoba
R3C 4K5 Canada
(204) 945-2548
www.msc.gov.mb.ca/

**MARYLAND**
Ms. Melanie Senter Lubin
Securities Commissioner
Office of the Attorney General
Division of Securities
200 Saint Paul Place
Baltimore, MD 21202-2020
(410) 576-6360
www.oag.state.md.us/securities/

**MASSACHUSETTS**
Mr. Bryan Lantagne
Director
Securities Division
One Ashburton Place, Room 1701
Boston, MA 02108
(617) 727-3548
www.sec.state.ma.us/sct/sctidx.htm

**MEXICO**
Ms. Angelica Gonzalez-Saravia
Vice President, International Affairs
Comision Nacional Bancaria y de
  Valores
Direccion General de Asuntos Int'l
Av. Insurgentes Sur 1971
Torre Sur, Piso 8
Plaza Inn, Col. Guadalupe Inn, C.P.
01020 Mexico
011 (52) 55-1454-6020
www.cnbv.gob.mx

**MICHIGAN**
Mr. Ken Ross
Commissioner
Conduct Review & Securities Division
Office of Financial & Insurance
  Services
Dept. of Labor & Economic Growth
611 West Ottawa, 3rd fl.
Lansing, MI 48933
(877) 999-6442
www.michigan.gov/ofis

**MINNESOTA**
Mr. Mike Rothman
Commissioner
Department of Commerce
85 East 7th Place, Suite 500

St. Paul, MN 55101
(651) 296-4026
www.state.mn.us/portal/mn/jsp/
  home.do?agency=Commerce

**MISSISSIPPI**
Ms. Tanya Webber
Assistant Secretary of State
Office of the Secretary of State
Business Regulation & Enforcement
  Division
700 North Street
Jackson, MS 39202
(601) 359-9055
www.sos.ms.gov/

**MISSOURI**
Mr. Matt Kitzi
Securities Commissioner
Office of the Secretary of State
600 West Main Street
Jefferson City, MO 65101
(573) 751-4136
www.sos.mo.gov/securities/

**MONTANA**
Ms. Lynne Egan
Deputy Securities Commissioner
Office of the State Auditor
Securities Department
840 Helena Avenue
Helena, MT 59601
(406) 444-2040
sao.mt.gov/securities/index.asp

**NEBRASKA**
Mr. Jack E. Herstein
Assistant Director
Department of Banking & Finance
Commerce Court
1230 "O" Street, Suite 400
P.O. Box 95006
Lincoln, NE 68509-5006
(402) 471-3445
www.ndbf.ne.gov/index.shtml

**NEVADA**
Ms. Carolyn Ellsworth
Securities Administrator
Secretary of State
Securities Division
555 E. Washington Ave., Suite 5200
Las Vegas, NV 89101
(702) 486-2440
nvsos.gov/index.aspx?page=6

**NEW BRUNSWICK**
Mr. Rick Hancox
Executive Director

# STATE SECURITIES ADMINISTRATORS

Department of Justice
Securities Administration Branch
85 Charlotte St., Suite 300
St. John, New Brunswick
E2L 2J2 Canada
(506) 658-3060
www.nbsc-cvmnb.ca/nbsc/

## NEWFOUNDLAND / LABRADOR
Mr. Winston Morris
Superintendent of Securities
Financial Services Regulation Division
P.O. Box 8700
St. Johns, Newfoundland
A1B 4J6 Canada
(709) 729-4189
www.gs.gov.nl.ca/

## NEW HAMPSHIRE
Mr. Joseph Long
Director of Securities Regulation
Bureau of Securities Regulation
State House Annex, Suite 317A
Concord, NH 03302
(603) 271-1463
www.sos.nh.gov/securities/

## NEW JERSEY
Ms. Abbe Tiger
Bureau Chief
Department of Law & Public Safety
Bureau of Securities
153 Halsey Street, 6th fl.
Newark, NJ 07102
(973) 504-3600
www.njconsumeraffairs.gov/bos/

## NEW MEXICO
Mr. Daniel Tanaka
Director of Securities
Regulation and Licensing Department
Securities Division
2550 Cerrillos Road
Santa Fe, NM 87505
(505) 476-4580
www.rld.state.nm.us/Securities/
   index.html

## NEW YORK
Mr. Marc Minor
Bureau Chief
Office of the Attorney General
Investor Protection Bureau
120 Broadway, 23rd fl.
New York, NY 10271
(212) 416-8222
www.ag.ny.gov/bureaus/investor_
   protection/about.html

## NORTH CAROLINA
Mr. David S. Massey
Deputy Securities Administrator
Department of the Secretary of State
Securities Division
2 South Salisbury Street
Raleigh, NC 27601
(919) 733-3924
www.secretary.state.nc.us/sec/

## NORTH DAKOTA
Ms. Karen Tyler
Commissioner
Securities Commission
600 E. Boulevard, 5th fl.
Bismarck, ND 58505-0510
(701) 328-2910
www.ndsecurities.com

## NORTHWEST TERRITORIES
Gary MacDougall
Superintendent of Securities
Department of Justice
5009 - 49th Street, 1st fl.
Yellowknife, Northwest Territories
X1A 2L9 Canada
(867) 873-7490
www.gov.nt.ca/

## NOVA SCOTIA
Mr. H. Leslie O'Brien
Vice-Chair
Securities Commission
1690 Hollis Street, 2nd fl.
Halifax, Nova Scotia
B3J 3J9 Canada
(902) 424-7768
www.gov.ns.ca/nssc

## NUNAVUT
Mr. Louis Arki
Director
Department of Justice
Legal Registries Division
P.O. Box 1000 - Station 570
1st fl., Brown Bldg.
Iqaluit, NU X0A 0H0
Canada
(867) 975-6590
www.gov.nu.ca

## OHIO
Ms. Andrea Seidt
Commissioner
Division of Securities
77 South High Street, 22nd fl.
Columbus, OH 43215
(614) 644-7381
www.com.ohio.gov/secu/

## OKLAHOMA
Mr. Irving Faught
Administrator
Department of Securities
120 N. Robinson, Suite 860
Oklahoma City, OK 73102
(405) 280-7700
www.securities.ok.us/

## ONTARIO
Ms. Kathryn Daniels
Deputy Director of Enforcement
Securities Commission
20 Queen Street West, Suite 190
Toronto, Ontario
M5H 3S8 Canada
(416) 593-8314
www.osc.gov.on.ca

## OREGON
Mr. David Tatman
Division Administrator
Department of Consumer and Business
   Services
Division of Finance and
   Corporate Securities
350 Winter Street NE, Rm. 410
Salem, OR 97301-3881
(503) 378-4140
www.cbs.state.or.us/external/dfcs

## PENNSYLVANIA
Mr. Steven D. Irwin
Commissioner
Securities Commission
1010 North 7th Street, 2nd fl.
Harrisburg, PA 17102-1410
(717) 787-8061
www.psc.state.pa.us/

## PRINCE EDWARD ISLAND
Mr. Steve Dowling
Corporate Counsel
Office of the Attorney General
95 Rochford Street, 4th fl.
Charlottetown, Prince Edward Island
C1A 7N8 Canada
(902) 368-4551
www.gov.pe.ca/jps/ccaid-
   info/dg.inc.php3

## PUERTO RICO
Mr. Asdrubal Aponte
Director of Enforcement
Commission of Financial Institutions
1492 Ponce de Leon Avenue, Suite 600

# STATE SECURITIES ADMINISTRATORS

San Juan, PR 00907
(787) 723-3131 x2222
www.cif.gov.pr/index_eng.html

## QUEBEC
Mr. Jean Lorrain
Director, International Affairs
  Regulation Directorate
Autorite des Marches Financiers
800 Square Victoria, 22nd fl.
Montreal, Quebec
H4Z 1G3 Canada
(514) 395-0337
www.lautorite.qc.ca/en/corpo-en.html

## RHODE ISLAND
Ms. Maria D'Alessandro
Associate Director & Superintendent of
  Securities
Department of Business Regulation
1511 Pontiac Ave.
Providence, RI 02903-4232
(401) 462-9527
www.dbr.state.ri.us

## SASKATCHEWAN
Ms. Barbara Shourounis
Director
Securities Commission
800-1920 Broad Street
Regina, Saskatchewan
S4P 3V7 Canada
(306) 787-5645
www.sfsc.gov.sk.ca/ssc/

## SOUTH CAROLINA
Mr. T. Stephen Lynch
Deputy Securities Commissioner
Office of the Attorney General
Securities Division
1000 Assembly Street
Columbia, SC 29201
(803) 734-4731
www.scag.gov/

## SOUTH DAKOTA
Mr. Michael Youngberg
Director
Division of Securities
445 East Capitol Avenue
Pierre, SD 57501-2000
(605) 773-4823
www.state.sd.us/drr2/reg/
  securities/index.htm

## TENNESSEE
Ms. Daphne D. Smith
Assistant Commissioner for Securities
Department of Commerce and Insurance

Securities Division
500 James Robertson Pkwy., Suite 680
Nashville, TN 37243-0575
(615) 741-2947
tn.gov/commerce/securities/index.shtml

## TEXAS
Mr. Benette Zivley
Securities Commissioner
State Securities Board
208 E. 10th Street, 5th fl.
Austin, TX 78701
(512) 305-8300
www.ssb.state.tx.us/

## UTAH
Mr. Keith Woodwell
Director
Department of Commerce
Division of Securities
160 East 300 South, 2nd fl.
Salt Lake City, UT 84111
(801) 530-6600
www.securities.state.ut.us

## VERMONT
Mr. Thomas Candon
Deputy Commissioner of Securities
Department of Banking, Insurance,
  Securities & Health Care
  Administration
89 Main Street, Drawer 20
Montpelier, VT 05620-3101
(802) 828-3420
www.bishca.state.vt.us/

## VIRGINIA
Mr. Ronald W. Thomas
Director
State Corporation Commission
Division of Securities & Retail
  Franchising
1300 E. Main Street, 9th fl.
Richmond, VA 23219
(804) 371-9051
www.scc.virginia.gov/srf/index.aspx

## WASHINGTON
Mr. William Beatty
Director of Securities
Department of Financial Institutions
Securities Division
150 Israel Rd. SW
Tumwater, WA 98501
(360) 902-8760
www.dfi.wa.gov/sd

## WEST VIRGINIA
Ms. Lisa Hopkins
Senior Deputy Commissioner of
  Securities
Office of the State Auditor
Securities Division
Building 1, Room W-100
Charleston, WV 25305-0230
(304) 558-2257
www.wvsao.gov/securitiescommission/

## WISCONSIN
Ms. Patricia D. Struck
Administrator
Department of Financial Institutions
Division of Securities
345 W. Washington Ave., 4th fl.
Madison, WI 53703
(608) 266-1064
www.wdfi.org/fi/securities/

## WYOMING
Ms. Karen Wheeler
Division Director
Secretary of State
Securities Division
200 W. 24th Street, Rm. 109
Cheyenne, WY 82002-0020
(307) 777-7370
soswy.state.wy.us/

## YUKON TERRITORIES
Mr. Frederick Pretorius
Superintendent of Securities
Department of Justice
P.O. Box 2703
Corporate Affairs J-9
Whitehorse, Yukon Territories
Y1A 2C6 Canada
(867) 667-5314
www.gov.yk.ca

# STATE REVENUE COMMISSIONERS

## Revenue

Administers state tax laws and the collection and processing of state taxes.

### ALABAMA
Ms. Julie P. McGee
Commissioner
Department of Revenue
50 North Ripley Street
Montgomery, AL 36132
P: (334) 242-1170
F: (334) 242-0550

### ALASKA
Mr. Bryan Butcher
Commissioner
Department of Revenue
550 West 7th Avenue, Suite 1820
Juneau, AK 99501
P: (907) 465-2301
F: (907) 465-2389
E: bryan.butcher@alaska.gov

### AMERICAN SAMOA
Hon. Magalei Logovi'i
Treasurer
Department of the Treasury
American Samoa Government
Pago Pago, AS 96799
P: (684) 633-4155
F: (684) 633-4100

### ARIZONA
Mr. Gale Garriott
Director
Department of Revenue
1600 West Monroe
Phoenix, AZ 85007
P: (602) 716-6090
F: (602) 542-2072
E: ggarriott@azdor.gov

### ARKANSAS
Mr. John H. Theis
Assistant Commissioner of Revenue
Department of Finance & Administration
P.O. Box 1272
Little Rock, AR 72203
P: (501) 682-7000
F: (501) 682-1161
E: john.theis
@rev.state.ar.us

### CALIFORNIA
Mr. Selvi Stanislaus
Executive Officer
Franchise Tax Board
P.O. Box 1468
Sacramento, CA 95812
P: (916) 845-4543
F: (916) 845-3191

### COLORADO
Ms. Roxy Huber
Executive Director
Department of Revenue
1375 Sherman Street
Denver, CO 80261
P: (303) 866-5610
F: (303) 866-2400

### CONNECTICUT
Mr. Kevin B. Sullivan
Commissioner
Department of Revenue
25 Sigourney Street, Suite 2
Hartford, CT 06106
P: (860) 297-5612
F: (860) 297-5698

### DELAWARE
Mr. Patrick T. Carter
Director
Division of Revenue
820 North French Street, 8th Floor
Wilmington, DE 19801
P: (302) 577-8686
F: (302) 577-8656
E: patrick.carter
@state.de.us

### DISTRICT OF COLUMBIA
Mr. Stephen M. Cordi
Deputy Chief Financial Officer
Office of Tax & Revenue
1101 4th Street, Southwest, Suite W270
Suite 203
Washington, DC 20024
P: (202) 727-4829
F: (202) 727-1643
E: stephen.cordi@dc.gov

### FLORIDA
Ms. Lisa Vickers
Executive Director
Department of Revenue
5050 West Tennessee Street
Tallahassee, FL 32399
P: (850) 617-8600
E: vickersl@dor.state.fl.us

### GEORGIA
Mr. Doug MacGinnite
Commissioner
Department of Revenue
1800 Century Center Boulevard
Suite 15300
Atlanta, GA 30345
P: (404) 417-2100
F: (404) 417-2101

### GUAM
Mr. Artemio B. Ilagan
Director
Department of Revenue & Taxation
P.O. Box 23607
GMF, GU 96921
P: (671) 635-1835
F: (671) 633-2643
E: ilagan@revtax.gov.gu

### HAWAII
Mr. Frederick D. Pablo
Director
Department of Taxation
Princess Ruth Keelikolani Building
830 Punchbowl Street
Honolulu, HI 96813
P: (808) 587-1510
F: (808) 587-1560
E: Tax.Directors.Office
@hawaii.gov

### IDAHO
Mr. Robert L. Geddes
Chair
Tax Commission
P.O. Box 36
Boise, ID 83722
P: (208) 334-7660
E: robert.geddes
@tax.idaho.gov

### ILLINOIS
Mr. Brian A. Hamer
Director of Revenue
Department of Revenue
Willard Ice Building
101 West Jefferson Street
Springfield, IL 62794
P: (217) 785-7570
F: (217) 782-6337

### INDIANA
Mr. John Eckart
Commissioner
Department of Revenue
100 North Senate Avenue, Room N248
Indianapolis, IN 46204
P: (317) 232-8039
F: (317) 232-2103
E: jeckart@dor.in.gov

### IOWA
Ms. Courtney M. Kay-Decker
Director
Department of Revenue
Hoover State Office Building
1305 East Walnut Street
Des Moines, IA 50319
P: (515) 281-3204
E: courtney.decker@iowa.gov

### KANSAS
Mr. Nick Jordan
Secretary
Department of Revenue
Docking State Office Building, Room 230
915 Southwest Harrison Street
Topeka, KS 66612
P: (785) 296-3909
F: (785) 296-7928

### KENTUCKY
Mr. Thomas B. Miller
Commissioner
Department of Revenue
501 High Street
Frankfort, KY 40620
P: (502) 564-3226
F: (502) 564-3875

### LOUISIANA
Ms. Cynthia Bridges
Secretary
Department of Revenue
1702 North 3rd Street
P.O. Box 94214
Baton Rouge, LA 70804
P: (225) 219-2700
F: (225) 219-2708

### MAINE
Mr. Jerome D. Gerard
Acting Executive Director
Revenue Services
24 State House Station
26 Edison Drive
Augusta, ME 04333
P: (207) 626-8475
E: Jerome.D.Gerard
@maine.gov

### MARYLAND
Mr. James M. Arnie
Director
Revenue Administration Division
Comptroller of Maryland
110 Carroll Street, Room 105
Annapolis, MD 21411
P: (410) 260-7445
F: (410) 974-3456
E: jarnie@comp.state.md.us

### MASSACHUSETTS
Ms. Navjeet Bal
Commissioner
Department of Revenue
100 Cambridge Street, 8th Floor
Boston, MA 02114
P: (617) 626-2201
F: (617) 626-2299

# STATE REVENUE COMMISSIONERS

**MICHIGAN**
Mr. Jeff Guilfoyle
Administrator
Office of Revenue & Tax
Analysis
Richard H. Austin Building
430 West Allegan Street
Lansing, MI 48922
P: (517) 373-2158
F: (517) 335-3298

**MINNESOTA**
Mr. Myron Frans
Commissioner
Department of Revenue
600 North Robert Street, 4th
Floor
St. Paul, MN 55146
P: (651) 556-6003
F: (651) 556-3133
E: myron.frans@state.mn.us

**MISSISSIPPI**
Mr. Ed Morgan
Commissioner
Department of Revenue
P.O. Box 1033
Jackson, MS 39215
P: (601) 923-7000
F: (601) 923-7423

**MISSOURI**
Ms. Alana M. Barragan-Scot
Director
Department of Revenue
301 West High Street
P.O. Box 311
Jefferson City, MO 65105
P: (573) 751-4450
F: (573) 751-7150
E: dormail@dor.mo.gov

**MONTANA**
Mr. Dan Bucks
Director
Department of Revenue
P.O. Box 5805
Helena, MT 59604
P: (406) 444-0761
F: (406) 444-1505
E: dbucks@mt.gov

**NEBRASKA**
Mr. Doug Ewald
Tax Commissioner
Department of Revenue
P.O. Box 94818
Lincoln, NE 68509
P: (402) 471-5605
F: (402) 471-5608
E: doug.ewald@nebraska.gov

**NEVADA**
Mr. Christopher Nielsen
Interim Executive Director
Department of Taxation
1550 College Parkway, Suite
115
Carson City, NV 89706
P: (775) 684-2070
F: (775) 684-2020
E: cnielsen@tax.state.nv.us

**NEW HAMPSHIRE**
Mr. Kevin A. Clougherty
Commissioner
Department of Revenue
Administration
109 Pleasant Street
P.O. Box 457
Concord, NH 03302
P: (603) 271-2318
F: (603) 271-6121
E: kevin.clougherty
  @rev.state.nh.us

Ms. Margaret Fulton
Assistant Commissioner
Department of Revenue
Administration
109 Pleasant Street
P.O. Box 457
Concord, NH 03302
P: (603) 271-2318
F: (603) 271-6121
E: MFulton@rev.state.nh.us

**NEW JERSEY**
Mr. Michael J. Bryan
Acting Director
Division of Taxation
P.O. Box 281
Trenton, NJ 08695
P: (609) 292-5185

**NEW MEXICO**
Ms. Demesia Padilla
Secretary
Taxation & Revenue
Department
1100 South St. Francis Drive
Santa Fe, NM 87504
P: (505) 827-0700
F: (505) 827-1759

**NEW YORK**
Mr. Thomas H. Mattox
Commissioner
Department of Taxation &
Finance
W.A. Harriman Campus,
Building 9
Albany, NY 12227

**NORTH CAROLINA**
Mr. David Hoyle
Secretary
Department of Revenue
P.O. Box 25000
Raleigh, NC 27640
P: (919) 733-7211
F: (919) 733-0023

**NORTH DAKOTA**
Hon. Cory Fong (R)
Commissioner
Office of State Tax
Commissioner
600 East Boulevard Avenue
Department 127
Bismarck, ND 58505
P: (701) 328-7088
F: (701) 328-3700
E: cfong@nd.gov

**NORTHERN MARIANA
ISLANDS**
Ms. Estrellita S. Ada
Director of Revenue & Tax
Division of Revenue & Taxation
Caller Box 10007, Capitol Hill
Saipan, MP 96950
P: (670) 664-1000
F: (670) 664-1015
E: revtax@gtepacifica.net

**OHIO**
Mr. Joseph W. Testa
Tax Commissioner
Department of Taxation
30 East Broad Street, 22nd Floor
P.O. Box 530
Columbus, OH 43216
P: (614) 466-2166
F: (614) 466-6401

**OKLAHOMA**
Mr. Thomas Kemp Jr.
Chair
Tax Commission
2501 North Lincoln Boulevard
Oklahoma City, OK 73194
P: (405) 521-3160
F: (405) 522-0074

**OREGON**
Ms. Karen S. Gregory
Acting Director
Department of Revenue
Room 457, Revenue Building
Salem, OR 97301
P: (503) 945-8214
F: (503) 945-8290
E: karen.s.gregory
  @state.or.us

**PENNSYLVANIA**
Mr. Dan Meuser
Secretary
Department of Revenue
11th Floor, Stawberry Square
Harrisburg, PA 17128
P: (717) 783-3680
F: (717) 787-3990

**RHODE ISLAND**
Ms. Rosemary Booth Gallogly
State Budget Officer
Department of Revenue
One Capitol Hill
Providence, RI 02908
P: (401) 574-8999
F: (401) 574-8997

**SOUTH CAROLINA**
Mr. James F. Etter
Director
Department of Revenue
P.O. Box 125
Columbia, SC 29214
P: (803) 898-5040
E: Director@sctax.org

**SOUTH DAKOTA**
Mr. Andy Gerlach
Secretary of Revenue &
Regulation
Department of Revenue &
Regulation
445 East Capital Avenue
Pierre, SD 57501
P: (605) 773-3311
F: (605) 773-5129

Mr. David Wiest
Interim Secretary of Revenue &
Regulation
Department of Revenue &
Regulation
445 East Capital Avenue
Pierre, SD 57501
P: (605) 773-3311
F: (605) 773-5129

**TENNESSEE**
Mr. Richard H. Roberts
Commissioner
Department of Revenue
500 Deaderick Street
Andrew Jackson Building
Nashville, TN 37242
P: (615) 741-2461
F: (615) 741-2883

# STATE REVENUE COMMISSIONERS

**TEXAS**
Ms. Susan Combs
Comptroller of Public Accounts
Office of the Comptroller of
Public Accounts
111 East 17th
P.O.Box 13528
Austin, TX 78711
P: (512) 463-4444
F: (512) 463-4965
E: susan.combs
   @cpa.state.tx.us

**U.S. VIRGIN ISLANDS**
Ms. Claudette J.
   Watson-Anderson
Director
Internal Revenue Bureau
9601 Estate Thomas
St. Thomas, VI 00802
P: (340) 774-5865
F: (340) 714-9345

**UTAH**
Mr. Barry C. Conover
Executive Director
State Tax Commission
210 North 1950 West
Salt Lake City, UT 84134
P: (801) 297-3820
F: (801) 297-6358
E: bconover@utah.gov

**VERMONT**
Mr. James B. Reardon
Commissioner
Department of Finance &
Management
109 State Street
Montpelier, VT 05602
P: (802) 828-2376
F: (802) 828-2428
E: jim.reardon@state.vt.us

**VIRGINIA**
Mr. Craig M. Burns
Tax Commissioner
Department of Taxation
Main Street Centre
600 East Main Street, 23rd Floor
Richmond, VA 23219
P: (804) 786-3301
F: (804) 786-4208
E: craig.burns
   @tax.virginia.gov

**WEST VIRGINIA**
Mr. Charles O. Lorensen
Cabinet Secretary
Department of Revenue
Building 1, W-300
P.O. Box 963
Charleston, WV 25324
P: (304) 558-0211
F: (304) 558-2324
E: Charles.O.Lorensen
   @wv.gov

**WISCONSIN**
Mr. Richard Chandler
Secretary
Department of Revenue
P.O. Box 8933
Mail Stop #624-A
Madison, WI 53708
P: (608) 266-6466
F: (608) 266-5718
E: dorsecretary
   @revenue.wi.gov

**WYOMING**
Mr. Edmund J. Schmidt
Director
Department of Revenue
Herschler Building
122 West 25th Street, 2nd West
Cheyenne, WY 82002
P: (307) 777-5287
F: (307) 777-7722
E: Ed.Schmidt@wyo.gov

# STATE ENVIRONMENTAL PROTECTION AGENCIES

## Environmental Protection

Oversees the overall quality of the environment by coordinating and managing the state's pollution control programs and planning, permit granting and regulation of standards.

Information provided by:

**Environmental Council of the States**
R. Steven Brown
Executive Director
444 North Capitol Street, NW
Suite 445
Washington, DC 20001
P: (202) 624-3660
F: (202) 624-3666
sbrown@sso.org
www.ecos.org

---

**ALABAMA**
Mr. Lance LeFleur
Director
Department of Environmental
Management
1400 Coliseum Boulevard
P.O. Box 301463
Montgomery, AL 36130
P: (334) 271-7710
F: (334) 271-7950

**ALASKA**
Mr. Larry Hartig
Commissioner
Department of Environmental
Conservation
410 Willoughby, Suite 303
P.O. Box 111800
Juneau, AK 99811
P: (907) 465-5065
F: (907) 465-5070
E: larry.hartig@alaska.gov

**ARIZONA**
Mr. Henry Darwin
Director
Deaprtment of Environmental
Quality
1110 West Washington Street
Phoenix, AZ 85007
P: (602) 771-2203
F: (602) 771-2218
E: hrd@azdeq.gov

**ARKANSAS**
Ms. Teresa Marks
Director
Department of Environmental
Quality
5301 Northshore Drive
P.O. Box 8913
North Little Rock, AR 72118
P: (501) 682-0959
F: (501) 682-0798
E: marks@adeq.state.ar.us

**CALIFORNIA**
Ms. Linda Adams
Secretary
Environmental Protection
Agency
1001 I Street, 25th Floor
Sacramento, CA 95814
P: (916) 445-3846
F: (916) 445-6401
E: ladams@calepa.ca.gov

Ms. Cindy Tuck
Under Secretary
Environmental Protection
Agency
1001 I Street, 25th Floor
Sacramento, CA 95814
P: (916) 323-3708
F: (916) 445-6401
E: ctuck@calepa.ca.gov

**COLORADO**
Dr. Christopher E. Urbina
Executive Director
Department of Public Health &
Environment
4300 Cherry Creek Drive, South
Denver, CO 80246
P: (303) 692-2000
F: (303) 691-7702
E: christopher.urbina
@state.co.us

**CONNECTICUT**
Mr. Daniel C. Esty
Commissioner
Department of Environmental
Protection
79 Elm Street
Hartford, CT 06106
P: (860) 424-3009
F: (860) 424-4054
E: daniel.esty@ct.gov

**DELAWARE**
Mr. Collin O'Mara
Secretary
Department of Natural
Resources & Environmental
Control
89 Kings Highway
P.O. Box 1401
Dover, DE 19903
P: (302) 739-9000
F: (302) 739-6242

**DISTRICT OF COLUMBIA**
Mr. Christophe A. G. Tulou
Acting Director
Department of the Environment
1200 First Street, Northeast, 5th
Floor
Washington, DC 20002
P: (202) 535-2600
F: (202) 535-2881
E: ddoe@dc.gov

**FLORIDA**
Mr. Herschel T. Vinyard
Secretary
Department of Environmental
Protection
3900 Commonwealth Boulevard
Mail Station 49
Tallahassee, FL 32399
P: (850) 245-2011
F: (850) 245-2128
E: herschel.vinyard
@dep.state.fl.us

**GEORGIA**
Mr. F. Allen Barnes
Director, Environmental
Protection Division
Department of Natural
Resources
2 Martin Luther King Jr. Drive,
SE
Suite 1252, East Tower
Atlanta, GA 30334
P: (404) 656-4713
F: (404) 651-5778

**HAWAII**
Mr. Gary Gill
Deputy Director for
Environmental Health
Department of Health
1250 Punchbowl Street, 3rd
Floor
Honolulu, HI 96801
P: (808) 586-4424
F: (808) 586-4368
E: gary.gill@doh.hawaii.gov

**IDAHO**
Ms. Toni Hardesty
Director
Department of Environmental
Quality
1410 North Hilton
Boise, ID 83706
P: (208) 373-0240
F: (208) 373-0417
E: toni.hardesty
@deq.idaho.gov

**ILLINOIS**
Ms. Lisa Bonnett
Acting Director
Environmental Protection
Agency
1021 North Grand Avenue, East
P.O. Box 19276
Springfield, IL 62794
P: (217) 782-3397
F: (217) 782-9039

**INDIANA**
Mr. Thomas Easterly
Commissioner
Department of Environmental
Management
100 North Senate Avenue, MC
50-01
P.O. Box 6015
Indianapolis, IN 46206
P: (317) 232-8611
F: (317) 233-6647
E: teasterl@idem.in.gov

**IOWA**
Mr. Wayne Gieselman
Division Administrator
Environmental Services
Division
4th Floor Wallace Building
502 East 9th Street
Des Moines, IA 50319
P: (515) 281-5817
F: (515) 281-8895
E: wayne.gieselman
@dnr.iowa.gov

**KANSAS**
Mr. John Mitchell
Director
Division of Environment
Department of Health &
Environment
1000 Southwest Jackson, Suite
400
Topeka, KS 66612
P: (785) 296-1535
F: (785) 296-8464
E: jmitchell@kdheks.gov

**KENTUCKY**
Ms. Valerie Hudson
Deputy Commissioner
Department for Environmental
Protection
14 Reilly Road
Frankfort, KY 40601
P: (502) 564-2150
F: (502) 564-2145
E: valerie.hudson@ky.gov

# STATE ENVIRONMENTAL PROTECTION AGENCIES

Mr. Bruce Scott
Commissioner
Department for Environmental
Protection
300 Fair Oaks Lane
Frankfort, KY 40601
P: (502) 564-2150 Ext. 152
F: (502) 564-3354
E: bruce.scott@ky.gov

## LOUISIANA
Ms. Peggy Hatch
Secretary
Department of Environmental
Quality
602 North Fifth Street, #1022
P.O. Box 4301
Baton Rouge, LA 70821
P: (225) 219-3950
F: (225) 219-3970
E: peggy.hatch@la.gov

## MAINE
Mr. James Brooks
Acting Commissioner
Department of Environmental
Protection
17 State House Station
Augusta, ME 04333
P: (207) 287-2812
F: (207) 287-2814
E: james.p.brooks@maine.gov

## MARYLAND
Mr. Robert Summers
Acting Secretary
Department of the Environment
1800 Washington Boulevard
Baltimore, MD 21230
P: (410) 537-3084
F: (410) 537-3888
E: bsummers@mde.state.md.us

## MASSACHUSETTS
Mr. Kenneth Kimmell
Commissioner
Department of Environmental
Protection
One Winter Street, #1022
Boston, MA 02108
P: (617) 292-5856
F: (617) 574-6880
E: ken.kimmell@state.ma.us

## MICHIGAN
Mr. Jim Sygo
Deputy Director for
Environmental Protection
Department of Environmental
Quality
P.O. Box 30473
525 West Allegan Street
Lansing, MI 48909
P: (517) 373-7917
F: (517) 241-7401

## MINNESOTA
Mr. Paul Aasen
Commissioner
Pollution Control Agency
520 Lafayette Road North, 6th
Floor
St. Paul, MN 55155
P: (651) 757-2016
F: (651) 296-6334
E: paul.aasen@state.mn.us

## MISSISSIPPI
Ms. Trudy H. Fisher
Executive Director
Department of Environmental
Quality
2380 Highway 80 West
P.O. Box 2369
Jackson, MS 39289
P: (601) 961-5001
F: (601) 961-5093
E: trudy_fisher
    @deq.state.ms.us

## MISSOURI
Ms. Sara Parker Pauley
Director
Department of Natural
Resources
P.O. Box 176
Jefferson City, MO 65102
P: (573) 751-4732
F: (573) 751-7627
E: sara.pauley@dnr.mo.gov

## MONTANA
Mr. Richard H. Opper
Director
Department of Environmental
Quality
1520 East 6th Avenue
P.O. Box 200901
Helena, MT 59620
P: (406) 444-6815
F: (406) 444-4386
E: ropper@mt.gov

## NEBRASKA
Mr. Michael J. Linder
Director
Department of Environmental
Quality
1200 N Street, Suite 400
P.O. Box 98922
Lincoln, NE 68509
P: (402) 471-3585
F: (402) 471-2909
E: mike.linder@nebraska.gov

## NEVADA
Ms. Colleen Cripps
Administrator
Division of Environmental
Protection
901 South Stewart Street, Suite
4001
Carson City, NV 89701
P: (775) 687-9302
F: (775) 687-5856
E: cripps@ndep.nv.gov

## NEW HAMPSHIRE
Mr. Thomas S. Burack
Commissioner
Department of Environmental
Services
29 Hazen Drive
P.O. Box 95
Concord, NH 03302
P: (603) 271-2958
F: (603) 271-2867
E: thomas.burack@des.nh.gov

## NEW JERSEY
Mr. Bob Martin
Commissioner
Department of Environmental
Protection
401 East State Street
P.O. Box 402
Trenton, NJ 08625
P: (609) 292-2885
F: (609) 292-7695

## NEW MEXICO
Mr. F. David Martin
Secretary
Environment Department
1190 Saint Francis Drive
Harold Runnels Building
Santa Fe, NM 87503
P: (505) 827-2855
F: (505) 827-2836

## NEW YORK
Mr. Joe Martens
Commissioner
Department of Environmental
Conservation
625 Broadway, 14th Floor
Albany, NY 12233
P: (518) 402-8540
F: (518) 402-8541
E: joemartens
    @gw.dec.state.ny.us

## NORTH CAROLINA
Ms. Dee A. Freeman
Secretary
Department of Environment &
Natural Resources
512 North Salisbury Street
1601 Mail Service Center
Raleigh, NC 27699
P: (919) 733-4984
F: (919) 715-3060
E: dee.freeman@ncdenr.gov

## NORTH DAKOTA
Mr. L. David Glatt
Chief
Environmental Health Section
Department of Health
1200 Missouri Avenue, P.O. Box
5520
Bismarck, ND 58506
P: (701) 328-5152
F: (701) 328-5200
E: dglatt@nd.gov

## OHIO
Mr. Scott Nally
Director
Environmental Protection
Agency
122 South Front Street, 6th
Floor
Columbus, OH 43215
P: (614) 644-2782
F: (614) 644-3184
E: scott.nally
    @epa.state.oh.us

## OKLAHOMA
Mr. Steven A. Thompson
Executive Director
Department of Environmental
Quality
707 North Robinson, Suite 7100
P.O.Box 1677
Oklahoma City, OK 73101
P: (405) 702-7163
F: (405) 702-7101

## OREGON
Mr. Dick Pedersen
Director
Department of Environmental
Quality
811 Southwest 6th Avenue
Portland, OR 97204
P: (503) 229-5300
F: (503) 229-5850
E: pedersen.dick
    @deq.state.or.us

# STATE ENVIRONMENTAL PROTECTION AUTHORITIES

**PENNSYLVANIA**
Mr. Michael Krancer
Secretary
Department of Environmental
Protection
Carson State Office Building,
16th Floor
400 Market Street
Harrisburg, PA 17101
P: (717) 787-2814
F: (717) 705-4980

**RHODE ISLAND**
Ms. Janet Coit
Director
Department of Environmental
Management
235 Promenade Street, 4th Floor
Providence, RI 02908
P: (401) 222-2771
F: (401) 222-6802
E: janet.coit@dem.ri.gov

**SOUTH CAROLINA**
Mr. Robert W. King Jr.
Deputy Commissioner
Department of Health &
Environmental Control
2600 Bull Street
Columbia, SC 29201
P: (803) 896-8940
F: (803) 896-8941

**SOUTH DAKOTA**
Mr. Steve M. Pirner
Secretary
Department of Environment &
Natural Resources
Joe Foss Building
523 East Capital Avenue
Pierre, SD 57501
P: (605) 773-3151
F: (605) 773-6035
E: steve.pirner@state.sd.us

**TENNESSEE**
Mr. Robert J. Martineau Jr.
Commissioner
Department of Environment and
Conservation
401 Church Street
1st Floor, L&C Annex
Nashville, TN 37243

Mr. Paul Sloan
Deputy Commissioner
Department of Environment &
Conservation
401 Church Street, Annex
Nashville, TN 37243
P: (615) 532-0102
F: (615) 532-0120
E: paul.sloan@state.tn.us

**TEXAS**
Dr. Bryan W. Shaw
Chairman
Commission on Environmental
Quality
12100 Park 35 Circle
P.O. Box 13087
Austin, TX 78711
P: (512) 239-5510
F: (512) 239-6377

**UTAH**
Ms. Amanda Smith
Executive Director
Department of Environmental
Quality
168 North 1950 West
P.O. Box 144810
Salt Lake City, UT 84114
P: (801) 538-1000
F: (801) 538-1557
E: amandasmith@utah.gov

**VERMONT**
Mr. David K. Mears
Commissioner
Department of Environmental
Conservation
103 South Main Street, Center
Building
Waterbury, VT 05671
P: (802) 241-3808
F: (802) 244-5141
E: david.mears@state.vt.us

**VIRGINIA**
Mr. David K. Paylor
Director
Department of Environmental
Quality
629 East Main Street
P.O. Box 1105
Richmond, VA 23218
P: (804) 698-4390
F: (804) 698-4019
E: dkpaylor
   @deq.virginia.gov

**WASHINGTON**
Mr. Ted L. Sturdevant
Director
Department of Ecology
P.O. Box 47600
Olympia, WA 98504
P: (360) 407-7001
F: (360) 407-6989
E: tstu461@ecy.wa.gov

**WEST VIRGINIA**
Mr. Randy Huffman
Cabinet Secretary
Department of Environmental
Protection
601 57th Street, Southeast
Charleston, WV 25304
P: (304) 926-0440
F: (304) 926-0447
E: randy.c.huffman@wv.gov

**WISCONSIN**
Ms. Cathy Stepp
Secretary
Department of Natural
Resources
101 South Webster Street
P.O. Box 7921
Madison, WI 53707
P: (608) 267-7556
F: (608) 266-6983
E: cathy.stepp
   @wisconsin.gov

**WYOMING**
Mr. John V. Corra
Director
Department of Environmental
Quality
Herschler Building
122 West 25th Street, 4th Floor,
West
Cheyenne, WY 82002
P: (307) 777-7937
F: (307) 777-7682
E: jcorra@wyo.gov

# STATE DATA CENTERS

## State Data Center

Center that acts as an information clearinghouse for the Census Bureau and other data sources within the state.

### ALABAMA
Ms. Annette Watters
Director
State Data Center
University of Alabama
P.O. Box 870221
Tuscaloosa, AL 35487
P: (205) 348-6191
F: (205) 348-2951
E: awatters@cba.ua.edu

### ALASKA
Mr. Click Bishop
Commissioner
Department of Labor &
Workforce Development
P.O. Box 21149
Juneau, AK 99802
P: (907) 465-2700
F: (907) 465-2784
E: commissioner.labor
@ak.gov

### AMERICAN SAMOA
Mr. Vai Filiga
Statistician
Department of Commerce
American Samoa Government
Pago Pago, AS 96799
P: (684) 633-5155
F: (684) 633-4195
E: JRScanlan@samoatelco.com

### ARIZONA
Mr. Allen L. Barnes
State Data Center Lead
Population Statistics Unit
Commerce Authority
1700 West Washington Street,
Suite 600
Phoenix, AZ 85007
P: (602) 542-5746
F: (602) 771-1207
E: AllenB@azcommerce.com

### ARKANSAS
Ms. Phyllis Poche
Director
Census State Data Center
2801 South University
Little Rock, AR 72204
P: (501) 569-8530
F: (501) 569-8538
E: pnpoche@ualr.edu

### CALIFORNIA
Mr. John Malson
Acting Chief
Demographic Research Unit
915 L Street
Sacramento, CA 95814
P: (916) 323-4086
F: (916) 327-0222
E: john.malson@dof.ca.gov

### COLORADO
Ms. Elizabeth Garner
State Demographer
Demography Office
Department of Local Affairs
1313 Sherman Street, Room 521
Denver, CO 80203
P: (303) 866-3096
F: (303) 866-2660
E: elizabeth.garner
@state.co.us

### CONNECTICUT
Mr. Orlando Rodriguez
Manager and Demographer
State Data Center
University of Connecticut
341 Mansfield Road, Room 401
Storrs, CT 06269
P: (860) 486-9269
E: Orlando.Rodriguez
@uconn.edu

### DELAWARE
Mr. Michael B. Mahaffie
GIS/Spatial Data
Coordinator/Webmaster
Office of State Planning
Coordination
122 William Penn Street, Suite
302
Haslet Building, Third Floor
Dover, DE 19901
P: (302) 739-3090
F: (302) 739-6958
E: mike.mahaffie
@state.de.us

### DISTRICT OF COLUMBIA
Ms. Joy E. Phillips
Associate Director
State Data Center
801 North Capitol Street,
Northeast
Suite 4000
Washington, DC 20002
P: (202) 442-7600
F: (202) 442-7637

### FLORIDA
Mr. David W. Taylor
Executive Director & Chief
Information Officer
Agency for Enterprise
Information Technology
4030 Esplanade Way, Suite 135
Tallahassee, FL 32399
P: (850) 922-7502
F: (850) 487-9937
E: David.Taylor
@aeit.myflorida.com

### GEORGIA
Mr. Robert Giacomini
Director of Research
Office of Planning & Budget
270 Washington Street,
Southwest
8th Floor
Atlanta, GA 30334
P: (404) 653-4445
F: (404) 656-3828
E: robert.giacomini
@opb.state.ga.us

### GUAM
Mr. Alberto C. Lamorena V
Acting Director
Bureau of Statistics & Plans
P.O. Box 2950
Hagatna, GU 96932
P: (671) 472-4201
F: (671) 477-1812

### HAWAII
Ms. Jan Nakamoto
Research & Economic Analysis
Division
State Data Center
P.O. Box 2359
Honolulu, HI 96804
P: (808) 586-2493
F: (808) 586-8449
E: jnakamot
@dbedt.hawaii.gov

### IDAHO
Mr. Donald A. Dietrich
Director
Department of Commerce
700 West State Street
P.O. Box 83720
Boise, ID 83720
P: (208) 334-2470
F: (208) 334-2631
E: don.dietrich
@commerce.idaho.gov

### ILLINOIS
Ms. Suzanne Ebetsch
Coordinator
Information Management
Commerce & Economic
Opportunity
620 East Adams
Springfield, IL 62701
P: (217) 524-0187
F: (217) 524-4876

### INDIANA
Ms. Roberta L. Brooker
State Librarian
State Library
315 West Ohio Street, Room
407
Indianapolis, IN 46202
P: (317) 232-3692
E: rbrooker@library.in.gov

### IOWA
Mr. Gary Krob
Data Warehouse Analyst
State Data Center
Ola Babcock Miller Building
1112 East Grand Avenue
Des Moines, IA 50319
P: (515) 281-6618
F: (515) 242-6543
E: gary.krob
@lib.state.ia.us

### KENTUCKY
Mr. Michael Price
Interim Director
State Data Center
University of Louisville
426 West Bloom Street
Louisville, KY 40208
P: (502) 852-7990
F: (502) 852-7386

### LOUISIANA
Mr. Neal Underwood
Program Management Director
Office of Information
Technology
Division of Administration
P.O. Box 94095
Baton Rouge, LA 70804
P: (225) 219-9470
F: (225) 219-9465
E: neal.underwood@la.gov

### MAINE
Mr. Michael LeVert
State Economist
State Planning Office
38 State House Station
Augusta, ME 04333
P: (207) 287-1479
F: (207) 287-6489
E: michael.levert@maine.gov

# STATE DATA CENTERS

**MARYLAND**
Ms. Jane Traynham
Manager
Research & State Data Center
Department of Planning
301 West Preston Street
Baltimore, MD 21201
P: (410) 767-4450
F: (410) 767-4480
E: jtraynham
    @mdp.state.md.us

**MASSACHUSETTS**
Mr. John Gaviglio
Data Manager
State Data Center
UMASS Donahue Institute
100 Venture Way, Suite 9
Hadley, MA 02035
P: (413) 545-0176
F: (413) 545-3420
E: jgaviglio
    @donahue.umassp.edu

**MICHIGAN**
Mr. David Behen
Director & CIO
Department of Technology,
Management & Budget
320 South Walnut Street, 2nd
Floor
Lansing, MI 48933
P: (517) 373-1006
F: (517) 373-8213

**MINNESOTA**
Mr. Spencer Cronk
Commissioner
Department of Administration
50 Sherburne Avenue
200 Administration Building
St. Paul, MN 55155
P: (651) 201-2555
F: (651) 297-7909
E: Spencer.Cronk
    @state.mn.us

**MISSISSIPPI**
Mr. Cliff Holley
Director
Center for Population Studies
Leavel Hall, Room 101
University, MS 38677
P: (662) 232-7288
F: (662) 915-7736
E: saholley@olemiss.edu

**MISSOURI**
Ms. Katina Jones
Statistical Research Analyst
Census Data Center
State Library
P.O. Box 387
Jefferson City, MO 65101
P: (573) 526-1087
E: katina.jones@sos.mo.gov

**MONTANA**
Mr. Richard Clark
Chief Information Officer
Information Technology
Services Division
Department of Administration
P.O. Box 200113
Helena, MT 59620
P: (406) 444-2700
F: (406) 444-2701
E: dclark@mt.gov

**NEBRASKA**
Mr. Jerome Deichart
Director
Center for Public Affairs
Research
University of Nebraska Omaha
Omaha, NE 68182
P: (402) 554-2134
F: (402) 554-4946
E: jdeicher@unomaha.edu

**NEVADA**
Mr. William D. Anderson
Chief Economist
Department of Employment,
Training & Rehabilitation
Research & Analysis Bureau
500 East Third Street
Carson City, NV 89713
P: (775) 684-0387
F: (775) 684-3850
E: wdanderson@nvdetr.org

**NEW HAMPSHIRE**
Ms. Joanne L. Cassulo
Senior Planner
State Data Center
Office of Energy & Planning
4 Chenell Drive
Concord, NH 03301
P: (603) 271-1755
F: (603) 271-2615
E: joanne.cassulo@nh.gov

**NEW JERSEY**
Mr. Len Preston
Director
State Data Center
P.O. Box 388
Trenton, NJ 08625
P: (609) 984-2595
F: (609) 984-6833
E: lpreston@dol.state.nj.us

**NEW MEXICO**
Ms. Elizabeth Davis
Research Program Officer
Economic Development
Department
1100 St. Francis Drive
P.O. Box 20003
Santa Fe, NM 87504
P: (505) 827-0264
F: (505) 827-0211
E: Elizabeth.Davis
    @state.nm.us

**NEW YORK**
Mr. Robert Scardamalia
Chief Demographer
State Data Center
30 South Pearl Street
Albany, NY 12207
P: (518) 292-5300
E: rscardamalia
    @empire.state.ny.us

**NORTH CAROLINA**
Ms. Francine Stephenson
Manager
Office of State Budget &
Management
State Data Center
116 West Jones Street
Raleigh, NC 27603
P: (919) 807-4700
E: francine.stephenson
    @osbm.nc.gov

**NORTH DAKOTA**
Dr. Lisa Feldner
Chief Information Officer
Information Technology
Department
600 East Boulevard Avenue
Department 112
Bismarck, ND 58505
P: (701) 328-1000
F: (701) 328-3000
E: lfeldner@nd.gov

**NORTHERN MARIANA
ISLANDS**
Mr. Sixto Igisomar
Acting Secretary
Department of Commerce
Caller Box 10007
Saipan, MP 96950
P: (670) 664-3064
F: (670) 664-3067

**OHIO**
Mr. James A. Leftwich
Director
Department of Development
77 South High Street
P.O. Box 1001
Columbus, OH 43216
P: (614) 466-3379
F: (614) 644-0745
E: jim.leftwich
    @development.oh.gov

**OKLAHOMA**
Ms. Deidre Myers
Division Director
Policy, Research & Economic
Analysis
900 North Stiles Avenue
Oklahoma City, OK 73104
P: (405) 815-5383
F: (405) 605-2807
E: deidre_myers
    @okcommerce.gov

**OREGON**
Ms. Julie Bozzi
Administrator
State Data Center
530 Airport Road
Salem, OR 97301
P: (503) 378-4578
E: julie.bozzi@state.or.us

**PENNSYLVANIA**
Ms. Sue Copella
Director
State Data Center
777 West Harrisburg Pike
Middletown, PA 17057
P: (717) 948-6427
F: (717) 948-6754
E: sdc3@psu.edu

**PUERTO RICO**
Mr. Juan C. Pavia
Director
Office of Budget &
Management
P.O. Box 9023228
San Juan, PR 00902
P: (787) 725-9420
F: (787) 721-8329

# STATE DATA CENTERS

**RHODE ISLAND**
Mr. Mark Brown
Principal Planner
Division of Planning,
Geographic & Demographic
Data Center
Department of Administration
One Capitol Hill
Providence, RI 02908
P: (401) 222-6183
F: (401) 222-2083
E: mbrown@doa.ri.gov

**SOUTH CAROLINA**
Mr. Bobby M. Bowers
Office Director
Office of Research & Statistics,
Budget & Control Board
1201 Main Street, Suite 715
P.O. Box 27
Columbia, SC 29201
P: (803) 734-3798
E: bobby@drss.state.sc.us

**SOUTH DAKOTA**
Ms. Nancy Nelson
Director
State Data Center
University of South Dakota
132 Patterson Hall, 414 East
Clark
Vermillion, SD 57069
P: (605) 677-5287
F: (605) 677-5427
E: nnelson@usd.edu

**TENNESSEE**
Mr. Mark Bengel
Chief Information Officer
Office for Information
Resources
312 Rosa L. Parks Avenue
16th Floor, Tennessee Tower
Nashville, TN 37343
P: (615) 741-7951
F: (615) 532-0471

**TEXAS**
Ms. Karen W. Robinson
Chief Technology Officer
Department of Information
Resources
300 West 15th Street, Suite 1300
P.O. Box 13564
Austin, TX 78711
P: (512) 475-4720
F: (512) 475-4759

**U.S. VIRGIN ISLANDS**
Mr. Dayle Barry
Coordinator
Conservation Data Center
Eastern Caribbean Center, UVI
#2 John Brewer Bay
St. Thomas, VI 00802
P: (340) 693-1030
F: (340) 693-1025

**UTAH**
Mr. Ron Bigelow
Executive Director
Governor's Office of Planning &
Budget
State Capitol, Suite 150
P.O. Box 132210
Salt Lake City, UT 84114
P: (801) 538-1555
F: (801) 538-1547
E: ronbigelow@utah.gov

**VERMONT**
Mr. Will Sawyer
Program Manager & State Data
Center Manager
State Data Center
Center for Rural Studies
207 Morrill Hall, University of
Vermont
Burlington, VT 05405
P: (802) 656-0892
E: william.sawyer@uvm.edu

**VIRGINIA**
Mr. John R. Broadway
Commissioner
Employment Commission
703 East Main Street
Richmond, VA 23219
P: (804) 786-1485
E: john.broadway
   @vec.virginia.gov

**WEST VIRGINIA**
Mr. J. Keith Burdette
Secretary of Commerce
Department of Commerce
Capitol Complex Building 6,
Room 525
1900 Kanawha Boulevard East
Charleston, WV 25305
P: (304) 558-2234
F: (304) 558-1189
E: J.Keith.Burdette@wv.gov

**WISCONSIN**
Mr. Phil Wells
Census Data Consultant
Demographic Services Center
101 East Wilson, 9th Floor
Madison, WI 53703
P: (608) 266-1927
F: (608) 267-6931
E: philip.wells
   @wisconsin.gov

**WYOMING**
Mr. Buck McVeigh
Administrator
Economic Analysis Division
Dept. of Administration &
Information
1807 Capitol Avenue, Suite 206
Cheyenne, WY 82002
P: (307) 777-7504
F: (307) 632-1819
E: bmcvei@wyo.gov

# Vital Statistics

**Maintains a statewide file of birth, death, marriage and divorce records, and issues certified copies of those records.**

**ALABAMA**
Ms. Dorothy S. Harshbarger
Director
Center for Health Statistics
RSA Tower, 201 Monroe Street,
Suite 1150
P.O. Box 5625
Montgomery, AL 36103
P: (334) 206-5426
F: (334) 206-2659

**ALASKA**
Mr. Phillip Mitchell
Section Chief
Bureau of Vital Statistics
Department of Health & Social
Services
P.O. Box 110675
Juneau, AK 99801
P: (907) 465-3391
F: (907) 465-3618
E: phillip.mitchell
@alaska.gov

**ARIZONA**
Mr. Will Humble
Director
Department of Health Services
150 North 18th Avenue
Phoenix, AZ 85007
P: (602) 542-1025
F: (602) 542-1062

**ARKANSAS**
Mr. Michael Adams
Director
Division of Vital Records
4815 West Markham Street
Little Rock, AR 72205
P: (501) 661-2371
F: (501) 661-2717
E: mike.adams@arkansas.gov

**CALIFORNIA**
Ms. Janet McKee
Chief
Office of Vital Records
1616 Capitol Avenue, Suite 317,
MS 5000
P.O. Box 997377
Sacramento, CA 95899
P: (916) 552-8129
E: janet.mckee@cdph.ca.gov

**COLORADO**
Mr. Bob O'Doherty
Director and Chief Information
Officer
Center for Health and
Environmental Information &
Statistics
4300 Cherry Creek Drive South
Denver, CO 80246
P: (303) 692-2160
F: (303) 691-7704

**CONNECTICUT**
Ms. Jane Purtill
State Registrar of Vital Records
Health Information Systems &
Reporting
Department of Public Health
410 Capitol Avenue
Hartford, CT 06134
P: (860) 509-7895
F: (860) 509-7160
E: jane.purtill@ct.gov

**DELAWARE**
Ms. Judy Chaconas
Director
Bureau of Health Planning &
Resources Management
Jesse Cooper Building
417 Federal Street
Dover, DE 19901
P: (302) 744-4776
F: (302) 739-3313

**DISTRICT OF COLUMBIA**
Mr. David A. Berns
Director
Department of Human Services
64 New York Avenue, Northeast
6th Floor
Washington, DC 20002
P: (202) 671-4200
E: dhs@dc.gov

**FLORIDA**
Mr. Ken T. Jones
Deputy State Registrar
Department of Health
1217 Pearl Street
P.O. Box 210
Jacksonville, FL 32231
P: (904) 359-6900
F: (904) 359-6931
E: ken_jones
@doh.state.fl.us

**GEORGIA**
Dr. Brenda Fitzgerald
Director
Division of Public Health
Two Peachtree Street, Northwest
Atlanta, GA 30303
P: (404) 657-2700

**HAWAII**
Dr. Alvin T. Onaka
Chief & State Registrar
Office of Health Status
Monitoring
P.O. Box 3378
Honolulu, HI 96801
P: (808) 586-4600
F: (808) 586-4606

**IDAHO**
Ms. Jane S. Smith
Division Administrator for
Health
Bureau of Health Policy & Vital
Statistics
450 West State Street
4th Floor, Pete T. Cenarrusa
Building
Boise, ID 83720
P: (208) 334-5932
F: (208) 334-6581
E: smithj2@dhw.idaho.gov

**ILLINOIS**
Dr. Damon T. Arnold
Director
Department of Public Health
535 West Jefferson Street
Springfield, IL 62761
P: (217) 557-2556
F: (217) 785-3209

**INDIANA**
Ms. Erin Kellam
Director
Vital Records Division
2 North Meridian Street, Room
2NLL077
Indianapolis, IN 46204
P: (317) 233-7523
F: (317) 233-5956
E: ekellam@isdh.IN.gov

**IOWA**
Ms. Jill France
Bureau Chief
Bureau of Health Statistics
Lucas State Office Building
321 East 12th Street
Des Moines, IA 50319
P: (515) 281-4944
E: jill.france
@idph.iowa.gov

**KANSAS**
Dr. Elizabeth W. Saadi
Acting Bureau Director & State
Registrar
Office of Vital Statistics
Curtis State Office Building
1000 Southwest Jackson
Topeka, KS 66612
P: (785) 296-1400
F: (785) 296-8075
E: Vital.Records@kdheks.gov

**KENTUCKY**
Dr. William D. Hacker
Commissioner
Department for Public Health
275 East Main Street
Mailstop 4W-A
Frankfort, KY 40621
P: (502) 564-3970
F: (502) 564-3866

**LOUISIANA**
Ms. Darlene W. Smith
State Registrar & Center
Director
Vital Records & Statistics
Vital Records Registry
P.O. Box 60630
New Orleans, LA 70160
P: (504) 593-5100
F: (504) 568-8716
E: _dhh-vitalweb@la.gov

**MAINE**
Mr. Marty Henson
State Registrar & Director
Office of Data, Research &
Vital Statistics
11 State House Station
244 Water Street
Augusta, ME 04333
P: (207) 287-5500
F: (207) 287-5470
E: marty.henson@maine.gov

**MARYLAND**
Dr. Isabelle L. Horon
Director
Vital Statistics Administration
Department of Health & Mental
Hygiene
4201 Patterson Avenue
Baltimore, MD 21215
P: (410) 764-3513
F: (410) 767-6840
E: horoni@dhmh.state.md.us

**MASSACHUSETTS**
Mr. John Auerbach
Commissioner
Department of Public Health
250 Washington Street
Boston, MA 02108
P: (617) 624-6000

# VITAL STATISTICS

**MICHIGAN**
Mr. Glenn Copeland
State Registrar & Division
Director
Division for Vital Records &
Health Statistics
Capitol View Building, Second
Floor
201 Townsend Street
Lansing, MI 48913
P: (517) 335-8677
F: (517) 335-9264
E: CopelandG@michigan.gov

**MINNESOTA**
Dr. Edward Ehlinger
Commissioner
Department of Health
625 Robert Street North
Box 64975
St. Paul, MN 55164
P: (651) 201-5810
F: (651) 201-4986
E: edward.ehlinger
    @state.mn.us

**MISSISSIPPI**
Ms. Judy Moulder
State Registrar
Public Health Statistics
571 Stadium Drive
P.O. Box 1700
Jackson, MS 39216
P: (601) 576-7960
F: (601) 576-7505
E: jmoulder
    @msdh.state.ms.us

**MISSOURI**
Ms. Ivra J. Cross
State Registrar
Bureau of Vital Records
Department of Health & Senior
Services
930 Wildwood Drive, P.O. Box
570
Jefferson City, MO 65102
P: (573) 526-0348
F: (573) 526-3846
E: ivra.cross@dhss.mo.gov

**MONTANA**
Mr. Jim Edgar
Section Supervisor
Office of Vital Statistics
111 North Sanders, Room 205
Helena, MT 59604
P: (406) 444-4250
F: (406) 444-1803

**NEBRASKA**
Dr. Joann Schaefer
Director
Division of Public Health
Department of Health & Human
Services
P.O. Box 95007
Lincoln, NE 68509
P: (402) 471-8566
F: (402) 471-9449
E: joann.schaefer
    @nebraska.gov

**NEVADA**
Dr. Luana J. Ritch
Bureau Chief
Bureau of Health Statistics,
Planning & Emergency
Response
Department of Health & Human
Services
4150 Technology Way, Suite 200
Carson City, NV 89706
P: (775) 684-4242
F: (775) 684-4156
E: lritch@health.nv.gov

**NEW HAMPSHIRE**
Mr. Steven M. Wurtz
Supervisor
Division of Vital Records
Department of State
71 South Fruit Street
Concord, NH 03301
P: (603) 271-4655
F: (603) 271-3447
E: swurtz@sos.state.nh.us

**NEW JERSEY**
Ms. Mary E. O'Dowd
Acting Commissioner
Department of Health & Senior
Services
P.O. Box 360
Trenton, NJ 08625
P: (609) 292-7837
F: (609) 292-0053

**NEW YORK**
Mr. Peter Carucci
Director
Bureau of Production Systems
Management
800 North Pearl Street
Albany, NY 12204
P: (518) 474-5245

**NORTH CAROLINA**
Ms. Linda Brinkley
Director & State Registrar
Department of Health & Human
Services
Vital Records Division
1903 Mail Service Center
Raleigh, NC 27699
P: (919) 733-3000
F: (919) 733-1511

**NORTH DAKOTA**
Mr. Darin J. Meschke
State Registrar, Director
Division of Vital Records
600 East Boulevard Avenue
Department 301
Bismarck, ND 58505
P: (701) 328-2360
F: (701) 328-1850
E: dmeschke@nd.gov

**NORTHERN MARIANA
ISLANDS**
Mr. John G. Moore
Commonwealth Recorder
Vital Records Section
P.O. Box 500307
Saipan, MP 96950
P: (670) 236-9830
F: (670) 236-9831

**OHIO**
Mr. Robert J. Campbell
Deputy Director
Center for Public Health
Statistics & Informatics
Department of Health
246 North High Street
Columbus, OH 43215
P: (614) 995-5591
F: (614) 728-4638

**OKLAHOMA**
Ms. Kelly Baker
M.P.H. Director
Department of Health
Center for Health Statistics
1000 NE 10th Street
Oklahoma City, OK 73117
P: (405) 271-6225
F: (405) 270-9061
E: kellyb@health.ok.gov

**OREGON**
Ms. Jennifer Woodward
Program Manager/State
Registrar
Center for Health Statistics
Department Of Human Services
800 Northeast Oregon Street,
Suite 205
Portland, OR 97232
P: (971) 673-1190
F: (971) 673-1203
E: jennifer.a.woodward
    @state.or.us

**PENNSYLVANIA**
Ms. Linda Caniglia
Director
Division of Vital Records
101 South Mercer Street
P.O. Box 1528
New Castle, PA 16103
P: (724) 656-3286
F: (724) 656-3079

**PUERTO RICO**
Mr. Nicolas
    Fernandez-Cornier
Executive Director
Demographic Registry
P.O. Box 11854
San Juan, PR 00910
P: (787) 281-8867
F: (787) 751-5003

**RHODE ISLAND**
Ms. Colleen Fontana
Chief, State Registrar
Office of Vital Records
Department of Health
3 Capitol Hill, Room 101
Providence, RI 02908
P: (401) 222-7841
F: (401) 222-6548
E: colleen.fontana
    @health.ri.gov

**SOUTH CAROLINA**
Dr. Guang Zhao
Director & Assistant State
Registrar
Public Health Statistics &
Information Services
Dept. of Health &
Environmental Control
2600 Bull Street
Columbia, SC 29201
P: (803) 898-4144

# VITAL STATISTICS

**SOUTH DAKOTA**
Mr. Anthony Nelson
State Registrar
Vital Records
Hayes Building
600 East Capitol Avenue
Pierre, SD 57501
P: (605) 773-5303
F: (605) 773-5683
E: anthony.nelson
  @state.sd.us

**TENNESSEE**
Ms. Sharon Leinbach
State Registrar & Director
Vital Records
425 5th Avenue, North
Cordell Hull Building, 3rd Floor
Nashville, TN 37243
P: (615) 532-2600

**TEXAS**
Ms. Geraldine Harris
Vital Statistics
Department of State Health
Services
P.O. Box 12040
Austin, TX 78711
P: (888) 963-7111
F: (512) 458-7711

Dr. Yvonne Howze
Health Information & Vital
Statistics
1100 West 49th Street
P.O.Box 149347
Austin, TX 78714
P: (512) 458-7437
F: (512) 458-7711

**U.S. VIRGIN ISLANDS**
Ms. Fern P. Clarke
Acting Commissioner
Department of Health
1303 Hospital Grounds, Suite 10
Charlotte Amalie
St. Thomas, VI 00802
P: (340) 774-9000

**UTAH**
Ms. Janice Houston
Director
Office of Vital Records &
Statistics
288 North 1460 West
P.O. Box 141012
Salt Lake City, UT 84114
P: (801) 538-6262
F: (801) 538-7012
E: jlhouston@utah.gov

**VERMONT**
Dr. William K. Apao
Director
Division of Health Surveillance
Department of Health
108 Cherry Street
Burlington, VT 05402
P: (802) 863-7300
F: (802) 865-7754

**VIRGINIA**
Ms. Karen Remley
Commissioner
Department of Health
109 Governor Street, 13th Floor
Richmond, VA 23219
P: (804) 864-7009
F: (804) 864-7022
E: karen.remley
  @vdh.virginia.gov

**WASHINGTON**
Ms. Jennifer Tebaldi
Assistant Secretary
Epidemiology, Health Statistics
& Public Health Laboratories
Division
P.O. Box 47811
Olympia, WA 98504
P: (360) 236-4204
F: (360) 236-4245
E: jennifer.tebaldi
  @doh.wa.gov

**WEST VIRGINIA**
Mr. Gary L. Thompson
State Registrar
Health Statistics Center
350 Capitol Street, Room 165
Charleston, WV 25301
P: (304) 558-2931
F: (304) 558-1051
E: Gary.L.Thompson@wv.gov

**WISCONSIN**
Mr. Brett H. Davis
Medicaid Director
Division of Health Care
Financing
1 West Wilson Street, Room 350
Madison, WI 53701
P: (608) 266-1271
F: (608) 266-1096

**WYOMING**
Ms. Gladys Breeden
Manager
Vital Statistics Services
Rural & Frontier Health
Division
6101 Yellowstone Road, Suite
510
Cheyenne, WY 82002
P: (307) 777-7264
F: (307) 777-8545

# STATE CHAMBERS OF COMMERCE

Note: The following states have no state Chamber of Commerce: Rhode Island, and Wyoming.

U.S. Chamber of Commerce
1615 H Street, NW
Washington, DC 20062
(202) 659-6000; (800) 638-6582
www.uschamber.com

Business Council of Alabama
2 N. Jackson St., P.O. Box 76
Montgomery, AL 36104-0076
(334) 834-6000; (800) 665-9647
FAX (334) 241-5984
www.bcatoday.org

Alaska State Chamber of Commerce
217 2nd Street, #201
Juneau, AK 99801-1267
(907) 586-2323
FAX (907) 463-5515
www.alaskachamber.com

Arizona Chamber of Commerce
1850 N. Central Ave., #1433
Phoenix, AZ 85004
(602) 248-9172
FAX (602) 265-1262
www.azchamber.com

Arkansas State Chamber of Commerce
1200 W. Capitol Ave., P.O. Box 3645
Little Rock, AR 72203-3645
(501) 372-2222
FAX (501) 372-2722
www.arkansasstatechamber.com

California Chamber of Commerce
1215 K Street, #1400, P.O. Box 1736
Sacramento, CA 95812-1736
(916) 444-6670
FAX (916) 325-1272
www.calchamber.com

Colorado Assn. of Commerce &
Industry
1600 Broadway, #1000
Denver, CO 80202-4935
(303) 831-7411
FAX (303) 860-1439
www.cochamber.com

Connecticut Business & Industry Assn.
350 Church Street
Hartford, CT 06103-1126
(860) 244-1900
FAX (860) 278-8562
www.cbia.com

Delaware State Chamber of Commerce
1201 N. Orange Street, #200
P.O. Box 671
Wilmington, DE 19899-0671
(302) 655-7221
FAX (302) 654-0691
www.dscc.com

District of Columbia Chamber of
Commerce
506 9th St., NW
Washington, DC 20004
(202) 347-7201
FAX (202) 638-6762
www.dcchamber.org

Florida Chamber of Commerce
136 S. Bronough St., P.O. Box 11309
Tallahassee, FL 32302-3309
(850) 521-1200
FAX (850) 521-1219
www.flchamber.com

Georgia Chamber of Commerce
233 Peachtree Street, NE #2000
Atlanta, GA 30303-1564
(404) 223-2264
(800) 241-2286 (GA only)
FAX (404) 223-2290
www.gachamber.com

Guam Chamber of Commerce
173 Aspinall Ave., #101
Hagatna, GU 96910
(671) 472-6311; (671) 472-8001
FAX (671) 472-6202
www.guamchamber.com.gu

Chamber of Commerce of Hawaii
1132 Bishop Street, #402
Honolulu, HI 96813-2830
(808) 545-4300
FAX (808) 545-4369
www.cochawaii.org

Idaho Chamber of Commerce
250 S. 5th St., Suite 300
Boise, ID 83702
(208) 472-5200
FAX (208) 472-5201
www.boisechamber.org

Illinois State Chamber of Commerce
300 S. Wacker Drive, Suite 1600
Chicago, IL 60606-6619

(312) 983-7100
FAX (312) 983-7101
www.ilchamber.org

Indiana Chamber of Commerce
115 W. Washington St., #850 S
Indianapolis, IN 46204-3497
(317) 264-3110
FAX (317) 264-6855
www.indianachamber.com

Iowa Assn. of Business and Industry
400 E. Court Ave., Suite100
Des Moines, IA 50309-3503
(515) 280-8000
(800) 383-4224
FAX (515) 244-3285
www.iowaabi.org

Kansas Chamber of Commerce and
Industry
835 SW Topeka Blvd.
Topeka, KS 66612-1671
(785) 357-6321
FAX (785) 357-4732
www.kansaschamber.org

Kentucky Chamber of Commerce
464 Chenault Rd.
Frankfort, KY 40601
(502) 695-4700
FAX (502) 695-5051
www.kychamber.com

Louisiana Assn. of Business &
Industry
3113 Valley Creek Dr.
P.O. Box 80258
Baton Rouge, LA 70898-0258
(225) 928-5388; (888) 816-5224
FAX (225) 929-6054
www.labi.org

Maine State Chamber of Commerce
125 Community Dr., Suite 101
Augusta, ME 04330-9412
(207) 623-4568
FAX (207) 622-7723
www.mainechamber.org

Maryland Chamber of Commerce
60 West St., #100
Annapolis, MD 21401-2479
(410) 269-0642; (301) 261-2858
FAX (410) 269-5247

# STATE CHAMBERS OF COMMERCE

www.mdchamber.org

Massachusetts Chamber of Business & Industry
143 Shaker Rd.
E. Longmeadow, MA 01028
(413) 426-3850
FAX (413) 525-1184
www.masscbi.com

Michigan Chamber of Commerce
600 S. Walnut Street
Lansing, MI 48933-2200
(517) 371-2100; (800) 748-0266
FAX (517) 371-7224
www.michamber.com

Minnesota State Chamber of Commerce
400 Robert St. N., #1500
St. Paul, MN 55101-4901
(651) 292-4650
(800) 821-2230
FAX (651) 292-4656
www.mnchamber.com

Mississippi Economic Council
248 E. Capitol St., Suite 940
P.O. Box 23276
Jackson, MS 39225-3276
(601) 969-0022; (800) 748-7626
FAX (601) 353-0247; (888) 717-2809
www.mec.ms

Missouri Chamber of Commerce
428 E. Capitol Ave., P.O. Box 149
Jefferson City, MO 65101-0149
(573) 634-3511
FAX (573) 634-8855
mochamber.com

Montana Chamber of Commerce
P.O. Box 1730
Helena, MT 59624-1730
(406) 442-2405
FAX (406) 442-2409
montanachamber.com

Nebraska Chamber of Commerce & Industry
1320 Lincoln Mall
P.O. Box 95128
Lincoln, NE 68509-5128
(402) 474-4422
FAX (402) 474-5681
www.nechamber.com

Nevada State Chamber of Commerce
449 S. Virginia St., 2nd fl.
Reno, NV 89501

(775) 337-3030
FAX (775) 337-3038
www.renosparkschamber.org

Business & Industry Assn. of New Hampshire
122 N. Main St.
Concord, NH 03301
(603) 224-5388
FAX (603) 224-2872
www.nhbia.org

New Jersey Chamber of Commerce
216 W. State Street
Trenton, NJ 08608
(609) 989-7888
FAX (609) 989-9696
www.njchamber.com

Assn. of Commerce & Industry of New Mexico
2201 Buena Vista Dr. SE, #410
Albuquerque, NM 87106
(505) 842-0644
FAX (505) 842-0734
www.aci-nm.org

Business Council of New York State, Inc.
152 Washington Ave
Albany, NY 12210
(518) 465-7511
(800) 358-1202
FAX (518) 465-4389
www.bcnys.org

North Carolina Citizens for Business & Industry
701 Corporate Dr., Suite 400
Raleigh, NC 27607
(919) 836-1400
FAX (919) 836-1425
www.ncchamber.net

Greater North Dakota Assn.
2000 Schafer St., P.O. Box 2639
Bismarck, ND 58502-2639
(701) 222-0929; (800) 382-1405
FAX (701) 222-1611
www.ndchamber.com

Ohio Chamber of Commerce
230 E. Town St., P.O. Box 15159
Columbus, OH 43215-0159
(614) 228-4201; (800) 622-1893
FAX (614) 228-6403
www.ohiochamber.com

The State Chamber of Oklahoma's Association of Business & Industry

330 NE 10th Street
Oklahoma City, OK 73104-3200
(405) 235-3669
FAX (405) 235-3670
www.okstatechamber.com

Associated Oregon Industries
1149 Court St., NE
Salem, OR 97301-4030
(503) 588-0050
FAX (503) 588-0052
www.aoi.org

Pennsylvania Chamber of Business & Industry
417 Walnut Street
Harrisburg, PA 17101-1918
(717) 255-3252
(800) 225-7224
FAX (717) 255-3298
www.pachamber.org

Puerto Rico Chamber of Commerce
P.O. Box 9024033
San Juan, PR 00902-4033
(787) 721-6060; (787) 721-6082
FAX (787) 723-1891
www.camarapr.org

South Carolina Chamber of Commerce
1201 Main Street, #1700
Columbia, SC 29201
(803) 799-4601
FAX (803) 779-6043
www.scchamber.net

South Dakota Chamber of Commerce and Industry
P.O. Box 190
Pierre, SD 57501-0190
(605) 224-6161
(800) 742-8112 (SD only)
FAX (605) 224-7198
www.sdchamber.biz

Tennessee Chamber of Commerce & Industry
611 Commerce St. #3030
Nashville, TN 37203-3742
(615) 256-5141
FAX (615) 256-6726
www.tnchamber.org

Texas Association of Business & Chamber of Commerce
1209 Nueces St.
Austin, TX 78701-1209
(512) 477-6721
FAX (512) 477-0836; (512) 320-0280
www.txbiz.org

# STATE CHAMBERS OF COMMERCE

Utah State Chamber of Commerce
175 E. 400 S, #600
Salt Lake City, UT 84111
(801) 328-5090
FAX (801) 328-5098
www.utahstatechamber.org

Vermont State Chamber of Commerce
P.O. Box 37
Montpelier, VT 05602
(802) 223-3443
FAX (802) 223-4257
www.vtchamber.com

St. Thomas-St. John Chamber of
 Commerce
P.O. Box 324
Charlotte Amalie, VI 00804-0324
(340) 776-0100
FAX (340) 776-0588
www.usvichamber.com

Virginia Chamber of Commerce
9 S. Fifth Street
Richmond, VA 23219
(804) 644-1607
FAX (804) 783-6112
www.vachamber.com

Assn. of Washington Business
1414 Cherry St. SE, P.O. Box 658
Olympia, WA 98501-0658
(360) 943-1600
FAX (360) 943-5811
www.awb.org

West Virginia Chamber of Commerce
1624 Kanawha Blvd. East
Charleston, WV 25311
(304) 342-1115
FAX (304) 342-1130
www.wvchamber.com

Wisconsin Manufacturers & Commerce
501 E. Washington Ave., P.O. Box 352
Madison, WI 53703
(608) 258-3400
FAX (608) 258-3413
www.wmc.org

# STATE CHIEF LIBRARIANS

**ALABAMA**
Rebecca Mitchell, Director
Alabama Public Library Service
6030 Monticello Drive
Montgomery, AL 36130
(334) 213-3901
FAX (334) 213-3993
rmitchell@apls.state.al.us
www.apls.state.al.us

**ALASKA**
Linda Thibodeau, Director
Alaska State Library & Archives
P.O. Box 110571
Juneau, AK 99811-0571
(907) 465-2911
FAX (907) 465-2151
linda.thibodeau@alaska.gov
www.library.state.ak.us

**ARIZONA**
Janet Fisher, Acting State Librarian
Department of Library, Archives
 & Public Records
1700 W. Washington, Suite 200
Phoenix, AZ 85007
(602) 926-4035
FAX (602) 256-7983
jfisher@lib.az.us
www.lib.az.us

**ARKANSAS**
Carolyn Ashcraft, State Librarian
Arkansas State Library
900 W. Capitol, Suite 100.
Little Rock, AR 72201
(501) 682-1526
FAX (501) 682-1899
carolyn@library.arkansas.gov
www.asl.lib.ar.us

**CALIFORNIA**
Stacey A. Aldrich, State Librarian
California State Library
P.O. Box 942837
Sacramento, CA 94237-0001
(916) 654-0266
FAX (916) 654-0064
saldrich@library.ca.gov
www.library.ca.gov

**COLORADO**
Eugene Hainer, Director
Colorado State Library
Colorado Department of Education
201 E. Colfax Ave., Rm. 309
Denver, CO 80203
(303) 866-6733
FAX (303) 866-6940
hainer_g@cde.state.co.us
www.cde.state.co.us/cdelib

**CONNECTICUT**
Kendall F. Wiggin, State Librarian
Connecticut State Library
231 Capitol Avenue
Hartford, CT 06106
(860) 757-6510
FAX (860) 757-6503
kwiggin@cslib.org
www.cslib.org

**DELAWARE**
Anne Norman, Director & State
 Librarian
Division of Libraries
121 Duke of York Street
Dover, DE 19901
(302) 739-4748 x5126
FAX (302) 739-6787
annie.norman@state.de.us
www.state.lib.de.us

**DISTRICT OF COLUMBIA**
Ginnie Cooper, Chief Librarian
District of Columbia Public Library
901 G St. NW
Washington, DC 20001
(202) 727-1101
FAX (202) 727-1129
ginnie.cooper@dc.gov
www.dclibrary.org

**FLORIDA**
Judith Ring, State Librarian
Division of Library and Information
 Services
500 S. Bronough St.
Tallahassee, FL 32399-0250
(850) 245-6600
FAX (850) 245-6282
jring@dos.state.fl.us
dlis.dos.state.fl.us

**GEORGIA**
Dr. Lamar Veatch, State Librarian
Georgia Public Library Service
1800 Century Place, Suite 150
Atlanta, GA 30345
(404) 235-7200
FAX (404) 235-7201
lveatch@georgialibraries.org
www.georgialibraries.org

**HAWAII**
Richard Burns, State Librarian
Hawaii State Public Library System
44 Merchant Street, Rm. B-1
Honolulu, HI 96813
(808) 586-3704
FAX (808) 586-3715
richard_burns@librarieshawaii.org
www.librarieshawaii.org

IDAHO
Ann Joslin, State Librarian
Idaho Commission for Libraries
325 W. State Street
Boise, ID 83702
(208) 334-2150
FAX (208) 334-4016
ann.joslin@libraries.idaho.gov
libraries.idaho.gov

**ILLINOIS**
Anne Craig, Director
Illinois State Library
300 S. 2nd St.
Springfield, IL 62701
(217) 782-2994
FAX (217) 785-4326
acraig@ilsos.net
www.cyberdriveillinois.com/
 departments/library/home.html

**INDIANA**
Roberta Brooker, Director and
 State Librarian
Indiana State Library
315 W. Ohio Street
Indianapolis, IN 46202
(317) 232-3693
FAX (317) 232-3713
rbrooker@library.in.gov
www.library.in.gov

**IOWA**
Mary Wegner, State Librarian
State Library of Iowa
1112 East Grand Ave.
Des Moines, IA 50319
(515) 281-4105
FAX (515) 281-6191
mary.wegner@lib.state.ia.us
www.statelibraryofiowa.org

**KANSAS**
Jo Budler, State Librarian
State Library of Kansas
300 SW 10th Ave.
Topeka, KS 66612
(785) 506-4563
FAX (785) 368-7291
jo.budler@library.ks.gov
www.skyways.org/KSL/

**KENTUCKY**
Wayne Onkst, State Librarian
 and Commissioner
Department for Library and Archives
300 Coffee Tree Road
Frankfort, KY 40601
(502) 564-8300 x312
FAX (502) 564-5773
wayne.onkst@ky.gov

# STATE CHIEF LIBRARIANS

www.kdla.ky.gov

**LOUISIANA**
Rebecca Hamilton, State Librarian
State Library of Louisiana
P.O. Box 131
Baton Rouge, LA 70821-0131
(225) 342-4923
FAX (225) 219-4804
rhamilton@crt.state.la.us
www.state.lib.la.us/

**MAINE**
Linda Lord
Maine State Library
64 State House Station
Augusta, ME 04333
(207) 287-5600
FAX (207) 287-5624
linda.lord@maine.gov
www.maine.gov/msl/

**MARYLAND**
Irene Padilla, Assistant State
 Superintendent for Library Development
 & Services
Maryland State Department of Education
200 W. Baltimore Street
Baltimore, MD 21201
(410) 767-0435
FAX (410) 333-2507
ipadilla@msde.state.md.us
www.marylandpublicschools.org/
 MSDE/divisions/library/

**MASSACHUSETTS**
Robert C. Maier, Director
Board of Library Commissioners
98 N. Washington St., Suite 401
Boston, MA 02114
(617) 725-1860
FAX (617) 725-0140
robert.maier@state.ma.us
mblc.state.ma.us

**MICHIGAN**
Nancy Robertson, State Librarian
Library of Michigan
702 W. Kalamazoo
P.O. Box 30007
Lansing, MI 48909-7507
(517) 373-5511
FAX (517) 373-4480
robertsonn@michigan.gov
www.michigan.gov/libraryofmichigan/

**MINNESOTA**
Nancy Walton, Director and State
Librarian
State Library Services
1500 Highway 36 West
Roseville, MN 55113-4266

(651) 582-8881
FAX (651) 582-8752
mde.lst@state.mn.us
education.state.mn.us/MDE/Learning_
Support/Library_Services/index.html

**MISSISSIPPI**
Sharman Bridges Smith, Executive
 Director
Mississippi Library Commission
3881 Eastwood Drive
Jackson, MS 39211
(601) 961-4039
FAX (601) 432-4480
sharman@mlc.lib.ms.us
www.mlc.lib.ms.us/

**MISSOURI**
Margaret Conroy, State Librarian
Missouri State Library
P.O. Box 387, 600 West Main Street
Jefferson City, MO 65102-0387
(573) 526-4783
FAX (573) 751-3612
margaret.conroy@sos.mo.gov
www.sos.state.mo.gov/library

**MONTANA**
Darlene Staffeldt, State Librarian
Montana State Library
1515 E. 6th Avenue
Helena, MT 59620-1800
(406) 444-3115
FAX (406) 444-0266
dstaffeldt@mt.gov
msl.mt.gov/

**NEBRASKA**
Rod Wagner, Director
Nebraska Library Commission
1200 N St., Suite 120
Lincoln, NE 68508
(402) 471-4001
FAX (402) 471-2083
rod.wagner@nebraska.gov
www.nlc.state.ne.us/

**NEVADA**
Daphne DeLeon, Administrator
Nevada State Library and Archives
100 N. Stewart Street
Carson City, NV 89701
(775) 684-3315
FAX (775) 684-3311
ddeleon@nevadaculture.org
www.nevadaculture.org/nsla/

**NEW HAMPSHIRE**
Michael York, State Librarian
New Hampshire State Library
20 Park Street

Concord, NH 03301
(603) 271-2397
FAX (603) 271-6826
michael.york@dcr.nh.gov
www.nh.gov/nhsl

**NEW JERSEY**
Norma Blake, State Librarian
Division of State Library
New Jersey Department of Education
185 W. State Street
P.O. Box 520
Trenton, NJ 08625-0520
(609) 278-2640
FAX (609) 278-2652
nblake@njstatelib.org
www.njstatelib.org

**NEW MEXICO**
Ben Wakashige, Interim State Librarian
New Mexico State Library
1209 Camino Carlos Rey
Santa Fe, NM 87507
(505) 476-9762
ben.wakashige@state.nm.us
www.nmstatelibrary.org/

**NEW YORK**
Bernard A. Margolis, State Librarian
 and Assistant Commissioner
 for Libraries
New York State Library
10C34 Cultural Education Center
Albany, NY 12230
(518) 474-5930
FAX (518) 486-6880
bmargolis@mail.nysed.gov
www.nysl.nysed.gov

**NORTH CAROLINA**
Mary Boone, State Librarian
State Library of North Carolina
4640 Mail Service Center
109 E. Jones Street
Raleigh, NC 27699-4640
(919) 807-7410
FAX (919) 733-8748
mary.boone@ncdcr.gov
statelibrary.ncdcr.gov

**NORTH DAKOTA**
Hulen Bivins, State Librarian
North Dakota State Library
604 E. Boulevard Ave.
Bismarck, ND 58505-0800
(701) 328-4654
FAX (701) 328-2040
hbivins@nd.gov
www.library.nd.gov

# STATE CHIEF LIBRARIANS

**OHIO**
Beverly Cain, State Librarian
State Library of Ohio
274 E. 1st Avenue
Columbus, OH 43201
(614) 644-6843
FAX (614) 466-3584
bcain@library.ohio.gov
www.library.ohio.gov/

**OKLAHOMA**
Susan McVey, Director
Oklahoma Department of Libraries
200 NE 18th Street
Oklahoma City, OK 73105
(405) 521-2502
FAX (405) 521-1077
smcvey@oltn.odl.state.ok.us
www.odl.state.ok.us

**OREGON**
Jim Scheppke, State Librarian
Oregon State Library
250 Winter St. NE
Salem, OR 97301-3950
(503) 378-4367
FAX (503) 585-8059
jim.b.scheppke@state.or.us
oregon.gov/OSL/

**PENNSYLVANIA**
Mary Clare Zales, Secretary of Education
 for Commonwealth Libraries &
 Commissioner for Libraries
Office of Commonwealth Libraries
333 Market Street
Harrisburg, PA 17126-1745
(717) 787-2646
FAX (717) 772-3265
mzales@state.pa.us
www.statelibrary.state.pa.us

**RHODE ISLAND**
Howard Boksenbaum, Chief Library
 Officer
Office of Library & Information
 Services
1 Capitol Hill, 4th fl.
Providence, RI 02908-5803
(401) 574-9301
FAX (401) 574-9320
howard.boksenbaum@olis.ri.gov
www.olis.ri.gov/

**SOUTH CAROLINA**
David S. Goble, State Librarian
South Carolina State Library
P.O. Box 11469
Columbia, SC 29211
(803) 734-8656
FAX (803) 734-8676

dgoble@statelibrary.sc.gov
www.statelibrary.sc.gov

**SOUTH DAKOTA**
Dan Siebersma, State Librarian
South Dakota State Library
800 Governors Drive
Pierre, SD 57501-2294
(605) 773-3131
FAX (605) 773-6962
dan.siebersma@state.sd.us
www.sdstatelibrary.com

**TENNESSEE**
Charles Sherrill, State Librarian
 and Archivist
Tennessee State Library and
 Archives
403 Seventh Avenue N.
Nashville, TN 37243-0312
(615) 741-7996
FAX (615) 532-9293
chuck.sherrill@tn.gov
www.tennessee.gov/tsla

**TEXAS**
Peggy Rudd, Director & State Librarian
Texas State Library & Archives
 Commission
P.O. Box 12927
Austin, TX 78711-2927
(512) 463-5460
FAX (512) 463-5436
dir.lib@tsl.state.tx.us
www.tsl.state.tx.us/

**UTAH**
Donna Jones Morris, Director & State
 Librarian
Utah State Library
250 N. 1950 West, Suite A
Salt Lake City, UT 84116-7901
(801) 715-6770
FAX (801) 715-6767
dmorris@utah.gov
library.utah.gov/

**VERMONT**
Martha Reid, State Librarian
Vermont Department of Libraries
109 State Street
Montpelier, VT 05609-0601
(802) 828-3265
FAX (802) 828-2199
martha.reid@state.vt.us
libraries.vermont.gov

**VIRGIN ISLANDS**
Ingrid Bough, Territorial Director of
 Libraries, Archives & Museums
1122 Kings St.

Christiansted, St. Croix, VI 00820
(340) 773-5715
FAX (340) 773-5327
www.virginislandspubliclibraries.org/
 usvi/

**VIRGINIA**
Sandra G. Treadway, Librarian of
 Virginia
The Library of Virginia
800 E. Broad St.
Richmond, VA 23219-8000
(804) 692-3535
FAX (804) 692-3594
sandra.treadway@lva.virginia.gov
www.lva.virginia.gov

**WASHINGTON**
Rand Simmons, State Librarian
Washington State Library
Office of the Secretary of State
6880 Capitol Blvd.
Tumwater, WA 98504
(360) 57-05585
FAX (360) 586-7575
rand.simmons@sos.wa.gov
www.sos.wa.gov/library

**WEST VIRGINIA**
Karen Goff, Interim Secretary
West Virginia Library Commission
1900 Kanawha Blvd. E.
Charleston, WV 25305
(304) 558-2041
FAX (304) 558-2044
karen.e.goff@wv.gov
www.librarycommission.lib.wv.us

**WISCONSIN**
Kurt Kiefer, Librarian
Div. for Libraries, Technology and
 Community Learning
125 S. Webster Street, P. O. Box 7841
Madison, WI 53707-7841
(608) 266-2205
FAX (608) 266-8770
kurt.kiefer@dpi.wi.gov
www.dpi.wi.gov/dltcl/index.html

**WYOMING**
Lesley Boughton, State Librarian
Wyoming State Library Division
2800 Central Ave.
Cheyenne, WY 82002
(307) 777-5911
FAX (307) 777-5920
lesley.boughton@wyo.gov
will.state.wy.us/

# STATE LAW LIBRARIES

# Law Library

**Legal resource for the state's highest court.**

## ALABAMA
Mr. Timothy A. Lewis
Director & State Law Librarian
State Law Library
300 Dexter Avenue
Montgomery, AL 36104
P: (334) 229-0560
F: (334) 242-4484
E: director@alalinc.net

## ALASKA
Ms. Catherine Lemann
Law Librarian
State Court Law Library
303 K Street
Anchorage, AK 99501
P: (907) 264-0583
F: (907) 264-0733
E: clemann
@courts.state.ak.us

## AMERICAN SAMOA
Hon. Fepulea'i A.
Ripley Jr.
Attorney General
Office of the Attorney General
American Samoa Government
Executive Office Building,
Utulei
Pago Pago, AS 96799
P: (684) 633-4163
F: (684) 633-1838

## ARIZONA
Ms. Janet Fisher
Acting Director
State Library, Archives &
Public Records
1700 West Washington Street,
Suite 200
Phoenix, AZ 85007
P: (602) 926-4035
F: (602) 256-7983

## ARKANSAS
Ms. Ava Hicks
Director
Supreme Court Library
Justice Building, 1st Floor North
625 Marshall
Little Rock, AR 72201
P: (501) 682-2147
F: (501) 682-6877
E: ava.hicks
@mail.state.ar.us

## CALIFORNIA
Mr. Mark Linneman
Manager
Witkin State Law Library
P.O. Box 942837
Sacramento, CA 94237
P: (916) 653-3883
E: mlinneman@library.ca.gov

## COLORADO
Mr. Dan Cordova
Librarian
State Law Library, Judicial
Branch
State Judicial Building, #B112
2 East 14th Avenue
Denver, CO 80203
P: (303) 837-3720
F: (303) 864-4510

## CONNECTICUT
Ms. Maureen Well
Deputy Director
Law Libraries
Judicial Branch
90 Washington Street, Third
Floor
Hartford, CT 06106
P: (860) 706-5145
F: (860) 706-5086
E: maureen.well@jud.ct.gov

## DELAWARE
Ms. Karen Parrott
Law Librarian
State Law Library
414 Federal Street, #100
Dover, DE 19901
P: (302) 739-5467
F: (302) 739-6721

## DISTRICT OF COLUMBIA
Ms. Letty Limbach
Librarian
Court of Appeals
500 Indiana Avenue, Northwest
Washington, DC 20001
P: (202) 879-2767

## FLORIDA
Ms. Billie J. Blaine
Librarian
Supreme Court Library
500 South Duvall Street
Tallahassee, FL 32399
P: (850) 488-8919
F: (850) 922-5219

## GUAM
Mr. Andrew Quenga
Executive Director/Librarian
Law Library
141 San Ramon Street
Hagatna, GU 96910
P: (671) 477-7623
F: (671) 472-1246
E: gllexecdir@teleguam.net

## HAWAII
Ms. Jenny Fujinaka
Law Librarian
Supreme Court Law Library
Ali'iolani Hale, Room 115
417 South King Street
Honolulu, HI 96813
P: (808) 539-4964
F: (808) 539-4974
E: jenny.r.fujinaka
@courts.state.hi.us

## IDAHO
Mr. John Keay
Acting Director
Law Library
702 West Idaho
P.O. Box 83720
Boise, ID 83720
P: (208) 334-2117
F: (208) 334-2467
E: jkeaye@idcourts.net

## ILLINOIS
Ms. Brenda Larison
Librarian
Courts of Illinois
Supreme Court Building
200 East Capitol Avenue
Springfield, IL 62701
P: (217) 782-2424
F: (217) 782-5287

## INDIANA
Ms. Terri Ross
Law Librarian
Supreme Court Law Library
200 West Washington Street
State House 316
Indianapolis, IN 46204
P: (317) 232-2557
F: (317) 233.8693
E: tross@courts.state.in.us

## IOWA
Mr. Cory Quist
Law Librarian
State Law Library
State Library
1007 East Grand Avenue
Des Moines, IA 50319
P: (515) 281-4307
F: (515) 281-5405
E: cory.quist
@lib.state.ia.us

## KENTUCKY
Ms. Jennifer Frazier
Manager
State Law Library
State Capitol, Suite 200
700 Capitol Avenue
Frankfort, KY 40601
P: (502) 564-4848
F: (502) 564-5041

## LOUISIANA
Ms. Georgia Chadwick
Director
Law Library
Supreme Court
400 Royal Street, 2nd Floor
New Orleans, LA 70130
P: (504) 310-2400
F: (504) 310-2419
E: library@lasc.org

## MAINE
Mr. John R. Barden
Director
State Law & Legislative
Reference Library
43 State House Station
Augusta, ME 04333
P: (207) 287-1600
F: (207) 287-6467
E: john.barden
@legislature.maine.gov

## MARYLAND
Mr. Steve P. Anderson
Director
State Law Library
Murphy Courts of Appeal
Building
361 Rowe Boulevard
Annapolis, MD 21401
P: (410) 260-1432
F: (410) 974-2063

## MICHIGAN
Ms. Susan Adamczak
Administrator
State Law Library
702 West Kalamazoo Street
P.O. Box 30007
Lansing, MI 48909
P: (517) 373-0630
F: (517) 373-7130
E: AdamczakS@michigan.gov

# STATE LAW LIBRARIES

**MINNESOTA**
Ms. Judy Rehak
Acting State Law Librarian
State Law Library
Room G25, Judicial Center
25 Rev. Dr. Martin Luther King
Jr. Dr.
St. Paul, MN 55155
P: (651) 297-7800
F: (651) 296-6740
E: judy.rehak
@courts.state.mn.us

**MISSISSIPPI**
Ms. Clara Joorfetz
State Librarian
State Law Library
P.O. Box 1040
Jackson, MS 39215
P: (601) 359-3672
F: (601) 359-2912
E: cjoorfetz
@mssc.state.ms.us

**MISSOURI**
Mr. Bryan Dunlap
Assistant Librarian
Supreme Court Library
207 West High Street
P.O. Box 150
Jefferson City, MO 65102
P: (573) 751-2636
F: (573) 751-2573

**MONTANA**
Ms. Judith A. Meadows
Director & State Law Librarian
State Law Library
P.O. Box 203004
Helena, MT 59620
P: (406) 444-3660
F: (406) 444-3603
E: jmeadows@mt.gov

**NEBRASKA**
Ms. Janice K. Walker
State Court Administrator
Supreme Court
1445 "K" Street, 1213 State
Capitol
P.O. Box 98910
Lincoln, NE 68509
P: (402) 471-3730
F: (402) 471-2197
E: nsc.info@nebraska.gov

**NEVADA**
Ms. Kathleen L. Harrington
Law Librarian
Supreme Court Law Library
201 South Carson Street
Carson City, NV 89701
P: (775) 684-1671
F: (775) 684-1662
E: harrington
@nvcourts.nv.gov

**NEW HAMPSHIRE**
Ms. Mary S. Searles
Director, Cataloging
State Law Library
Supreme Court Building
One Charles Doe Drive
Concord, NH 03301
P: (603) 271-3777
F: (603) 513-5450
E: msearles
@courts.state.nh.us

**NEW MEXICO**
Mr. Robert Mead
State Law Librarian
Supreme Court Law Library
237 Don Gaspar
Santa Fe, NM 87501
P: (505) 827-4850
F: (505) 827-4852

**NORTH CAROLINA**
Mr. Tom Davis
Librarian
Supreme Court Library
500 Justice Building
2 East Morgan Street
Raleigh, NC 27601
P: (919) 831-5709
E: tpd@sc.state.nc.us

**NORTH DAKOTA**
Mr. Ted Smith
Law Librarian
Supreme Court Law Library
600 East Boulevard Avenue, 2nd
Floor
Judicial Wing
Bismarck, ND 58505
P: (701) 328-4594
F: (701) 328-3609
E: TSmith@ndcourts.gov

**NORTHERN MARIANA
ISLANDS**
Ms. Margarita M. Palacios
Court Administrator
Supreme Court
P.O. Box 2165
Saipan, MP 96950
P: (670) 236-9800
F: (670) 236-9701
E: supreme.court@saipan.com

**OHIO**
Mr. Kenneth Kozlowski
Director
Law Library
Supreme Court of Ohio
65 South Front Street, 11th Floor
Columbus, OH 43215
P: (614) 387-9650
F: (614) 387-9689
E: libref@sc.ohio.gov

**OKLAHOMA**
Ms. Susan Gilley
Administrator
Cartwright Memorial Library
2300 North Lincoln Boulevard,
Room B-8
Oklahoma City, OK 73105
P: (405) 522-3213
F: (405) 521-2753

**OREGON**
Mr. Joe Stephens
Law Librarian
State Law Library
1163 State Street
Salem, OR 97301
P: (503) 986-5644
F: (503) 986-5623
E: joe.k.stephens
@ojd.state.or.us

**PENNSYLVANIA**
Ms. Alice Lubrecht
Director
Bureau of State Library
333 Market Street
Harrisburg, PA 17126
P: (717) 783-5968
F: (717) 772-8258
E: alubrecht@state.pa.us

**RHODE ISLAND**
Ms. Karen Quinn
Chief Law Librarian
State Law Library
Frank Licht Judicial Complex
250 Benefit Street
Providence, RI 02903
P: (401) 222-3275
F: (401) 222-3865
E: kquinn
@courts.state.ri.us

**SOUTH CAROLINA**
Ms. Janet Meyer
Librarian
Supreme Court Library
Supreme Court Building
1231 Gervais Street
Columbia, SC 29211
P: (803) 734-1080
F: (803) 734-0519

**SOUTH DAKOTA**
Ms. Sheridan Anderson
Director
Supreme Court Law Library
500 East Capitol Avenue
Pierre, SD 57501
P: (605) 773-4898
F: (605) 773-6128
E: sheri.anderson
@ujs.state.sd.us

**TEXAS**
Mr. Dale W. Propp
Director
State Law Library
205 West 14th , Room G01
P.O. Box 12367
Austin, TX 78711
P: (512) 463-1722
F: (512) 463-1728

**U.S. VIRGIN ISLANDS**
Ms. Janet Lloyd
Law Librarian
Law Library
5400 Veteran's Drive
St. Thomas, VI 00802
P: (340) 774-6680
F: (340) 776-9889

**UTAH**
Ms. Jessica Van Buren
Director
State Law Library
450 South State Street
Salt Lake City, UT 84114
P: (801) 238-7991
F: (801) 238-7993
E: JESSICAVB
@email.utcourts.gov

**VERMONT**
Ms. Martha Reid
State Librarian
Department of Libraries
Agency of Adminstration
109 State Street
Montpelier, VT 05609
P: (802) 828-3265
F: (802) 828-2199
E: martha.reid@state.vt.us

**VIRGINIA**
Mr. Karl Hade
Executive Secretary
Supreme Court
Supreme Court of Virginia
100 North Ninth Street
Richmond, VA 23219
P: (804) 786-6455
F: (804) 786-4542
E: khade@courts.state.va.us

**WASHINGTON**
Ms. Kay E. Newman
State Law Librarian
State Law Library
415 12th Avenue, Southwest
P.O. Box 40751
Olympia, WA 98504
P: (360) 357-2136
E: kay.newman@courts.wa.gov

**WEST VIRGINIA**
Ms. Kaye L. Maerz
State Law Librarian
State Law Library
State Capitol, Room E-404
1900 Kanawha Boulevard, East
Charleston, WV 25305
P: (304) 558-2607
F: (304) 558-3673
E: kaye.maerz@courtswv.gov

**WISCONSIN**
Ms. Jane Colwin
State Law Librarian
State Law Library
120 Martin Luther King Jr.
Boulevard
Madison, WI 53703
P: (608) 266-1600
F: (608) 267-2319
E: jane.colwin@wicourts.gov

**WYOMING**
Ms. Kathy Carlson
State Law Librarian
State Law Library
Supreme Court & Library
Building
2301 Capitol Avenue
Cheyenne, WY 82002
P: (307) 777-7509
F: (307) 777-7040
E: kcarls@state.wy.us

# HOTLINE NUMBERS FOR BILL STATUS AND LEGISLATIVE INFORMATION

| | | | |
|---|---|---|---|
| Alabama | (334) 242-7600 (House) | Nevada | (775) 684-5545; (775) 684-6827 |
| | (334) 242-7800 (Senate) | | (between sessions) |
| Alaska | (907) 465-4648 | New Hampshire | (603) 271-2239 |
| Arizona | (602) 542-4221 (House) | New Jersey | (609) 292-4840; (800) 792-8630 |
| | (602) 542-3559 (Senate) | New Mexico | (505) 986-4600 |
| Arkansas | (501) 682-7771 (House) | New York | (518) 455-7545; (800) 342-9860 |
| | (501) 682-6107 (Senate) | North Carolina | (919) 733-7044 |
| California | (916) 319-2856 (House) | North Dakota | (701) 328-2916 |
| | (916) 445-2323 | | (between sessions) |
| Colorado | (303) 866-3055 (during sessions) | | (701) 328-2000; (800) 422-1439 |
| | (303) 866-3521 | | (during sessions) |
| | (between sessions) | Ohio | (614) 466-8842; (800) 282-0253 |
| Connecticut | (860) 240-8400 | Oklahoma | (405) 521-2711 (House) |
| Delaware | (302) 739-4114; (800) 282-8545 | | (405) 521-5642 (Senate) |
| District of | | Oregon | (503) 986-1180; (800) 332-2313 |
| Columbia | (202) 724-8050 | Pennsylvania | (717) 787-2342 |
| Florida | (850) 488-4371 | Rhode Island | (401) 751-8833; (401) 222-3580 |
| Georgia | (404) 656-5015 (House) | South Carolina | (803) 212-6720; (800) 922-1539 |
| | (404) 656-5040; (800) 282-5803 | South Dakota | (605) 773-3251 |
| | (Senate) | Tennessee | (615) 741-1552 |
| Hawaii | (808) 587-0478 | Texas | (512) 463-1252 |
| Idaho | (208) 334-2475 | | (800) 253-9693 |
| Illinois | (217) 782-3944 | Utah | (801) 538-1029 (House) |
| Indiana | (317) 232-9856 | | (801) 538-1035 (Senate) |
| Iowa | (515) 281-5129 | Vermont | (802) 828-2231 |
| Kansas | (785) 296-3296; (800) 432-3924 | Virginia | (804) 698-1500 |
| Kentucky | (502) 564-8100 | Washington | (360) 786-7573; (800) 562-6000 |
| Louisiana | (225) 342-2430 | West Virginia | (304) 347-4836; (800) 642-8650 |
| | (800) 256-3793 | Wisconsin | (608) 266-9960; (800) 362-9472 |
| Maine | (207) 287-1692 | Wyoming | (307) 777-6185 |
| Maryland | (410) 946-5400 | | (800) 342-9570 (during sessions) |
| | (800) 492-7122 (x5400) | | (307) 777-7881 |
| Massachusetts | (617) 722-2000 (House) | | (between sessions) |
| | (617) 722-1455 (Senate) | Puerto Rico | (787) 721-5200 |
| Michigan | (517) 373-0135 (House) | Virgin Islands | (340) 774-0880 |
| | (517) 373-2400 (Senate) | Guam | (671) 472-3465 |
| Minnesota | (651) 296-0504 (Senate) | American Samoa | (684) 633-5231 |
| | (651) 296-2146 (House) | | |
| Mississippi | (601) 359-3719 (during sessions) | United States | (202) 225-1772 |
| | (601) 359-3770 (Senate) | | |
| | (601) 359-3360 (House) | | |
| | (between sessions) | | |
| Missouri | (573) 751-4633 | | |
| Montana | (406) 444-4800 | | |
| | (during sessions) | | |
| | (406) 444-3064 | | |
| | (between sessions) | | |
| Nebraska | (402) 471-2271 | | |
| | (between sessions) | | |
| | (402) 471-0769; (800)742-7456 | | |
| | (during sessions) | | |

Note: Toll-free numbers are for in-state use only.

# STATE PUBLIC DEFENDERS

# Public Defender

Represents indigent criminal defendants who desire to appeal their convictions to the state's intermediate appellate court or court of last resort.

## ALASKA
Mr. Quinlan Steiner
Director
Public Defender Agency
Department of Administration
900 West 5th Avenue, Suite 200
Anchorage, AK 99501
P: (907) 334-4400
F: (907) 269-5746
E: quinlan.steiner
@alaska.gov

## ARKANSAS
Ms. Didi Sallings
Director
Public Defender Commission
101 East Capitol, Suite 201
Little Rock, AR 72201
P: (501) 682-9070
F: (501) 682-9073

## CALIFORNIA
Mr. Michael J. Hersek
State Public Defender
Office of the State Public Defender
221 Main Street, 10th Floor
San Francisco, CA 94105
P: (415) 904-5600
F: (415) 904-5635

## COLORADO
Mr. Douglas Wilson
State Public Defender
Office of the State Public Defender
110 16th Street
Petroleum Building, Suite 800
Denver, CO 80202
P: (303) 620-4888
F: (303) 620-4931

## CONNECTICUT
Ms. Susan O. Storey
Chief Public Defender
Division of Public Defender Services
30 Trinity Street, 4th Floor
Hartford, CT 06106
P: (860) 509-6429
E: susan.storey@jud.ct.gov

## DELAWARE
Mr. Brendan O'Neill
Public Defender
Office of the Public Defender
Carvel State Office Building
820 North French Street, 3rd Floor
Wilmington, DE 19801
P: (302) 577-5200
F: (302) 577-3995

## DISTRICT OF COLUMBIA
Ms. Avis Buchanan
Director
Public Defender Service
633 Indiana Avenue, Northwest
Washington, DC 20004
P: (202) 628-1200
F: (202) 824-2423
E: abuchanan@pdsdc.org

## FLORIDA
Mr. Sheldon Gusky
Executive Director
Public Defender Association
103 North Gadsden Street
P.O. Box 11057
Tallahassee, FL 32302
P: (850) 488-6850
F: (850) 488-4720
E: sgusky@st.flpda.org

## GEORGIA
Hon. Sam S. Olens (R)
Attorney General
Office of the Attorney General
40 Capitol Square, Southwest
Atlanta, GA 30334
P: (404) 656-3300
F: (404) 657-8733

## GUAM
Mr. Mike Nisperos
Executive Director
Public Defender Service Corporation
Judicial Center, 2nd Floor
110 West O'Brien Drive
Agana, GU 96910
P: (671) 475-3100
F: (671) 477-5844
E: mnisperos@guampdsc.net

## HAWAII
Mr. John M. Tonaki
Public Defender
Office of the Public Defender
1130 North Nimitz Highway
Suite A-254
Honolulu, HI 96817
P: (808) 586-2200
F: (808) 586-2222

## IDAHO
Ms. Molly J. Huskey
State Appellate Public Defender
Appellate Public Defender
3647 Lake Harbor Lane
Boise, ID 83703
P: (208) 334-2712
F: (208) 334-2985
E: mhusky@sapd.state.id.us

## ILLINOIS
Mr. Michael J. Pelletier
State Appellate Defender
Office of the State Appellate Defender
400 West Monroe, Suite 202
P.O. Box 5240
Springfield, IL 62704
P: (217) 782-7203
F: (217) 782-5385
E: Michael.Pelletier
@osad.state.il.us

## IOWA
Mr. Tomas Rodriguez
State Public Defender
State Public Defender Office
Lucas Building, 4th Floor
321 East 12th Street
Des Moines, IA 50319
P: (515) 242-6158
F: (515) 281-7289
E: tomas.rodriguez
@spd.state.ia.us

## KANSAS
Ms. Patricia A. Scalia
Executive Director
Board of Indigents' Defense Services
714 Southwest Jackson, Suite 200
Topeka, KS 66603
P: (785) 296-4505
F: (785) 291-3082

## KENTUCKY
Mr. Edward C. Monahan
Public Advocate
Department of Public Advocacy
100 Fair Oaks Lane, Suite 302
Frankfort, KY 40601
P: (502) 564-8006
F: (502) 564-7890

## LOUISIANA
Ms. Jean M. Faria
State Public Defender
Public Defender Board
5000 Laurel Street, Suite 300
Baton Rouge, LA 70801
P: (225) 219-9305
F: (225) 219-9326
E: jfaria@lpdb.la.gov

## MARYLAND
Mr. Paul B. DeWolfe Jr.
Public Defender
Public Defender System
William Donald Schefer Tower
6 St. Paul Street, Suite 1400
Baltimore, MD 21202
P: (410) 767-8479
F: (410) 333-8496
E: pdewolfe@opd.state.md.us

## MASSACHUSETTS
Mr. Anthony Benedetti
Chief Counsel
Public Defender Division
Committee for Public Counsel Services
44 Bromfield Street
Boston, MA 02108
P: (617) 988-8322
F: (617) 988-8495

## MICHIGAN
Mr. James Neuhard
Director
State Appellate Defender Office
Suite 3300, Penobscot Building
645 Griswald
Detroit, MI 48226
P: (313) 256-9833

## MINNESOTA
Mr. John Stuart
State Public Defender
Office of the State Public Defender
331 Second Avenue South, Suite 900
Minneapolis, MN 55401
P: (612) 279-3512
E: John.Stuart@state.mn.us

## MISSOURI
Ms. Cathy R. Kelly
State Public Defender
State Public Defender System
Woodrail Centre
1000 West Nifong, Building 7, Suite 100
Columbia, MO 65203
P: (573) 882-9855
F: (573) 882-9740
E: public.defender
@mspd.mo.gov

## MONTANA
Ms. Randi M. Hood
Chief Public Defender
Office of the State Public Defender
44 West Park Street
Butte, MT 59701
P: (406) 496-6082
F: (406) 496-6098

# STATE PUBLIC DEFENDERS

**NEBRASKA**
Mr. James Mowbray
Chief Counsel
Commission on Public
Advocacy
P.O. Box 98932
Lincoln, NE 68509
P: (402) 471-7774
E: jmowbray@ncpa.ne.gov

**NEVADA**
Mr. Steven G. McGuire
State Public Defender
Office of the Public Defender
Department of Health & Human
Services
511 East Robinson Street, #1
Carson City, NV 89701
P: (775) 687-4880
F: (775) 687-4993
E: smcguire
   @govmail.state.nv.us

**NEW HAMPSHIRE**
Mr. Christopher Keating
Executive Director
Public Defender
10 Ferry Street, Suite 202
Concord, NH 03301
P: (603) 224-1236
F: (603) 227-9367
E: ckeating@nhpd.org

**NEW JERSEY**
Ms. Yvonne Smith Segars
Public Defender
Office of the Public Defender
25 Market Street, 1st Floor
N-Wing
P.O. Box 850
Trenton, NJ 08625
P: (609) 292-7087
F: (609) 777-1795
E: thedefenders
   @opd.state.nj.us

**NEW MEXICO**
Mr. Hugh Dangler
Chief Public Defender
Public Defender Department
301 North Guadalupe Street,
Suite 101
Santa Fe, NM 87501
P: (505) 827-3931
F: (505) 827-3999

**NORTH CAROLINA**
Mr. Thomas Maher
Executive Director
Office of Indigent Defense
Services
123 W. Main Street
Suite 400
Durham, NC 27701
P: (919) 560-3380
F: (919) 560-3332
E: Thomas.K.Maher
   @nccourts.org

**NORTH DAKOTA**
Hon. Wayne Stenehjem (R)
Attorney General
Office of the Attorney General
State Capitol, Department 125
600 East Boulevard Avenue
Bismarck, ND 58505
P: (701) 328-2210
F: (701) 328-2226
E: wstenehjem@nd.gov

**NORTHERN MARIANA
ISLANDS**
Ms. Adam Hardwicke
Public Defender
Office of the Public Defender
Caller Box 10007, Capitol Hill
Saipan, MP 96950
P: (670) 234-2421
F: (670) 234-1009

**OHIO**
Mr. Timothy Young
Director
Office of the Public Defender
250 East Broad Street, Suite
1400
Columbus, OH 43215
P: (614) 466-5394
F: (614) 644-9972

**OKLAHOMA**
Mr. Joe P. Robertson
Executive Director
Indigent Defense System
P.O. Box 926
Norman, OK 73070
P: (405) 801-2601

**OREGON**
Ms. Ingrid Swenson
Executive Director
Office of Public Defense
Services
1320 Capitol Street, Northeast
Suite 200
Salem, OR 97303
P: (503) 378-2515
F: (503) 378-4462
E: Ingrid.Swenson
   @opds.state.or.us

**RHODE ISLAND**
Mr. John J. Hardiman
Public Defender
Office of the Public Defender
160 Pine Street
Providence, RI 02903
P: (401) 222-3492
E: Information@ripd.org

**SOUTH DAKOTA**
Hon. Marty J. Jackley (R)
Attorney General
Office of the Attorney General
1302 East Highway 14,
Suite 1
Pierre, SD 57501
P: (605) 773-3215
F: (605) 773-4106
E: atghelp@state.sd.us

**U.S. VIRGIN ISLANDS**
Mr. Thurston McKelvin
Federal Public Defender
Office of the Public Defender
P.O. Box 3450
Christiansted
St. Croix, VI 00820
P: (340) 773-3585
F: (340) 773-3742

**VERMONT**
Mr. Matthew F. Valerio
Defender General
Office of the Defender General
6 Baldwin Street, 4th Floor
Montpelier, VT 05633
P: (802) 828-3168
F: (802) 828-3163
E: matthew.valerio
   @state.vt.us

**VIRGINIA**
Mr. David J. Johnson
Executive Director
Indigent Defense Commission
1604 Santa Rosa Road, Suite
109
Richmond, VA 23229
P: (804) 662-7249
F: (804) 662-7359
E: djohnson
   @idc.virginia.gov

**WASHINGTON**
Ms. Joanne Moore
Director
State Office of Public Defense
711 Capitol Way South, Suite
106
Evergreen Plaza Building, P.O.
Box 40957
Olympia, WA 98504
P: (360) 586-3164, Ext. 112
F: (360) 586-8165
E: opd@opd.wa.gov

**WEST VIRGINIA**
Mr. Russ Cook
Acting Executive Director
Public Defender Services
One Players Club Drive, Suite
301
Charleston, WV 25311
P: (304) 558-3905
F: (304) 558-1098
E: Russell.S.Cook@wv.gov

**WISCONSIN**
Ms. Kelli Thompson
State Public Defender
Office of the State Public
Defender
315 North Henry, 2nd Floor
Madison, WI 53707
P: (608) 266-0087
F: (608) 267-0584

**WYOMING**
Ms. Diane Lozano
State Public Defender
State Public Defenders Office
2020 Carey Avenue, 3rd Floor
Cheyenne, WY 82002
P: (307) 777-7137
F: (307) 777-6253

# CLERK OF STATE COURT OF LAST RESORT

# Clerk of the State's Highest Court

**Individual who keeps records of the state's highest court.**

**ALABAMA**
Mr. Robert G. Esdale Sr.
Clerk
Supreme Court
300 Dexter Avenue
Montgomery, AL 36104
P: (334) 229-0700

**ALASKA**
Ms. Marilyn May
Clerk of the Appellate Courts
Appellate Courts
303 K Street
Anchorage, AK 99501
P: (907) 264-0612
F: (907) 264-0878
E: mmay
@appellate.courts.state.ak.us

**AMERICAN SAMOA**
Mr. Robert Gorniak
Chief Clerk
High Court of American Samoa
American Samoa Government
Pago Pago, AS 96799
P: (684) 633-4131
F: (684) 633-1318

**ARIZONA**
Ms. Rachelle M. Resnick
Clerk of the Court
Supreme Court
1501 West Washington, Suite 402
Phoenix, AZ 85007
P: (602) 452-3396
E: scclerk@courts.az.gov

**ARKANSAS**
Mr. Leslie W. Steen
Clerk of the Courts
Supreme Court
1320 Justice Building
625 Marshall Street
Little Rock, AR 72201
P: (501) 682-6849

**CALIFORNIA**
Mr. Frederick K. Ohlrich
Clerk of the Court
Supreme Court
350 McAllister Street
San Francisco, CA 94102
P: (415) 865-7015

**COLORADO**
Ms. Susan J. Festag
Clerk of the Supreme Court
Supreme Court
2 East 14th Avenue. 4th Floor
Denver, CO 80203
P: (303) 837-3790
E: susan.festag
@judicial.state.co.us

**CONNECTICUT**
Ms. Michele T. Angers
Chief Clerk
Supreme Court
231 Capitol Avenue
Hartford, CT 06106
P: (860) 757-2200
F: (860) 757-2217

**DELAWARE**
Ms. Cathy L. Howard
Clerk of the Court
Supreme Court
Carvel State Office Building
820 North French Street, 11th Floor
Wilmington, DE 19801
P: (302) 739-4187
F: (302) 577-3702

**DISTRICT OF COLUMBIA**
Mr. Julio A. Castillo
Clerk of the Court
Court of Appeals
Historic Courthouse
430 E Street, Northwest
Washington, DC 20001
P: (202) 879-2725

**FLORIDA**
Mr. Thomas D. Hall
Clerk
Supreme Court
500 South Duval Street
Tallahassee, FL 32399
P: (850) 488-0125
E: supremecourt
@flcourts.org

**GEORGIA**
Ms. Therese S. Barnes
Clerk
Supreme Court
244 Washington Street
Room 572, State Office Annex Building
Atlanta. GA 30334
P: (404) 656-3470
F: (404) 656-2253

**GUAM**
Ms. Hannah M.
   Gutierrez-Arroyo
Supreme Court
Guam Judicial Center
120 West O'Brien Drive
Hagatna, GU 96910
P: (671) 475-3162
E: hgutierrezarroyo
@guamsupremecourt.com

**HAWAII**
Ms. Naomi Komenaka
Chief Clerk
Supreme Court
Aliiolani Hale
417 South King Street
Honolulu, HI 96813
P: (808) 539-4919
F: (808) 539-4928

**IDAHO**
Mr. Stephen W. Kenyon
Clerk of the Supreme Court
Supreme Court
P.O. Box 83720
Boise, ID 83720
P: (208) 334-2210
F: (208) 947-7590

**ILLINOIS**
Ms. Carolyn Taft Grosboll
Clerk of the Supreme Court
Supreme Court
Supreme Court Building
200 East Capitol
Springfield, IL 62701
P: (217) 782-2035

**INDIANA**
Mr. Kevin Smith
Clerk of Supreme Court, Court of Appeals & Tax Court
State Courts
200 West Washington Street
216 State House
Indianapolis, IN 46204
P: (317) 232-1930
F: (317) 232-8365

**IOWA**
Ms. Donna Humpal
Clerk
Supreme Court
Iowa Judicial Branch Building
1111 East Court Avenue
Des Moines, IA 50319
P: (515) 281-5911
E: Donna.Humpal
@iowacourts.gov

**KANSAS**
Ms. Carol Gilliam Green
Clerk of the Appellate Courts
Office of the Clerk of the Appellate Courts
Judicial Center
301 Southwest 10th Avenue,
Room 374
Topeka, KS 66612
P: (785) 296-3229
F: (785) 296-1028
E: appellateclerk
@kscourts.org

**KENTUCKY**
Ms. Susan Stokley Clary
Clerk of the Supreme Court
Supreme Court
State Capitol
700 Capitol Avenue, Room 235
Frankfort, KY 40601
P: (502) 564-5444
F: (502) 564-2665

**LOUISIANA**
Mr. John Tarlton Olivier
Clerk of Court
Supreme Court
400 Royal Street, Suite 4200
New Orleans, LA 70130
P: (504) 310-2300

**MAINE**
Mr. Matthew Pollack
Clerk of the Law Court
Supreme Court
205 Newbury Street, Room 139
Portland, ME 04101
P: (207) 822-4146

**MARYLAND**
Ms. Bessie M. Decker
Clerk of Court of Appeals
Judiciary of Maryland
Robert Murphy Courts of Appeal Building
361 Rowe Boulevard
Annapolis, MD 21401
P: (410) 260-1508

**MASSACHUSETTS**
Ms. Susan Mellen
Clerk
Supreme Judicial Court of Commonwealth
John Adams Courthouse, Suite 1-400
One Pemberton Square
Boston, MA 02108
P: (617) 557-1020
F: (617) 557-1145

**MICHIGAN**
Mr. Corbin R. Davis
Clerk
Supreme Court
P.O. Box 30052
Lansing, MI 48909
P: (517) 373-0120
E: MSC_Clerk@courts.mi.gov

**MINNESOTA**
Mr. Frederick K. Grittner
Clerk of Appellate Courts
Supreme Court
305 Minnesota Judicial Center
25 Rev. Martin Luther King Jr Boulevard
St. Paul, MN 55155
P: (651) 296-2581

**MISSISSIPPI**
Ms. Kathy Gillis
Clerk
Supreme Court
P.O. Box 117
Jackson, MS 39205
P: (601) 359-2175
F: (601) 359-2407
E: sctclerk
@mssc.state.ms.us

**MISSOURI**
Mr. Thomas F. Simon
Supreme Court Clerk
Supreme Court
P. O. Box 150
Jefferson City, MO 65102
P: (573) 751-4144
F: (573) 751-7514

**MONTANA**
Mr. Ed Smith
Clerk
Supreme Court
215 North Sanders, Room 323
P.O. Box 203003
Helena, MT 59620
P: (406) 444-3858
F: (406) 444-5705

**NEBRASKA**
Ms. Lanet S. Asmussen
Clerk
Supreme Court
2413 State Capitol
P.O. Box 98910
Lincoln, NE 68509
P: (402) 471-3731
F: (402) 471-3480

# CLERK OF STATE COURT OF LAST RESORT

**NEVADA**
Ms. Tracie K. Lindeman
Chief Clerk
Supreme Court
201 South Carson Street
Carson City, NV 89701
P: (775) 684-1600
F: (775) 684-1601
E: tlindeman
@nvcourts.nv.gov

**NEW HAMPSHIRE**
Ms. Eileen Fox
Clerk of Court
Supreme Court
Supreme Court Building
One Charles Doe Drive
Concord, NH 03301
P: (603) 271-2646
F: (603) 271-6630

**NEW JERSEY**
Mr. Mark Neary
Clerk
Supreme Court
Richard J. Hughes Justice
Complex
P.O. Box 970
Trenton, NJ 08625
P: (609) 292-4837

**NEW MEXICO**
Ms. Kathleen Jo Gibson
Chief Clerk
Supreme Court
237 Don Gaspar Avenue
Santa Fe, NM 87501
P: (505) 827-4860
F: (505) 827-4837

**NEW YORK**
Mr. Andrew Klein
Clerk of the Court
Court of Appeals
20 Eagle Street
Albany, NY 12207
P: (518) 455-7700
F: (518) 463-6869

**NORTH CAROLINA**
Ms. Christie Speir Cameron
Clerk
Supreme Court
Clerk's Office
2 East Morgan Street, P.O. Box 2170
Raleigh, NC 27602
P: (919) 831-5700

**NORTH DAKOTA**
Ms. Penny Miller
Clerk of Supreme Court
Supreme Court
State Capitol
600 East Boulevard Avenue
Bismarck, ND 58505
P: (701) 328-2221
F: (701) 328-4480
E: PMiller@ndcourts.gov

**NORTHERN MARIANA ISLANDS**
Mr. Chris Kaipat
Clerk
Supreme Court
P.O. Box 502165
Saipan, MP 96950
P: (670) 236-9700
F: (670) 236-9702
E: supreme.court@saipan.com

**OHIO**
Ms. Kristina D. Frost
Clerk of the Court
Supreme Court
65 South Front Street, 8th Floor
Columbus, OH 43215
P: (614) 387-9530
F: (614) 387-9539

**OKLAHOMA**
Mr. Michael S. Richie
Supreme Court Clerk
Supreme Court
P.O. Box 53126
Oklahoma City, OK 73152
P: (405) 521-2163

**OREGON**
Ms. Kingsley W. Click
State Court Administrator
Judicial Department
Supreme Court Building
1163 State Street
Salem, OR 97301
P: (503) 986-5500
F: (503) 986-5503
E: kingsley.w.click
@state.or.us

**PENNSYLVANIA**
Ms. Patricia Johnson
Chief Clerk
Supreme Court
468 City Hall
Philadelphia, PA 19107
P: (215) 560-6370

Ms. Patricia A. Niccola
Chief Clerk
Supreme Court
801 City-County Building
Pittsburgh, PA 15219
P: (412) 565-2816

Ms. Elizabeth Zisk
Chief Clerk
Supreme Court
601 Commonwealth Avenue,
Suite 4500
P.O. Box 62575
Harrisburg, PA 17106
P: (717) 787-6181

**PUERTO RICO**
Ms. Patricia Oton Oliveri
Secretary of Supreme Court
Supreme Court
P.O. Box 9022392
San Juan, PR 00902
P: (787) 723-6033
F: (787) 723-9199

**RHODE ISLAND**
Ms. Debra A. Saunders
Supreme Court Clerk
Supreme Court
Frank Licht Judicial Complex
250 Benefit Street
Providence, RI 02903
P: (401) 222-3599

**SOUTH CAROLINA**
Mr. Daniel E. Shearouse
Clerk of Court
Supreme Court
1231 Gervais Street
P.O. Box 11330
Columbia, SC 29211
P: (803) 734-1080
F: (803) 734-1499

**SOUTH DAKOTA**
Ms. Shirley A.
    Jameson-Fergel
Clerk
Supreme Court
500 East Capitol Avenue
Pierre, SD 57501
P: (605) 773-3511
F: (605) 773-6128

**TENNESSEE**
Mr. Mike Catalano
Appellate Court Clerk
Appellate Courts
Supreme Court Building
401 7th Avenue, North
Nashville, TN 37219
P: (615) 741-2681
F: (615) 532-8757

**TEXAS**
Mr. Blake A. Hawthorne
Clerk of the Court
Supreme Court
Supreme Court Building-A
P.O. Box 12248
Austin, TX 78711
P: (512) 463-1312
F: (512) 463-1365

**U.S. VIRGIN ISLANDS**
Ms. Veronica J. Handy
Clerk of the Court
Supreme Court
P.O. Box 590
St. Thomas, VI 00804
P: (340) 774-2237
F: (340) 774-2258

**UTAH**
Ms. Pat H. Bartholomew
Clerk of Court
Supreme Court
450 South State Street, 5th Floor
P.O. Box 140210
Salt Lake City, UT 84114
P: (801) 238-7974
F: (801) 238-7980
E: pathb@email.utcourts.gov

**VERMONT**
Mr. Robert Greemore
Court Administrator and Clerk
Supreme Court
109 State Street
Montpelier, VT 05609
P: (802) 828-3278
F: (802) 828-4750
E: bob.greemore@state.vt.us

**VIRGINIA**
Ms. Patricia L. Harrington
Clerk
Supreme Court
100 North 9th Street, 5th Floor
Richmond, VA 23219
P: (804) 786-2251

**WASHINGTON**
Mr. Ronald R. Carpenter
Clerk
Supreme Court
415 12th Avenue, Southwest
P.O. Box 40929
Olympia, WA 98504
P: (360) 357-2077
F: (360) 357-2102
E: supreme@courts.wa.gov

**WEST VIRGINIA**
Mr. Rory L. Perry II
Clerk of Court
Supreme Court of Appeals
State Capitol, Room E-317
Charleston, WV 25305
P: (304) 558-2601
F: (304) 558-3815

**WISCONSIN**
Mr. A. John Voelker
Director of State Courts/Acting
Clerk
Supreme Court
16 East State Capitol
P.O. Box 1688
Madison, WI 53701
P: (608) 266-6828
F: (608) 267-0980
E: john.voelker
@courts.state.wi.us

**WYOMING**
Ms. Judy Pacheco
Clerk of Court
Supreme Court
2301 Capitol Avenue
Cheyenne, WY 82001
P: (307) 777-7316
F: (307) 777-6129
E: jpacheco
@courts.state.wy.us

# STATE COURT ADMINISTRATORS

**ALABAMA**
Ms. Callie Dietz
Administrative Director of
 the Courts
300 Dexter Ave.
Montgomery, AL 36104-3741
(334) 954-5080

**ALASKA**
Ms. Christine Johnson
Administrative Director of the
 Courts
Alaska Court System
303 K Street
Anchorage, Alaska 99501
(907) 264-0547

**AMERICAN SAMOA**
Mr. Otto Thompson
Court Administrator
High Court of American Samoa
P.O. Box 309
Pago Pago, American Samoa 96799
011 (684) 633-1150

**ARIZONA**
Mr. David K. Byers
Administrative Director of the Courts
Arizona Supreme Court
1501 W. Washington St., Suite 411
Phoenix, AZ 85007
(602) 452-3301

**ARKANSAS**
Mr. James D. Gingerich
Director, Administrative Office of
 the Courts
Supreme Court of Arkansas
Justice Building
625 Marshall St.
Little Rock, AR 72201
(501) 682-9400

**CALIFORNIA**
Mr. William C. Vickrey
Administrative Director of the
 Courts
Administrative Office of the
 Courts
455 Golden Gate Ave.
San Francisco, CA 94102
(415) 865-4235

**COLORADO**
Mr. Gerald A. Marroney

State Court Administrator
Colorado Judicial Department
101 West Colfax, Suite 500
Denver, CO 80202
(303) 837-3668

**CONNECTICUT**
Honorable Barbara M. Quinn
Chief Court Administrator
Supreme Court of Connecticut
231 Capitol Avenue
Hartford, CT 06106
(860) 757-2100

**DELAWARE**
Hon. Patricia W. Griffin
State Court Administrator
Administrative Office of the Courts
1 S. Race Street
Georgetown, DE 19947
(302) 856-5406

**DISTRICT OF COLUMBIA**
Ms. Anne B. Wicks
Executive Officer
Courts of the District of Columbia
500 Indiana Ave. NW, Room 6680
Washington, DC 20001
(202) 879-1700

**FLORIDA**
Ms. Elisabeth H. Goodner
State Courts Administrator
Supreme Court Building
500 South Duval Street
Tallahassee, FL 32399-1900
(850) 922-5081

**GEORGIA**
Ms. Marla S. Moore
Director, Administrative Office of
 the Courts
244 Washington Street, SW,
 Suite 300
Atlanta, GA 30334
(404) 656-5171

**GUAM**
Mr. Perry C. Taitano
Administrator of the Courts
Judiciary of Guam
Guam Judicial Center
120 West O'Brien Drive
Hagatna, GU 96910
(671) 475-3330

**HAWAII**
Mr. Rodney A. Maile
Administrative Director of the
 Courts
The Judiciary, State of Hawaii
417 South King Street, Rm. 206
Honolulu, HI 96813
(808) 539-4900

**IDAHO**
Ms. Patricia Tobias
Administrative Director of the
 Courts
Supreme Court Building
451 West State Street
P.O. Box 83720
Boise, ID 83720-0101
(208) 334-2246

**ILLINOIS**
Ms. Cynthia Y. Cobbs
Director of the Administrative
 Office of the Illinois Courts
222 North LaSalle St., 13th fl.
Chicago, IL 60601
(312) 793-3250

**INDIANA**
Ms. Lilia G. Judson
Executive Director, Division of
 State Court Administration
Indiana Supreme Court
30 S. Meridian St., Suite 500
Indianapolis, IN 46204-3568
(317) 232-2542

**IOWA**
Mr. David K. Boyd
State Court Administrator
Iowa Judicial Branch Bldg.
1111 East Court Ave.
Des Moines, IA 50319
(515) 281-5241

**KANSAS**
Ms. Nancy Dixon
Judicial Administrator
Kansas Judicial Center
301 SW 10th Street
Topeka, KS 66612
(785) 296-4873

**KENTUCKY**
Ms. Laurie Dudgeon

# STATE COURT ADMINISTRATORS

Administrative Director
Administrative Office of the Courts
100 Millcreek Park
Frankfort, KY 40601
(502) 573-2350

## LOUISIANA
Mr. Timothy F. Averill
Judicial Administrator
Supreme Court of Louisiana
400 Royal St., Suite 1190
New Orleans, LA 70130
(504) 310-2605

## MAINE
Mr. James T. Glessner
State Court Administrator
Administrative Office of the Courts
P.O. Box 4820
Portland, ME 04112-4820
(207) 822-0710

## MARYLAND
Mr. Frank Broccolina
State Court Administrator
Administrative Office of the Courts
Maryland Judicial Center
580 Taylor Avenue
Annapolis, MD 21401
(410) 260-1295

## MASSACHUSETTS
Hon. Robert A. Mulligan
Chief Justice for Administration
 and Management
Massachusetts Trial Court
One Pemberton Square
Boston, MA 02108
(617) 878-0203

## MICHIGAN
Hon. Chad Schmucker
State Court Administrator
State Court Administrative Office
P.O. Box 30048
Lansing, MI 48909
(517) 373-0128

## MINNESOTA
Ms. Sue K. Dosal
State Court Administrator
Supreme Court of Minnesota
135 Minnesota Judicial Center
25 Rev. Dr. Martin Luther
 King Jr. Blvd.
St. Paul, MN 55155
(651) 296-2474

## MISSISSIPPI
Mr. Kevin Lackey
Director, Administrative Office of
 the Courts
Supreme Court of Mississippi
P.O. Box 117
Jackson, MS 39205
(601) 576-4636

## MISSOURI
Mr. Gregory J. Linhares
State Court Administrator
Supreme Court of Missouri
2112 Industrial Drive
P.O. Box 104480
Jefferson City, MO 65110
(573) 751-4377

## MONTANA
Ms. Lois Menzies
State Court Administrator
Montana Supreme Court
301 South Park Ave., Rm. 238
P.O. Box 203005
Helena, MT 59620-3005
(406) 841-2957

## NEBRASKA
Ms. Janice K. Walker
State Court Administrator
Nebraska Supreme Court
State Capitol Building
P.O. Box 98910
Lincoln, NE 68509-8910
(402) 471-3730

## NEVADA
Ms. Robin Sweet
State Court Administrator
Administrative Office of the Courts
Supreme Court Building
201 S. Carson Street, Suite 250
Carson City, NV 89701-4702
(775) 684-1717

## NEW HAMPSHIRE
Mr. Donald D. Goodnow
Director, Administrative Office of
 the Courts
Two Charles Doe Drive
Concord, NH 03301
(603) 271-2521

## NEW JERSEY
Hon. Glenn A. Grant
Acting Administrative Director of
 the Courts

25 Market Street, 7th fl.
P.O. Box 037 RJH Justice Complex
Trenton, NJ 08625-0037
(609) 984-0275

## NEW MEXICO
Mr. Arthur W. Pepin
Director, Administrative Office of
 the Courts
237 Don Gaspar, Room 25
Santa Fe, NM 87501-2178
(505) 827-4800

## NEW YORK
Hon. Ann Pfau
Chief Administrative Judge
Office of Court Administration
25 Beaver St., 11th fl.
New York, NY 10004
(212) 428-2100

## NORTH CAROLINA
Mr. John W. Smith
Director, Administrative Office of
 the Courts
North Carolina Judicial Center
901 Corporate Center Drive
P.O. Box 2448
Raleigh, NC 27602
(919) 890-1391

## NORTH DAKOTA
Ms. Sally Holewa
State Court Administrator
Supreme Court of North Dakota
State Capitol Bldg., 1st fl.,
 Judicial Wing
600 East Blvd. Avenue, Dept. 180
Bismarck, ND 58505-0530
(701) 328-4216

## NORTHERN MARIANA
ISLANDS
Ms. Tracy M. Guerrero
Director of Courts
Supreme Court of the Northern
Mariana Islands
Guma Hustisia, 1st fl.
Susupe, P.O. Box 502165
Saipan, MP 96950
(670) 236-9807

## OHIO
Mr. Steven C. Hollon
Administrative Director
Supreme Court of Ohio
65 South Front Street

# STATE COURT ADMINISTRATORS

Columbus, OH 43215-3431
(614) 387-9500

**OKLAHOMA**
Mr. Michael D. Evans
Administrative Director of the
 Courts
1915 N. Stiles, Suite 305
Oklahoma City, OK 73105
(405) 522-7878

**OREGON**
Ms. Kingsley W. Click
State Court Administrator
Office of the State Court
 Administrator
Supreme Court Building
1163 State St.
Salem, OR 97301-2563
(503) 986-5500

**PENNSYLVANIA**
Mr. Zygmont Pines
Court Administrator of Pennsylvania
Administrative Office of PA Courts
Supreme Court of Pennsylvania
1515 Market Street, Suite 1414
Philadelphia, PA 19102
(215) 560-6337

**PUERTO RICO**
Hon. Sonia I. Velez
Administrative Director of the
 Courts
Office of Court Administration
P.O. Box 190917, Hato Rey Station
6 Vela St., Stop 35 - 1/2
San Juan, PR 00919-0917
(787) 641-6623

**RHODE ISLAND**
Mr. J. Joseph Baxter
State Court Administrator
Supreme Court of Rhode Island
Licht Judicial Complex
250 Benefit Street, Suite 705
Providence, RI 02903
(401) 222-3263

**SOUTH CAROLINA**
Ms. Rosalyn W. Frierson
Director, South Carolina Court
 Administration
1015 Sumter St., Suite 200
Columbia, SC 29201
(803) 734-1800

**SOUTH DAKOTA**
Ms. Patricia Duggan
State Court Administrator
Unified Judicial System
500 East Capitol Avenue
Pierre, SD 57501-5070
(605) 773-3474

**TENNESSEE**
Ms. Elizabeth A. Sykes
Director, Administrative Office of
 the Courts
Nashville City Center
511 Union Street, Suite 600
Nashville, TN 37219
(615) 741-2687

**TEXAS**
Mr. Carl Reynolds
Administrative Director
Office of Court Administration
Tom C. Clark State Courts Building
205 W. 14th Street, Suite 600
P.O. Box 12066
Austin, TX 78711-2066
(512) 463-1625

**UTAH**
Mr. Daniel Becker
State Court Administrator
450 South State
P.O. Box 140241
Salt Lake City, UT 84114-0241
(801) 578-3806

**VERMONT**
Mr. Robert Greemore
Court Administrator
State of Vermont
109 State Street
Montpelier, VT 05609-0701
(802) 828-3278

**VIRGINIA**
Mr. Karl R. Hade
Executive Secretary
Supreme Court of Virginia
100 North Ninth Street, Third Floor
Richmond, VA 23219-2334
(804) 786-6455

**VIRGIN ISLANDS**
Ms. Glenda L. Lake
Administrative Director
Superior Court of the Virgin
 Islands

P. O. Box 590
St. Thomas, VI 00805
(340) 774-2237

**WASHINGTON**
Mr. Jeff E. Hall
State Court Administrator
Administrative Office of the Courts
415 12th Ave., SW
P.O. Box 41170
Olympia, WA 98504-1170
(360) 357-2120

**WEST VIRGINIA**
Mr. Steven D. Canterbury
Administrative Director
West Virginia Supreme Court of
 Appeals
Administrative Office
Rm. E-100, State Capitol Building
Charleston, WV 25305-0832
(304) 558-0145

**WISCONSIN**
Mr. A. John Voelker
Interim Director of State Courts
Supreme Court of Wisconsin
16 East State Capitol
P. O. Box 1688
Madison, WI 53701-1688
(608) 266-6828

**WYOMING**
Ms. Joann Odendahl
State Court Administrator
Supreme Court of Wyoming
Supreme Court Building
2301 Capital Avenue
Cheyenne, WY 82002
(307) 777-7581

# STATE CHIEF JUSTICES

**ALABAMA**
Honorable Sue Bell Cobb
Chief Justice, Supreme Court of
 Alabama
300 Dexter Avenue
Montgomery, AL 36104-3741
(334) 242-0599

**ALASKA**
Honorable Walter L. Carpeneti
Chief Justice, Supreme Court of
 Alaska
123 4th St., Rm. 750
Juneau, AK 99801
(907) 463-4771

**AMERICAN SAMOA**
Honorable F. Michael Kruse
Chief Justice, The High Court of
 American Samoa
Courthouse, P.O. Box 309
Pago Pago, American Samoa 96799
011 (684) 633-1410

**ARIZONA**
Honorable Rebecca White Berch
Chief Justice, Supreme Court of
 Arizona
1501 W. Washington Street, 4th fl.
Phoenix, AZ 85007-3231
(602) 452-3535

**ARKANSAS**
Honorable Jim Hannah
Chief Justice, Supreme Court of
 Arkansas
Justice Building, 625 Marshall
 Street
Little Rock, AR 72201
(501) 682-6873

**CALIFORNIA**
Honorable Tani Cantil-Sakauye
Chief Justice, Supreme Court of
 California
350 McAllister Street
San Francisco, CA 94102
(415) 865-7060

**COLORADO**
Honorable Michael L. Bender
Chief Justice, Supreme Court of
 Colorado
State Judicial Building
101 W. Colfax Ave., Suite 800
Denver, CO 80203
(303) 837-3741

**CONNECTICUT**
Honorable Chase T. Rogers
Chief Justice, Supreme Court of
 Connecticut

Connecticut Judicial Branch
Supreme Court Building
231 Capitol Avenue
Drawer N, Station A
Hartford, CT 06106
(860) 757-2120

**DELAWARE**
Honorable Myron T. Steele
Chief Justice, Supreme Court of
 Delaware
57 The Green
Dover, DE 19901
(302) 739-4214

**DISTRICT OF COLUMBIA**
Honorable Eric T. Washington
Chief Judge, Court of Appeals of
 the District of Columbia
430 E St., NW, Suite 319
Washington, DC 20001
(202) 879-2770

**FLORIDA**
Honorable Charles T. Canady
Chief Justice, Supreme Court of
 Florida
Supreme Court Building
500 South Duval Street
Tallahassee, FL 32399-1925
(850) 410-8092

**GEORGIA**
Honorable Carol W. Hunstein
Chief Justice, Supreme Court of
 Georgia
244 Washington St. SW
Atlanta, GA 30334
(404) 656-3475

**GUAM**
Honorable F. Philip Carbullido
Chief Justice, Supreme Court of
 Guam
Guam Judicial Center, Suite 300
120 West O'Brien Drive
Hagatna, GU 96910-5174
(671) 475-3413

**HAWAII**
Honorable Mark E. Recktenwald
Chief Justice, Supreme Court of
 Hawaii
417 South King Street
Honolulu, HI 96813
(808) 539-4700

**IDAHO**
Honorable Daniel T. Eismann
Chief Justice, Supreme Court of
 Idaho
451 West State Street

Boise, ID 83720-0101
(208) 334-2149

**ILLINOIS**
Honorable Thomas L. Kilbride
Chief Justice, Supreme Court of
 Illinois
1819 Fourth Ave.
Rock Island, IL 61201
(309) 794-3608

**INDIANA**
Honorable Randall T. Shepard
Chief Justice, Supreme Court of
 Indiana
304 Indiana State House
200 W. Washington St.
Indianapolis, IN 46204
(317) 233-8682

**IOWA**
Honorable Mark S. Cady
Chief Justice, Supreme Court of
 Iowa
State Capitol
1111 East Court Avenue
Des Moines, IA 50319
(515) 281-3952

**KANSAS**
Honorable Lawton R. Nuss
Chief Justice, Supreme Court of
 Kansas
Kansas Judicial Center, 301 West
 Tenth Ave.
Topeka, KS 66612-1507
(785) 296-5322

**KENTUCKY**
Honorable John D. Minton, Jr.
Chief Justice, Supreme Court of
 Kentucky
State Capitol Building, Room 231
700 Capitol Avenue
Frankfort, KY 40601
(502) 564-4162

**LOUISIANA**
Honorable Catherine D. Kimball
Chief Justice, Supreme Court of
 Louisiana
Supreme Court Building
400 Royal St.
New Orleans, LA 70130-8102
(504) 310-2340

**MAINE**
Honorable Leigh I. Saufley
Chief Justice, Supreme Judicial
 Court of Maine
205 Newbury St, Rm. 139
Portland, ME 04101-4125

# STATE CHIEF JUSTICES

(207) 822-4286

**MARYLAND**
Honorable Robert M. Bell
Chief Judge, Court of Appeals of
  Maryland
634 Courthouse East
111 North Calvert Street
Baltimore, MD 21202
(410) 333-6396

**MASSACHUSETTS**
Honorable Roderick L. Ireland
Chief Justice, Supreme Judicial
  Court of Massachusetts
One Pemberton Square, Suite 2200
Boston, MA 02108-1735
(617) 557-1131

**MICHIGAN**
Honorable Robert P. Young, Jr.
Chief Justice, Supreme Court of
  Michigan
3034 W. Grand Blvd., Suite 8-500
Detroit, MI 48202
(313) 972-3250

**MINNESOTA**
Honorable Lorie Skjerven Gildea
Chief Justice, Supreme Court of
  Minnesota
424 Minnesota Judicial Center
25 Rev. Dr. Martin Luther
  King, Jr. Blvd.
St. Paul, MN 55155
(651) 296-3380

**MISSISSIPPI**
Honorable William L. Waller, Jr.
Chief Justice, Supreme Court of
  Mississippi
450 High Street
P.O. Box 117
Jackson, MS 39205-0117
(601) 359-2139

**MISSOURI**
Honorable Richard B. Teitelman
Chief Justice, Supreme Court of
  Missouri
207 West High Street
P.O. Box 150
Jefferson City, MO 65101
(573) 751-1004

**MONTANA**
Honorable Mike McGrath
Chief Justice, Supreme Court of
  Montana
215 North Sanders
P.O. Box 203001
Helena, MT 59620-3001
(406) 444-5490

**NEBRASKA**
Honorable Michael G. Heavican
Chief Justice, Supreme Court of

Nebraska
2214 State Capitol
1445 K Street
Lincoln, NE 68508
(402) 471-3738

**NEVADA**
Honorable Michael L. Douglas
Chief Justice, Supreme Court of
  Nevada
201 S. Carson Street
Carson City, NV 89701-4702
(702) 486-3225

**NEW HAMPSHIRE**
Honorable Linda Steward Dalianis
Chief Justice, Supreme Court of
  New Hampshire
One Charles Doe Drive
Concord, NH 03301
(603) 271-3751

**NEW JERSEY**
Honorable Stuart Rabner
Chief Justice, Supreme Court of
  New Jersey
Richard J. Hughes Justice Complex
25 Market Street
P.O. Box 023
Trenton, NJ 08625-0023
(609) 292-2448

**NEW MEXICO**
Honorable Charles W. Daniels
Chief Justice, Supreme Court of
  New Mexico
237 Don Gaspar Ave.
Santa Fe, NM 87501
(505) 827-4889

**NEW YORK**
Honorable Jonathan Lippman
Chief Judge, New York State
  Unified Justice System
230 Park Avenue, Suite 826
New York, NY 10169
(212) 661-6787 (New York)
(518) 455-7741 (Albany)

**NORTH CAROLINA**
Honorable Sarah Parker
Chief Justice, Supreme Court of
  North Carolina
2 East Morgan St.
P.O. Box 1841
Raleigh, NC 27602
(919) 831-5711

**NORTH DAKOTA**
Honorable Gerald W. VandeWalle
Chief Justice, Supreme Court of
  North Dakota
State Capitol Building
600 East Boulevard Ave., Dept. 180
Bismarck, ND 58505-0530
(701) 328-4211

**NORTHERN MARIANA
ISLANDS**
Honorable Miguel S. Demapan
Chief Justice, Supreme Court of the
  Commonwealth of the Northern
  Mariana Islands
P.O. Box 502165
Saipan, MP 96950
(670) 236-9708

**OHIO**
Honorable Maureen O'Connor
Chief Justice, Supreme Court of
  Ohio
65 South Front Street
Columbus, OH 43215-3431
(614) 387-9000

**OKLAHOMA**
Honorable Steven W. Taylor
Chief Justice, Supreme Court of
  Oklahoma
245 State Capitol Building
2300 North Lincoln Boulevard
Oklahoma City, OK 73105
(405) 521-3845

Honorable Arlene Johnson
Presiding Judge, Court of Criminal
  Appeals of Oklahoma
230 State Capitol Building
2300 N. Lincoln Blvd.
Oklahoma City, OK 73105
(405) 521-2157

**OREGON**
Honorable Paul J. DeMuniz
Chief Justice, Supreme Court of
  Oregon
Supreme Court Building
1163 State Street
Salem, OR 97301
(503) 986-5709

**PENNSYLVANIA**
Honorable Ronald D. Castille
Chief Justice, Supreme Court of
  Pennsylvania
1818 Market St., Suite 3730
Philadelphia, PA 19103
(215) 560-5663

**PUERTO RICO**
Honorable Federico Hernandez
  Denton
Chief Justice, Supreme Court of
  Puerto Rico
Ponce de Leon Avenue
P.O. Box 9022392
San Juan, PR 00902-2392
(787) 724-3535

**RHODE ISLAND**
Honorable Paul A. Suttell
Chief Justice, Supreme Court of
  Rhode Island
250 Benefit Street

# STATE CHIEF JUSTICES

Providence, RI 02903
(401) 222-3943

**SOUTH CAROLINA**
Honorable Jean Hoefer Toal
Chief Justice, Supreme Court of
  South Carolina
1231 Gervais St.
Columbia, SC 29201
(803) 734-1584

**SOUTH DAKOTA**
Honorable David Gilbertson
Chief Justice, Supreme Court of
  South Dakota
500 East Capitol Avenue
Pierre, SD 57501
(605) 773-6254

**TENNESSEE**
Honorable Cornelia A. Clark
Chief Justice, Supreme Court of
  Tennessee
401 Seventh Ave. N, Suite 318
Nashville, TN 37219-1407
(615) 741-2114

**TEXAS**
Honorable Wallace B. Jefferson
Chief Justice, Supreme Court of
  Texas
201 W. Fourteenth Street
P.O. Box 12248, Capitol Station
Austin, TX 78711
(512) 463-7899

Honorable Sharon Keller
Presiding Judge
Court of Criminal Appeals of Texas
201 W. Fourteenth St.
Capitol Station
Austin, TX 78701
(512) 463-1590

**UTAH**
Honorable Christine M. Durham
Chief Justice, Supreme Court of
  Utah
Scott Matheson Courthouse
450 South State Street
P.O. Box 140210
Salt Lake City, UT 84114-0210
(801) 238-7945

**VERMONT**
Honorable Paul L. Reiber
Chief Justice, Supreme Court of
  Vermont
109 State Street
Montpelier, VT 05609-0801
(802) 828-3278

**VIRGINIA**
Honorable Cynthia D. Kinser
Chief Justice, Supreme Court of
  Virginia

185 Redwood Ave., Suite 101
P.O. Box 457
Pennington Gap, VA 24277
(276) 546-4563

**VIRGIN ISLANDS**
Honorable Rhys S. Hodge
Chief Justice
Supreme Court of the Virgin Islands
1G1B Crown Bay
P.O. Box 590
St. Thomas, VI 00804
(340) 777-2237

**WASHINGTON**
Honorable Barbara A. Madsen
Chief Justice, Supreme Court of
  Washington
Temple of Justice
415 12th Ave., SW
P.O. Box 40929
Olympia, WA 98504-0929
(360) 357-2038

**WEST VIRGINIA**
Honorable Margaret L. Workman
Chief Justice, Supreme Court of
  Appeals of West Virginia
State Capitol Complex, Room E-306
1900 Kanawha Boulevard, East
Charleston, WV 25305
(304) 558-2606

**WISCONSIN**
Honorable Shirley S. Abrahamson
Chief Justice, Supreme Court of
  Wisconsin
16 East State Capitol
P.O. Box 1688
Madison, WI 53701-1688
(608) 266-1885

**WYOMING**
Honorable Marilyn S. Kite
Chief Justice, Supreme Court of
  Wyoming
2301 Capitol Avenue
Cheyenne, WY 82002
(307) 777-7422

# STATE COURT STRUCTURE CHARTS

## Alabama
### (Court structure as of Fiscal Year 2009)

**Supreme Court** — COLR / S
*9 justices sit in panels of 5 or en banc*
*Assigns cases to the Court of Civil Appeals*

CSP Case Types:
- Appeal by right tort, contract, and real property, probate ($50,000 – no maximum), limited administrative agency.
- Appeal by permission criminal, civil, administrative agency. Interlocutory appeals in criminal, civil, administrative agency.
- Death penalty appeal by permission.
- Original proceeding writ application, bar/judiciary, certified question. Exclusive discipline/eligibility, advisory opinion.

link

**Court of Civil Appeals** — IAC / S
*5 judges sit en banc*

CSP Case Types:
- Appeal by right in civil ($0 - $50,000), administrative agency.

link

**Court of Criminal Appeals** — IAC / S
*5 judges sit en banc*

CSP Case Types:
- Appeal by right criminal, juvenile. Interlocutory appeals in criminal, juvenile.
- Death penalty appeal by right, writ application.
- Original proceeding writ *application, bar admission,* judicial qualification, certified question.

link

**Circuit Court** (41 circuits) — GJC / A / M
*144 judges*
*Jury trials*

CSP Case Types:
- Tort, contract, real property ($3,000 – no maximum). Exclusive civil appeals.
- Domestic relations.
- Felony, misdemeanor, and criminal appeals.
- Juvenile.

link

**District Court** (67 districts) — LJC / M
*106 judges*
*No jury trials*

CSP Case Types:
- Tort, contract, real property ($3,000 - 10,000). Exclusive small claims (up to $3,000).
- Paternity, custody, support, visitation, adoption.
- Preliminary hearings, misdemeanor.
- Juvenile.
- Traffic infractions.

**Probate Court** (68 courts) — LJC / £
*68 judges*
*No jury trials*

CSP Case Types:
- Exclusive mental health, probate/estate. Real property.
- Adoption.

**Municipal Court** (274 courts) — LJC / £
*275 judges*
*No jury trials*

CSP Case Types:
- Misdemeanor.
- Exclusive ordinance violations. Traffic infractions, parking.

### Legend

| | |
|---|---|
| ▭ (bold outline) | = Appellate level |
| ▭ (thin outline) | = Trial level |
| ↑ | = Route of appeal |

**COLR** = Court of Last Resort
**IAC** = Intermediate Appellate Court
**GJC** = General Jurisdiction Court
**LJC** = Limited Jurisdiction Court

**A** = Appeal from Admin. Agency
**S** = State funded
**£** = Locally funded
**M** = Mixed (state and locally) funded

**AOC Web site:**
**www.judicial.alabama.gov**

# Alaska
(Court structure as of Fiscal Year 2009)

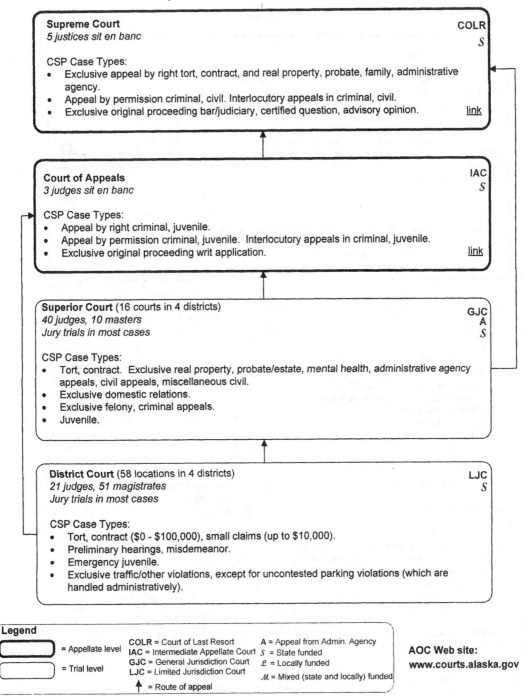

**Supreme Court**                                                                     COLR
*5 justices sit en banc*                                                                  *S*

CSP Case Types:
- Exclusive appeal by right tort, contract, and real property, probate, family, administrative agency.
- Appeal by permission criminal, civil. Interlocutory appeals in criminal, civil.
- Exclusive original proceeding bar/judiciary, certified question, advisory opinion.        link

**Court of Appeals**                                                                   IAC
*3 judges sit en banc*                                                                   *S*

CSP Case Types:
- Appeal by right criminal, juvenile.
- Appeal by permission criminal, juvenile.  Interlocutory appeals in criminal, juvenile.
- Exclusive original proceeding writ application.                                        link

**Superior Court** (16 courts in 4 districts)                                           GJC
*40 judges, 10 masters*                                                                   A
*Jury trials in most cases*                                                               *S*

CSP Case Types:
- Tort, contract.  Exclusive real property, probate/estate, *mental health, administrative agency* appeals, civil appeals, miscellaneous civil.
- Exclusive domestic relations.
- Exclusive felony, criminal appeals.
- Juvenile.

**District Court** (58 locations in 4 districts)                                        LJC
*21 judges, 51 magistrates*                                                               *S*
*Jury trials in most cases*

CSP Case Types:
- Tort, contract ($0 - $100,000), small claims (up to $10,000).
- Preliminary hearings, misdemeanor.
- Emergency juvenile.
- Exclusive traffic/other violations, except for uncontested parking violations (which are handled administratively).

**Legend**

☐ = Appellate level
☐ = Trial level

**COLR** = Court of Last Resort
**IAC** = Intermediate Appellate Court
**GJC** = General Jurisdiction Court
**LJC** = Limited Jurisdiction Court
↑ = Route of appeal

**A** = Appeal from Admin. Agency
*S* = State funded
*L* = Locally funded
*M* = Mixed (state and locally) funded

**AOC Web site:**
**www.courts.alaska.gov**

# Arizona

(Court structure as of Fiscal Year 2009)

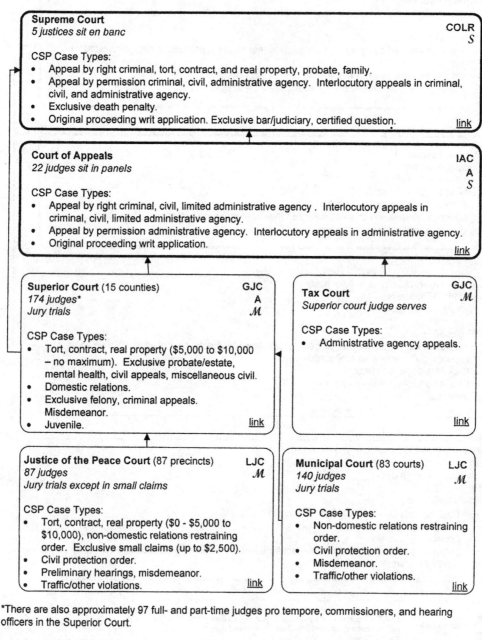

**Supreme Court**
*5 justices sit en banc*

COLR
*S*

CSP Case Types:
- Appeal by right criminal, tort, contract, and real property, probate, family.
- Appeal by permission criminal, civil, administrative agency. Interlocutory appeals in criminal, civil, and administrative agency.
- Exclusive death penalty.
- Original proceeding writ application. Exclusive bar/judiciary, certified question.

link

**Court of Appeals**
*22 judges sit in panels*

IAC
*A*
*S*

CSP Case Types:
- Appeal by right criminal, civil, limited administrative agency . Interlocutory appeals in criminal, civil, limited administrative agency.
- Appeal by permission administrative agency. Interlocutory appeals in administrative agency.
- Original proceeding writ application.

link

**Superior Court** (15 counties)
*174 judges\**
*Jury trials*

GJC
*A*
*M*

CSP Case Types:
- Tort, contract, real property ($5,000 to $10,000 – no maximum). Exclusive probate/estate, mental health, civil appeals, miscellaneous civil.
- Domestic relations.
- Exclusive felony, criminal appeals. Misdemeanor.
- Juvenile.

link

**Tax Court**
*Superior court judge serves*

GJC
*M*

CSP Case Types:
- Administrative agency appeals.

link

**Justice of the Peace Court** (87 precincts)
*87 judges*
*Jury trials except in small claims*

LJC
*M*

CSP Case Types:
- Tort, contract, real property ($0 - $5,000 to $10,000), non-domestic relations restraining order. Exclusive small claims (up to $2,500).
- Civil protection order.
- Preliminary hearings, misdemeanor.
- Traffic/other violations.

link

**Municipal Court** (83 courts)
*140 judges*
*Jury trials*

LJC
*M*

CSP Case Types:
- Non-domestic relations restraining order.
- Civil protection order.
- Misdemeanor.
- Traffic/other violations.

link

\*There are also approximately 97 full- and part-time judges pro tempore, commissioners, and hearing officers in the Superior Court.

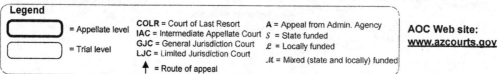

**Legend**

☐ = Appellate level
☐ = Trial level
↑ = Route of appeal

**COLR** = Court of Last Resort
**IAC** = Intermediate Appellate Court
**GJC** = General Jurisdiction Court
**LJC** = Limited Jurisdiction Court

A = Appeal from Admin. Agency
*S* = State funded
*L* = Locally funded
*M* = Mixed (state and locally) funded

**AOC Web site:**
**www.azcourts.gov**

# STATE COURT STRUCTURE CHARTS

## Arkansas
### (Court structure as of Calendar Year 2009)

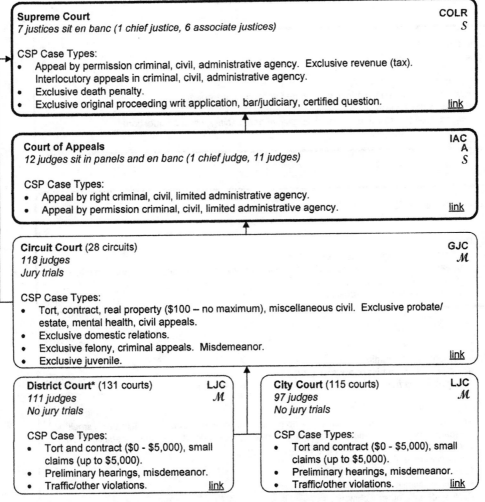

**Supreme Court**           COLR   S
*7 justices sit en banc (1 chief justice, 6 associate justices)*

CSP Case Types:
- Appeal by permission criminal, civil, administrative agency. Exclusive revenue (tax). Interlocutory appeals in criminal, civil, administrative agency.
- Exclusive death penalty.
- Exclusive original proceeding writ application, bar/judiciary, certified question.    link

**Court of Appeals**          IAC   A   S
*12 judges sit in panels and en banc (1 chief judge, 11 judges)*

CSP Case Types:
- Appeal by right criminal, civil, limited administrative agency.
- Appeal by permission criminal, civil, limited administrative agency.    link

**Circuit Court** (28 circuits)          GJC   M
*118 judges*
*Jury trials*

CSP Case Types:
- Tort, contract, real property ($100 – no maximum), miscellaneous civil. Exclusive probate/ estate, mental health, civil appeals.
- Exclusive domestic relations.
- Exclusive felony, criminal appeals. Misdemeanor.
- Exclusive juvenile.    link

**District Court\*** (131 courts)    LJC   M
*111 judges*
*No jury trials*

CSP Case Types:
- Tort and contract ($0 - $5,000), small claims (up to $5,000).
- Preliminary hearings, misdemeanor.
- Traffic/other violations.    link

**City Court** (115 courts)    LJC   M
*97 judges*
*No jury trials*

CSP Case Types:
- Tort and contract ($0 - $5,000), small claims (up to $5,000).
- Preliminary hearings, misdemeanor.
- Traffic/other violations.    link

\*Act 663 of 2007 created pilot state district court judgeships. These judges have jurisdiction to hear tort and contract cases up to $25,000 as well as probate/estate and domestic relations cases pending in Circuit Court. In 2008, there were 16 state district court judgeships in 19 courts.

Note: In 2001, Arkansas combined the Chancery and Probate Court with the Circuit Court and reduced the number of limited jurisdiction courts from six to two by combining the County, Police, Common Pleas, and Justice of the Peace courts into the Municipal Court which was renamed and is now the District Court.

AOC Web site: **www.courts.arkansas.gov**

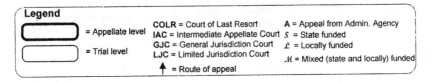

**Legend**

|  |  |  |
|---|---|---|
| ⬛ = Appellate level | **COLR** = Court of Last Resort | **A** = Appeal from Admin. Agency |
| ⬜ = Trial level | **IAC** = Intermediate Appellate Court | *S* = State funded |
|  | **GJC** = General Jurisdiction Court | *L* = Locally funded |
|  | **LJC** = Limited Jurisdiction Court | *M* = Mixed (state and locally) funded |
|  | ⬆ = Route of appeal |  |

Reprinted with permission. Court Statistics Project.
National Center for State Courts.

# California

(Court structure as of Fiscal Year 2009)

---

**Supreme Court**
*7 justices sit en banc*

CSP Case Types:
- Appeal by permission criminal, civil, limited administrative agency.
- Exclusive death penalty.
- Original proceeding writ application. Exclusive bar/judiciary, certified question.

COLR
A
*S*

link

---

**Courts of Appeal** (6 districts)
*105 justices sit in panels*

CSP Case Types:
- Appeal by right criminal, civil, administrative agency.
- Appeal by permission criminal, civil, administrative agency. Interlocutory appeals in criminal, civil, administrative agency.
- Original proceeding writ application.

IAC
A
*S*

link

---

**Superior Court** (58 counties)
*1,630 judges, 392 commissioners and referees\**
*Jury trials except in appeals, domestic relations, and juvenile cases*

CSP Case Types:
- Tort, contract, real property ($25,000 – no maximum), miscellaneous civil. Exclusive small claims (up to $5,000), probate/estate, mental health, civil appeals. [Limited jurisdiction: tort, contract, real property ($0 - $25,000).]
- Exclusive domestic relations.
- Exclusive criminal.
- Exclusive juvenile.
- Exclusive traffic/other violations.

GJC
A
*S*

link

---

*Includes 50 new judgeships effective 2008, but not funded.

**AOC Web site: www.courts.ca.gov**

**Legend**

| | | |
|---|---|---|
| ▭ = Appellate level | **COLR** = Court of Last Resort | **A** = Appeal from Admin. Agency |
| ▭ = Trial level | **IAC** = Intermediate Appellate Court | *S* = State funded |
| | **GJC** = General Jurisdiction Court | *£* = Locally funded |
| | **LJC** = Limited Jurisdiction Court | *M* = Mixed (state and locally) funded |
| | ↑ = Route of appeal | |

# STATE COURT STRUCTURE CHARTS

## Colorado
(Court structure as of Fiscal Year 2009)

**Supreme Court**  COLR A S
*7 justices sit en banc*

CSP Case Types:
- Appeal by right criminal, civil. Interlocutory appeals in criminal, civil.
- Appeal by permission in criminal, civil. Exclusive administrative agency. Interlocutory appeals in criminal, civil, administrative agency.
- Exclusive death penalty.
- Exclusive original proceeding writ application, bar/judiciary, certified question, advisory opinion.

link

**Court of Appeals**  IAC A S
*19 judges sit in panels of 3*

CSP Case Types:
- Appeal by right criminal, civil, administrative agency.

link

**District, Denver Juvenile, and Denver Probate Court**
153 judges

**District Court (22 districts)**  GJC A *M*
149 judges
*Jury trials except in appeals*

CSP Case Types:
- Tort, contract, real property, probate/estate, civil appeals, mental health, miscellaneous civil.
- Exclusive domestic relations.
- Felony, criminal appeals.
- Exclusive juvenile.

link

**Denver Juvenile Court**  GJC S
3 judges
*Jury trials*

CSP Case Types:
- Exclusive adoption, custody, support in Denver.
- Exclusive juvenile in Denver.  link

**Denver Probate Court**  GJC *M*
1 judge
*Jury trials*

CSP Case Types:
- Exclusive probate/estate, mental health in Denver.  link

**Water Court** (7 courts)  GJC *M*
*District court judges serve*

CSP Case Types:
- Real property.

link

**County Court** (64 counties)  LJC *M*
123 judges
*Jury trials except in small claims and appeals*

CSP Case Types:
- Tort, contract, real property ($0 - $15,000). Exclusive small claims (up to $7,500).
- Felony, preliminary hearings, misdemeanor, criminal appeals.
- Traffic infractions.  link

**Municipal Court** (206 courts)  LJC *L*
~250 judges
*Jury trials*

CSP Case Types:
- DWI/DUI, domestic violence.
- Traffic infractions, parking, other violations. Exclusive ordinance violations.

AOC Web site:
www.courts.state.co.us

Reprinted with permission. Court Statistics Project.
National Center for State Courts.

# Connecticut
### (Court structure as of Fiscal Year 2009)

---

**Supreme Court**    COLR  *S*
*7 justices sit in panels of 5 (membership rotates daily); upon order of chief justice, may sit en banc*

CSP Case Types:
- Appeal by right criminal, tort, contract, and real property, probate, family.
- Appeal by permission criminal, tort, contract, and real property, administrative agency.
- Exclusive death penalty appeal by right.
- Exclusive original proceeding judicial qualification.    link

---

**Appellate Court**    IAC  A  *S*
*9 judges sit in panels of 3 (membership rotates daily, may sit en banc)*

CSP Case Types:
- Appeal by right criminal, civil, administrative agency.
- Appeal by permission limited administrative agency. Interlocutory appeals in administrative agency.
- Exclusive original proceeding bar discipline/eligibility.    link

---

**Superior Court** (13 districts and 20 geographical areas for civil, domestic relations, criminal, and traffic matters; 13 districts for juvenile matters; and 7 housing session locations)    GJC  A  *S*
*201 judges*
*Jury trials in most cases*

CSP Case Types:
- Mental health, miscellaneous civil. Exclusive tort, contract, real property rights, small claims (up to $5,000), administrative agency appeals (except workers' compensation).
- Support, custody, paternity. Exclusive marriage dissolution.
- Exclusive criminal.
- Juvenile.
- Exclusive traffic/other violations, except for uncontested parking (which is handled administratively).    link

---

**Probate Court** (133 courts)    LJC  *£*
*54 judges*
*No jury trials*

CSP Case Types:
- Mental, health, miscellaneous civil. Exclusive probate/estate.
- Support, custody, paternity. Exclusive adoption.
- Juvenile.    link

---

**Legend**

☐ = Appellate level
☐ = Trial level

COLR = Court of Last Resort
IAC = Intermediate Appellate Court
GJC = General Jurisdiction Court
LJC = Limited Jurisdiction Court

↑ = Route of appeal

A = Appeal from Admin Agency
*S* = State funded
*£* = Locally funded
*M* = Mixed (state and locally) funded

**AOC Web site:**
**www.jud.ct.gov**

---

# STATE COURT STRUCTURE CHARTS

## Delaware
### (Court structure as of Fiscal Year 2009)

**Supreme Court** — COLR — S
*5 justices sit in panels and en banc*

CSP Case Types:
- Exclusive appeal by right criminal, civil, administrative agency.
- Exclusive appeal by permission criminal, tort, contract, and real property, probate, family, administrative agency. Interlocutory appeals in criminal, tort, contract, and real property, probate, family, administrative agency.
- Exclusive death penalty.
- Exclusive original proceeding writ application, bar/judiciary, certified question, advisory opinion. link

---

**Court of Chancery** — GJC — S
(3 counties)
*1 chancellor and 4 vice-chancellors*
*No jury trials*

CSP Case Types:
- Tort, contract, real property.
- Exclusive probate/estate. link

**Superior Court** (3 counties) — GJC — A — S
*19 judges*
*Jury trials except in appeals*

CSP Case Types:
- Tort, contract, real property, mental health, civil
- appeals, miscellaneous civil.
- Exclusive felony. Misdemeanor, criminal appeals. link

---

**Court of Common Pleas*** — LJC — A — S
(3 counties)
*9 judges*
*Jury trials in some cases*

CSP Case Types:
- Tort, contract, real property rights ($0-$50,000), civil appeals, miscellaneous civil.
- Preliminary hearings, misdemeanor, criminal appeals. link

**Family Court** (3 counties) — LJC — S
*17 judges,*
*No jury trials*

CSP Case Types:
- Exclusive domestic relations.
- Misdemeanor.
- Exclusive juvenile.
- Traffic infractions (juvenile). link

---

**Justice of the Peace Court*** — LJC — S
(18 courts)
*57 justices of the peace, 1 chief magistrate and 3 deputy chief magistrates*
*Jury trials in some cases*

CSP Case Types:
- Tort, contract, real property ($0-$15,000).
- Misdemeanor.
- Traffic/other violations. link

**Alderman's Court** (6 courts) — LJC — £
*~9 alderman*
*No jury trials*

CSP Case Types:
- Misdemeanor.
- Traffic/other violations. link

---

\* The Municipal Court of Wilmington was eliminated effective May 1, 1998, and a new Justice of the Peace Court was created in Wilmington.

**AOC Web site: http://courts.state.de.us**

---

**Legend**

☐ = Appellate level

☐ = Trial level

↑ = Route of appeal

COLR = Court of Last Resort
IAC = Intermediate Appellate Court
GJC = General Jurisdiction Court
LJC = Limited Jurisdiction Court

A = Appeal from Admin. Agency
S = State funded
£ = Locally funded
ℳ = Mixed (state and locally) funded

Reprinted with permission. Court Statistics Project.
National Center for State Courts.

## District of Columbia
### (Court structure as of Calendar Year 2009)

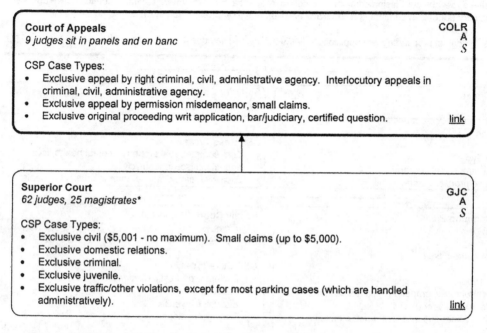

**Court of Appeals**
*9 judges sit in panels and en banc*

COLR
A
S

CSP Case Types:
- Exclusive appeal by right criminal, civil, administrative agency. Interlocutory appeals in criminal, civil, administrative agency.
- Exclusive appeal by permission misdemeanor, small claims.
- Exclusive original proceeding writ application, bar/judiciary, certified question.

link

**Superior Court**
*62 judges, 25 magistrates\**

GJC
A
S

CSP Case Types:
- Exclusive civil ($5,001 - no maximum). Small claims (up to $5,000).
- Exclusive domestic relations.
- Exclusive criminal.
- Exclusive juvenile.
- Exclusive traffic/other violations, except for most parking cases (which are handled administratively).

link

\*Does not include senior judges that serve on a part-time basis.

AOC Web site: www.dccourts.gov/
dccourts/index.jsp

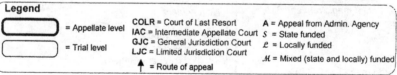

**Legend**

| | |
|---|---|
| ☐ | = Appellate level |
| ☐ | = Trial level |

**COLR** = Court of Last Resort
**IAC** = Intermediate Appellate Court
**GJC** = General Jurisdiction Court
**LJC** = Limited Jurisdiction Court

↑ = Route of appeal

**A** = Appeal from Admin. Agency
*S* = State funded
*£* = Locally funded

*M* = Mixed (state and locally) funded

# Florida
**(Court structure as of Fiscal Year 2009)**

---

**Supreme Court**  COLR A S
*7 justices sit en banc*

CSP Case Types:
- Appeal by right criminal, civil, administrative agency.
- Appeal by permission criminal, civil, administrative agency.
- Exclusive death penalty.
- Original proceeding writ application. Exclusive bar/judiciary, certified question, advisory opinion.

link

---

**District Courts of Appeal** (5 courts)  IAC A S
*62 judges sit in panels of 3*

CSP Case Types:
- Appeal by right criminal, civil, administrative agency. Interlocutory appeals in criminal, civil, interlocutory agency.
- Appeal by permission criminal, civil, administrative agency.
- Original proceeding writ application.

link

---

**Circuit Court** (20 circuits)  GJC M
*599 judges*
*Jury trials except in appeals*

CSP Case Types:
- Tort, contract, real property ($15,001 – no maximum), miscellaneous civil. Exclusive mental health, probate/estate, civil appeals.
- Domestic relations.
- Exclusive felony, criminal appeals.
- Exclusive juvenile.

link

---

**County Court** (67 counties)  LJC M
*322 judges*

CSP Case Types:
- Tort contract, real property ($5,001 - $15,000), miscellaneous civil. Exclusive small claims (up to $5,000).
- Dissolution/divorce.
- Preliminary hearings. Exclusive misdemeanor.
- Exclusive traffic/other violations, except parking (which is handled administratively).

link

**AOC Web site: www.flcourts.org**

---

**Legend**

|  | = Appellate level |
|---|---|
|  | = Trial level |

**COLR** = Court of Last Resort
**IAC** = Intermediate Appellate Court
**GJC** = General Jurisdiction Court
**LJC** = Limited Jurisdiction Court

↑ = Route of appeal

**A** = Appeal from Admin. Agency
*S* = State funded
*L* = Locally funded
*M* = Mixed (state and locally) funded

---

# Georgia

(Court structure as of Calendar Year 2009)

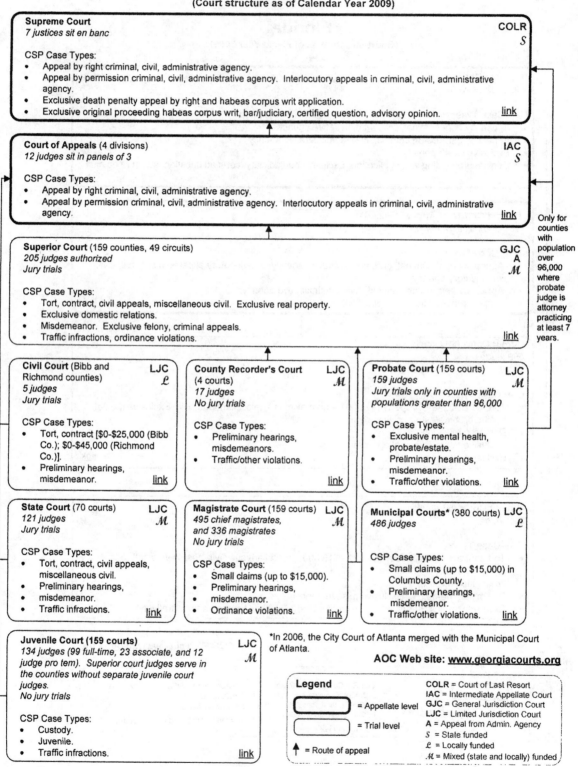

**Supreme Court**
*7 justices sit en banc*

COLR
*S*

CSP Case Types:
- Appeal by right criminal, civil, administrative agency.
- Appeal by permission criminal, civil, administrative agency. Interlocutory appeals in criminal, civil, administrative agency.
- Exclusive death penalty appeal by right and habeas corpus writ application.
- Exclusive original proceeding habeas corpus writ, bar/judiciary, certified question, advisory opinion.

link

**Court of Appeals** (4 divisions)
*12 judges sit in panels of 3*

IAC
*S*

CSP Case Types:
- Appeal by right criminal, civil, administrative agency.
- Appeal by permission criminal, civil, administrative agency. Interlocutory appeals in criminal, civil, administrative agency.

link

**Superior Court** (159 counties, 49 circuits)
*205 judges authorized*
*Jury trials*

GJC
A
*M*

CSP Case Types:
- Tort, contract, civil appeals, miscellaneous civil. Exclusive real property.
- Exclusive domestic relations.
- Misdemeanor. Exclusive felony, criminal appeals.
- Traffic infractions, ordinance violations.

link

Only for counties with population over 96,000 where probate judge is attorney practicing at least 7 years.

**Civil Court** (Bibb and Richmond counties)
*5 judges*
*Jury trials*

LJC
*L*

CSP Case Types:
- Tort, contract [$0-$25,000 (Bibb Co.); $0-$45,000 (Richmond Co.)].
- Preliminary hearings, misdemeanor.

link

**County Recorder's Court**
(4 courts)
*17 judges*
*No jury trials*

LJC
*M*

CSP Case Types:
- Preliminary hearings, misdemeanors.
- Traffic/other violations.

link

**Probate Court** (159 courts)
*159 judges*
*Jury trials only in counties with populations greater than 96,000*

LJC
*M*

CSP Case Types:
- Exclusive mental health, probate/estate.
- Preliminary hearings, misdemeanor.
- Traffic/other violations.

link

**State Court** (70 courts)
*121 judges*
*Jury trials*

LJC
*M*

CSP Case Types:
- Tort, contract, civil appeals, miscellaneous civil.
- Preliminary hearings,
- misdemeanor.
- Traffic infractions.

link

**Magistrate Court** (159 courts)
*495 chief magistrates, and 336 magistrates*
*No jury trials*

LJC
*M*

CSP Case Types:
- Small claims (up to $15,000).
- Preliminary hearings,
- misdemeanor.
- Ordinance violations.

link

**Municipal Courts*** (380 courts)
*486 judges*

LJC
*L*

CSP Case Types:
- Small claims (up to $15,000) in Columbus County.
- Preliminary hearings, misdemeanor.
- Traffic/other violations.

link

**Juvenile Court (159 courts)**
*134 judges (99 full-time, 23 associate, and 12 judge pro tem). Superior court judges serve in the counties without separate juvenile court judges.*
*No jury trials*

LJC
*M*

CSP Case Types:
- Custody.
- Juvenile.
- Traffic infractions.

link

*In 2006, the City Court of Atlanta merged with the Municipal Court of Atlanta.

AOC Web site: **www.georgiacourts.org**

**Legend**

= Appellate level

= Trial level

↑ = Route of appeal

COLR = Court of Last Resort
IAC = Intermediate Appellate Court
GJC = General Jurisdiction Court
LJC = Limited Jurisdiction Court
A = Appeal from Admin. Agency
*S* = State funded
*L* = Locally funded
*M* = Mixed (state and locally) funded

Reprinted with permission. Court Statistics Project.
National Center for State Courts.

# Hawaii

**(Court structure as of Fiscal Year 2009)**

---

**Supreme Court**                                                          COLR
*5 justices sit en banc*                                                    S

CSP Case Types:
- Appeal by right criminal, civil, administrative agency.
- Exclusive appeal by permission criminal, civil, administrative agency.  Interlocutory appeals in criminal, civil, administrative agency.
- Original proceeding writ application. Exclusive bar/judiciary, certified question.                    link

---

**Intermediate Court of Appeals**                                          IAC
*6 judges sit in panels of 3*                                               A
                                                                            S

CSP Case Types:
- Appeal by right criminal, civil, administrative agency.  Interlocutory in criminal, civil, administrative agency.
- Original proceeding writ application.                                      link

---

**Circuit Court and Family Court** (4 circuits)                            GJC
*33 circuit judges, 4 of which are designated Family Court judges,*          A
*plus 15 District Family Court judges*                                       S
*Jury trials*

CSP Case Types:
- Tort contract, real property ($10,000 – no maximum) [concurrent from $10,000-$25,000], miscellaneous civil.  Exclusive mental health, probate/estate, administrative agency appeals
- Exclusive domestic relations.                                    Circuit Court link
- Exclusive juvenile.
- Traffic infractions.                                             Family Court link

---

**District Court** (4 circuits)                                            LJC
*22 judges**                                                                S
*No jury trials*

CSP Case Types:
- Tort, contract, real property ($0 - $25,000) [concurrent from $10,000-$25,000 (civil nonjury)], miscellaneous civil.  Exclusive small claims up to ($3,500).
- Preliminary hearings, misdemeanor.
- Traffic infractions.  Exclusive parking, ordinance violations.

*Excludes per diem judges.                                                  link

---

**AOC Web site: www.courts.state.hi.us**

---

**Legend**

| | |
|---|---|
| = Appellate level | |
| = Trial level | |

COLR = Court of Last Resort          A = Appeal from Admin. Agency
IAC = Intermediate Appellate Court   S = State funded
GJC = General Jurisdiction Court     L = Locally funded
LJC = Limited Jurisdiction Court
                                     M = Mixed: state and locally funded
↑ = Route of appeal

# STATE COURT STRUCTURE CHARTS

## Idaho
(Court structure as of Calendar Year 2009)

**Supreme Court**
*5 justices sit en banc*
*Assigns cases to the Court of Appeals*

COLR
A
*S*

CSP Case Types:
- Appeal by right criminal, civil. Exclusive administrative agency.
- Exclusive appeal by permission criminal, civil, administrative agency. Interlocutory appeals in criminal, civil, administrative agency.
- Exclusive death penalty.
- Original proceeding writ application. Exclusive bar discipline/eligibility, judicial qualification, certified question.

link

**Court of Appeals**
*4 judges sit en banc*

IAC
*S*

CSP Case Types:
- Appeal by right criminal, civil.
- Original jurisdiction writ application.

**District Court** (7 districts)
*43 district judges*
*Jury trials*

GJC
A
*M*

CSP Case Types:
- Tort, contract, real property rights ($10,000 – no maximum), probate/estate, mental health, miscellaneous civil.
- Domestic relations.
- Exclusive felony and criminal appeals. Misdemeanor.
- Juvenile.

link

**Magistrates Division**
*87 full-time magistrate judges*

LJC
A
*M*

CSP Case Types:
- Tort, contract, real property rights ($0 - $10,000), small claims (up to $5,000), probate/estate, mental health, miscellaneous civil.
- Domestic relations.
- Preliminary hearings, misdemeanor.
- Juvenile.
- Exclusive traffic/other violations.

Notes: The Magistrates Division of the District Court functions as a limited jurisdiction court. There are an additional 44 senior judges that serve the judicial branch.

AOC Web site: www.isc.idaho.gov

**Legend**
= Appellate level
= Trial level
COLR = Court of Last Resort
IAC = Intermediate Appellate Court
GJC = General Jurisdiction Court
LJC = Limited Jurisdiction Court
↑ = Route of appeal
A = Appeal from Admin. Agency
*S* = State funded
*£* = Locally funded
*M* = Mixed: state and locally funded

# Illinois
### (Court structure as of Calendar Year 2009)

**Supreme Court**                                                                COLR
*7 justices sit en banc*                                                            S

CSP Case Types:
- Appeal by right criminal, civil, administrative agency. Interlocutory appeals in criminal, civil, administrative agency.
- Appeal by permission in criminal, civil, administrative agency. Interlocutory appeals in criminal, civil, administrative agency.
- Exclusive death penalty.
- Original proceeding writ application. Exclusive bar admission, bar discipline/eligibility, certified question.                                                            link

**Appellate Court** (5 districts)                                                  IAC
*54 authorized judges, with 12 circuit court judges assigned to the appellate court*   A
                                                                                     S

CSP Case Types:
- Appeal by right criminal, civil, limited administrative agency. Interlocutory appeals in criminal, civil, limited administrative agency.
- Appeal by permission criminal, civil, limited administrative agency. Interlocutory appeals in criminal, civil, limited administrative agency.
- Original proceeding writ application.                                              link

**Circuit Court** (23 circuits)                                                    GJC
*517 circuit judges, 389 associate judges*                                           A
*Jury trials permissible in most cases*                                              ℳ

CSP Case Types:
- Exclusive civil (including administrative agency appeals), small claims (up to $10,000).
- Exclusive domestic relations.
- Exclusive criminal.
- Exclusive juvenile.
- Exclusive traffic/other violations.                                               link

**AOC Web site: www.state.il.us/court**

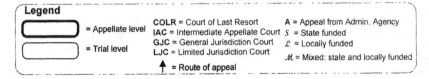

**Legend**

| | | |
|---|---|---|
| = Appellate level | **COLR** = Court of Last Resort | **A** = Appeal from Admin. Agency |
| | **IAC** = Intermediate Appellate Court | **S** = State funded |
| = Trial level | **GJC** = General Jurisdiction Court | **ℒ** = Locally funded |
| | **LJC** = Limited Jurisdiction Court | **ℳ** = Mixed: state and locally funded |
| | ↑ = Route of appeal | |

# Indiana
(Court structure as of Calendar Year 2009)

**Supreme Court**                                                                                   COLR
*5 justices sit en banc*                                                                               *S*

CSP Case Types:
- Appeal by right felony, tort, contract, and real property, probate, family.
- Appeal by permission criminal, civil, limited administrative agency.
- Exclusive death penalty.
- Exclusive original proceeding writ application, bar/judiciary, certified question, advisory opinion.          link

**Court of Appeals** (5 districts)                        IAC
*15 judges*                                                  A
CSP Case Types:                                              *S*
- Appeal by right criminal, civil, limited administrative agency.
- Appeal by permission interlocutory appeals in criminal, civil, limited administrative agency.          link

**Tax Court**                     IAC
*1 judge*                          A
                                   *S*
CSP Case Types:
- Appeal by right revenue (tax).          link

**Superior, Circuit, and Probate Court**
315 Judges

**Superior Court** (196 divisions)*          GJC
*210 judges*                                   A
*Jury trials except small claims, probate/estate,*   *M*
*mental health, domestic relations, and juvenile*

CSP Case Types:
- Tort, contract, real property, small claims (up to $6,000), mental health, probate/estate, civil appeals, miscellaneous civil.
- Domestic relations.
- Felony, misdemeanor, criminal appeals, preliminary hearings.
- Juvenile.
- Traffic infractions.          link

**Circuit Court** (91 circuits)          GJC
*104 judges*                               A
*Jury trials except small claims*          *M*

CSP Case Types:
- Tort, contract, real property, small claims (up to $6,000), mental health, probate/estate, civil appeals, miscellaneous civil.
- Domestic relations.
- Felony, misdemeanor, criminal appeals, preliminary hearings.
- Juvenile.
- Traffic infractions.          link

**Probate Court**          GJC
(St. Joseph)                *M*
*1 judge*
*Jury trials*

CSP Case Types:
- Probate/estate, miscellaneous civil.
- Adoption.
- Miscellaneous criminal.
- Juvenile.          link

**City and Town Court**
75 judges

**City Court** (47 courts)          LJC
*47 judges*                           *£*
*Jury trials*

CSP Case Types:
- Tort, contract ($0-$500 to $3,000), small claims (up to $3,000).
- Misdemeanor.
- Traffic/other violations.          link

**Town Court**          LJC
(28 courts)              *£*
*28 judges*
*Jury trials*

CSP Case Types:
- Misdemeanor.
- Traffic/other violations.          link

**Small Claims Court of Marion County**          LJC
(9 courts)                                         *£*
*9 judges*

CSP Case Types:
- Small claims (up to $6,000), miscellaneous civil.

\* Effective January 1, 1996, all Municipal Courts became Superior Court.  Effective January 1, 2009, all County Courts merged with Superior Court.

**Legend**

▢ = Appellate level
▢ = Trial level

COLR = Court of Last Resort
IAC = Intermediate Appellate Court
GJC = General Jurisdiction Court
LJC = Limited Jurisdiction Court
↑ = Route of appeal

A = Appeal from Admin. Agency
*S* = State funded
*£* = Locally funded
*M* = Mixed: state and locally funded

AOC Web site: www.in.gov/judiciary/

# Iowa
(Court structure as of Calendar Year 2009)

**Supreme Court**        COLR
*7 justices sit en banc\**
*Assigns cases to the Court of Appeals*    S

CSP Case Types:
- Appeal by right criminal, civil, administrative agency.
- Exclusive appeal by permission criminal, civil, administrative agency. Interlocutory appeals in criminal, civil, administrative agency.
- Original proceeding writ application. Exclusive bar/judiciary, certified question, advisory opinion.

link

**Court of Appeals**        IAC
*9 judges sit in panels and en banc*    S

CSP Case Types:
- Appeal by right criminal, civil, administrative agency. Interlocutory appeals in criminal, civil, administrative agency.
- Original proceeding writ application.

link

**District Court** (8 districts in 99 counties)     GJC
*116 authorized district judges, 60 district associate judges, 9 FTE\*\* senior judges,*    A
*12 associate juvenile judges, 152 part-time magistrates, and 1 associate probate judge*    $\mathcal{M}$
*Jury trials except in small claims, juvenile, equity cases, city and county ordinance violations, mental health cases*

CSP Case Types:
- Exclusive civil. Small claims (up to $5,000).
- Exclusive domestic relations.
- Exclusive criminal.
- Exclusive juvenile.
- Exclusive traffic/other violations, except for uncontested parking.

link

\* As of January 2000, the court no longer sits in panels; it decides en banc.
\*\* Includes 37 senior judges who work ¼ time (13 weeks/year).

AOC Web site: **www.iowacourts.gov**

**Legend**

| | |
|---|---|
| ☐ = Appellate level | |
| ☐ = Trial level | |

COLR = Court of Last Resort    A = Appeal from Admin. Agency
IAC = Intermediate Appellate Court    S = State funded
GJC = General Jurisdiction Court    $\mathcal{L}$ = Locally funded
LJC = Limited Jurisdiction Court    $\mathcal{M}$ = Mixed: state and locally funded
↑ = Route of appeal

# Kansas

(Court structure as of Fiscal Year 2009)

**Supreme Court** COLR
*7 justices sit en banc* *S*

CSP Case Types:
- Appeal by right criminal, tort, contract, and real property, probate, family, administrative agency.
- Appeal by permission criminal, civil, administrative agency. Interlocutory appeals in criminal, civil, administrative agency.
- Exclusive death penalty.
- Original proceeding writ application. Exclusive bar/judiciary, certified question, advisory opinion.

link

**Court of Appeals** IAC
*12 judges generally sit in panels* A
*S*

CSP Case Types:
- Appeal by right criminal, civil, limited administrative agency. Interlocutory appeals in criminal, limited administrative agency.
- Appeal by permission interlocutory appeals in tort, contract, and real property, probate, family.
- Original proceeding limited writ application.

link

**District Court** (31 districts) GJC
*246 judges (includes 79 magistrates)* A
*Jury trials except in small claims* *M*

CSP Case Types:
- Exclusive civil (including civil appeals). Small claims (up to $4,000).
- Exclusive domestic relations.
- DWI/DUI. Exclusive felony, misdemeanor, criminal appeals.
- Exclusive juvenile.
- Traffic infractions.

link

**Municipal Court** (385 cities) LJC
*259 judges* *L*
*No jury trials*

CSP Case Types:
- DWI/DUI.
- Traffic infractions. Exclusive ordinance violations, parking.

**AOC Web site: www.kscourts.org**

**Legend**

| | | |
|---|---|---|
| ▭ = Appellate level | **COLR** = Court of Last Resort | **A** = Appeal from Admin. Agency |
| | **IAC** = Intermediate Appellate Court | *S* = State funded |
| ▭ = Trial level | **GJC** = General Jurisdiction Court | *L* = Locally funded |
| | **LJC** = Limited Jurisdiction Court | *M* = Mixed: state and locally funded |
| | ↑ = Route of appeal | |

# STATE COURT STRUCTURE CHARTS

## Kentucky
### (Court structure as of Fiscal Year 2009)

**Supreme Court**        COLR
*7 justices sit en banc*        *S*

CSP Case Types:
- Appeal by right felony (limited to 20 yr+ sentence), workers' compensation. Interlocutory appeals in felony, workers' compensation.
- Appeal by permission criminal, civil, administrative agency. Interlocutory appeals in criminal, civil, administrative agency.
- Exclusive death penalty.
- Original proceeding writ application. Exclusive bar/judiciary, certified question, advisory opinion.   link

**Court of Appeals**        IAC
*14 judges generally sit in panels, but sit en banc in a policy-making capacity*        *S*

CSP Case Types:
- Appeal by right criminal (limited to less than 20 year sentence), civil, limited administrative agency.
- Appeal by permission misdemeanor, civil, limited administrative agency. Interlocutory appeals in misdemeanor, civil, limited administrative agency.
- Original proceeding limited writ application.   link

**Circuit Court** (57 judicial circuits)     GJC
*95 judges plus domestic relations commissioners*     A
*Jury trials except in appeals*     *S*

CSP Case Types:
- Tort, contract, real property ($4,001-no maximum), interstate support, probate/estate. Exclusive civil appeals, miscellaneous civil.
- Domestic relations.
- Misdemeanor. Exclusive felony, criminal appeals.
- Juvenile.   link

**Family Court** (71 counties)     GJC
*51 judges*     *S*

CSP Case Types:
- Domestic relations.
- Domestic violence.
- Juvenile.

  link

**District Court** (60 judicial districts)     LJC
*116 judges plus trial commissioners*     *S*
*Jury trials in most cases*

CSP Case Types:
- Tort, contract, real property ($0 - $4,000), probate/estate. Exclusive mental health, small claims (up to $1,500).
- Domestic relations.
- Preliminary hearings, misdemeanor.
- Juvenile.
- Exclusive traffic/other violations.   link

Note: There are also 67 senior status judges that can serve on any court except the Supreme Court.

**Legend**

☐ = Appellate level
☐ = Trial level

COLR = Court of Last Resort
IAC = Intermediate Appellate Court
GJC = General Jurisdiction Court
LJC = Limited Jurisdiction Court
↑ = Route of appeal

A = Appeal from Admin. Agency
*S* = State funded
*£* = Locally funded
*M* = Mixed: state and locally funded

**AOC Web site:**
**www.courts.ky.gov**

# Louisiana
### (Court structure as of Calendar Year 2009)

**Supreme Court**
*7 justices sit en banc*

COLR
*S*

CSP Case Types:
- Appeal by right limited criminal, civil, administrative agency.
- Exclusive appeal by permission criminal, civil, administrative agency. Interlocutory appeals in criminal, civil, administrative agency.
- Exclusive death penalty.
- Original proceeding application for writ. Exclusive bar/judiciary, certified question.

link

---

**Court of Appeals** (5 courts)
*53 judges sit in panels*

IAC
A
*S*

CSP Case Types:
- Appeal by right criminal, civil, administrative agency.
- Original proceeding application for writ.

link

---

**District Court**
*236 judges, 11 commissioners*

**District Court** (64 parishes)
*236 judges, 21 commissioners*
*Jury trials in most cases*

GJC
A
*M*

CSP Case Types:
- Tort, contract, real property, mental health. Exclusive probate/estate, civil trial court appeals, miscellaneous civil.
- Domestic relations.
- Misdemeanor. Exclusive felony, criminal appeals.
- Juvenile.
- Traffic/other violations.

link

---

**Juvenile Court** (4 courts)
*14 judges*
*No jury trials*

GJC
*M*

CSP Case Types:
- Mental health.
- Support, adoption.
- Juvenile.

link

**Family Court** (1 in East Baton Rouge)
*4 judges*
*No jury trials*

GJC
*M*

CSP Case Types:
- Mental health.
- Domestic relations.
- Domestic violence.
- Juvenile.

link

---

**Justice of the Peace Court**
(~385 courts)
*~385 justices of the peace*
*No jury trials*

LJC
*M*

CSP Case Types:
- Tort, contract ($0-$5,000), small claims (up to $2,000).
- Traffic/other violations.

**Mayor's Court** (~250 courts)
*~250 judges (mayors)*
*No jury trials*

LJC
*L*

CSP Case Types:
- Traffic/other violations.

**City and Parish Courts** (52 courts)
*73 judges*
*No jury trials*
CSP Case Types:

LJC
*M*

- Tort, contract ($0-$50,000, varies by court), small claims (up to $3,000), civil appeals.
- Paternity.
- Preliminary hearings, misdemeanor.
- Juvenile.
- Traffic/other violations.

---

**Legend**

= Appellate level

= Trial level

COLR = Court of Last Resort
IAC = Intermediate Appellate Court
GJC = General Jurisdiction Court
LJC = Limited Jurisdiction Court
↑ = Route of appeal

A = Appeal from Admin. Agency
*S* = State funded
*L* = Locally funded
*M* = Mixed: state and locally funded

AOC Web site: **www.lasc.org**

# STATE COURT STRUCTURE CHARTS

## Maine
(Court structure as of Fiscal Year 2009)

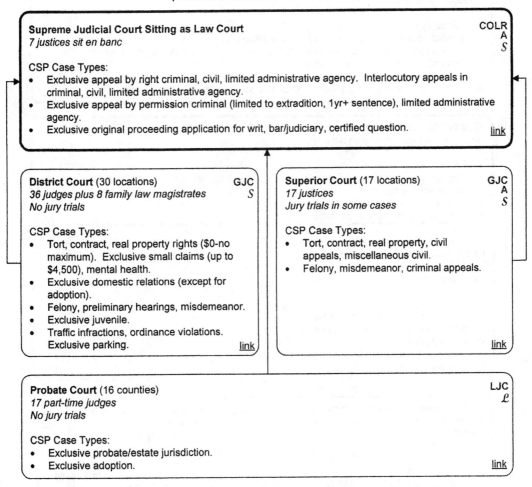

**Supreme Judicial Court Sitting as Law Court**
*7 justices sit en banc*

COLR
A
*S*

CSP Case Types:
- Exclusive appeal by right criminal, civil, limited administrative agency. Interlocutory appeals in criminal, civil, limited administrative agency.
- Exclusive appeal by permission criminal (limited to extradition, 1yr+ sentence), limited administrative agency.
- Exclusive original proceeding application for writ, bar/judiciary, certified question.

link

---

**District Court** (30 locations)
*36 judges plus 8 family law magistrates*
*No jury trials*

GJC
*S*

CSP Case Types:
- Tort, contract, real property rights ($0-no maximum). Exclusive small claims (up to $4,500), mental health.
- Exclusive domestic relations (except for adoption).
- Felony, preliminary hearings, misdemeanor.
- Exclusive juvenile.
- Traffic infractions, ordinance violations. Exclusive parking.

link

---

**Superior Court** (17 locations)
*17 justices*
*Jury trials in some cases*

GJC
A
*S*

CSP Case Types:
- Tort, contract, real property, civil appeals, miscellaneous civil.
- Felony, misdemeanor, criminal appeals.

link

---

**Probate Court** (16 counties)
*17 part-time judges*
*No jury trials*

LJC
*£*

CSP Case Types:
- Exclusive probate/estate jurisdiction.
- Exclusive adoption.

link

Note: The Administrative Court was eliminated effective March 15, 2001, with the caseload absorbed by the District Court.

AOC Web site: **www.courts.state.me.us**

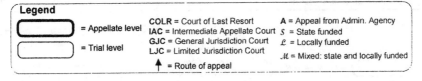

| Legend | | |
|---|---|---|
| ▢ = Appellate level | **COLR** = Court of Last Resort | **A** = Appeal from Admin. Agency |
| ▢ = Trial level | **IAC** = Intermediate Appellate Court | *S* = State funded |
| | **GJC** = General Jurisdiction Court | *£* = Locally funded |
| | **LJC** = Limited Jurisdiction Court | *M* = Mixed: state and locally funded |
| | ↑ = Route of appeal | |

# Maryland

(Court structure as of Fiscal Year 2009)

---

**Court of Appeals**                                                    COLR
*7 judges sit en banc*                                                   S

CSP Case Types:
- Limited appeal by right.  Limited interlocutory appeals.
- Appeal by permission criminal, civil, administrative agency.  Interlocutory appeals in criminal, civil, administrative agency.
- Exclusive death penalty.
- Original proceeding writ application. Exclusive bar/judiciary, certified question.

link

---

**Court of Special Appeals**                                            IAC
*13 judges sit in panels and en banc*                                    S

CSP Case Types:
- Appeal by right criminal, civil, administrative agency.  Interlocutory appeals in criminal, civil, administrative agency.
- Appeal by permission criminal, civil.
- Original proceeding writ application.

link

---

**Circuit Court** (8 circuits in 24 counties)                          GJC
*153 judges*                                                            A
*Jury trials in most cases*                                             M

CSP Case Types:
- Tort, contract, real property ($5,000-no maximum), probate/estate, miscellaneous civil. Exclusive mental health, civil appeals.
- Domestic relations.
- Felony, misdemeanor.  Exclusive criminal appeals.
- Exclusive juvenile.

link

---

**District Court** (12 districts in 24 counties)     LJC       **Orphan's Court** (22 counties)    LJC
*111 judges (plus 1 chief judge with administrative*  S        *66 judges*                          £
*duties)*                                                      *No jury trials*
*No jury trials*

CSP Case Types:                                                CSP Case Types:
- Tort, contract ($5,000-$30,000), real property,             - Probate/estate, except where
  miscellaneous civil. Exclusive small claims (up to            such cases are handled by
  $5,000).                                                       circuit court in Montgomery
- Civil protection/restraining orders.                          and Harford counties.
- Felony, preliminary hearings, misdemeanor.
- Exclusive traffic/other violations.        link                                                   link

---

AOC Web site: www.courts.state.md.us

---

**Legend**

| | |
|---|---|
| (thick box) = Appellate level | **COLR** = Court of Last Resort |
| (thin box) = Trial level | **IAC** = Intermediate Appellate Court |
| | **GJC** = General Jurisdiction Court |
| | **LJC** = Limited Jurisdiction Court |
| | ↑ = Route of appeal |

**A** = Appeal from Admin. Agency
*S* = State funded
*£* = Locally funded
*M* = Mixed: state and locally funded

# Massachusetts
(Court structure as of Fiscal Year 2009)

**Supreme Judicial Court** — COLR / A / S
*7 justices sit en banc and in panels of 5\**

CSP Case Types:
- Appeal by permission criminal, civil, administrative agency. Interlocutory appeals in criminal, civil, administrative agency.
- Exclusive original proceeding application for writ, bar/judiciary, certified question, advisory opinion.   link

**Appeals Court** — IAC / A / S
*25 justices sit in panels of 3\**

CSP Case Types:
- Exclusive appeal by right criminal, civil, administrative agency.
- Appeal by permission interlocutory appeals in criminal, civil, administrative agency.   link

**Superior Court Department** (14 divisions) — GJC / A / S
*82 justices*
*Jury trials*

CSP Case Types:
- Tort, contract, real property ($25,000 – no maximum), civil appeals, miscellaneous civil.
- Civil protection/restraining orders.
- Felony, misdemeanor.   link

**District Court Department** (62 divisions) — LJC / S
*158 justices*
*Jury trials*

CSP Case Types:
- Tort, contract, real property ($0-$25,000), small claims (up to $2,000), mental health, civil appeals, miscellaneous civil.
- Civil protection/restraining orders.
- Felony, preliminary hearings, misdemeanor.
- Traffic/other violations.   link

**Boston Municipal Court Department** (8 divisions) — LJC / S
*30 justices*
*Jury trials*

CSP Case Types:
- Tort, contract, real property rights ($0-$25,000), small claims (up to $2,000), mental health, civil appeals, miscellaneous civil.
- Civil protection/restraining orders.
- Felony, preliminary hearings, misdemeanor.
- Traffic/other violations.   link

**Juvenile Court Department** — LJC / S
(11 divisions)
*41 justices*
*Jury trials*

CSP Case Types:
- Guardianship.
- Adoption.
- Juvenile.   link

**Housing Court Department** — LJC / S
(5 divisions)
*10 justices*
*Jury trials except in small claims*

CSP Case Types:
- Contract, small claims (up to $2,000).
- Preliminary hearings, misdemeanor.
- Ordinance violations. link

**Land Court Department** — LJC / S
(1 statewide court)
*7 justices*
*Jury trials*

CSP Case Types:
- Mortgage foreclosure, real property.   link

**Probate & Family Court Department** — LJC / S
(14 divisions)
*51 justices*
*No jury trials*

CSP Case Types:
- Exclusive probate/estate, miscellaneous civil.
- Domestic relations. Exclusive divorce/dissolution.
- Juvenile dependency. link

Note: All Departments (general and limited jurisdiction trial courts) make up the Trial Court of Massachusetts. The Administrative Office of the Trial Court reports caseload data by Department; thus, each Department is treated as a unique CSP reporting unit.

**Legend**
- ▭ = Appellate level
- ▭ = Trial level
- COLR = Court of Last Resort
- IAC = Intermediate Appellate Court
- GJC = General Jurisdiction Court
- LJC = Limited Jurisdiction Court
- ↑ = Route of appeal
- A = Appeal from Admin. Agency
- S = State funded
- £ = Locally funded
- M = Mixed: state and locally funded

\*The justices also sit individually in the "single justice" side of the court, on a rotating basis.

AOC Web site: www.mass.gov/courts

# Michigan

(Court structure as of Calendar Year 2009)

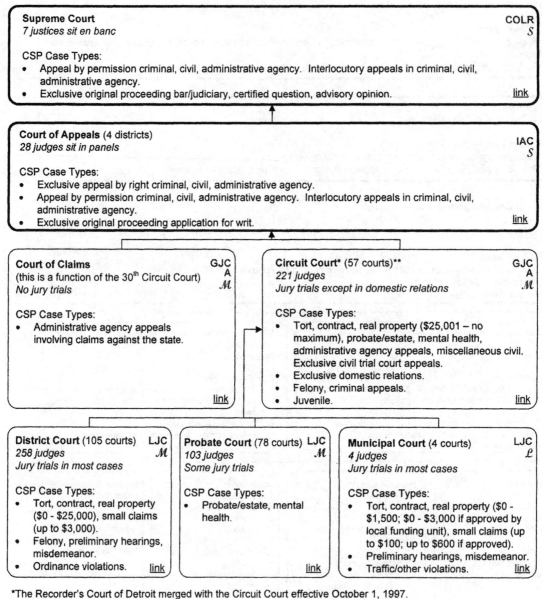

**Supreme Court**
*7 justices sit en banc*

COLR
*S*

CSP Case Types:
- Appeal by permission criminal, civil, administrative agency. Interlocutory appeals in criminal, civil, administrative agency.
- Exclusive original proceeding bar/judiciary, certified question, advisory opinion.

link

**Court of Appeals** (4 districts)
*28 judges sit in panels*

IAC
*S*

CSP Case Types:
- Exclusive appeal by right criminal, civil, administrative agency.
- Appeal by permission criminal, civil, administrative agency. Interlocutory appeals in criminal, civil, administrative agency.
- Exclusive original proceeding application for writ.

link

**Court of Claims**
(this is a function of the 30th Circuit Court)
*No jury trials*

GJC
A
*M*

CSP Case Types:
- Administrative agency appeals involving claims against the state.

link

**Circuit Court*** (57 courts)**
*221 judges*
*Jury trials except in domestic relations*

GJC
A
*M*

CSP Case Types:
- Tort, contract, real property ($25,001 – no maximum), probate/estate, mental health, administrative agency appeals, miscellaneous civil. Exclusive civil trial court appeals.
- Exclusive domestic relations.
- Felony, criminal appeals.
- Juvenile.

link

**District Court** (105 courts)
*258 judges*
*Jury trials in most cases*

LJC
*M*

CSP Case Types:
- Tort, contract, real property ($0 - $25,000), small claims (up to $3,000).
- Felony, preliminary hearings, misdemeanor.
- Ordinance violations. link

**Probate Court** (78 courts)
*103 judges*
*Some jury trials*

LJC
*M*

CSP Case Types:
- Probate/estate, mental health.

link

**Municipal Court** (4 courts)
*4 judges*
*Jury trials in most cases*

LJC
*L*

CSP Case Types:
- Tort, contract, real property ($0 - $1,500; $0 - $3,000 if approved by local funding unit), small claims (up to $100; up to $600 if approved).
- Preliminary hearings, misdemeanor.
- Traffic/other violations. link

*The Recorder's Court of Detroit merged with the Circuit Court effective October 1, 1997.
**A Family Division of Circuit Court became operational on January 1, 1998.

AOC Web site: **www.courts.michigan.gov**

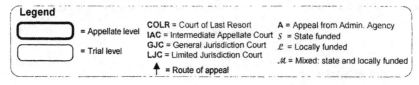

**Legend**

▭ = Appellate level

▭ = Trial level

**COLR** = Court of Last Resort
**IAC** = Intermediate Appellate Court
**GJC** = General Jurisdiction Court
**LJC** = Limited Jurisdiction Court

↑ = Route of appeal

**A** = Appeal from Admin. Agency
*S* = State funded
*L* = Locally funded

*M* = Mixed: state and locally funded

# Minnesota
### (Court structure as of Calendar Year 2009)

**Supreme Court**
*7 justices sit en banc*

COLR
A
*S*

CSP Case Types:
- Appeal by right felony, administrative agency.
- Appeal by permission criminal, civil, limited administrative agency.
- Original proceeding application for writ, certified question. Exclusive bar discipline/eligibility, advisory opinion.

link

**Court of Appeals**
*19 judges sit en banc and in panels*

IAC
A
*S*

CSP Case Types:
- Appeal by right criminal, civil, workers' compensation. Interlocutory appeals in criminal, civil, workers' compensation.
- Appeal by permission criminal, civil. Exclusive workers' compensation. Interlocutory appeals in criminal, civil, workers' compensation.
- Original proceeding application for writ, certified question.

link

**District Court** (10 districts)
*289 judges*
*Jury trials except in small claims and non-extended juvenile jurisdiction cases*

GJC
*M*

CSP Case Types:
- Exclusive civil (conciliation division: $0 - $7,500).
- Exclusive domestic relations.
- Exclusive criminal.
- Exclusive juvenile.
- Exclusive traffic/other violations.

link

AOC Web site: www.mncourts.gov/
default.aspx

**Legend**

| | |
|---|---|
| ☐ = Appellate level | |
| ☐ = Trial level | |

COLR = Court of Last Resort    A = Appeal from Admin. Agency
IAC = Intermediate Appellate Court  *S* = State funded
GJC = General Jurisdiction Court  *L* = Locally funded
LJC = Limited Jurisdiction Court

↑ = Route of appeal    *M* = Mixed: state and locally funded

# Mississippi
(Court structure as of Fiscal Year 2009)

**Supreme Court**
*9 justices sit en banc*
*Assigns cases to the Court of Appeals*

COLR
S

CSP Case Types:
- Appeal by right criminal, civil, administrative agency.  Interlocutory appeals in criminal, civil, administrative agency.
- Exclusive appeal by permission criminal, civil, administrative agency.  Interlocutory appeals in criminal, civil, administrative agency.
- Exclusive death penalty.
- Original proceeding application for writ.  Exclusive bar/judiciary, certified question, advisory opinion.link

**Court of Appeals** (5 districts)
*10 judges sit in panels and en banc*

IAC
S

CSP Case Types:
- Appeal by right criminal, civil, administrative agency.  Interlocutory appeals in criminal, civil, administrative agency.
- Original proceeding application for writ.                                                          link

**Circuit Court** (22 districts)
*51 judges*
*Jury trials*

GJC
A
M

CSP Case Types:
- Tort, contract, real property ($201 – no maximum), civil law appeals.
- Criminal.                                                                                          link

**Chancery Court** (20 districts)
*48 chancellors*
*Jury trials (limited)*

LJC
M

CSP Case Types:
- Tort, contract, real property ($0 – no maximum), probate/estate, mental health, civil equity appeals.
- Domestic relations.
- Juvenile (if no County Court).
- Appeals from Justice and Municipal Courts (if no County Court).                 link

**County Court** (20 counties)
*29 judges*
*Jury trials (limited)*

LJC
£

CSP Case Types:
- Tort, contract, real property ($0 - $200,000), civil appeals.  Probate/estate and mental health (as assigned by Chancery Court).
- Domestic relations (as assigned by Chancery Court).
- Preliminary hearings, misdemeanor.
- Juvenile.                                                                                          link

**Justice Court** (82 courts)
*197 judges*
*Jury trials*

LJC
£

CSP Case Types:
- Small claims ($0 - $3,500).
- Preliminary hearings, misdemeanor.     link

**Municipal Court** (226 courts)
*227 judges*
*No jury trials*

LJC
£

CSP Case Types:
- Preliminary hearings, misdemeanor.
- Traffic/other violations.                link

The Family Court was abolished July 1, 1999 and merged into County Court.

**Legend**

| | |
|---|---|
| ▭ = Appellate level | |
| ▭ = Trial level | |

COLR = Court of Last Resort
IAC = Intermediate Appellate Court
GJC = General Jurisdiction Court
LJC = Limited Jurisdiction Court

↑ = Route of appeal

A = Appeal from Admin. Agency
S = State funded
£ = Locally funded

M = Mixed: state and locally funded

AOC Web site:
**www.courts.ms.gov**

# Missouri

(Court structure as of Fiscal Year 2009)

**Supreme Court**         COLR *S*
*7 justice sit en banc*

CSP Case Types:
- Appeal by right limited criminal, civil (except juvenile). Interlocutory appeals in criminal, civil.
- Appeal by permission criminal, civil, administrative agency. Interlocutory appeals in criminal, civil, administrative agency.
- Exclusive death penalty.
- Original proceeding application for writ. Exclusive bar/judiciary.

link

**Court of Appeals** (3 districts)     IAC A S
*32 judges sit in panels*

CSP Case Types:
- Appeal by right criminal, civil, administrative agency. Interlocutory appeals in criminal, civil, administrative agency.
- Original proceeding application for writ.

link

**Circuit Court** (45 circuits)     GJC A *M*
*141 circuit judges, 193 associate circuit judges, 32 commissioners and 3 deputy commissioners*
*Jury trials in most cases*

CSP Case Types:
- Exclusive civil (circuit division: $0 – no maximum; associate division: $0 - $25,000), small claims (up to $3,000).
- Exclusive domestic relations.
- Exclusive criminal.
- Exclusive juvenile.
- Traffic/other violations.

link

**Municipal Court** (460 courts)     LJC *M*
*399 municipal judges*
*Jury trials in Springfield Municipality only*

CSP Case Types:
- Traffic/other violations.

link

AOC Web site: **www.courts.mo.gov**

**Legend**

| | |
|---|---|
| (rounded box) | = Appellate level |
| (box) | = Trial level |

COLR = Court of Last Resort    A = Appeal from Admin. Agency
IAC = Intermediate Appellate Court    *S* = State funded
GJC = General Jurisdiction Court    *L* = Locally funded
LJC = Limited Jurisdiction Court
↑ = Route of appeal    *M* = Mixed: state and locally funded

## Montana
### (Court Structure as of Calendar Year 2009)

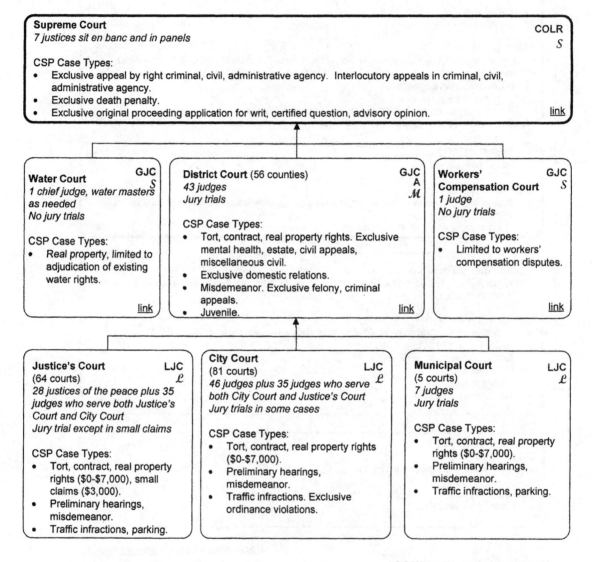

**Supreme Court**
*7 justices sit en banc and in panels*

COLR
*S*

CSP Case Types:
- Exclusive appeal by right criminal, civil, administrative agency. Interlocutory appeals in criminal, civil, administrative agency.
- Exclusive death penalty.
- Exclusive original proceeding application for writ, certified question, advisory opinion.

link

**Water Court**
*1 chief judge, water masters as needed*
*No jury trials*

GJC
*S*

CSP Case Types:
- Real property, limited to adjudication of existing water rights.

link

**District Court** (56 counties)
*43 judges*
*Jury trials*

GJC
A
*M*

CSP Case Types:
- Tort, contract, real property rights. Exclusive mental health, estate, civil appeals, miscellaneous civil.
- Exclusive domestic relations.
- Misdemeanor. Exclusive felony, criminal appeals.
- Juvenile.

link

**Workers' Compensation Court**
*1 judge*
*No jury trials*

GJC
*S*

CSP Case Types:
- Limited to workers' compensation disputes.

link

**Justice's Court**
(64 courts)
*28 justices of the peace plus 35 judges who serve both Justice's Court and City Court*
*Jury trial except in small claims*

LJC
*L*

CSP Case Types:
- Tort, contract, real property rights ($0-$7,000), small claims ($3,000).
- Preliminary hearings, misdemeanor.
- Traffic infractions, parking.

**City Court**
(81 courts)
*46 judges plus 35 judges who serve both City Court and Justice's Court*
*Jury trials in some cases*

LJC
*L*

CSP Case Types:
- Tort, contract, real property rights ($0-$7,000).
- Preliminary hearings, misdemeanor.
- Traffic infractions. Exclusive ordinance violations.

**Municipal Court**
(5 courts)
*7 judges*
*Jury trials*

LJC
*L*

CSP Case Types:
- Tort, contract, real property rights ($0-$7,000).
- Preliminary hearings, misdemeanor.
- Traffic infractions, parking.

**AOC Web site: www.courts.mt.gov**

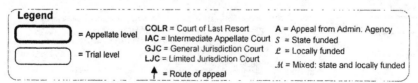

**Legend**

☐ = Appellate level

☐ = Trial level

↑ = Route of appeal

**COLR** = Court of Last Resort
**IAC** = Intermediate Appellate Court
**GJC** = General Jurisdiction Court
**LJC** = Limited Jurisdiction Court

**A** = Appeal from Admin. Agency
*S* = State funded
*L* = Locally funded
*M* = Mixed: state and locally funded

# STATE COURT STRUCTURE CHARTS

## Nebraska
### (Court structure as of Calendar Year 2009)

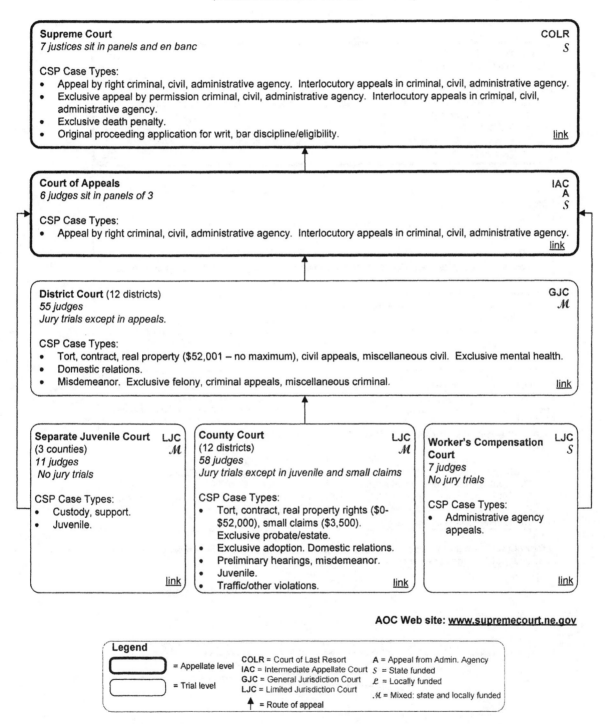

**Supreme Court**  COLR  *S*
*7 justices sit in panels and en banc*

CSP Case Types:
- Appeal by right criminal, civil, administrative agency. Interlocutory appeals in criminal, civil, administrative agency.
- Exclusive appeal by permission criminal, civil, administrative agency. Interlocutory appeals in criminal, civil, administrative agency.
- Exclusive death penalty.
- Original proceeding application for writ, bar discipline/eligibility.  link

**Court of Appeals**  IAC  A  *S*
*6 judges sit in panels of 3*

CSP Case Types:
- Appeal by right criminal, civil, administrative agency. Interlocutory appeals in criminal, civil, administrative agency.  link

**District Court** (12 districts)  GJC  *M*
*55 judges*
*Jury trials except in appeals.*

CSP Case Types:
- Tort, contract, real property ($52,001 – no maximum), civil appeals, miscellaneous civil. Exclusive mental health.
- Domestic relations.
- Misdemeanor. Exclusive felony, criminal appeals, miscellaneous criminal.  link

**Separate Juvenile Court**  LJC  *M*
(3 counties)
*11 judges*
*No jury trials*

CSP Case Types:
- Custody, support.
- Juvenile.  link

**County Court**  LJC  *M*
(12 districts)
*58 judges*
*Jury trials except in juvenile and small claims*

CSP Case Types:
- Tort, contract, real property rights ($0-$52,000), small claims ($3,500). Exclusive probate/estate.
- Exclusive adoption. Domestic relations.
- Preliminary hearings, misdemeanor.
- Juvenile.
- Traffic/other violations.  link

**Worker's Compensation Court**  LJC  *S*
*7 judges*
*No jury trials*

CSP Case Types:
- Administrative agency appeals.  link

**AOC Web site: www.supremecourt.ne.gov**

**Legend**
- ▢ = Appellate level
- ▢ = Trial level
- **COLR** = Court of Last Resort
- **IAC** = Intermediate Appellate Court
- **GJC** = General Jurisdiction Court
- **LJC** = Limited Jurisdiction Court
- ↑ = Route of appeal
- **A** = Appeal from Admin. Agency
- *S* = State funded
- *L* = Locally funded
- *M* = Mixed: state and locally funded

Reprinted with permission. Court Statistics Project.
National Center for State Courts.

# Nevada

(Court structure as of Fiscal Year 2009)

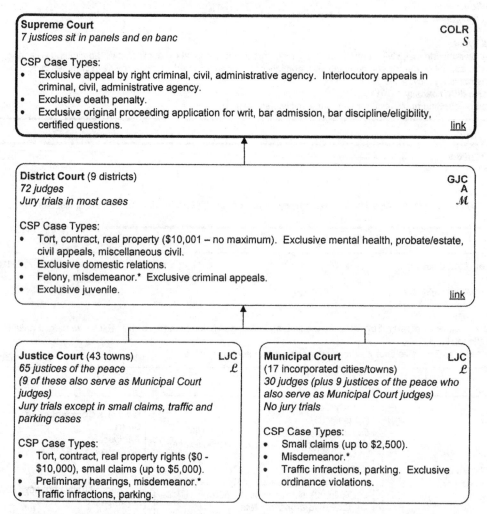

**Supreme Court**                                                                    COLR
*7 justices sit in panels and en banc*                                                  *S*

CSP Case Types:
- Exclusive appeal by right criminal, civil, administrative agency. Interlocutory appeals in criminal, civil, administrative agency.
- Exclusive death penalty.
- Exclusive original proceeding application for writ, bar admission, bar discipline/eligibility, certified questions.                                          link

**District Court** (9 districts)                                                      GJC
*72 judges*                                                                             A
*Jury trials in most cases*                                                             *M*

CSP Case Types:
- Tort, contract, real property ($10,001 – no maximum). Exclusive mental health, probate/estate, civil appeals, miscellaneous civil.
- Exclusive domestic relations.
- Felony, misdemeanor.* Exclusive criminal appeals.
- Exclusive juvenile.                                                                link

**Justice Court** (43 towns)                          LJC
*65 justices of the peace*                              *£*
*(9 of these also serve as Municipal Court judges)*
*Jury trials except in small claims, traffic and parking cases*

CSP Case Types:
- Tort, contract, real property rights ($0 - $10,000), small claims (up to $5,000).
- Preliminary hearings, misdemeanor.*
- Traffic infractions, parking.

**Municipal Court**                                    LJC
*(17 incorporated cities/towns)*                        *£*
*30 judges (plus 9 justices of the peace who also serve as Municipal Court judges)*
*No jury trials*

CSP Case Types:
- Small claims (up to $2,500).
- Misdemeanor.*
- Traffic infractions, parking. Exclusive ordinance violations.

*District Court hears gross misdemeanor cases; Justice & Municipal Courts hear misdemeanors with fines under $1,000 and/or sentence of less than six months.

**AOC Web site: www.nevadajudiciary.us**

**Legend**

☐ = Appellate level
☐ = Trial level

COLR = Court of Last Resort
IAC = Intermediate Appellate Court
GJC = General Jurisdiction Court
LJC = Limited Jurisdiction Court
↑ = Route of appeal

A = Appeal from Admin. Agency
*S* = State funded
*£* = Locally funded
*M* = Mixed: state and locally funded

# STATE COURT STRUCTURE CHARTS

## New Hampshire
(Court structure as of Calendar Year 2009)

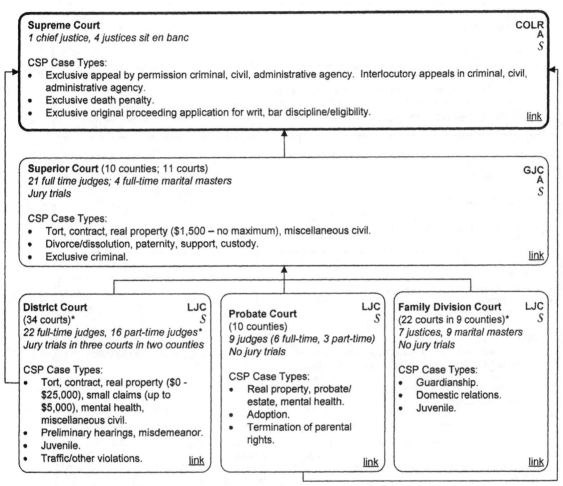

**Supreme Court**
*1 chief justice, 4 justices sit en banc*

CSP Case Types:
- Exclusive appeal by permission criminal, civil, administrative agency. Interlocutory appeals in criminal, civil, administrative agency.
- Exclusive death penalty.
- Exclusive original proceeding application for writ, bar discipline/eligibility.

COLR
A
*S*

link

**Superior Court** (10 counties; 11 courts)
*21 full time judges; 4 full-time marital masters*
*Jury trials*

CSP Case Types:
- Tort, contract, real property ($1,500 – no maximum), miscellaneous civil.
- Divorce/dissolution, paternity, support, custody.
- Exclusive criminal.

GJC
A
*S*

link

**District Court**
(34 courts)*
*22 full-time judges, 16 part-time judges**
*Jury trials in three courts in two counties*

CSP Case Types:
- Tort, contract, real property ($0 - $25,000), small claims (up to $5,000), mental health, miscellaneous civil.
- Preliminary hearings, misdemeanor.
- Juvenile.
- Traffic/other violations.

LJC
*S*

link

**Probate Court**
(10 counties)
*9 judges (6 full-time, 3 part-time)*
*No jury trials*

CSP Case Types:
- Real property, probate/ estate, mental health.
- Adoption.
- Termination of parental rights.

LJC
*S*

link

**Family Division Court**
(22 courts in 9 counties)*
*7 justices, 9 marital masters*
*No jury trials*

CSP Case Types:
- Guardianship.
- Domestic relations.
- Juvenile.

LJC
*S*

link

* The Family Division Court was created in 2005. The Municipal Court merged with the District Court in May, 2000. Eleven per diem judges also serve the District Court.

AOC Web site: www.courts.state.nh.us

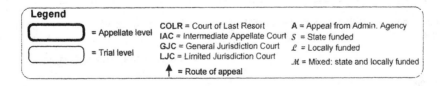

**Legend**

| | | |
|---|---|---|
| ☐ = Appellate level | **COLR** = Court of Last Resort | **A** = Appeal from Admin. Agency |
| ☐ = Trial level | **IAC** = Intermediate Appellate Court | *S* = State funded |
| | **GJC** = General Jurisdiction Court | *£* = Locally funded |
| | **LJC** = Limited Jurisdiction Court | *M* = Mixed: state and locally funded |
| ↑ = Route of appeal | | |

# STATE COURT STRUCTURE CHARTS

## New Jersey

(Court structure as of Fiscal Year 2009)

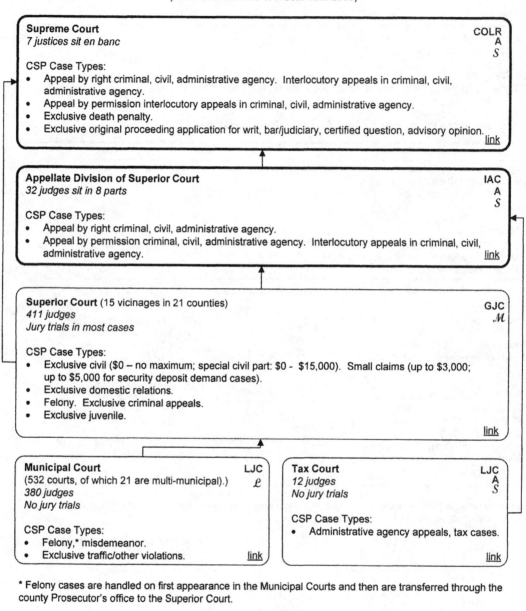

**Supreme Court**
*7 justices sit en banc*

COLR
A
*S*

CSP Case Types:
- Appeal by right criminal, civil, administrative agency. Interlocutory appeals in criminal, civil, administrative agency.
- Appeal by permission interlocutory appeals in criminal, civil, administrative agency.
- Exclusive death penalty.
- Exclusive original proceeding application for writ, bar/judiciary, certified question, advisory opinion.

link

**Appellate Division of Superior Court**
*32 judges sit in 8 parts*

IAC
A
*S*

CSP Case Types:
- Appeal by right criminal, civil, administrative agency.
- Appeal by permission criminal, civil, administrative agency. Interlocutory appeals in criminal, civil, administrative agency.

link

**Superior Court** (15 vicinages in 21 counties)
*411 judges*
*Jury trials in most cases*

GJC
*M*

CSP Case Types:
- Exclusive civil ($0 – no maximum; special civil part: $0 - $15,000). Small claims (up to $3,000; up to $5,000 for security deposit demand cases).
- Exclusive domestic relations.
- Felony. Exclusive criminal appeals.
- Exclusive juvenile.

link

**Municipal Court**
(532 courts, of which 21 are multi-municipal).)
*380 judges*
*No jury trials*

LJC
*£*

CSP Case Types:
- Felony,* misdemeanor.
- Exclusive traffic/other violations.

link

**Tax Court**
*12 judges*
*No jury trials*

LJC
A
*S*

CSP Case Types:
- Administrative agency appeals, tax cases.

link

\* Felony cases are handled on first appearance in the Municipal Courts and then are transferred through the county Prosecutor's office to the Superior Court.

**AOC Web site: www.judiciary.state.nj.us**

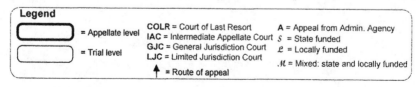

**Legend**

| | | |
|---|---|---|
| ▭ = Appellate level | **COLR** = Court of Last Resort | **A** = Appeal from Admin. Agency |
| ▭ = Trial level | **IAC** = Intermediate Appellate Court | *S* = State funded |
| | **GJC** = General Jurisdiction Court | *£* = Locally funded |
| | **LJC** = Limited Jurisdiction Court | |
| | ↑ = Route of appeal | *M* = Mixed: state and locally funded |

Reprinted with permission. Court Statistics Project.
National Center for State Courts.

# New Mexico
(Court structure as of Fiscal Year 2009)

**Supreme Court**  COLR
*5 justices sit en banc*  A
  *S*

CSP Case Types:
- Appeal by right felony, limited administrative agency. Interlocutory appeals in criminal, administrative agency.
- Appeal by permission criminal, civil, administrative agency. Interlocutory appeals in criminal, civil, administrative agency.
- Exclusive death penalty.
- Original proceeding application for writ. Exclusive bar discipline/eligibility, judicial qualification, certified question.  link

**Court of Appeals**  IAC
*10 judges sit in panels of 3*  A
  *S*

CSP Case Types:
- Appeal by right criminal, limited administrative agency. Exclusive civil.
- Appeal by permission criminal, civil. Interlocutory appeals in criminal, civil.
- Original proceeding application for writ.  link

**District Court** (13 districts)  GJC
*88 judges*  *M*
*Jury trials*

CSP Case Types:
- Tort, contract, real property, probate/estate. Exclusive mental health, civil appeals, miscellaneous civil.
- Exclusive domestic relations.
- Felony, misdemeanor. Exclusive criminal appeals.
- Exclusive juvenile.  link

**Magistrate Court** (49 courts)  LJC
*66 judges*  *M*
*Jury trials in some cases*

CSP Case Types:
- Small claims (up to $10,000).
- Preliminary hearings, misdemeanor.
- Traffic infractions.  link

**Bernalillo County Metropolitan Court**  LJC
*19 judges*  *£*
*Jury trials in some cases*

CSP Case Types:
- Small claims (up to $10,000).
- Preliminary hearings, misdemeanor.
- Traffic/other violation.  link

**Municipal Court** (81 courts)  LJC
*85 judges*  *£*
*No jury trials*

CSP Case Types:
- Misdemeanor.
- Traffic/other violations.

**Probate Court** (33 counties)  LJC
*33 judges*  *£*
*No jury trials*

CSP Case Types:
- Probate/estate (uncontested cases).

AOC Web site: **www.nmcourts.gov**

**Legend**

| | |
|---|---|
| ⬭ = Appellate level | |
| ▭ = Trial level | |

**COLR** = Court of Last Resort  **A** = Appeal from Admin. Agency
**IAC** = Intermediate Appellate Court  *S* = State funded
**GJC** = General Jurisdiction Court  *£* = Locally funded
**LJC** = Limited Jurisdiction Court  *M* = Mixed: state and locally funded

↑ = Route of appeal

# STATE COURT STRUCTURE CHARTS

## New York
### (Court structure as of Calendar Year 2009)

**Court of Appeals** — COLR *S*
7 judges

CSP Case Types:
- Appeal by right civil, administrative agency. Interlocutory appeals in civil, administrative agency.
- Appeal by permission criminal, civil, administrative agency. Interlocutory appeals in criminal, civil, administrative agency.
- Exclusive death penalty.
- Exclusive original proceeding judicial qualification, certified question.

link

---

**Appellate Divisions of Supreme Court** — IAC A *S*
56 justices sit in panels in 4 departments

CSP Case Types:
- Appeal by right criminal, civil, administrative agency. Interlocutory appeals in criminal, civil, administrative agency.
- Appeal by permission criminal, civil, administrative agency. Interlocutory appeals in criminal, civil, administrative agency.
- Exclusive original proceeding application for writ, bar/judiciary.

link

**Appellate Terms of Supreme Court** — IAC *S*
14 justices sit in panels in 2 departments

CSP Case Types:
- Appeal by right criminal, civil. Interlocutory appeal in criminal, civil.
- Appeal by permission criminal, juvenile. Interlocutory appeals in criminal, juvenile.

link

---

**Supreme and County Court** 326 justices, 134 judges

**Supreme Court** (12 districts) — GJC A *S*
326 justices plus 59 judges from the Court of Claims
Jury trials

CSP Case Types:
- Tort, contract, real property, miscellaneous civil.
- Exclusive marriage dissolution.
- Felony, misdemeanor.

link

**County Court** (57 counties outside NYC) — GJC *S*
129 judges (50 serve the Surrogates' Court and 6 serve the Family Court)
Jury trials

CSP Case Types:
- Tort, contract, real property ($0 - $25,000), civil appeals, miscellaneous civil.
- Criminal.

link

---

**Court of Claims** (1 court) — LJC *S*
86 judges (of which 59 act as Supreme Court justices)
No jury trials

CSP Case Types:
- Tort, contract, real property involving the state.

link

**Family Court** (62 counties) — LJC *S*
127 judges plus 6 judges from the County Court and 81 quasi-judicial staff
No jury trials
CSP Case Types:
- Guardianship.
- Domestic relations.
- Exclusive domestic violence.
- Exclusive juvenile.

**Surrogates' Court** (62 counties) — LJC *S*
31 surrogates plus 50 judges from the County Court
Jury trials in probate/estate
CSP Case Types:
- Probate/estate.
- Adoption.

**District and City Court** 208 judges

**District Court** (Nassau and Suffolk counties) — LJC *S*
50 judges
Jury trials except in traffic
CSP Case Types:
- Tort, contract, real property ($0 - $15,000), small claims (up to $5,000)
- Felony, preliminary hearings, misdemeanor.
- Traffic infractions, ordinance violations.

**City Court** (79 courts in 61 cities) — LJC *S*
158 judges
Jury trials for highest level misdemeanor
CSP Case Types:
- Tort, contract, real property ($0 - $15,000), small claims (up to $5,000)
- Felony, preliminary hearings, misdemeanor.
- Traffic infractions, ordinance violations.

**Civil Court of the City of New York** — LJC *S*
120 judges
Jury trials
CSP Case Types:
- Tort, contract, real property ($0 - $25,000), small claims, (up to $5,000), miscellaneous civil.

link

**Criminal Court of the City of New York** — LJC *S*
107 judges
Jury trials for highest level misdemeanor
CSP Case Types:
- Preliminary hearings, misdemeanor.
- Traffic infractions, ordinance violations.

link

**Town and Village Justice Court** — LJC *M*
(1,487 courts)
2,300 justices
Jury trials in most cases

CSP Case Types:
- Tort, contract, real property ($0 - $3,000), small claims (up to $3,000)
- Preliminary hearings, misdemeanor.
- Traffic/other violations. link

---

**Legend**

☐ = Appellate level

☐ = Trial level

↑ = Route of appeal

COLR = Court of Last Resort
IAC = Intermediate Appellate Court
GJC = General Jurisdiction Court
LJC = Limited Jurisdiction Court

A = Appeal from Admin. Agency
*S* = State funded
*£* = Locally funded
*M* = Mixed: state and locally funded

**AOC Web site:**
**www.courts.state.ny.us**

Reprinted with permission. Court Statistics Project.
National Center for State Courts.

# North Carolina
(Court structure as of Fiscal Year 2009)

**Supreme Court**       COLR A S
*7 justices sit en banc*

CSP Case Types:
- Appeal by right criminal, civil, administrative agency. Interlocutory appeals in criminal, civil, administrative agency.
- Appeal by permission criminal, civil, administrative agency. Interlocutory appeals in criminal, civil, administrative agency.
- Exclusive death penalty.
- Original proceeding application for writ, bar/judiciary.    link

**Court of Appeals**       IAC A S
*15 judges sit in panels*
CSP Case Types:
- Appeal by right criminal, civil, administrative agency.
- Appeal by permission criminal, civil, administrative agency. Interlocutory appeals in criminal, civil, administrative agency.
- Original proceeding application for writ, bar/judiciary.    link

**Superior Court** (49 districts for administrative purposes; 65 districts for elective purposes)    GJC A M
*111 judges (includes 13 special judges) and 100 clerks serve as ex officio judges of probate with jurisdiction in estate cases and with certain other judicial authorities*
*Jury trials*

CSP Case Types:
- Tort, contract, real property ($10,001 – no maximum), miscellaneous civil. Exclusive probate/estate, administrative agency appeals.
- Criminal.    link

**District Court** (41 districts for administrative purposes; 40 districts for elective purposes)    LJC M
*262 judges and 737 magistrates*
*Jury trials in civil cases only*

CSP Case Types:
- Tort, contract, real property ($0 - $10,000), miscellaneous civil. Exclusive small claims (up to $5,000), mental health.
- Exclusive domestic relations.
- Preliminary hearings, misdemeanor.
- Exclusive juvenile.
- Traffic/other violations.    link

**AOC Web site: www.nccourts.org**

**Legend**

| | | |
|---|---|---|
| ▭ = Appellate level | **COLR** = Court of Last Resort | **A** = Appeal from Admin. Agency |
| ▭ = Trial level | **IAC** = Intermediate Appellate Court | **S** = State funded |
| | **GJC** = General Jurisdiction Court | **L** = Locally funded |
| | **LJC** = Limited Jurisdiction Court | **M** = Mixed: state and locally funded |
| | ↑ = Route of appeal | |

# North Dakota

(Court structure as of Calendar Year 2009)

**Supreme Court**                                                                    COLR
*5 justices sit en banc*                                                                 *S*
Assigns cases to the Temporary Court of Appeals

CSP Case Types:
- Appeal by right criminal, civil, administrative agency. Interlocutory appeals in criminal, civil, administrative agency.
- Original proceeding application for writ. Exclusive bar/judiciary, certified question, advisory opinion.                                                         link

**Temporary Court of Appeals***                                                      IAC
*3 judges sit in panels*                                                                 *S*

CSP Case Types:
- Appeal by right criminal, civil, administrative agency. Interlocutory appeals in criminal, civil, administrative agency.
- Original proceeding application for writ.

**District Court** (7 judicial districts in 53 counties)                              GJC
*44 judges, 8 judicial referees*                                                          A
*Jury trials in many cases*                                                               *S*

CSP Case Types:
- Exclusive civil.
- Exclusive domestic relations.
- Criminal.
- Exclusive juvenile.
- Traffic/other violations.                                                          link

**Municipal Court** (80 municipalities)                                              LJC
*73 judges*                                                                               *£*
*No jury trials*

CSP Case Types:
- DWI/DUI.
- Traffic/other violations.                                                          link

*Note: A temporary Court of Appeals was established July 1, 1987, to exercise appellate and original jurisdiction as delegated by the Supreme Court. *Authorization for the Court of Appeals extends to January 1, 2012.

AOC Web site: www.ndcourts.gov

**Legend**

| | | | |
|---|---|---|---|
| = Appellate level | **COLR** = Court of Last Resort | **A** = Appeal from Admin. Agency | |
| | **IAC** = Intermediate Appellate Court | *S* = State funded | |
| = Trial level | **GJC** = General Jurisdiction Court | *£* = Locally funded | |
| | **LJC** = Limited Jurisdiction Court | *M* = Mixed: state and locally funded | |
| | ↑ = Route of appeal | | |

# Ohio
### (Court structure as of Calendar Year 2009)

---

**Supreme Court**                                                                COLR A *S*
*7 justices sit en banc*

CSP Case Types:
- Appeal by right criminal, civil, administrative agency.
- Exclusive appeal by permission criminal, civil, limited administrative agency. Interlocutory appeals in criminal, civil, administrative agency.
- Exclusive death penalty.
- Original proceeding application for writ. Exclusive bar/judiciary, certified question.          link

---

**Court of Appeals** (12 courts)                                                IAC A *S*
*69 judges sit in panels of 3 members each*

CSP Case Types:
- Appeal by right criminal, civil, administrative agency. Interlocutory appeals in criminal, civil, administrative agency.
- Original proceeding application for writ.          link

---

**Court of Common Pleas** (88 courts)                                            GJC A *M*
*394 judges*
*Jury trials in most cases*

CSP Case Types:
- Tort, contract, real property ($500 – no maximum), administrative agency appeals, miscellaneous civil. Exclusive mental health, probate/estate.
- Exclusive domestic relations.
- Felony, misdemeanor.
- Exclusive juvenile.
- Traffic/other violations (juvenile only).          link

---

**Municipal Court** (128 courts)          LJC *M*
*212 judges*
*Jury trials in most cases*

CSP Case Types:
- Tort, contract, real property ($0 - $15,000), small claims (up to $3,000), miscellaneous civil.
- Criminal.
- Traffic infractions, ordinance violations.          link

---

**County Court** (38 courts)          LJC *M*
*44 judges*
*Jury trials in most cases*

CSP Case Types:
- Tort, contract, real property ($0 - $15,000), small claims (up to $3,000), miscellaneous civil.
- Criminal.
- Traffic infractions, ordinance violations.          link

---

**Court of Claims**          LJC *S*
*Judges assigned by the Chief Justice*
*Jury trials in some cases*

CSP Case Types:
- Civil (actions against the state, victims of crime cases).          link

---

**Mayors Court** (~335 courts)          LJC *£*
*~335 mayors or magistrates*
*No jury trials*

CSP Case Types:
- DWI/DUI, other misdemeanors.
- Traffic/other violations.          link

---

**Legend**

|  |  |  |  |
|---|---|---|---|
| ▭ = Appellate level | **COLR** = Court of Last Resort | **A** = Appeal from Admin. Agency | |
| ▭ = Trial level | **IAC** = Intermediate Appellate Court | *S* = State funded | |
| | **GJC** = General Jurisdiction Court | *£* = Locally funded | |
| | **LJC** = Limited Jurisdiction Court | *M* = Mixed: state and locally funded | |
| ↑ = Route of appeal | | | |

**AOC Web site:**
**www.sconet.state.oh.us**

# Oklahoma
### (Court structure as of Fiscal Year 2009)

**Supreme Court**                                          COLR
*9 justices sit en banc*                                       A
*Assigns cases to the Court of Civil Appeals*                  S

CSP Case Types:
- Appeal by right civil, administrative agency. Interlocutory appeals in civil, administrative agency.
- Appeal by permission civil, administrative agency. Interlocutory appeals in civil, administrative agency.
- Exclusive original proceeding bar/judiciary, certified question.                                          link

**Court of Criminal Appeals**                              COLR
*5 judges sit en banc*                                         S

CSP Case Types:
- Exclusive appeal by right criminal, juvenile. Interlocutory appeals in criminal, juvenile.
- Exclusive appeal by permission criminal, juvenile. Interlocutory appeals in criminal, juvenile.
- Exclusive death penalty.
- Original proceeding application for writ.          link

**Court of Civil Appeals**                                 IAC
*12 judges sit in 4 permanent divisions of 3 members each*     S

CSP Case Types:
- Appeal by right civil, administrative agency. Interlocutory appeals in civil, administrative agency.
- Original proceeding application for writ.                 link

**District Court** (77 courts in 26 districts)             GJC
*75 district, 77 associate district, and 89 special judges*    A
*Jury trials*                                                  S

CSP Case Types:
- Exclusive civil (except administrative agency appeals), small claims (up to $6,000).
- Exclusive domestic relations.
- Exclusive criminal.
- Exclusive juvenile.
- Traffic infractions, ordinance violations.               link

**Court of Tax Review**                      LJC
*3 District Court judges serve*               A
*No jury trials*                              S

CSP Case Types:
- Administrative agency appeals.
                                            link

**Municipal Court Not of Record**           LJC
(340 courts)                                  £
*~350 full- and part-time judges*
*Jury trials*

CSP Case Types:
- Traffic/other violations.

**Municipal Court of Record**               LJC
(2 courts)                                    £
*~8 full-time and 18 part-time judges*
*Jury trials*

CSP Case Types:
- Traffic/other violations.

Note: Oklahoma has a workers' compensation court, which hears complaints that are handled exclusively by administrative agencies in other states.

**AOC Web site: www.oscn.net**

**Legend**

☐ = Appellate level

☐ = Trial level

**COLR** = Court of Last Resort
**IAC** = Intermediate Appellate Court
**GJC** = General Jurisdiction Court
**LJC** = Limited Jurisdiction Court

↑ = Route of appeal

**A** = Appeal from Admin. Agency
*S* = State funded
*£* = Locally funded
*M* = Mixed: state and locally funded

# STATE COURT STRUCTURE CHARTS

# Oregon

(Court structure as of Calendar Year 2009)

**Supreme Court**                                                                    COLR
*7 justices sit en banc*                                                               A
                                                                                       *S*
CSP Case Types:
- Exclusive appeal by right revenue (tax).
- Exclusive appeal by permission criminal, civil, limited administrative agency.
- Exclusive death penalty.
- Exclusive original proceeding application for writ, bar/judiciary, certified question, advisory opinion.      link

**Court of Appeals**                                                                 IAC
*10 judges sit in panels and en banc*                                                  A
                                                                                       *S*
CSP Case Types:
- Exclusive appeal by right criminal, civil, limited administrative agency.           link

---

**Tax Court**                                            GJC
*1 judge*                                                  A
*No jury trials*                                           *S*

CSP Case Types:
- Administrative agency appeals.
                                                         link

---

**Circuit Court** (27 judicial districts in 36 counties; 36 courts)      GJC
*173 judges*                                                              *M*
*Jury trials for most case types*

CSP Case Types:
- Exclusive tort, contract, real property, probate/estate, civil appeals, civil miscellaneous. Small claims (up to $7,500), mental health.
- Exclusive domestic relations (except adoption).
- Exclusive felony, criminal appeals. Misdemeanor.
- Juvenile. Exclusive termination of parental rights.
- Traffic/other violations.                                             link

---

**County Court** (7 courts)          LJC
*7 judges*                            *L*
*No jury trials*

CSP Case Types:
- Probate/estate, mental health.
- Adoption.
- Juvenile (except termination of parental rights).
                                      link

---

**Justice Court**                     LJC
(30 courts/19 counties)               *L*
*30 justices of the peace*
*Jury trials for some case types*

CSP Case Types:
- Landlord/tenant, small claims (up to $7,500).
- Misdemeanor.
- Traffic/other violations.          link

---

**Municipal Court**                   LJC
(144 courts)                          *L*
*225 judges*
*Jury trials for some case types*

CSP Case Types:
- Misdemeanor.
- Traffic/other violations.
                                      link

---

Note: Effective January 15, 1998 all District Courts were eliminated and District judges became Circuit judges.

AOC Web site:
www.courts.oregon.gov/OJD/courts/index.page

## Legend

|  |  |  |  |
|---|---|---|---|
| ☐ = Appellate level | **COLR** = Court of Last Resort | **A** = Appeal from Admin. Agency | |
| ☐ = Trial level | **IAC** = Intermediate Appellate Court | *S* = State funded | |
|  | **GJC** = General Jurisdiction Court | *L* = Locally funded | |
|  | **LJC** = Limited Jurisdiction Court | *M* = Mixed: state and locally funded | |
|  | ↑ = Route of appeal | | |

# Pennsylvania

(Court structure as of Calendar Year 2009)

**Supreme Court**                                                                                                    COLR
*7 justices sit en banc*                                                                                              *S*

CSP Case Types:
- Appeal by right criminal, civil, administrative agency.  Interlocutory appeals in criminal, civil, administrative agency.
- Appeal by permission criminal, civil, administrative agency.  Interlocutory appeals in criminal, civil, administrative agency.
- Exclusive death penalty.
- Original proceeding application for writ.  Exclusive bar/judiciary, certified question.                          link

**Commonwealth Court***                    IAC
*9 judges sit in panels and en banc*        A
                                            *S*

CSP Case Types:
- Appeal by right criminal, civil, administrative agency.  Interlocutory appeals in criminal, civil, administrative agency.
- Appeal by permission civil, limited administrative agency.  Interlocutory appeals in civil, administrative agency.
- Original proceeding application for writ.    link

**Superior Court**                          IAC
*15 judges sit in panels and en banc*        *S*

CSP Case Types:
- Appeal by right criminal, civil.  Interlocutory appeal in criminal, civil.
- Appeal by permission criminal, civil.  Interlocutory appeal in criminal, civil.
- Original proceeding application for writ.

link

**Court of Common Pleas** (60 districts in 67 counties)                                                            GJC
*439 judges*                                                                                                          A
*Jury trials in most cases*                                                                                          *M*

CSP Case Types:
- Tort, contract, real property, probate/estate, administrative agency appeals, miscellaneous civil.
- Domestic relations.
- Felony, miscellaneous criminal.
- Exclusive juvenile.                                                                                               link

**Philadelphia Municipal Court**  LJC
*25 judges*                         *M*
*No jury trials*

CSP Case Types:
- Landlord/tenant, real property ($0 - $15,000), small claims (up to $10,000), miscellaneous civil.
- Felony, preliminary hearings, misdemeanor.
- Ordinance violations.    link

**Philadelphia Traffic Court**  LJC
*7 judges*                        *M*
*No jury trials*

CSP Case Types:
- Traffic infraction, parking violation.

link

**Magisterial District Judge Court**** (546 courts)  LJC
*546 judges*                                           *M*
*No jury trials*

CSP Case Types:
- Small claims (up to $8,000).
- Felony, preliminary hearings, misdemeanor.
- Traffic/other violations.    link

*Commonwealth Court hears cases brought by and against the Commonwealth.
**Effective January 1, 2005, the Pittsburgh Municipal Court merged with the Allegheny County Magisterial District Judge Court.

**Legend**

☐ = Appellate level
☐ = Trial level

**COLR** = Court of Last Resort
**IAC** = Intermediate Appellate Court
**GJC** = General Jurisdiction Court
**LJC** = Limited Jurisdiction Court
↑ = Route of appeal

**A** = Appeal from Admin. Agency
*S* = State funded
*L* = Locally funded
*M* = Mixed: state and locally funded

**AOC Web site:**
**www.aopc.org**

# Puerto Rico

(Court structure as of Fiscal Year 2009)

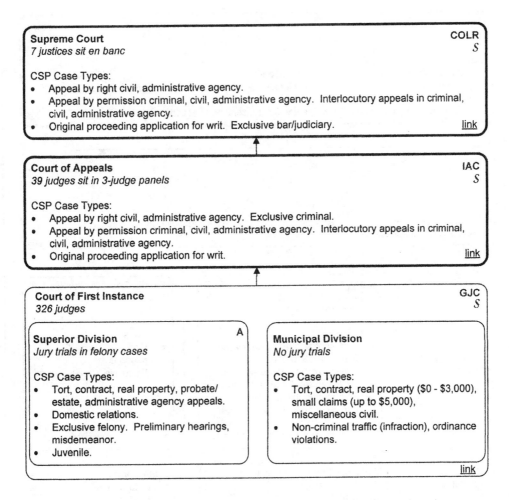

**Supreme Court** — COLR — *S*

*7 justices sit en banc*

CSP Case Types:
- Appeal by right civil, administrative agency.
- Appeal by permission criminal, civil, administrative agency. Interlocutory appeals in criminal, civil, administrative agency.
- Original proceeding application for writ. Exclusive bar/judiciary.

link

**Court of Appeals** — IAC — *S*

*39 judges sit in 3-judge panels*

CSP Case Types:
- Appeal by right civil, administrative agency. Exclusive criminal.
- Appeal by permission criminal, civil, administrative agency. Interlocutory appeals in criminal, civil, administrative agency.
- Original proceeding application for writ.

link

**Court of First Instance** — GJC — *S*

*326 judges*

**Superior Division** — A

*Jury trials in felony cases*

CSP Case Types:
- Tort, contract, real property, probate/ estate, administrative agency appeals.
- Domestic relations.
- Exclusive felony. Preliminary hearings, misdemeanor.
- Juvenile.

**Municipal Division**

*No jury trials*

CSP Case Types:
- Tort, contract, real property ($0 - $3,000), small claims (up to $5,000), miscellaneous civil.
- Non-criminal traffic (infraction), ordinance violations.

link

Note: The Judicial Law 2001, renamed the Judicial Reform Act of 1994, changed the name of the intermediate appellate court from the Circuit Court of Appeals to the Court of Appeals and abolished the District Division of the Court of First Instance. The District Division was abolished in 2002, and its functions were transferred to the Superior Division.

**AOC Web site: www.ramajudicial.pr**

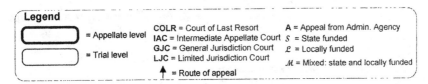

**Legend**

☐ = Appellate level

☐ = Trial level

COLR = Court of Last Resort
IAC = Intermediate Appellate Court
GJC = General Jurisdiction Court
LJC = Limited Jurisdiction Court
↑ = Route of appeal

A = Appeal from Admin. Agency
*S* = State funded
*L* = Locally funded
*M* = Mixed: state and locally funded

# Rhode Island

**(Court structure as of Calendar Year 2009)**

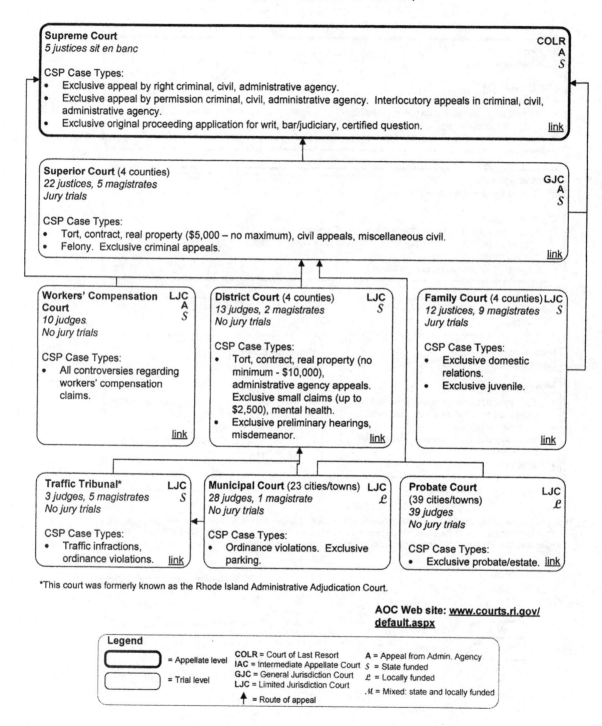

**Supreme Court**
*5 justices sit en banc*

COLR
A
*S*

CSP Case Types:
- Exclusive appeal by right criminal, civil, administrative agency.
- Exclusive appeal by permission criminal, civil, administrative agency. Interlocutory appeals in criminal, civil, administrative agency.
- Exclusive original proceeding application for writ, bar/judiciary, certified question.

link

**Superior Court** (4 counties)
*22 justices, 5 magistrates*
*Jury trials*

GJC
A
*S*

CSP Case Types:
- Tort, contract, real property ($5,000 – no maximum), civil appeals, miscellaneous civil.
- Felony. Exclusive criminal appeals.

link

**Workers' Compensation Court**
*10 judges.*
*No jury trials*

LJC
A
*S*

CSP Case Types:
- All controversies regarding workers' compensation claims.

link

**District Court** (4 counties)
*13 judges, 2 magistrates*
*No jury trials*

LJC
*S*

CSP Case Types:
- Tort, contract, real property (no minimum - $10,000), administrative agency appeals. Exclusive small claims (up to $2,500), mental health.
- Exclusive preliminary hearings, misdemeanor.

link

**Family Court** (4 counties)
*12 justices, 9 magistrates*
*Jury trials*

LJC
*S*

CSP Case Types:
- Exclusive domestic relations.
- Exclusive juvenile.

link

**Traffic Tribunal***
*3 judges, 5 magistrates*
*No jury trials*

LJC
*S*

CSP Case Types:
- Traffic infractions, ordinance violations.

link

**Municipal Court** (23 cities/towns)
*28 judges, 1 magistrate*
*No jury trials*

LJC
*£*

CSP Case Types:
- Ordinance violations. Exclusive parking.

**Probate Court**
(39 cities/towns)
*39 judges*
*No jury trials*

LJC
*£*

CSP Case Types:
- Exclusive probate/estate. link

*This court was formerly known as the Rhode Island Administrative Adjudication Court.

AOC Web site: **www.courts.ri.gov/default.aspx**

**Legend**

= Appellate level

= Trial level

**COLR** = Court of Last Resort
**IAC** = Intermediate Appellate Court
**GJC** = General Jurisdiction Court
**LJC** = Limited Jurisdiction Court

↑ = Route of appeal

A = Appeal from Admin. Agency
*S* = State funded
*£* = Locally funded
*.M.* = Mixed: state and locally funded

# South Carolina
(Court structure as of Fiscal Year 2009)

---

**Supreme Court**                                                          COLR
*5 justices sit en banc*                                                      S
*Assigns cases to the Court of Appeals*

CSP Case Types:
- Appeal by right criminal, civil.  Interlocutory appeals in criminal, civil.
- Exclusive appeal by permission criminal, civil, administrative agency.  Interlocutory appeals in criminal, civil, administrative agency.
- Exclusive death penalty.
- Exclusive original proceeding application for writ , bar/judiciary, certified question.          link

---

**Court of Appeals**                                                         IAC
*9 judges sit in panels and en banc*                                          S

CSP Case Types:
- Appeal by right criminal, civil.  Exclusive administrative agency.          link

---

**Circuit Court** (16 circuits, 46 counties)                                 GJC
*46 judges and 21 masters-in-equity*                                          A
*Jury trials except in appeals*                                               M

CSP Case Types:
- Tort, contract, real property, miscellaneous civil. Exclusive civil appeals.
- Misdemeanor.  Exclusive felony, criminal appeals.                          link

---

**Family Court**                              LJC
(16 circuits, 46 counties)                     M
*52 judges*
*No jury trials*

CSP Case Types:
- Exclusive domestic relations.
- Juvenile.
- Traffic/other violations (juvenile cases only).                        link

---

**Magistrate Court** (286 courts, 46          LJC
counties)                                      M
*310 magistrates*
*Jury trials*
CSP Case Types:
- Small claims (up to $7,500).
- Preliminary hearings, misdemeanor.
- Traffic/other violations.                                              link

---

**Probate Court** (46 courts, 46 counties)    LJC
*46 judges*                                     M
*No jury trials*

CSP Case Types:
- Exclusive probate/estate, mental health.                               link

---

**Municipal Court** (~200 courts)             LJC
*300 judges*                                    M
*Jury trials*

CSP Case Types:
- Preliminary hearings, misdemeanor.
- Traffic/other violations.                                              link

---

**AOC Web site: www.sccourts.org**

**Legend**

☐ = Appellate level

☐ = Trial level

COLR = Court of Last Resort
IAC = Intermediate Appellate Court
GJC = General Jurisdiction Court
LJC = Limited Jurisdiction Court

↑ = Route of appeal

A = Appeal from Admin. Agency
S = State funded
L = Locally funded

M = Mixed: state and locally funded

# South Dakota
### (Court structure as of Fiscal Year 2009)

---

**Supreme Court**                                          COLR
*5 justices sit en banc*                                      *S*

CSP Case Types:
- Exclusive appeal by right criminal, civil, administrative agency.
- Exclusive appeal by permission criminal, civil, administrative agency.  Interlocutory appeals in criminal, civil, administrative agency.
- Exclusive death penalty.
- Exclusive original proceeding application for writ, bar/judiciary, certified question, advisory opinion.                                      link

↑

**Circuit Court** (7 circuits)                               GJC
*41 judges*                                                    A
*Jury trials except in small claims*                         *M*

CSP Case Types:
- Tort, contract, real property ($12,000 – no maximum), small claims (up to $12,000).
- Exclusive domestic relations.
- Criminal.
- Exclusive juvenile.
- Exclusive traffic/other violations (except uncontested parking, which is handled administratively).                                     link

↑

**Magistrate Court** (7 circuits)                            LJC
*12 full-time and 1 part-time magistrates*                   *M*
*No jury trials*

CSP Case Types:
- Tort, contract, real property ($0 - $10,000), small claims (up to $12,000).
- Preliminary hearings, misdemeanor.                         link

---

**AOC Web site: www.sdjudicial.com**

**Legend**

| | |
|---|---|
| ☐ = Appellate level | |
| ☐ = Trial level | |

**COLR** = Court of Last Resort    **A** = Appeal from Admin. Agency
**IAC** = Intermediate Appellate Court    *S* = State funded
**GJC** = General Jurisdiction Court    *ℒ* = Locally funded
**LJC** = Limited Jurisdiction Court    *ℳ* = Mixed: state and locally funded

↑ = Route of appeal

# STATE COURT STRUCTURE CHARTS

## Tennessee
(Court structure as of Fiscal Year 2009)

**Supreme Court**      COLR / S
*5 justices sit en banc*
CSP Case Types:
- Exclusive appeal by right workers' compensation.
- Appeal by permission criminal, civil, administrative agency. Interlocutory appeals in criminal, civil, administrative agency.
- Death penalty.
- Exclusive original proceeding bar admission, bar discipline/eligibility, certified question.    link

**Court of Appeals** (3 divisions)     IAC / A / *S*
*12 judges sit in panels*

CSP Case Types:
- Exclusive appeal by right civil, limited administrative agency.
- Appeal by permission interlocutory appeals in civil, administrative agency.      link

**Court of Criminal Appeals** (3 divisions)     IAC / S
*12 judges sit in panels*

CSP Case Types:
- Exclusive appeal by right criminal.
- Appeal by permission interlocutory appeals in criminal.
- Death penalty.
- Exclusive original proceeding limited application for writ.    link

**Circuit, Criminal, Chancery and Probate Court** (31 districts)
120 judges, 34 chancellors

**Circuit Court**    GJC / A / *M*
(95 counties)
*85 judges*
*Jury trials*

CSP Case Types:
- Tort, contract, real property ($50 – no maximum), probate/estate, civil appeals.
- Domestic relations.
- Criminal.

**Chancery Court**    GJC / *M*
*34 chancellors*
*Jury trials*

CSP Case Types:
- Tort, contract, real property ($50 – no maximum), probate/estate, civil appeals.
- Domestic relations.

**Probate Court**    GJC / *M*
*2 judges*
*No jury trials*

CSP Case Types:
- Probate/estate, civil appeals.

**Criminal Court**    GJC / *M*
*33 judges*
*Jury trials*

CSP Case Types:
- Criminal.

**Juvenile Court**    LJC / *M*
(98 courts)
*17 judges No jury trials*
CSP Case Types:
- Mental health.
- Support, custody, paternity.
- Juvenile.    link

**General Session Court**    LJC / *M*
(93 counties;
2 additional counties have a trial justice court)
*151 judges*
*No jury trials*

CSP Case Types:
- Landlord/tenant, probate/estate, mental health. Exclusive small claims (up to $25,000).
- Marriage dissolution, support, custody.
- Preliminary hearings, misdemeanor.
- Juvenile.
- Traffic/other violations.

**Municipal Court**    LJC / *M*
(~300 courts)
*251 judges*
*No jury trials*

CSP Case Types:
- Preliminary hearings, misdemeanor.
- Traffic/other violations.

**Legend**

☐ = Appellate level
☐ = Trial level

**COLR** = Court of Last Resort
**IAC** = Intermediate Appellate Court
**GJC** = General Jurisdiction Court
**LJC** = Limited Jurisdiction Court
↑ = Route of appeal

**A** = Appeal from Admin. Agency
*S* = State funded
*£* = Locally funded
*M* = Mixed: state and locally funded

**AOC Web site:**
**www.tncourts.gov**

# STATE COURT STRUCTURE CHARTS

## Texas
### (Court structure as of Fiscal Year 2009)

---

**Supreme Court**
*9 justices sit en banc*

COLR
*S*

CSP Case Types:
- Exclusive appeal by permission civil, administrative agency.
- Original proceeding application for writ, certified question. Exclusive bar/judiciary.

link

---

**Court of Criminal Appeals**
*9 judges sit en banc*

COLR
*S*

CSP Case Types:
- Exclusive appeal by permission criminal.
- Exclusive death penalty.
- Original proceeding application for writ, certified question.

link

---

**Court of Appeals** (14 courts)
*80 justices sit in panels*

IAC
*S*

CSP Case Types:
- Appeal by right criminal, civil, administrative agency. Interlocutory appeals in criminal, civil, administrative agency.
- Original proceeding application for writ.

link

---

**District Courts*** (449 courts) *449 judges*

**District Court** (436 courts)
*436 judges*
*Jury trials*

GJC
A
*M*

CSP Case Types:
- Tort, contract, real property ($201 – no maximum), probate/estate, miscellaneous civil. Exclusive administrative agency appeal.
- Domestic relations.
- Felony, misdemeanor.
- Juvenile.

**Criminal District Court**
(13 courts)
*13 judges*
*Jury trials*

GJC
*M*

CSP Case Types:
- Felony, misdemeanor.

---

**County-Level Courts** (499 courts) *499 judges*

**Constitutional County Court**
(254 courts)
*254 judges*
*Jury trials*

LJC
*S*

CSP Case Types:
- Tort, contract, real property ($200 - $10,000), probate/estate, mental health, civil trial court appeals, miscellaneous civil.
- Misdemeanor, criminal appeals.
- Juvenile.
- Traffic infractions.

link

**Probate Court**
(18 courts)
*18 judges*
*Jury trials*

LJC
*M*

CSP Case Types:
- Probate/estate, mental health.

link

**County Court at Law** (227 courts)
*227 judges*
*Jury trials*

LJC
*S*

CSP Case Types:
- Tort, contract, real property ($200 - $100,000), probate/estate, mental health, civil trial court appeals, miscellaneous civil.
- Misdemeanor, criminal appeals.
- Juvenile.
- Traffic infractions.

---

**Municipal Court**** (916 courts)
*1,414 judges*
*Jury trials*

LJC
*£*

CSP Case Types:
- Misdemeanor.
- Traffic infractions. Exclusive ordinance violations.

link

**Justice Courts**** (821 courts)
*821 judges*
*Jury trials*

LJC
*£*

CSP Case Types:
- Tort, contract, real property ($0 - $10,000), small claims (up to $10,000).
- Misdemeanor.
- Traffic infractions, parking.

link

---

**Some Municipal and Justice of the Peace courts may appeal to the District court.

---

**Legend**

| | = Appellate level |
| --- | --- |
| | = Trial level |

COLR = Court of Last Resort
IAC = Intermediate Appellate Court
GJC = General Jurisdiction Court
LJC = Limited Jurisdiction Court

↑ = Route of appeal

A = Appeal from Admin. Agency
*S* = State funded
*£* = Locally funded
*M* = Mixed: state and locally funded

AOC Web site:
**www.courts.state.tx.us**

---

Reprinted with permission. Court Statistics Project.
National Center for State Courts.

# Utah

**(Court structure as of Fiscal Year 2009)**

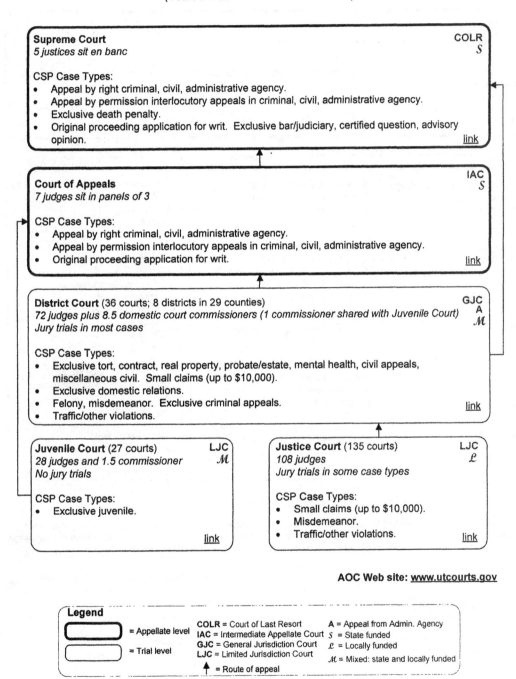

**Supreme Court** — COLR — *S*
*5 justices sit en banc*

CSP Case Types:
- Appeal by right criminal, civil, administrative agency.
- Appeal by permission interlocutory appeals in criminal, civil, administrative agency.
- Exclusive death penalty.
- Original proceeding application for writ. Exclusive bar/judiciary, certified question, advisory opinion.

link

**Court of Appeals** — IAC — *S*
*7 judges sit in panels of 3*

CSP Case Types:
- Appeal by right criminal, civil, administrative agency.
- Appeal by permission interlocutory appeals in criminal, civil, administrative agency.
- Original proceeding application for writ.

link

**District Court** (36 courts; 8 districts in 29 counties) — GJC — A — *M*
*72 judges plus 8.5 domestic court commissioners (1 commissioner shared with Juvenile Court)*
*Jury trials in most cases*

CSP Case Types:
- Exclusive tort, contract, real property, probate/estate, mental health, civil appeals, miscellaneous civil. Small claims (up to $10,000).
- Exclusive domestic relations.
- Felony, misdemeanor. Exclusive criminal appeals.
- Traffic/other violations.

link

**Juvenile Court** (27 courts) — LJC — *M*
*28 judges and 1.5 commissioner*
*No jury trials*

CSP Case Types:
- Exclusive juvenile.

link

**Justice Court** (135 courts) — LJC — *£*
*108 judges*
*Jury trials in some case types*

CSP Case Types:
- Small claims (up to $10,000).
- Misdemeanor.
- Traffic/other violations.

link

**AOC Web site: www.utcourts.gov**

**Legend**
| | | |
|---|---|---|
| ☐ = Appellate level | **COLR** = Court of Last Resort | **A** = Appeal from Admin. Agency |
| | **IAC** = Intermediate Appellate Court | *S* = State funded |
| ☐ = Trial level | **GJC** = General Jurisdiction Court | *£* = Locally funded |
| | **LJC** = Limited Jurisdiction Court | *M* = Mixed: state and locally funded |
| | ↑ = Route of appeal | |

# Vermont
(Court structure as of Fiscal Year 2009)

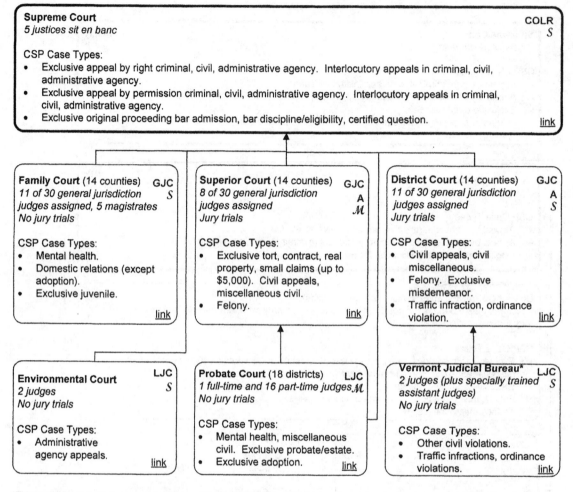

**Supreme Court**                                                                    COLR
*5 justices sit en banc*                                                                 *S*

CSP Case Types:
- Exclusive appeal by right criminal, civil, administrative agency. Interlocutory appeals in criminal, civil, administrative agency.
- Exclusive appeal by permission criminal, civil, administrative agency. Interlocutory appeals in criminal, civil, administrative agency.
- Exclusive original proceeding bar admission, bar discipline/eligibility, certified question.                                    link

**Family Court** (14 counties)   GJC
*11 of 30 general jurisdiction*     *S*
*judges assigned, 5 magistrates*
*No jury trials*

CSP Case Types:
- Mental health.
- Domestic relations (except adoption).
- Exclusive juvenile.
                                    link

**Superior Court** (14 counties)   GJC
*8 of 30 general jurisdiction*      *A*
*judges assigned*                   *M*
*Jury trials*

CSP Case Types:
- Exclusive tort, contract, real property, small claims (up to $5,000). Civil appeals, miscellaneous civil.
- Felony.                           link

**District Court** (14 counties)   GJC
*11 of 30 general jurisdiction*     *A*
*judges assigned*                   *S*
*Jury trials*

CSP Case Types:
- Civil appeals, civil miscellaneous.
- Felony. Exclusive misdemeanor.
- Traffic infraction, ordinance violation.
                                    link

**Environmental Court**            LJC
*2 judges*                          *S*
*No jury trials*

CSP Case Types:
- Administrative agency appeals.
                                    link

**Probate Court** (18 districts)   LJC
*1 full-time and 16 part-time judges* *M*
*No jury trials*

CSP Case Types:
- Mental health, miscellaneous civil. Exclusive probate/estate.
- Exclusive adoption.              link

**Vermont Judicial Bureau***       LJC
*2 judges (plus specially trained*  *S*
*assistant judges)*
*No jury trials*

CSP Case Types:
- Other civil violations.
- Traffic infractions, ordinance violations.                       link

*This court was formerly known as the Vermont Traffic and Municipal Ordinance Bureau.

Note: An additional 28 assistant judges participate in findings of fact in the Superior and Family courts. Some assistant judges, after special training, may hear small claims cases and traffic complaints, conduct criminal arraignments, and decide child support, parentage, and uncontested divorce proceedings. These assistant judges (who need not be attorneys) are elected to four-year terms by voters in Vermont's 14 counties.

AOC Web site: www.vermontjudiciary.org

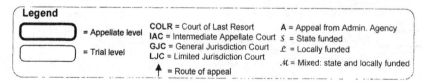

**Legend**

☐ = Appellate level

☐ = Trial level

↑ = Route of appeal

**COLR** = Court of Last Resort
**IAC** = Intermediate Appellate Court
**GJC** = General Jurisdiction Court
**LJC** = Limited Jurisdiction Court

*A* = Appeal from Admin. Agency
*S* = State funded
*L* = Locally funded
*M* = Mixed: state and locally funded

# Virginia

(Court structure as of Calendar Year 2009)

**Supreme Court**  COLR  *S*
*7 justices sit in panels and en banc*

CSP Case Types:
- Appeal by right administrative agency. Exclusive criminal.
- Appeal by permission criminal, civil, administrative agency. Interlocutory appeals in criminal, civil, administrative agency.
- Exclusive death penalty.
- Original proceeding application for writ, bar/judiciary, and certified question..    link

**Court of Appeals**  IAC  *S*
*11 judges sit in panels and en banc*

CSP Case Types:
- Appeal by right administrative agency. Exclusive family. Interlocutory appeals in family, administrative agency.
- Appeal by permission criminal. Interlocutory appeals in criminal.    link

**Circuit Court** (31 circuits, 120 courts)  GJC  A  *M*
*157 judges*
*Jury trials*

CSP Case Types:
- Tort, contract, real property ($4,500 – no maximum), probate/estate, mental health, civil appeals, miscellaneous civil.
- Domestic relations.
- Criminal.    link

**District Court\*** (32 districts, 191 courts)  LJC  *M*
*127 FTE general district and 117 FTE juvenile and domestic relations judges*
*No jury trials*

CSP Case Types:
- Tort, contract, real property ($0 - $15,000), small claims (up to $5,000), mental health.
- Support, custody.
- Preliminary hearings, misdemeanor. Exclusive DWI/DUI.
- Exclusive juvenile.
- Exclusive traffic infractions. Ordinance violations.    link

\*The District Court is referred to as the Juvenile and Domestic Relations Court when hearing juvenile and domestic relations cases and as the General District Court for the balance of the cases.

AOC Web site: **www.courts.state.va.us**

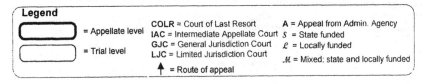

**Legend**

| | |
|---|---|
| ☐ = Appellate level | |
| ☐ = Trial level | |

**COLR** = Court of Last Resort
**IAC** = Intermediate Appellate Court
**GJC** = General Jurisdiction Court
**LJC** = Limited Jurisdiction Court

**↑** = Route of appeal

**A** = Appeal from Admin. Agency
*S* = State funded
*£* = Locally funded
*M* = Mixed: state and locally funded

# Washington
(Court structure as of Calendar Year 2009)

**Supreme Court**        COLR
*9 justices sit en banc*     *S*

CSP Case Types:
- Appeal by permission criminal, civil, administrative agency. Interlocutory appeals in criminal, civil, administrative agency.
- Exclusive death penalty.
- Original proceeding application for writ. Exclusive bar/judiciary, certified question.

link

**Court of Appeals** (3 courts/divisions)    IAC
*24 judges sit in panels*    *S*

CSP Case Types:
- Exclusive appeal by right criminal, civil, administrative agency.
- Appeal by permission criminal, civil, administrative agency. Interlocutory appeals in criminal, civil, administrative agency.
- Original proceeding application for writ.

link

**Superior Court** (32 districts in 39 counties)    GJC
*188 judges*    A
*Jury trials*    *M*

CSP Case Types:
- Tort, contract. Exclusive real property, probate/estate, mental health, civil appeals, miscellaneous civil.
- Exclusive domestic relations.
- Exclusive felony, criminal appeals.
- Exclusive juvenile.

link

**Municipal Court** (~121 courts)   LJC
*96 judges (including 65 part-time*   *£*
*judges)*
*Jury trials except in traffic*
*infractions and parking violations*

CSP Case Types:
- Misdemeanor.
- Traffic/other violations.

link

**District Court*** (~48 courts)   LJC
*112 judges (including 24 part-time judges)*   *£*
*Jury trials except in traffic infractions and parking violations*

CSP Case Types:
- Tort, contract ($0 - $75,000). Exclusive small claims (up to $5,000).
- Preliminary hearings, misdemeanor.
- Traffic/other violations.

link

*District Court provides services to municipalities that do not have a Municipal Court.

AOC Web site: www.courts.wa.gov

**Legend**

| | = Appellate level |
| | = Trial level |

COLR = Court of Last Resort
IAC = Intermediate Appellate Court
GJC = General Jurisdiction Court
LJC = Limited Jurisdiction Court

↑ = Route of appeal

A = Appeal from Admin. Agency
*S* = State funded
*£* = Locally funded
*M* = Mixed: state and locally funded

# STATE COURT STRUCTURE CHARTS

## West Virginia
(Court structure as of Calendar Year 2009)

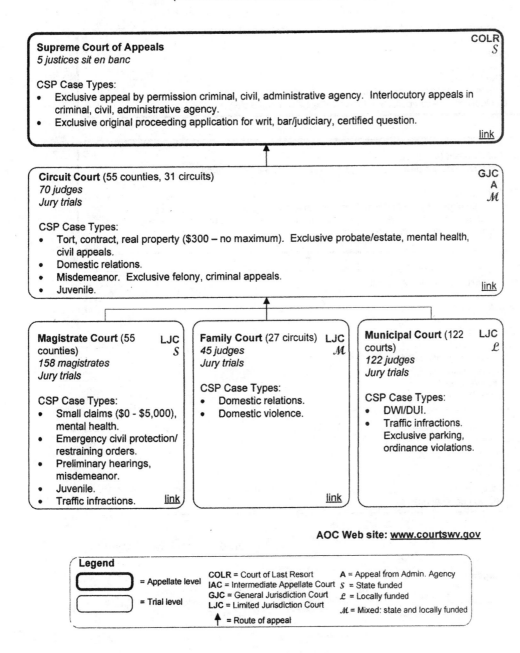

**Supreme Court of Appeals**    COLR *S*
*5 justices sit en banc*

CSP Case Types:
- Exclusive appeal by permission criminal, civil, administrative agency. Interlocutory appeals in criminal, civil, administrative agency.
- Exclusive original proceeding application for writ, bar/judiciary, certified question.

link

**Circuit Court** (55 counties, 31 circuits)    GJC A *M*
*70 judges*
*Jury trials*

CSP Case Types:
- Tort, contract, real property ($300 – no maximum). Exclusive probate/estate, mental health, civil appeals.
- Domestic relations.
- Misdemeanor. Exclusive felony, criminal appeals.
- Juvenile.

link

**Magistrate Court** (55 counties)   LJC *S*
*158 magistrates*
*Jury trials*

CSP Case Types:
- Small claims ($0 - $5,000), mental health.
- Emergency civil protection/ restraining orders.
- Preliminary hearings, misdemeanor.
- Juvenile.
- Traffic infractions.   link

**Family Court** (27 circuits)   LJC *M*
*45 judges*
*Jury trials*

CSP Case Types:
- Domestic relations.
- Domestic violence.

link

**Municipal Court** (122 courts)   LJC *£*
*122 judges*
*Jury trials*

CSP Case Types:
- DWI/DUI.
- Traffic infractions. Exclusive parking, ordinance violations.

AOC Web site: www.courtswv.gov

**Legend**

| | |
|---|---|
| ▭ = Appellate level | |
| ▭ = Trial level | |

COLR = Court of Last Resort    A = Appeal from Admin. Agency
IAC = Intermediate Appellate Court    *S* = State funded
GJC = General Jurisdiction Court    *£* = Locally funded
LJC = Limited Jurisdiction Court
↑ = Route of appeal    *M* = Mixed: state and locally funded

# Wisconsin

(Court structure as of Calendar Year 2009)

---

**Supreme Court**                                                    COLR
*7 justices sit en banc*                                               S

CSP Case Types:
- Appeal by permission criminal, civil, administrative agency.
- Original proceeding application for writ. Exclusive bar/judiciary, certified question.          link

---

**Court of Appeals** (4 districts)                                    IAC
*16 judges (two 4-judge districts, one 3-judge district, one 5-judge district)*     S

CSP Case Types:
- Exclusive appeal by right criminal, civil, administrative agency.
- Appeal by permission interlocutory appeals in criminal, civil, administrative agency.
- Original proceeding application for writ.                          link

---

**Circuit Court** (69 circuits/72 counties)                          GJC
*248 judges*                                                           A
*Jury trials in most cases*                                            M

CSP Case Types:
- Exclusive civil.
- Exclusive domestic relations.
- Exclusive criminal.
- Exclusive juvenile.
- Traffic/other violations.                                          link

---

**Municipal Court** (244 courts)                                     LJC
*246 judges*                                                           ℒ
*No jury trials*

CSP Case Types:
- Traffic/other violations.                                          link

---

AOC Web site: **www.wicourts.gov**

---

**Legend**

| | = Appellate level |
| | = Trial level |

**COLR** = Court of Last Resort         **A** = Appeal from Admin. Agency
**IAC** = Intermediate Appellate Court  *S* = State funded
**GJC** = General Jurisdiction Court    *ℒ* = Locally funded
**LJC** = Limited Jurisdiction Court    *M* = Mixed: state and locally funded

↑ = Route of appeal

# Wyoming

**(Court structure as of Fiscal Year 2009)**

**Supreme Court**                                                                    COLR
*5 justices sit en banc*                                                               A
                                                                                       *S*

CSP Case Types:
- Exclusive appeal by right criminal, civil, administrative agency.  Interlocutory appeals in criminal, civil, administrative agency.
- Exclusive death penalty.
- Exclusive original proceeding application for writ, bar/judiciary, certified question, advisory opinion.                                                    link

**District Court** (9 districts)                                                     GJC
*21 judges*                                                                            A
*Jury trials*                                                                         *M*

CSP Case Types:
- Tort, contract, real property ($7,001 – no maximum), civil miscellaneous.  Exclusive probate/ estate, mental health, civil appeals.
- Exclusive domestic relations.
- Exclusive felony, criminal appeals.
- Exclusive juvenile.                                                                link

**Circuit Court*** (24 courts in 9 districts)        LJC
*24 judges, 6 magistrates*                            *M*
*Jury trials except in small claims*

CSP Case Types:
- Tort, contract, real property ($0 - $7,000), small claims (up to $5,000), non-domestic relations restraining order.
- Civil protection/restraining order.
- Preliminary hearings.
- Traffic infractions.                          link

**Municipal Court**                          LJC
(82 cities and towns)                         *£*
*78 judges*
*Jury trials*

CSP Case Types:
- Traffic infractions, parking. Exclusive ordinance violations.

                                             link

*In January 2003, Justice of the Peace courts were combined with County courts, and County Court was renamed Circuit Court.

**AOC Web site: www.courts.state.wy.us**

**Legend**

| | |
|---|---|
| = Appellate level | |
| = Trial level | |

COLR = Court of Last Resort          A = Appeal from Admin. Agency
IAC = Intermediate Appellate Court   *S* = State funded
GJC = General Jurisdiction Court     *£* = Locally funded
LJC = Limited Jurisdiction Court
                                     *M* = Mixed: state and locally funded
↑ = Route of appeal

# NATIONAL REPORTER SYSTEM

## ATLANTIC REPORTER

Connecticut
Delaware
District of Columbia
Maine
Maryland

New Hampshire
New Jersey
Pennsylvania
Rhode Island
Vermont

## NORTHEASTERN REPORTER

Illinois
Indiana
Massachusetts
New York
Ohio

## NORTHWESTERN REPORTER

Iowa
Michigan
Minnesota
Nebraska
North Dakota
South Dakota
Wisconsin

## PACIFIC REPORTER

Alaska
Arizona
California
Colorado
Hawaii
Idaho
Kansas
Montana
Nevada
New Mexico
Oklahoma
Oregon
Utah
Washington
Wyoming

## SOUTHEASTERN REPORTER

Georgia
North Carolina
South Carolina
Virginia
West Virginia

## SOUTHWESTERN REPORTER

Arkansas
Kentucky
Missouri
Tennessee
Texas

## SOUTHERN REPORTER

Alabama
Florida
Louisiana
Mississippi

# STATE CODES, REPORTERS, REGULATIONS AND REGISTERS

For live, updated links go to http://www.infosourcespub.com/leg_researchers.cfm

## ALABAMA

### Statutes:

1. Michie's Alabama Code (annotated)-1975
   Lexis - 38 vols.
   annual pocket parts
   legislative service
   *http://www.legislature.state.al.us/CodeofAlabama/
   1975/coatoc.htm*
   *http://alisondb.legislature.state.al.us/acas/
   acaslogin.asp*
2. Code of Alabama (official code)-1975
   West - 45 vols.
   annual supp.
   legislative service

### Cases:

Alabama Reporter 3d (West)
Southern 3d (West)
   Supreme Court/Court of Appeals
*http://www.alalinc.net*
*http://caselaw.findlaw.com/courts/Alabama*

### Regulations:

Alabama Administrative Code-1984
   Legis. Ref. Service
   Admin. Procedure Div.
   Alabama State House, Suite 435
   Montgomery, AL 36130
   (334) 242-7570; FAX (334) 242-0888
38 vols.; looseleaf; quarterly supp.; on Westlaw;
   Lexis; on CD-ROM
*http://www.alabamaadministrativecode.state.al.us/*

### Register:

Alabama Administrative Monthly
began 10/82; monthly
*http://www.alabamaadministrativecode.state.al.us/
   monthly.html*

## ALASKA

### Statutes:

1. Alaska Statutes-2010
   Lexis - 13 vols.
   biennial supp.
   legislative service
2. West's Alaska Statutes Annotated-2007
   West - 27 vols.
   pocket parts
   legislative service
*http://www.legis.state.ak.us/basis/folio.asp*

### Cases:

Alaska Reporter 3d (West)
Pacific 3d (West)
   Supreme Court (1991-)
*http://www.touchngo.com/sp/sp.htm*
   Supreme Court/Court of Appeals (1960-)

*http://government.westlaw.com/akcases/*
   Court of Appeals (1991-)
*http://www.touchngo.com/ap/ap.htm*

### Regulations:

1. Alaska Administrative Code
   publ. by West
   10 vols.; looseleaf; quarterly supp.
2. Alaska Administrative Code-1990
   publ. by Lexis
   10 vols.; looseleaf; quarterly supp.; on
   Lexis, Westlaw; on CD-ROM
*http://old-www.legis.state.ak.us/
   cgi-bin/folioisa.dll/aac?*
*http://www.touchngo.com/lglcntr/akstats/aac.htm*

### Register:

Alaska Administrative Journal
began 1983 in print, 1986-5/00 on web, replaced
   by Online Public Notice system
*http://notes4.state.ak.us/pn/pubnotic.nsf/?Open*
*http://old-www.legis.state.ak.us/cgi-
   bin/folioisa.dll/adjr?*

## ARIZONA

### Statutes:

1. Arizona Revised Statutes Annotated-1956
   West - 66 vols.
   annual pocket parts
   legislative service
2. Annotated Arizona Revised Statutes-2010
   Lexis - 14 vols.
   annual edition
   legislative service
3. Arizona Revised Statutes-2010
   West - 6 vols., paperbound, annual ed.
*http://www.azleg.state.az.us/
   arizonarevisedstatutes.asp*

### Cases:

Arizona Reports (West)
Pacific 3d (West)
   Supreme Court (1997-)
*http://azcourts.gov/opinions*
   Court of Appeals Division One (1999-)
*http://azcourts.gov/coa1/Decisions.aspx*
   Court of Appeals Division Two (1999-)
*http://www.appeals2.az.gov/ODSPlus/
   recentdecisions.cfm*
   Supreme Court/Court of Appeals (1997-)
*http://caselaw.findlaw.com/courts/Arizona*

### Regulations:

Arizona Admin. Code-1986
   Office of Secy. of State
   Publications Div.
   1700 W. Washington, 7th fl.

# STATE CODES, REPORTERS, REGULATIONS AND REGISTERS

Phoenix, AZ 85007
(602) 542-4086; FAX (602) 542-4366
20 vols.; looseleaf; quarterly supp.; on Lexis;
Westlaw; on CD-ROM
*http://www.azsos.gov/public_services/*
*table_of_contents.htm*
Register:
Arizona Admin. Register
began 10/76; weekly
*http://www.azsos.gov/aar/contents.htm*


## ARKANSAS
**Statutes:**
1. Arkansas Code of 1987 Annotated-1987
   Lexis - 55 vols.
   biennial pocket parts
   legislative service
2. West's Arkansas Code Annotated-2004
   West - 54 vols.
   annual pocket parts
*http://www.lexisnexis.com/hottopics/arcode/*
*Default.asp*
**Cases:**
Arkansas Cases (West)
Southwest 3d (West)
   Supreme Court/Court of Appeals (1996-)
*http://courts.state.ar.us/opinions/opmain.htm*
**Regulations:**
Arkansas Administrative Code-2000
   publ. by Lexis; 23 vols.; looseleaf;
   monthly supp.; on Lexis, Westlaw
*http://www.sos.arkansas.gov/rules_and_regs/*
*index.php/rules/search/new/*
**Register:**
1. Arkansas Government Register
   Publ. by Lexis
   began 1969; monthly; on Lexis
2. Arkansas Register
   began 1977; by Secy. of State; monthly
*http://www.sos.arkansas.gov/rulesRegs/Pages/*
*ArkansasRegister.aspx*


## CALIFORNIA
**Statutes:**
1. Deering's California Codes Annotated-
   1992
   Lexis - 219 vols. (or 4 vols. annual ed.)
   annual supp.
   legislative service
2. West's Annotated California Codes-1954
   West - 350 vols.
   annual pocket parts
   legislative service
3. West's California Codes compact ed.
   (unannotated)

West - 25 vols., available separately,
   annual edition
*http://www.leginfo.ca.gov/calaw.html*
**Cases:**
California Reports (West)
California Appellate Reports (Bancroft-Whitney)
California Reporter 3d (West)
Pacific 3d (West)
   Supreme Court/Court of Appeals (1850-)
*http://www.courts.ca.gov/opinions.htm*
*http://caselaw.findlaw.com/cacases/*
**Regulations:**
Official California Code of Regulations-1945
   publ. by Office of Admin. Law / Thomson
   West; order from (800) 537-2707
38 vols.; looseleaf; weekly supp.; on Lexis,
   Westlaw; on CD-ROM
*http://ccr.oal.ca.gov/*
*http://www.calregs.com/*
**Register:**
Calif. Regulatory Notice Register
   publ.by West
began 1974; weekly; on Westlaw
*http://www.oal.ca.gov/California_Regulatory_*
*Notice_Online.htm*


## COLORADO
**Statutes:**
1. Colorado Revised Statutes-2010
   Bradford - 2 vols.
   annual edition
2. Colorado Revised Statutes Annotated-
   2001
   West - 78 vols.
   annual pocket parts
   legislative service
3. Colorado Revised Statutes-2010
   Lexis-20 vols.
   annual editions
*http://www.michie.com/colorado/*
*lpext.dll?f=templates&fn=main_h.htm&cp=*
**Cases:**
Colorado Reporter 3d (West)
Pacific 3d (West)
   Supreme Court/Court of Appeals (1996-)
*http://www.cobar.org/ors.cfm*
*http://www.cocourts.com* (subscribers only)
   Supreme Court/Court of Appeals (case
   announcements 2007-)
*http://www.courts.state.co.us/Courts/*
*Supreme_Court/Case_Announcements/Index.cfm*
*http://www.courts.state.co.us/Courts/*
*Court_of_Appeals/Case_Announcements/*
*Index.cfm*

# STATE CODES, REPORTERS, REGULATIONS AND REGISTERS

**Regulations:**
Code of Colorado Regulations (CCR)
    publ. by Lexis
30 vols., looseleaf; monthly supp. by Register; on
    Westlaw
*http://www.sos.state.co.us/CCR/*
    **Register:**Colorado Register
began 1978; monthly
*http://www.sos.state.co.us/CCR/RegisterHome.do*


## CONNECTICUT
    **Statutes:**
1.    Connecticut General Statutes Annotated-
    2004
    West - 61 vols.
    annual pocket parts
    legislative service
2.    Connecticut General Statutes-2011
    (unannotated)
    Conn. Secy. of State - 16 vols. biennial
*http://www.cslib.org/psaindex.htm*
*http://www.cga.ct.gov/asp/menu/statutes.asp*
    **Cases:**
Connecticut Reports
Connecticut Appellate Reports
Connecticut Supplement
Connecticut Law Journal
(all published by the Commission on Official
    Legal Publications)
Connecticut Reporter 3d (West)
Atlantic 3d (West)
*http://www.jud.state.ct.us/opinions.htm*
    **Regulations:**
Regulations of Connecticut State Agencies-1962
    Commission on Official Legal
    Publications
    111 Phoenix Ave.
    Enfield, CT 06082
    (860) 741-3027; FAX (860) 745-2178
18 vols.; looseleaf; annual supp.; on Westlaw
    Lexis; on CD-ROM
    **Register:**
1.    Connecticut Law Journal
    began 1935; monthly; on Lexis
2.    Connecticut Government Register
    publ. by Lexis
    began 2001; monthly


## DELAWARE
    **Statutes:**
1.    Delaware Code Annotated-1974
    Lexis - 20 vols.
    annual pocket parts
    interim supp.
    legislative service

2.    West's Delaware Code Annotated-2006
    West - 31 vols.
    annual pocket parts
*http://www.michie.com/delaware/*
*lpext.dll?f=templates&fn=main_h.htm&cp=decode*
*http://delcode.delaware.gov/index.shtml*
    **Cases:**
Delaware Reporter 3d (West)
Atlantic 3d (West)
    Supreme Court (11/98-)
*http://www.virtualdocket.com*
*http://courts.state.de.us/opinions/*
    *(osaxc4zslw1b0xejtl3agjeu)/*
    *List.aspx?ag=AllCourts*
*http://caselaw.findlaw.com/courts/Delaware*
    **Regulations:**
Code of Delaware Regulations-1996
    publ. by Lexis
15 vols.; monthly supp.; on Lexis, Westlaw;
    on CD-ROM
*http://regulations.delaware.gov/AdminCode*
    **Register:**
1.    Delaware Government Register
    publ. by Lexis
2.    Delaware Register of Regulations
    publ.by Delaware General Assembly
began 12/96; weekly; on Lexis, Westlaw
*http://regulations.delaware.gov/services/*
    *register.shtml*


## DISTRICT OF COLUMBIA
    **Statutes:**
1.    District of Columbia Code (Annotated)-
    2001
    West - 26 vols.
    annual pocket parts
    legislative service
2.    District of Columbia Code-2004
    Lexis - 17 vols.
    annual pocket parts
    legislative service
*http://www.michie.com/dc/*
*lpext.dll?f=templates&fn=main_h.htm&cp=dccode*
*http://government.westlaw.com/linkedslice/*
    *default.asp?SP=DCC-1000*
    **Cases:**
D.C. Appeals Reports (West)
Atlantic 3d (West)
Court of Appeals (1998-)
*http://www.dcappeals.gov/dccourts/appeals/*
    *opinions_mojs.jsp*
    **Regulations:**
Code of District of Columbia Municipal
    Regulations-1999
    publ. by Lexis

17 vols.; looseleaf; monthly supp.; on Lexis,
Westlaw; on CD-ROM
*http://www.dcregs.dc.gov*
**Register:**
District of Columbia Register
  publ. by Office of Docs. & Admin.
  Issuances, only on web
began 1954; weekly; on Lexis, Westlaw
*http://www.dcregs.dc.gov*

## FLORIDA
**Statutes:**
1.  Florida Statutes Annotated-1961
    West - 131 vols.
    annual pocket parts
    legislative service
2.  LexisNexis Florida Annotated Statutes-
    2010
    Lexis - 49 vols.
    biennial editions
3.  Florida Statutes (unannotated)-2010
    Law Book Distrib. Office - 6 vols.
    biennial
    (850) 488-2323
*http://www.leg.state.fl.us/Statutes
  /index.cfm?Mode=ViewStatutes
  &Submenu=1&Tab=statutes*
*http://flsenate.gov/statutes/index.cfm*
**Cases:**
Florida Cases 3d (West)
Southern 3d (West)
  Supreme Court (1999-)/Courts of Appeal
  (2001-)
*http://www.flcourts.org/*
  Supreme Court (1846-)
*http://www.law.fsu.edu/library/flsupct/index.html*
  Supreme Court/Courts of Appeal (1/97-)
*http://caselaw.findlaw.com/courts/Florida*
**Regulations:**
Florida Admin. Code Annotated-2004
  publ. by Lexis
15 vols.; looseleaf; monthly supp.; on Lexis,
  Westlaw; on CD-ROM
*http://www.flrules.org/*
**Register:**
Florida Admin. Weekly
  publ. by Lexis
began 1/75; weekly; on Lexis
*http://www.flrules.org*

## GEORGIA
**Statutes:**
1.  Official Code of Georgia Annotated-1982
    Lexis - 48 vols.
    annual pocket parts

2.  Code of Georgia Annotated-2003
    West - 75 vols.
    annual pocket parts
    legislative service
*http://www.lexis-nexis.com/hottopics/gacode/
  default.asp*
**Cases:**
Georgia Reports (Darby)
Georgia Appeals Reports (Darby)
Georgia Cases 2d (West)
Southeast 2d (West)
  Supreme Court (1996-)
*http://www.gasupreme.us/sc-op/index10.php*
*http://www.lexisone.com/caselaw/freecaselaw?
  action=FCLDisplayCaseSearchForm*
**Regulations:**
Official Compilation of Rules and
  Regulations of the State of
  Georgia-1982
  Georgia Admin. Procedure Division
  (404) 656-2865
  order from Darby (404) 344-2665
18 vols.; looseleaf; monthly supp., on Westlaw,
Lexis; on CD-ROM
*http://rules.sos.state.ga.us/cgi-bin/page.cgi?d=1*
**Register:**
Georgia Government Register
  publ. by Lexis
began 2001; monthly

## HAWAII
**Statutes:**
1.  Michie's Hawaii Revised Statutes
    Annotated-2004
    Lexis - 25 vols.
    annual pocket parts
    legislative service
2.  Hawaii Revised Statutes-1993
    Office of the Lt. Governor - 14 vols.
    annual supp.
3.  West's Hawaii Revised Statutes-2008
    West - 28 vols.
    annual pocket parts
    legislative service
*http://www.capitol.hawaii.gov/site1/hrs/
  default.asp*
**Cases:**
Hawaii Reports (West)
Hawaii Appellate Reports (Library of
  Supreme Court)
Pacific 3d (West)
  Supreme Court/Court of Appeals (1/98-)
*http://www.state.hi.us/jud/ctops.htm*
*http://caselaw.findlaw.com/courts/Hawaii*
**Regulations:**
Hawaii Administrative Code-1997

publ. by Lexis; 21 vols.; monthly supp.; on Lexis, Westlaw; on CD-ROM
*http://www.hawaii.gov/ltgov/office/adminrules/*
**Register:**
Hawaii Government Register
    publ. by Lexis
began 1997; monthly; on Lexis


## IDAHO
**Statutes:**
1.     Idaho Code (annotated)-1947
    Lexis - 25 vols.
    annual pocket parts
    legislative service
2.     Idaho Code (unannotated)-2008
    Thornton - 4 vols. (888) 977-9339
    annual editions
3.     West's Idaho Code Annotated-2006
    West - 29 vols.
    annual pocket parts
*http://www.legislature.idaho.gov/idstat/TOC/ idstTOC.htm*
**Cases:**
Idaho Reports (West)
Pacific 3d (West)
    Supreme Court/Court of Appeals (3/99-)
*http://www.isc.idaho.gov/search/*
    Supreme Court/Court of Appeals (1/97-)
*http://caselaw.findlaw.com/courts/Idaho*
**Regulations:**
Idaho Administrative Code
on Lexis, Westlaw; on CD-ROM; no print
*http://adm.idaho.gov/adminrules/agyindex.htm*
**Register:**
Idaho Administrative Bulletin
began 1993; monthly; on Lexis
*http://adm.idaho.gov/adminrules/bulletin/ mstrtoc.htm*


## ILLINOIS
**Statutes:**
1.     Smith-Hurd Illinois Compiled Statutes Annotated-1993
    West - 145 vols.
    annual pocket parts
    legislative service
2.     Illinois Compiled Statutes (unannotated) - 2011
    West - 9 vols. (compact ed.)
    biennial edition and supp. in alternate yrs.
3.     Illinois Compiled Statutes Annotated-1993
    Lexis - 55 vols.
    annual pocket parts
    legislative service

*http://www.ilga.gov/legislation/ilcs/ilcs.asp*
**Cases:**
Illinois Reports 2d (West)
Illinois Appellate Court Reports 3d (West)
Illinois Court of Claims Reports (Court of Claims)
West's Illinois Decisions 2d (West)
Northeast 2d (West)
    Supreme Court (1/97-)/Appellate Court (1970-)
*http://www.state.il.us/court/*
*http://caselaw.findlaw.com/courts/Illinois*
**Regulations:**
Code of Illinois Rules-1999
    publ. by Lexis
22 vols.; looseleaf; monthly supp.; on CD-ROM; on Lexis, Westlaw
*http://www.ilga.gov/commission/jcar/admincode/ titles.html*
**Register:**
Illinois Register
    publ. by Secretary of State (217) 782-6537
began 1977; weekly; on Westlaw, Lexis
*http://www.cyberdriveillinois.com/departments/ index/register/home.html*


## INDIANA
**Statutes:**
1.     Burns Indiana Statutes Annotated-1972
    Lexis - 47 vols.
    annual pocket parts
    legislative service
2.     West's Annotated Indiana Code-1998
    West - 83 vols.
    annual pocket parts
    legislative service
*http://www.state.in.us/legislative/ic/code/*
**Cases:**
Indiana Cases (West)
Northeast 2d (West)
    Supreme Court/Court of Appeals/Tax Court (1/97-)
*http://www.in.gov/judiciary/opinions*
*http://caselaw.findlaw.com/courts/Indiana*
**Regulations:**
Indiana Admin. Code-2006
    publ. by West
14 vols.; paperbound; annual supp.; on Lexis, Westlaw
*http://www.state.in.us/legislative/iac/*
**Register:**
Indiana Register
    publ. by Indiana Legislative Council
no print, web only
began 7/78; monthly; on Lexis
*http://www.in.gov/legislative/iac/irtoc.htm*

# STATE CODES, REPORTERS, REGULATIONS AND REGISTERS

## IOWA

**Statutes:**

1.  Iowa Code Annotated-1992
    West - 89 vols.
    annual pocket parts
    legislative service
2.  Iowa Code (unannotated) - 2011
    State Printing Div. (515) 281-8871
    7 vols. - biennial editions; interim supp.
*http:/www.legis.state.ia.us/IowaLaw.html*

**Cases:**

Northwest 2d (West)
> Supreme Court/Court of Appeals (1998-)
*http://www.iowacourts.gov/Supreme_Court/*
> *Opinions/*
*http://www.iowacourts.gov/Court_of_Appeals/*
> *Opinions/*
*http://caselaw.findlaw.com11stategov/ia/iaca.html*
> SupremeCourt/Court of Appeals (1/97-)
*http://caselaw.findlaw.com/courts/Iowa*

**Regulations:**

Iowa Admin. Code-1975-76
biweekly supp. by IAC Bulletin on web; no print,
only on web; on CD-ROM; on Lexis, Westlaw
*http://www.legis.iowa.gov/IowaLaw/AdminCode/*
> *adminLaw.aspx*

**Register:**

Iowa Admin. Bulletin
began 7/1/75; biweekly; on Lexis
no print, web only
*http://www.legis.iowa.gov/IowaLaw/AdminCode/*
> *adminLaw.aspx*

## KANSAS

**Statutes:**

1.  Kansas Statutes Annotated-1989
    Kansas Secretary of State - 15 vols.
    annual pocket parts
2.  West's Kansas Statutes Annotated-2008
    West - 45 vols.
    annual pocket parts
*http://www.kslegislature.org/li/statute/*

**Cases:**

Kansas Reports (Sup. Ct. Library)
Kansas Court of Appeals Reports 2d (Sup. Ct.
> Library)
Kansas Cases (West)
Pacific 3d (West)
> Supreme Court/Court of Appeals
> (10/25/96-)
*http://www.kscourts.org/cases-and-opinions/*
> *opinions*
*http://caselaw.findlaw.com/courts/Kansas* (1/97-)

**Regulations:**

Kansas Admin. Regulations-2009
> Secy. of State

120 SW 10th Ave.
Memorial Hall, 1st fl.
Topeka, KS 66612
(785) 296-2114
order from (785) 296-4557
6 vols.; annual cum. supp.; on CD-ROM; on Lexis,
> Westlaw
*http://da.state.ks.us/ps/documents/regs/default.htm*
*http://www.kssos.org/pubs/pubs_kar.aspx*

**Register:**

Kansas Register
began 1/82; weekly; on Lexis
*http://www.kssos.org/pubs/pubs_kansas_*
> *register.asp*

## KENTUCKY

**Statutes:**

1.  Michie's Kentucky Revised Statutes
    Annotated, Certified Version-1971
    Lexis - 33 vols.
    annual pocket parts
    legislative service
2.  Baldwin's Kentucky Revised Statutes
    Annotated-2006
    West - 40 vols. (looseleaf)
    annual pocket parts
*http://www.lrc.state.ky.us/statrev/frontpg.htm*

**Cases:**

Kentucky Decisions 3d (West)
Southwest 3d (West)
> Supreme Court (1997-)
*http://apps.kycourts.net/courtrecordsKBA*

**Regulations:**

Kentucky Admin. Regulations Service-2008-09
> Legis. Research Comm.
> Rm. 64, State Capitol
> Frankfort, KY 40601
> (502) 564-8100; FAX (502) 564-5947
12 vols.; paperbound; annual edition; monthly supp.
> in Register; on Westlaw; on CD-ROM
*http://www.lrc.state.ky.us/kar/frntpage.htm*

**Register:**

Admin. Register of Kentucky
began 1974; monthly
*http://www.lrc.state.ky.us/kar/frntpage.htm*

## LOUISIANA

**Statutes:**

1.  West's Louisiana Statutes Annotated-1951
    West - 190 vols.
    annual pocket parts
    legislative service
2.  West's Louisiana Statutes-2011

# STATE CODES, REPORTERS, REGULATIONS AND REGISTERS

West - 9 vols. (compact ed.)
*http://www.legis.state.la.us/searchweb.asp*
**Cases:**
Louisiana Cases (West)
Southern 3d (West)
    Supreme Court (1995-)
*http://www.lasc.org/opinion_search.asp*
    Court of Appeal (1st cir.) (2003-)
*http://www.la-fcca.org/index.php/opinions*
    Court of Appeal (2nd cir.) (2001-)
*http://lacoa2.org/*
**Regulations:**
1.    Louisiana Admin. Code-1984
    Office of the State Register
    P.O. Box 94095
    Baton Rouge, LA 70804
    (225) 342-5015; FAX (225) 342-0284
92 vols.; paperbound; on CD-ROM; on Lexis,
    Westlaw
*http://doa.louisiana.gov/osr/lac/books.htm*
**Register:**
Louisiana Register
began 1975; monthly; on Lexis, Westlaw
*http://doa.louisiana.gov/osr/reg/register.htm*

## MAINE
**Statutes:**
1.    Maine Revised Statutes Annotated-1964
    West - 53 vols.
    annual pocket parts
    legislative service
2.    West's Maine Statutes-2010
    West - 8 vols.
*http://www.mainelegislature.org/legis/statutes/*
**Cases:**
Maine Reporter (West)
Atlantic 3d (West)
    Supreme Judicial Court (1/1/97-)
*http://www.courts.state.me.us/court_info/opinions/*
*http://caselaw.findlaw.com/courts/Maine*
**Regulations:**
Code of Maine Rules-1986
    publ. by Lexis
21 vols.; looseleaf; monthly supp.; on Lexis,
    Westlaw; on CD-ROM
*http://www.maine.gov/sos/cec/rules/rules.html*
**Register:**
Maine Government Register (not official)
    publ. by Lexis
began 2/91; monthly; on Lexis
*http://www.maine.gov/sos/cec/rules/rules.html*

## MARYLAND
**Statutes:**

1.    Michie's Annotated Code of Maryland-1957
    & 1974
    Lexis - 50 vols.
    annual pocket parts
    legislative service
2.    West's Annotated Code of Maryland-2002
    West - 73 vols.
    annual pocket parts
    legislative service
*http://mlis.state.md.us/asp/web_statutes.asp*
*http://www.michie.com/maryland/*
*lpext.dll?f=templates&fn=main_h.htm&cp=mdcode*
**Cases:**
Maryland Reports (West)
Maryland Reporter 3d (West)
Maryland Appellate Reports (West)
Atlantic 3d (West)
    Court of Appeals/Court of Special Appeals
    (1995-)
*http://www.courts.state.md.us/opinions.html*
*http://caselaw.findlaw.com/courts/Maryland*
**Regulations:**
Code of Maryland Regulations (COMAR)-1977
    Div. of State Documents
    State House
    100 State Circle
    Annapolis, MD 21401-1924
    (410) 974-2486; FAX (410) 974-2546
35 vols.; looseleaf; annual supp.; on Westlaw,
    Lexis; on CD-ROM
*http://www.dsd.state.md.us/comar/*
**Register:**
Maryland Register (biweekly)
Maryland Contract Weekly
began 1974; on Lexis; on CD-ROM; on DVD
*http://www.dsd.state.md.us/MDregister/*
    *mdregister.aspx*

## MASSACHUSETTS
**Statutes:**
1.    Annotated Laws of Massachusetts-1978
    Lexis - 102 vols.
    annual pocket parts
    legislative service
2.    Massachusetts General Laws Annotated-
    1958
    West - 85 vols.
    annual pocket parts
    legislative service
3.    General Laws of Massachusetts official
    ed. (unannotated)
    West - 25 vols.
    biennial edition and supp. in alternate yrs.
*http://www.lawlib.state.ma.us/source/mass/*
    *mgl.html*
*http://www.malegislature.gov/Laws/GeneralLaws*

**Cases:**
Massachusetts Reports (West)
Massachusetts Decisions (West)
Massachusetts Appeals Court Reports (West)
Massachusetts Appellate Division Reports (Mass.
    Lawyers Weekly)
Northeast 2d (West)
    Supreme Judicial Court (1999-)
*http://socialaw.com/slips.htm?sid=120*
*http://massreports.com/OpinionArchive/*
    *Default.aspx*
    Appeals Court (1999-)
*http://socialaw.com/slips.htm?sid=119*
*http://ma-appellatecourts.org/search.php*
*http://massreports.com/OpinionArchive/*
    *Default.aspx*
**Regulations:**
1.    Code of Massachusetts Regulations
      (CMR) -1993
      Mass. Secy. of State
      Regulations Division
      1 Ashburton Place, Rm. 1613
      Boston, MA 02108
      (617) 727-2831
25 vols.; looseleaf; biweekly supp. in Register;
    on CD-ROM; on Lexis, Westlaw
*http://www.lawlib.state.ma.us/source/mass/cmr/*
    *index.html*
2.    Code of Massachusetts Regulations-1995
      publ. by Lexis
28 vols; monthly supp.; looseleaf; on Lexis,
    Westlaw
**Register:**
Mass. Register
    publ. by Secretary of State
began 1976; biweekly; on Lexis


# MICHIGAN
**Statutes:**
1.    Michigan Compiled Laws Annotated-
      1967
      West - 102 vols.
      annual pocket parts
      legislative service
2.    Michigan Compiled Laws Service-2001
      Lexis - 76 vols.
      annual pocket parts
      legislative service
3.    Michigan Compiled Laws (unannotated)-
      2011
      West - 8 vols. (compact ed.)
*http://www.legislature.mi.gov/*
**Cases:**
Michigan Reports (West)
Michigan Appeals Reports (West)
Northwest 2d (West)

Michigan Reporter 2d (West)
    Supreme Court (1942-)/ Court of Appeals
    (1965-)
*http://www.icle.org/help/mlo.htm*
*http://www.milawyersweekly.com/* (1996-)
*http://www.michbar.org/opinions/* (1998-)
*http://caselaw.findlaw.com/courts/Michigan*
    (1995-)
    Court of Appeals (2001-)
*http://coa.courts.mi.gov/resources/opinions.htm*
**Regulations:**
Michigan Administrative Code
no print, only on web; on CD-ROM, on Lexis,
    Westlaw
*http://www.michigan.gov/lara/*
    *0,1607,7-154-10576_35738_5698---,00.html*
**Register:**
Michigan Register
Office of Administrative Hearings & Rules
    (517) 241-1671
began 1984; semimonthly
*http://www.michigan.gov/lara/*
    *0,1607,7-154-10576_35738_40280---,00.html*


# MINNESOTA
**Statutes:**
1.    Minnesota Statutes Annotated-1950
      West - 117 vols.
      annual pocket parts
      legislative service
2.    Minnesota Statutes (unannotated)-2008
      Documents Div., Dept. of Administration
      15 vols.; biennial eds. with pocket parts
*https://www.revisor.leg.mn.gov/pubs/*
**Cases:**
Minnesota Reporter (West)
Northwest 2d (West)
    Supreme Court/ Court of Appeals (5/96-)
*http://www.mncourts.gov/*
*http://www.lawlibrary.state.mn.us/archive/*
    *index. html*
*http://caselaw.findlaw.com/courts/Minnesota*
    (1/97-)
**Regulations:**
Minnesota Rules-2007
    Revisor of Statutes
    700 State Office Bldg.
    St. Paul, MN 55155
    (651) 296-2868 FAX (651) 296-0569
    order from (651) 297-3000
11 vols.; hardbound; biennial editions with
    semiannual pocket part supp. in even yrs.;
    on Lexis, Westlaw; on CD-ROM
*http://www.revisor.mn.gov/rules/*
**Register:**
Minnesota State Register

# STATE CODES, REPORTERS, REGULATIONS AND REGISTERS

began 7/76; weekly; no print, only on web; on Lexis
*http://www.comm.media.state.mn.us/bookstore/
state_register.asp*

## MISSISSIPPI
### Statutes:
1.  Mississippi Code of 1972 Annotated-1999
    Lexis - 32 vols.
    annual pocket parts
    legislative service
2.  West's Annotated Mississippi Code-1999
    West - 50 vols.
    annual pocket parts
*http://www.michie.com/mississippi/
lpext.dll?f=templates&fn=main_h.htm&cp=mscode*
*http://www.mscode.com/*
### Cases:
Mississippi Cases (West)
Southern 3d (West)
    Supreme Court/Court of Appeals (1996-)
*http://www.mssc.state.ms.us/appellate_courts/sc/
scdecisions.html*
*http://www.mslawyer.com/mssc*
*http://www.mssc.state.ms.us/appellate_courts/coa/
coadecisions.html*
### Regulations:
Code of Mississippi Rules-1996
    publ. by Lexis
19 vols; monthly supp.; on Lexis, Westlaw;
    on CD-ROM
*http://www.mscode.com/regs/regsin.htm*
### Register:
Mississippi Government Register
    publ. by Lexis
began 1996; monthly; on Lexis

## MISSOURI
### Statutes:
1.  Vernon's Annotated Missouri Statutes-1951
    West - 84 vols.
    annual pocket parts
    legislative service
2.  Missouri Revised Statutes (unannotated)-
    2010
    Revisor of Statutes  (573) 751-4223
20 vols.; annual cum. supplement
*http://www.moga.mo.gov/STATUTES/
STATUTES.HTM*
### Cases:
Missouri Cases 3d (West)
Southwest 3d (West)
    Supreme Court/ Court of Appeals
*http://www.sos.mo.gov/archives/judiciary/
supremecourt/ (*historical-1783-1871)
*http://www.courts.mo.gov/page.asp?id=
12086&dist=Opinions*

*http://caselaw.findlaw.com/courts/Missouri* (1/97-)
### Regulations:
Code of State Regulations Annotated-1988
    Secy. of State - Admin. Rules
    600 W. Main
    Jefferson City, MO 65109
    (573) 751-4015; FAX (573) 751-3032
14 vols.; looseleaf; monthly; on CD-ROM;
    on Lexis, Westlaw
*http://www.sos.mo.gov/adrules/csr/csr.asp*
### Register:
Missouri Register
began 1975; semimonthly; on Lexis
*http://www.sos.mo.gov/adrules/moreg/moreg.asp*

## MONTANA
### Statutes:
1.  Montana Code Annotated-2009
    Montana Legis. Services (406) 444-3064
    15 vols. and 12 vols. of annotations
    reprinted biennially (odd years); on
    CD-ROM
2.  West's Montana Code Annotated-2009
    West - 43 vols.
    annual pocket parts
    legislative service
*http://data.opi.state.mt.us/bills/mca_toc/index.htm*
### Cases:
Montana Reports (State Publ. Co.)
Pacific 3d (West)
    Supreme Court (1/97-)
*http://caselaw.findlaw.com/courts/Montana*
### Regulations:
Admin. Rules of Montana-1988
    Secy. of State
    P.O. Box 202801
    Helena, MT 59620
    (406) 444-2055; FAX (406) 444-4263
29 vols.; looseleaf; quarterly supp.; on CD-ROM; on
    Lexis, Westlaw
*http://www.mtrules.org*
### Register:
Montana Admin. Register
began 1/73; semimonthly
*http://sos.mt.gov/ARM/Register/index.asp*

## NEBRASKA
### Statutes:
1.  Revised Statutes of Nebraska-1943
    Nebraska State Library - 15 vols.
    annual supp. (odd years) (402) 471-3189
    cum. supp. (even years)
2.  Revised Statutes of Nebraska Annotated-
    1995
    Lexis - 27 vols.

annual pocket parts
3.    West's Revised Statutes of Nebraska
Annotated-2009
West - 45 vols.
annual pocket parts
*http://uniweb.legislature.ne.gov/laws/*
*browse-statutes.php*
**Cases:**
Nebraska Reports (Nebraska Sup. Ct.)
Nebraska Court of Appeals Decisions (Nebraska
    Sup. Ct.)
Northwest 2d (West)
    Supreme Court/Court of Appeals (90 days)
*http://court.nol.org/opinions/*
    Supreme Court/Court of Appeals (1997-)
*http://caselaw.findlaw.com/courts/Nebraska*
**Regulations:**
Nebraska Admin. Rules and Regulations-1983
    Office of Secy. of State/Rules & Regs.
    State Capitol, Suite 1305
    Lincoln, NE 68509
    (402) 471-2385; FAX (402) 471-2530
35 vols.; looseleaf; monthly supp.; on
    Westlaw; Lexis; on CD-ROM
*http://www.sos.state.ne.us/rules-and-*
*regs/regsearch/*
**Register:**
Nebraska Administrative Code Updates
    publ. by Legis. Council (402) 471-2385
began 2001; monthly; on Lexis

## NEVADA
**Statutes:**
1.    Nevada Revised Statutes-2009
Nevada Legis. Counsel Bureau
(775) 684-6835 - 57 vols.
looseleaf & paperbound
biennial supp. (odd years)
2.    Michie's Nevada Revised Statutes
Annotated-1999
Lexis - 25 vols.
biennial pocket parts
3.    West's Nevada Revised Statutes
Annotated-2000
West - 40 vols.
biennual pocket parts
legislative service
*http://www.leg.state.nv.us/nrsIndex/index.html*
**Cases:**
Nevada Reports (Legis. Counsel Bureau)
Pacific 3d (West)
    Supreme Court (latest 3 mos.)
*http://www.leg.state.nv.us/law1.cfm*
**Regulations:**
Nevada Admin. Code-1986
    Legis. Counsel Bureau

401 S. Carson St.
Carson City, NV 89701
(775) 684-6835; FAX (775) 684-6663
15 vols.; looseleaf; bimonthly supp.; on Lexis,
    Westlaw; on CD-ROM
*http://www.leg.state.nv.us/nac/*
**Register:**
Nevada Administrative Code Register
began 1997; monthly; on Lexis
*http://www.leg.state.nv.us/register/*

## NEW HAMPSHIRE
**Statutes:**
1.    New Hampshire Revised Statutes
Annotated-1955
Lexis - 31 vols.
annual pocket parts
2.    New Hampshire Revised Statutes
Annotated-2000 (official code)
West - 39 vols.
annual pocket parts
legislative service
*http://www.gencourt.state.nh.us/rsa/html/indexes/*
*default.html*
**Cases:**
New Hampshire Reports (Lexis)
Atlantic 3d (West)
    Supreme Court (11/95-)
*http://www.courts.state.nh.us/supreme/opinions/*
*index.htm*
*http://caselaw.findlaw.com/courts/New-Hampshire*
    (1/97-)
**Regulations:**
Code of New Hampshire Rules-1996
    publ. by Lexis
15 vols.; monthly supp.; looseleaf; on Lexis,
    Westlaw
*http://gencourt.state.nh.us/rules/listagencies.html*
**Register:**
1.    New Hampshire Rulemaking Register
Admin. Rules Office (603) 271-3680
began 1980; weekly
2.    New Hampshire Government Register
publ. by Lexis
began 1996; monthly supp.; on Lexis
*http://www.gencourt.state.nh.us/rules/index.html*

## NEW JERSEY
**Statutes:**
1.    New Jersey Statutes Annotated-1939
West - 106 vols.
annual pocket parts
legislative service
2.    New Jersey Statutes-2011
West - 8 vols. (compact ed.)

annual editions
*http://lis.njleg.state.nj.us/cgi-bin/om_isapi.dll?clien tID=97041&depth=2&expandheadings=of f&headingswithhits=on&infobase= s tatutes.nfo&softpage=TOC_Frame_Pg42*
**Cases:**
New Jersey Reports (West)
New Jersey Superior Court Reports (West)
Atlantic 2d (West)
    Supreme Court (3/94-)
*http://lawlibrary.rutgers.edu/search.shtml*
    Appellate Division/Tax Court (9/95-)
*http://lawlibrary.rutgers.edu/search.shtml*
**Regulations:**
New Jersey Administrative Code-2006
    publ. by Lexis
38 vols.; looseleaf; monthly supp.; on CD-ROM;
    on Lexis, Westlaw
*http://www.lexisnexis.com/njoal/*
**Register:**
New Jersey Register
    publ. by Lexis
began 9/69; semimonthly; on Westlaw, Lexis
*http://www.lexisnexis.com/njoal/*


## NEW MEXICO
**Statutes:**
1.    West's New Mexico Statutes Annotated-2003
    West - 39 vols.
    annual supp.
    legislative service
2.    Michie's Annotated Statutes of New Mexico - 2006
    Lexis - 18 vols.
    annual pocket parts
3.    New Mexico Statutes Annotated-1978
    New Mexico Compilation Commission
    order from (505) 363-3116
    17 vols.; looseleaf
*http://www.nmcompcomm.us*
*http://www.conwaygreene.com/nmsu/ lpext.dll?f=templates&fn=main-h.htm&2.0*
**Cases:**
New Mexico Reports (New Mexico Compilation Commission)
Pacific 3d (West)
    Supreme Court (1998-)
*http://www.nmcompcomm.us*
    Supreme Court/Court of Appeals (1/97-)
*http://caselaw.findlaw.com/courts/New-Mexico*
*http://www.conwaygreene.com/nmsu/ lpext.dll?f=templates&fn=main-h.htm&2.0*
**Regulations:**
Code of New Mexico Rules-2000
    publ. by Lexis

19 vols; looseleaf; monthly supp.; on DVD; on
    Lexis, Westlaw
*http://www.nmcpr.state.nm.us/nmac/*
**Register:**
New Mexico Register
    publ. by Commission of Public Records
    (505) 476-7907
began 1990; semimonthly; on Lexis
*http://www.nmcpr.state.nm.us/nmregister*


## NEW YORK
**Statutes:**
1.    New York Consolidated Law Service-1978
    Lexis - 150+ vols.
    annual pocket parts and quarterly updates
    legislative service
2.    McKinney's Consolidated Laws of New York Annotated-1948
    West - 309 vols.
    annual pocket parts
    legislative service
3.    McKinney's Consolidated Laws of New York-2011
    West - 15 vols.
    annual editions
*http://codes.lp.findlaw.com/nycode/*
*http://public.leginfo.state.ny.us/menugetf.cgi?*
    COMMONQUERY=LAWS
**Cases:**
New York Reports 3d (West)
New York Appellate Division Reports 3d (West)
New York Miscellaneous Reports 3d (West)
New York Supplement 2d (West)
Northeast 2d (West)
    Supreme Court (1999-)
*http://www.nycourts.gov/library/queens/ decisions.shtml*
    Supreme Court/Court of Appeals (1/97-)
*http://caselaw.findlaw.com/courts/New-York*
    Court of Appeals
*http://www.nycourts.gov/decisions/index.shtml*
**Regulations:**
Official Compilation of Codes, Rules
    and Regulations (NYCRR)
    publ. by West
85 vols.; looseleaf; semimonthly supp.; on
    CD-ROM; on Lexis, Westlaw
*http://government.westlaw.com/linkedslice/ default.asp?SP=nycrr-1000*
**Register:**
New York State Register
    publ. by Dept. of State (518) 474-6957
began 1979; weekly; on Lexis, Westlaw
*http://www.dos.state.ny.us/info/register.htm*

# STATE CODES, REPORTERS, REGULATIONS AND REGISTERS

**NORTH CAROLINA**

**Statutes:**
1. General Statutes of North Carolina-2009
Lexis - 21 vols. (paperback or hardbound)
biennial editions
legislative service
2. West's North Carolina General Statutes
Annotated-2000
West - 67 vols.
annual pocket parts
*http://www.ncleg.net/gascripts/statutes/*
*statutes.asp*

**Cases:**
North Carolina Reports (Admin. Office of the
Courts)
North Carolina Court of Appeals Reports (Admin.
Office of the Courts)
North Carolina Reporter (West)
Southeast 2d (West)
Supreme Court/Court of Appeals (1997-)
*http://appellate.nccourts.org/opinions/*
*http://caselaw.findlaw.com/courts/North-Carolina*

**Regulations:**
North Carolina Administrative Code-2000
publ. by West
33 vols.; paperbound; monthly supp.; on CD-ROM;
on Lexis, Westlaw
*http://reports.oah.state.nc.us/ncac.asp*

**Register:**
North Carolina Register
publ. by Office of Admin. Hearings
(919) 431-3075
began 4/86; semimonthly; on Lexis, Westlaw
*http://www.oah.state.nc.us/rules/register/*

**NORTH DAKOTA**

**Statutes:**
1. North Dakota Century Code Annotated-
1960
Lexis - 24 vols.
biennial pocket parts and interim supp.
legislative service
2. West's North Dakota Century Code
Annotated-2008
West - 31 vols.
annual supplements
*http://www.legis.nd.gov/information/*
*statutes/cent-code.html*

**Cases:**
North Dakota Reports (West) - out-of-print
Northwest 2d (West)
Supreme Court (1971-)
*http://www.ndcourts.org/Court/Opinions.htm*
Supreme Court (1/97-)/Court of Appeals
(7/98-)
*http://caselaw.findlaw.com/courts/North-Dakota*

**Regulations:**
North Dakota Admin. Code-1978
Legislative Council
State Capitol
Bismarck, ND 58505
(701) 328-2916
19 vols.; looseleaf; quarterly supp.; on CD-ROM; on
Westlaw
*http://www.legis.nd.gov/information/rules/*
*admincode.html*

**Register:**
None in print
Rulemaking Notices:
*http://www.legis.nd.gov/information/rules/*
*hearings.html*

**OHIO**

**Statutes:**
1. Baldwin's Ohio Revised Code Annotated-
1993
West - 69 vols.
annual supp.
legislative service
2. Page's Ohio Revised Code Annotated-1953
Lexis - 39 vols.
annual pocket parts
legislative service
*http://codes.ohio.gov/orc*

**Cases:**
Ohio Cases (West)
Ohio State Reports 3d (West)
Ohio Appellate Court Reports 3d (West)
Northeast 2d (West)
Supreme Court (1992-)
*http://www.sconet.state.oh.us/rod/*
Supreme Court/Court of Appeals (1997-)
*http://caselaw.findlaw.com/courts/Ohio*

**Regulations:**
Ohio Admin. Code-1994
publ. by West
18 vols.; paperback; supp. as needed; on
CD-ROM; on Lexis, Westlaw
*http://codes.ohio.gov/oac*

**Register:**
Ohio Monthly Record
publ. by West
began 1/77; monthly; on Lexis
*http://www.registerofohio.state.oh.us*

**OKLAHOMA**

**Statutes:**
1. Oklahoma Statutes Annotated-1981
West - 92 vols.
annual pocket parts
legislative service

# STATE CODES, REPORTERS, REGULATIONS AND REGISTERS

2.    Oklahoma Statutes-2001
      West - 12 vols.
      annual supp.
*http://www.lsb.state.ok.us/*
*http://oklegal.onenet.net/statutes.basic.html*
*http://www.oscn.net/applications/oscn/*
      *index.asp?ftdb=STOKST&level=1*
      **Cases:**
Oklahoma Decisions (West)
Pacific 3d (West)
      Supreme Court (1909-)/Court of Appeals
      (1968-)
*http://oklegal.onenet.net/sample.basic.html*
*http://www.oscn.net*
      Supreme Court/Court of Appeals (1/97-)
*http://caselaw.findlaw.com/courts/Oklahoma*
      **Regulations:**
Oklahoma Admin. Code-2006
      Secy. of State
      Office of Admin. Rules
      2401 N. Lincoln Blvd., Rm. 220
      Oklahoma City, OK 73105
      (405) 521-4911, FAX (405) 522-3555
21 vols; looseleaf; annual supp.; on CD-ROM; on
      Lexis, Westlaw
*http://204.87.112.100/oar/codedoc02.nsf/frm*
*Main?OpenFrameSet&Frame=Main&Src=*
      **Register:**
The Oklahoma Register
began 1982; semimonthly; on CD-ROM; on Lexis
*http://204.87.112.100/oar/codedoc02.nsf/frm*
*Main?OpenFrameSet&Frame=Main&Src=*


## OREGON
      **Statutes:**
1.    Oregon Revised Statutes with Annotations
      Oregon Legis. Counsel  (503) 986-1243 -
      21 vols.
      biennial editions (odd years)
2.    West's Oregon Revised Statutes
      Annotated-2003
      West - 54 vols.; annual pocket parts
*http://landru.leg.state.or.us/ors/*
      **Cases:**
Oregon Cases (West)
Oregon Reports
Court of Appeals Reports
Tax Court Reports
      (State Court Administrator)
Pacific 3d (West)
      Supreme Court (1/98-)
*http://www.publications.ojd.state.or.us/*
      *supreme.htm*
      Court of Appeals (1/98-)
*http://www.publications.ojd.state.or.us/*
      *appeals.htm*

      Supreme Court/Court of Appeals (1/97-)
*http://caselaw.findlaw.com/courts/Oregon*
      **Regulations:**
Oregon Admin. Rules Compilation-2011
      Secy. of State/Archives Div.
      800 NE Summer Street
      Salem, OR 97310
      (503) 378-5199
19 vols.; paperbound; monthly supp.; on CD-ROM;
on Westlaw, Lexis
*http://arcweb.sos.state.or.us/banners/rules.htm*
      **Register:**
Oregon Bulletin
began 1958; monthly; no print, only on web; on
      Lexis
*http://arcweb.sos.state.or.us/rules/*
      *bulletin_default.html*


## PENNSYLVANIA
      **Statutes:**
1.    Purdon's Pennsylvania Statutes Annotated-
      1930
      West - 137 vols.
      annual pocket parts
      legislative service
2.    Pennsylvania Consolidated Statutes-1975
      Legislative Ref. Bureau (717) 787-4223
      12 vols.; looseleaf; semiannual supp.
3.    Purdon's Pennsylvania Statutes and
      Consolidated Statutes-2011
      West - 8 vols.
      annual editions
*http://government.westlaw.com/linkedslice/*
      *default.asp?SP=pac-1000*
      **Cases:**
Pennsylvania Reports 2d (West)
Pennsylvania State Reports (West)
Atlantic 3d (West)
Pennsylvania Superior Court Reports (West)
Pennsylvania District and County Reports (Legal
      Intelligencer)
      Supreme Court/ Superior Court/
      Commonwealth Court (1997-)
*http://www.aopc.org/*
*http://caselaw.findlaw.com/courts/Pennsylvania*
      **Regulations:**
Pennsylvania Code
      publ. by Fry Communications, Inc.
      800 W. Church Rd.
      Mechanicsburg, PA 17055
      (800) 334-1429 x2340
62 vols; looseleaf; monthly supp.; on CD-ROM;
      on Lexis, Westlaw
*http://www.pacode.com/*
      **Register:**
Pennsylvania Bulletin

began 1970; weekly; on Westlaw, Lexis
*http://www.pabulletin.com/*

## RHODE ISLAND
### Statutes:
1.    General Laws of Rhode Island-1956
    Lexis - 30 vols.
    annual pocket parts
    legislative service
2.    West's General Laws of Rhode Island
    Annotated-2006
    West - 34 vols.
    annual pocket parts
    legislative service
*http://www.rilin.state.ri.us/statutes/statutes.html*
### Cases:
Rhode Island Reporter (West)
Atlantic 3d (West)
    Supreme Court (1997-)
*http://caselaw.findlaw.com/courts/Rhode-Island*
### Regulations:
Code of Rhode Island Rules-1992
    publ. by Lexis
27 vols.; looseleaf; monthly supp., on Lexis,
    Westlaw; on CD-ROM
*http://sos.ri.gov/rules/*
### Register:
Rhode Island Govt. Register
    publ. by Lexis
began 9/92; monthly; on Lexis

## SOUTH CAROLINA
### Statutes:
Code of Laws of South Carolina Annotated-1976
West - 49 vols.
annual pocket parts
*http://www.scstatehouse.gov/code/statmast.htm*
### Cases:
South Carolina Reports (West)
Southeast 2d (West)
    Supreme Court/Court of Appeals  (1997-)
*http://caselaw.findlaw.com/courts/South-Carolina*
*http://www.judicial.state.sc.us/opinions/*
    *indexSCPub.cfm*

*http://www.judicial.state.sc.us/opinions/*
    *indexCOAPub.cfm*
### Regulations:
Code of Regulations of South Carolina(vols. 23-27
    of Code of Laws - see above)-1976
    publ. by West
9 vols.; looseleaf; annual supp.; on CD-ROM; on
    Westlaw, Lexis
*http://www.scstatehouse.gov/coderegs/statmast.htm*
### Register:

South Carolina State Register
    publ. by Legislative Council
    P.O. Box 11489
    Columbia, SC 29211
    (803) 212-4500
began 1977; monthly; on Lexis
*http://www.scstatehouse.gov/archives/aregist.htm*

## SOUTH DAKOTA
### Statutes:
South Dakota Codified Laws (annotated)-2004
West - 40 vols.
annual pocket parts
*http://legis.state.sd.us/statutes/index.aspx*
### Cases:
South Dakota Reports (West)
Northwest 2d (West)
    Supreme Court (1996-)
*http://www.sdjudicial.com/sc/scopinions.aspx*
*http://caselaw.findlaw.com/courts/South-Dakota*
### Regulations:
Administrative Rules of South Dakota-1978
    Legis. Research Council
    Capitol Building, 3rd fl.
    500 East Capitol Avenue
    Pierre, SD 57501-5070
    (605) 773-3251; FAX (605) 773-4576
order from Property Mgmt. (605) 773-4935
13 vols.; looseleaf; periodic supp.; on CD-ROM;
    on Lexis, Westlaw
*http://legis.state.sd.us/rules/index.aspx*
### Register:
South Dakota Register
    publ. by Legislative Research Council
    (605) 773-3251
began 7/74; weekly; on Lexis
*http://legis.state.sd.us/rules/RegisterArchive.aspx*

## TENNESSEE
### Statutes:
1.    Tennessee Code Annotated-1999
    Lexis - 35 vols.
    annual pocket parts
    legislative service
2.    West's Tennessee Code Annotated-2002
    West - 51 vols.
    annual pocket parts
    legislative service
*http://www.michie.com/tennessee/*
*lpext.dll?f=templates&fn=main_h.htm&cp=tncode*
### Cases:
Tennessee Decisions 3d (West)
Southwest 3d (West)
    Supreme Court (1995-)
*http://www.tsc.state.tn.us/opinions/tsc/oplsttsc.htm*

# STATE CODES, REPORTERS, REGULATIONS AND REGISTERS

Court of Appeals (1995-)
*http://www.tsc.state.tn.us/opinions/tca/oplsttca.htm*
Supreme Court/Court of Appeals (1/97-)
*http://caselaw.findlaw.com/courts/Tennessee*
### Regulations:
no print, only on web; also on Lexis,
Westlaw; on CD-ROM
*http://www.state.tn.us/sos/rules/index.htm*
### Register:
Tennessee Administrative Register
no print, only on web, on Lexis, on CD-ROM
*http://www.state.tn.us/sos/pub/tar/index.htm*


## TEXAS
### Statutes:
Vernon's Texas Statutes Annotated-1926
West - 192 vols.
annual pocket parts
biennial legislative service
*http://www.statutes.legis.state.tx.us*
### Cases:
Texas Cases (West)
Southwest 3d (West)
Supreme Court (1997-)
*http://www.supreme.courts.state.tx.us/*
Supreme Court/Court of Appeals
Criminal/Court of Appeals (1/97-)
*http://caselaw.findlaw.com/courts/Texas*
### Regulations:
Official Texas Administrative Code-1998
publ. by West
24 vols.; paperbound; annual editions; on CD-ROM; on Lexis, Westlaw
*http://www.sos.state.tx.us/tac/*
### Register:
Texas Register
publ. by Secy. of State
P.O. Box 13824
Austin, TX 78711-3824
(512) 463-5561
began 1/76; weekly; on Lexis, Westlaw
*http://www.sos.state.tx.us/texreg*
*http://texinfo.library.unt.edu/texasregister*


## UTAH
### Statutes:
1.    Utah Code Annotated-1986
Lexis - 28 vols.
annual pocket parts
legislative service
2.    West's Utah Code Annotated-2004
West - 37 vols.
annual pocket parts
legislative service
3.    Utah Code Unannotated-2009

Lexis - 5 vols.
paperbound; annual editions
*http://www.le.state.ut.us/Documents/
code_const.htm*
*http://www.michie.com/utah/
lpext.dll?f=templates&fn=main_h.htm&cp=utcode*
*http://www.code-co.com/utah* (subscribers only)
### Cases:
Pacific 3d (West)
Utah Reporter 3d (West)
Supreme Court/Court of Appeals (9/96-)
*http://www.utcourts.gov/opinions/*
*http://caselaw.findlaw.com/courts/Utah*
### Regulations:
Utah Administrative Code Annotated-2008
publ. by Lexis
10 vols.; paperbound; semiannual supp.; on CD-ROM; on Lexis, Westlaw
*http://www.rules.utah.gov/publicat/code.htm*
*http://www.code-co.com/utah*
### Register:
Utah State Bulletin
print discontinued 4/1/03; only on web; on Lexis
*http://www.rules.utah.gov/publicat/bulletin.htm*


## VERMONT
### Statutes:
1.    Vermont Statutes Annotated-1959
Lexis - 31 vols.
annual pocket parts
legislative service
2.    West's Vermont Statutes Annotated-2007
West - 28 vols.
annual pocket parts
*http://www.leg.state.vt.us/statutesMain.cfm*
*http://www.michie.com/vermont/
lpext.dll?f=templates&fn=main_h.htm&cp=vtcode*
### Cases:
Vermont Reports (Lexis)
Atlantic 3d (West)
Supreme Court (1989-)
*http://libraries.vermont.gov/law/supct/*
Supreme Court (1/97-)
*http://caselaw.findlaw.com/courts/Vermont*
### Regulations:
Code of Vermont Rules-1990
publ. by Lexis
13 vols.; looseleaf; monthly supp.; on CD-ROM; on Lexis, Westlaw
### Register:
Vermont Government Register
publ. by Lexis
began 2/91; monthly; on Lexis

# STATE CODES, REPORTERS, REGULATIONS AND REGISTERS

## VIRGINIA

**Statutes:**
1. Code of Virginia (Annotated)-1950
   Lexis - 32 vols.
   annual pocket parts
   legislative service
   *http://leg1.state.va.us/000/src.htm*
2. West's Annotated Code of Virginia-1999
   West - 50 vols.
   annual pocket parts
   semiannual legislative service

**Cases:**
Virginia Reports (Darby)
Virginia Court of Appeals Reports (West)
Southeast 2d (West)
   Supreme Court (6/95-)
*http://www.courts.state.va.us/search/*
   *textopinions.html*
   Court of Appeals (5/95-)
*http://www.courts.state.va.us/txtcap.htm*
   Supreme Court/ Court of Appeals (1/97-)
*http://www.valawyersweekly.com/*
*http://caselaw.findlaw.com/courts/Virginia*

**Regulations:**
Virginia Administrative Code-2001
   publ. by West
22 vols. looseleaf; semiannual supp.; on CD-ROM;
   on Lexis, Westlaw
*http://leg1.state.va.us/000/srr.htm*

**Register:**
The Virginia Register of Regulations
   publ. by Lexis since 6/2/03
began 10/1/84; monthly; on Lexis
*http://legis.state.va.us/codecomm/register/*
   *regindex.htm*


## WASHINGTON

**Statutes:**
1. Revised Code of Washington Annotated-
   1962
   West - 121 vols.
   annual pocket parts
   legislative service
2. Revised Code of Washington
   (unannotated)-2010
   Office of Code Reviser (866) 650-6369
   9 vols.; biennial ed.
3. Annotated Revised Code of Washington-
   1994
   Lexis - 28 vols.
   paperbound; annual supp.
*http://apps.leg.wa.gov/rcw*
*http://www.mrsc.org/mc/_toc/rcw.htm*

**Cases:**
Washington Reports 2d (West)
Washington Appellate Reports (West)

Pacific 3d (West)
   Supreme Court/Court of Appeals
   (90 days)
*http://www.courts.wa.gov/opinions/index.cfm*
   Supreme Court/Court of Appeals (1889-)
*http://www.legalwa.org*
   Supreme Court/Court of Appeals (1/97-)
*http://caselaw.findlaw.com/courts/Washington*

**Regulations:**
Washington Administrative Code (WAC)-2009
   Code Revisor's Office
   P.O. Box 40551
   Olympia, WA 98504
   (360) 786-6777; FAX (360) 786-1529
13 vols.; paperbound; annual supp.; biennial
   editions; on CD-ROM; on Lexis, Westlaw
*http://www.mrsc.org/mc/_toc/wac.htm*
*http://apps.leg.wa.gov/wac/*

**Register:**
Washington State Register
began 1/78; biweekly; on Lexis; on CD-ROM
*http://www1.leg.wa.gov/codereviser/pages/*
   *washington_state_register.aspx*


## WEST VIRIGINIA

**Statutes:**
1. Michie's West Virginia Code Annotated-
   1998
   Lexis - 29 vols.
   annual pocket parts
   legislative service
2. West's Annotated Code of West Virginia-
   2002
   West - 39 vols.
   annual pocket parts
*http://www.legis.state.wv.us/WVCODE/Code.cfm*

**Cases:**
West Virginia Reports (West)
West Virginia Court of Claims Reports (Court of
   Claims)
Southeast 2d (West)
   Supreme Court (9/91-)
*http://www.state.wv.us/wvsca/opinions.htm*
*http://caselaw.findlaw.com/courts/West-Virginia*
   (2/97-)

**Regulations:**
Code of State Rules-1990
   Administrative Law Div.-Secy. of State
   1900 Kanawha Blvd. E.
   Charleston, WV 25305
   (304) 558-6000; FAX (304) 558-0900
14 vols.; looseleaf; monthly supp.; on CD-ROM; on
   Lexis, Westlaw
*http://apps.sos.wv.gov/adlaw/csc/index.aspx*

**Register:**

# STATE CODES, REPORTERS, REGULATIONS AND REGISTERS

West Virginia Register
began 6/83; weekly
*http://www.sos.wv.gov/*
  *administrative-law/register/Pages/default.aspx*


## WISCONSIN
### Statutes:
1.  West's Wisconsin Statutes Annotated-1957
    West - 75 vols.
    annual pocket parts
    biennial legislative service
2.  Wisconsin Statutes (unannotated)-2009-10
    Revisor of Statutes - 5 vols.- biennial
    order from Doc. Sales (608) 264-9419
*http://legis.wisconsin.gov/rsb/stats.html*
### Cases:
Wisconsin Reports 2d (West)
Wisconsin Reporter 2d (West)
Northwest 2d (West)
    Supreme Court (9/95-)
*http://www.wisbar.org/AM/Template.cfm?*
    *Section=Legal_Research*
    Court of Appeals (6/95-)
*http://www.wisbar.org/WisCtApp/index.html*
    Supreme Court/Court of Appeals (1/97-)
*http://caselaw.findlaw.com/courts/Wisconsin*
### Regulations:
Wisconsin Administrative Code-1978
    Revisor of Statutes Bureau
    Document Sales
    4622 University Avenue
    Madison, WI 53705
    (608) 266-3358
18 vols.; looseleaf; monthly supp.; on CD-ROM; on
    Lexis, Westlaw
*http://legis.wisconsin.gov/rsb/code.html*
### Register:
Wisconsin Administrative Register
began 1/56; semimonthly; on Lexis, Westlaw
*http://legis.wisconsin.gov/rsb/regindex.htm*


## WYOMING
### Statutes:
1.  Wyoming Revised Statutes-2009
    Lexis - 12 vols. (paperbound)
    annual supp.
    biennial eds.
2.  West's Wyoming Statutes Annotated-2007
    West - 24 vols.
    annual pocket parts
    legislative service
*http://legisweb.state.wy.us/titles/statutes.htm*
### Cases:
Wyoming Reporter 3d (West)
Pacific 3d (West)

Supreme Court (1/97-)
*http://courts.state.wy.us/Opinions.aspx*
*http://caselaw.findlaw.com/courts/Wyoming*
### Regulations:
Code of Wyoming Rules-1995
    publ. by Lexis
11 vols.; looseleaf; monthly supp.; on Lexis,
    Westlaw; on CD-ROM
*http://soswy.state.wy.us/Rules/Rule_Search_Main.asp*
### Register:
Wyoming Government Register
began 1995; monthly; on Lexis

# HISTORICAL COVERAGE OF FEDERAL AND STATE APPELLATE COURT DECISIONS ON ONLINE RESEARCH SERVICES

| | Westlaw | Lexis-Nexis | Bloomberg Law | CaseClerk | Casemaker | Fastcase | Loislaw | TheLaw.net America | VersusLaw | Google Scholar | FindLaw | Official site* |
|---|---|---|---|---|---|---|---|---|---|---|---|---|
| U.S. Supreme Court | 1790- | 1790- | 1789- | 1900- | 1754- | 1754- | 1790 | 1900- | 1900- | 1791- | 1893- | 1991- |
| 1st Circuit | 1891- | 1912- | 1891- | 1930- | 1950- | 1950- | 1924- | 1930- | 1930- | 1923- | 1995- | 2000- |
| 2d Circuit | 1891- | 1912- | 1891- | 1930- | 1950- | 1924- | 1924- | 1930- | 1930- | 1923- | 1995- | 30 days |
| 3d Circuit | 1891- | 1912- | 1891- | 1930- | 1950- | 1950- | 1924- | 1930- | 1930- | 1923- | 1994- | 1994- |
| 4th Circuit | 1891- | 1912- | 1891- | 1930- | 1950- | 1950- | 1924- | 1930- | 1930- | 1923- | 1995- | 1996- |
| 5th Circuit | 1891- | 1912- | 1891- | 1930- | 1950- | 1950- | 1924- | 1930- | 1930- | 1923- | 1996- | 1992- |
| 6th Circuit | 1891- | 1912- | 1891- | 1930- | 1950- | 1950- | 1924- | 1930- | 1930- | 1923- | 1995- | 1999- |
| 7th Circuit | 1891- | 1912- | 1891- | 1930- | 1950- | 1950- | 1924- | 1930- | 1930- | 1923- | 1995- | 30 days |
| 8th Circuit | 1891- | 1912- | 1891- | 1930- | 1950- | 1950- | 1924- | 1930- | 1930- | 1923- | 1995- | 1995- |
| 9th Circuit | 1891- | 1912- | 1891- | 1941- | 1950- | 1950- | 1924- | 1941- | 1941- | 1923- | 1996- | 1995- |
| 10th Circuit | 1929- | 1912- | 1929- | 1930- | 1950- | 1950- | 1924- | 1930- | 1930- | 1923- | 19 97- | 1995- |
| 11th Circuit | 1891- | 1912- | 1980- | 1981- | 1981- | 1981- | 1981- | 1981- | 1981- | 1981- | 1995- | 1995- |
| D.C. Circuit | 1919- | 1919- | 1893- | 1950- | 1950- | 1950- | 1922- | 1950- | 1950- | 1923- | 1997- | 1997- |
| Federal Circuit | 1856- | 1982- | 1982- | 1982- | 1982- | 1982- | 1929- | 1982- | 1982- | 1982- | 1997- | 2004- |
| Alabama | 1820- | 1820- | 1840- | 1955- | 1939- | 1950- | 1916- | 1955- | 1955- | 1950- | 1998- | 1994- |
| Alaska | 1959- | 1960- | 1960- | 1960- | 1950- | 1950- | 1923- | 1960- | 1960- | 1950- | 1991- | 1991- |
| Arizona | 1866- | 1866- | 1866- | 1930- | 1950- | 1950- | 1925- | 1930- | 1930- | 1950- | 1997- | 1998- |
| Arkansas | 1837- | 1837- | 1837- | 1957- | 1950- | 1950- | 1924- | 1957- | 1957- | 1950- | 1996- | 1996- |
| California | 1850- | 1850- | 1850- | 1930- | 1950- | 1950- | 1899- | 1930- | 1930- | 1950- | 1934- | 1996- |
| Colorado | 1864- | 1864- | 1864- | 1930- | 1856- | 1950- | 1924- | 1930- | 1930- | 1950- | 1998- | 1996- |
| Connecticut | 1785- | 1785- | j1814- | 1950- | 1900- | 1950- | 1899- | 1950- | 1950- | 1950- | 2000- | 2000- |
| Delaware | 1792- | 1814- | 1790- | 1950- | 1950- | 1950- | 1949- | 1950- | 1950- | 1950- | 1998- | 2000- |
| D.C. | 1942- | 1942- | 2004- | 1945- | 1950- | 1950- | 1942- | 1945- | 1945- | 1950- | 1998- | 1998- |
| Florida | 1846- | 1846- | 1846- | 1950- | 1950- | 1950- | 1925- | 1950- | 1950- | 1950- | 1995- | 1985- |
| Georgia | 1846- | 1846- | 1846- | 1940- | 1939- | 1950- | 1939- | 1940- | 1940- | 1950- | 2006- | 2008- |
| Hawaii | 1847- | 1847- | 1847- | 1930- | 1950- | 1950- | 1924- | 1930- | 1930- | 1950- | 1998- | 1998- |
| Idaho | 1866- | 1866- | 1866- | 1965- | 1890- | 1950- | 1922- | 1965- | 1965- | 1950- | 1998- | 2006- |
| Illinois | 1819- | 1819- | 1819- | 1985- | 1950- | 1950- | 1925- | 1985- | 1985- | 1950- | 1996- | 1996- |
| Indiana | 1817- | 1817- | 1817- | 1940- | 1925- | 1950- | 1923- | 1940- | 1940- | 1950- | 1998- | 1999- |
| Iowa | 1839- | 1855- | 1839- | 1995- | 1950- | 1950- | 1923- | 1995- | 1995- | 1950- | 1998- | 1998- |
| Kansas | 1858- | 1858- | 1858- | 1982- | 1945- | 1950- | 1949- | 1982- | 1982- | 1950- | 1997- | 1997- |

| | | | | | | | | | | | | |
|---|---|---|---|---|---|---|---|---|---|---|---|---|
| Kentucky | 1785- | 1785- | 1785- | 1945- | 1925- | 1950- | 1924- | 1945- | 1945- | 1950- | 1997- | 1999- |
| Louisiana | 1813- | 1809- | 1809- | 1980- | 1950- | 1950- | 1921- | 1980- | 1980- | 1950- | 1996- | 1996- |
| Maine | 1820- | 1820- | 1820- | 1996- | 1849- | 1950- | 1923- | 1996- | 1996- | 1950- | 1997- | 1997- |
| Maryland | 1787- | 1770- | 1851- | 1950- | 1950- | 1950- | 1899- | 1950- | 1950- | 1950- | 1995- | 1995- |
| Massachusetts | 1804- | 1804- | 1804- | 1930- | 1929- | 1950- | 1899- | 1930- | 1930- | 1950- | 1998- | Recent |
| Michigan | 1805- | 1843- | 1847- | 1930- | 1942- | 1950- | 1923- | 1930- | 1930- | 1950- | 1995- | 1942- |
| Minnesota | 1851- | 1851- | 1851- | 1930- | 1950- | 1950- | 1924- | 1930- | 1930- | 1950- | 1986- | Recent |
| Mississippi | 1818- | 1818- | 1818- | 1954- | 1919- | 1950- | 1924- | 1954- | 1954- | 1950- | 1985- | 1996- |
| Missouri | 1821- | 1821- | 1821- | 1960- | 1930- | 1950- | 1919- | 1960- | 1960- | 1950- | 1997- | 1997- |
| Montana | 1868- | 1868- | 1868- | 1993- | 1950- | 1950- | 1924- | 1993- | 1993- | 1950- | 1997- | 1988- |
| Nebraska | 1871- | 1871- | 1860- | 1965- | 1929- | 1950- | 1919- | 1965- | 1965- | 1950- | 1997- | last 90 days |
| Nevada | 1865- | 1865- | 1865- | 1950- | 1950- | 1950- | 1924- | 1950- | 1950- | 1950- | 1998- | last 90 days |
| New Hampshire | 1816- | 1816- | 1816- | 1930- | 1872- | 1950- | 1874- | 1930- | 1930- | 1950- | 1995- | 1996- |
| New Jersey | 1790- | 1790- | 1790- | 1930- | 1950- | 1950- | 1948- | 1930- | 1930- | 1950- | 1999- | 1994- |
| New Mexico | 1852- | 1852- | 1883- | 1930- | 1950- | 1950- | 1921- | 1930- | 1930- | 1950- | 1998- | 2001- |
| New York | 1799- | 1794- | 1796- | 1955- | 1950- | 1950- | 1924- | 1955- | 1955- | 1950- | 1992- | 1990- |
| N. Carolina | 1778- | 1778- | 1778- | 1945- | 1939- | 1950- | 1778- | 1945- | 1945- | 1950- | 1994- | 1997- |
| N. Dakota | 1867- | 1867- | 1890- | 1930- | 1950- | 1950- | 1924- | 1930- | 1930- | 1950- | 1996- | 1971- |
| Ohio | 1821- | 1821- | 1852- | 1950- | 1914- | 1950- | 1923- | 1950- | 1950- | 1950- | 1997- | 1992- |
| Oklahoma | 1890- | 1890- | 1890- | 1954- | 1890- | 1950- | 1934- | 1954- | 1954- | 1950- | 1934- | 1909- |
| Oregon | 1853- | 1847- | 1853- | 1950- | 1939- | 1950- | 1924- | 1950- | 1950- | 1950- | 1998- | 1998- |
| Pennsylvania | 1754- | 1791- | 1845- | 1950- | 1950- | 1950- | 1924- | 1950- | 1950- | 1950- | 1997- | 1996- |
| Rhode Island | 1828- | 1828- | 1828- | 1950- | 1828- | 1950- | 1828- | 1950- | 1950- | 1950- | 1997- | 1999- |
| S. Carolina | 1868- | 1868- | 1868- | 1996- | 1899- | 1950- | 1900- | 1996- | 1996- | 1950- | 1998- | 1997- |
| S. Dakota | 1867- | 1867- | 1890- | 1965- | 1950- | 1950- | 1949- | 1965- | 1965- | 1950- | 1996- | 1996- |
| Tennessee | 1811- | 1791- | 1791- | 1950- | 1950- | 1950- | 1925- | 1950- | 1950- | 1950- | 1995- | 1995- |
| Texas | 1840- | 1840- | 1846- | 1950- | 1924- | 1950- | 1890- | 1950- | 1950- | 1950- | 1998- | 1998- |
| Utah | 1861- | 1861- | 1873- | 1950- | 1939- | 1950- | 1923- | 1950- | 1950- | 1950- | 1996- | 1996- |
| Vermont | 1789- | 1826- | 1826- | 1930- | 1929- | 1950- | 1924- | 1930- | 1930- | 1950- | 1997- | 1994- |
| Virginia | 1729- | 1730- | 1790- | 1930- | 1950- | 1950- | 1931- | 1930- | 1930- | 1950- | 1995- | 1995- |
| Washington | 1854- | 1854- | 1889- | 1935- | 1854- | 1950- | 1925- | 1935- | 1935- | 1950- | 1997- | last 90 days |
| West Virginia | 1864- | 1864- | 1864- | 1991- | 1864- | 1950- | 1923- | 1991- | 1991- | 1950- | 1991- | 1991- |
| Wisconsin | 1839- | 1839- | 1839- | 1945- | 1950- | 1950- | 1939- | 1945- | 1945- | 1950- | 1995- | 1995- |
| Wyoming | 1870- | 1870- | 1870- | 1993- | 1950- | 1950- | 1924- | 1993- | 1993- | 1950- | 1996- | 1990- |

# THE DEATH PENALTY AND THE STATES

**States That Have
Capital Punishment Statutes**

Alabama
Arizona
Arkansas
California
Colorado
Connecticut
Delaware
Florida
Georgia
Idaho
Indiana
*Kansas
Kentucky
Louisiana
Maryland
Mississippi
Missouri
Montana
Nebraska
Nevada
New Hampshire
North Carolina
Ohio
Oklahoma
Oregon
Pennsylvania
South Carolina
South Dakota
Tennessee
Texas
Utah
Virginia
Washington
Wyoming
U.S. Government
U.S. Military

**States That Do Not Have
Capital Punishment Statutes**
(with year abolished)

Alaska (1957)
District of Columbia (1981)
Hawaii (1948)
Illinois (2011)
Iowa (1965)
Maine (1887)
Massachusetts (1984)
Michigan (1846)
Minnesota (1911)
New Jersey (2007)
New Mexico (2009)
New York (2007)
North Dakota (1973)
Rhode Island (1984)
Vermont (1964)
West Virginia (1965)
Wisconsin (1853)

* Kansas statute was declared unconstitutional in 2004.

# RECORD OF PASSAGE OF UNIFORM AND MODEL ACTS, AS OF SEPTEMBER 30, 2011

Legend:
- ● Amended Version Enacted
- ■ Substantially Similar
- ★ Enacted

Column headers (left to right): Wyoming, Wisconsin, West Virginia, Washington, Virginia, Vermont, Utah, U.S. Virgin Islands, Texas, Tennessee, South Dakota, South Carolina, Rhode Island, Puerto Rico, Pennsylvania, Oregon, Oklahoma, Ohio, North Dakota, North Carolina, New York, New Mexico, New Jersey, New Hampshire, Nevada, Nebraska, Montana, Missouri, Mississippi, Minnesota, Michigan, Massachusetts, Maryland, Maine, Louisiana, Kentucky, Kansas, Iowa, Indiana, Illinois, Idaho, Hawaii, Georgia, Florida, District of Columbia, Delaware, Connecticut, Colorado, California, Arkansas, Arizona, Alaska, Alabama

## Table I – Uniform Acts

| Count | Act |
| --- | --- |
| 46 | Anatomical Gift (2006) (2007) |
| 15 | Arbitration (2000) |
| 3 | Assignment of Rents (2005) |
| 42 | Athlete Agents (2000) |
| 53 | Attendance of Out of State Witnesses (1931) (1936) |
| 0 | Business Organizations Code (2011) |
| 0 | Certificate of Title (2005) (2006) |
| 0 | Certificate of Title for Vessels (2011) |
| 8 | Certification of Questions of Law (1995) |
| 12 | Child Abduction Prevention (2006) |
| 51 | Child Custody Jurisdiction and Enforcement (1997) |
| 3 | Collaborative Law (2009) (2010) |
| 1 | Collateral Consequences of Conviction (2009) (2010) |
| 53 | Commercial Code (1951) (1957) (1962) (1966) |
| 41 | Commercial Code – Article 1 (2001) |
| 51 | Commercial Code – Article 2A (1987) (1990) |
| 52 | Commercial Code – Article 3 (1990) |
| 10 | Commercial Code – Article 3 (2002) |
| 52 | Commercial Code – Article 4 (1990) |
| 10 | Commercial Code – Article 4 (2002) |
| 53 | Commercial Code – Article 4A (1989) |
| 52 | Commercial Code – Article 5 (1995) |
| 51 | Commercial Code – Article 6 (1989) |
| 40 | Commercial Code – Article 7 (2003) |
| 53 | Commercial Code – Article 8 (1977) (1994) |
| 53 | Commercial Code – Article 9 (1972) (1999) |
| 9 | Commercial Code – Article 10 (2010) |
| 1 | Common Interest Owners Bill of Rights (2008) |
| 3 | Common Interest Ownership (2008) |
| 2 | Computer Information Transactions (1999) (2000) (2002) |
| 16 | Condominium (1977) (1980) |
| 25 | Conservation Easement (1981) |
| 47 | Controlled Substances (1970)(1974) |
| 20 | Custodial Trust (1987) |
| 8 | Debt-Management Services (2005) (2008) (2011) |
| 45 | Declaratory Judgments (1922) |
| 43 | Determination of Death (1978) (1980) |
| 14 | Disposition of Community Property Rights at Death (1971) |
| 36 | Division of Income for Tax Purposes (1957) (1966) |
| 0 | Electronic Legal Materials (2011) |
| 1 | Electronic Recordation of Custodial Interrogations (2010) |
| 49 | Electronic Transactions (1999) |
| 14 | Emergency Volunteer Health Practitioners (2006) (2007) |
| 50 | Enforcement of Foreign Judgments (1948) (1964) |
| 25 | Environmental Covenants (2003) |
| 1 | Faithful Presidential Electors (2010) |
| 36 | Federal Lien Registration (1978) (1982) |
| 17 | Foreign-Country Money Judgments Recognition (2005) |
| 24 | Foreign Money Claims (1989) |
| 44 | Fraudulent Transfer (1984) |
| 9 | Health-Care Decisions (1993) |
| 20 | Interstate Depositions and Discovery (2007) |
| 19 | Interstate Enforcement of Domestic-Violence Protection Orders (2000) (2002) |

# RECORD OF PASSAGE OF UNIFORM AND MODEL ACTS

Column headers (left to right): Wyoming, Wisconsin, West Virginia, Washington, Virginia, Vermont, Utah, U.S. Virgin Islands, Texas, Tennessee, South Dakota, South Carolina, Rhode Island, Puerto Rico, Pennsylvania, Oregon, Oklahoma, Ohio, North Dakota, North Carolina, New York, New Mexico, New Jersey, New Hampshire, Nevada, Nebraska, Montana, Missouri, Mississippi, Minnesota, Michigan, Massachusetts, Maryland, Maine, Louisiana, Kentucky, Kansas, Iowa, Indiana, Illinois, Idaho, Hawaii, Georgia, Florida, District of Columbia, Delaware, Connecticut, Colorado, California, Arkansas, Arizona, Alaska, Alabama.

Legend:
- ● Amended Version Enacted
- ■ Substantially Similar
- ★ Enacted

## Table I - Uniform Acts (Continued)

| # | WY | WI | WV | WA | VA | VT | UT | VI | TX | TN | SD | SC | RI | PR | PA | OR | OK | OH | ND | NC | NY | NM | NJ | NH | NV | NE | MT | MO | MS | MN | MI | MA | MD | ME | LA | KY | KS | IA | IN | IL | ID | HI | GA | FL | DC | DE | CT | CO | CA | AR | AZ | AK | AL | Act |
|---|----|----|----|----|----|----|----|----|----|----|----|----|----|----|----|----|----|----|----|----|----|----|----|----|----|----|----|----|----|----|----|----|----|----|----|----|----|----|----|----|----|----|----|----|----|----|----|----|----|----|----|----|----|-----|
| 10 | | ★ | | | | | | ★ | | | | ★ | | | | | ★ | | | | | ★ | | | ★ | | | | | ★ | | | ★ | | | | | | ★ | | | | | | | | ★ | | | | | | | Interstate Family Support (2008) |
| 0 | | | | | | | | | | | | | | | | | | | | | | | | | | | | | | | | | | | | | | | | | | | | | | | | | | | | | | Law Enforcement Access to Entity Information (2009) |
| 5 | | | | | | | ★ | | | | | | | | | | | ★ | | | | | | | | | ★ | | | | | | | | | | | | | | | | | | | ★ | | ★ | | | | | | Limited Cooperative Association (2007) |
| 4 | ★ | | | | | | ★ | | | | | | | | | | | | | | | | | | | | ★ | | | | | | | ★ | | ★ | | | | | | | | | | | ★ | | | | | | | Limited Liability Company (2006) |
| 19 | | | | ★ | | | ★ | | | | | | | | | | | | | ★ | | ★ | | | | ★ | | ★ | | ★ | | | | ★ | | ★ | | ★ | ★ | | ★ | | | ★ | ★ | | | ★ | ★ | | | | ★ | Limited Partnership (2001) |
| 11 | | | | ★ | | | ★ | ★ | | | | | ★ | | | | | | | | ★ | | | | | ★ | | | | ★ | | | | | | ★ | | ★ | | ★ | | | ★ | | | ★ | | | | | | | | Mediation (2001) (2003) |
| 6 | | | | | | | ★ | | | | | | | | | | | ★ | | | ★ | ★ | | | | ★ | | | | ★ | | | | | | | | | | | | | | | | ★ | | | | | | | Military and Overseas Voters (2010) |
| 8 | | | | ★ | | ★ | | ● | ★ | | | | | | | ■ | | | | | | | | | | | | | | | | | | ★ | | | | | | | | | | | | ● | | ● | | | | | Money Services (2000) (2004) |
| 1 | | | | | | | | | | | | | | | | | | | | ★ | | | | | | | | | | | | | | | | | | | | | | | | | | | | | | | | | | Notarial Acts (2010) |
| 9 | ● | | | ★ | | | ● | | ● | | ● | | | | | ● | | | | ● | | | ● | | | | | | | | | | | | | | | | | | | | | | | | ● | | | | | | ★ | Parentage (2000) (2002) |
| 1 | | | | | | | | | | | | | | | | | | | | | ★ | | | | | | | | | | | | | | | | | | | | | | | | | | | | | | | | | Partition of Heirs Property (2010) |
| 40 | ★ | | ★ | ★ | ★ | | ★ | ★ | ★ | ★ | ■ | ■ | | ★ | | ★ | ★ | | ★ | ★ | | ★ | ★ | ★ | | ■ | | ★ | | ★ | ★ | | ★ | | ★ | ★ | | ★ | | ★ | ★ | | ★ | ★ | ★ | ★ | ★ | | ★ | ★ | ★ | ★ | ★ | Partnership (1994) (1997) |
| 27 | | ■ | | ★ | | ★ | | ★ | | ★ | | ★ | | | ★ | | ★ | | ★ | | | ★ | ★ | | ★ | | | ★ | | ★ | ★ | | | ★ | | ★ | | ★ | ★ | ★ | ★ | ★ | | ★ | | ★ | ★ | ■ | | ★ | ★ | ★ | | Premarital Agreement (1983) |
| 44 | ★ | ★ | ● | ● | ● | | | | ● | | ● | | | | ★ | | | ● | ● | | ★ | ● | ● | ● | ● | | ● | | | ● | ● | ★ | ★ | | | ● | | ● | ● | ● | | | ★ | | ● | | | | ● | ● | ● | ● | ● | Principal and Income (1997) (2000) (2008) |
| 20 | | ■ | ★ | | | | | | | | ● | ● | | | ★ | | ★ | | ■ | | | ● | | | ● | ● | | | | ★ | | ★ | ★ | ● | | | | | | ★ | | ● | | | | | | ● | | | ★ | ★ | Probate Code (1969)(1975)(1982)(1989)(1990)(1991)(1997)(1998)(2003)(2008)(2010) |
| 22 | | | ★ | | ★ | | | ★ | | | | ★ | | | | | | ★ | | | ★ | | | | ★ | | ★ | ★ | | | | ★ | | ★ | ★ | | | | ★ | | | | | ★ | | | | ★ | ★ | | ★ | ★ | ★ | ★ | Testamentary Additions to Trusts (1991) *UPC Article II, 2-511 (1991)* |
| 20 | | ★ | | ★ | | | ★ | | | | | ★ | | | | | | ★ | | | | | | | ★ | ★ | ★ | | ★ | | | | ★ | | ★ | | | | ★ | ★ | | | | | ★ | | ★ | | ★ | ★ | ★ | ★ | ★ | Simultaneous Death (1991/1993) *UPC Article II, 2-702 (1991/1993)* |
| 28 | | | ★ | | ★ | | | | | | | | | | | | | ★ | | | | ★ | | | ★ | | | | | ★ | | ★ | ★ | | | | ★ | | | ★ | ★ | | ★ | | | ★ | | ★ | ★ | ★ | ★ | ★ | ★ | Disclaimer of Property Interests (1999/2002/2006) *UPC Article II, Part 11 (2002) (2006)* |
| 28 | | | ● | | ● | | | | | | | | | | | | | ● | | | | ★ | | | ● | | | | ★ | ★ | ★ | | | | ● | | | ● | | ● | | | ● | ● | ● | ● | | ● | | ● | ● | ● | ● | Statutory Rule Against Perpetuities (1986) 1990 *UPC Article II, Part 9 (1990)* |
| 18 | | | | | ★ | | | | | | | | | | | | | | | | | ★ | ★ | | | | ★ | ★ | | | | | ★ | ★ | | | | ★ | | | | | ★ | | | | ★ | ★ | ★ | | | | | International Wills (1977) *UPC Article II, Part 10 (1977)* |
| 7 | | | | ★ | | | | | | | | | | | | | | | | | | | | | | | | | | | | | | | ★ | | | | | | | | | ★ | | ★ | | | | ★ | | | | Estate Tax Apportionment (2003) *UPC Article III, Part 9A (2003)* |
| 19 | | | | | | | | ★ | ● | | | ★ | | | | ★ | | | | | ★ | | | | | | | | | ★ | | ● | | ● | | | | | | ● | ● | | | ★ | | ● | | | ■ | | | ● | | | ★ | ★ | ● | Guardianship and Protective Proceedings (1997) *UPC Article V, Parts 1-4 (1998)* |
| 30 | | | ★ | ★ | ★ | | ★ | ★ | | | ★ | | | ★ | ★ | | ★ | | | | ★ | | | | ★ | | | | ★ | ★ | ★ | ★ | | | ★ | | | | ★ | | ★ | ★ | ★ | ★ | | | | | ★ | ★ | | ★ | | ★ | ★ | ★ | ★ | Adult Guardianship and Protective Proceedings Jurisdiction (2007) *UPC Article V, Part 5A (2010)* |
| 12 | | ★ | | ★ | | ★ | | | | | ★ | | ★ | | | | | | | | | | | | ★ | | | ★ | | ★ | | ★ | | | | | | ■ | | ★ | | | | | | | ★ | | ★ | | | ★ | Power of Attorney (2006) *UPC Article V, Part 5B (2010)* |
| 11 | | | | | | | | | | | | ★ | | | | | | | | | | ★ | | | ★ | ● | | | | | ★ | | | | | | | ★ | | | | | | | | | | | ★ | | | ★ | ★ | ★ | | Nonprobate Transfers on Death (1989) (1998) *UPC Article VI, Parts 1-3 (1989) (1998)* |
| 13 | | | | | | | | | | | ★ | | | ■ | | | | | | | | | ★ | | | ★ | | | | | ★ | ★ | | | | | | ★ | | | | | | | | | | ★ | ★ | | | ★ | ★ | ★ | ★ | Multiple-Person Accounts (1989) (1998) *UPC Article VI, Part 2 (1989)* |
| 50 | ★ | ★ | ★ | ★ | ★ | | | | ★ | ★ | | ★ | ★ | | ★ | | ★ | ★ | ★ | | ★ | | | | ★ | ★ | | ★ | ★ | ★ | ★ | ★ | | | | ■ | | | ★ | ★ | ★ | ★ | ★ | | ★ | ★ | ★ | ★ | ★ | ★ | ★ | ★ | ★ | TOD Security Registration (1989) (1998) *UPC Article VI, Part 3 (1989) (1998)* |
| 5 | | | | | | | | | | | | | | | | | | | | | | ★ | | | | | ★ | | | | | | ★ | | | | | | ★ | | | | | | | ★ | | | | | | | | | Real Property Transfer on Death (2009) *UPC Article VI, Part 4 (2010)* |
| 0 | | | | | | | | | | | | | | | | | | | | | | | | | | | | | | | | | | | | | | | | | | | | | | | | | | | | | | Protection of Genetic Information in Employment (2010) |
| 45 | ★ | ★ | ★ | ★ | ★ | | | | ★ | ★ | ★ | ★ | ★ | | ★ | ★ | | | ★ | ★ | | ★ | ★ | ★ | | ★ | ★ | | ★ | ★ | ★ | ★ | ★ | ★ | | ★ | ■ | ★ | | | ★ | ★ | ★ | ★ | ★ | | ★ | ★ | ★ | ★ | ★ | ★ | ★ | Prudent Investor (1994) |
| 50 | ★ | ★ | ★ | ★ | ★ | | | | ★ | ★ | ★ | ★ | ★ | | ★ | ★ | | | ★ | ★ | | ★ | ★ | ★ | ■ | ★ | ★ | | ★ | ★ | ★ | ★ | ★ | | | ★ | ★ | ■ | ★ | ★ | ★ | ★ | ★ | ★ | ★ | ★ | | ★ | ★ | ★ | ★ | ★ | ★ | Prudent Management of Institutional Funds (2006) |
| 27 | | ★ | | ★ | ★ | | | | ★ | ★ | ★ | | ★ | | | | | | ★ | | | | ★ | | ★ | ■ | ★ | ★ | | ★ | | | | ★ | | ★ | | | | ★ | | ★ | ★ | ★ | ★ | ★ | ★ | | | ★ | ★ | | ★ | Real Property Electronic Recording (2004) (2005) |
| 0 | | | | | | | | | | | | | | | | | | | | | | | | | | | | | | | | | | | | | | | | | | | | | | | | | | | | | | Representation of Children in Abuse, Neglect, and Custody Proceedings (2006) (2007) |
| 21 | | | | ■ | ★ | | | | | | ★ | | ★ | ★ | | | ★ | ★ | | | | | | ★ | | | | | ★ | ★ | | ★ | | ★ | | | | ★ | ★ | | | | | ★ | ★ | | ★ | | | | | ★ | ★ | Residential Landlord and Tenant (1972)(1974) |
| 18 | | ★ | | | | ★ | | ★ | ★ | | ★ | | | | ★ | | | | | | | | | ★ | | | | | ★ | ★ | | ★ | ★ | | ★ | | ★ | ★ | | ★ | | | ★ | ★ | | | | | | | | | | Securities (2002) |
| 1 | | | | | | | | | | | | | | | | | | | | | | | | | | | | | | | | | | | | | | | | | | | | | | | ★ | | | | | | | Statutory Trust Entity (2009) |
| 48 | ● | ● | ● | ● | ● | | | | ● | ● | | ● | | | ● | ● | | ★ | ★ | ● | ● | ● | | | ● | | ● | | ● | ● | ● | ● | ● | | ● | | | ● | ● | ★ | | | ● | ● | ● | ● | ● | | ● | ★ | ● | ● | ● | Trade Secrets (1979) (1985) |
| 50 | ● | ● | ★ | ● | ● | | | | ● | ● | ● | ● | | ● | ★ | | ● | ● | ★ | ● | ■ | ● | ● | ● | ● | ● | ● | | ★ | ★ | ● | ● | ● | ● | | ● | ● | ● | ● | ★ | ★ | ● | ● | ● | ● | ● | | ● | ★ | ● | ● | ● | ● | Transfers to Minors (1983) (1986) |
| 24 | | ★ | | ★ | | ★ | | ★ | ★ | | ★ | ★ | | ★ | | | ★ | | ★ | ★ | | ★ | ★ | ★ | | ★ | | ★ | | ★ | ★ | | ★ | | ★ | | | | ★ | | | | | ★ | ★ | | | | ★ | ★ | | ★ | ★ | ★ | Trust Code (2000) (2001) (2003) (2004) (2005) |
| 4 | | | | | | | | | | | | | | | | | | | | | ★ | | | | ★ | | | | | | | | ★ | | | | | | | | | | ★ | | | | | | ★ | | | | | UTC Insurable Interest Amendment (2010) |
| 16 | | | ★ | | | | ★ | | ★ | | ★ | | | | | | ★ | | ★ | | | | ★ | | | ★ | | ★ | | | ★ | | ★ | ★ | | ★ | | ★ | | | | | ★ | | | | | | | ★ | ★ | | ★ | Unclaimed Property (1995) |
| 4 | | | | | | | | | | | | | | | | | | | | | ★ | | | | | | ★ | | | | | | | ★ | | | | | | | | ★ | | | | | ★ | | | | ★ | | | Unincorporated Nonprofit Association (2008) |
| 15 | | ★ | | ★ | | | ★ | | | | ★ | | ★ | | | | | | | | ★ | | ★ | | | ★ | | ★ | ★ | | | ★ | | | | | | ★ | | | | | | | ★ | ★ | ★ | | ★ | | | | ★ | Unsworn Foreign Declarations (2008) |

# RECORD OF PASSAGE OF UNIFORM AND MODEL ACTS

Legend:
- ● Amended Version Enacted
- ■ Substantially Similar
- ★ Enacted

Column headers (states, read top to bottom), left to right:
Wyoming, Wisconsin, West Virginia, Washington, Virginia, Vermont, Utah, U.S. Virgin Islands, Texas, Tennessee, South Dakota, South Carolina, Rhode Island, Puerto Rico, Pennsylvania, Oregon, Oklahoma, Ohio, North Dakota, North Carolina, New York, New Mexico, New Jersey, New Hampshire, Nevada, Nebraska, Montana, Missouri, Mississippi, Minnesota, Michigan, Massachusetts, Maryland, Maine, Louisiana, Kentucky, Kansas, Iowa, Indiana, Illinois, Idaho, Hawaii, Georgia, Florida, District of Columbia, Delaware, Connecticut, Colorado, California, Arkansas, Arizona, Alaska, Alabama

## Table II – Model Acts
(Uniformity not necessary but helpful if state desires legislation on the subject)

| Count | Act |
|---|---|
| 1 | Adoption (1994) |
| 3 | Anti-Discrimination (1966) |
| 0 | Apportionment of Tort Responsibility (2002) (2003) |
| 3 | Audio-Visual Deposition (1978) |
| 3 | Child Witness Testimony by Alternative Methods (2002) |
| 4 | Class Actions (1976) (1987) |
| 1 | Construction Lien (1987) |
| 10 | Consumer Credit Code (1968) (1974) |
| 1 | Consumer Leases (2001) |
| 3 | Consumer Sales Practices (1970) (1971) |
| 3 | Controlled Substances (1990)(1994) |
| 1 | Correction or Clarification of Defamation (1993) |
| 0 | Criminal Procedure, Rules of (1974) (1987) |
| 1 | Discovery of Electronically Stored Information (2007) |
| 2 | Dormant Mineral Interests (1986) |
| 0 | Drug Dependence Treatment and Rehabilitation (1973) |
| 2 | Eminent Domain Code (1974) |
| 0 | Employment Termination (1991) |
| 2 | Entity Transactions (2005) (2007) |
| 34 | Evidence, Rules of (1953) (1974/1986/1988) |
| 1 | Evidence, Rules of (1999) |
| 1 | Exemptions (1976) (1979) |
| 1 | Extradition and Rendition (1980) |
| 1 | Insanity Defense and Post-Trial Disposition (1984) |
| 9 | Land Sales Practices (1966) |
| 2 | Management of Public Employee Retirement Systems (1997) |
| 8 | Mandatory Disposition of Detainers (1958) |
| 1 | Marital Property (1983) |
| 1 | Marketable Title (1990) |
| 8 | Marriage and Divorce (1970) (1973) |
| 6 | Minor Student Capacity to Borrow (1969) |
| 0 | Motor Vehicle Accident Reparations (1972) |
| 0 | Nonjudicial Foreclosure (2002) |
| 0 | Periodic Payment of Judgments (1990) |
| 1 | Planned Community (1980) |
| 1 | Post-Conviction Procedure (1980) |
| 0 | Protection of Charitable Assets (2011) |
| 0 | Punitive Damages (1996) |
| 1 | Real Estate Cooperative (1981) |
| 5 | Real Estate Time-Share (1980) (1982) |
| 11 | Registered Agents (2006) |
| 2 | Residential Mortgage Satisfaction (2004) |
| 0 | State Administrative Procedure (2010) |
| 1 | Statute and Rule Construction (1995) |
| 0 | Surface Use and Mineral Development Accommodation (1990) |
| 7 | Transboundary Pollution Reciprocal Access (1982) |
| 0 | Transfer of Litigation (1991) |
| 1 | Victims of Crime (1992) |
| 0 | Wage Withholding and Unemployment Insurance Procedure (2004) |

## Table III – Other Acts
(Recommended for consideration in states having need for legislation in field involved)

| Count | Act |
|---|---|
| 13 | Act to Provide for the Appointment of Commissioners (1944) |
| 10 | Alcoholism and Intoxication Treatment (1971) |
| 0 | Commercial Code – Article 2 (2003) |
| 0 | Commercial Code – Article 2A (2003) |
| 3 | Comparative Fault (1977) (1979) |
| 1 | Criminal History Records (1986) |
| 7 | Duties to Persons with Medical ID Devices (1972) |
| 23 | Facsimile Signatures of Public Officials (1958) |
| 1 | Information Practices Code (1980) |
| 0 | Land Transactions (1975) (1977) (1983) |
| 0 | Simplification of Land Transfers (1976) (1977) (1983) (1990) |
| 13 | Vendor and Purchaser Risk (1935) |

# INTERNATIONAL INFORMATION

## SELECTED INTERNATIONAL GOVERNMENTAL ORGANIZATIONS

Inter-American Development Bank
1300 New York Avenue, NW
Washington, DC 20577
(202) 623-1000
FAX (202) 623-3096
www.iadb.org

International Atomic Energy Agency
P.O. Box 100
Wagramer Strasse 5
A-1400 Vienna, Austria
(431) 2600-0
FAX (431) 2600-7
www.iaea.org

Intl. Centre for Settlement of Investment Disputes
1818 H St., NW
Washington, DC 20433
(202) 458-1534
FAX (202) 522-2615
www.worldbank.org/icsid

International Chamber of Commerce
38, Cours Albert 1er
75008 Paris, France
+33(1) 49532828
FAX +33(1) 49532859
www.iccwbo.org

International Court of Justice
Peace Palace
2517 KJ The Hague, Netherlands
31 (0) (70) 302-2323
FAX 31 (0) (70) 364-9928
www.icj-cij.org

International Finance Corporation
2121 Pennsylvania Ave. NW
Washington, DC 20433
(202) 473-1000
FAX (202) 974-4384
www.ifc.org

International Monetary Fund
700 19th St., NW
Washington, DC 20431
(202) 623-7000
FAX (202) 623-4661
www.imf.org

North Atlantic Treaty Organization
Blvd. Leopold III
1110 Brussels, Belgium
www.nato.int

Organization of American States
17th St. & Constitution Ave., NW
Washington, DC 20006
(202) 458-3000
FAX (202) 458-3967
www.oas.org

Organization for Economic Cooperation and
  Development
2, rue André Pascal
F-75775 Paris Cedex 16, France
(33) 01 45248200;  FAX (33) 01 45248500
2001 L Street, NW, Suite 650
Washington, DC 20036-4922
(202) 785-6323; FAX (202) 785-0350
www.oecd.org / www.oecdwash.org

United Nations
760 United Nations Plaza
New York, NY 10017
(212) 963-1234
FAX (212) 758-2718
www.un.org

The World Bank
1818 H Street, NW
Washington, DC 20433
(202) 473-1000
FAX (202) 477-6391
www.worldbank.org

World Health Organization
20 Avenue Appia
1211 Geneva 27, Switzerland
(41-22) 791-2111
FAX (41-22) 791-3111
www.who.int

World Intellectual Property Organization
34, chemin des Colombettes
CH- 1211 Geneva 20, Switzerland
(4122) 338-9111
FAX (4122) 733-5428
www.wipo.int

World Trade Organization
Rue de Lausanne 154
CH-1211 Geneva 21, Switzerland
(4122) 7395111
FAX (4122) 7314206
www.wto.org

# EUROPEAN UNION

## MEMBER COUNTRIES

| | | |
|---|---|---|
| Austria | Greece | Portugal |
| Belgium | Hungary | Romania |
| Bulgaria | Ireland | Slovakia |
| Cyprus | Italy | Slovenia |
| Czech Republic | Latvia | Spain |
| Denmark | Lithuania | Sweden |
| Estonia | Luxembourg | United Kingdom |
| Finland | Malta | |
| France | Netherlands | |
| Germany | Poland | |

### UNION INSTITUTIONS

European Commission
200 rue de la Loi
B-1049 Brussels, Belgium
(32-2) 299-1111
FAX (32-2) 295-0138
europa.eu

Committee of the Regions of the EU
Rue Belliard, 99-101
B-1040 Brussels, Belgium
Tel. (32-2) 282-2211
FAX (32-2) 282-2325
www.cor.europa.eu

Council of the European Union
Rue de la Loi 175
B-1048 Brussels, Belguim
(32-2) 281-6111
FAX (32-2) 281-6934
www.consilium.europa.eu

Court of Justice of the EC
Cour de Justice
L-2925 Luxembourg
Tel. (352) 4303-1
FAX (352) 43-03-2600
curia.europa.eu

European Court of Auditors
12, rue Alcide de Gaspari
L-1615 Luxembourg
Tel. (352) 43-98-4398-1
FAX (352) 43-98-46410
www.eca.europa.eu

Economic and Social Committee
99, rue Belliard
B-1040 Brussels, Belgium
Tel. (32-2) 546-9011
FAX (32-2) 513-4893
eesc.europa.eu

European Ombudsman
1 Ave. du President Robert Schuman, CS 30403
F-67001 Strasbourg Cedex, France
Tel. (33-3) 8817-2313
FAX (33-3) 8817-9062
www.ombudsman.europa.eu

European Investment Bank
100 blvd. Konrad Adenauer
L-2950 Luxembourg
Tel. (352) 43791
FAX (352) 437704
www.eib.org

European Central Bank
Kaiserstrasse 29
60311 Frankfurt am Main, Germany
Tel. (49-69) 13440
FAX (49-69) 13446000
www.ecb.int/

European Parliament
Allee du Printemps, BP 1024/F
F-67070 Strasbourg Cedex, France
Tel. (33-3) 8817-4001
FAX (33-3) 8817-5184
www.europarl.europa.eu

Office for Official Publications of the EC
2, rue Mercier
L-2985 Luxembourg
Tel. (352) 2929-1
FAX (352) 44637
publications.europa.eu

European Data Protection Supervisor
Rue Wiertz 60
B-1047 Brussels, Belgium
Tel. (32-2) 283-1900
FAX (32-2) 283-1950
www.edps.europa.int

# UNITED NATIONS

## GENERAL ASSEMBLY

The General Assembly is composed of all 193 United Nations Member States.

## SECURITY COUNCIL

The Security Council has 15 members. The United Nations Charter designates five States as permanent members, and the General Assembly elects 10 other members for two-year terms. The term of office for each non-permanent member of the Council ends on December 31 of the year indicated in parentheses next to its name.

The five permanent members of the Security Council are China, France, Russian Federation, the United Kingdom and the United States.

The 10 non-permanent members of the Council in 2011are Bosnia and Herzegovina (2011), Brazil (2011), Colombia (2012), Gabon (2011), Germany (2012), India (2012), Lebanon (2011), Nigeria (2011), Portugal (2012) and South Africa (2012).

## ECONOMIC AND SOCIAL COUNCIL

The Economic and Social Council has 54 members, elected for three-year terms by the General Assembly. The term of office for each member expires on December 31 of the year in parentheses next to its name. Voting in the Council is by simple majority; each member has one vote. In 2011the Council is composed of the following 54 States:

| | | |
|---|---|---|
| Argentina (2012) | Ghana (2012) | Pakistan (2013) |
| Australia (2013) | Guatemala (2011) | Peru (2011) |
| Bahamas (2012) | Guinea-Bissau (2011) | Philippines (2012) |
| Bangladesh (2012) | Hungary (2013) | Qatar (2013) |
| Belgium (2012) | India (2011) | Republic of Korea (2013) |
| Cameroon (2013) | Iraq (2012) | Russian Federation (2013) |
| Canada (2012) | Italy (2012) | Rwanda (2012) |
| Chile (2012) | Japan (2011) | Saint Kitts and Nevis (2011) |
| China (2013) | Latvia (2013) | Saudi Arabia (2011) |
| Comoros (2012) | Malawi (2013) | Senegal (2013) |
| Cote d'Ivoire (2011) | Malta (2011) | Slovakia (2012) |
| Ecuador (2013) | Mauritius (2011) | Spain (2011) |
| Egypt (2012) | Mexico (2013) | Switzerland (2011) |
| Estonia (2011) | Mongolia (2012) | Ukraine (2012) |
| Finland (2013) | Morocco (2011) | United Kingdom (2013) |
| France (2011) | Namibia (2011) | United States (2012) |
| Gabon (2013) | Nicaragua (2013) | Venezuela (2011) |
| Germany (2011) | Norway (2013) | Zambia (2012) |

## INTERNATIONAL COURT OF JUSTICE

The International Court of Justice has 15 members, elected by both the General Assembly and the Security Council. Judges hold nine-year terms.

The current composition of the court is as follows: President Hisashi Owada (Japan); Vice-President Peter Tomka (Slovakia). Judges: Xue Hanqin (China), Abdul G. Koroma (Sierra Leone), Awn Shawkat Al-Khasawneh (Jordan), Joan E. Donoghue (United States of America), Bruno Simma (Germany), Ronny Abraham (France), Kenneth Keith (New Zealand), Bernardo Sepulveda-Amor (Mexico), Mohamed Bennouna (Morocco), Leonid Skotnikov (Russian Federation), Antonio A. Cancado Trindade (Brazil), Abdulqawi Ahmed Yusuf (Somalia) and Christopher Greenwood (United Kingdom of Great Britain and Northern Ireland)

The Registrar of the Court is Mr. Philippe Couvreur (Belgium).

## UNITED NATIONS SECRETARIAT

One United Nations Plaza, New York NY 10017, (212) 963-1234, http://www.un.org

*Secretary General* - Ban Ki-moon (Republic of Korea)
*Deputy Secretary* - Dr. Asha-Rose Migiro (Tanzania)

# COUNTRIES OF THE WORLD

| Country | Capital | Currency | Official language(s) |
|---------|---------|----------|----------------------|
| Afghanistan | Kabul | Afghani | Pashtu; Dari |
| Albania | Tirana | Lek | Albanian |
| Algeria | Algiers | Algerian Dinar | Arabic |
| American Samoa | Pago Pago | U.S. Dollar | Samoan; English; Tongan |
| Andorra | Andorra la Vella | Euro | Catalan |
| Angola | Luanda | Kwanza | Portuguese |
| Anguilla | The Valley | E. Caribbean Dollar | English |
| Antigua and Barbuda | St. John's | E. Caribbean Dollar | English |
| Argentina | Buenos Aires | Argentine Peso | Spanish |
| Armenia | Yerevan | Dram | Armenian |
| Aruba | Oranjestad | Aruban Guilder/Florin | Dutch; Papiamento; Spanish; English |
| Australia | Canberra | Australian Dollar | English |
| Austria | Vienna | Euro | German |
| Azerbaijan | Baku | Azerbaijani Manat | Azerbaijani (Azeri) |
| Bahamas, The | Nassau | Bahamian Dollar | English |
| Bahrain | Manama | Bahrain Dinar | Arabic |
| Bangladesh | Dhaka | Taka | Bangla |
| Barbados | Bridgetown | Barbadian Dollar | English |
| Belarus, | Minsk | Belarusian Ruble | Belarusian |
| Belgium | Brussels | Euro | Dutch, French |
| Belize | Belmopan | Belizan Dollar | English |
| Benin | Porto-Novo | Franc CFA | French |
| Bermuda | Hamilton | Bermudian Dollar | English |
| Bhutan | Thimphu | Ngultrum | Dzongkha |
| Bolivia | La Paz | Boliviano | Spanish; Quechua; Aymara |
| Bosnia and Herzogovina | Sarajevo | Konvertibilina Marka | Serbian, Croatian, Bosnian |
| Botswana | Gaborone | Pula | English |
| Brazil | Brasilia | Real | Portuguese |
| Brunei | Bandar Seri Begawan | Brunei Dollar | Malay |
| Bulgaria | Sofia | Lev | Bulgarian |
| Burkina Faso | Ouagadougou | Franc CFA | French |
| Burundi | Bujumbura | Burundi Franc | Kirundi; French |
| Cambodia | Phnom Penh | Riel | Khmer |
| Cameroon | Yaounde | Franc CFA | French; English |
| Canada | Ottawa, Ontario | Canadian Dollar | English; French |
| Cape Verde | Praia | Cape Verdean Escudo | Portuguese, Crioulo |
| Cayman Islands | George Town | Caymanian Dollar | English |
| Central African Rep. | Bangui | Franc CFA | French |
| Chad | N'Djamena | Franc CFA | French; Arabic |
| Chile | Santiago | Chilean Peso | Spanish |
| China, People's Republic of | Beijing | Yuan Renminbi | Mandarin |
| Christmas Island | The Settlement | Australian Dollar | English |
| Cocos (Keeling) Islands | West Island | Australian Dollar | Malay; English |
| Colombia | Bogota | Colombian Peso | Spanish |
| Comoros | Moroni | Comoran Franc | Arabic; French |
| Congo, Democratic Republic of | Kinshasa | Congolese Franc | French |
| Congo, Republic of | Brazzaville | Franc CFA | French |

# COUNTRIES OF THE WORLD

| Country | Capital | Currency | Official language(s) |
|---|---|---|---|
| Cook Islands | Avarua | New Zealand Dollar | English |
| Costa Rica | San Jose | Costa Rican Colon | Spanish |
| Croatia | Zagreb | Kuna | Croatian |
| Cuba | Havana | Cuban Peso | Spanish |
| Cyprus | Nicosia | Cypriot Pound, Euro | Greek; Turkish; English |
| Czech Republic | Prague | Czech Koruna | Czech |
| Denmark | Copenhagen | Danish Krone | Danish |
| Djibouti | Djibouti | Djiboutian Franc | Arabic; French |
| Dominica | Roseau | E. Caribbean Dollar | English |
| Dominican Republic | Santo Domingo | Dominican Peso | Spanish |
| Ecuador | Quito | U.S. Dollar | Spanish |
| Egypt | Cairo | Egyptian Pound | Arabic |
| El Salvador | San Salvador | U.S. Dollar | Spanish |
| Equatorial Guinea | Malabo | Franc CFA | Spanish; French |
| Eritrea | Asmara | Nakfa | Tigrinya; Tigre; Afar; Arabic; Kunama |
| Estonia | Tallinn | Estonian Kroon | Estonian |
| Ethiopia | Addis Ababa | Birr | Amarigna; English |
| Falkland Islands | Stanley | Falkland Pound | English |
| Faroe Islands | Torshavn | Danish Krone | Faroese; Danish |
| Fiji | Suva | Fijian Dollar | English; Fijian |
| Finland | Helsinki | Euro | Finnish; Swedish |
| France | Paris | Euro | French |
| French Polynesia | Papeete | Comptoirs Francais du Pacifique Franc | French |
| Gabon | Libreville | Franc CFA | French |
| Gambia | Banjul | Dalasi | English |
| Georgia, Rep. of | Tbilisi | Lari | Georgian |
| Germany | Berlin | Euro | German |
| Ghana | Accra | Ghana Cedi | English |
| Gibraltar | Gibraltar | Gibraltar Pound | English |
| Greece | Athens | Euro | Greek |
| Grenada | St. George's | E. Caribbean Dollar | English |
| Greenland | Nuuk | Danish Krone | Greenlandic; Danish; English |
| Guam | Hagatna | U.S. Dollar | English |
| Guatemala | Guatemala City | Quetzal | Spanish |
| Guinea | Conakry | Guinean Franc | French |
| Guinea-Bissau | Bissau | Franc CFA | Portuguese |
| Guyana | Georgetown | Guyanese Dollar | English |
| Haiti | Port-au-Prince | Gourde | French; Creole |
| Honduras | Tegucigalpa | Lempira | Spanish |
| Hong Kong | | HK Dollar | English; Chinese |
| Hungary | Budapest | Forint | Hungarian |
| Iceland | Reykjavik | Icelandic Krona | Icelandic |
| India | New Delhi | Indian Rupee | Hindi; English |
| Indonesia | Jakarta | Indonesian Rupiah | Bahasa Indonesian |
| Iran | Tehran | Iranian Rial | Persian |

# COUNTRIES OF THE WORLD

| Country | Capital | Currency | Official language(s) |
|---------|---------|----------|----------------------|
| Iraq | Baghdad | New Iraqi Dinar | Arabic |
| Ireland | Dublin | Euro | Irish; English |
| Israel | Jerusalem | New Israeli Shekel | Hebrew |
| Italy | Rome | Euro | Italian |
| Ivory Coast | Yamoussoukro | Franc CFA | French; African |
| | | | |
| Jamaica | Kingston | Jamaican Dollar | English |
| Japan | Tokyo | Yen | Japanese |
| Jordan | Amman | Jordanian Dinar | Arabic |
| | | | |
| Kazakhstan | Astana | Tenge | Kazakh; Russian |
| Kenya | Nairobi | Kenyan Shilling | English; Kiswahili |
| Kiribati | Tarawa | Australian Dollar | English |
| Korea, North | Pyongyang | North Korean Won | Korean |
| Korea, South | Seoul | South Korean Won | Korean |
| Kosovo | Pristina | Euro | Albanian; Serbian |
| Kuwait | Kuwait City | Kuwaiti Dinar | Arabic |
| Kyrgyzstan | Bishkek | Som | Kyrgyz; Russian |
| | | | |
| Laos | Vientiane | New Kip | Lao |
| Latvia, Rep. of | Riga | Lat | Latvian |
| Lebanon | Beirut | Lebanese Pound | Arabic |
| Lesotho | Maseru | Maloti; S. African Rand | English |
| Liberia | Monrovia | Liberian Dollar | English |
| Libya | Tripoli | Libyan Dinar | Arabic |
| Liechtenstein | Vaduz | Swiss franc | German |
| Lithuania, Rep. of | Vilnius | Litas | Lithuanian |
| Luxembourg | Luxembourg | Euro | Luxembourgish French; German |
| | | | |
| Macau | Macao | Pataca | Chinese |
| Macedonia | Skopje | Macedonian Denar | Macedonian; Albanian |
| Madagascar | Antananarivo | Ariary | Malagasy; French; English |
| Malawi | Lilongwe | Malawian Kwacha | Chichewa |
| Malaysia | Kuala Lumpur | Ringgit | Bahasa Malaysia |
| Maldives | Male | Rufiyaa | Dhivehi; English |
| Mali | Bamako | Franc CFA | French |
| Malta | Valletta | Euro | Maltese; English |
| Marshall Islands | Majuro | U.S. Dollar | Marshallese; English |
| Mauritania | Nouakchott | Ouguiya | Arabic; Wolof |
| Mauritius | Port Louis | Mauritian Rupee | English; Creole |
| Mayotte | Mamoudzou | Euro | French |
| Mexico | Mexico City | Mexican Peso | Spanish |
| Micronesia,Federated States of | Palikir | U.S. Dollar | English |
| Moldova | Chisinau | Moldovan Leu | Moldovan |
| Monaco | Monaco | Euro | French |
| Mongolia | Ulaanbaatar | Tugrik | Khalkha Mongol |
| Montenegro | Podgorica | Euro | Montenegrin |
| Montserrat | Plymouth | E. Caribbean Dollar | English |
| Morocco | Rabat | Moroccan Dirham | Arabic |
| Mozambique | Maputo | Metical | Portuguese |
| Myanmar | Yangon | Kyat | Burmese |

# COUNTRIES OF THE WORLD

| Country | Capital | Currency | Official language(s) |
|---|---|---|---|
| Namibia | Windhoek | Namibian Dollar | English; Afrikaans |
| Nauru | Yaren | Australian Dollar | Nauruan |
| Nepal | Kathmandu | Nepalese Rupee | Nepali |
| Netherlands | Amsterdam | Euro | Dutch; Frisian |
| New Caledonia | Noumea | Comptoirs Francais du Pacifique Franc | French |
| New Zealand | Wellington | New Zealand Dollar | English; Maor |
| Nicaragua | Managua | Gold Cordoba | Spanish |
| Niger | Niamey | Franc CFA | French |
| Nigeria | Abuja | Naira | English |
| Niue | Alofi | New Zealand Dollar | Niuean; English |
| Norfolk Island | Kingston | Australian Dollar | English |
| Northern Cyprus | Lefkosa | Turkish Lira | Turkish |
| Northern Mariana Islands | Saipan | U.S. Dollar | Philippine languages; Chinese |
| Norway | Oslo | Norwegian Krone | Norwegian |
| Oman | Muscat | Omani Rial | Arabic |
| Pakistan | Islamabad | Pakistani Rupee | Urdu; English |
| Palau | Melekeok | U.S. Dollar | English; Palauan |
| Panama | Panama City | Balboa; US Dollar | Spanish |
| Papua New Guinea | Port Moresby | Kina | English; Tok Pisin; Motu |
| Paraguay | Asuncion | Guarani | Spanish; Guarani |
| Peru | Lima | Nuevo Sol | Spanish; Quechua |
| Philippines | Manila | Philippine Peso | Filipino; English |
| Pitcairn Islands | Adamstown | New Zealand Dollar | English |
| Poland | Warsaw | Zloty | Polish |
| Portugal | Lisbon | Euro | Portuguese; Mirandese |
| Qatar | Doha | Qatari Rial | Arabic |
| Romania | Bucharest | "New" Leu | Romanian |
| Russia | Moscow | Russian Ruble | Russian |
| Rwanda | Kigali | Rwanda Franc | French; English Kinyarwanda |
| St. Kitts and Nevis | Basseterre | E. Caribbean Dollar | English |
| St. Helena | Jamestown | St. Helenian Pound | English |
| St. Lucia | Castries | E. Caribbean Dollar | English |
| St. Pierre and Miquelon | St. Pierre | Euro | French |
| St. Vincent and The Grenadines | Kingstown | E. Caribbean Dollar | English; French Patois |
| Samoa | Apia | Tala | Samoan; English |
| San Marino | San Marino | Euro | Italian |
| Sao Tome e Principe | Sao Tome | Dobra | Portuguese |
| Saudi Arabia | Riyadh | Saudi Rial | Arabic |
| Senegal | Dakar | Franc CFA | French |
| Serbia and Montenegro | Belgrade | Serbian Dinar | Serbian |
| Seychelles | Victoria | Seychelles Rupee | English; Creole |

# COUNTRIES OF THE WORLD

| Country | Capital | Currency | Official lamguage(s) |
|---|---|---|---|
| Sierra Leone | Freetown | Leone | English |
| Singapore | Singapore City | Singapore Dollar | Mandarin; English |
| Slovakia | Bratislava | Slovak Koruna | Slovak |
| Slovenia | Ljubljana | Euro | Slovenian |
| Solomon Islands | Honiara | Solomon Islands Dollar | English |
| Somalia | Mogadishu | Somali Shilling | Somali |
| South Africa, Rep. of | Pretoria | Rand | Isizulu; Isixhosa; Afrikaans; English |
| Spain | Madrid | Euro | Castilian Spanish |
| Sri Lanka | Colombo | Sri Lankan Rupee | Sinhala; Tamil |
| Sudan | Khartoum | Sudanese Pound | Arabic; English |
| Svalbard | Longyearbyen | Norwegian Krone | Norwegian; Russian |
| Suriname | Paramaribo | Surinam Dollar | Dutch; English |
| Swaziland | Mbabane | Lilangeni | English; siSwati |
| Sweden | Stockholm | Swedish Krona | Swedish |
| Switzerland | Bern | Swiss Franc | German; French; Italian; Romansch |
| Syria | Damascus | Syrian Pound | Arabic |
| Taiwan | Taipei | Taiwan Dollar | Mandarin |
| Tajikistan | Dushanbe | Somoni | Tajik |
| Tanzania | Dodoma | Tanzanian Shilling | English; Swahili |
| Thailand | Bangkok | Baht | Thai; English |
| Timor-Leste (East Timor) | Dili | U.S. Dollar | Tetum; Portuguese |
| Togo | Lome | Franc CFA | French |
| Tokelau | None | New Zealand Dollar | Tokelauan; English |
| Tonga | Nuku'alofa | Pa'anga | Tongan; English |
| Trinidad and Tobago | Port-of-Spain | Trinidad and Tobago Dollar | English |
| Tunisia | Tunis | Tunisian Dinar | Arabic |
| Turkey | Ankara | Turkish Lira | Turkish |
| Turkmenistan | Ashgabat | Turkmen Manat | Turkmen |
| Turks and Caicos Islands | Grand Turk | U.S. Dollar | English |
| Tuvalu | Funafuti | Australian Dollar | Tuvaluan; English; Samoan |
| Uganda | Kampala | Ugandan Shilling | English |
| Ukraine | Kiev | Hryvnia | Ukrainian |
| United Arab Emirates | Abu Dhabi | Emirati Dirham | Arabic |
| United Kingdom | London | British Pound | English; Welsh; Gaelic |
| United States | Washington, D.C. | U.S. Dollar | English |
| Uruguay | Montevideo | Uruguayan Peso | Spanish |
| Uzbekistan | Tashkent | Soum | Uzbek; Russian |
| Vanuatu | Port-Vila | Vatu | Bislama; English |
| Vatican City | | Euro | Italian; Latin |
| Venezuela | Caracas | Bolivar | Spanish |
| Vietnam | Hanoi | Dong | Vietnamese |
| Virgin Islands, British | Road Town | U.S. Dollar | English |
| Yemen | Sanaa | Yemeni Rial | Arabic |
| Zambia | Lusaka | Zambian Kwacha | English |
| Zimbabwe | Harare | Zimbabwean Dollar | English |

# CANADIAN COURT SYSTEM

Supreme Court of Canada
Supreme and Federal Courts Bldg.
301 Wellington Street
Ottawa, Ontario K1A 0J1
Canada
(613) 995-4330
FAX (613) 996-9138
www.scc-csc.gc.ca/

Federal Court of Canada
90 Elgin Street
Ottawa, Ontario K1A 0H9
Canada
(613) 992-4238
FAX (613) 952-3653
www.fct-cf.gc.ca/

Federal Court of Appeal
90 Elgin Street
Ottawa, Ontario K1A 0H9
Canada
(613) 996-6795
FAX (613) 952-7226
www.fca-caf.gc.ca/

Tax Court of Canada
200 Kent Street
Ottawa, Ontario K1A 0H9
Canada
(613) 992-0901
(800) 927-5499
FAX (613) 957-9034
www.tcc-cci.gc.ca/

Court Martial Appeal Court of
  Canada
Supreme and Federal Court Bldg.
Ottawa, Ontario K1A 0H9
Canada
(613) 996-6795
FAX (613) 941-9454
www.cacm-cmac.ca

## ALBERTA

Court of Appeal
Law Courts Bldg.
1A Sir Winston Churchill Square
Edmonton, T5J OR2
Canada
(780) 422-2416
FAX (780) 422-4127
www.albertacourts.ab.ca/ca/

Court of Queen's Bench
Law Courts Bldg.

1A Sir Winston Churchill Square
Edmonton, T5J OR2
Canada
(780) 422-2492
FAX (780) 427-9742
www.albertacourts.ab.ca/qb/

## BRITISH COLUMBIA

Court of Appeal
Law Courts
400-800 Hornby St.
Vancouver, V6Z 2C5
Canada
(604) 660-2468
FAX (604) 660-1951
www.courts.gov.bc.ca/Court_of_
  Appeal/index.aspx

Supreme Court
Law Courts
850 Burdett Ave.
Victoria, V8W 1B4
Canada
(250) 356-1478
FAX (250) 356-6279
www.courts.gov.bc.ca/supreme_
  court/index.aspx

## MANITOBA

Court of Appeal
Law Courts
100E, 408 York Avenue
Winnipeg, R3C OP9
Canada
(204) 945-2647
FAX (204) 948-2072
www.manitobacourts.mb.ca/

Court of Queen's Bench
Law Courts
408 York Avenue
Winnipeg, R3C OP9
Canada
(204) 945-0344
FAX (204) 948-2369
www.manitobacourts.mb.ca/

## NEW BRUNSWICK

Court of Appeal
Justice Bldg., Box 6000, Rm. 202
427 Queen Street
Fredericton, E3B 5H1
Canada

(506) 453-2452
FAX (506) 453-7921
www.gnb.ca/cour/

Court of Queen's Bench
Justice Bldg., Box 6000
427 Queen Street
Fredericton, E3B 1B7
Canada
(506) 453-2015
FAX (506) 444-5675
www.gnb.ca/cour/04CQB/
  index-e.asp

## NEWFOUNDLAND and
## LABRADOR

Court of Appeal
287 Duckworth Street
St. John's, A1C 5M3
Canada
(709) 729-0066
FAX (709) 729-7909
www.court.nl.ca/supreme/appeal/
  default.htm

Trial Division
309 Duckworth Street
St. John's, A1C 5M3
Canada
(709) 729-1137
FAX (709) 729-6623
www.court.nl.ca/supreme/trial/
  default.htm

## NORTHWEST TERRITORIES

Court of Appeal
Court House, Box 550
Yellowknife, X1A 2N4
Canada
(867) 873-7602
FAX (867) 873-0291
www.nwtcourts.ca/courts/ca.htm

Supreme Court
Court House, Box 550
Yellowknife, X1A 2N4
Canada
(867) 873-7105
FAX (867) 873-0287
www.nwtcourts.ca/courts/sc.htm

# CANADIAN COURT SYSTEM

## NOVA SCOTIA

Court of Appeal
The Law Courts
1815 Upper Water St.
Halifax, B3J 1S7
Canada
(902) 424-6937
FAX (902) 424-0646
www.courts.ns.ca/Appeals/
    index_ca.htm

Supreme Court
The Law Courts Bldg.
1815 Upper Water St.
Halifax, B3J 1S7
(902) 424-4900
FAX (902) 424-0524
www.courts.ns.ca/supreme/
    index_sc.htm

## ONTARIO

Court of Appeal
130 Queen Street West
Toronto, M5H 2N5
Canada
(416) 327-5020
FAX (416) 327-5032
www.ontariocourts.on.ca/coa/en/

Superior Court of Justice
130 Queen Street West
Toronto, M5H 2N5
Canada
(416) 327-5100
FAX (416) 327-6187
www.ontariocourts.on.ca/scj/en

## PRINCE EDWARD ISLAND

Supreme Court (Appeal and
    Trial Divs.)
Box 2000
42 Water Street
Charlottetown, C1A 7N8
Canada
(902) 368-4000
FAX (902) 368-0266
www.gov.pe.ca/courts/supreme/
    index.php3

## QUEBEC

Court of Appeal
Palais de Justice
100, rue Notre Dame E.
Montreal, H2Y 4B6
Canada
(514) 393-2022
FAX (514) 864-7270
www.justice.gouv.qc.ca

Superior Court
Palais de Justice
1, rue Notre Dame E.
Montreal, H2Y 1B6
Canada
(514) 393-2721
FAX (514) 873-4760
www.justice.gouv.qc.ca

## SASKATCHEWAN

Court of Appeal
Court House
2425 Victoria Avenue
Regina, S4P 3V7
Canada
(306) 787-5382
FAX (306) 787-0505
www.sasklawcourts.ca

Court of Queen's Bench
Court House
2425 Victoria Avenue
Regina, S4P 3V7
Canada
(306) 787-5377
FAX (306) 787-7217
www.sasklawcourts.ca

## YUKON

Court of Appeal of Yukon Territory
The Law Courts
2134 Second Ave.
Whitehorse, Y1A 5H6
Canada
(867) 667-3429
FAX (867) 393-6212
www.yukoncourts.ca/courts/
    appeal.html

Supreme Court of Yukon Territory
The Law Courts
P.O. Box 2703, J-3
Whitehorse, Y1A 5H6
Canada
(867) 667-5937
FAX (867) 393-6212
www.yukoncourts.ca/courts/
    supreme.html

Territorial Court of Yukon
    Territory
Box 2703, J-3E
Whitehorse, Y1A 2C6
Canada
(867) 667-5441
FAX (867) 393-6212
www.yukoncourts.ca/courts/
    territorial.html

Federal Court of Yukon Territory
Box 2703, J-3E
Whitehorse, Y1A 2C6
Canada
(867) 667-5441
FAX (867) 393-6212
www.yukoncourts.ca/courts/
    federal.html

# LAW LIBRARY SUPPLIERS DIRECTORY

## PUBLISHERS

This directory lists selected publishers of: legal and law related materials; books on library science; general reference works; and any materials of interest and usefulness to the legal researcher. Publishers of most state codes are included. For a more comprehensive listing of publishers, consult LEGAL LOOSELEAFS IN PRINT and LEGAL NEWSLETTERS IN PRINT (both are published annually).

Access Intelligence
4 Choke Cherry Rd., 2nd fl.
Rockville, MD 20850
(301) 354-2000
(800) 777-5006
FAX (301) 309-3847
www.accessintel.com

Alert Publications, Inc.
65 E. Scott St., #12E
Chicago, IL 60610
(312) 337-1362
FAX (312) 337-1388
www.alertpub.com

ALI-ABA Committee on Continuing
 Professional Education
4025 Chestnut St.
Philadelphia, PA 19104
(800) CLE-NEWS
FAX (215) 243-1664
www.ali-aba.org

American Arbitration Association
1633 Broadway, 10th fl.
New York, NY 10019
(212) 716-5870
(800) 778-7879
FAX (212) 716-5905
www.adr.org

American Bankers Association
1120 Connecticut Ave., NW
Washington, DC 20036
(202) 663-5378
(800) BANKERS
FAX (202) 828-4540
www.aba.com

American Bar Association
321 N. Clark St.
Chicago, IL 60610
(312) 988-5522
(800) 285-2221
FAX (312) 988-5528
www.americanbar.org

American Bar Foundation

750 N. Lake Shore Drive
Chicago, IL 60611
(312) 988-6500
(800) 285-2221
FAX (312) 988-6579
www.americanbarfoundation.org

American Enterprise Institute for
 Public Policy Research
1150 17th St., NW
Washington, DC 20036
(202) 862-5800
(800) 862-5801
FAX (202) 862-7177
www.aei.org

American Institute of Certified
 Public Accountants
1211 Ave. of the Americas
New York, NY 10036-8775
(212) 596-6200
(888) 777-7077
FAX (212) 596-6213
www.aicpa.org

ALM
120 Broadway, 5th fl.
New York, NY 10271
(800) 888-8300
FAX (646) 822-5146
www.alm.com

American Legal Publishing Corp.
432 Walnut Street, 12th fl.
Cincinnati, OH 45202
(800) 445-5588
FAX (513) 763-3562
www.amlegal.com

American Library Association
50 East Huron
Chicago, IL 60611
(312) 944-6780
(800) 545-2433
FAX (312) 440-9372
www.ala.org

American Society of International

Law
2223 Massachusetts Ave., NW
Washington, DC 20008
(202) 939-6000
FAX (202) 797-7133
www.asil.org

Aspen Publishers
76 Ninth Ave., 7th fl.
New York, NY 10011
(212) 771-0849
www.aspenpublishers.com

Atlantic Law Book Co.
22 Grassmere Ave.
West Hartford, CT 06110
(860) 231-9300
(800) 259-5534
FAX (860) 231-9242
www.atlanticlawbooks.com

Bernan
15200 NBN Way
Blue Ridge Summit, PA 17214
(301) 459-7666
(800) 865-3457
FAX (800) 865-3450
www.bernan.com

George T. Bisel Company, Inc.
710 South Washington Square
Philadelphia, PA 19106-3591
(215) 922-5760
(800) 247-3526
FAX (215) 922-2235
www.bisel.com

BNA
1801 S. Bell Street
Arlington, VA 22202
(703) 341-3500
(800) 372-1033
FAX (800) 253-0332
www.bna.com

Bradford Publishing
1743 Wazee St.
Denver, CO 80202

# PUBLISHERS

(303) 292-2590
(800) 446-2831
FAX (303) 298-5014
www.bradfordpublishing.com

BRB Publications, Inc.
P.O. Box 27869
Tempe, AZ 85285
(800) 929-3811
FAX (800) 929-4981
www.brbpublications.com

Bridge Publishing Group LLC
39 Concetta Court
Getzville, NY 14068
(716) 445-4852
(800) 758-3010
FAX (800) 758-3010
www.bridgepublishinggroup.com

The Brookings Institution
1775 Massachusetts Ave., NW
Washington, DC 20036
(202) 797-6000
FAX (202) 797-6004
www.brookings.edu

Business Publishers, Inc.
2222 Sedwick Drive, Suite 101
Durham, NC 27713
(800) 223-8720
www.bpinews.com

Cambridge University Press
32 Avenue of the Americas
New York, NY 10013
(212) 924-3900
FAX (212) 691-3239
www.cambridge.org/us

Canada Law Book
2075 Kennedy Blvd.
Toronto, Ontario, M1T 3V4
CANADA
(416) 609-3800
(800) 387-5351
FAX (416) 298-5082
www.canadalawbook.ca

Carolina Academic Press
700 Kent St.
Durham, NC 27701
(919) 489-7486
FAX (919) 493-5668
www.cap-press.com

Carroll Publishing
4701 Sangamore Rd., Suite S-155

Bethesda, MD 20816
(301) 263-9800
(800) 336-4240
FAX (301) 263-9801
www.carrollpub.com

Carswell
2075 Kennedy Road
Toronto, Ontario, M1T 3V4
CANADA
(416) 609-8000
(800) 387-5164; (800) 363-3783
FAX (416) 298-5094
www.carswell.com

CBA-CLE
1900 Grant St., 5th fl.
Denver, CO 80203
(303) 860-0608
(888) 860-2531
FAX (303) 894-0821
www.cobar.org/CLE

CCH, Inc.
2700 Lake Cook Road
Riverwoods, IL 60015
(847) 267-7000
(800) 344-3734
(888) 224-7377
FAX (773) 866-3726
www.cch.com

Cengage Learning
P.O. Box 6904
Florence, KY 41022
(800) 334-9706
www.gale.cengage.com

Claitor's Law Books and Publishing
  Division
P.O. Box 261333
Baton Rouge, LA 70826-1333
(225) 344-0476
(800) 274-1403
FAX (225) 344-0480
www.claitors.com

CLE Alabama
P.O. Box 870384
Tuscaloosa, AL 35487
(205) 348-6230
(800) 627-6514
FAX (205) 348-1072
www.clealabama.org

Code-Co Law Publishers
P.O. Box 826
Payson, UT 84651603-1471

(801) 226-6876
(800) 255-5294
FAX (801) 226-1733
www.code-co.com

Columbia University Press
61 W. 62nd St.
New York, NY 10023
(212) 459-0600
FAX (800) 351-5073
cup.columbia.edu

Congressional Quarterly, Inc.
77 K St., NE, 8th fl.
Washington, DC 20002
(202) 650-6500
(800) 432-2250
FAX (800) 380-3810
corporate.cqrollcall.com

Continuing Education of the Bar,
  California
300 Frank H. Ogawa Plaza,
  Suite 410
Oakland, CA 94612-2001
(510) 302-2000
(800) 232-3444
www.ceb.com

The Council of State Governments
2760 Research Park Dr.
Lexington, KY 40578
(859) 244-8000
(800) 800-1910
FAX (859) 244-8001
www.csg.org

Dahlstrom Legal Publishing
113 E. Bare Hill Road
Harvard, MA 01451-1856
(978) 456-9042FAX (978) 456-9247
www.legalpub.com

Daily Journal Corp.
915 E. First St.
Los Angeles, CA 90012
(213) 229-5300
(800) 487-8262
FAX (213) 229-5481
www.dailyjournal.com

Darby Printing Co.
6215 Purdue Drive
Atlanta, GA 30336
(800) 241-5292
FAX (404) 346-3332
www.darbyprinting.com

# PUBLISHERS

Data Trace Publishing Company
P.O. Box 1239
Brooklandville, MD 21022
(410) 494-4994
(800) 342-0454
FAX (410) 494-0515
www.datatrace.com

Dolan Media
222 S. Ninth St., Suite 2300
Minneapolis, MN 55402
(612) 317-9420
FAX (612) 321-0563
www.dolanmedia.com

DRI
55 W. Monroe, Suite 2000
Chicago, IL 60603
(312) 795-1101
FAX (312) 795-0749
www.dri.org

Edward Elgar Publishing, Inc.
9 Dewey Court
Northampton, MA 01060
(413) 584-5551
FAX (413) 584-9933
www.e-elgar.com

Elsevier Business Intelligence
685 Route 202/206
Bridgewater, NJ 08807
(908) 547-2159
(800) 332-2181
www.elsevierbi.com

Environmental Law Institute
2000 L St., NW, Suite 620
Washington, DC 20036
(202) 939-3800
FAX (202) 939-3868
www.eli.org

Euromoney Legal Media Group
Nestor House, Playhouse Yard
London, EC4V 5EX
ENGLAND
+44 020 7779 8999
FAX +44 020 7779 8602
www.legalmediagroup.com

Executive Press, Inc.
P.O. Box 21639
Concord, CA 94521-0639
(925) 685-5111
FAX (925) 930-9284
www.executivepress.net

Federal Bar Council
123 Main St., Suite L100
White Plains, NY 10601-3104
(914) 682-8800
FAX (914) 682-4400
www.federalbarcouncil.com

Financial Accounting Standards
  Board
401 Merritt 7
Norwalk, CT 06856
(203) 847-0700
(800) 748-0659
FAX (203) 849-9714
www.fasb.org

Financial Publishing Co.
1251 N. Eddy St., Suite 202
South Bend, IN 46617
(800) 247-3214
FAX (574) 243-6060
www.financial-publishing.com

Forster-Long, Inc.
12160 N. Abrams, Suite 576
Dallas, TX 75243
(214) 838-5745
(800) 328-5091
FAX (214) 838-5754
www.forster-long.com

FTC: Watch
604 Cameron St.
Alexandria, VA 22314
(703) 684-7171
FAX (202) 478-0260
www.ftcwatch.com

Gann Law Books
1 Washington Park, Suite 1300
Newark, NJ 07102
(973) 268-1200
FAX (973) 268-1330
www.gannlaw.com

Gaunt
3011 Gulf Drive
Holmes Beach, FL 34217-2199
(941) 778-5211
(800) 942-8683
FAX (941) 778-5252
www.gaunt.com

General Code
781 Elmgrove Rd.
Rochester, NY 14624
(855) 436-2133
FAX (585) 328-8189

www.generalcode.com

Globe Law and Business
New Hibernia House
Winchester Walk
London Bridge
London SE1 9AG ENGLAND
+44 20 7234 0606
www.gbplawbooks.com

Government Research Service
P.O. Box 2067
Topeka, KS 66601
(785) 232-7720
(800) 346-6898
FAX (785) 232-1615
www.thinktankdirectory.com

Greenwood Publishing Group
ABC-CLIO
130 Cremona Drive
Santa Barbara, CA 93117
(805) 968-1911
(800) 368-6868
FAX (866) 270-3856
www.greenwood.com

Grey House Publishing
4949 Route 22
Amenia, NY 12501
(518) 789-8700
(800) 562-2139
FAX (518) 789-0556
www.greyhouse.com

HarperCollins Publishers
10 East 53 St.
New York, NY 10022
(212) 207-7000
(800) 242-7737
FAX (800) 822-4090
www.harpercollins.com

Harvard Law Review
Gannett House
Cambridge, MA 02138
(617) 495-7889
FAX (617) 496-5053
www.harvardlawreview.org

Harvard University Press
79 Garden St.
Cambridge, MA 02138
(401) 531-2800
(800) 405-1619
FAX (800) 406-9145
www.hup.harvard.edu

# PUBLISHERS

William S. Hein & Co., Inc.
1285 Main St.
Buffalo, NY 14209-1987
(716) 882-2600
FAX (716) 883-8100
www.wshein.com

Hoover's Inc.
5800 Airport Blvd.
Austin, TX 78752-3812
(512) 374-4500
(866) 281-6092
FAX (512) 374-4501
www.hoovers.com

Houghton Mifflin
222 Berkeley St.
Boston, MA 02116
(617) 351-5000
(800) 225-1464
FAX (800) 458-9501
www.hmco.com

Infobase Publishing
132 W. 31st St., 17th fl.
New York, NY 10001
(800) 322-8755
FAX (800) 678-3633
www.infobase.com

Information Today, Inc.
143 Old Marlton Pike
Medford, NJ 08055-8750
(609) 654-6266
(800) 300-9868
FAX (609) 654-4309
www.infotoday.com

Infosources Publishing
140 Norma Road
Teaneck, NJ 07666
(201) 836-7072
FAX (201) 357-5575
www.infosourcespub.com

Institute of Continuing Legal
  Education
1020 Greene St.
Ann Arbor, MI 48109-1444
(734) 764-0533
(877) 229-4350
FAX (877) 229-4351
www.icle.org/

International Bureau of Fiscal
  Documentation
P.O. Box 20237
1000 HE

Amsterdam, NETHERLANDS
3120-5540100
FAX 3120-6208626
www.ibfd.org

International Law Institute
1055 Thomas Jefferson St., NW
Washington, DC 20007
(202) 247-6006
FAX (202) 247-6010
www.ili.org

James Publishing
3505 Cadillac Ave., Suite H
Costa Mesa, CA 92626
(714) 755-5450
(800) 440-4780
FAX (714) 751-2709
www.jamespublishing.com

Jones McClure Publishing, Inc.
3131 Eastside St., Suite 300
Houston, TX 77098
(713) 335-8200
(800) 626-6667
FAX (713) 335-8201
www.jonesmcclure.com

Juris Publishing, Inc.
71 New St.
Huntington, NY 11743
(631) 351-5712
(800) 887-4064
FAX (631) 351-5712
www.jurispub.com

J. J. Keller & Associates, Inc.
3003 W. Breezewood Lane
Neenah, WI 54957
(877) 564-2333
FAX (800) 727-7516
www.jjkeller.com

Knowles Publishing, Inc.
5535 Airport Freeway
Ft. Worth, TX 76117
(817) 838-0202
(800) 299-0202
FAX (817) 831-0019
www.knowlespublishing.com

Land Development Institute, Ltd.
1401 16th St. NW
Washington, DC 20036
(202) 232-2144
FAX (202) 232-8924

Law Bulletin Publishing Co.

415 N. State St.
Chicago, IL 60610
(312) 644-7800
FAX (312) 644-4255
www.lawbulletin.com

Law Reporters
1601 Connecticut Ave., NW
Washington, DC 20009
(202) 462-5755
FAX (202) 328-2430
www.lawreporters.com

Lawpress Corporation
P.O. Box 29
Alameda, CA 94501-0329
(800) 622-1181
FAX (510) 217-6600
www.lawpresscorp.com

Lawyers & Judges Publishing Co.
917 N. Swan Rd., Suite 300
Tucson, AZ 85711
(520) 323-1500
(800) 209-7109
FAX (520) 323-0055
www.lawyersandjudges.com

Lawyers USA
Dolan Media
10 Milk St., 10th fl.
Boston, MA 02108
(800) 444-5297
www.lawyersusaonline.com

Leadership Directories, Inc.
104 Fifth Ave.
New York, NY 10011
(212) 627-4140
FAX (212) 645-0931
www.leadershipdirectories.com

Legal Directories Publishing Co.
9111 Garland Road
Dallas, TX 75218
(214) 321-3238
FAX (214) 321-3157
www.legaldirectories.com

LexisNexis Academic & Library
  Solutions
7500 Old Georgetown Rd.
Bethesda, MD 20814-6126
(301) 654-1550
(800) 638-8380
FAX (301) 657-3203
www.lexisnexis.com/academic

# PUBLISHERS

LexisNexis Canada, Inc.
123 Commerce Valley Drive East
Markham, Ontario, L3T 7W8
CANADA
(905) 479-2665
(800) 668-6481
FAX (905) 479-4082
www.butterworths.ca

LexisNexis Group
9433 Springboro Pike
Dayton, OH 45342
(800) 227-4908
www.lexisnexis.com

LexisNexis Mealey's
1016 W. Ninth Ave.
King of Prussia, PA 19406-1225
(610) 768-7800
(800) MEALEYS
FAX (610) 768-0880
www.lexisnexis.com/

Libraries Unlimited
An Imprint of ABC-CLIO
130 Cremona Drive
Santa Barbara, CA 93116
(800) 368-6868
FAX (866) 270-3858
www.lu.com

LRP Publications
P.O. Box 24668
West Palm Beach, FL 33416
(215) 784-0860
(800) 341-7874
FAX (561) 622-2423
www.lrp.com

Mariposa Publishing
1865 Buerkle Rd.
St. Paul, MN 55110
(651) 773-5230
(800) 442-1419
FAX (651) 773-5233
www.mariposapublishing.com

Massachusetts Continuing Legal
   Education, Inc.
10 Winter Place
Boston, MA 02108
(617) 482-2205
(800) 966-6253
FAX (617) 482-9498
www.mcle.org

McGraw-Hill Inc.
P.O. Box 182604

Columbus, OH 43272
(877) 833-5524
FAX (614) 759-3759
www.mcgraw-hill.com

The MIT Press
55 Hayward Street
Cambridge, MA 02142-1493
(617) 253-5646
(800) 405-1619
FAX (617) 258-6779
mitpress.mit.edu

Municipal Code Corp.
P.O. Box 2235
Tallahassee, FL 32316
(850) 576-3171
FAX (850) 575-8852
www.municode.com

National Business Institute, Inc.
P.O. Box 3067
Eau Claire, WI 54702
(800) 930-6182
www.nbi-sems.com/

National Legal Research Group,
   Inc.
2421 Ivy Road
Charlottesville, VA 22903
(800) 727-6574
FAX (434) 817-6570
www.nlrg.com

National Technical Information
   Service
5301 Shawnee Rd.
Alexandria,VA 22312
(703) 605-6585
(888) 584-8332
FAX (703) 605-6900
www.ntis.gov

The National Underwriter Co.
5081 Olympic Blvd.
Erlanger, KY 41018
(800) 543-0874
www.nuco.com

Neal-Schuman Publishers, Inc.
100 William St., Suite 2004
New York, NY 10038
(212) 925-8650
FAX (212) 219-8916
www.neal-schuman.com

New England LawPress
P.O. Box 331

Westerly, RI 02891
(800) 955-4089
FAX (860) 535-0378
www.nelawpress.com

New Jersey Institute for Continuing
   Legal Education
One Constitution Square
New Brunswick, NJ 08901-1500
(732) 214-8500
FAX (732) 249-0383
www.njicle.com

New York Legal Publishing
136 Railroad Ave. Extension
Albany, NY 12205
(518) 459-1100
(800) 541-2681
FAX (518) 459-9718
www.nylp.com

New York State Bar Association
1 Elk St.
Albany, NY 12207
(518) 463-3200
FAX (518) 487-5517
www.nysba.org

New York University Press
838 Broadway, 3rd fl.
New York, NY 10003-4812
(212) 998-2575
FAX (212) 995-3833
www.nyupress.org/

Nolo Press
950 Parker St.
Berkeley, CA 94710-2524
(800) 728-3555
FAX (800) 645-0895
www.nolo.com

Oceana Publications, Inc. / Oxford
198 Madison Ave.
New York, NY 10016
(800) 334-4249 x6469
FAX (212) 726-6476
www.oceanalaw.com

O'Reilly
1005 Gravenstein Hwy. North
Sebastopol, CA 95472
(707) 827-7000
(800) 998-9938
FAX (707) 829-0104
www.oreilly.com

Organization for Economic

# PUBLISHERS

Cooperation and Development
Center
2001 L St., NW, Suite 650
Washington, DC 20036-4922
(202) 785-6323
FAX (202) 785-0350
www.oecdwash.org

Oxford University Press
198 Madison Ave.
New York, NY 10016
(212) 726-6000
(800) 445-9714
www.oup.com/us

Practising Law Institute
810 Seventh Ave., 21st fl
New York, NY 10019-5818
(212) 824-5700
(800) 260-4PLI
www.pli.edu

Primary Source Media
12 Lunar Drive
Woodbridge, CT 06525
(203) 397-2600
(800) 444-0799
FAX (203) 397-3893
gale.cengage.com/psm

Public Utilities Reports
8229 Boone Blvd., Suite 400
Vienna, VA 22182-2623
(703) 847-7720
(800) 368-5001
FAX (703) 847-0683
www.pur.com

Record Press
229 W. 36th St., 8th fl.
New York, NY 10018
(212) 619-4949
www.recordpress.com

Routledge-Cavendish
Taylor & Francis Group
2 Park Square, Milton Park
Abingdon
Oxford OX14 4RN UK
+44 (0) 20 7017 6000
+44 (0) 20 7017 6699
www.routledge.com

Rowman & Littlefield Publishers
4501 Forbes Blvd., Suite 200
Lanham, MD 20706
(301) 459-3366
(800) 462-6420

FAX (301) 429-5748
www.rowmanlittlefield.com

The Rutter Group
15760 Ventura Blvd., Suite 630
Encino, CA 91436-3022
(800) 747-3161
(818) 990-3260
FAX (818) 377-7842
www.ruttergroup.com

St. Martin's Press
175 Fifth Ave.
New York, NY 10010
(212) 674-5151
(800) 221-7945
FAX (212) 420-9314
www.stmartins.com

Scarecrow Press, Inc.
4501 Forbes Blvd., Suite 200
Lanham, MD 20706
(301) 459-3366
(800) 462-6420
FAX (301) 429-5748
www.scarecrowpress.com

Self-Counsel Press, Inc.
1481 Charlotte Rd.
North Vancouver, BC V7J 1H1
Canada
(604) 986-3366
(800) 663-3007
www.self-counsel.com

Sheshunoff Information Services
412 Freidrich Lane, Suite 100
Austin, TX 78744
(512) 305-6500
(800) 456-2340
FAX (512) 365-6575
www.sheshunoff.com

M. Lee Smith Publishers LLC
P.O. Box 5094
Brentwood, TN 37024-5094
(800) 274-6774
www.mleesmith.com

Special Libraries Association
331 S. Patrick St.
Alexandria, VA 22314-3501
(703) 647-4900
FAX (703) 647-4901
www.sla.org

Springer
233 Spring Street

New York, NY 10013
(212) 460-1500
(800) SPRINGER
FAX (212) 460-1575
www.springer.com

STP Specialty Technical Publishers
1750 Grant Ave.
Blaine, WA 98230
(604) 983-3434
(800) 251-0381
FAX (604) 983-3445
www.stpub.com

Sweet & Maxwell, Ltd.
100 Avenue Road
London NW3 3PF
ENGLAND
020 7393 7000
020 7449 1111 (customer services)
FAX 020 7393 7010
www.smlawpub.co.uk

Tax Analysts
400 S. Maple Ave., Suite 400
Falls Church, VA 22046
(703) 533-4400
(800) 955-2444
FAX (703) 533-4444
www.taxanalysts.com

Taylor & Francis Group Ltd
2 Park Square
Milton Park
Abingdon
Oxford OX14 4RN
ENGLAND
44(0) 20-7071 6000
FAX 44(0) 20-7017 6699
www.taylorandfrancis.com

Thomson Reuters
3 Times Square
New York, NY 10036
(646) 223-4000
www.thomsonreuters.com

Thompson Publishing Group
805 15th St.
Washington, DC 20005
(202) 872-4000
(800) 677-3789
FAX (800) 759-7179
www.thompson.com

Thompson Tax & Accounting (was
  RIA)
195 Broadway

# PUBLISHERS

New York, NY 10007
(800) 431-9025
ria.thomsonreuters.com

United Nations Publications
c/o National Book Network
P.O. Box 190
Blue Ridge Summit, PA 17214

(888) 254-4281
FAX (800) 338-4550
unp.un.org

U.S. Government Printing Office
Superintendent of Documents
710 N. Capitol St., NW
Washington, DC 20401
(866) 512-1800
FAX (202) 512-2104
www.access.gpo.gov

University of California Press
2120 Berkeley Way
Berkeley, CA 94704
(510) 642-4247
(800) 777-4726
FAX (510) 643-7127
www.ucpress.edu

University of Chicago Press
1427 East 60th St.
Chicago, IL 60637
(773) 702-7700
FAX (773) 702-9756
www.press.uchicago.edu

Urban Land Institute
1025 Thomas Jefferson St., NW,
 Suite 500 West
Washington, DC 20007
(202) 624-7000
(800) 321-5011
FAX (202) 624-7140
www.uli.org

West, a ThomsonReuters Co.
610 Opperman Drive
Eagan, MN 55123-1396
(651) 687-7000
(800) 344-5009
FAX (800) 213-2323
west.thomson.com

Wiley & Sons
111 River St.
Hoboken, NJ 07030
(201) 748-6000
FAX (800) 597-3299

www.wiley.com

H. W. Wilson Company
950 University Ave.
Bronx, NY 10452
(718) 588-8400
(800) 367-6770
FAX (718) 590-1617
(800) 590-1617
www.hwwilson.com

Yale University Press
P.O. Box 209040
New Haven, CT 06520-9040
(203) 432-0960
FAX (203) 432-0948
yalepress.yale.edu

# USED AND RARE LAW BOOK DEALERS

The Advanced Book Exchange, Inc.
500-655 Tyee Rd.
Victoria, BC V9A 6X5
CANADA
(250) 412-3258
www.abebooks.com

Meyer Boswell Books, Inc.
2141 Mission Street
San Francisco, CA 94110
(415) 255-6400
FAX (415) 255-6499
rarelaw@meyerbos.com
www.meyerbos.com

Claitor's Law Books
P.O. Box 261333
Baton Rouge, LA 70826-1333
(225) 344-0476
(800) 274-1403
FAX (225) 344-0480
www.claitors.com

A. Gerits & Sons
Distelvlinerweg 37d
1113 LA Diemen
The Netherlands
+31(0) 20-698-1375
FAX +31(0) 20-625 89 70
www.agerits.com

Wm. S. Hein & Co., Inc.
1285 Main Street
Buffalo, NY 14209-1987
(716) 882-2600
(800) 828-7571
FAX (716) 883-8100
www.wshein.com

The Lawbook Exchange, Ltd.
33 Terminal Ave.
Clark, NJ 07066-1321
(732) 382-1800
(800) 422-6686
FAX (732) 382-1887
www.lawbookexchange.com

LEGIBUS
Box 809
La Grange, IL 60525
(708) 352-3039
www.concentric.net/~drb7949/

Linda Montemaggi
244 W. 101st St.
New York, NY 10025
(212) 662-5712
montemag@earthlink.net

# BOOKBINDERS

ACME Bookbinding
P.O. Box 290699
Charlestown, MA 02129-0212
(617) 242-1100
FAX (617) 242-3764
www.acmebook.com

Bound to Stay Bound Books, Inc.
1880 West Morton Ave.
Jacksonville, IL 62650-2697
(800) 637-6586
FAX (800) 747-2872
www.btsb.com

Bridgeport National Bindery, Inc.
P.O. Box 289
Agawam, MA 01001-0289
(413) 789-1981
(800) 223-5083
FAX (413) 789-4007
www.bnbindery.com

Campbell-Logan Bindery, Inc.
212 North Second Street
Minneapolis, MN 55401-1423
(612) 332-1313
(800) 942-6224
FAX (612) 332-1316
www.campbell-logan.com

Denver Bookbinding Co. Inc.
2715 17th Street
Denver, CO 80211-3995
(303) 455-5521
(800) 727-4752
FAX (303) 455-2677
www.denverbook.com

The HF Group
8844 Mayfield Rd.
Chesterland, OH 44026-2632
(440) 729-9411
(888) 485-5415
FAX (440) 729-9415
www.thehfgroup.com

The HF Group - Indiana
1010 N. Sycamore St.
North Manchester, IN 46962
(260) 982-2107
(800) 334-3628
FAX (260) 982-1130
www.thehfgroup.com

The HF Group - North Carolina
6204 Corporate Park Drive
Brown Summit, NC 27214
(336) 931-0800
(800) 444-7534
FAX (336) 931-0711
www.thehfgroup.com

The HF Group - Pennsylvania
63 East Broad Street
Hatfield, PA 19440-2464
(215) 855-2293
(800) 230-2253
FAX (215) 368-7308
www.thehfgroup.com

The HF Group - Virginia
1440 Hickory Hill Road
Petersburg, VA 23803-4778
(804) 732-8970
(800) 831-9400
FAX (800) 732-7474
www.thehfgroup.com

The HF Group - Washington
121 Avery St.
Walla Walla, WA 99362-1669
(509) 529-4220
(800) 253-5456
FAX (509) 529-6880
www.thehfgroup.com

Kater-Crafts Bookbinding
4860 Gregg Road
Pico Rivera, CA 90660-2199
(562) 692-0665
FAX (562) 692-7920
www.katercrafts.com

Mutual Library Bindery, Inc.
P.O. Box 6026
Syracuse, NY 13217-6026
(315) 455-6638

National Library Bindery Co. of GA
100 Hembree Park Drive
Roswell, GA 30076
(770) 442-5490
FAX (770) 442-0183

Ocker & Trapp Library Bindery, Inc.
662 Silver St.
Agawam, MA 01001

(800) 223-5083
www.ockerandtrapp.com

Perma-Bound Books
A Division of Hertzberg-New
Method, Inc.
617 E. Vandalia Road
Jacksonville, IL 62650-3544
(217) 243-5451
FAX (217) 243-7505
www.perma-bound.com

Roswell Bookbinding
2614 N. 29th Avenue
Phoenix, AZ 85009-1611
(602) 272-9338
(888) 803-8883
FAX (602) 272-9786
www.roswellbookbinding.com

Utah Bookbinding Co.
573 W. 4800 South
Murray, UT 84123
(801) 685-6151
(888) 700-3871
FAX (801) 685-0182
www.utahbookbinding.com

Wert Bookbinding, Inc.
9975 Allentown Blvd.
Grantville, PA 17028-8709
(717) 469-0626
(800) 344-9378
FAX (717) 469-0629
www.wertbookbinding.com

# SUBSCRIPTION AGENTS AND BOOK WHOLESALERS

Ambassador Book Service, Inc.
445 Broad Hollow Rd., Suite 206
Melville, NY 11747
(631) 770-1010
(800) 431-8913
FAX (631) 770-1041
www.absbook.com

American Overseas Book Co., Inc.
550 Walnut Street
Norwood, NJ 07648
(201) 767-7600
FAX (201) 784-0263
www.aobc.com

Baker & Taylor, Inc.
2550 W. Tyvola Rd., Suite 300
Charlotte, NC 28217
(704) 998-3100
(800) 775-1800
www.btol.com

Basch Subscriptions, Inc.
10 Ferry St., Suite 425
Concord, NH 03301
(603) 229-0662
(800) 226-5310
FAX (603) 226-9443
www.basch.com

Bernan Associates
15200 NBN Way
Blue Ridge Summit, PA 17214
(301) 459-7666
(800) 865-3457
FAX (301) 459-6988
www.bernan.com

Blackwell's Book Services
6024 Jean Rd., Bldg G.
Lake Oswego, OR 97035
(503) 684-1140
(800) 547-6426
FAX (503) 639-2481
(or)
100 University Court
Blackwood, NJ 08012
(856) 228-8900
FAX (856) 228-6097
www.blackwell.com

The Book House, Inc.
208 W. Chicago Street
Jonesville, MI 49250

(517) 849-2117
(800) 248-1146
FAX (800) 858-9716
www.thebookhouse.com

Brodart Automation
500 Arch Street
Williamsport, PA 17701
(800) 474-9802 x6772
FAX (800) 999-6799
www.brodart.com

Coutts Library Services Inc.
3 Ingram Blvd.
La Vergne, TN 37086
(905) 356-6382
(800) 263-1686
FAX (905) 356-5064
www.couttsinfo.com

Eastern Book Company
55 Bradley Dr.
Westbrook, ME 04092
(800) 937-0331
FAX (800) 214-3895
www.ebc.com

EBSCO Subscription Services
Box 1943
Birmingham, AL 35201-1943
(205) 991-6600
FAX (205) 995-1518
www.ebsco.com
(or)
10 Estes St.
Ipswich, MA 01938-0682
(978) 356-6500
(800) 653-2726
FAX: (978) 356-6565

Emery Pratt Co.
1966 W. M21
Owosso, MI 48867-1397
(989) 723-5291
(800) 248-3887
FAX (800) 523-6379
www.emery-pratt.com

Gaunt
3011 Gulf Drive
Holmes Beach, FL 34217-2199
(941) 778-5211
(800) 942-8683
FAX (941) 778-5252

www.gaunt.com

William. S. Hein & Co., Inc.
1285 Main Street
Buffalo, NY 14209-1987
(716) 882-2600
(800) 828-7571
FAX (716) 883-8100
www.wshein.com

Ingram Library Services, Inc.
One Ingram Blvd.
LaVergne, TN 37086-1986
(800) 937-5300
www.ingramlibrary.com

The Lawbook Exchange, Ltd.
33 Terminal Ave.
Clark, NJ 07066-1321
(732) 382-1800
(800) 422-6686
FAX (732) 382-1887
www.lawbookexc.com

Midwest Library Service
11443 St. Charles Rock Road
Bridgeton, MO 63044-2789
(314) 739-3100
(800) 325-8833
FAX (314) 739-1326
www.midwestls.com

Research Periodicals & Book
  Services, Inc.
P.O. Box 720728
Houston, TX 77272
(713) 779-2999
(800) 521-0061
FAX (713) 779-2992
www.rpbs.com

SerialHive LLC
330 W. Diversey Pkwy., Suite 1808
Chicago, IL 60657
(773) 244-2487
FAX (773) 913-0680
www.serialhive.com

Swets Subscription Service
904 Black Horse Pike
Runnemede, NJ 08078
(856) 312-2690
(800) 645-6595
FAX (856) 312-2000

# SUBSCRIPTION AGENTS AND BOOK WHOLESALERS

www.swets.com

Tatnuck Bookseller
18 Lyman Street
Westborough, MA 01602
(508) 366-4959
FAX (508) 366-7929
www.tatnuck.com

W.T. Cox Subscriptions
201 Village Rd.
Shallotte, NC 28470
(800) 571-9554
FAX (910) 755-6274
www.wtcox.com

Wolper Subscription Services
6 Centre Square, Suite 202
Easton, PA 18042
(610) 559-9550
FAX (610) 559-9898
www.wolper.com

YBP Library Services
999 Maple Street
Contoocock, NH 03229
(603) 746-3102
(800) 258-3774
FAX (603) 746-5628
www.ybp.com

# AUDIO-VISUAL PUBLISHERS OF LEGAL AND LAW-RELATED MATERIALS

AAJ
777 6th St., NW, Suite 200
Washington, DC 20001
(202) 965-3500
(800) 424-2725
FAX (202) 342-5484
www.justice.org

ALI-ABA
Committee on Continuing
Professional Education
4025 Chestnut Street
Philadelphia, PA 19104
(800) CLE-NEWS
FAX (215) 243-1664
www.ali-aba.org

American Bar Association
321 N. Clark St.
Chicago, IL 60654
(312) 988-5522
(800) 285-2221
www.americanbar.org

CCH, Inc.
2700 Lake Cook Rd.
Riverwoods, IL 60015
(888) 224-7377
www.cch.com

Commonwealth Films
223 Commonwealth Avenue
Boston, MA 02116-1700
(617) 262-5634
FAX (617) 262-6948

www.commonwealthfilms.com

Continuing Education of the Bar,
  California
300 Frank H. Ogawa Plaza,
  Suite 410
Oakland, CA 94612-2001
(510) 302-2000
(800) 232-3444
www.ceb.com

National Institute for Trial
  Advocacy
1685 38th St., Suite 200
Boulder, CO 80301
(800) 225-6482
FAX (720) 890-7069
www.nita.org

Practising Law Institute
810 Seventh Avenue
New York, NY 10019
(212) 824-5700
(800) 260-4PLI
FAX (800) 321-0093
www.pli.edu

Professional Education Group, Inc.
12401 Minnetonka Blvd.
Minnetonka, MN 55305-3994
(952) 933-9990
(800) 229-2531
FAX (952) 933-7784
www.proedgroup.com

Rampion Visual Productions LLC
125 Walnut Street
Watertown, MA 02472

(617) 972-1777
FAX (617) 972-9157
www.rampion.com

Seak Inc.
P.O. Box 729
Falmouth, MA 02540
(508) 457-1111
FAX (508) 540-8304
www.seak.com

State Bar of Wisconsin
P.O. Box 7158
Madison, WI 53707-7158
(800) 728-7788
(608) 257-3838
FAX (608) 257-5502
www.wisbar.org

West, a Thomson Co.
610 Opperman Dr.
Eagan, MN 55164-0832
(651) 687-7000
(800) 937-8529
FAX (800) 340-9378
west.thomson.com

# CONTINUING LEGAL EDUCATION SPONSORS

(Note: Most State Bar Assns. offer CLE courses. For a complete list, consult the list of State Bar Assns. on page 315.)
*Online CLE

*American Bar Association
Center for CLE
321 N. Clark St.
Chicago, IL 60610
(312) 988-5000
(800) 285-2221
FAX (312) 988-5368
www.americanbar.org

*American Law Institute
4025 Chestnut Street
Philadelphia, PA 19104
(215) 243-1604
(800) CLE-NEWS
FAX (215) 243-1664
www.ali-aba.org

*Celesq
6421 Congress Ave., Suite 100
Boca Raton, FL 33487
(561) 241-1919
FAX (561) 241-1969
www.celesq.com

AAJ Education
777 6th St., NW, Suite 200
Washington, DC 20001
(800) 424-2725
FAX (202) 625-7084
www.justice.org

*CLEonline.com
P.O. Box 80947
Austin, TX 78708
(512) 778-5665
FAX (512) 287-5300
www.cleonline.com

DigiLearn Systems, Inc.
245 East Cheyenne Mountain Blvd.
Colorado Springs, CO 80906
(888) 619-8883
FAX (719) 785-5770
www.digilearnonline.com

Federal Publications Seminars, Inc.
1100 13th St. NW, Suite 200
Washington, DC 20005
(202) 772-8295
(888) 494-3696
FAX (202) 772-8298
www.fedpubseminars.com

*Lawline.com
61 Broadway, Suite 1105
New York, NY 10006
(212) 514-8035
(800) LAWLINE
www.lawline.com

*Law.com Online CLE
120 Broadway, 6th fl.
New York, NY 10005
(800) 348-0466
clecenter.com

*New York State Bar Association
One Elk Street
Albany, NY 12207
(518) 463-3200
FAX (518) 487-5517
www.nysba.org

*OSBA
Ohio CLE Institute
1700 Lake Shore Drive
Columbus, OH 43204
(800) 282-6556
FAX (614) 487-1008
www.ohiobar.org

*Practising Law Institute
810 Seventh Avenue
New York, NY 10019-5818
(212) 824-5710
(800) 260-4PLI
www.pli.edu

Professional Education Systems
P.O. Box 1000
Eau Claire, WI 54702
(800) 844-8260
FAX (800) 554-9775
www.pesi.com/

The Rutter Group
15760 Ventura Blvd., Suite 630
Encino, CA 91436
(818) 990-3260
(800) 747-3161
FAX (818) 377-7839
www.ruttergroup.com

*Taecan.com
1530 Westlake Ave. N., Suite 1

Seattle, WA 98109
(206) 285-3411
FAX (206) 285-8300
www.taecan.com/

University of Texas School of Law
   Office of CLE
727 E. Dean Keeton St.
Austin, TX 78705
(512) 475-6700
FAX (512) 475-6876
www.utcle.org

*West LegalEdCenter
610 Opperman Drive
St. Paul, MN 55123
(800) 495-9378
www.westlegaledcenter.com

# MICROFORM READER-PRINTERS

BMI Imaging Systems
1115 E. Arques Avenue
Sunnyvale, CA 94085
(408) 736-7444
(800) 359-3456
FAX (408) 736-4397
www.bmiimaging.com

Canon U.S.A. Inc.
Image Filing Systems Div.
1 Canon Plaza
Lake Success, NY 11042-1198
(516) 328-5000
(800) OK-CANON
www.usa.canon.com

Eye Communication Systems, Inc.
P.O. Box 620
Hartland, WI 53029
(262) 367-1360
(800) 558-2153
FAX (262) 367-1362
www.eyecom.com

Hudson Microimaging
P.O. Box 640, Route 9W
Port Ewen, NY 12466
(845) 338-5785
FAX (845) 338-2556
www.hudsonmicroimaging.com

Indus International, Inc.
340 S. Oak Street
West Salem, WI 54669
(608) 786-0300
(800) 843-9377
FAX (608) 786-0786
www.indususa.com

The Library Store Ltd.
10528 St. Paul Street
Kensington, MD 20895
(301) 652-8811
(800) 858-8117
FAX (301) 654-4960
www.librarystoreltd.com

Northern Micrographics
2004 Kramer St.
La Crosse, WI 54603
(608) 781-0850
(800) 236-0850
www.normicro.com

PMI Technologies
1931 Olney Ave., Suite 600
Cherry Hill, NJ 08003
(800) 750-0110
www.pmitechnologies.com

S-T Imaging, Inc.
630 Dundee Rd., Suite 210
Northbrook, IL 60012
(847) 501-3344
FAX (847) 501-3377
www.stimaging.com

# GENERAL LIBRARY SUPPLIES/FURNITURE

Bretford, Inc.
11000 Seymour Ave.
Franklin Park, 1L 60131
(847) 678-2545
(800) 521-9614
FAX (847) 678-0852
FAX (800) 343-1779
www.bretford.com

Brodart, Inc.
500 Arch St.
Williamsport, PA 17705
(888) 820-4377
FAX (800) 283-6087
www.brodart.com

The Buckstaff Co.
P.O. Box 2506
Oshkosh, WI 54903-2506
(920) 235-5890
(800) 755-5890
www.buckstaff.com

Demco, Inc.
P.O. Box 7488
Madison, WI 53707-7488
(800) 279-1586
FAX (800) 245-1329
www.demco.com

Gaylord Bros., Inc.
P.O. Box 4901
Syracuse, NY 13221-4901
(315) 634-8243
(800) 962-9580
FAX (800) 272-3412
www.gaylord.com

Highsmith, Inc.
P.O. Box 7820
Madison, WI 53707
(920) 563-9571
(800) 558-2110
FAX (800) 835-2329
www.highsmith.com

Library Bureau
172 Industrial Rd.
Fitchburg, MA 01420-0004
(978) 345-7942
(800) 221-6638
FAX (978) 345-0188
www.librarybureau.com

The Library Store Inc.
P.O. Box 964
301 E. South St.
Tremont, IL 61568
(800) 548-7204
FAX (800) 320-7706
www.thelibrarystore.com

Library Suppliers.com
517 Main St.
Holyoke, MA 01040
(800) 628-1912
FAX (800) 532-9281
www.librarysuppliers.com

Oblique Filing Systems
411 Western Lane
Irmo, SC 29063
(803) 749-6900
(800) 845-7068
FAX (803) 749-6904
www.obliquefilingsystems.com

Russ Bassett
8189 Byron Road
Whittier, CA 90606-2615
(562) 945-2445
(800) 350-2445
FAX (562) 698-8972
www.russbassett.com

Vernon Library Supplies
2851 Cole Court
Norcross, GA 30071
(770) 446-1128
(800) 878-0253
FAX (800) 446-1165
www.vernlib.com

The Worden Company
199 E. 17 Street
Holland, MI 49423
(616) 392-1848
(800) 748-0561
FAX (616) 392-2542
www.wordencompany.com

# SHELVING

Adjustable Shelving Products Co.,
Inc.
54-54 43rd St.
Maspeth, NY 11378
(718) 784-2949
FAX (718) 784-9169
www.adjustableshelving.com

Borroughs Corporation
3002 N. Burdick Street
Kalamazoo, MI 49004
(800) 748-0227
FAX (269) 342-4161
www.borroughs.com

Demco Library Interiors
P.O. Box 8548
Madison, WI 53708-8548
(800) 747-7561
FAX (800) 730-8094
www.demcoservices.com

Flexible Montisa
323 Acorn St.
Plainwell, MI 49080
(269) 685-6831
(800) 875-6836
FAX (269) 685-9195
www.flexiblemontisa.com

Gressco, Ltd
328 Moravian Valley Rd.
P.O. Box 339
Waunakee, WI 53597-0339
(608) 849-6300
(800) 345-3480
FAX (608) 849-6304
www.gressco.com

Ironbound Metal Products, Inc.
1600 Lower Rd.
Linden, NJ 07036
(908) 862-7999

J.P. Jay Associates, Inc.
1313 Roth Ave.
Allentown, PA 18102
(610) 435-9666
FAX (610) 435-9216
www.jpjay.com

Kardex Remstar
41 Eisenhower Dr.
Westbrook, ME 04092
(800) 639-5805
www.kardexremstar.com

Library Bureau, Inc.
P.O. Box 400
172 Industrial Rd.
Fitchburg, MA 01420-0004
(978) 345-7942
(800) 221-6638
FAX (978) 345-0188
www.librarybureau.com

MJ Industries
P.O. Box 259, 4 Carleton Drive
Georgetown, MA 01833
(978) 352-6190
(800) 247-4353
FAX (866) 352-6964
www.mjshelving.com

Montel - High Density Storage
 Systems
225, 4th Avenue
C.P. 130
Montmagny, QC G5V 3S5
CANADA
(418) 248-0235
FAX  (418) 248-7266
www.montel.com

Jim Quinn & Associates
P.O. Box 641
Altamount, NY 12009
(518) 861-7125
FAX (518) 861-7125
www.jimquinn.com

Spacesaver Corp.
1450 Janesville Avenue
Ft. Atkinson, WI 53538-2798
(920) 563-6362
(800) 492-3434
FAX (920) 563-2702
www.spacesaver.com

Tennsco
P.O. Box 1888
Dickson, TN 37056-1888
(615) 446-8000
(800) 251-8184
FAX (800) 722-0134
www.tennsco.com

The Worden Company
199 East 17 Street
Holland, MI 49423
(800) 748-0561
FAX (616) 392-2542
www.wordencompany.com

# MOVABLE SHELVING SYSTEMS

ASRS of America, Inc.
304 Park Ave. South., 11th fl.
New York, NY 10010
(212) 760-1607
FAX (212) 714-2084
www.elecompack.com

Creative Library Concepts
535 Boulevard
Kenilworth, NJ 07033
(908) 276-9200
FAX (908) 276-9217
www.creativelibraryconcepts.com

Kardex Remstar
41 Eisenhower Dr.
Westbrook, ME 04092
(800) 639-5805
www.kardexremstar.com

Kwik-File Systems
619 N. Commerce St.
P.O. Box 728
Sheboygan, WI 53082
(920) 457-5537
(800) 822-8037
FAX (920) 457-7388
www.mayline.com

Montel - High Density Storage
 Systems
225, 4th Avenue
C.P. 130
Montmagny, QC G5V 3S5
CANADA
(877) 935-0236
FAX  (418) 248-7266
www.montel.com

Richards-Wilcox, Inc.
600 S. Lake Street
Aurora, IL 60506
(630) 897-6951
(800) 253-5668
FAX (630) 897-6994
www.richardswilcox.com

Spacesaver Corp.
1450 Janesville Ave.
Ft. Atkinson, WI 53538-2798
(920) 563-6362
(800) 492-3434
FAX (920) 563-2702
www.spacesaver.com

SpaceNow! Corp.
234 Emmet St.
Newark, NJ 07114
(973) 504-8585
(800) 504-8585
FAX (973) 504-8330
www.spacenowcorp.com

Tab
605 Fourth Street
Mayville, WI 53050
(888) 466-8228
FAX (800) 304-4947
www.tab.com

# AUTOMATED LIBRARY SYSTEM VENDORS

Brodart Automation
500 Arch St.
Williamsport, PA 17707
(570) 326-2461
(800) 474-9802 x6772
FAX (800) 999-6799
www.brodart.com

CyberTools for Libraries
249 Ayer Rd., Suite 302
Harvard, MA 01451
(978) 772-9200
(800) 894-9206
FAX (978) 772-9400
www.cybertoolsforlibraries.com

EOS International (EOS.Web)
2292 Faraday Avenue, Suite 350
Carlsbad, CA 92008-7258
(760) 431-8400
(800) 876-5484
FAX (760) 431-8448
www.eosintl.com

Ex Libris (Aleph, SFX, Metalib)
1350 E. Touhy Ave., Suite 200 East
Des Plaines, IL 60018
(847) 296-2200
(800) 762-6300
FAX (847) 296-5636
www.exlibrisgroup.com

Follett Software Co. (Destiny)
1391 Corporate Dr.
McHenry, IL 60050
(815) 344-8700
(800) 323-3397
FAX (815) 578-5575
www.fsc.follett.com

Infor Library & Information
Solutions (Vubis Smart)
550 Cochituate Rd.
Framingham, MA 01701
(508) 598-4064
(800) 825-2574
FAX (508) 598-4215
www.vubis-smart.com

Infovision Software (Amlib)
3830 Valley Centre Drive
San Diego, CA 92130
(800) 849-1655
FAX (815) 642-8541

www.infovisionsoftware.com

INMAGIC Inc. (Genie)
200 Unicorn Park Dr.
Woburn, MA 01801-6357
(781) 938-4444; (800) 229-TEXT
FAX (781) 938-4446
www.inmagic.com

Innovative Interfaces, Inc.
 (Millennium)
5850 Shellmound Way
Emeryville, CA 94608
(510) 655-6200
(800) 444-2344
FAX (510) 450-6350
www.iii.com

Kelowna Software Ltd. (Library 4
 Universal)
#400-1632 Dickson Ave.
Kelowna, BC, V1Y 7T2 CANADA
(250) 712-4644; (800) 667-3634
FAX (800) 856-4036
www.L4U.com

Library Corporation (CARL
Solution; CARL-X)
Research Park
Inwood, WV 25428-9733
(304) 229-0100; (800) 325-7759
FAX (304) 229-0295
www.TLCdelivers.com

Mandarin Library Automation, Inc.
 (Mandarin M3 / Oasis)
P.O. Box 272308
Boca Raton, FL 33427-2308
(800) 426-7477
FAX (561) 994-4065
www.mlasolutions.com

New Generation Technologies Inc.
 (Librarysoft)
P.O. Box 34069
Seattle, WA 98124
(800) 661-7112
FAX (604) 327-4670
www.librarysoft.com

Open Text Corp. (Livelink ECM)
275 Frank Tompa Dr.
Waterloo, ON N2L 0A1 CANADA
(519) 888-7111

(800) 499-6544
FAX (519) 888-0677
www.opentext.com

Polaris Library Systems
P.O. Box 4903
Syracuse, NY 13221-4901
(800) 272-3414
FAX (315) 457-5883
www.polarislibrary.com

Robert A. Schless & Co. Inc.
 (NOTEbookS)
43 Mary Catherine Lane
Sudbury, MA 01776
(978) 443-2996
FAX (978) 443-7602
www.rasco.com

SIMA, Inc. (Camelot)
P.O. Box 248
Springfield, VA 22150-0248
(703) 569-0993
FAX (703) 569-5161
www.simainc.com

SirsiDynix (UNICORN)
400 W. Dynix Dr.
Provo, UT 84604
(800) 288-8020
FAX (801) 223-5202
www.sirsidynix.com

Softlink (Liberty 3)
720 Third Ave., Suite 2230
Seattle, WA 98104
(877) 454-2725
FAX (310) 943-2393
www.softlinkamerica.com

SydneyPLUS International
5138-13562 Maycrest Way
Richmond, BC V6V 2J7 CANADA
(604) 278-6717
FAX (604) 278-9161
www.sydneyplus.com

VTLS (Virtua)
1701 Kraft Drive
Blacksburg, VA 24060
(540 557-1200
(800) 468-8857
FAX (540) 557-1210
www.vtls.com

# ELECTRONIC RESOURCE MANAGEMENT SYSTEMS

Name of company -  product name - URL


Colorado Alliance - Gold Rush - goldrush.coalliance.org

Cybertools - ERM Module - www.cybertoolsforlibraries.com

Ex Libris - Verde - www.exlibrisgroup.com/verde.htm

Harrassowitz - HERMIS 3.0 - www.harrassowitz.de/subscription_services/hermis.html

Innovative Interfaces - Electronic Resource Management Module -
   www.iii.com/products/electronic_resource.shtml

Proquest SerialsSolutions - ERMS - www.serialssolutions.com/promotion/ERMS/default.asp

Serials Solutions - 360 Resource Manager - www.serialssolutions.com/360-resource-manager

TDNet - e-Resource Manager - www.tdnet.com


# CONTENT  MANAGEMENT  SYSTEMS


Auto-Graphics, Inc. - Content Management System CMS - www.auto-graphics.com

Drupal - drupal.org (open source)

Ex Libris - Primo - www.exlibrisgroup.com

Infor Library Solutions - V-spaces - www.v-spaces.com

Inmagic, Inc. - Inmagic Presto - www.inmagic.com

Innovative Interfaces, Inc. - Encore - www.iii.com

Joomla! - www.joomla.org (open source)

SirsiDynix - EPS/ Enterprise Portal Solution - www.sirsidynix.com

Springshare - LibGuides - www.springshare.com

Vivisimo - Velocity - www.vivisimo.com

# INFORMATION SERVICES
(Research and/or document retrieval)

Access Information
234 Columbine Street, Suite 310
Denver, CO 80206
(303) 778-7677
(800) 827-7607
FAX (303) 778-7691
www.access-information.com

Air Data Research
9865 Tower View
Helotes, TX 78023
(210) 695-2204
FAX (210) 695-2301
www.airsafety.com

Airline Information Research, Inc.
343 Round Hill Rd.
Sapphire, NC 28774
(703) 489-9801
www.airlineinfo.com

Bates Information Services Inc.
8494 Boulder Hills Dr.
Niwot, CO 80503
(303) 772-7095
www.batesinfo.com

BNA Plus
1801 S. Bell Street
Arlington, VA 22202
(703) 341-3303
(800) 372-1033
FAX (800) 253-0332
www.bnaplus.com

Boalt Express
Boalt Hall Law Library, Rm 227A
Berkeley, CA 94720-7210
(510) 642-0950
FAX (510) 642-9122
www.law.berkeley.edu/library/
  services/bex/index.html

British Library Document Supply
  Centre
Boston Spa, Wetherby
West Yorkshire LS23 7BQ
ENGLAND
44 (0) 843208 1144
(800) 932-3575
FAX (800) 325-2221

www.bl.uk

Cal Info, Inc.
316 West 2nd St., Suite 1102
Los Angeles, CA 90012
(213) 687-8710
FAX (213) 687-8778
www.calinfo.net

CCH Corsearch
111 Eighth Ave.
New York, NY 10011
(800) 732-7241
FAX (800) 233-2986
www.ctcorsearch.com
(trademark and copyright research)

CCH Washington Service Bureau,
  Inc.
1015 15th Street, NW,  Suite 1000
Washington, DC 20005
(202) 842-73550
(800) 289-1057
FAX (202) 962-0152
www.wsb.com

Columbia University Law School
Document Delivery Services
435 West 116th St.
New York, NY 10027
(212) 854-7851; (800) 332-4529
FAX (212) 854-1359
www.law.columbia.edu/library/
  services/fee/docdel/

Judy Diamond Associates, Inc.
1301 Connecticut Ave. NW, Ste 300
Washington, DC 20036
(202) 728-0840
(800) 231-0669
FAX (202) 728-0845
www.judydiamond.com
(pension plan research)

Gallagher Law Library Copy & Send
University of Washington
William H. Gates Hall
Box 353025
Seattle, WA 98195-3025
(206) 616-2370
FAX (206) 616-9903

copysend@uwashington.edu
lib.law.washington.edu/copy&send/
  copy&send.html

Global Information Research &
  Retrieval, LLC
1577- D New Garden Rd., Suite 700
Greensboro, NC 27410
(336) 665-0977
www.searchitright.com

InfoNOW
University of Minnesota Libraries
305 Diehl Hall
505 Essex St., SE
Minneapolis, MN 55455
(612) 626-3940
(800) 477-6689
www.lib.umn.edu/infonow

Infotrieve
P.O. Box 7102
Wilton, CT 06897
(203) 423-2175
(800) 422-4633
FAX (203) 423-2155
www.infotrieve.com

Information Express
565 Middlefield Rd.
Bldg. 108, 2nd fl.
Menlo Park, CA 94025
(650) 812-3588
FAX (650) 812-3573
www.ieonline.com

Jenkins Law Library
Document Express
833 Chestnut East, Suite 1220
Philadelphia, PA 19107-4429
(215) 574-7900
FAX (215) 574-7920
www.jenkinslaw.org/

Legislative Intent Service
712 Main Street, Suite 200
Woodland, CA 95695
(800) 666-1917
FAX (530) 668-5866
www.legintent.com

# INFORMATION SERVICES

Legislative Research, Inc.
1107 9th St., Suite 220
Sacramento, CA 95814
(916) 442-7660
(800) 530-7613
FAX (916) 442-1529
www.lrihistory.com

Library Consultants, LLC
201 St. Charles Ave., Suite 114-262
New Orleans, LA 70170
(504) 885-5926
www.libraryconsultants.com

Market Research
11200 Rockville Pike, Suite 504
Rockville, MD 20852
(800) 298-5699
FAX (240) 747-3004
www.marketresearch.com

Michigan Information Transfer
  Source (MITS)
University of Michigan
106 North Hatcher Grad. Lib.
Ann Arbor, MI 48109-1205
(734) 763-5060
FAX (877) 329-6487
www.lib.umich.edu/mits/

National Corporate Research
1100 G St., NW, Suite 420
Washington, DC 20005
(800) 494-5225
FAX (800) 494-7512
www.nationalcorp.com

New York Legislative Services, Inc.
15 Maiden Lane, Suite 1000
New York, NY 10007
(212) 962-2826
FAX (212) 962-1420
www.nyls.org

Penco Information Retrieval
6560 Backlick Rd., Suite 250
Springfield, VA 22150
(703) 912-9080
(800) 690-7362
FAX (800) 607-3626
www.penco-info.com

Pinpoint Documents
1524 Cloverfield Blvd., Suite E
Santa Monica, CA 90404
(310) 477-0354
FAX (323) 375-1576
www.pinpointdocuments.com

Research & Retrieval LLC
1301 Manhattan Avenue #E
Hermosa Beach, CA 90254
(310) 798-8100
(800) 707-8771
FAX (310) 421-0344
www.researchandretrieval.com

Research Solutions
P.O. Box 3117
Chico, CA 95927
(866) 933-4634
www.researchsolutions.com

San Diego County Public Law
  Library
1168 Union Street
San Diego, CA 92101-3904
(619) 531-3900
FAX (619) 238-7716
www.sdcpll.org

Social Law Library
1 Pemberton Square, Suite 4100
Boston, MA 02108
(617) 226-1500
FAX (617) 523-2458
www.socialaw.com

Thomson Scientific
1500 Spring Garden St., 4th fl.
Philadelphia, PA 19130
(215) 386-0100
(800) 336-4474
FAX (215) 386-2911
scientific.thomson.com

Wisconsin Techsearch
140B Wendt Library
215 N. Randall Ave.
Madison, WI 53706
(608) 262-5917
FAX (800) 514-1423
www.wisc.edu/techsearch

# PROFESSIONAL SERVICES
## (Consultants, filing, employment, cataloguing services, etc.)

Aaron Cohen Associates, Ltd.
159 Teatown Rd.
Croton-on-Hudson, NY 10520
(914) 271-8170
FAX (914) 271-2434
www.acohen.com

Accufile Incorporated
75 Central St., 5th fl.
Boston, MA 02109
(617) 728-3500
FAX (617) 728-3511
www.accufile.com

Andornot Consulting Inc.
1700-808 Nelson St.
Vancouver, BC V6Z 2H2
CANADA
(604) 269-2525; (866) 266-2525
FAX (604) 269-2527
www.andornot.com

Associated Library Service, Inc.
325 W. 38th St.
New York, NY 10018
(212) 748-1800
FAX (212) 346-9420
associatedlibraryservice.com

Axelroth & Associates
2409 Dexter Avenue
Silver Spring, MD 20902
(301) 681-1660
FAX (301) 681-1543
www.axelrothandassociates.com

Balkin Library & Information
  Services
295 Hurstbourne Road
Rochester, NY 14609-5504
(585) 482-1506
FAX (585) 654-5325
www.balkininfo.com

C. Berger Group, Inc.
327 E. Gundersen Dr.
Carol Stream , IL 60188
(630) 653-1115
(800) 382-4CBC
FAX (630) 653-1691
www.cberger.com

Cassidy Cataloguing Services, Inc.
248 W. Main St., Suite 200
Rockaway, NJ 07866

(973) 586-3200
FAX (973) 586-3201
www.cassidycat.com

Everlove & Associates, Inc.
412 65th St. North
St. Petersburg, FL 33710
(727) 345-8180; (800) 487-6672
FAX (727) 345-9525
www.everlove.net

Integrated Management Services
P.O. Box 1448
Hoboken, NJ 07030
(917) 539-7835
www.integratedmgt.com

Law Library Management, Inc.
38 Bunkerhill Drive
Huntington, NY 11743
(631) 266-1093
FAX (631) 266-6923
www.lawlib.com

Library Associates
6500 Wilshire Blvd., Suite 2240
Los Angeles, CA 90048
(323) 852-1083
(800) 987-6794
FAX (323) 852-1093
www.libraryassociates.com

Library Specialists, Inc.
P.O. Box 666100
Marietta, GA 30066
(678) 290-8001
(800) 578-6200
FAX (678) 290-8004
www.libraryspecialists.com

Library Systems & Services, LLC
12850 Middlebrook Rd., Suite 400
Germantown, MD 20874
(301) 540-5100
(800) 638-8725
FAX (301) 540-5522
www.lssi.com

Library Update
332 Terrace Avenue
Hasbrouck Heights, NJ 07604
(201) 288-5883
FAX (201) 288-7976
www.libraryupdate.com

Macdonald Information Consultants
360 Bloor St. E, Suite 1212
Toronto, ON M4W 3M3
CANADA
(416) 972-6195
FAX (416) 972-6265
janetmac@inforamp.ca

McCaughtry & Associates
10 Depot Rd., #1004
Willington, CT 06279
(860) 429-7637
FAX (860) 429-7930
www.mccaughtryassociates.com

Pro Libra Associates Inc.
436 Springfield Ave., Suite 3
Summit, NJ 07901
(908) 918-0077
(800) 262-0070
FAX (908) 918-0977
www.prolibra.com

SIMA, Inc.
P.O. Box 248
Springfield, VA 22150-0248
(703) 569-0993
FAX (703) 569-5161
www.simainc.com

# ONLINE SERVICES

ABC-Clio
P.O. Box 1911
Santa Barbara, CA 93116-1911
(805) 968-1911; (800) 368-6868
FAX (866) 270-3856
www.abc-clio.com

ALM Legal Intelligence
120 Broadway, 5th fl.
New York, NY 10271
(888) 770-5647
almlegalintel.com

American LegalNet, Inc.
16501 Ventura Blvd., Suite 615
Encino, CA 91436
(818) 817-9225
(800) 293-2771
FAX (818) 817-9239
www.americanlegalnet.com

America Online
770 Broadway
New York, NY 10003
(212) 652-6400
www.aol.com

BloombergLaw
(888) 560-2529
bloomberglaw.com

Burrelle's Broadcast Database
75 East Northfield Road
Livingston, NJ 07039
(800) 631-1160
FAX (973) 992-7675
www.burrellesluce.com

CaseClerk.com
P.O. Box 1519
Dandridge, TN 37725
(865) 397-7900
FAX (865) 387-5900
www.caseclerk.com

CasemakerElite
Lawriter LLC
1467 Greenbrier Place
Charlottesville, VA 22903
(877) 659-0801
www.lawriter.net

CCH, Inc.
2700 Lake Cook Road
Riverwoods, IL 60015
(800) 835-0105

FAX (773) 866-3095
www.cch.com

CompuServe, Inc.
P.O. Box 65834
Sterling, VA 20165
(800) 848-8990
www.compuserve.com

CourtLink
(888) 311-1966
courtlinklearning.lexisnexis.com

CQ Roll Call
77 K St., NE, 8th fl.
Washington, DC 20002
(202) 650-6500
(800) 432-2250
corporate.cqrollcall.com

The Dialog Corporation
2250 Perimeter Park Dr., Suite 300
Morrisville, NC 27560
(919) 804-6400
(800) 334-2564
FAX (919) 804-6410
www.dialog.com

The D & B Corporation
103 JFK Pkwy.
Short Hills, NJ 07078
(973) 921-5500
(800) 234-3867
www.dnb.com

EDGAR Online
50 Washington St., 9th fl.
Norwalk, CT 06854
(203) 852-5666
(888) 870-2316
FAX (203) 852-5667
www.edgar-online.com

Factiva
P.O. Box 300
Princeton, NJ 08543-0300
(800) 369-0166
dowjones.com/factiva

Fastcase, Inc.
1155 15th St. NW, Suite 1000
Washington, DC 20005
(866) 773-2782
FAX (703) 740-5960
www.fastcase.com

The Globe and Mail
444 Front Street West
Toronto, ON M5V 2S9
CANADA
(416) 585-5000
www.theglobeandmail.com

HeinOnline
1285 Main St.
Buffalo, NY 14209
(716) 882-2600
(800) 828-7571
heinonline.org

IndexMaster Inc.
P.O. Box 335
Avon, OH 44011
(440) 327-1607
(800) 829-1836
FAX (440) 327-9301
www.indexmaster.com

Infomart Dialog Ltd.
1450 Don Mills Rd.
Toronto, ON M3B 2X7
CANADA
(416) 442-2121
(800) 661-7678
FAX (416) 442-2968
www.fpinfomart.ca

JuriSearch
1467 Greenbrier Place
Charlottesville, VA 22903
(877) 587-4732
FAX (434) 220-6091
www.jurisearch.com

Law.com
120 Broadway, 5th fl.
New York, NY 10271
(877) 256-2472
FAX (415) 558-9380
www.law.com

Law Journal Press Online
120 Broadway, 5th fl.
New York, NY 10271
(877) 807-8076
lawjournalpress.com

Law Resources Online
Oxford University Press
198 Madison Ave.
New York, NY 10016
(800) 624-0153

# ONLINE SERVICES

www.oup.com/online/us/law

TheLawNet
P.O. Box 928106
San Diego, CA 92192
(877) 4 LAWNET
www.thelaw.net

LexisNexis
9433 Springboro Pike
Dayton, OH 45342
(937) 865-6800
(800) 227-4908
www.lexisnexis.com

Loislaw.com, div. Of Wolters
    Kluwer Law & Business
4025 W. Peterson Ave.
Chicago, IL 60646
(877) 471-5632
FAX (866) 887-5232
www.loislaw.com

Mergent
(800) 342-5647
www.mergent.com

National Library of Medicine
8600 Rockville Pike
Bethesda, MD 20894
(301) 594-5983
(888) FIND-NLM
FAX (301) 402-1384
www.nlm.nih.gov

OCLC Online Computer Library
    Center, Inc.
6565 Kilgour Place
Dublin, OH 43017-3395
(614) 764-6000
(800) 848-5878
FAX (614) 764-6096
www.oclc.org

Ovid
333 Seventh Ave, 20th fl.
New York, NY 10001
(646) 674-6300
(800) 950-2035
FAX (646) 674-6301
www.ovid.com

Practical Law Company, Inc.
747 Third Avenue, 36th fl.
New York, NY 10017
(646) 562-3405
us.practicallaw.com

Questel Orbit
1725 Duke Street
Alexandria, VA 22314
(703) 519-1820
(800) 456-7248
FAX (703) 519-1821
www.questel.orbit.com

Smart Litigator
120 Broadway, 5th fl.
New York, NY 10271
(877) 807-8076
smartlitigator.com

State Net
444 N Capitol St. NW, Suite 725
Washington, DC 20001
(202) 638-7999
FAX (202) 638-7292
www.statenet.com

Thomson Financial Securities Data
22 Thomson Place
Boston, MA 02210
(617) 856-2000
(877) 882-4373
www.thomson.com/solutions/
    financial

VersusLaw
P.O. Box 1435
Bellevue, WA 98009
(425) 250-0142
FAX (425) 250-0157
www.versuslaw.com

Westlaw
610 Opperman Drive
Eagan, MN 55123
(651) 687-7000
(800) 328-9352
www.westlaw.com

WilsonWeb
950 University Avenue
Bronx, NY 10452
(718) 588-8400
www.hwwilson.com

# LITIGATION SUPPORT COMPANIES AND SOFTWARE

Access Data
425 Market St., 7th fl.
San Francisco, CA 94105
(801) 377-5410
accessdata.com

Advocate Software
4575 Gallery Rd.
Colorado Springs, CO 80915
(800) 825-8763
(888) 216-4374
FAX (719) 548-4477
www.advocatesoftware.com

C2 Legal
45 W. 45th St., 2nd fl.
New York, NY 10036
(212) 871-5190
FAX (917) 289-9197
www.c2legal.com

Chicago Partners
30 S. Wacker, 34th fl.
Chicago, IL 60606
(312) 251-5200
FAX (312) 251-5201
www.chipar.com

Compex Legal Services
352 Maple Ave.
Torrance, CA 90503
(310) 782-1801
(800) 669-5170
FAX (800) 479-3365
www.compexlegal.com

CompuLaw LLC
10277 W. Olympic Boulevard
Los Angeles, CA 90067
(310) 553-3355
(800) 444-0215
FAX (310) 553-7660
www.compulaw.com

Concordance
13427 NE 16th St., Suite 100
Bellevue, WA 98005
(425) 467-3515
(800) 421-8398
FAX (425) 974-1419
www.lexisnexis.com/concordance

Doar Litigation Consulting
170 Earle Ave.
Lynbrook, NY 11563
(516) 823-4000
(800) 875-8705
FAX (516) 823-4400
www.doar.com

DocuWorks, Inc.
17311 Dallas Pkwy.
Dallas, TX 75248
(877) 342-0698
FAX (972) 267-8565
www.docuworks.com/

EED
11 Stott Ave.
Norwich, CT 06360
(860) 823-4400; (800) 676-2215
FAX (860) 823-4401
eed-dt.com

InMagic, Inc.
200 Unicorn Park Dr., 4th fl.
Woburn, MA 01801
(781) 938-4444
(800) 229-8398
FAX (781) 938-4446
www.inmagic.com

ISYS Search Software
8765 E. Orchard Rd., Suite 702
Englewood, CO 80111
(303) 689-9998
(800) 992-4797
FAX (303) 689-9997
www.isysdev.com

Kroll Ontrack
9023 Columbine Rd.
Eden Prairie, MN 55347
(800) 347-6105
www.krollontrack.com

Litigation Risk Analysis, Inc.
P.O. Box 1085
Kenwood, CA 95452
(707) 833-1093
FAX (707) 833-0084
www.litigationrisk.com

Lockheed Martin Aspen Systems
2277 Research Blvd.
Rockville, MD 20850
(301) 519-5000
FAX (301) 330-8946
www.aspensys.com

SuperiorGlacier
42 Broadway, 2nd fl.
New York, NY 10004
(212)514-6500
Fax (212) 635-2499
www.superiorglacier.com

TechLaw Solutions, Inc.
14500 Avion Pkwy., Suite 301
Chantilly, VA 20151
(703) 818-3225
FAX (703) 817-1149
www.techlawsolutions.com

# URLs OF LEADING LAW-RELATED WEB SITES

### Law-Related Index Pages

| | |
|---|---|
| FindLaw | http://www.findlaw.com |
| Legal Information Institute | http://www.law.cornell.edu |
| Hieros Gamos | http://www.hg.org |
| WashLaw Web | http://www.washlaw.edu |
| Justia | http://www.justia.com |

### Search Engines

| | |
|---|---|
| Google | http://www.google.com |
| Yahoo | http://www.yahoo.com |
| Bing | http://www.bing.com |
| Ask | http://www.ask.com |
| Internet Archive | http://www.archive.org |

### State Law Index Pages

| | |
|---|---|
| Cornell Univ. Legal Information Institute | http://www.law.cornell.edu/states/ |
| FindLaw | http://www.findlaw.com/11stategov/ |
| Hieros Gamos | http://www.hg.org/usstates.html |
| Municipal Codes: Municode.com | http://www.municode.com/library/library.aspx |
| E-Codes | http://www.generalcode.com/webcode2.html |
| American Legal Pub. | http://www.amlegal.com/library/ |
| National Conf. of State Legislatures Bill Tracking | http://www.ncsl.org/default.aspx?tabid=21583 |
| Uniform Law Commissioners | http://www.nccusl.org/Acts.aspx |

### Federal Government Sites

Links for all federal agencies:

| | |
|---|---|
| US Government Official Web Portal | http://www.usa.gov |
| Louisiana State University Libraries | http://www.lib.lsu.edu/gov/index.html |
| Government Information Locator Service | http://www.gpoaccess.gov/gils/index.html |
| Executive: White House | http://www.whitehouse.gov |
| Legislative: Thomas | http://thomas.loc.gov |
| FDSys | http://www.gpo.gov/fdsys/ |
| U.S. House of Representatives | http://www.house.gov |
| U.S. Senate | http://www.senate.gov |
| Federal Judiciary | http://www.uscourts.gov |
| U.S. Supreme Court | http://www.supremecourtus.gov |
| Library of Congress | http://lcweb.loc.gov |
| U.S. Code | http://1.usa.gov/nhXWKF |
| Code of Federal Regulations | http://1.usa.gov/qrAaVM |
| | http://www.regulations.gov/ |
| Federal Register | http://1.usa.gov/neDpcE |
| | http://www.federalregister.gov |
| Congressional Record | http://1.usa.gov/mXe3PQ |
| U. S. Government Manual | http://usgovernmentmanual.gov/ |
| Congressional Directory | http://bioguide.congress.gov/biosearch/biosearch.asp |
| U.S. Constitution | http://1.usa.gov/p8FCe0 |
| Administrative Decisions & Other Actions | http://bit.ly/qzTUcZ |

### Blawgs

| | |
|---|---|
| Blawg | http://www.blawg.com/ |
| Blawg Directory (ABA) | http://www.abajournal.com/blawgs |
| Justia Blawg Search | http://blawgsearch.justia.com/ |

### Case Law

| | |
|---|---|
| LexisONE | http://www.lexisone.com/caselaw/freecaselaw/ |
| Google Advanced Scholar Search | http://scholar.google.com/advanced_scholar_search |
| FindACase | http://findacase.com/ |
| Public Library of Law | http://www.plol.org/Pages/Search.aspx |
| Justia | http:///law.justia.com/cases/ |

# ASSOCIATIONS AND ORGANIZATIONS

## AMERICAN BAR ASSOCIATION
321 N. Clark St.
Chicago, IL 60610
(312) 988-5000; (800) 285-2221
FAX (312) 988-6281, 6282, 6283
URL: www.americanbar.org

**SECTIONS, DIVISIONS, AND FORUMS OF THE AMERICAN BAR ASSOCIATION**
Administrative Law and Regulatory Practice (202) 662-1582 adminlaw@americanbar.org
Antitrust Law (312) 988-5550 antitrust@americanbar.org
Business Law (312) 988-5588 businesslaw@americanbar.org
Criminal Justice (202) 662-1500 crimjustice@americanbar.org
Dispute Resolution (202) 662-1680 dispute@americanbar.org
Division for Bar Services (312) 988-5343 barservices@americanbar.org
Division for Media Relations and Communication Services (312) 988-6137 abanews@americanbar.org
Environment, Energy & Resources (312) 988-5724 environ@americanbar.org
Family Law (312) 988-5145 familylaw@americanbar.org
Forums:  Affordable Housing and Community Development Law (312) 988-5660 dawn.holiday@americanbar.org
         Air and Space Law (312) 988-5660 dawn.holiday@americanbar.org
         Communications Law (312) 988-5580 Teresa.Ucok@americanbar.org
         Construction Industry (312) 988-5579 amanda.raible@americanbar.org
         Entertainment and Sports Industries (312) 988-5580 Teresa.Ucok@americanbar.org
         Franchising (312) 988-5794 kelly.rodenberg@americanbar.org
General Practice Solo and Small Firm Section (312) 988-5648 genpractice@americanbar.org
Government and Public Sector Lawyers Division (202) 662-1020 gpsld@americanbar.org
Health Law Section (312) 988-5548 healthlaw@americanbar.org
Individual Rights and Responsibilities (202) 662-1030 irr@americanbar.org
Intellectual Property Law (312) 988-5598 iplaw@americanbar.org
International Law and Practice (202) 662-1660 intlaw@americanbar.org
Judicial Division (312) 988-5700 abajd@americanbar.org
         Appellate Judges' Conference
         Lawyers Conference
         National Conference of Administrative Law Judiciary
         National Conference of Federal Trial Judges
         National Conference of Specialized Court Judges
         National Conference of State Trial Judges
Labor and Employment Law (312) 988-5813 laborempllaw@americanbar.org
Law Practice Management (312) 988-5661 lpm@americanbar.org
Law Student Division (312) 988-5624 abalsd@americanbar.org
Legal Education and Admissions to the Bar (312) 988-6738 legaled@americanbar.org
Legal Services (312) 988-5749 legalservices@americanbar.org
Litigation (312) 988-5662 abalit@americanbar.org
Public Contract Law (312) 988-5596 pubcontract@americanbar.org
Public Education Division (312) 988-5735 publiceducation@americanbar.org
Public Services Division (202) 662-1691 pubservices@americanbar.org
Public Utility, Communications & Transportation Law (312) 988-6238 pubutil@americanbar.org
Real Property, Probate and Trust Law (312) 988-5670 rpte@americanbar.org
Science and Technology (312) 988-5599 sciencetech@americanbar.org
Senior Lawyers Division (312) 988-5582 abasrlawyers@americanbar.org
State and Local Government Law (312) 988-5649 statelocal@americanbar.org
Taxation (202) 662-8670 tax@americanbar.org
Tort, Trial and Insurance Practice (312) 988-5673 tips@americanbar.org
Young Lawyers Division (312) 988-5611 yld@americanbar.org

# SELECTED ASSOCIATIONS

Advanced Medical Technology
  Association (AdvaMed)
701 Pennsylvania Ave., NW, Ste 800
Washington, DC 20004
(202) 783-8700
FAX (202) 783-8750
www.advamed.org

American Academy of Actuaries
1850 M St., NW, Suite 300
Washington, DC 20036
(202) 223-8196
FAX (202) 872-1948
www.actuary.org

American Academy of Matrimonial
  Lawyers
150 N. Michigan Avenue, Ste. 2040
Chicago, IL 60601
(312) 263-6477
FAX (312) 263-7682
www.aaml.org

American Advertising Federation
1101 Vermont Ave., NW, Ste. 500
Washington, DC 20005-6306
(202) 898-0089; (800) 999-2231
FAX (202) 898-0159
www.aaf.org

American Arbitration Association
1633 Broadway, 10th fl.
New York, NY 10019
(212) 716-5800
(800) 778-7879
FAX (212) 716-5905
www.adr.org

American Association for Justice
777 6th St., NW, Suite 200
Washington, DC 20001
(202) 965-3500
(800) 424-2725
FAX (202) 333-2861
www.justice.org

American Bankers Association
1120 Connecticut Ave., NW
Washington, DC 20036
(202) 663-5000
(800) BANKERS
FAX (202) 663-7453
www.aba.com

American Bankruptcy Institute
44 Canal Center Plaza, Suite 400
Alexandria, VA 22314
(703) 739-0800
(703) 739-1060
www.abiworld.org

American Bar Association
321 N. Clark St.
Chicago, IL 60610
(312) 988-5000
(800) 285-2221
FAX (312) 988-6281
www.americanbar.org

American Bar Foundation
750 N. Lake Shore Drive, 4th fl.
Chicago, IL 60611-4403
(312) 988-6500
FAX (312) 988-6579
www.abf-sociolegal.org

American Chemistry Council
700 2nd St. NE
Washington, DC 20002
(202) 249-7000
FAX (202) 249-6100
www.americanchemistry.com/

American College of Trust and
  Estate Counsel
901 15th St., NW
Washington, DC 20005
(202) 684-8460
FAX (202) 684-8459
www.actec.org

American Corporate Counsel Assn.
1025 Connecticut Ave. NW, Ste. 200
Washington, DC 20036
(202) 293-4103
FAX (202) 293-4701
www.acca.com

American Council of Life Insurance
101 Constitution Ave. NW, Suite 700
Washington, DC 20001-2133
(202) 624-2000
(877) 674-4659
www.acli.com

American Enterprise Institute
1150 Seventeenth St. NW
Washington, DC 20036

(202) 862-5800
FAX (202) 862-7177
www.aei.org

American Financial Services
  Association
919 18th Street, NW, Suite 300
Washington, DC 20006
(202) 296-5544
FAX (202) 223-0321
www.afsaonline.com

American Health Lawyers Assn.
1620 Eye St., NW, 6th fl.
Washington, DC 20006
(202) 833-1100
FAX (202) 833-1105
www.healthlawyers.org

American Immigration Lawyers
  Association
1331 G St, NW, Suite 300
Washington, DC 20005-3142
(202) 507-7600
FAX (202) 783-7853
www.aila.org

American Institute of Architects
1735 New York Ave., NW
Washington, DC 20006-5292
(800) AIA-3837
FAX (202) 626-7547
www.aia.org/

American Institute of Certified
  Public Accountants
2200 Leigh Farm Rd.
Durham, NC 27707
(201) 938-3000; (877) 242-7212
FAX (800) 362-5066
www.aicpa.org

American Insurance Association
2101 L St. NW, Suite 400
Washington, DC 20037
(202) 828-7100
FAX (202) 293-1219
www.aiadc.org

American Intellectual Property Law
  Association
241 18th St. South, Suite 700
Arlington, VA 22202
(703) 415-0780

FAX (703) 415-0786
www.aipla.org

American Judges Association
300 Newport Ave.
Williamsburg, VA 23185-4147
(757) 259-1841
(800) 616-6165
FAX (757) 259-1520
aja.ncsc.dni.us/

American Judicature Society
2700 University Ave.
Des Moines, Iowa 50311
(515) 271-2281; (800) 626-4089
FAX (515) 279-3090
www.ajs.org

American Law Institute
4025 Chestnut Street
Philadelphia, PA 19104
(215) 243-1600
FAX (215) 243-1636
www.ali.org

American Management Association
1601 Broadway
New York, NY 10019
(212) 586-8100
(800) 262-9699
FAX (212) 903-8168
www.amanet.org

American Marketing Association
311 S. Wacker Drive, Suite 5800
Chicago, IL 60606
(312) 542-9000
(800) AMA-1150
FAX (312) 542-9001
www.marketingpower.com

American Medical Association
515 N. State Street
Chicago, IL 60654
(312) 464-5000
(800) 621-8335
FAX (312) 464-4184
www.ama-assn.org

American Petroleum Institute
1220 L Street, NW, 9th fl.
Washington, DC 20005-4070
(202) 682-8000
FAX (202) 682-8099
www.api.org

American Prepaid Legal Services
 Institute
321 N. Clark St., 19th fl.

Chicago, IL 60654
(312) 988-5751
FAX (312) 988-5785
www.aplsi.org

American Society of Composers,
 Authors and Publishers
One Lincoln Plaza
New York, NY 10023
(212) 621-6000
FAX (212) 621-8453
www.ascap.com

American Society of International
Law
2223 Massachusetts Avenue NW
Washington, DC 20008
(202) 939-6000
FAX (202) 797-7133
www.asil.org

American Tort Reform Association
1101 Connecticut Ave. NW, Ste. 400
Washington, DC 20036
(202) 682-1163
FAX (202) 682-1022
www.atra.org

Appraisal Institute
550 W. Van Buren Street, Suite 1000
Chicago, IL 60607
(312) 335-4100
FAX (312) 335-4400
www.appraisalinstitute.org

Association of American Law
 Schools
1201 Connecticut Ave. NW, Ste. 800
Washington, DC 20036-2717
(202) 296-8851
FAX (202) 296-8869
www.aals.org

Association for Conflict Resolution
12100 Sunset Hills Rd., Suite 130
Reston, VA 20190
(703) 234-4141
FAX (703) 435-4390
www.acrnet.org

Association of Legal Administrators
75 Tri-State International, Suite 222
Lincolnshire, IL 60069-4435
(847) 267-1252
FAX (847) 267-1329
www.alanet.org

Bank Administration Institute
115 S. LaSalle St, Suite 3300

Chicago, IL 60606-3801
(312) 683-2464
(888) 284-4078
FAX (312) 683-2373
www.bai.org

Commercial Finance Association
370 7th Ave., Suite 1801
New York, NY 10001
(212) 792-9390
FAX (212) 564-6053
www.cfa.com

Commercial Law League of America
205 N. Michigan, Suite 2212
Chicago, IL 60601
(312) 240-1400
FAX (312) 240-1408
www.clla.org

Conference of Chief Justices
300 Newport Avenue
Williamsburg, VA 23185-4147
(757) 259-1841
FAX (757) 259-1520
ccj.ncsc.dni.us/

Conference of State Bank
 Supervisors
1129 20th St., NW, 9th fl.
Washington, DC 20036
(202) 296-2840
FAX (202) 296-1928
www.csbs.org

Copyright Clearance Center
222 Rosewood Drive
Danvers, MA 01923
(978) 750-8400
FAX (978) 646-8600
www.copyright.com

Copyright Society of the U.S.A.
352 7th Ave., Suite 739
New York, NY 10001
(212) 354-6401
www.csusa.org

Council of State Governments
P.O. Box 11910
Lexington, KY 40578-1910
(859) 244-8000
FAX (859) 244-8001
www.csg.org

Direct Marketing Association, Inc.
1120 Ave. of the Americas
New York, NY 10036-6700
(212) 768-7277

FAX (212) 302-6714
www.the-dma.org

Education Law Association
300 College Park
Dayton, OH 45469-0528
(937) 229-3589
FAX (937) 229-3845
www.educationlaw.org

Energy Bar Association
1990 M St, NW, Suite 350
Washington, DC 20036
(202) 223-5625
FAX (202) 833-5596
www.eba-net.org

Environmental Law Institute
2000 L St., NW, Suite 620
Washington, DC 20036
(202) 939-3800
FAX (202) 939-3868
www.eli.org

The Federal Bar Association
1220 N. Fillmore St., Suite 444
Arlington, VA 22201
(571) 481-9100
(571) 481-9090
www.fedbar.org

Federation of Tax Administrators
444 N. Capitol Street, Suite 348
Washington, DC 20001
(202) 624-5890
www.taxadmin.org

Financial Industry Regulatory
  Authority, Inc.
1735 K Street, NW
Washington, DC 20006
(202) 728-8000
FAX (202) 728-8882
www.nasd.com

Food and Drug Law Institute
1155 15th St., NW, Suite 800
Washington, DC 20005
(202) 371-1420
FAX (202) 371-0649
www.fdli.org

Futures Industry Association
2001 Pennsylvania Ave., NW,
  Suite 600
Washington, DC 20006
(202) 466-5460
FAX (202) 296-3184
www.futuresindustry.org

Independent Community Bankers of
  America
1615 L St., NW, Suite 900
Washington, D. C. 20036
(800) 422-8439
FAX (202) 659-3604
www.icba.org

Institute of Judicial Administration
40 Washington Sq. South, Rm. 413
New York, NY 10012
(212) 998-6217
FAX (212) 995-4881
www.law.nyu.edu/institutes/judicial

Insurance Information Institute
110 William Street
New York, NY 10038
(212) 346-5500
www.iii.org

Inter-American Bar Association
1211 Connecticut Ave. NW, Ste. 202
Washington, DC 20036
(202) 466-5944
FAX (202) 466-5946
www.iaba.org

International Association of Defense
  Counsel
303 W. Madison, Suite 925
Chicago, IL 60606
(312) 368-1494
FAX (312) 368-1854
www.iadclaw.org

International Code Council
500 New Jersey Ave NW, 6th fl.
Washington, DC 20001-2070
(202) 783-2348
(800) 422-7233
www.iccsafe.org

International Law Institute
1055 Thomas Jefferson St., NW,
  Suite M100
Washington, DC 20007
(202) 247-6006
FAX (202) 247-6010
www.ili.org/

International Municipal Lawyers
  Association
7910 Woodmont Ave., Suite 1440
Bethesda, MD 20814
(202) 466-5424
FAX (202) 785-0152
www.imla.org

International Technology Law
  Association
401 Edgewater Place, Suite 600
Wakefield, MA 01880
(781) 876-8877
FAX (781) 224-1239
www.itechlaw.org

International Trademark Association
655 Third Ave, 10th fl.
New York, NY 10017-5617
(212) 642-1700
FAX (212) 768-7796
www.inta.org

Investment Company Institute
1401 H St., NW, Suite 1200
Washington, DC 20005
(202) 326-5800
FAX (202) 326-5985
www.ici.org

Justice Research & Statistics Assn.
777 N. Capitol Street, NE, Suite 801
Washington, DC 20002
(202) 842-9330
FAX (202) 842-9329
www.jrsa.org

Law School Admission Council
662 Penn Street
Newtown, PA 18940
(215) 968-1001
FAX (215) 968-1119
www.lsac.org

Lawyers' Committee For Civil
  Rights Under Law
1401 New York Ave. NW, Ste. 400
Washington, DC 20005
(202) 662-8600
FAX (202) 783-0857
www.lawyerscommittee.org

Media Law Resource Center
520 8th Ave., North Tower, 20th fl.
New York, NY 10018
(212) 337-0200
FAX (212) 337-9893
www.medialaw.org

Mortgage Bankers Association of
  America
1717 Rhode Island Ave., Suite 400
Washington, DC 20036
(202) 557-2700
www.mbaa.org

National Association for Legal
Career Professionals
1220 20th St., NW, Suite 401
Washington, DC 20036
(202) 835-1001
FAX (202) 835-1112
www.nalp.org

National Association of Attorneys
 General
2030 M St., NW, 8th fl.
Washington, DC 20036
(202) 326-6000
FAX (202) 331-1427
www.naag.org

National Assocation.of Bar
Executives
321 N. Clark St., Suite 2000
Chicago, IL 60610
(312) 988-6008
FAX (312) 988-5492
www.americanbar.org/nabe/

National Association of Broadcasters
1771 N Street, NW
Washington, DC 20036
(202) 429-5300
FAX (202) 429-4199
www.nab.org

National Association of College and
 University Attorneys
One Dupont Circle, Suite 620
Washington, DC 20036
(202) 833-8390
FAX (202) 296-8379
www.nacua.org

National Association of Criminal
 Defense Lawyers
1660 L Street, NW, 12th fl.
Washington, DC 20036
(202) 872-8600
FAX (202) 872-8690
www.nacdl.org

National Association of Insurance
 Commissioners
2301 McGee Street, Suite 800
Kansas City, MO 64108-2662
(816) 842-3600
FAX (816) 783-8175
www.naic.org

National Association of Legal
Assistants
1516 S. Boston, Suite 200
Tulsa, OK 74119

(918) 587-6828
FAX (918) 582-6772
www.nala.org

National Association of Legal
Secretaries
8159 E. 41st St.
Tulsa, OK 74145
(918) 582-5188
FAX (918) 582-5907
www.nals.org

National Association of Realtors
430 N. Michigan Avenue
Chicago, IL 60611
(800) 874-6500
www.realtor.org

National Association of Regulatory
 Utility Commissioners
1101 Vermont Ave NW, Suite 200
Washington, DC 20005
(202) 898-2200
FAX (202) 898-2213
www.naruc.org

National Association of Secretaries
 of State
444 N. Capitol St., NW, Suite 401
Washington, DC 20001
(202) 624-3525
FAX (202) 624-3527
www.nass.org

National Association of Women
 Lawyers
321 N. Clark St.
Chicago, IL 60610
(312) 988-6186
FAX (312) 988-5491
www.nawl.org

National Bar Association
1225 11th Street, NW
Washington, DC 20001
(202) 842-3900
FAX (202) 289-6170
www.nationalbar.org

National Center for State Courts
300 Newport Avenue
Williamsburg, VA 23185-4147
(800) 616-6164
FAX (757) 564-2022
www.ncsc.org

National Conference of Bar
 Examiners
302 S. Bedford Street

Madison, WI 53703-3622
(608) 280-8550
FAX (608) 280-8552
www.ncbex.org

National Conference of Black
 Lawyers
P.O. Box 10024
New York, NY 10024
(866) 266-5091
FAX (212) 222-2680
www.ncbl.org

National Conference of
 Commissioners on Uniform State
 Laws
111 N. Wabash Ave., Suite 1010
Chicago, IL 60602
(312) 450-6600
FAX (312) 450-6601
www.nccusl.org

National Conference of Insurance
 Legislators
385 Jordan Rd.
Troy, NY 12180
(518) 687-0178
FAX (518) 687-0401
www.ncoil.org/

National Conference of State
 Legislatures
7700 E. 1st Place
Denver, CO 80230
(303) 364-7700
FAX (303) 364-7800
www.ncsl.org

National Conference of States on
 Building Codes and Standards, Inc.
505 Huntmar Park Drive, Suite 210
Herndon, VA 20170
(703) 437-0100
FAX (703) 481-3596
www.ncsbcs.org

National Conference of Women's
 Bar Associations
P.O. Box 82366
Portland, OR 97282
(503) 657-3813
FAX (503) 657-3932
www.ncwba.org

National Council of Juvenile and
 Family Court Judges
P.O. Box 8970
Reno, NV 89507
(775) 784-6012

FAX (775) 784-6628
www.ncjfcj.org/

National Court Reporters Assn.
8224 Old Courthouse Rd.
Vienna, VA 22182-3808
(703) 556-NCRA
(800) 272-NCRA
FAX (703) 556-6291
msic@ncrahq.org
www.verbatimreporters.com

National Criminal Justice Assn.
720 7th Street, NW, 3rd fl.
Washington, DC 20001-3716
(202) 628-8550
FAX (202) 448-1723
www.ncja.org

National District Attorneys Assn.
44 Canal Center Plaza, Suite 510
Alexandria, VA 22314
(703) 549-9222
FAX (703) 836-3195
www.ndaa.org

National Education Association
1201 16th Street, NW
Washington, DC 20036-3290
(202) 833-4000
FAX (202) 822-7974
www.nea.org

National Federation of Paralegal
 Associations
P.O. Box 2016
Edmonds, WA 98020
(425) 967-0045
FAX (425) 771-9588
www.paralegals.org

National Futures Association
300 S. Riverside Plaza, Suite 1800
Chicago, IL 60606-6615
(312) 781-1300
(800) 621-3570
FAX (312) 781-1467
www.nfa.futures.org

National Governors' Association
444 N. Capitol Street
Washington, DC 20001-1512
(202) 624-5300
FAX (202) 624-5313
www.nga.org

National Institute for Trial
 Advocacy
1685 38th St., Suite 200

Boulder, CO 80301
(800) 225-6482
FAX (720) 890-7069
www.nita.org

National Judicial College
University of Nevada
Judicial College Building #358
Reno, NV 89557
(775) 784-6747
(800) 255-8343
FAX (775) 784-1253
www.judges.org

National Lawyers Guild
132 Nassau St., Suite 922
New York, NY 10038
(212) 679-5100
FAX (212) 679-2811
www.nlg.org/

National League of Cities
1301 Pennsylvania Avenue, NW,
 Suite 550
Washington, DC 20004
(202) 626-3000
FAX (202) 626-3043
www.nlc.org

National Legal Aid and Defender
 Association
1140 Connecticut Ave. NW, Ste. 900
Washington, DC 20036
(202) 452-0620
FAX (202) 872-1031
www.nlada.org/

National Notary Association
9350 De Soto Ave.
Chatsworth, CA 91311
(800) 876-6827
FAX (800) 833-1211
www.nationalnotary.org/

National Paralegal Association
Box 406
Solebury, PA 18963
(215) 297-8333
FAX (215) 297-8358
www.nationalparalegal.org

North American Securities
 Administrators Association, Inc.
750 First St., Suite 1140
Washington, DC 20002
(202) 737-0900
FAX (202) 783-3571
www.nasaa.org

Puerto Rican Bar Association
303 Park Avenue South, Suite 1405
New York, NY 10010
(347) 244-7132
www.prba.net

Securities Industry and Financial
 Markets Association
120 Broadway, 35th fl..
New York, NY 10271
(212) 313-1200
FAX (212) 313-1301
www.sifma.org

Society of Actuaries
475 N. Martingale, Suite 600
Schaumburg, IL 60173
(847) 706-3500
FAX (847) 706-3599
www.soa.org

Sports Lawyers Association
12100 Sunset Hills Rd., Suite 130
Reston, VA 20190
(703) 437-4377
FAX (703) 435-4390
www.sportslaw.org

U.S. Chamber of Commerce
1615 H Street, NW
Washington, DC 20062-2000
(202) 659-6000
www.uschamber.com

United States Conference of Mayors
1620 I Street, NW
Washington, DC 20006
(202) 293-7330
FAX (202) 293-2352
www.usmayors.org/

Vera Institute of Justice
233 Broadway, 12th fl.
New York, NY 10279
(212) 334-1300
FAX (212) 941-9407
www.vera.org

# SELECTED FOREIGN LAW ASSOCIATIONS

Australian Bar Association
Level 5 Inns of Court
North Quay, Brisbane
Queeensland 4001, Australia
617-3238-5100
www.austbar.asn.au

The Bar Council
289-293 High Holborn
London, WC1V 7HZ England
44(71) 242-0082
FAX 44(71) 831-9217
www.barcouncil.org.uk

Barreau du Quebec
445 boul. Saint-Laurent
Montreal, QC H2Y 3T8
Canada
(514) 954-3400
www.barreau.qc.ca/

Canadian Bar Association
500-865 Carling Ave.
Ottawa, Ontario, K1S 5S8
Canada
(613) 237-2925
(800) 267-8860
FAX (613) 237-0185
www.cba.org

Chambre des Notaires du Quebec
600-1801, avenue McGill College
Montreal, Quebec H3A 0A7
Canada
(514) 879-1793
(800) 263-1793
FAX (514) 879-1923
www.cdnq.org/

Confederation Nationale des
  Avocats
15, rue Soufflot
75005 Paris,
France
(1) 43-54-65-48
FAX (1) 43-54-75-09
www.cna-avocats.fr

Federation of Law Societies of
  Canada
45 O'Connor St., Suite 1810
Ottawa, Ontario K1P 1A4
Canada
(613) 236-7272

FAX (613) 236-7233
www.flsc.ca/

General Council of the Bar of
  Ireland
P.O. Box 4460
The Four Courts
Dublin 7, Ireland
353 (1) 8175000
FAX 353 (1) 8175150
www.lawlibrary.ie

General Council of the Bar of
  Northern Ireland
Royal Court of Justice
91 Chichester Street
P.O. Box 414
Belfast BT1 3JP
Northern Ireland
(01232) 562349
FAX (01232) 562350
www.barlibrary.com

General Council of the Bar of South
  Africa
P.O. Box 786878
Sandton 2146
South Africa
+27 (0) 11 784-0175
FAX +27 (0) 11 784-0182
www.sabar.co.za/

International Bar Association
1 Stephen St., 10th fl.
London, W1T 1AT
England
44-0207-691-6868
FAX 44-0207-691-6544
www.ibanet.org/

Japan Federation of Bar Associations
1-1-3- Kasumigaseki
Chiyoda-ku, Tokyo 100-D013
Japan
81 (3) 3580-9741
FAX 81 (3) 3580-9840
www.nichibenren.or.jp/en

Law Council of Australia
GPO Box 1989
Canberra ACT 2601
Australia
02 6246-3788
FAX 02 6248-0639

www.lawcouncil.asn.au/

The Law Institute of Victoria
470 Bourke St.
Melbourne, Victoria 3000
Australia
(3) 9607-9311
FAX (3) 9602-5270
www.liv.asn.au/

The Law Society of Alberta
500-919-11th Avenue, SW
Calgary, Alberta T2R 1P3
Canada
(403) 229-4700
(800) 661-9003
FAX (403) 228-1728
www.lawsocietyalberta.com

The Law Society of British
  Columbia
845 Cambie Street
Vancouver, BC V6B 4Z9
Canada
(604) 669-2533
(800) 903-5300 (BC)
FAX (604) 669-5232
www.lawsociety.bc.ca/

Law Society of England & Wales
113 Chancery Lane
London WC2A 1PL
England
44 207 242-1222
FAX 44 207 831-0344
www.lawsoc.org.uk/

The Law Society of Hong Kong
3/F., Wing On House,
71 Des Voeux Rd., Central,
Hong Kong
(852) 28460500
FAX (852) 28450387
www.hklawsoc.org.hk/

Law Society of Ireland
Blackhall Place
Dublin 7, Ireland
(353) 1-672-4800
FAX (353) 1-672-4801
www.lawsociety.ie/

The Law Society of Manitoba
219 Kennedy Street

# SELECTED FOREIGN LAW ASSOCIATIONS

Winnipeg, MB R3C 1S8
Canada
(204) 942-5571
FAX (204) 956-0624
www.lawsociety.mb.ca/

Law Society of New Brunswick
68 Avonlea Court
Fredericton, NB E3C 1N8
Canada
(506) 458-8540
FAX (506) 451-1421
www.lawsociety.nb.ca

The Law Society of New South
  Wales
170 Philip Street
Sydney NSW 2000
Australia
+61-2-9926-0333
FAX +61-2-9231-5809
www.lawsociety.com.au/

Law Society of Newfoundland and
  Labrador
P.O. Box 1028
St. John's, Newfoundland A1C 5M3
Canada
(709) 722-4740
FAX (709) 722-8902
www.lawsociety.nf.ca/

The Law Society of Northern
  Ireland
96 Victoria St.
Belfast BT1 3GN
Northern Ireland, United Kingdom
44-028-9023-1614
FAX 44-028-9023-2606
www.lawsoc-ni.org

The Law Society of Prince Edward
  Island
49 Water Street
Box 128
Charlottetown, PE C1A 7K2
Canada
(902) 566-1666
FAX (902) 368-7557
www.lspei.pe.ca

Law Society of Saskatchewan
2425 Victoria Avenue
Regina, SK S4P 0R7
Canada
(877) 989-4999
FAX (306) 352-2989
www.lawsociety.sk.ca/

The Law Society of Scotland
LP1-EDINBURGH1
26 Drumsheugh Gardens
Edinburgh EH3 7YR
Scotland
+440 (131) 226-7411
FAX +440 (131) 225-2934
www.lawscot.org.uk

Law Society of Singapore
39 South Bridge Rd.
Singapore 058673
(65) 6538-2500
FAX (65) 6533-5700
www.lawsoc.org.sg/

Law Society of South Africa
304 Brooks Street
Menlo Park, Pretoria
South Africa
27 (12) 366-8800
FAX 27 (12) 362-0969
lssa.org.za

Law Society of Tasmania
28 Murray St.
Hobart, Tasmania,
Australia 7000
+61 (03) 6234-4133
FAX +61 (03) 6223 8240
www.taslawsociety.asn.au/

Law Society of the Australian
  Capital Territory
11 London Circuit, Level 3
Canberra ACT,
Australia 2601
(02) 6247-5700
FAX (02) 6247-3754
actlawsociety.asn.au

Law Society of the Northwest
  Territories
P.O. Box 1298
5004-50th Ave., Main fl.
Yellowknife, NT X1A 2N9
Canada
(867) 873-3828
FAX (867) 873-6344
www.lawsociety.nt.ca/

The Law Society of Upper Canada
Osgoode Hall
130 Queen Street W.
Toronto, M5H 2N6
Canada
(416) 947-3300
(800) 668-7380

FAX (416) 947-3924
www.lsuc.on.ca

The Law Society of Yukon Territory
302 Steele Street, Suite 202
Whitehorse, Yukon Y1A 2C5
Canada
(867) 668-4231
FAX (867) 667-7556
www.lawsocietyyukon.com

The New South Wales Bar
  Association
Selbourne Chambers
174 Philip Street
Sydney NSW 2000
Australia
(2) 9232-4055
FAX (2) 9221-1149
www.nswbar.asn.au/

New Zealand Law Society
P.O. Box 5041, Lambton Quay
Wellington, 6145
New Zealand
+64 (4) 4727-837
FAX +64 (4) 4737-909
www.nz-lawsoc.org.nz/

Netherlands Orde van Advocaten
P.O. Box 30851
2500 GW Den Haag
Netherlands
(70) 335-3535
FAX (70) 335-3531
www.advocatenorde.nl

Nova Scotia Barristers' Society
1101-1645 Granville St.
Halifax, NS B3J 1X3
Canada
(902) 422-1491
FAX (902) 429-4869
www.nsbs.ns.ca

Ordre des Avocats de Paris
11, place Dauphine
75053 Paris, France
01-80-27 19 20
www.avocatparis.org

# STATE BAR ASSOCIATIONS

Alabama State Bar
415 Dexter Ave.
Montgomery, AL 36104
(334) 269-1515
FAX (334) 261-6310
Exec. Dir.: Keith B. Norman
www.alabar.org

Alaska Bar Association
P.O. Box 100279
Anchorage, AK 99501-0279
(907) 272-7469
FAX (907) 272-2932
Exec. Dir.: Deborah O'Regan
www.alaskabar.org

State Bar of Arizona
4201 N. 24th St., Suite 200
Phoenix, AZ 85016-6288
(602) 252-4804
FAX (602) 271-4930
Exec. Dir.: John Phelps
www.azbar.org

Arkansas Bar Association
2224 Cottondale Lane
Little Rock, AR 72202
(501) 375-4606
(800) 609-5668
FAX (501) 375-4901
Exec. Dir.: Karen Hutchins
www.arkbar.com

State Bar of California
180 Howard Street
San Francisco, CA 94105-1639
(415) 538-2000
Exec. Dir.: Judy Johnson
www.calbar.ca.gov

Colorado Bar Association
1900 Grant Street, 9th fl.
Denver, CO 80203
(303) 860-1115
(800) 332-6736
FAX (303) 894-0821
Exec. Dir.: Charles C. Turner
www.cobar.org

Connecticut Bar Association
30 Bank Street
New Britain, CT 06050-0350
(860) 223-4400
FAX (860) 223-4488
Interim Exec. Dir.: Norman James
www.ctbar.org

Delaware State Bar Association
301 North Market Street
Wilmington, DE 19801
(302) 658-5279
FAX (302) 658-5212
Exec. Dir.: Rina Marks
www.dsba.org

Bar Association of the District of
  Columbia
1016 16th St. NW
Washington, DC 20036
(202) 223-6600
FAX (202) 293-3388
Exec. Dir.: Mary Eva Candon
www.badc.org

District of Columbia Bar
1101 K St., NW, Suite 200
Washington, DC 20005-5937
(202) 737-4700
FAX (202) 626-3475
Exec. Dir.: Katherine A. Mazzaferri
www.dcbar.org

The Florida Bar
651 E. Jefferson Street
Tallahassee, FL 32399-2300
(850) 561-5600
FAX (850) 561-5827
Exec. Dir.: John F. Harkness, Jr.
www.flabar.org

State Bar of Georgia
104 Marietta Street, NW, Suite 100
Atlanta, GA 30303
(404) 527-8700
(800) 334-6865
FAX (404) 527-8717
Exec. Dir.: Cliff Brashier
www.gabar.org

Hawaii State Bar Association
1100 Alaska St., Suite 1000
Honolulu, HI 96813
(808) 537-1868
FAX (808) 521-7936
Exec. Dir.: Lyn Flanigan
www.hsba.org

Idaho State Bar
P.O. Box 895
Boise, ID 83701
(208) 334-4500
FAX (208) 334-4515
Exec. Dir.: Diane K. Minnich
www.idaho.gov/isb

Illinois State Bar Association
424 South 2nd Street
Springfield, IL 62701
(217) 525-1760; (800) 252-8908
FAX (217) 525-0712
Exec. Dir.: Robert E. Craghead
www.isba.org

Indiana State Bar Association
1 Indiana Square, Suite 530
Indianapolis, IN 46204-2199
(317) 639-5465; (800) 266-2581
FAX (317) 266-2588
Exec. Dir.: Thomas A. Pyrz
www.inbar.org

Iowa State Bar Association
625 East Court Avenue
Des Moines, IA 50309-1939
(515) 243-3179
FAX (515) 243-2511
Exec. Dir.: Dwight Dinkla
www.iowabar.org

Kansas Bar Association
1200 SW Harrison Street
Topeka, KS 66612-1806
(785) 234-5696
FAX (785) 234-3813
Exec. Dir.: Jeffrey Alderman
www.ksbar.org

Kentucky Bar Association
514 West Main Street

# STATE BAR ASSOCIATIONS

Frankfort, KY 40601-1883
(502) 564-3795
FAX (502) 564-3225
Interim Exec. Dir.:John D. Meyers
www.kybar.org

Louisiana State Bar Association
601 St. Charles Ave.
New Orleans, LA 70130-3404
(504) 566-1600; (800) 421-5722
FAX (504) 566-0930
Exec. Dir.: Loretta L. Larsen
www.lsba.org

Maine State Bar Association
P.O. Box 788
Augusta, ME 04332-0788
(207) 622-7523
FAX (207) 623-0083
Exec. Dir.: Julie G. Rowe
www.mainebar.org

Maryland State Bar Assn.
520 W. Fayette Street
Baltimore, MD 21201
(410) 685-7878
(800) 492-1964
FAX (410) 685-1016
Exec. Dir.: Paul V. Carlin
www.msba.org

Massachusetts Bar Association
20 West Street
Boston, MA 02111-1204
(617) 338-0500
FAX (617) 338-0650
Exec. Dir.: Martin W. Healy
www.massbar.org

State Bar of Michigan
306 Townsend Street
Lansing, MI 48933-2012
(517) 346-6300
(800) 968-1442
FAX (517) 482-6248
Exec. Dir.: Janet K. Welch
www.michbar.org

Minnesota State Bar Association
600 Nicollet Mall, Suite 380
Minneapolis, MN 55402
(612) 333-1183
(800) 882-MSBA
FAX (612) 333-4927

Exec. Dir.: Timothy Groshens
www.mnbar.org

Mississippi State Bar
P.O. Box 2168
Jackson, MS 39225-2168
(601) 948-4471
FAX (601) 355-8635
Exec. Dir.: Larry Houchins
www.msbar.org

The Missouri Bar
P.O. Box 119
Jefferson City, MO 65102-0119
(573) 635-4128
FAX (573) 635-2811
Exec. Dir.: Keith A. Birkes
www.mobar.org

State Bar of Montana
P.O. Box 577
Helena, MT 59624
(406) 442-7660
FAX (406) 442-7763
Exec. Dir.: Chris Manos
www.montanabar.org

Nebraska State Bar Association
635 S. 14th Street, Suite 200
P.O. Box 81809
Lincoln, NE 68508
(402) 475-7091; (800) 927-0117
FAX (402) 475-7098
Exec. Dir.: Jane L. Schoenike
www.nebar.com

State Bar of Nevada
600 E. Charleston Blvd.
Las Vegas, NV 89014
(702) 382-2200
(800) 254-2797
FAX (702) 385-2878
Exec. Dir.: Kimberly Farmer
www.nvbar.org

New Hampshire Bar Association
2 Pillsbury St., Suite 300
Concord, NH 03301
(603) 224-6942
FAX (603) 224-2910
Exec. Dir.: Jeannine McCoy
www.nhbar.org

New Jersey State Bar Association
One Constitution Square
New Brunswick, NJ 08901-1520
(732) 249-5000
FAX (732) 249-2815
Exec. Dir.: Angela C. Schnek
www.njsba.com

State Bar of New Mexico
5121 Masthead NE
P.O. Box 92860
Albuquerque, NM 87199-2860
(505) 797-6000; (800) 816-6227
FAX (505) 828-3765
Exec. Dir.: Joe Conte
www.nmbar.org

New York State Bar Association
One Elk Street
Albany, NY 12207
(518) 463-3200
FAX (518) 487-5517
Exec. Dir.: Patricia R. Bucklin
www.nysba.org

North Carolina State Bar
P.O. Box 25908
208 Fayetteville Street Mall
Raleigh, NC 27611-5908
(919) 828-4620
FAX (919) 821-9168
Exec. Dir.: L. Thomas Lunsford II
www.ncbar.com

North Carolina Bar Association
P.O. Box 3688
Cary, NC 27519
(919) 677-0561; (800) 662-7407
FAX (919) 677-0761
Exec. Dir.: Allan B. Head
www.ncbar.org

State Bar Assn. of North Dakota
P.O. Box 2136
Bismarck, ND 58502-2136
(701) 255-1404
(800) 472-2685 (ND)
FAX (701) 224-1621
Exec. Dir.: Bill Neumann
www.sband.org

Ohio State Bar Association
1700 Lake Shore Dr.
Columbus, OH 43204

# STATE BAR ASSOCIATIONS

(614) 487-2050
(800) 282-6556
FAX (614) 487-1008
Exec. Dir.: Denny L. Ramey
www.ohiobar.org

Oklahoma Bar Association
P.O. Box 53036
Oklahoma City, OK 73152-3036
(405) 416-7000
FAX (405) 416-7001
Exec. Dir.: John Morris Williams
www.okbar.org

Oregon State Bar
16037 SW Upper Boones Ferry Rd.
P.O. Box 231935
Tigard, OR 97224
(503) 620-0222
FAX (503) 684-1366
Exec. Dir.: Teresa Schmid
www.osbar.org

Pennsylvania Bar Association
100 South Street, P.O. Box 186
Harrisburg, PA 17101
(717) 238-6715; (800) 432-0311
FAX (717) 238-1204
Exec. Dir.: Barry M. Simpson, Esq.
www.pabar.org

Puerto Rico Bar Association
P.O. Box 9021900
San Juan, PR 00902-1900
(787) 725-3358
FAX (787) 721-0330
Exec. Dir.: Madi Pacheco

Rhode Island Bar Association
115 Cedar St.
Providence, RI 02903
(401) 421-5740
FAX (401) 421-2703
Exec. Dir.: Helen Desmond
 McDonald
www.ribar.com

South Carolina Bar
950 Taylor Street
Columbia, SC 29201
(803) 799-6653
FAX (803) 799-4118
Exec. Dir.: Robert S. Wells
www.scbar.org

State Bar of South Dakota
222 East Capitol Avenue
Pierre, SD 57501
(605) 224-7554
(800) 952-2333
FAX (605) 224-0282
Exec. Dir.: Thomas C. Barnett, Jr.
www.sdbar.org

Tennessee Bar Association
221 Fourth Avenue N., Suite 400
Nashville, TN 37219-2198
(615) 383-7421
FAX (615) 297-8058
Exec. Dir.: Allan F. Ramsaur
www.tba.org

State Bar of Texas
Post Office Box 12487
Austin, TX 78711
(512) 427-1463; (800) 204-2222
FAX (512) 427-4100
Exec. Dir.: John Edwards, Michelle
 Hunter
www.texasbar.com

Utah State Bar
645 South 200 East
Salt Lake City, UT 84111
(801) 531-9077
FAX (801) 531-0660
Exec. Dir.: John Baldwin
www.utahbar.org

Vermont Bar Association
P.O.Box 100
Montpelier, VT 05601-0100
(802) 223-2020
FAX (802) 223-1573
Exec. Dir.: Robert M. Paolini
www.vtbar.org

Virgin Islands Bar Association
P.O. Box 224108
Christiansted, VI 00822
(340) 778-7497
FAX (340) 773-5060
Exec. Dir.: Hinda Carbon
www.vibar.org

Virginia State Bar
707 East Main Street, Suite 1500
Richmond, VA 23219-2800
(804) 775-0500

FAX (804) 775-0501
Exec. Dir.: Karen Gould
www.vsb.org

Virginia Bar Association
701 E. Franklin Street, Suite 1120
Richmond, VA 23219
(804) 644-0041
FAX (804) 644-0052
Dir. of Programs: Guy K. Tower
www.vba.org

Washington State Bar Association
1325 Fourth Ave, Suite 600
Seattle, WA 98101-2539
(206) 443-WSBA
(800) 945-WSBA
FAX (206) 727-8319
Exec. Dir.: Paula Littlewood
www.wsba.org

West Virginia State Bar
2006 Kanawha Blvd. E.
Charleston, WV 25311-2204
(304) 558-2456
FAX (304) 558-2467
Exec. Dir.: Anita Casey
www.wvbar.org

West Virginia Bar Association
P.O. Box 2162
Huntington, WV 25722
(304) 522-2652; (800) 944-9822
FAX (304) 522-2795
Exec. Dir.: Pryce M. Haynes II
www.wvbarassociation.org

State Bar of Wisconsin
P.O. Box 7158
Madison, WI 53707-7158
(608) 257-3838; (800) 728-7788
FAX (608) 257-5502
Exec. Dir.: George Brown
www.wisbar.org

Wyoming State Bar
P.O. Box 109
Cheyenne, WY 82003-0109
(307) 632-9061
FAX (307) 632-3737
Exec. Dir.: Sleeter C. Dover
www.wyomingbar.org

# SELECTED LOCAL BAR ASSOCIATIONS

**ALABAMA**
Birmingham Bar Association
2021 2nd Ave. North
Birmingham, AL 35203
(205) 251-8006
FAX (205) 251-7193
www.birminghambar.org/

**ARIZONA**
Maricopa County Bar Association
303 East Palm Lane
Phoenix, AZ 85004
(602) 257-4200
FAX (602) 682-8601
www.maricopabar.org/

**CALIFORNIA**
Alameda County Bar Association
70 Washington St., Suite 200
Oakland, CA 94607
(510) 302-2222
FAX (510) 452-2224
www.acbanet.org

Bar Association of San Francisco
301 Battery St., 3rd fl.
San Francisco, CA 94111
(415) 982-1600
www.sfbar.org

Beverly Hills Bar Association
P.O. Box 7277
Beverly Hills, CA 90212
(310) 601-2422
FAX (310) 601-2423
www.bhba.org

Los Angeles County Bar Assn.
P.O. Box 55020
Los Angeles, CA 90055
(213) 627-2727
www.lacba.org

Orange County Bar Association
P.O. Box 6130
Newport Beach, CA 92658
(949) 440-6700
FAX (949) 440-6710
www.ocbar.org

Sacramento County Bar Association
1329 Howe Ave., Suite 100

Sacramento, CA 95825
(916) 564-3780
FAX (916) 564-3787
www.sacbar.org/

San Diego County Bar Association
1333 Seventh Avenue
San Diego, CA 92101
(619) 231-0781
FAX (619) 338-0042
www.sdcba.org

Santa Clara County Bar Association
31 N. Second Street, 4th fl.
San Jose, CA 95113
(408) 287-2557
FAX (408) 287-6083
www.sccba.com/

**COLORADO**
Boulder County Bar Association
1942 Broadway, Suite 205
Boulder, CO 80302
(303) 440-4758
FAX (303) 402-6958
www.boulder-bar.org/

Denver Bar Association
1900 Grant Street, 9th fl.
Denver, CO 80203
(303) 860-1115; (800) 332-6736
FAX (303) 894-0821
www.denbar.org

**CONNECTICUT**
Hartford County Bar Association
100 Pearl St., 4th fl.
Hartford, CT 06103
(860) 525-8106
FAX (860) 293-1345
www.hartfordbar.org

**FLORIDA**
Orange County Bar Association
880 North Orange Avenue
Orlando, FL 32801
(407) 422-4551
FAX (407) 843-3470
www.orangecountybar.org

Dade County Bar Association
123 NW First Avenue, Suite 214

Miami, FL 33128
(305) 371-2220
FAX (305) 373-6210
www.dadecountybar.org/

**GEORGIA**
Atlanta Bar Association
229 Peachtree Street, NE , #400
Atlanta, GA 30303-1601
(404) 521-0781
FAX (404) 522-0269
www.atlantabar.org

**ILLINOIS**
The Chicago Bar Association
321 S. Plymouth Court
Chicago, IL 60604-3997
(312) 554-2000
FAX (312) 554-2054
www.chicagobar.org/

The Chicago Council of Lawyers
750 N. Lake Shore Drive, 4th fl.
Chicago, IL 60611
(312) 988-6565
FAX (312) 654-8644
www.chicagocouncil.org

DuPage County Bar Association
126 S. County Farm Rd.
Wheaton, IL 60187-4597
(630) 653-7779
FAX (630) 653-7870
www.dcba.org

**INDIANA**
Indianapolis Bar Association
135 N. Pennsylvania St., Suite 1500
Indianapolis, IN 46204
(317) 269-2000
FAX (317) 269-1915
www.indybar.org

**KENTUCKY**
Louisville Bar Association
600 W. Main Street
Louisville, KY 40202-4917
(502) 583-5314
FAX (502) 583-4113
www.loubar.org

# SELECTED LOCAL BAR ASSOCIATIONS

**LOUISIANA**
New Orleans Bar Association
650 Poydras St., Suite 1505
New Orleans, LA 70130
(504) 525-7453
FAX (504) 525-6549
www.neworleansbar.org

**MARYLAND**
Baltimore County Bar Association
401 Bosley Avenue, Rm. 100
Towson, MD 21204
(410) 337-9103
www.bcba.org

Bar Association of Baltimore City
111 N. Calvert St., Suite 627
Baltimore, MD 21202
(410) 539-5936
FAX (410) 685-3420
www.baltimorebar.org

Bar Association of Montgomery
County
27 W. Jefferson Street
Rockville, MD 20850
(301) 424-3454
FAX (301) 217-9327
www.montbar.org

**MASSACHUSETTS**
Boston Bar Association
16 Beacon Street
Boston, MA 02108
(617) 742-0615
FAX (617) 523-0127
www.bostonbar.org

**MICHIGAN**
Detroit Metropolitan Bar Assn.
645 Griswold, Suite 1356
Detroit, MI 48226
(313) 961-6120
FAX (313) 965-0842
www.detroitlawyer.org

Oakland County Bar Association
1760 S. Telegraph Rd., Suite 100
Bloomfield Hills, MI 48302
(248) 334-3400
FAX (248) 334-7757
www.ocba.org

**MINNESOTA**
Hennepin County Bar Association

600 Nicollet Mall, Suite 390
Minneapolis, MN 55402
(612) 752-6600
FAX (612) 752-6601
www.hcba.org/

Ramsey County Bar Association
332 Minnesota St., Suite E1401
St. Paul, MN 55101
(651) 222-0846
FAX (651) 223-8344
www.ramseybar.org

**MISSOURI**
Kansas City Metropolitan Bar Assn.
2300 Main St., Suite 100
Kansas City, MO 64108
(816) 474-4322
FAX (816) 474-0103
www.kcmba.org

Bar Association of Metropolitan St.
  Louis
720 Olive, Suite 2900
St. Louis, MO 63101-2308
(314) 421-4134
FAX (314) 421-0013
www.bamsl.org/

**NEVADA**
Clark County Bar Association
725 S. Eighth Street
Las Vegas, NV 89101
(702) 333-2270
FAX (702) 387-7867
www.ccba.net

**NEW JERSEY**
Bergen County Bar Association
15 Bergen Street
Hackensack, NJ 07601
(201) 488-0032
FAX (201) 488-0073
www.bergenbar.org

Essex County Bar Association
470 Dr. Martin Luther King Jr. Blvd,
  Rm. B01
Newark, NJ 07020
(973) 622-6207
FAX (973) 622-4341
www.essexbar.com

**NEW YORK**
Association of the Bar of the City

of New York
42 West 44th Street
New York, NY 10036
(212) 382-6600
FAX (212) 768-8116
www.abcny.org

Bar Association of Erie County
438 Main Street, 6th fl.
Buffalo, NY 14202-2992
(716) 852-8687
FAX (716) 852-7641
www.eriebar.org

Brooklyn Bar Association
123 Remsen Street
Brooklyn, NY 11201
(718) 624-0675
FAX (718) 797-1713
www.brooklynbar.org/

Legal Aid Society of New York
199 Water St.
New York, NY 10038
(212) 577-3300
FAX (212) 509-8761
www.legal-aid.org/

Nassau County Bar Association
15th & West Streets
Mineola, NY 11501
(516) 747-4070
FAX (516) 747-4147
www.nassaubar.org

New York County Lawyers' Assn.
14 Vesey Street
New York, NY 10007
(212) 267-6646
FAX (212) 406-9252
www.nycla.org/

Queens County Bar Association
90-35 148th Street
Jamaica, NY 11435
(718) 291-4500
FAX (718) 657-1789
www.qcba.com

Suffolk County Bar Association
560 Wheeler Rd.
Hauppauge, NY 11788-4357
(631) 234-5511
FAX (631) 234-5899
www.scba.org/

# SELECTED LOCAL BAR ASSOCIATIONS

Westchester County Bar
 Association
One N. Broadway, Suite 512
White Plains, NY 10601
(914) 761-3707
FAX (914) 761-9402
www.wcbany.org

## OHIO

Cleveland Bar Association
1301 E. 9th St., 2nd fl.
Cleveland, OH 44114-1253
(216) 696-3525
FAX (216) 696-2413
www.clevelandbar.org

Cincinnati Bar Association
225 East 6th Street, 2nd fl.
Cincinnati, OH 45202-2492
(513) 381-8213
FAX (513) 381-0528
www.cincybar.org

Columbus Bar Association
175 South Third Street, Suite 1100
Columbus, OH 43215-5193
(614) 221-4112
FAX (614) 221-4850
www.cbalaw.org

## OKLAHOMA

Oklahoma Bar Association
1901 N. Lincoln Boulevard
P. O. Box 53036
Oklahoma City, OK 73152-3036
(405) 416-7000
FAX (405) 416-7001
www.okbar.org

Tulsa County Bar Association
1446 S. Boston
Tulsa, OK 74119-3612
(918) 584-5243
FAX (918) 592-0208
www.tulsabar.com

## OREGON

Multnomah Bar Association
620 SW Fifth Ave., Suite 1220
Portland, OR 97204
(503) 222-3275
FAX (503) 243-1881
www.mbabar.org

## PENNSYLVANIA

Allegheny County Bar Association
400 Koppers Building
436 Seventh Avenue
Pittsburgh, PA 15219
(412) 261-6161
FAX (412) 261-3622
www.acba.org

Philadelphia Bar Association
1101 Market Street, 11th fl.
Philadelphia, PA 19107-2911
(215) 238-6300
FAX (215) 238-1159
www.philabar.org

## TENNESSEE

Chattanooga Bar Association
801 Broad Street, Suite 420
Chattanooga, TN 37402
(423) 756-3222
FAX (423) 265-6602
www.chattbar.org

Knoxville Bar Association
505 Main St., Suite 50
P. O. Box 2027 (37901-2027)
Knoxville, TN 37902
(865) 522-6522
FAX (865) 523-5662
www.knoxbar.org/

Memphis Bar Association
80 Monroe, Suite 220
Memphis, TN 38103
(901) 527-3573
FAX (901) 527-3582
www.memphisbar.org

Nashville Bar Association
150 4th Ave.
North Nashville, TN 37219
(615) 242-9272
FAX (615) 255-3026
www.nashvillebar.org

## TEXAS

Dallas Bar Association
2101 Ross Avenue
Dallas, TX 75201
(214) 220-7400
FAX (214) 220-7465
www.dallasbar.org

Houston Bar Association

1001 Fannin, Suite 1300
Houston, TX 77002
(713) 759-1133
FAX (713) 759-1710
www.hba.org

San Antonio Bar Association
100 Dolorosa, 5th fl.
San Antonio, TX 78205
(210) 227-8822
FAX (210) 271-9614
www.sanantoniobar.org

## VIRGINIA

Fairfax Bar Association
4110 Chain Bridge Road, Suite 215
Fairfax, VA 22030
(703) 246-2740
FAX (703) 273-1274
www.fairfaxbar.org

## WASHINGTON

King County Bar Association
1200 5th Ave., Suite 600
Seattle, WA 98101
(206) 267-7100
FAX (206) 267-7099
www.kcba.org

## WISCONSIN

Milwaukee Bar Association
424 E. Wells St.
Milwaukee, WI 53202
(414) 274-6760
FAX (414) 274-6765
www.milwbar.org

# LAW LIBRARIANSHIP

## AMERICAN ASSOCIATION OF LAW LIBRARIES

105 W. Adams Street, Suite 3300
Chicago, IL 60603
(312) 939-4764
FAX (312) 431-1097
Email: aallhq@aall.org
URL: www.aallnet.org

**COMMITTEES**

AALL Lexis-Nexis Call for Papers
AALLNET Committee
Annual Meeting Local Arrangements Committee
Annual Meeting Program Committee
Appointments Committee
Awards
Bylaws and Resolutions
Conference on Newer Law Librarians (CONELL)
Continuing Professional Education Committee
Copyright
Council of Newsletter Editors (CONE)
CRIV (Relations with Information Vendors Committee)
Digital Access to Legal Information Committee
Diversity
Economic Status of Law Librarians Committee
Executive Board Administration Committee
Executive Board Executive Committee
Executive Board Finance and Budget Committee
Executive Board Strategic Directions Committee
Futures Summit Planning Special Committee
Government Relations
Grants
Index to Foreign Legal Periodicals (Advisory Committee)
Indexing of Periodical Literature (Advisory Committee)
Law Library Journal and AALL Spectrum
Law Student Research Competencies Task Force
Leadership Development
Membership Development Committee
Nominations
Placement
Price Index for Legal Publications (Advisory Committee)
Public Relations
Recruitment to Law Librarianship Committee
Research and Publications
Scholarships

# AMERICAN ASSOCIATION OF LAW LIBRARIES

**SPECIAL INTEREST SECTIONS**

Academic Law Libraries:  www.aallnet.org/sis/allsis/
Computing Services:  cssis.org/
Foreign, Comparative and International Law:  www.aallnet.org/sis/fcilsis/
Government Documents:  www.aallnet.org/sis/gd/
Legal History and Rare Books:  www.aallnet.org/sis/lhrb/
Legal Information Services to the Public:  www.aallnet.org/sis/lisp/
Micrographics and Audio-Visual
Online Bibliographic Services:  www.aallnet.org/sis/obssis/
Private Law Libraries:  www.aallnet.org/sis/pllsis/
Research Instruction and Patron Services:  www.aallnet.org/sis/ripssis/
Social Responsibilities:  www.aallnet.org/sis/srsis/
State, Court and County Law Libraries:  www.aallnet.org/sis/sccll/
Technical Services:  www.aallnet.org/sis/tssis/


**CHAPTERS**

Arizona Association of Law Libraries (AZALL)  www.aallnet.org/chapter/azll/
Association of Law Libraries of Upstate New York (ALLUNY)  www.aallnet.org/chapter/alluny/
Atlanta Law Libraries Association (ALLA)  www.aallnet.org/chapter/alla/
Chicago Association of Law Libraries (CALL)  www.aallnet.org/chapter/call
Colorado Association of Law Libraries (COALL)  www.aallnet.org/chapter/coall
Dallas Association of Law Librarians (DALL)  www.dallnet.org/
Greater Philadelphia Law Library Association (GPLLA)  www.gplla.org/
Houston Area Law Librarians (HALL)  www.houstonarealibrarians.com
Law Librarians Association of Wisconsin (LLAW)  www.aallnet.org/chapter/llaw/
Law Librarians of New England (LLNE)  www.aallnet.org/chapter/llne/
Law Librarians of Puget Sound (LLOPS)  www.llops.org
Law Librarians' Society of Washington DC (LLSDC)  www.llsdc.org/
Law Libraries Association of Alabama (LLAA)  www.aallnet.org/chapter/llaa/
Law Library Association of Greater New York (LLAGNY)  www.aallnet.org/chapter/llagny/
Law Library Association of Maryland (LLAM)  www.aallnet.org/chapter/llam/
Michigan Association of Law Libraries (Mich/ALL)  www.aallnet.org/chapter/michall/

Mid-America Association of Law Libraries (MAALL)  www.aallnet.org/chapter/maall/
Minnesota Association of Law Libraries (MALL)  www.aallnet.org/chapter/mall/
New Jersey Law Librarians Association (NJLLA)  www.njlla.org/
New Orleans Association of Law Librarians (NOALL)  www.aallnet.org/chapter/noall/
Northern California Association of Law Libraries (NOCALL)  www.nocall.org/
Ohio Regional Association of Law Libraries (ORALL)  www.orall.org/
San Diego Area Law Libraries (SANDALL)  www.aallnet.org/chapter/sandall/
South Florida Association of Law Libraries, Inc. (SFALL)  www.aallnet.org/chapter/sfall/
Southeastern Chapter of the AALL (SEAALL)  www.aallnet.org/chapter/seaall/
Southern California Association of Law Libraries (SCALL)  www.aallnet.org/chapter/scall/
Southern New England Law Librarians Association (SNELLA)  www.aallnet.org/chapter/snella/
Southwestern Association of Law Libraries (SWALL)  www.aallnet.org/chapter/swall/
Virginia Association of Law Libraries (VALL)  vall.pbworks.com
Western Pacific Chapter of the AALL (WestPac)  www.aallnet.org/chapter/westpac
Western Pennsylvania Law Library Association (WPLLA)  www.aallnet.org/chapter/wplla/

# AALL CHAPTERS AND PRESIDENTS
## 2011-2012

**Chair, Council of Chapter Presidents**
Sarah Mauldin, Law Librarian
Chamberlain, Hrdlicka, et al.
191 Peachtree St. NE, 34th fl.
Atlanta, GA 30303
(404) 658-5430
sarah.mauldin@chamberlainlaw.com

**ALLA – Atlanta Law Libraries**
**Association**
William Haines, Asst. Law Librarian
for Electronic Services
Emory University Law Library
1301 Clifton Rd
Atlanta, GA 30322-2780
(404) 727-4322
libwjh@law.emory.edu

**ALLUNY - Association of Law**
**Libraries of Upstate New York**
Jean-Paul Vivian, Principal Law Librarian
N.Y.S. Supreme Court Library - Nassau
100 Supreme Court Drive
Mineola, NY 11501
(516) 571-2757
jvivian@courts.state.ny.us

**AzALL - Arizona Association of Law**
**Libraries**
Karen Anderson, Info. Specialist
Quarles & Brady LLP
2 N Central Ave., Fl. 13
Phoenix, AZ 85004-2391
(602) 229-5388
karen.anderson@quarles.com

**CALL – Chicago Association of Law**
**Libraries**
Julia Jackson, Dir.of Library Services
Brinks, Hofer, Gilson & Lione
455 N. Cityfront Plaza Dr
Chicago, IL 60611-5599
(312) 321-7733
jjackson@brinkshofer.com

**CoALL – Colorado Association of**
**Law Libraries**

Robert M. Linz, Associate Director
& Head of Public Services
Univ. of Colorado Law Library
2405 Kittredge Loop Road
Boulder, CO 80309-0402
(303) 492-2504
robert.linz@colorado.edu

**DALL - Dallas Association of**
**Law Librarians**
David S. Matthewson
Director of Library Services
Haynes & Boone, LLP
2323 Victory Ave., Ste.700
Dallas, TX 75219
(214) 651-5712
david.matthewson@haynesboone.
com

**GPLLA - Greater Philadelphia**
**Law Library Association**
Kristen Rook
Morgan, Lewis & Bockius LLP
1701 Market St.
Philadelphia, PA 19103-2921
(215) 963-4692
krook@morganlewis.com

**HALL – Houston Area Law**
**Librarians**
Saskia Mehlhorn
Systems/Reference Librarian
Fulbright & Jaworski LLP
1301 McKinney St., Ste. 5100
Houston, TX 77010-3095
(713) 651-3670
smehlhorn@fulbright.com

**LLAA – Law Libraries**
**Association of Alabama**
John Hightower, Law Librarian
Lanier, Ford, Shaver & Payne
2101 West Clinton Ave., Ste. 102
Huntsville, AL 35805
(256) 535-1100
jhightower@lanierford.com

**LLAGNY - Law Library**
**Association of Greater New York**

Caren Biberman
Cahill, Gordon & Reindel
80 Pine Street
New York, NY 10005
(212) 701-3540
cbiberman@cahill.com

**LLAM - Law Library**
**Association of Maryland**
Sara Jane Witman, Research Lib.
Gordon, Feinblatt, et al.
233 E. Redwood St.
Baltimore, MD 21202-3332
(410) 576-4010
switman@gfrlaw.com

**LLAW - Law Librarians**
**Association of Wisconsin, Inc.**
Laura La Rose, Research Specialist
Reinhart, Boerner, Van Deuren
1000 N. Water St., Ste. 2100
Milwaukee, WI 53202-3186
(414) 298-8772
llarose@reinhartlaw.com

**LLNE - Law Librarians of New**
**England**
Katherine K. Coolidge
Bulkley, Richardson & Gelinas
1500 Main St.
Springfield, MA 01115
(413) 272-6275
kcoolidge@bulkley.com

**LLOPS - Law Librarians of**
**Puget Sound**
Crystal Sherman Norton
Director of Library Services
Riddell Williams PS
1001 4th Ave., Ste. 4500
Seattle, WA 98154-1065
(206) 624-3600 x717
cnorton@riddellwilliams.com

**LLSDC - Law Librarians Society**
**of Washington, D.C., Inc.**
Roger V. Skalbeck
Assoc. Law Librarian

# AALL CHAPTERS AND PRESIDENTS

Georgetown University Law Library
111 G St. NW
Washington, DC 20001-1489
(202) 662-9158
rvs5@law.georgetown.edu

**MAALL - Mid-America Association of Law Libraries**
Richard Leiter, Director
Schmid Law Library
Univ. of Nebraska College of Law
P.O. Box 830902
Lincoln, NE 68583-0902
(402) 472-3547
rleiter@unl.edu

**MALL - Minnesota Association of Law Libraries**
Elizabeth Reppe, Law Library Manager
Dakota County Law Library
1560 Highway 55
Hastings, MN 55033-2343
(651) 438-8244
liz.reppe@co.dakota.mn.us

**MichALL - Michigan Association of Law Libraries**
Virginia C. Thomas, Director
Wayne State University Law Library
474 Ferry Mall
Detroit, MI 48202-3620
(313) 577-6166
virginiathomas@wayne.edu

**NJLLA - New Jersey Law Librarians Association**
Gayle-Lynn Nelson
gayle.lynn-nelson@lexisnexis.com

**NOALL - New Orleans Association of Law Librarians**
Brent T. Hightower, Librarian
U.S. Court of Appeals, 5th Circuit Lib.
600 Camp St., Rm. 106
New Orleans, LA 70130-3425
(504) 310-7794
brent_hightower@ca5.uscourts.gov

**NOCALL - Northern California Association of Law Libraries**
Holly M. Riccio

Library/Calendar Manager for
Northern California
O'Melveny & Myers LLP
2 Embarcadero Center, Fl. 28
San Francisco, CA 34111-3903
(415) 984-8761
hriccio@omm.com

**ORALL - Ohio Regional Association of Law Libraries**
Steven R. Probst
Valparaiso Univ. Law Library
656 S. Greenwich St.
Valparaiso, IN 46383-4945
(219) 465-7820
steven.probst@valpo.edu

**SANDALL - San Diego Area Law Libraries**
Jane Larrington
Univ. of San Diego School of Law
Legal Research Center
5998 Alcala Park
San Diego, CA 92110
(619) 260-4766
jlarrington@sandiego.edu

**SCALL - Southern California Association of Law Libraries**
Mark A. Gediman
Director of Information Services
Best Best & Krieger LLP
3750 University Ave., Ste. 400
Riverside, CA 92501-3369
(951) 826-8230
mark.gediman@bbklaw.com

**SEAALL - Southeastern Chapter of the Am. Assn. of Law Libraries**
Carol Watson
Director of the Law Library
University of Georgia School of Law
225 Herty Drive
Athens, GA 30602-6018
(706) 542-5078
cwatson@uga.edu

**SFALL -South Florida Assn. of Law Libraries**
Stephanie Peace Hess
Assistant Head of Tech. Serv.
Nova SE Univ. Law Library

3305 College Ave
Ft. Lauderdale, FL 33314-7721
(954) 262-6216
hesss@nsu.law.nova.edu

**SNELLA - Southern New England Law Librarians Assn.**
Camilla Tubbs, Reference Librarian
Yale Law School Library
127 Wall St.
New Haven, CT 06520-8215
(203) 432-7535
camilla.tubbs@yale.edu

**SWALL - Southwestern Association of Law Libraries**
Mon Yin Lung, Associate Director
O'Quinn Law Library
University of Houston Law Center
Houston, TX 77204
(713) 743-2307
mlung@central.uh.edu

**VALL - Virginia Association of Law Libraries**
Michele Gernhardt, Ref. Librarian
Hunton & Wuilliams
951 E. Byrd St., Ste. 200
Richmond, VA 23219-4074
(804) 788-7355
mgernhardt@hunton.com

**WestPac - Western Pacific Chapter**
Robert Truman
Paul L. Boley Law Library
Lewis and Clark Law School
10015 SW Terwilliger Blvd
Portland, OR 97219-7768
(503) 768-6780
rtruman@lclark.edu

**WPLLA - Western Pennsylvania Law Library Association**
Louise A. Beswick
Senior Research Librarian
Reed Smith LLP
435 6th Ave.
Pittsburgh, PA 15219-1808
(412) 288-3207
lbeswick@reedsmith.com

# MAJOR LIBRARY-RELATED ASSOCIATIONS

American Assn. of Law Libraries
105 W. Adams St., Suite 3300
Chicago, IL 60603
(312) 939-4764
FAX (312) 431-1097
www.aallnet.org

American Assn. of School Libraries
50 E. Huron Street
Chicago, IL 60611-2795
(800) 545-2433 x4382
FAX (312) 280-5276
www.ala.org/aasl/

American Library Association
50 E. Huron Street
Chicago, IL 60611-2795
(800) 545-2433
FAX (312) 440-9374
www.ala.org

American Society for Information
 Science and Technology
1320 Fenwick Lane, Suite 510
Silver Spring, MD 20910
(301) 495-0900
FAX (301) 495-0810
www.asis.org

The American Society for Indexing
10200 West 44th Avenue, Suite 304
Wheat Ridge, CO 80033
(303) 463-2887
FAX (303) 422-8894
www.asindexing.org/

Aslib, The Assn. for Info. Mgmt.
Howard House
Wagon Lane
Bingley, BD16 1WA England
+44 (0) 1274 777700
FAX +44 (0) 1274 785201
www.aslib.com

Association of College and
 Research Libraries
50 E. Huron Street
Chicago, IL 60611-2795
(800) 545-2433 x2523
FAX (312) 280-2520
 www.ala.org/acrl.html

ARMA International
11880 College Blvd., Suite 450
Overland Park, KS 66210
(913) 341-3808
(800) 422-2762

FAX (913) 341-3742
www.arma.org

Association for Library and
 Information Science Education
65 E. Wacker Place, Suite 1900
Chicago, IL 60601-7246
(312) 795-0996
FAX (312) 419-8950
www.alise.org/

Association of Independent
 Information Professionals (AIIP)
8550 United Plaza Blvd., Suite
1001
Baton Rouge, LA 70809
(225) 408-4400
FAX (225) 408-4422
www.aiip.org

Association of Research Libraries
21 Dupont Circle, Suite 800
Washington, DC 20036
(202) 296-2296
FAX (202) 872-0884
www.arl.org

Australian Library and Information
 Association (ALIA)
P.O. Box 6335
Kingston 2604, Australia
+612 6215 8222
FAX +612 6282 2249
www.alia.org.au/

Canadian Assn. of Law Libraries
4 Cataraqui St., Suite 310
Kingston, ON, Canada K7L 5C8
(613) 531-9338
FAX (866) 303-0626
www.callacbd.ca/

Canadian Library Association
1150 Morrison Drive, Suite 400
Ottawa, ON, Canada K2H 8S9
(613) 232-9625
FAX (613) 563-9895
www.cla.ca/

Chartered Institute of Library and
 Informational Professionals
 (CILIP)
7 Ridgmount St.
London, WC1E 7AE England
44-20-7255-0500
FAX 44-20-7255-0501
www.cilip.org.uk

International Federation of Library
 Associations and Institutions
P.O. Box 95312
2509 CH The Hague, Netherlands
+31 70 3140884
FAX +31 70 3834827
www.ifla.org

Library and Information Technology
 Association
50 E. Huron Street
Chicago, IL 60611-2795
(800) 545-2433 x4270
FAX (312) 280-3257
www.lita.org

Library Leadership and
 Management Association
50 E. Huron Street
Chicago, IL 60611-2795
(800) 545-2433 x5032
FAX (312) 280-2169
www.ala.org/lama/

Medical Library Association
65 E. Wacker Place, Suite 1900
Chicago, IL 60601-7246
(312) 419-9094
FAX (312) 419-8950
www.mlanet.org

OCLC
6565 Kilgour Place
Dublin, OH 43017-3395
(614) 764-6000
(800) 848-5878
FAX (614) 764-6096
www.oclc.org

Public Library Association
50 E. Huron Street
Chicago, IL 60611-2795
(800) 545-2433 x5752
FAX (312) 280-5029
www.pla.org

Special Libraries Association
331 South Patrick Street
Alexandria, VA 22314-3501
(703) 647-4900
FAX (703) 647-4901
www.sla.org

# ALA—ACCREDITED GRADUATE LIBRARY EDUCATION PROGRAMS

## NORTHEAST

Catholic University of America[1]
Master of Science in Library
 Science
School of Library and Information
 Science
Washington, DC 20064
(202) 319-5085
slis.cua.edu/

Clarion University of Pennsylvania[1]
**OFFERS 100% ONLINE PROGRAM**
Master of Science in Library
 Science
Dept. of Library Science
Clarion, PA 16214
(866) 272-5612
www.clarion.edu/libsci

Drexel University[1,2]
**OFFERS 100% ONLINE PROGRAM**
Master of Science (Library and
 Information Science)
College of Information Science
 and Technology
Philadelphia, PA 19104-2875
(215) 895-2474
www.ischool.drexel.edu

Long Island University[1,2]
Master of Science in Library and
 Information Studies
Palmer School of Library and
 Information Science
Brookville, NY 11548
(516) 299-2866
www.liu.edu/palmer

University of Maryland[2]
**OFFERS 100% ONLINE PROGRAM**
Master of Library Science
College of Information Studies
College Park, MD 20742
(301) 405-2033
ischool.umd.edu

State University of New York,
 Albany[1,2]
Master of Science in Information
 Science
College of Computing and Information
Dept. of Information Science
Albany, NY 12222
(518) 442-5110
infostudies@albany.edu
www.albany.edu/
 /informationstudies/index.php

State University of New York at
 Buffalo[1]
Master of Library Science
Graduate School of Education, Library
 and Information Studies
Buffalo, NY 14260
(716) 645-2412
www.gse.buffalo.edu/lis/

University of Pittsburgh[1,2]
Master of Library and Information
 Science
School of Information Sciences,
 Library and Information Science
 Program
Pittsburgh, PA 15260
(412) 624-9420
www.ischool.pitt.edu

Pratt Institute[1]
Master of Science in Library and
 Information Science
School of Information and Library
 Science
New York, NY 10011
(212) 647-7682
www.pratt.edu/academics/
 information_and_library_sciences/

Queens College, City University of
 New York[1]
Master of Library Studies
Graduate School for Library and
 Information Studies
Flushing, NY 11367-1597
(718) 997-3790
www.qc.edu/GSLIS

University of Rhode Island[1]
Master of Library and Information
 Studies
Graduate School of Library and
 Information Studies
Kingston, RI 02881
(401) 874-2878
www.uri.edu/artsci/lsc/

Rutgers, The State University of New
 Jersey[1,2]
**OFFERS 100% ONLINE PROGRAM**
Master of Library and Information
 Science
School of Communication and
 Information
New Brunswick, NJ 08901-1071
(732) 932-7500 x8218
comminfo.rutgers.edu

St. John's University[1]
Master of Library Science
Division of Library and Information
 Science
Jamaica, NY 11439
(718) 990-6200
DLIS@stjohns.edu
www.stjohns.edu/libraryscience

Simmons College[1,2]
Master of Science
Graduate School of Library and
 Information Science
Boston, MA 02115
(617) 521-2800
www.simmons.edu/gslis

Southern Connecticut State
 University[1]
**OFFERS 100% ONLINE PROGRAM**
Master of Library Science
School of Education, Dept. of
 Information and Library Science
New Haven, CT 06515
(203) 392-5781
www.southernct.edu/ils/

Syracuse University[1,2]
Master of Science in Library and
 Information Science
School of Information Studies
Syracuse, NY 13244
(315) 443-2911
ischool.syr.edu

## SOUTHEAST

University of Alabama[1,2]
**OFFERS 100% ONLINE PROGRAM**
Master of Library and Information
 Studies
School of Library and Information
 Studies
Tuscaloosa, AL 35487-0252
(205) 348-4610
www.slis.ua.edu

Florida State University[1,2]
**OFFERS 100% ONLINE PROGRAM**
Master of Science; Master of Arts
College of Information
Tallahassee, FL 32306-2100
(850) 644-5775
slis.su.edu

University of Kentucky[1,2]
**OFFERS 100% ONLINE PROGRAM**
Master of Science in Library
 Science; Master of Arts

---

1. Offers post-Master's specialist or certificate program. (The ALA does not accredit post-Master's specialist or certificate programs.)
2. Offers program for Doctoral degree. (The ALA does not accredit programs leading to the Doctoral degree.)
Credit: American Library Association

# ALA-ACCREDITED GRADUATE
# LIBRARY EDUCATION PROGRAMS

School of Library and Information
   Science
Lexington, KY 40506-0039
(859) 257-8876
www.uky.edu/CIS/SLIS/

Louisiana State University[1]
Master of Library and Information
   Science
School of Library and Information
   Science
Baton Rouge, LA 70803
(225) 578-3158
slis@lsu.edu
slis.lsu.edu

University of North Carolina at
   Chapel Hill [1,2]
Master of Science in Library
   Science; Master of Science in
   Information Science
School of Information and Library
   Science
Chapel Hill, NC 27599-3360
(919) 962-8366
info@ils.unc.edu
sils.unc.edu

University of North Carolina at
   Greensboro[1]
Master of Library and Information
   Studies
Department of Library and
   Information Studies
Greensboro, NC 27401-6170
(336) 334-3477
lis.uncg.edu/

North Carolina Central University[1]
**OFFERS 100% ONLINE PROGRAM**
Master of Library Science
School of Library and Information
   Sciences
Durham, NC 27707
(919) 530-6485
www.nccuslis.org

University of Puerto Rico[1]
**OFFERS 100% ONLINE PROGRAM**
Master of Information Sciences
School of Information Sciences and
   Technologies
San Juan, Puerto Rico 00931-1906
(787) 763-6199
egcti.upr.edu

University of South Carolina[1]
**OFFERS 100% ONLINE PROGRAM**
Master of Library and Information
   Science
School of Library and Information
   Science
Columbia, SC 29208
(803) 777-3858
www.libsci.sc.edu

University of South Florida
Master of Arts in Library and
   Information Science
School of Library and Information
   Science
Tampa, FL 33620
(813) 974-3520
slis.usf.edu

University of Southern Mississippi
**OFFERS 100% ONLINE PROGRAM**
Master of Library and Information
   Science
School of Library and Information
   Science
Hattiesburg, MS 39406-0001
(601) 266-4228
www.usm.edu/slis

University of Tennessee [2]
**OFFERS 100% ONLINE PROGRAM**
Master of Science
School of Information Sciences
Knoxville, TN 37996-0341
(865) 974-2148
www.sis.utk.edu

Valdosta State University
Master of Library and Information
   Science
Department of Information Studies
Valdosta, GA 31698-0133
(229) 333-5966
www.valdosta.edu/mlis/

**MIDWEST**
Emporia State University[1,2]
Master of Library Science
School of Library and Information
   Management
Emporia, KS 66801
(316) 341-5203
slim.emporia.edu

University of Illinois at Urbana-
   Champaign [1,2]
Master of Science
Graduate School of Library and
   Information Science
Champaign, IL 61820-6211
(217) 333-3280
www.lis.uiuc.edu/

Indiana University[1,2]
Master of Library Science; Master
   of Information Science
School of Library and Information
   Science
Bloomington, IN 47405-3907
(812) 855-2018
slis@indiana.edu
www.slis.indiana.edu

University of Iowa

Master of Arts in Library and
   Information Science
School of Library and Information
   Science
Iowa City, IA 52242-1420
(319) 335-5707
slis.uiowa.edu/~slisweb/

Kent State University[1]
Master of Library and Information
   Science
School of Library and Information
   Science
Kent, OH 44242-0001
(330) 672-2782
www.slis.kent.edu

University of Michigan[2]
Master of Science in Information
School of Information
Ann Arbor, MI 48109
(734) 763-2285
www.si.umich.edu

University of Missouri-Columbia[1,2]
Master of Arts in Library Science
College of Education, Information
   Science and Learning Technologies
Columbia, MO 65211
(573) 747-5868
lis.missouri.edu

Dominican University [1,2]
Master of Library and Information
   Science
Graduate School of Library and
   Information Science
River Forest, IL 60305
(708) 524-6845
gslis@dom.edu
www.gslis.dom.edu

Wayne State University[1]
**OFFERS 100% ONLINE PROGRAM**
Master of Library and Information
   Science
School of Library and Information
   Science
Detroit, MI 48202
(313) 577-1825
slis.wayne.edu

St. Catherine University
Master of Library and Information
   Science
School of Professional Studies
MLIS Program/ Info. Mgmt. Dept.
St. Paul, MN 55105
(651) 690-6802
www.stkate.edu/academics/mlis/

University of Wisconsin-Madison[1,2]
Master of Arts in Library and
   Information Studies
School of Library and Information

# ALA-ACCREDITED GRADUATE
# LIBRARY EDUCATION PROGRAMS

Studies
Madison, WI 53706
(608) 263-2900
uw-slis@slis.wisc.edu
www.slis.wisc.edu

University of Wisconsin-
Milwaukee[1,2]
**OFFERS 100% ONLINE PROGRAM**
Master of Library and Information
Science
School of Information Studies
Milwaukee, WI 53201
(414) 229-4707
www4.uwm.edu/sois

## SOUTHWEST
University of Arizona [2]
Master of Arts
School of Information Resources
and Library Science
Tucson, AZ 85719
(520) 621-3565
sirls.arizona.edu

University of Denver[1]
Master of Library and Information
Science
College of Education, Library and
Information Science Program
Denver, CO 80208
(303) 871-2747
www.du.edu/LIS

University of North Texas [1,2]
Master of Science
Dept. of Library and Information
Sciences
Denton, TX 76203-5017
(940) 565-2445
www.ci.unt.edu

University of Oklahoma[1]
Master of Library and Information
Studies
School of Library and Information
Studies
Norman, OK 73019-6032
(405) 325-3921
www.ou.edu/cas/slis

University of Texas at Austin[1,2]
Master of Science in Information
Studies
School of Information
Austin, TX 78701-1213
(512) 471-3821
www.ischool.utexas.edu

Texas Woman's University[1,2]
**OFFERS 100% ONLINE PROGRAM**
Master of Arts in Library Science;
Master of Library Science
School of Library and Information
Studies

Denton, TX 76204-5438
(940) 898-2602/2603
www.twu.edu/library-studies/

**WEST**
University of California, Los
Angeles[1,2]
Master of Library and Information
Studies
Graduate School of Education and
Information Studies
Los Angeles, CA 90095-1520
(310) 825-8799
info@gseis.ucla.edu
is.gseis.ucla.edu/

University of Hawaii[1,2]
Library and Information Science
Program
Master of Library and Information
Science
Honolulu, HI 96822
(808) 956-7321
slis@hawaii.edu
www.hawaii.edu/lis

San Jose State University
**OFFERS 100% ONLINE PROGRAM**
Master of Library and Information
Science
School of Library and Information
Science
San Jose, CA 95192-0029
(408) 924-2490
slisweb.sjsu.edu

University of Washington[1,2]
**OFFERS 100% ONLINE PROGRAM**
Master of Library and Information
Science
The Information School
Seattle, WA 98195-2840
(206) 685-9937
ischool.uw.edu

**CANADA**
University of Alberta [2]
Master of Library and Information
Studies
School of Library and Information
Studies
Edmonton, Alberta T6G 2J4
(780) 492-4578
slis@ualberta.ca
www.slis.ualberta.ca

University of British Columbia [1,2]
Master of Library and Information
Studies
School of Library, Archival and
Information Studies
Vancouver, BC V6T 1Z1
(604) 822-2404
slais@interchange.ubc.ca
www.slais.ubc.ca

Dalhousie University
Master of Library and Information
Studies
School of Information Management
Halifax, Nova Scotia B3H 3J5
(902) 494-3656
sim@dal.ca
sim.management.dal.ca

McGill University [1,2]
Master of Library and Information
Studies
School of Information Studies
Montreal, Quebec H3A 1X1
(514) 398-4204
sis@mcgill.ca
www.mcgill.ca/sis/

Université de Montréal [2]
Maitrise en sciences de l'information
Ecole de bibliothéconomie
et des sciences de l'information
Montréal, Quèbec H3C 3J7
(514) 343-6044
www.ebsi.umontreal.ca/

University of Toronto [1,2]
Master of Information
Faculty of Information
Toronto, Ontario M5S 3G6
(416) 978-3202
www.ischool.utoronto.ca

University of Western Ontario[2]
Master of Library and Information
Science
Graduate Programs in Library and
Information Science
London, Ontario N6A 5B7
(519) 661-4017
www.fims.uwo.ca

**SCHOOLS WITH 100% ONLINE
ACCREDITED PROGRAMS**

1. Clarion University
2. Drexel University
3. Florida State University
4. North Carolina Central University
5. Rutgers - the State University of New
Jersey
6. San Jose State University
7. Southern Connecticut State University
8. Texas Women's University
9. University of Alabama
10. University of Kentucky
11. University of Maryland
12. University of Puerto Rico
13. University of South Carolina
14. University of Southern Mississippi
15. University of Tennessee
16.University of Washington
17. University of Wisconsin -
Milwaukee
18. Wayne State University

| | | | |
|---|---|---|---|
| JZ | | | Polticial Science, including JZ International Relations (Political aspects) |
| | JZ | 2-6530 | International relations |
| | JZ | 4835-5490 | International organizations and associations including the United Nations |
| | JZ | 5511-6300 | Promotion of peace |
| | JZ | 6360-6377 | Non-military coercion |
| | JZ | 6385-6530 | Armed conflict. War and order |
| K | | | Law in General : Comparative and Uniform Law - Jurisprudence |
| | K | 1-487 | Law in general, Jurisprudence |
| | K | 524-5582 | Comparative and Uniform law, Jurisprudence |
| | K | 7000-7720 | Private international law, Conflict of laws |
| KB | | | Religious Law – Comparative (includes different Christian religious legal systems) |
| | KBM | 1-4855 | Jewish law. Halakah |
| | KBP | 1-4860 | Islamic law. Shari'ah. Fiqh |
| | KBR | 27-4090 | History of Canon law |
| | KBS | 3-4130 | Canon law of the Eastern churches |
| | KBT | 3-280 | Canon law of Eastern Rite churches in communion with the Holy See of Rome |
| | KBU | 2-4820 | Law of the Roman Catholic Church. The Holy See |
| KD | | | Law of the United Kingdom and Ireland |
| | KD | | England and Wales |
| | KDC | | Scotland |
| | KDE | | Northern Ireland |
| | KDG | | Isle of Man, Channel Islands |
| | KDK | | Ireland (Eire) |
| KDZ | | | Law of the Americas: North America |
| | KDZ | 1101-1199 | Organization of American States (OAS) |
| | KDZ | | Bermuda, Greenland, St. Pierre and Miquelon |
| KE, KEA-KEZ | | | Law of Canada, Canadian provinces, cities |
| KG-KH | | | Law of Latin America, Mexico and Central America |
| | KG-KGH | | CENTRAL AMERICA |
| | KGA | | Belize |
| | KGB | | Costa Rica |
| | KGC | | El Salvador |
| | KGD | | Guatemala |
| | KGE | | Honduras |
| | KGF | | Mexico |
| | KGG | | Nicaragua |
| | KGH | | Panama, Panama Canal Zone |
| | KGJ-KGZ | | WEST INDIES, CARIBBEAN AREA |
| | KGJ | | Anguilla |
| | KGK | | Antigua, Barbuda, Aruba |
| | KGL | | Bahamas, Barbados, Bonaire, British Leeward Islands, British Virgin Islands, British West Indies, British Windward Islands |
| | KGM | | Cayman Islands |
| | KGN | | Cuba |
| | KGP | | Curacao |
| | KGQ | | Dominica, Dominican Republic |
| | KGR | | Dutch Leeward Islands, Dutch West Indies, Dutch Windward Islands, French West Indies, Grenada, Guadeloupe |
| | KGS | | Haiti |
| | KGT | | Jamaica, Martinique, Montserrat |
| | KGU | | Navassa Islands, Puerto Rico |
| | KGW | | Saba, St. Christopher (St. Kitts), Nevis, Anguilla, St. Lucia, St. Vincent, The Grenadines, St. Eustatius, St. Maarten |
| | KGX | | Trinidad and Tobago |
| | KGY | | Turks and Caicos Islands |
| | KGZ | | Virgin Islands of the United States |
| | KH-KHW | | SOUTH AMERICA |
| | KHA | | Argentina |
| | KHC | | Bolivia |
| | KHD | | Brazil |
| | KHF | | Chile |
| | KHH | | Colombia |
| | KHK | | Ecuador |
| | KHL | | Falkland Islands |
| | KHM | | French Guiana |

| | KHN | | Guyana |
|---|---|---|---|
| | KHP | | Paraguay |
| | KHQ | | Peru |
| | KHR | | South Georgia and South Sandwich Islands |
| | KHS | | Surinam |
| | KHU | | Uruguay |
| | KHW | | Venezuela |
| **KIA-KIX** | | | **Law of Indigenous Peoples in the Americas** |
| | KIA | | Arctic, Northern Canada, Inuit, Alaska |
| | KIB | | Eastern Canada |
| | KIC | | Western Canada |
| | KIE-KIK | | United States of America – lower 48 states |
| | KIL-KIP | | Mexico and Central America (currently explored) |
| | (KIS-KIX) | | South America |
| **KJ-KKZ** | | | **Law of Europe** |
| | KJ-KJA | | History of Law (Europe), Roman law |
| | KJC | | Regional comparative and uniform law (Europe) |
| | KJE | | Regional organization and integration (Europe) |
| | KJG | | Albania |
| | KJH | | Andorra |
| | KJJ | | Austria |
| | KJK | | Belgium, Bosnia and Hercegovina ( Republic, 1992- ) |
| | KJM | | Bulgaria, Croatia (1992- ) |
| | KJN | | Cyprus |
| | KJP | | Czechoslovakia to 1993, Czech Republic (1993- ) |
| | KJQ | | Slovakia (1993- ) |
| | KJR | | Denmark |
| | KJS | | Estonia |
| | KJT | | Finland |
| | KJV-KJW | | France |
| | KK-KKC | | Germany. East Germany. West Germany |
| | KKE | | Greece |
| | KKF | | Hungary |
| | KKG | | Iceland |
| | KKH | | Italy, Kosovo (2008- ) |
| | KKI | | Latvia |
| | KKJ | | Liechtenstein, Lithuania |
| | KKK | | Luxembourg, Macedonia (1992- ), Malta |
| | KKL | | Monaco, Montenegro (2006- ) |
| | KKM | | Netherlands |
| | KKN | | Norway |
| | KKP | | Poland |
| | KKQ | | Portugal |
| | KKR | | Romania |
| | KKS | | San Marino , Serbia (2006- ), Slovenia (1992- ) |
| | KKT | | Spain |
| | KKV | | Sweden |
| | KKW | | Switzerland |
| | KKX | | Turkey |
| | KKY | | Ukraine (1991- ) |
| | KKZ | | Yugoslavia (1956-2003). Serbia (to 2006). Montenegro (to 2006) |
| **KL-KWX** | | | **Law of Asia and Eurasia, Africa, Pacific Area, and Antarctica** |
| | KL | 2-9299 | History of Law. The Ancient Orient |
| | **KLA-KWX** | | **EURASIA** |
| | KLA-KLB | | Russia, Soviet Union, Russia (Federation, 1992- ) |
| | KLD | | Armenian SSR (to 1991) |
| | KLE | | Azerbaijan |
| | KLF | | Belarus (Republic) |
| | KLH | | Georgia (Republic) |

| | | |
|---|---|---|
| KLM | | Moldova |
| KLN | | Russian S.F.S.R. (to 1991) |
| KLP | | Ukraine (1919-1991), Zakavkazskaia Sotsialisticheskaia - Federativnaia Sovetskaia Respublika (to 1936) |
| KLQ | | Bukharskaia Narodnaia Sovetskaia Respublika (to 1924) |
| KLR | | Kazakhstan , Khorezmskaia Sovetskaia Sotsialisticheskaia Respublika (to 1924) |
| KLS | | Kyrgyzstan |
| KLT | | Tajikistan |
| KLV | | Turkmenistan |
| KLW | | Uzbekistan |
| KM | 1-999 | Asia (General) |
| KMC-KMY | | **MIDDLE EAST. SOUTHWEST ASIA** |
| KMC | | Regional comparative and uniform law, Palestine after 1948 |
| KME | | Regional organization & integration |
| KMF | | Armenia (Republic), Bahrain |
| KMG | | Gaza |
| KMH | | Iran |
| KMJ | | Iraq |
| KMK | | Israel |
| KML | | Jerusalem |
| KMM | | Jordan, West Bank |
| KMN | | Kuwait |
| KMP | | Lebanon |
| KMQ | | Oman, Palestine to 1948 |
| KMS | | Qatar |
| KMT | | Saudi Arabia |
| KMU | | Syria |
| KMV | | United Arab Emirates |
| KMX-KMY | | Yemen, Yemen (People's Democratic Republic) to 1990 |
| KNC-KPW | | **SOUTH ASIA. SOUTHEAST ASIA. EAST ASIA** |
| KNC | | Regional comparative and uniform law |
| KNE | | Regional organization and integration |
| KNF | | Afghanistan |
| KNG | | Bangladesh |
| KNH | | Bhutan |
| KNK | | Brunei |
| KNL | | Burma |
| KNM | | Cambodia |
| KNN | | China |
| KNP-KNQ | | China (Republic, 1949 - ). Taiwan, China (People's Republic) 1949 - |
| KNR | | Hong Kong to 1997 |
| KNS-KNU | | India |
| KNV | | French Indochina, Indochina (Federation) |
| KNW | | Indonesia, East Timor |
| KNX | | Japan |
| KNY | | Japan – Cities, etc. |
| KPA | | Korea. South Korea |
| KPC | | Democratic People's Republic of Korea. North Korea |
| KPE | | Laos |
| KPF | | Macau (to 1999) |
| KPG-KPH | | Malaysia, Maldives |
| KPJ | | Mongolia |
| KPK | | Nepal |
| KPL | | Pakistan |
| KPM | | Philippines |
| KPP | | Singapore |
| KPS | | Sri Lanka |
| KPT | | Thailand |
| KPV | | Vietnam, North Vietnam |

| | | | |
|---|---|---|---|
| | KPW | | Vietnam (Republic). South Vietnam |
| | KQ-KTZ | | **AFRICA** |
| | KQ | | History of the law of Africa,   Law of indigenous peoples (Africa) |
| | KQC | | Regional comparative and uniform law (Africa) |
| | KQE | | Regional organization and integration (Africa) |
| | KQG | | Algeria |
| | KQH | | Angola |
| | KQJ | | Benin |
| | KQK | | Botswana |
| | KQM | | British Central Africa Protectorate |
| | KQP | | British Indian Ocean Territory,   British Somaliland |
| | KQT | | Burkina Faso |
| | KQV | | Burundi |
| | KQW | | Cameroon |
| | KQX | | Cape Verde |
| | KRB | | Central African Republic |
| | KRC | | Chad |
| | KRE | | Comoros |
| | KRG | | Congo (Brazzaville) |
| | KRK | | Djibouti |
| | KRL | | East Africa Protectorate |
| | KRM | | Egypt (United Arab Republic) |
| | KRN | | Eritrea |
| | KRP | | Ethiopia |
| | KRR | | French Equatorial Africa |
| | KRS | | French West Africa |
| | KRU | | Gabon |
| | KRV | | Gambia |
| | KRW | | German East Africa |
| | KRX | | Ghana |
| | KRY | | Gibraltar |
| | KSA | | Guinea |
| | KSC | | Guinea-Bissau |
| | KSE | | Equatorial Guinea,   Ifni |
| | KSG | | Italian East Africa,   Italian Somaliland |
| | KSH | | Cote d'Ivoire (Ivory Coast) |
| | KSK | | Kenya |
| | KSL | | Lesotho |
| | KSN | | Liberia |
| | KSP | | Libya |
| | KSR | | Madagascar |
| | KSS | | Malawi |
| | KST | | Mali |
| | KSU | | Mauritania |
| | KSV | | Mauritius,   Mayotte |
| | KSW | | Morocco |
| | KSX | | Mozambique |
| | KSY | | Namibia |
| | KSZ | | Niger |
| | KTA | | Nigeria |
| | KTC | | Réunion |
| | KTD | | Rwanda |
| | KTE | | Saint Helena |
| | KTF | | Sao Tome and Principe |
| | KTG | | Senegal |
| | KTH | | Seychelles |
| | KTJ | | Sierra Leone |
| | KTK | | Somalia |
| | KTL | | South Africa, Republic of |
| | KTM | | South Sudan |
| | KTN | | Spanish West Africa (to 1958),   Spanish Sahara (to 1975) |
| | KTQ | | Sudan |
| | KTR | | Swaziland |
| | KTT | | Tanzania |
| | KTU | | Togo |

| | | | |
|---|---|---|---|
| | KTV | | Tunisia |
| | KTW | | Uganda |
| | KTX | | Congo (Democratic Republic) |
| | KTY | | Zambia, Zanzibar (to 1964) |
| | KTZ | | Zimbabwe |
| | KU | | Australia |
| | KUA-KUN | | Australian Territories |
| | KUQ | | New Zealand |
| | **KVB-KWW** | | **PACIFIC AREA JURISDICTIONS** |
| | KVC | | Regional comparative and uniform law: other Pacific area jurisdictions |
| | KVE | | Regional organization and integration: other Pacific area jurisdictions |
| | KVH | | American Samoa, British New Guinea (Territory of Papua) |
| | KVL | | Cook Islands |
| | KVM | | Easter Island |
| | KVN | | Fiji |
| | KVP | | French Polynesia, German New Guinea to 1914 |
| | KVQ | | Guam |
| | KVR | | Kiribati (inc. Gilbert, Phoenix, and Line Islands) |
| | KVS | | Marshall Islands, Micronesia (Federated States), Midway Islands |
| | KVU | | Nauru, Netherlands New Guinea to 1963 |
| | KVW | | New Caledonia |
| | KWA | | Niue |
| | KWC | | Northern Mariana Islands |
| | KWE | | Pacific Islands (Trust Territory) |
| | KWG | | Palau |
| | KWH | | Papua New Guinea |
| | KWL | | Pitcairn Island, Solomon Islands |
| | KWP | | Tonga |
| | KWQ | | Tuvalu |
| | KWR | | Vanuatu |
| | KWT | | Wake Island, Wallis and Futuna Islands |
| | KWW | | Samoa |
| | KWX | | Antarctica |
| **KZ** | | | **Law of Nations** |
| | KZ | 1-7500 | Law of nations – treaties, foreign affairs, international criminal law |
| | KZA | 1002-5205 | Law of the Sea |
| | KZD | 1002-6715 | Space Law, Law of Outer Space |
| **KF** | | | **Law of the United States (Federal)** |
| | KF | 1-8 | Bibliography |
| | KF | 11-49 | Congressional documents |
| | KF | 47 | Presidential messages. By date |
| | KF | 50-70 | Statutes and administrative regulations. Session law. Statutes at Large |
| | KF | 60 | Compilations of statutes |
| | KF | 70 | Administrative regulations. Proclamations and executive orders |
| | KF | 75 | Digests of statutes |
| | KF | 78 | Citators to statutes and/or administrative regulations |
| | KF | 80 | Indexes to statutes |
| | KF | 85 | Digests of and indexes to state legislation |
| | KF | 90 | Other bibliographic aids. Table of popular names |
| | KF | 101-153 | Law reports and related materials |
| | KF | 154-156 | Encyclopedias. Law dictionaries. Words and phrases |
| | KF | 159 | Legal maxims. Quotations |
| | KF | 165 | Uniform state law |
| | KF | 170 | Form books |
| | KF | 178 | Yearbooks |
| | KF | 180-185 | Judicial statistics. Criminal statistics |
| | KF | 190-195 | Directories |
| | KF | 200 | Society and bar association journals |
| | KF | 219-224 | Criminal trials |
| | KF | 226-228 | Civil trials |
| | KF | 240-247 | Legal research. Legal bibliography |
| | KF | 242.A1 | Electronic data processing. Information retrieval |
| | KF | 245 | System citation |
| | KF | 246 | Legal abbreviations |

| | | | |
|---|---|---|---|
| KF | 247 | Abstracting and indexing systems | |
| KF | 250-251 | Legal composition and draftsmanship | |
| KF | 255 | Law reporting | |
| KF | 261-292 | Legal education | |
| KF | 294 | Law societies | |
| KF | 297-334 | The legal profession. Practice of law. Bar associations. | |
| KF | 336-337.5 | Community legal services. Legal aid. Legal services to the poor | |
| KF | 338 | Lawyer referral services | |
| KF | 350-374 | History of American law | |
| kF | 379-382 | Jurisprudence and philosophy of American law | |
| KF | 384 | Relationship of law to other disciplines, subjects | |
| KF | 390.A-Z | Works for particular groups of users, A-Z [Accounts – Women] | |
| KF | 394 | Common law in the United States | |
| KF | 395.A2 | Restatement of the common law | |
| KF | 398-400 | Equity | |
| KF | 410-418 | Conflict of laws | |
| KF | 420 | Retroactive law. Intertemporal law | |
| KF | 422 | Retroactive judicial decisions. Prospective overruling | |
| KF | 445-450 | Concepts applying to several branches of law | |
| KF | 465-553 | Persons | |
| KF | 501-553 | Domestic relations. Family law | |
| KF | 560-720 | Property | |
| KF | 566-698 | Real property. Land law (Private use) | |
| KF | 656-685 | Transfer of rights in land | |
| KF | 691-698 | Mortgages | |
| KF | 701-720.2 | Personal property | |
| KF | 726-745 | Trusts and trustees | |
| KF | 733-742 | Trusts. Private trusts | |
| KF | 744-746 | Trustees. Trust companies | |
| KF | 746-780 | Estate planning. Succession upon death | |
| KF | 801-1241 | Contracts. General and comprehensive works. | |
| KF | 960-962 | Checks | |
| KF | 966-1032 | Banks and Banking | |
| KF | 1033 | Foreign-exchange brokerage | |
| KF | 1035-1040 | Loan of money | |
| KF | 1045 | Suretyship. Guaranty | |
| KF | 1046-1062 | Secured transactions | |
| KF | 1065-1084 | Marketing of securities. Stock exchange transactions | |
| KF | 1085-1087 | Commodity exchanges. Produce exchanges | |
| KF | 1091-1137 | Carriers. Carriage of goods and passengers | |
| KF | 1146-1238 | Insurance. Including regulation of insurance business | |
| KF | 1241 | Aleatory contracts | |
| KF | 1244 | Restitution. Quasi contracts. Unjust enrichment | |
| KF | 1246-1327 | Torts (Extracontractual liability). Remedies. Defenses | |
| KF | 1328 | Compensation to victims of crime. Reparation | |
| KF | 1329 | Assistance in emergencies. Good Samaritan laws | |
| KF | 1341-1348 | Agency | |
| KF | 1355-1481 | Associations. Unincorporated associations | |
| KF | 1365-1382 | Business associations. Partnership | |
| KF | 1384-1486 | Corporations. Juristic persons | |
| KF | 1388-1390 | Nonprofit corporations | |
| KF | 1396-1477 | Business corporations | |
| KF | 1419 | Foreign corporations | |
| KF | 1431-1440 | Issuing of securities | |
| KF | 1441-1446 | Particular types of stocks | |
| KF | 1448-1454 | Shares and shareholders' rights. Stock transfers | |
| KF | 1456 | Debentures. Bonds. Preferred stocks | |
| KF | 1457 | Trust indentures | |
| KF | 1465 | Holding companies | |
| KF | 1466 | Close corporations including family-owned businesses | |
| KF | 1470 | Cooperative societies | |
| KF | 1475 | Dissolution. Liquidation including spin-offs, sale | |
| KF | 1477 | Consolidation and merger including tender offers | |
| KF | 1478 | Divestiture. Spinoffs | |
| KF | 1480 | Government-owned corporations & organizations | |
| KF | 1501-1548 | Insolvency and bankruptcy. Creditors' rights | |

| | KF | 1570-1575 | Economic policy. Economic planning |
|---|---|---|---|
| | KF | 1600-2940 | Regulation of industry, trade, and commerce. Occupational law |
| | KF | 1601-1611 | Unfair trade practices. Work of the Federal Trade Commission |
| | KF | 1614-1617 | Advertising |
| | KF | 1619-1620 | Labeling |
| | KF | 1624-1625 | Restraint of trade |
| | KF | 1626-1629 | Price fixing. Price discrimination. Basing-point pricing |
| | KF | 1631-1657 | Monopolies. Antitrust laws |
| | KF | 1659 | Small business |
| | KF | 1661 | Trade associations |
| | KF | 1663 | State jurisdiction. Trade barriers |
| | KF | 1665-1666 | Weights and measures. Containers |
| | KF | 1668 | Standard time |
| | KF | 1681-1755 | Agriculture. Forestry. Work of the Dept. of Agriculture |
| | KF | 1760 | Aquaculture |
| | KF | 1770-1773 | Fishery |
| | KF | 1801-1873 | Mining. Quarrying including Oil and gas. Bureau of Mines |
| | KF | 1841-1850 | Petroleum. Oil and gas |
| | KF | 1870 | Natural gas |
| | KF | 1875 | Chemical industries |
| | KF | 1879 | Drug and pharmaceutical industries |
| | KF | 1881 | Textile industries |
| | KF | 1893 | Consumer products. Light industries |
| | KF | 1900-1944 | Food processing industries |
| | KF | 1902-1910 | Agricultural products |
| | KF | 1911-1917 | Meat industry |
| | KF | 1921-1924 | Dairy industry. Dairy products industry |
| | KF | 1930-1933 | Fishery products. Seafood industry |
| | KF | 1935-1936 | Vegetable oils and fats |
| | KF | 1939 | Spices. Herbs |
| | KF | 1940 | Beverages |
| | KF | 1950 | Construction and building industry. Contractors |
| | KF | 1975-1984 | International trade |
| | KF | 1987-1990 | Export trade. Export controls and regulations |
| | KF | 1993-1996 | Import trade. Import controls and regulations |
| | KF | 1998-1999 | Wholesale trade |
| | KF | 2005-2038 | Retail trade |
| | KF | 2041-2042 | Service trades |
| | KF | 2050-2057 | Warehouses |
| | KF | 2076-2140 | Public utilities |
| | KF | 2161-2849 | Transportation and communication |
| | KF | 2635-2640 | Merchant fleet |
| | KF | 2246-2462 | Carriage of passengers and goods |
| | KF | 2471-2480 | United States Space law |
| | KF | 2531-2654 | Water transportation. Navigation and shipping |
| | KF | 2661-2738 | Postal service |
| | KF | 2740-2743 | Express companies |
| | KF | 2745 | Forwarding agents. Freight forwarders |
| | KF | 2750 | Press law |
| | KF | 2761- | Telecommunication |
| | KF | 2847 | Electronic mail |
| | KF | 2900-2940 | Regulation of professionals |
| | KF | 2971-3194 | Intellectual property |
| | KF | 2983 | Intellectual property litigation |
| | KF | 2986-3080 | Copyright |
| | KF | 3084 | Author and publisher. The publishing contract |
| | KF | 3086 | Design protection |
| | KF | 3091-3193 | Patent law and trademarks |
| | KF | 3195-3198 | Unfair competition |
| | KF | 3301-3580 | Labor law. Protection of labor. Labor hygiene and safety |
| | KF | 3600-3686 | Social insurance. Pension trusts |
| | KF | 3720-3745 | Public welfare. Public assistance |
| | KF | 3750 | Disaster relief |
| | KF | 3775-3816 | Environmental law and damages. Public health. Toxic torts |
| | KF | 3821-3829 | Medical legislation |
| | KF | 3828 | Psychiatric hospitals and mental health facilities |

| | KF | 3830-3831 | Human reproductive technology |
|---|----|-----------|-------------------------------|
| | KF | 3835-3838 | Veterinary medicine & hygiene. Veterinary public health |
| | KF | 3841-3845 | Animal protection. Animal welfare. Animal rights |
| | KF | 3861-3896.2 | Food. Drugs. Cosmetics |
| | KF | 3901-3925 | Alcohol. Alcoholic beverages. Prohibition |
| | KF | 3941-3977 | Public safety |
| | KF | 3941-3942 | Weapons. Firearms. Munitions |
| | KF | 3945-3965 | Hazardous articles and processes |
| | KF | 3959 | Pesticides, herbicides, etc. |
| | KF | 3970 | Accident control |
| | KF | 3975-3977 | Fire prevention and control. Explosives |
| | KF | 3985-3995 | Control of social activities |
| | KF | 3987 | Amusements |
| | KF | 3989 | Sports. Prizefighting. Horse racing |
| | KF | 3992 | Lotteries. Gaming |
| | KF | 4101-4257 | Education. Public education |
| | KF | 4270-4330 | Science and the arts. Research |
| | KF | 4280.S7 | Space exploration |
| | KF | 4288-4305 | The arts. Museums and galleries |
| | KF | 4310-4312 | Historical buildings and monuments |
| | KF | 4315-4319 | Libraries and library services |
| | KF | 4325 | Archives. Historical documents |
| | KF | 4330 | Educational, scientific, and cultural exchanges |
| | KF | 4501-5130 | Constitutional law |
| | KF | 5150 | National emblem. Flag. Seal. National anthem |
| | KF | 5152 | Patriotic customs and observances |
| | KF | 5153-5154 | Decorations of honor. Awards |
| | KF | 5155-5156 | Commemorative medals |
| | KF | 5300-5332 | Local government |
| | KF | 5336-5398 | Civil service. Government officials and employees |
| | KF | 5399 | Police and power of the police |
| | KF | 5401-5425 | Administrative organization and procedure |
| | KF | 5500-5865 | Public property. Public restraints on private property |
| | KF | 5505-5510 | Conservation of natural resources |
| | KF | 5521-5536 | Roads |
| | KF | 5540-5541 | Bridges |
| | KF | 5551-5590 | Water resources. Watersheds. Rivers. Lakes |
| | KF | 5594 | Weather control. Meteorology. Weather stations |
| | KF | 5599 | Eminent domain |
| | KF | 5601-5646 | Public land law |
| | KF | 5616-5620 | Land reclamation |
| | KF | 5660-5662 | Indian lands |
| | KF | 5670-5673 | Homesteads |
| | KF | 5675-5677 | Land grants |
| | KF | 5691-5710 | Regional and city planning. Zoning. Building |
| | KF | 5721-5740 | Housing. Slum clearance. City redevelopment |
| | KF | 5750-5857 | Government property |
| | KF | 5820-5857 | Government use of personal property |
| | KF | 5865 | Public works |
| | KF | 5900-6075.52 | Government measures in time of war, national emergency, or economic crisis. Wartime and emergency legislation |
| | KF | 6200-6795 | Public finance |
| | KF | 6219 | Federal Reserve Board |
| | KF | 6201-6219 . | Money. Currency. Coinage |
| | KF | 6221-6239 | Budget. Government expenditures. Public auditing |
| | KF | 6241-6245 | Public debts. Loans. Bond issues |
| | KF | 6251-6708 | National revenue |
| | KF | 6271-6645 | Taxation |
| | KF | 6651-6708 | Tariff. Trade agreements. Customs |
| | KF | 6720-6795.2 | State and local finance |
| | KF | 7201-7755 | National defense. Military law |
| | KF | 7298 | Armed Forces hospitals |
| | KF | 7305-7479 | Particular branches of service |
| | KF | 7485-7488.7 | Auxiliary services during war or emergency |
| | KF | 7590 | Military discipline |
| | KF | 7597-7596 | Law enforcement. Criminal investigation |

| | KF | 7601-7679 | Military criminal law and procedure |
|---|---|---|---|
| | KF | 7680 | Criminal status of members of the Armed Forces |
| | KF | 7682-7683 | Other defense and intelligence agencies |
| | KF | 7685 | Civil defense |
| | KF | 7701-7755 | War veterans |
| | KF | 7739.M35 | Veteran's hospitals (1939-1945) |
| | KF | 7749.M35 | Veteran's hospitals (1945- ) |
| | KF | 8201-8228 | Indians |
| | KF | 8699-9075 | Court organization and procedure |
| | KF | 8810-9075 | Civil procedure |
| | KF | 8944 | Evidence |
| | KF | 9084 | Negotiated settlement. Compromise |
| | KF | 9085-9086 | Arbitration and award. Commercial arbitration |
| | KF | 9201-9461 | Criminal law |
| | KF | 9601-9763 | Criminal procedure |
| | KF | 9771-9795 | Juvenile courts |
| | KF | 9800-9822 | Juvenile criminal law and procedure |
| | KF | 9825 | Juvenile detention homes |
| | KF | 9827 | Probation |
| | KFA-KFW | | Law of the individual states : Alabama – Wyoming |
| | KFX | | Individual cities, A-Z |
| | KFZ | | Northwest Territory,  Confederate States of America |

Classification summaries reviewed by:

*Cassidy*
cataloguing
services
*The Ivy League of Information Retrieval*

# LEGAL RESEARCH BIBLIOGRAPHY–GENERAL

Armstrong, J.D.S. and Christopher A. Knott. **Where the Law Is: An Introduction to Advanced Legal Research**. 3rd ed. St. Paul: Thomson/West, 2009.

Barber, Steve. **Legal Research.** Albany: Delmar, 1996.

Bast, Carol M. and Margie Hawkins. **Foundations of Legal Research and Writing**. 4th ed. Clifton Park, NY: Delmar Cengage Learning,, 2010.

Berring, Robert C. **Finding the Law.** 12th ed. St. Paul: West, 2005.

Berring, Robert C. and Elizabeth Edinger. **Legal Research Survival Manual.** St. Paul: West, 2002.

Biehl, Kathy and Tara Calishain. **The Lawyer's Guide to Internet Research.** Lanham, MD: Scarecrow Press, 2000.

Botluk, Diana. **The Legal List: Research on the Internet.** St. Paul: West, 2004.

Bourdeau, John. **Legal Research for Beginners.** Hauppauge, NY: Barron's, 1997.

Bouchoux, Deborah E. **A Concise Guide to Legal Research and Writing.** New York: Aspen Publishers, 2011.

---. **Legal Research and Writing for Paralegals.** 6th ed. New York: Aspen Law & Business, 2011.

---. **Legal Research Explained.** 2nd ed. New York: Aspen Publishers, 2010.

Brown, Valerie J. Atkinson. **Legal Research Via the Internet.** Albany, NY: West/Thomson Learning, 2001.

Cane, Peter and Mark Tushnet, eds. **The Oxford Handbook of Legal Studies.** New York: Oxford University Press, 2003.

Cane, Peter and Herbert M. Kritzer, eds. **The Oxford Handbook of Empirical Legal Research.** New York: Oxford University Press, 2010.

Carson, Bryan M. **Finding the Law: Legal Research for Librarians and Paralegals.** Lanham, MD: Scarecrow Press, 2011.

Chandler, Yvonne. **Neal-Schuman Guide to Finding Legal and Regulatory Information on the Internet.** 2nd. ed. New York: Neal-Schuman, 2001.

Cochard, Susan. **Computer-Assisted Legal Research.** Chicago: ABA, 1997.

Cohen, Morris L., et al. **How To Find the Law.** 8th ed. St. Paul: West, 2003.

Cohen, Morris L and Ken C. Olson. **Legal Research in a Nutshell.** 10th ed. St. Paul: West, 2010.

Corbin, John. **Find the Law in the Library.** Chicago: American Library Assn., 1989.

Danner, Richard A. and Jules Winterton, eds. **The IALL International Handbook of Legal Information Management.** Burlington, VT: Ashgate, 2011.

Delaney, Stephanie. **Electronic Legal Research: An Integrated Approach.** 2nd ed. Clifton Park, NY: Delmar Cengage Learning, 2009.

Donahoe, Diana R. **Experiential Legal Research: Sources, Strategies, and Citation.** New York: Wolters Kluwer Law & Business, 2011.

Doyle, Francis R. **Searching the Law.** 3rd ed. Dobbs Ferry, NY: Transnational Publishers, 2005.

Dykes, Christopher C. **Federal Income Tax Law: A Legal Research Guide.** Buffalo, NY: Hein, 2010.

---. **International Tax Law: A Legal Research Guide.** Buffalo, NY: Hein, 2011.

Edwards, Linda L. and J. Stanley. **Guide to Factual Investigations.** Albany, NY: West/Thomson Learning, 2002.

Elias, Stephen. **Legal Research Online and in the Library.** Berkeley: Nolo Press, 1998.

---. **Legal Research: How to Find and Understand the Law.** 15th ed. Berkeley: Nolo Press, 2009.

Evans, James. **Law on the Net.** 2nd ed. Berkeley: Nolo Press, 1997.

Fine, Toni M. **American Legal Systems: A Resource and Reference Guide.** Cincinnati, OH: Anderson, 1997.

Fishman, Joel. **Navigating Legal Research & Technology: Quick Reference Guide to the 1,500 Most Common Questions about Traditional and Online Legal Research.** Getzville, NY: Bridge Pub. Group, 2010.

Foster, Lynn, and Nancy P. Johnson. **Legal Research Exercises.** Rev. 4th ed. St. Paul: West, 1995.

Gardner, Robert L., et al. **Tax Research Techniques.** 7th ed. New York: AICPA, 2005.

Germain, Claire M. **Germain's Transnational Law Research: A Guide for Attorneys.** Irvington-on-Hudson, New York: Transnational Juris Publications, 1992.

Gilman, Wesley. **Legal Research, Writing and Advocacy: a Sourcebook.** 2nd ed. Cincinnati: Anderson, 1987.

Glaser, Cathy, et al. **The Lawyer's Craft: An Introduction to Legal Analysis, Writing, Research and Advocacy.** Cincinnati: Anderson, 2002.

Gordon, Stacey L. **Online Legal Research: A Guide to Legal Research Services and Other Internet Tools.** Buffalo, NY: Hein, 2003.

Griffith, Cary. **Griffith's Guide to Computer Assisted Legal Research.** Cincinnati: Anderson, 1992.

Grossman, George, ed. **Legal Research: Historical Foundations of the Electronic Age.** New York: Oxford University Press, 1994.

**Guide to International Legal Research.** 2nd ed. Salem, NH: Butterworth, 1993.

Hames, Joanne Banker and Yvonne Ekern. **Legal Research, Analysis, and Writing: An Integrated Approach.** 4th ed. Upper Saddle River, NJ: Prentice Hall, 2012.

Harris, Myra A. **Legal Research.** Englewood Cliffs, NJ: Prentice Hall, 1997.

Hazelton, Penny A. **Computer Assisted Legal Research: The Basics.** St. Paul: West, 1993.

---. **Specialized Legal Research.** New York: Aspen Law & Business, 2001.

Heels, Erik. **Law, Law, Law on the Internet.** Chicago: ABA, 1998.

Hein, Edward H. **Legal Research for Paralegals.** St. Paul: West, 1996.

Helewitz, Jeffrey A. **The Legal Research and Writing Handbook.** New York: Aspen Law & Business, 1997.

Herman, Theodor. **How to Research Less and Find More: The Essential Guide to Computer -Assisted LegalResearch.** St. Paul: West, 1996.

Herskowitz, Suzan and James F. Duggan, **Legal Research Made Easy.** 4th ed. Naperville, IL: Sphinx Publishing, 2005.

Hodes, W. William. **Legal Research.** 2nd ed. St. Paul: Natl. Institute for Trial Advocacy, 1988.

Hoffman, Marci. **International Legal Research in a Nutshell.** St. Paul: Thomson/West, 2008.

Honigsberg, Peter Jan. **Legal Research Writing and Analysis.** 7th ed. Chicago: Harcourt Brace Legal and Professional Publications, 1995.

Howland, Joan S. **Principles of Power Research: Integrating Manual and Online Legal Research to Maximize Results and Minimize Costs.** St. Paul: West, 1992.

**Internet Legal Research.** Mechanicsburg, PA: Pennsylvania Bar Institute, 2010.

Jacobstein, J. Myron. **Legal Research Illustrated.** 7th ed. Westbury, NY: Foundation Press, 1998.

---. **Fundamentals of Legal Research.** 7th ed. Westbury, NY: Foundation Press, 1998.

Johnson, Nancy P. **Legal Research Exercises Following the Bluebook, A Uniform System of Citation**. St. Paul: West, 2005.

Johnson, Nancy P., et al. **Winning Research Skills**. 5th ed. St. Paul: West, 2002.

Johnsrud, Karin and Sarah Jaramillo. **New Jersey State Documents: A Bibliography of Legal Resources.** Chicago: AALL, 2011.

Jones, Rachel, ed. **Federal Regulatory Research: Selected Agency Knowledge Paths.** Binghamton, NY: Haworth Information Press, 2002.

Karlin, Barbara H. **Tax Research.** 4th ed. Upper Saddle River, NJ: Prentice Hall, 2009.

Kelso, J. Clark. **Studying Law: An Introduction to Legal Research.** 2nd ed. New York: Bender, 1995.

Klein, Deborah J. **Legal Research Materials.** 3rd ed. Dubuque, IA: Kendall/Hunt Publ. Co., 1991.

Kozlowski, Ken. **The Internet Guide for the Legal Researcher.** 3rd ed. Teaneck, NJ: Infosources Publishing, 2001.

Kunz, Christina L., et al. **The Process of Legal Research**. 7th ed. New York: Aspen Publishers, 2008.

Larsen, Sonya. **Legal Research for Beginners.** Hauppauge, NY: Barron's, 1997.

Larson, Joni and Dan Shaeffer. **Federal Tax Research**. 2nd ed. Durham, NC: Carolina Academic Press, 2011.

**Legal Research: Techniques and Strategies for Associates.** New York: Practising Law Institute, 1991.

Levitt, Carole A. **The Lawyering Guide to Fact Finding on the Internet**. 3rd ed. Chicago: ABA, 2006.

Levitt, Carole A. and Mark E. Rosch. **How to Use the Internet for Legal, Business and Investigative Research: A Guide for Legal Professionals.** 6th ed. Culver City, CA: Internet for Lawyers, 2002.

---. **Google for Lawyers: Essential Search Tips and Productivity Tools.** Chicago: ABA, 2010.

---. **Find Info Like a Pro: Mining the Internet's Publicly Available Resources for Investigative Research.** Chicago: ABA, 2010.

Lewis, Alfred J. **Using American Law Books.** 4th ed. Dubuque, IA: Kendall/Hunt Pub. Co. 1995.

Long, Judy A. **Computer Aided Legal Research.** Clifton Park, NY: Thomson/Delmar Learning 2003.

Manz, William H. **Guide to State Legislative and Administrative Materials**. Littleton, CO: Rothman, 2002.

Marke, Julius, et al. **Legal Research and Law Library Management.** New York: Law Journal Press, 1994.

Mays, Antje. **Federal, State, Local and International Laws on the Internet.** 2nd ed. Buffalo, NY: Hein, 2003.

---. **Legal Research On the Internet.** Buffalo, NY: Hein, 1999.

McCully, Brian J. and Grace I. Robinson. **The Legal Research Workbook.** Cincinnati: Anderson, 1996.

McKinney, Ruth Ann. **Legal Research: A Practical Guide and Self-Instructional Workbook.** 5th ed. St. Paul: West, 2008.

McNamara, Gayle E. **Legal Research: Tools and Methods for Legal Professionals.** Los Angeles: Yager, 2001.

Mersky, Roy M. and Donald J. Dunn. **Fundamentals of Legal Research.** 9th ed. New York: Foundation Press, 2009.

---. **Legal Research Illustrated.** 8th ed. New York: Foundation Press, 2002.

Merzon, Melvin S. **Legal Research.** Eau Claire, WI: Professional Education Systems, 1988.

Moscowitz, Ellyn. **Legal Research and Writing for Paralegals**. Cincinnati: Anderson, 1994.

Murray, Michael D. and Christy Hallam DeSanctis. **Legal Research and Writing**. NY: Foundation Press. 2005.

---. **Legal Research Methods**. New York: Thomson Reuters/Foundation Press, 2009.

# LEGAL RESEARCH BIBLIOGRAPHY–GENERAL

---. **Legal Research, Writing and Analysis.** NY: Foundation Press. 2006.

Neascu, Dana E. **Introduction to American Law and Legal Research**. Ardsley, NY: Transnational Publishers, 2005.

Nemeth, Charles. P. And Hope I. Haywood. **Learning Legal Research: A How-To Manual.** Upper Saddle River, NJ: Pearson Prentice-Hall, 2005.

Nolfi, Edward A. **Basic Legal Research**. New York: Glencoe, 1993.

---. **Basic Legal Research for Paralegals.** 2nd ed. New York: McGraw-Hill, 2008.

Oates, Laurel Currie. **The Legal Writing Handbook: Research, Analysis, and Writing.** 5th ed. New York: Aspen Law & Business, 2010.

Oates, Laurel Currie and Anne Enquist. **Just Research**. 3rd ed. New York: Aspen Publishers, 2011.

Olson, Kent C. **Legal Information: How to Find It, How to Use It.** Phoenix: Oryx Press, 1999.

---. **Practical Approaches to Legal Research.** New York: Haworth Press, 1988.

---. **Principles of Legal Research.** St. Paul, MN: West, 2009.

Osbeck, Mark K. **Impeccable Research: A Concise Guide to Mastering Legal Research Skills.** St. Paul, MN: Thomson/West, 2010.

Price, Miles O. **Effective Legal Research.** 4th ed. Boston: Little Brown, 1979.

Putman, William H. **Legal Research.** 2nd ed. Clifton Park, NY: Delmar Cengage Learning, 2010.

---. **Legal Research, Analysis and Writing.** 2nd ed. Clifton Park, NY: Delmar Cengage Learning, 2010.

---. **Pocket Guide to Legal Research.** Clifton Park, NY: Delmar Learning, 2008.

---. **Pocket Guide to Legal Writing.** Clifton Park, NY: Delmar Learning, 2006.

Raabe, William A. **Federal Tax Research.** 8th ed. Mason, OH: South-Western//Cengage Learning, 2009.

Ramy, Herbert N. and Samantha A. Moppett. **Navigating the Internet: Legal Research on the World Wide Web.** Buffalo: Hein, 2000.

Richmond, Gail Levin. **Federal Tax Research.** 8th ed. New York: Foundation Press, 2010.

Roberts, Bonita K. **Legal Research Guide: Patterns and Practice.** 6th ed. New Providence, NJ: LexisNexis, 2011.

Romantz, David S. and Kathleen Elliott Vinson. **Legal Analysis: The Fundamental Skill.** 2nd ed. Durham, NC: Carolina Academic Press, 2009.

Rombauer, Marjorie Dick. **Legal Problem Solving.** 5th ed. St. Paul: West, 1991

Simonsen, Craig B. **Computer-Aided Legal Research (CALR) on the Internet.** Upper Saddle River, NJ: Pearson Education, 2006.

Sloan, Amy. **Basic Legal Research: Tools and Strategies.** 4th ed. New York: Aspen Publishers, 2009.

Sloan, Amy E. and Steven D. Schwinn. **Basic Legal Research Workbook**. 2nd ed. New York: Aspen Publishers, 2005.

Smith, David J. **Legal Research and Writing.** Albany: Delmar, 1996.

Statsky, William P. **Legal Research and Writing.** 5th ed. Albany: West Legal Studies, 1999.

---. **Case Analysis and Fundamentals of Legal Writing.** 4th ed. St. Paul: West, 1995.

Stevens, Anne M. **Finding, Reading and Using the Law.** Albany, NY: West/Thomson Learning, 2002.

Teply, Larry L. **Legal Research and Citation.** 4th ed. St. Paul: West, 1992.

Thomas, Terry. **Computer-Assisted Legal and Tax Research.** Paramus, NJ: Prentice-Hall Information Services, 1986.

# LEGAL RESEARCH BIBLIOGRAPHY–GENERAL

Tyburski, Genie, ed. **Introduction to Online Legal, Regulatory & Intellectual Property Research: Search Strategies, Research Case Study, Research Problems, and Data Source Evaluations and Reviews**. Mason, Ohio: Thomson, 2004.

**Using the Internet for Legal Research**. Mechanicsburg, PA: Pennsylvánia Bar Institute, 2008.

Van Buren, Jessica C., et al. **Utah Legal Research.** Buffalo, NY: Hein, 2011.

van Hoecke, Mark, ed. **Methodologies of Legal Research: Which Kind of Method for What Kind of discipline?** Portland, OR: Hart, 2011.

Walston-Dunham, Beth. **Practical Legal Research: Skills and Strategies for the Legal Assistant.** St. Paul: West, 1995.

Wren, Christopher G. & Jill R. **The Legal Research Manual.** 2nd ed. Madison, WI: Adams & Ambrose, 1988.

Yelin, Andrea B. **The Legal Research and Writing Handbook: A Basic Approach for Paralegals.** 5th ed. New York: Aspen Law and Business, 2009.

Zich, Joanne and Gary McCann. **The Lawyer's Research Companion: A Concise Guide to Sources.** Buffalo, NY: Hein, 1998.

# LEGAL RESEARCH BIBLIOGRAPHY–STATE

Houdek, Frank G., ed. **State Practice Materials: Annotated Bibliographies**. Buffalo, NY: Hein, 2002.

## ALABAMA
Johnson, Hazel L. and Timothy Coggins. **Guide to Alabama State Documents and Selected Law-Related Materials.** Chicago: AALL, 1993.

## ALASKA
Ruzicka, Aimee T. **Alaska Legal and Law-Related Publications: A Guide for Law Librarians.** Chicago: AALL, 1984.

## ARIZONA
Herrara, Tamara S. **Arizona Legal Research.** Durham, NC: Carolina Academic Press, 2008.
Shimpock-Vieweg, Kathy. **Arizona Legal Research Guide.** Buffalo: Hein, 1992.
Teenstra, Richard, et al. **Survey of Arizona State Legal and Law-Related Documents.** Chicago: AALL, 1984.

## ARKANSAS
Barger, Coleen. **Arkansas Legal Research.** Durham, NC: Carolina Academic Press, 2007.
Foster, Lynn. **Arkansas Legal Bibliography: Documents and Selected Commercial Titles.** Chicago: AALL, 1988.

## CALIFORNIA
Castetter, Karla. **Locating the Law: A Handbook for Non-Law Librarians.** 2nd ed. Southern California Association of Law Libraries, 1989.
Dershem, Larry. **California Legal Research Handbook.** 2nd ed. Buffalo, NY: Hein, 2008.
Hanft, John K. **Legal Research in California.** 6th ed. St. Paul: Thomson West, 2007.
Macfarlane, Hether C. And Suzanne E. Rowe. **California Legal Research.** Durham, NC: Carolina Academic Press, 2008.
Maclay, Veronica and Laura Peritore. **California Government Publications and Legal Resources.** Chicago: AALL, 1991.
Martin, Daniel. **Henke's California Law Guide.** 8th ed. Newark, NJ: Matthew Bender, 2006.
McCully, Brian J. **The Legal Research Workbook: California Supplement.** Cincinnati: Anderson, 1996.
Ranharter, Kathryn W. **The State of California: An Introduction to Its Government Publications and Related Information.** Chicago: AALL, 1979.

## COLORADO
Alexander, Gary, et al. **Colorado Legal Resources: An Annotated Bibliography.** Chicago: AALL, 1987.
Craigmile, Kathleen E. **Internet Basics for the Colorado Attorney.** Eau Claire, WI: National Business Institute, 2000.
Linz, Robert M. **Colorado Legal Research.** Durham, NC: Carolina Academic Press, 2010.
McDavid, Wanda. **Legal Resources on the Internet.** Denver: Univ. of Denver College of Law, 1999.

## CONNECTICUT
Bysiewicz, Shirley K. **Sources of Connecticut Law.** Salem, NH: Butterworth, 1987.
Cheeseman, Lawrence G. and Arlene G. Bielefeld. **The Connecticut Legal Research Handbook.** Guilford, CT: Connecticut Law Book Co., 1992.
Hynes, Jessica G. **Connecticut Legal Research.** Durham, NC: Carolina Academic Press, 2009.
**Legal Research Handbook.** Enfield, CT: Comm. on Official Legal Publications, 1997.
Voisinet, David, et al. **Connecticut State Legal Documents: A Selective Bibliography.** Chicago: AALL, 1985.

## DISTRICT OF COLUMBIA
Ahearn, Carolyn P., et al. **Selected Information Sources for the District of Columbia.** 2nd ed. Chicago: AALL, 1985.
Chanin, Leah, et al. **Legal Research in D.C., Maryland and Virginia.** 2nd ed. Buffalo: Hein, 2000.

## FLORIDA
Bucharis, Barbara J. and Suzanne E. Rowe. **Florida Legal Research: Sources, Process, and Analysis.** 3rd ed. Durham, NC: Carolina Academic Press, 2007.
French, Harriet L. **Research in Florida Law.** 2nd ed. Dobbs Ferry, NY: Oceana, 1965.
Martin, Nikki L. **Florida Legal Research and Source Book.** Salem, NH: Butterworth, 1989.
Roehrenbeck, Carol A. **Florida Legislative Histories: A Practical Guide to Their Preparation and Use.**

Clearwater, FL: D & S Publishers, 1986.

Slupski, Betsy L., et al. **Guide to Florida Legal Research**. 7th ed. Tallahassee: Florida Bar, Continuing Legal Education, 2008.

## GEORGIA

Chanin, Leah F. and Suzanne L. Cassidy. **Guide to Georgia Legal Research and Legal History.** Norcross, GA: Harrison Company, 1990.

Johnson, Nancy P., et al. **Georgia Legal Research.** Rev. ed. Durham, NC: Carolina Academic Press, 2007.

Stillwagon, Rebecca Simmons. **Georgia Legal Documents: An Annotated Bibliography.** Chicago: AALL, 1991.

## HAWAII

Kahle, Richard F. **How to Research Constitutional, Legislative and Statutory History in Hawaii.** Rev. Ed. Honolulu: Hawaii Legislative Reference Bureau, 1997.

Seeger, Leina'ala R. **Hawaii State Documents: A Selective Bibiography of Legal Publications and Related Materials.** Chicago: AALL, 2010.

## IDAHO

Fordyce-Ruff, Tenielle and Suzanne E. Rowe. **Idaho Legal Research.** Durham, NC: Carolina Academic Press, 2008.

Greenlee, Michael J. **Idaho State Documents: Bibliography of Legal Publications.** Chicago: AALL, 2003.

## ILLINOIS

Davies, Bernita J. and F. J. Rooney. **Research in Illinois Law.** Dobbs Ferry, NY: Oceana, 1954.

Jacobs, Roger F., et al. **Illinois Legal Research Sourcebook.** Springfield, IL: Illinois Institute for Continuing Legal Education, 1977.

LeBlanc, Mary Ellen and John M. Rossi, eds. **The Internet Guide for Illinois Lawyers.** Springfield, IL: ICLE, 1997.

Nyberg, Cheryl Rae, et al. **Illinois State Documents: A Selective Annotated Bibliography for Law Librarians.** Chicago: AALL, 1986.

Simon, Michael S. **Internet Basics for the Illinois Attorney.** Eau Claire, WI: National Business Institute, 2000.

Wendt, Laurel A. **Illinois Legal Research Manual.** Salem, NH: Butterworth, 1988.

---. **Illinois Legal Research Guide**. 2nd ed. Buffalo, NY: Hein, 2006.

Wojcik, Mark E. **Illinois Legal Research.** 2nd ed. Durham, NC: Carolina Academic Press, 2009.

## INDIANA

Fariss, Linda K. and K. A. Buckley. **An Introduction to Indiana State Publications for the Law Librarian.** Chicago: AALL, 1982.

## IOWA

Burns, Paul David. **Internet Basics for the Iowa Attorney.** Eau Claire, WI: National Business Institute, 2000.

Edwards, John, ed. **Iowa Legal Research Guide.** Buffalo, NY: Hein, 2003.

Edwards, John, et al. **Iowa Legal Research.** Durham, NC: Carolina Academic Press, 2011.

Secrest, Angela K. **Iowa Legal Documents Bibliography.** Chicago: AALL, 1990.

## KANSAS

Custer, Joseph A. **Kansas Legal Research and Reference Guide**. 3rd ed. Topeka: Kansas Bar Assn., 2003.

Custer, Joseph A. and Christopher L. Steadham. **Kansas Legal Research.** Durham, NC: Carolina Academic Press, 2008.

**Internet Basics for the Kansas Attorney.** Eau Claire, WI: National Business Institute, 2002.

Snyder, Fritz. **A Guide to Kansas Legal Research.** Topeka: Kansas Bar Association, 1986.

Wisnecki, Martin E. **Kansas State Documents for Law Libraries: Publications Related to Law and State Government.** Chicago: AALL, 1984.

## KENTUCKY

Gilmer, Wesley, Jr. **Guide to Kentucky Legal Research 2nd: A State Bibliography.** Frankfort, KY: State Law Library, 1985.

Metzmeier, Kurt X., et al. **Kentucky Legal Research Manual.** 2nd ed. Lexington, KY: Univ. of Kentucky CLE, 2003.

Valentin, Ryan and Michelle Cosby. **Kentucky State Documents: A Bibliography of Legal and Law-Related Material.** Chicago: AALL, 2008.

## LOUISIANA

Algero, Mary Garvey. **Louisiana Legal Research**. Durham, NC: Carolina Academic Press, 2009.

Chiang, W. S. **Louisiana Legal Research.** 2nd ed. Salem, NH: Butterworth, 1990.

Corneil, Charlotte and M. Hebert. **Louisiana Legal Documents and Related Publications: A Selected Annotated Bibliography.** Chicago: AALL, 1984.

Hebert, Madeline. **Louisiana Legal Documents and Related Publications.** Chicago: AALL, 1990.

Wallach, Kate. **Louisiana Legal Research Manual.** Baton Rouge: Louisiana State University Law School, Institute of Continuing Legal Education, 1972.

## MAINE

Hepler, Christine I. and Maureen P. Quinlan. **Maine State Documents: A Bibliography of Legal and Law-Related Materials.** Chicago: AALL, 2003.

Wells, William W., Jr. **Maine Legal Research Guide.** Salem, NH: Butterworth, 1989.

## MARYLAND

Calia, Lauren R. and Maura L. DeMouy. **Practical Legal Research and Analysis for the Paralegal in Maryland.** Eau Claire, WI: Institute for Paralegal Education, 2000.

Chanin, Leah, et al. **Legal Research in D.C., Maryland and Virginia.** 2nd ed. Buffalo: Hein, 2000.

Davis, L. C. **An Introduction to Maryland State Publications for the Law Librarian.** Chicago: AALL, 1981.

Miller, Michael S. **Ghost Hunting: Finding Legislative Intent in Maryland.** Annapolis: Maryland State Law Library, 1984.

Taylor, William L. **Maryland State Publications in Law and Related Fields.** Chicago: AALL, 1996.

## MASSACHUSETTS

Blum, E. Joan. **Massachusetts Legal Research.** Durham, NC: Carolina Academic Press, 2009.

**Guide to Legislative and Government Research.** Boston: State Library of Massachusetts, 1977.

**Handbook of Legal Research in Massachusetts.** Rev. ed. Boston: Massachusetts Continuing Legal Education, 2009.

**How to Do Massachusetts Legal Research.** Boston: Mass. CLE, 1998.

McAuliffe, Leo and S. Z. Steinway. **Massachusetts: Annual State Bibliography.** Chicago: AALL, 1985.

Neary, Mary Ann. **Massachusetts Legal Research: Maximizing New and Old Tools for Effective Searching.** Boston: MCLE, 2001.

Withers, Kenneth J., ed. **The Internet Guide for Massachusetts Lawyers.** 2nd ed. Boston: MCLE Books, 1999.

## MICHIGAN

Beer, Richard L. and Judith J. Field. **Michigan Legal Literature: An Annotated Guide.** 2nd ed. Buffalo: Hein, 1991.

Bisard, Mark W., et al. **Internet Basics for the Michigan Attorney.** Eau Claire, WI: National Business Institute, 2002.

Bosh, Nancy L. **Research Edge: Finding Law and Facts Fast.** Ann Arbor, MI: Institute of Continuing Legal Education, 1993.

LeBlanc, Mary Ellen. **The Internet Guide for Michigan Lawyers.** Ann Arbor, MI: ICLE, 1998.

Lysaght, Pamela. **Michigan Legal Research.** 2nd ed. Durham, NC: Carolina Academic Press, 2011.

Selberg, Janice K. **Legal Research Sources: A Process Approach.** Detroit: Arthur Neef Law Library, Wayne State University, 1997.

Tillman-Davis, Michael W., ed. **Michigan Legal Documents: A Bibliography of Legal and Law-Related Documents.** Chicago: AALL, 2006.

## MINNESOTA

Hackerson, Deborah K. **A Bibliography of Minnesota Legal Documents.** Chicago: AALL, 2010.

Jack, Bill. **Internet Basics for the Minnesota Attorney.** Eau Claire, WI: National Business Institute, 2002.

Tessner, John, et al. **Minnesota Legal Research Guide.** 2nd ed. Buffalo: Hein, 2002.

Thorpe, Suzanne. **Minnesota Legal Research.** Durham, NC: Carolina Academic Press, 2010.

## MISSISSIPPI

Cole, B. **Mississippi Legal Documents and Related Publications: A Selected Annotated Bibliography.** Chicago: AALL, 1987.

Gilliland, Kris. **Mississippi Legal Research.** Durham, NC: Carolina Academic Press, 2011.

## MISSOURI

Aldrich, P., et al. **A Law Librarian's Introduction to Missouri State Publications.** Chicago: AALL, 1980.

**Internet Basics for the Missouri Attorney.** Eau Claire, WI: National Business Institute, 2001.

Nelson, Mary Ann. **Guide to Missouri State Documents and Selected Law-Related Materials.** Chicago: AALL, 1990.

# LEGAL RESEARCH BIBLIOGRAPHY–STATE

Temm, Wanda and Julie M. Cheslik. **Missouri Legal Research.** 2nd ed. Durham, NC: Carolina Academic Press, 2011.
**West's Missouri Law Finder.** St. Paul: West, 1993.

## MONTANA

Chansler, Margaret Ann. **Montana State Documents: A Bibliography of Legal and Law-Related Material.** Chicago: AALL, 2004.

Jordan, Stephen R. **A Guide to Montana Legal Research.** 7th ed. Helena, MT: State Law Library, 2002.

----. **Bibliography of Selective Legal and Law-Related Materials.** Chicago: AALL, 1990.

## NEBRASKA

Charles, Patrick J., et al. **LexisNexis's Research Guide to Nebraska Law.** Charlottesville: LexisNexis, 2006.

Fontenot, Mitchell J., et al. **Nebraska State Documents Bibliography.** Chicago: AALL, 1988.

Hill, Paul F. **Nebraska Legal Research and Reference Manual.** St. Paul: Mason, 1983.

## NEVADA

Gross, Jennifer. **Nevada Legal Research Guide.** Buffalo: Hein, 2005.

Henderson, K. **Nevada State Documents Bibliography, Part I: Legal Publications and Related Material.** 2nd ed. Chicago: AALL, 2000.

## NEW JERSEY

Allen, C. **A Guide to New Jersey Legal Bibliography and Legal History.** Littleton, CO.: Rothman, 1984.

Axel-Lute, Paul. **New Jersey Legal Research Handbook.** 4th ed. New Brunswick, NJ: New Jersey Institute for Continuing Legal Education, 1998.

Senezak, C. M. **New Jersey State Publications: A Guide for Law Librarians.** Chicago: AALL, 1984.

## NEW MEXICO

Poldervaart, A. W. **Manual for Effective New Mexico Legal Research.** Albuquerque: University of New Mexico Press, 1955.

Strike, Theresa. **Guide to New Mexico State Publications.** 3rd ed. Chicago: AALL, 2009.

Warden, D. and H. S. Carter. **Basic List of State Legal Documents for the State of New Mexico.** Albuquerque: University of New Mexico, School of Law Library, 1978.

## NEW YORK

Adelman, Elizabeth G. and Suzanne E. Rowe. **New York Legal Research.** Durham, NC: Carolina Academic Press, 2008.

Carter, Robert A. **Legislative Intent in New York State: Materials, Cases and Annotated Bibliography.** Albany: New York State Library, 1981.

---. **New York State Constitution: Sources of Legislative Intent.** Littleton, CO: Rothman, 1988.

Gibson, Ellen M. **Gibson's New York Legal Research Guide.** 3rd ed. Buffalo: Hein, 2004.

**New York Lawyer's Deskbook.** 2nd ed. Albany, NY: NYSBA, 2004.

Whittemore, Gail F. **New York Legal Documents: A Selective Annotated Bibliography.** Chicago: AALL, 2007.

## NORTH CAROLINA

Baer, Miriam. **A Guide to Legal Research in North Carolina.** Durham, NC: Carolina Academic Press, 2006.

Childs, Scott. **North Carolina Legal Research.** Durham, NC: Carolina Academic Press, 2010.

---. **North Carolina Legal Research Guide.** 2nd ed. Buffalo, NY: Hein, 2009.

Corbett, Mary Louise, et al. **Guide to North Carolina Legal and Law-Related Materials.** 2nd ed. Chicago: AALL, 2006.

Kavass, Igor I. and B. A. Christensen. **Guide to North Carolina Legal Research.** Buffalo: Hein, 1973.

Nixon, Donna, et al. **State Documents Bibliography: North Carolina.** Chicago: AALL, 2010.

## NORTH DAKOTA

**For All Intents and Purposes: Essentials in Researching Legislative Histories.** North Dakota Legislative Council, 1981.

Schwartz, Rhonda R. **North Dakota State Documents: A Selective Annotated Bibliography of Legal and Law-Related Material.** Chicago: AALL, 2009.

## OHIO

Corcos, Christine. **Ohio State Legal Documents and Related Publications: A Selected, Annotated Bibliography.** Chicago: AALL, 1986.

Gold, D. M. **A Guide to Legislative History in Ohio.** Columbus: Ohio Legislative Service Commission, 1985.

Hall, Katherine L. and Sara Sampson. **Ohio Legal Research.** Durham, NC: Carolina Academic Press, 2009.

**Internet Basics for the Ohio Attorney**. Eau Claire, WI: National Business Institute, 2001.

**Ohio Legal Resources: An Annotated Bibliography and Guide**. 4th ed. Columbus: Ohio Regional Association of Law Libraries and Ohio Library Association, 1996.

Putnam, Melanie K. **Ohio Legal Research Guide.** 2nd ed. Buffalo: Hein, 2010.

## OKLAHOMA

Fox, Darin. **State Documents Bibliography-Oklahoma: A Guide to Legal Research in Oklahoma.** Chicago: AALL, 2009.

## OREGON

Midkiff, Stephanie and Wendy Schroeder Hitchcock. **State Documents Bibliography: Oregon.** Chicago, AALL, 2009.

Rowe, Suzanne E. **Oregon Legal Research.** 2nd ed. Durham, NC: Carolina Academic Press, 2007.

Siegel, Timothy E. **Internet Basics for the Oregon Attorney.** Eau Claire, WI: National Business Institute, 2000.

## PENNSYLVANIA

Busharis, Barbara J. and Bonny L. Tavares. **Pennsylvania Legal Research.** Durham, NC: Carolina Academic Press, 2007.

Fishman, Joel. **Pennsylvania State Documents: A Bibliography of Legal and Law-Related Material.** Chicago: AALL, 2007.

Fitzpatrick, F. Emmett. **Internet Essentials for the Pennsylvania Attorney and Other Legal Professionals.** Philadelphia: Bisel, 2000.

**The Internet Guide for Pennsylvania Lawyers.** Mechanicsburg, PA: Pennsylvania Bar Institute, 1999.

Liu, Frank Y., et al. **Pennsylvania Legal Research Handbook.** Philadelphia: American Lawyer Media, 2008.

Moreland, Carroll and E. C. Surrency. **Research in Pennsylvania Law.** 2nd ed. Dobbs Ferry, NY: Oceana, 1965.

## RHODE ISLAND

Reavis, James O. **Internet Basics for the Rhode Island Attorney.** Eau Claire, WI: National Business Institute, 2002.

Winson, Gail I. **State of Rhode Island and Providence Plantations: Survey of State Documents and Law-Related Materials.** Chicago: AALL, 2004.

## SOUTH CAROLINA

Benson, Paula G. and D.A. Davis. **A Guide to South Carolina Legal Research and Citation**. Columbia, SC: South Carolina Bar CLE, 1991.

Conroy, Terrye, et al. **State Documents Bibliography: South Carolina.** Chicago: AALL, 2009.

Mills, Robin K. and J. S. Schultz. **South Carolina Legal Research Handbook.** Buffalo: Hein, 1976.

## SOUTH DAKOTA

Jorgensen, Delores A. **South Dakota Legal Documents: A Selective Bibliography.** Chicago: AALL, 1988.

---. **South Dakota Legal Research Guide.** 2nd ed. Buffalo: Hein, 1999.

## TENNESSEE

Best, Reba A. **Tennessee State Documents: A Bibliography of State Publications and Related Materials.** Chicago: AALL, 2009.

**The Internet Guide for Tennessee Lawyers.** Nashville: Vanderbilt Univ. Law School, 1998.

Laska, Lewis L. **Tennessee Legal Research Handbook.** Buffalo: Hein, 1977.

Marshall, Sibyl and Carol Parker. **Tennessee Legal Research.** Durham, NC: Carolina Academic Press, 2007.

Picquet, Cheryn and R. A. Best. **Law and Government Publications of the State of Tennessee.** Chicago: AALL, 1988.

## TEXAS

Allison, Malinda and K. Schlueter. **Texas State Documents for Law Libraries.** Chicago: AALL, 1983.

Brandt, Lydia M.V. **Texas Legal Research.** Dallas: Texas Lawyer Press, 1995.

Cordon, Matthew C. and Brandon D. Quarles. **Researching Texas Law.** 2nd ed. Buffalo, NY: Hein, 2008.

---. **Specialized Topics in Texas Legal Research.** Buffalo, NY: Hein, 2004.

Gruben, Karl T. and J. E. Hambleton, eds. **A Reference Guide to Texas Law and Legal History: Sources and Documentation.** 2nd ed. Salem, NH: Butterworth, 1987.

Permenter, Paris and S. F. Ratliff. **Guide to Texas Legislative History.** Austin: Legislative Reference Library, 1986.

Simons, Spencer L. **Texas Legal Research.** Durham, NC: Carolina Academic Press, 2009.

Tepper, Pamela R. **Texas Legal Research.** 2nd ed. Albany: Delmar, 1997.

## UTAH
Cheney, Mari. **Utah Legal Resources Bibiography.** Chicago: AALL, 2009.
**Internet Basics for the Utah Attorney.** Eau Claire, WI: National Business Institute, 2000.
Staheli, Kory D. **Utah Practice Materials.** Orem, UT: Code-Co, 1995.

## VERMONT
Wise, Virginia. **A Bibliographic Guide to the Vermont Legal System.** 2nd ed. Chicago: AALL, 1991.

## VIRGINIA
Chanin, Leah, et al. **Legal Research in D.C., Maryland and Virginia.** 2nd ed. Buffalo: Hein, 2000.
Eure, John D., ed. **A Guide to Legal Research in Virginia.** 6th ed. Charlottesville: Virginia CLE Publications, 2008.
Lichtman, Jacqueline and J. Stinson. **A Law Librarian's Introduction to Virginia State Publications.** Chicago: AALL, 1988.

## WASHINGTON
Burson, S. F. **Washington State Law-Related Publications: A Selective Bibliography with Commentary.** Chicago: AALL, 1984.
Heintz-Cho, Julie A., et al. **Washington Legal Research.** 2nd ed. Durham, NC: Carolina Academic Press, 2009.
Hazelton, Penny A., et al. **Washington Legal Researcher's Deskbook 3d.** Seattle: Gallagher Law Library, 2002.

## WEST VIRGINIA
Stemple, Sandra, et al. **West Virginia Legal Bibliography.** Chicago: AALL, 1990.

## WISCONSIN
Cervenka, Patricia A. and Leslie Behroozi. **Wisconsin Legal Research.** Durham, NC: Carolina Academic Press, 2010.
Danner, Richard A. **Legal Research in Wisconsin.** Madison: University of Wisconsin, Extension Law Department, 1980.
Fritschel, Barbara. **State Documents Bibliography: Wisconsin.** Chicago: AALL, 2009.
Knudson, W. **Wisconsin Legal Research Guide.** Madison: University of Wisconsin, Extension Law Department, 1972.
Potter, Theodore A., Gen. Ed. Legal Research in Wisconsin.. 2nd ed. Buffalo, NY: Hein, 2008.

## WYOMING
Person, Debora A. **Wyoming State Documents: A Bibliography of State Publications and Related Materials.** Chicago: AALL, 2006.

# LAW SCHOOLS IN THE U.S. AND CANADA

## LAW SCHOOLS APPROVED BY THE AMERICAN BAR ASSOCIATION

### ALABAMA

Samford University
Cumberland School of Law
800 Lakeshore Drive
Birmingham, AL 35229
(205) 726-2702; (800) 888-7213
(Approved in 1949; Private)
Lib. (205) 726-2714
cumberland.samford.edu

University of Alabama
School of Law
P.O. Box 870382
Tuscaloosa, AL 35487-0382
(205) 348-5440
(Approved in 1926; Public)
Lib. (205) 348-5925
www.law.ua.edu

Faulkner University
Thomas Goode Jones School of Law
5345 Atlanta Hwy.
Montgomery, AL 36109
(334) 272-5820
(Provisionally approved in 2006;
 Private)
Lib. (334) 386-7219
www.faulkner.edu/law/

### ARIZONA

Arizona State University
Sandra Day O'Connor College of
Law
P.O. Box 877906
Tempe, AZ 85287-7906
(480) 965-6184
(Approved in 1969; Public)
Lib. (480) 965-6141
www.law.asu.edu

University of Arizona
James E. Rogers College of Law
P.O. Box 210176, 1201 E. Speedway
Tucson, AZ 85721-0176
(520) 621-9949
(Approved in 1930; Public)
Lib. (520) 626-8023
www.law.arizona.edu

Phoenix School of Law
4041 N. Central Ave., Suite 100
Phoenix, AZ 85012

(602) 682-6800; (888) 749-5291
(Provisionally approved in 2007;
 Private)
Lib. (602) 682-6897
www.phoenixlaw.edu

### ARKANSAS

University of Arkansas
School of Law
Robert A. Leflar Law Center
Fayetteville, AR 72701
(479) 575-5601
(Approved in 1926; Public)
Lib. (479) 575-5834
law.uark.edu/

University of Arkansas at Little
 Rock
William H. Bowen School of Law
1201 McMath Ave.
Little Rock, AR 72202-5142
(501) 324-9434
(Approved in 1969; Public)
Lib. (501) 324-9444
www.law.ualr.edu

### CALIFORNIA

California Western School of Law
225 Cedar St.
San Diego, CA 92101
(619) 239-0391
(Approved in 1962; Private)
Lib. (619) 525-1419
www.cwsl.edu

Chapman University
School of Law
One University Drive
Orange, CA 92866
(714) 628-2500; (877) CHAPLAW
(Approved in 1998; Private)
Lib. (714) 628-2595
www.chapman.edu/law

Golden Gate University
School of Law
536 Mission St.
San Francisco, CA 94105-2968
(415) 442-7800
(Approved in 1956; Private)
Lib. (415) 442-6680

www.ggu.edu/school_of_law

Loyola Marymount University
Loyola Law School
919 S. Albany St.
Los Angeles, CA 90015
(213) 736-1000
(Approved in 1935; Private)
Lib. (213) 736-1177
www.lls.edu

Pepperdine University
School of Law
24255 Pacific Coast Highway
Malibu, CA 90263
(310) 506-4611
(Approved in 1972; Private)
Lib. (310) 506-4641
law.pepperdine.edu

Santa Clara University
School of Law
500 El Camino Real
Santa Clara, CA 95053
(408) 554-4361
(Approved in 1937; Private)
Lib. (408) 554-4072
www.scu.edu/law

Southwestern University
School of Law
3050 Wilshire Blvd.
Los Angeles, CA 90010
(213) 738-6700
(Approved in 1970; Private)
Lib. (213) 738-6725
www.swlaw.edu

Stanford University Law School
559 Nathan Abbott Way
Stanford, CA 94305-8610
(650) 723-2465
(Approved in 1923; Private)
Lib. (650) 723-0800
www.law.stanford.edu

Thomas Jefferson School of Law
1155 Island Ave.
San Diego, CA 92101
(619) 297-9700; (800) 956-5070
(Approved in 1996; Private)
Lib. (619) 297-4333
www.tjsl.edu

# LAW SCHOOLS

University of California
Berkeley School of Law
215 Boalt Hall
Berkeley, CA 94720-7200
(510) 642-1741
(Approved in 1923; Public)
Lib. (510) 642-0900
www.law.berkeley.edu

University of California-Davis
School of Law
400 Mrak Hall Drive
Davis, CA 95616-5201
(530) 752-6477
(Approved in 1968; Public)
Lib. (530) 752-3327
www.law.ucdavis.edu

University of California-Los Angeles
School of Law
Box 951476
Los Angeles, CA 90095-1476
(310) 825-4841
(Approved in 1950; Public)
Lib. (310) 825-4743
www.law.ucla.edu

University of California
Hastings College of the Law
200 McAllister St.
San Francisco, CA 94102
(415) 565-4600
(Approved in 1939; Public)
Lib. (415) 565-4750
www.uchastings.edu

University of La Verne
College of Law
320 East D St.
Ontario, CA 91764
(909) 460-2000
(Provisionally approved in 2006;
 Private)
Lib. (909) 460-2070
law.laverne.edu

University of San Diego
School of Law
5998 Alcala Park
San Diego, CA 92110-2492
(619) 260-4600
(Approved in 1961; Private)
Lib. (619) 260-4542
www.sandiego.edu/law/

University of San Francisco
School of Law
2130 Fulton St.

San Francisco, CA 94117-1080
(415) 422-6307
(Approved in 1935; Private)
Lib. (415) 422-6773
www.usfca.edu/law

University of Southern California
USC Law School
Los Angeles, CA 90089-0071
(213) 740-7331
(Approved in 1924; Private)
Lib. (213) 740-6482
lawweb.usc.edu

University of the Pacific
McGeorge School of Law
3200 Fifth Ave.
Sacramento, CA 95817
(916) 739-7191
(Approved in 1969; Private)
Lib. (916) 739-7164
www.mcgeorge.edu

Western State University
College of Law
1111 North State College Blvd.
Fullerton, CA 92831
(714) 738-1000
(Approved in 2005; Private)
Lib. (714) 459-1175
www.wsulaw.edu

Whittier Law School
3333 Harbor Blvd.
Costa Mesa, CA 92626
(714) 444-4141
(Approved in 1978; Private)
Lib. (714) 444-4141x480
www.law.whittier.edu

## COLORADO

University of Colorado
School of Law
UCB 403
Boulder, CO 80309-0403
(303) 492-8047
(Approved in 1923; Public)
Lib. (303) 492-7534
www.colorado.edu/law

University of Denver
Sturm College of Law
2255 E. Evans Ave.
Denver, CO 80208
(303) 871-6000
(Approved in 1923; Private)
Lib. (303) 871-6188

www.law.du.edu

## CONNECTICUT

Quinnipiac College
School of Law
275 Mt. Carmel Ave.
Hamden, CT 06518
(203) 582-8200
(Approved in 1992; Private)
Lib. (203) 582-3301
law.quinnipiac.edu

University of Connecticut
School of Law
45 Elizabeth St.
Hartford, CT 06105
(860) 570-5000
(Approved in 1933; Public)
Lib. (860) 570-5200
www.law.uconn.edu

Yale Law School
P.O. Box 208215
New Haven, CT 06520-8215
(203) 432-4995
(Approved in 1923; Private)
Lib. (203) 432-1600
www.law.yale.edu

## DELAWARE

Widener University-Delaware
School of Law
4601 Concord Pike, P.O. Box 7474
Wilmington, DE 19803-0474
(302) 477-2162
(Approved in 1975; Private)
Lib. (302) 477-2115
law.widener.edu

## DISTRICT OF COLUMBIA

American University
Washington College of Law
4801 Massachusetts Ave., NW
Washington, D.C. 20016
(202) 274-4000
(Approved in 1940; Private)
Lib. (202) 274-4350
www.wcl.american.edu

Catholic University of America
Columbus School of Law
620 Michigan Ave. NE
Washington, D.C. 20064
(202) 319-5140
(Approved in 1925; Private)

# LAW SCHOOLS

Lib. (202) 319-5156
www.law.edu

George Washington University Law
 School
2000 H St., NW
Washington, D.C. 20052
(202) 994-6261
(Approved in 1923; Private)
Lib. (202) 994-6647
www.law.gwu.edu

Georgetown University
Law Center
600 New Jersey Ave., NW
Washington, D.C. 20001
(202) 662-9000
(Approved in 1924; Private)
Lib. (202) 662-9131
www.law.georgetown.edu

Howard University
School of Law
2900 Van Ness St., NW
Washington, D.C. 20008
(202) 806-8000
(Approved in 1931; Private)
Lib. (202) 806-8045
www.law.howard.edu

University of The District of
 Columbia
David A. Clarke School of Law
4200 Connecticut Ave., NW
Washington, DC 20008
(202) 274-7400
(Approved in 1991; Public)
Lib. (202) 274-7310
www.law.udc.edu

## FLORIDA

Ave Maria School of Law
1025 Commons Circle
Naples, FL 34119
(239) 687-5300
(Approved in 2002; Private)
Lib. (239) 687-5504
www.avemarialaw.edu

Barry University
Dwayne O. Andreas School of Law
6441 East Colonial Drive
Orlando, FL 32807
(321) 206-5600
(Approved in 2002; Private)
Lib. (407) 206-5700
www.barry.edu/law

Florida A&M University
College of Law
201 Beggs Ave.
Orlando, FL 32801-3216
(407) 254-2450
(Approved in 2004; Public)
Lib. (407) 254-3263
law.famu.edu

Florida Coastal School of Law
8787 Baypine Rd.
Jacksonville, FL 32256
(904) 680-7700; (877) 210-2591
(Approved in 1999; Private)
Lib. (904) 680-7612
www.fcsl.edu

Florida International University
College of Law
RDB 1055
Miami, FL 33199
(305) 348-8006
(Approved in 2004; Public)
Lib. (305) 348-3542
law.fiu.edu/

Florida State University
College of Law
425 W. Jefferson St.
Tallahassee, FL 32306-1601
(850) 644-3400
(Approved in 1968; Public)
Lib. (850) 644-7288
www.law.fsu.edu

Nova Southeastern University
Shepard Broad Law Center
3305 College Ave.
Fort Lauderdale, FL 33314-7721
(954) 262-6100
(Approved in 1975; Private)
Lib. (954) 262-6211
www.nsulaw.nova.edu

St. Thomas University
School of Law
16401 NW 37th Ave.
Miami, FL 33054
(305) 623-2310; (800) 245-4569
(Approved in 1988; Private)
Lib. (305) 623-2330
www.stu.edu/lawschool/

Stetson University
College of Law
1401 61st St. South
Gulfport, FL 33707
(727) 562-7800

(Approved in 1930; Private)
Lib. (727) 562-7820
www.law.stetson.edu

University of Florida
Levin College of Law
P.O. Box 117620
Gainesville, FL 32611
(352) 273-0890; (877) 429-1297
(Approved in 1925; Public)
Lib. (352) 273-0700
www.law.ufl.edu

University of Miami
School of Law
1311 Miller Drive
Coral Gables, FL 33146
(305) 284-2339
(Approved in 1941; Private)
Lib. (305) 284-3585
www.law.miami.edu

## GEORGIA

Emory University
School of Law
Gambrell Hall, 1301 Clifton Road
Atlanta, GA 30322-2770
(404) 727-6816
(Approved in 1923; Private)
Lib. (404) 727-6824
www.law.emory.edu

Georgia State University
School of Law
140 Decatur St.
Atlanta, GA 30303
(404) 413-9200
(Approved in 1984; Public)
Lib. (404) 413-9100
law.gsu.edu

Mercer University
Walter F. George School of Law
1021 Georgia Ave.
Macon, GA 31207
(478) 301-2605
(Approved in 1925; Private)
Lib. (478) 301-2334
www.law.mercer.edu

University of Georgia
School of Law
225 Herty Drive
Athens, GA 30602-6012
(706) 542-5191
(Approved in 1930; Public)
Lib. (706) 542-8480

# LAW SCHOOLS

www.law.uga.edu

John Marshall Law School
1422 W. Peachtree St. NW
Atlanta, GA 30309
(404) 872-3593
(Approved in 2005; Private)
Lib. (404) 872-3593 x118
www.johnmarshall.edu

## HAWAII

University of Hawaii at Manoa
William S. Richardson School of
 Law
2515 Dole St.
Honolulu, HI 96822
(808) 956-7966
(Approved in 1974; Public)
Lib. (808) 956-7583
www.law.hawaii.edu

## IDAHO

University of Idaho
College of Law
709 Deakin Ave.
Moscow, ID 83844-2321
(208) 885-6567
(Approved in 1925; Public)
Lib. (208) 885-6521
www.law.uidaho.edu

## ILLINOIS

Chicago-Kent College of Law
Illinois Institute of Technology
565 West Adams St.
Chicago, IL 60661
(312) 906-5000
(Approved in 1936; Private)
Lib. (312) 906-5600
www.kentlaw.edu

DePaul University
College of Law
25 East Jackson Blvd.
Chicago, IL 60604-2219
(312) 362-8701; (800) 428-7453
(Approved in 1925; Private)
Lib. (312) 362-8121
www.law.depaul.edu

John Marshall Law School
315 South Plymouth Court
Chicago, IL 60604
(312) 427-2737; (800) 537-4280
(Approved in 1951; Private)

Lib. (312) 427-2737 x729
www.jmls.edu

Loyola University-Chicago
School of Law
25 East Pearson St.
Chicago, IL 60611
(312) 915-7120; (800) 545-5744
(Approved in 1925; Private)
Lib. (312) 915-7200
www.luc.edu/law

Northern Illinois University
College of Law
Swen Parson Hall
DeKalb, IL 60115
(815) 753-8595; (800) 892-3050
(Approved in 1978; Public)
Lib. (815) 753-0507
law.niu.edu

Northwestern University
School of Law
357 East Chicago Ave.
Chicago, IL 60611-3069
(312) 503-3100
(Approved in 1923; Private)
Lib. (312) 503-8450
www.law.northwestern.edu

Southern Illinois University-
 Carbondale
School of Law
1150 Douglas Drive
Carbondale, IL 62901
(618) 536-7711; (800) 739-9187
(Approved in 1974; Public)
Lib. (618) 453-8780
www.law.siu.edu

University of Chicago Law School
1111 East 60th St.
Chicago, IL 60637
(773) 702-9494
(Approved in 1923; Private)
Lib. (773) 702-9614
www.law.uchicago.edu

University of Illinois
College of Law
504 East Pennsylvania Ave.
Champaign, IL 61820
(217) 333-0931
(Approved in 1923; Public)
Lib. (217) 333-2914
www.law.uiuc.edu

## INDIANA

Indiana University-Bloomington
Maurer School of Law
211 S. Indiana Ave.
Bloomington, IN 47405-7001
(812) 855-7995
(Approved in 1923; Public)
Lib. (812) 855-9666
www.law.indiana.edu

Indiana University-Indianapolis
School of Law
530 West New York St.
Indianapolis, IN 46202-3225
(317) 274-8523
(Approved in 1944; Public)
Lib. (317) 274-4028
www.indylaw.indiana.edu

Notre Dame Law School
P.O. Box 780
Notre Dame, IN 46556-0959
(574) 631-6626
(Approved in 1925; Private)
Lib. (574) 631-7024
law.nd.edu

Valparaiso University
School of Law
656 S. Greenwich
Valparaiso, IN 46383-6493
(219) 465-7829; (888) 825-7652
(Approved in 1929; Private)
Lib. (219) 465-7827
www.valpo.edu/law/

## IOWA

Drake University Law School
2621 Carpenter Ave.
Des Moines, IA 50311-4505
(515) 271-2824
(800) 44DRAKE x2824
(Approved in 1923; Private)
Lib. (515) 271-3189
www.law.drake.edu

University of Iowa
College of Law
290 Boyd Law Building
Iowa City, IA 52242
(319) 335-9034
(800) 553-IOWA x9034
(Approved in 1923; Public)
Lib. (319) 335-9005
www.law.uiowa.edu

# LAW SCHOOLS

## KANSAS

University of Kansas
School of Law
1535 W. 15th St.
Lawrence, KS 66045-7577
(785) 864-4550; (866) 220-3654
(Approved in 1923; Public)
Lib. (785) 864-9250
www.law.ku.edu

Washburn University
School of Law
1700 SW College Ave.
Topeka, KS 66621-1140
(785) 670-1060; (800) WASHLAW
(Approved in 1923; Public)
Lib. (785) 670-1088
washburnlaw.edu

## KENTUCKY

Northern Kentucky University
Salmon P. Chase College of Law
Nunn Hall
Highland Heights, KY 41099
(859) 572-5490
(Approved in 1954; Public)
Lib. (859) 572-6484
chaselaw.nku.edu

University of Kentucky
College of Law
620 S. Limestone St.
Lexington, KY 40506-0048
(859) 257-1678
(Approved in 1925; Public)
Lib. (859) 257-8686
www.law.uky.edu

University of Louisville
Louis D. Brandeis School of Law
2301 South Third St.
Louisville, KY 40292
(502) 852-6358
(Approved in 1931; Public)
Lib. (502) 852-0729
www.law.louisville.edu

## LOUISIANA

Louisiana State University
Paul M. Hebert Law Center
202 Law Center, 1 E. Campus Dr.
Baton Rouge, LA 70803
(225) 578-8646
(Approved in 1926; Public)
Lib. (225) 578-4041

www.law.lsu.edu

Loyola University-New Orleans
School of Law
526 Pine St.
New Orleans, LA 70118
(504) 861-5550
(Approved in 1931; Private)
Lib. (504) 861-5545
law.loyno.edu

Southern University
Law Center
P.O. Box 9294
Baton Rouge, LA 70813-9294
(225) 771-2552; (800) 537-1135
(Approved in 1953; Public)
Lib. (225) 771-2139
www.sulc.edu

Tulane University Law School
6329 Freret St.
New Orleans, LA 70118
(504) 865-5939
(Approved in 1925; Private)
Lib. (504) 865-5952
www.law.tulane.edu

## MAINE

University of Maine
School of Law
246 Deering Ave.
Portland, ME 04102
(207) 780-4355
(Approved in 1962; Public)
Lib. (207) 780-4829
mainelaw.maine.edu

## MARYLAND

University of Baltimore
School of Law
1420 North Charles St.
Baltimore, MD 21201
(410) 837-4468
(Approved in 1972; Public)
Lib. (410) 837-4584
law.ubalt.edu

University of Maryland
School of Law
500 W. Baltimore St.
Baltimore, MD 21201
(410) 706-7214
(Approved in 1930; Public)
Lib. (410) 706-6502
www.law.umaryland.edu

## MASSACHUSETTS

Boston College Law School
885 Centre St.
Newton, MA 02459
(617) 552-8550
(Approved in 1932; Private)
Lib. (617) 552-4434
www.bc.edu/schools/law

Boston University
School of Law
765 Commonwealth Ave.
Boston, MA 02215
(617) 353-3100
(Approved in 1925; Private)
Lib. (617) 353-8881
www.bu.edu/law

Harvard Law School
1563 Massachusetts Ave.
Cambridge, MA 02138
(617) 495-3109
(Approved in 1923; Private)
Lib. (617) 495-3170
www.law.harvard.edu

New England School of Law
154 Stuart St.
Boston, MA 02116
(617) 451-0010
(Approved in 1969; Private)
Lib. (617) 422-7299
www.nesl.edu

Northeastern University
School of Law
400 Huntington Ave.
Boston, MA 02115
(617) 373-5149
(Approved in 1969; Private)
Lib. (617) 373-3332
www.northeastern.edu/law

Suffolk University Law School
120 Tremont St.
Boston, MA 02108-4977
(617) 573-8000
(Approved in 1953; Private)
Lib. (617) 573-8177
www.law.suffolk.edu

Western New England College
School of Law
1215 Wilbraham Road
Springfield, MA 01119-2684
(413) 782-3111; (800) 782-6665
(Approved in 1974; Private)

# LAW SCHOOLS

Lib. (413) 782-1457
www1.law.wne.edu

## MICHIGAN

Michigan State University
College of Law
368 Law College Building
East Lansing, MI 48824-1300
(517) 432-6800; (800) 844-9352
(Approved in 1941; Private)
Lib. (517) 432-6870
www.law.msu.edu

Thomas M. Cooley Law School
300 South Capitol Ave.
P.O. Box 13038
Lansing, MI 48901
(517) 371-5140 x2244
(Approved in 1975; Private)
Lib. (517) 371-5140 x3100
www.cooley.edu

University of Detroit Mercy
School of Law
651 East Jefferson
Detroit, MI 48226
(313) 596-0200
(Approved in 1933; Private)
Lib. (313) 596-0244
www.law.udmercy.edu

University of Michigan Law School
625 South State St., Hutchins Hall
Ann Arbor, MI 48109-1215
(734) 764-1358
(Approved in 1923; Public)
Lib. (734) 764-9324
www.law.umich.edu

Wayne State University Law School
471 W. Palmer St.
Detroit, MI 48202
(313) 577-3933
(Approved in 1937; Public)
Lib. (313) 577-3925
law.wayne.edu

## MINNESOTA

Hamline University
School of Law
1536 Hewitt Ave.
St. Paul, MN 55104
(651) 523-2600; (800) 388-3688
(Approved in 1975; Private)
Lib. (651) 523-2125
law.hamline.edu/

University of Minnesota Law School
Walter F. Mondale Hall
229 19th Ave. South
Minneapolis, MN 55455
(612) 625-1000
(Approved in 1923; Public)
Lib. (612) 625-4300
www.law.umn.edu

University of St. Thomas
Minneapolis School of Law
1000 LaSalle Ave.
Minneapolis, MN 55403
(651) 962-4892
(Approved in 2003; Private)
Lib. (651) 962-4902
www.stthomas.edu/law/

William Mitchell College of Law
875 Summit Ave.
St. Paul, MN 55105
(651) 227-9171
(Approved in 1938; Private)
Lib. (651) 290-6333
www.wmitchell.edu

## MISSISSIPPI

Mississippi College
School of Law
151 East Griffith St.
Jackson, MS 39201
(601) 925-7100; (800) 738-1236
(Approved in 1980; Private)
Lib. (601) 925-7120
law.mc.edu

University of Mississippi
School of Law
P.O. Box 1848
University, MS 38677-1848
(662) 915-7361
(Approved in 1930; Public)
Lib. (662) 915-6812
law.olemiss.edu

## MISSOURI

St. Louis University
School of Law
3700 Lindell Blvd.
St. Louis, MO 63108
(314) 977-2766
(Approved in 1924; Private)
Lib. (314) 977-3081
law.slu.edu

University of Missouri-Columbia
School of Law
203 Hulston Hall
Columbia, MO 65211
(573) 882-6487; (888) MULaw4u
(Approved in 1923; Public)
Lib. (573) 884-6362
www.law.missouri.edu

University of Missouri-Kansas City
School of Law
500 E. 52 St.
Kansas City, MO 64110
(816) 235-1644
(Approved in 1936; Public)
Lib. (816) 235-1650
law.umkc.edu

Washington University
School of Law
One Brookings Drive, Box 1120
St. Louis, MO 63130-4899
(314) 935-6400
(Approved in 1923; Private)
Lib. (314) 935-6450
law.wustl.edu

## MONTANA

University of Montana
School of Law
32 Campus Drive
Missoula, MT 59812
(406) 243-4311
(Approved in 1923; Public)
Lib. (406) 243-2699
www.umt.edu/law

## NEBRASKA

Creighton University
School of Law
2500 California Plaza
Omaha, NE 68178
(402) 280-2700
(Approved in 1924; Private)
Lib. (402) 280-2242
www.creighton.edu/law/

University of Nebraska-Lincoln
College of Law
1875 N. 42nd St.
P.O. Box 830902
Lincoln, NE 68583-0902
(402) 472-2161
(Approved in 1923; Public)
Lib. (402) 472-3547
law.unl.edu

# LAW SCHOOLS

## NEVADA

University of Nevada-Las Vegas
William S. Boyd School of Law
4505 Maryland Parkway
Box 451003
Las Vegas, NV 89154-1003
(702) 895-3671
(Approved in 2000; Public)
Lib. (702) 895-2420
www.law.unlv.edu

## NEW HAMPSHIRE

University of New Hampshire
  School of Law
2 White St.
Concord, NH 03301
(603) 228-1541
(Approved in 1974; Private)
Lib. (603) 513-5130
www.law.unh.edu

## NEW JERSEY

Rutgers University-Camden
School of Law
217 N. Fifth St.
Camden, NJ 08102
(856) 225-6375; (800) 466-7561
(Approved in 1950; Public)
Lib. (856) 225-6172
camlaw.rutgers.edu/

Rutgers University-Newark
School of Law
123 Washington St.
Newark, NJ 07102
(973) 353-5561
(Approved in 1941; Public)
Lib. (973) 353-5676
law.newark.rutgers.edu

Seton Hall University
School of Law
One Newark Center
Newark, NJ 07102-5210
(973) 642-8500
(Approved in 1951; Private)
Lib. (973) 642-8720
law.shu.edu

## NEW MEXICO

University of New Mexico
School of Law
1117 Stanford NE
Albuquerque, NM 87131-0001
(505) 277-2146
(Approved in 1948; Public)
Lib. (505) 277-6236
lawschool.unm.edu

## NEW YORK

Albany Law School of Union
  University
80 New Scotland Ave.
Albany, NY 12208
(518) 445-2311
(Approved in 1930; Private)
Lib. (518) 445-2340
www.albanylaw.edu

Brooklyn Law School
250 Joralemon St.
Brooklyn, NY 11201-9846
(718) 625-2200
(Approved in 1937; Private)
Lib. (718) 780-7973
www.brooklaw.edu

City University of New York
School of Law at Queens College
65-21 Main St.
Flushing, NY 11367-1300
(718) 340-4200
(Approved in 1985; Public)
Lib. (718) 340-4265
www.law.cuny.edu

Columbia University
School of Law
435 West 116th St.
New York, NY 10027
(212) 854-2640
(Approved in 1923; Private)
Lib. (212) 854-3922
www.law.columbia.edu

Cornell Law School
Myron Taylor Hall
Ithaca, NY 14853-5141
(607) 255-7190
(Approved in 1923; Private)
Lib. (607) 255-7236
www.lawschool.cornell.edu

Fordham University
School of Law
140 West 62nd St.
New York, NY 10023
(212) 636-6875
(Approved in 1936; Private)
Lib. (212) 636-6900
law.fordham.edu

Hofstra University
School of Law
121 Hofstra University
Hempstead, NY 11549
(516) 463-5916
(Approved in 1971; Private)
Lib. (516) 463-5898
law.hofstra.edu

New York Law School
185 W. Broadway
New York, NY 10013
(212) 431-2100
(Approved in 1954; Private)
Lib. (212) 431-2332
www.nyls.edu

New York University
School of Law
40 Washington Square South
New York, NY 10012
(212) 998-6100
(Approved in 1930; Private)
Lib. (212) 998-6312
www.law.nyu.edu

Pace University
School of Law
78 North Broadway
White Plains, NY 10603
(914) 422-4205
(Approved in 1978; Private)
Lib. (914) 422-4273
www.law.pace.edu

St. John's University
School of Law
8000 Utopia Parkway
Jamaica, NY 11439
(718) 990-6474
(Approved in 1937; Private)
Lib. (718) 990-6651
www.stjohns.edu/academics/
  graduate/law/

University at Buffalo Law School
The State University of New York
309 John Lord O'Brian Hall
Buffalo, NY 14260
(716) 645-2052
(Approved in 1936; Public)
Lib. (716) 645-2047
www.law.buffalo.edu

Syracuse University
College of Law
Syracuse, NY 13244-1030
(315) 443-1962

# LAW SCHOOLS

(Approved in 1923; Private)
Lib. (315) 443-9570
www.law.syr.edu

Touro College
Jacob D. Fuchsberg Law Center
225 Eastview Drive
Central Islip, NY 11722
(631) 761-7000
(Approved in 1983; Private)
Lib. (631) 761-7150
www.tourolaw.edu

Yeshiva University
Benjamin N. Cardozo School of
 Law
55 Fifth Ave.
New York, NY 10003
(212) 790-0200
(Approved in 1978; Private)
Lib. (212) 790-0220
www.cardozo.yu.edu/

## NORTH CAROLINA

Campbell University
Norman Adrian Wiggins School
 of Law
225 Hillsborough Street
Raleigh, NC 27603
(919) 865-4650
(Approved in 1979; Private)
Lib. (919) 865-5869
law.campbell.edu

Charlotte School of Law
2145 Suttle Ave.
Charlotte, NC 28208
(704) 971-8500
(Provisional approval in 2008;
 Private)
Lib. (704) 971-8573
www.charlottelaw.org

Duke University
School of Law
P.O. Box 90362
Durham, NC 27708
(919) 613-7006
(Approved in 1931; Private)
Lib. (919) 613-7114
www.law.duke.edu

Elon University
School of Law
201 N. Greene St.
Greensboro, NC 27401
(336) 279-9200; (800) ElonLaw

(Provisional approval in 2008;
Private)
Lib. (336) 279-9329
www.elon.edu/e-web/law/

North Carolina Central University
School of Law
640 Nelson St.
Durham, NC 27707
(919) 530-6333
(Approved in 1950; Public)
Lib. (919) 530-5189
web.nccu.edu/law

University of North Carolina
School of Law
Campus Box 3380
Chapel Hill, NC 27599-3380
(919) 962-5106
(Approved in 1923; Public)
Lib. (919) 962-1321
www.law.unc.edu

Wake Forest University
School of Law
P.O. Box 7206, Reynolda Station
Winston-Salem, NC 27109-7206
(336) 758-5437
(Approved in 1936; Private)
Lib. (336) 758-5438
law.wfu.edu

## NORTH DAKOTA

University of North Dakota
School of Law
P.O. Box 9003
Grand Forks, ND 58202-9003
(701) 777-2104
(Approved in 1923; Public)
Lib. (701) 777-3482
www.law.und.edu

## OHIO

Capital University Law School
303 E. Broad St.
Columbus, OH 43215-3200
(614) 236-6500
(Approved in 1950; Private)
Lib. (614) 236-6464
www.law.capital.edu

Case Western Reserve University
School of Law
11075 East Blvd.
Cleveland, OH 44106
(216) 368-3600

(Approved in 1923; Private)
Lib. (216) 368-2792
law.case.edu

Cleveland State University
Cleveland-Marshall College of Law
2121 Euclid Ave.
Cleveland, OH 44115-2214
(216) 687-2304
(Approved in 1957; Public)
Lib. (216) 687-6877
www.law.csuohio.edu

Ohio Northern University
Claude W. Pettit College of Law
525 S. Main St.
Ada, OH 45810
(419) 772-3051; (877) 452-9668
(Approved in 1948; Private)
Lib. (419) 772-2239
www.law.onu.edu

Ohio State University
Moritz College of Law
55 W. 12th Ave.
Columbus, OH 43210-1391
(614) 292-2631
(Approved in 1923; Public)
Lib. (614) 292-3987
moritzlaw.osu.edu

University of Akron
School of Law
150 University Ave.
Akron, OH 44325-2901
(330) 972-7331; (800) 4AKRON-U
(Approved in 1961; Public)
Lib. (330) 972-7330
www.uakron.edu/law

University of Cincinnati
College of Law
P.O. Box 210040
Cincinnati, OH 45221-0040
(513) 556-6805
(Approved in 1923; Public)
Lib. (513) 556-0163
www.law.uc.edu

University of Dayton
School of Law
300 College Park, 112 Keller Hall
Dayton, OH 45469-2760
(937) 229-3211
(Approved in 1975; Private)
Lib. (937) 229-2314
www.udayton.edu/law

# LAW SCHOOLS

University of Toledo
College of Law
2801 West Bancroft St.
Toledo, OH 43606-3390
(419) 530-4131
(Approved in 1939; Public)
Lib. (419) 530-2733
law.utoledo.edu

## OKLAHOMA

Oklahoma City University
School of Law
2501 North Blackwelder Ave.
Oklahoma City, OK 73106-1493
(405) 208-5337; (866) 529-6281
(Approved in 1960; Private)
Lib. (405) 208-5271
law.okcu.edu

University of Oklahoma
College of Law
Andrew M. Coats Hall
300 Timberdell Road
Norman, OK 73019
(405) 325-4699
(Approved in 1923; Public)
Lib. (405) 325-4311
www.law.ou.edu

University of Tulsa
College of Law
3120 East 4th Place
Tulsa, OK 74104-3189
(918) 631-2401
(Approved in 1950; Private)
Lib. (918) 631-2404
www.utulsa.edu/law

## OREGON

Lewis & Clark Law School
10015 SW Terwilliger Blvd.
Portland, OR 97219-7799
(503) 768-6600; (800) 303-4860
(Approved in 1970; Private)
Lib. (503) 768-6688
www.lclark.edu/law/

University of Oregon
School of Law
1515 Agate St.
Eugene, OR 97403-1221
(541) 346-3852
(Approved in 1923; Public)
Lib. (541) 346-3088
www.law.uoregon.edu

Willamette University
Truman Wesley Collins
  Legal Center
245 Winter St., SE
Salem, OR 97301
(503) 370-6282
(Approved in 1938; Private)
Lib. (503) 370-6386
www.willamette.edu/wucl

## PENNSYLVANIA

Drexel University
Earle Mack School of Law
3320 Market St.
Philadelphia, PA 19104
(215) 895-2000
(Provisional approval in 2008;
Private)
Lib. (215) 571-4772
earlemacklaw.drexel.edu

Duquesne University
School of Law
600 Forbes Ave.
Pittsburgh, PA 15282
(412) 396-6300
(Approved in 1960; Private)
Lib. (412) 396-4423
www.duq.edu/law

Penn State University
The Dickinson School of Law
333 W. South St.
Carlisle, PA 17013
(717) 240-5000; (800) 840-1122
(Approved in 1931; Public)
Lib. (717) 240-5229
www.dsl.psu.edu

Temple University
James E. Beasley School of Law
1719 North Broad St.
Philadelphia, PA 19122
(215) 204-7861
(Approved in 1933; Public)
Lib. (215) 204-7891
www.law.temple.edu

University of Pennsylvania
Law School
3400 Chestnut St.
Philadelphia, PA 19104-6204
(215) 898-7400
(Approved in 1923; Private)
Lib. (215) 898-4169
www.law.upenn.edu

University of Pittsburgh
School of Law
3900 Forbes Ave.
Pittsburgh, PA 15260
(412) 648-1490
(Approved in 1923; Public)
Lib. (412) 648-1325
www.law.pitt.edu

Villanova University
School of Law
299 North Spring Mill Road
Villanova, PA 19085
(610) 519-7000
(Approved in 1954; Private)
Lib. (610) 519-7020
www.law.villanova.edu

Widener University-Harrisburg
School of Law
3800 Vartan Way, P.O. Box 69381
Harrisburg, PA 17106-9381
(717) 541-3903
(Approved in 1988; Private)
Lib. (717) 541-3932
law.widener.edu

## PUERTO RICO

Inter American University
School of Law
P.O. Box 70351
San Juan, PR 00936-8351
(787) 751-1912
(Approved in 1969; Private)
Lib. (787) 751-1912
www.derecho.inter.edu

Pontifical Catholic University of
  Puerto Rico
School of Law
2250 Avenida Las Americas
Ponce, PR 00732
(787) 841-2000 x1836
(Approved in 1967; Private)
Lib. (787) 841-2000 x1853
www.pucpr.edu/derecho

University of Puerto Rico
School of Law
P.O. Box 23349
San Juan, PR 00931-3349
(787) 999-9595
(Approved in 1945; Public)
Lib. (787) 999-9684
www.law.upr.edu

# LAW SCHOOLS

**RHODE ISLAND**

Roger Williams University
Ralph R. Papitto School of Law
10 Metacom Ave.
Bristol, RI 02809-5171
(401) 254-4500; (800) 633-2727
(Approved in 1995; Private)
Lib. (401) 254-4546
www.rwu.edu

**SOUTH CAROLINA**

University of South Carolina
School of Law
701 South Main St.
Columbia, SC 29208
(803) 777-4155
(Approved in 1925; Public)
Lib. (803) 777-5902
www.law.sc.edu

Charleston School of Law
81 Mary St.
Charleston, SC 29402
(843) 329-1000
(Provisionally approved in 2006;
 Private)
Lib. (843) 329-2144
www.charlestonlaw.edu

**SOUTH DAKOTA**

University of South Dakota
School of Law
414 E. Clark St.
Vermillion, SD 57069-2390
(605) 677-5443
(Approved in 1923; Public)
Lib. (605) 677-5259
www.usd.edu/law

**TENNESSEE**

University of Memphis
Cecil C. Humphreys School of Law
1 N. Front St.
Memphis, TN 38103-2189
(901) 678-2421
(Approved in 1965; Public)
Lib. (901) 678-2426
www.memphis.edu/law/

University of Tennessee
College of Law
1505 W. Cumberland Ave.
Knoxville, TN 37996
(865) 974-2521

(Approved in 1925; Public)
Lib. (865) 974-7419
www.law.utk.edu

Vanderbilt University Law School
131 21st Ave. South
Nashville, TN 37203
(615) 322-2615
(Approved in 1925; Private)
Lib. (615) 322-2568
law.vanderbilt.edu

**TEXAS**

Baylor University
School of Law
1114 S. University Parks Dr.
Waco, TX 76798
(254) 710-1911; (800) BAYLOR-U
(Approved in 1931; Private)
Lib. (254) 710-2168
www.baylor.edu/law

St. Mary's University
School of Law
One Camino Santa Maria
San Antonio, TX 78228-8601
(210) 436-3011; (866) 639-5831
(Approved in 1948; Private)
Lib. (210) 436-3435
www.stmarytx.edu/law/

South Texas College of Law
1303 San Jacinto St.
Houston, TX 77002-7000
(713) 659-8040
(Approved in 1959; Private)
Lib. (713) 646-1792
www.stcl.edu

Southern Methodist University
Dedman School of Law
P.O. Box 750116
Dallas, TX 75275-0116
(214) 768-2550; (888) 768-5291
(Approved in 1927; Private)
Lib. (214) 768-1830
www.law.smu.edu

Texas Southern University
Thurgood Marshall School of Law
3100 Cleburne Ave.
Houston, TX 77004
(713) 313-4455
(Approved in 1949; Public)
Lib. (713) 313-7328
www.tsulaw.edu

Texas Tech University
School of Law
1802 Hartford Ave.
Lubbock, TX 79409
(806) 742-3990
(Approved in 1969; Public)
Lib. (806) 742-3957
www.law.ttu.edu

Texas Wesleyan University
School of Law
1515 Commerce St.
Ft. Worth, TX 76102
(817) 212-4000; (800) 733-9529
(Approved in 1994; Private)
Lib. (817) 212-3800
law.txwes.edu

University of Houston
Law Center
100 Law Center
Houston, TX 77204-6060
(713) 743-2100
(Approved in 1950; Public)
Lib. (713) 743-2300
www.law.uh.edu

University of Texas at Austin
School of Law
727 E. Dean Keeton St.
Austin, TX 78705
(512) 471-5151
(Approved in 1923; Public)
Lib. (512) 471-7726
www.utexas.edu/law/

**UTAH**

Brigham Young University
J. Reuben Clark Law School
P.O. Box 28000
Provo, UT 84602
(801) 422-4274
(Approved in 1974; Private)
Lib. (801) 422-3593
www.law.byu.edu

University of Utah
S.J. Quinney College of Law
332 South 1400 East, Rm 101
Salt Lake City, UT 84112-0730
(801) 581-6833
(Approved in 1927; Public)
Lib. (801) 581-6438
www.law.utah.edu

# LAW SCHOOLS

## VERMONT

Vermont Law School
164 Chelsea Street, P.O. Box 96
South Royalton, VT 05068-0096
(802) 831-1000; (888) 277-5985
(Approved in 1975; Private)
Lib. (802) 831-1441
www.vermontlaw.edu

## VIRGINIA

Appalachian School of Law
1169 Edgewater Drive
Grundy, VA 24614-7062
(276) 935-4349; (800) 895-7411
(Approved in 2001; Private)
Lib. (276) 935-6688 x1308
www.asl.edu

George Mason University
School of Law
3301 Fairfax Drive
Arlington, VA 22201
(703) 993-8000
(Approved in 1980; Public)
Lib. (703) 993-8120
www.law.gmu.edu

The Judge Advocate General's
  School
600 Massie Road
Charlottesville, VA 22903-1781
(Approved in 1958; Public)
www.jagcnet.army.mil/tjagsa

Liberty University
School of Law
1971 University Blvd.
Lynchburg, VA 24502
(434) 592-5300
(Approved in 2006; Private)
Lib. (434) 592-5350
law.liberty.edu

Regent University
School of Law
1000 Regent University Drive
Virginia Beach, VA 23464
(757) 226-4584
(Approved in 1989; Private)
Lib. (757) 352-4450
www.regent.edu/law

University of Richmond
School of Law
28 Westhampton Way
Richmond, VA 23173

(804) 289-8000
(Approved in 1928; Private)
Lib. (804) 289-8637
law.richmond.edu

University of Virginia
School of Law
580 Massie Rd.
Charlottesville, VA 22903-1789
(434) 924-7354
(Approved in 1923; Public)
Lib. (434) 924-3384
www.law.virginia.edu

Washington and Lee University
School of Law
1 Denny Circle
Lexington, VA 24450
(540) 458-8503
(Approved in 1923; Private)
Lib. (540) 463-8540
law.wlu.edu

William & Mary Law School
613 South Henry Street
P.O. Box 8795
Williamsburg, VA 23187-8795
(757) 221-3785
(Approved in 1932; Public)
Lib. (757) 221-3255
www.wm.edu/law

## WASHINGTON

Gonzaga University
School of Law
P.O. Box 3528
Spokane, WA 99220-3528
(509) 313-3700; (800) 793-1710
(Approved in 1951; Private)
Lib. (509) 313-5792
www.law.gonzaga.edu

Seattle University
School of Law
Sullivan Hall, 901 12th Ave.
Seattle, WA 98122-1090
(206) 398-4000
(Approved in 1994; Private)
Lib. (206) 398-4220
www.law.seattleu.edu

University of Washington
School of Law
William H. Gates Hall, Box 35-3020
Seattle, WA 98195-3020
(206) 543-4550
(Approved in 1924; Public)

Lib. (206) 543-6794
www.law.washington.edu

## WEST VIRGINIA

West Virginia University
College of Law
P.O. Box 6130
Morgantown, WV 26506-6130
(304) 293-5301
(Approved in 1923; Public)
Lib. (304) 293-6830
law.wvu.edu

## WISCONSIN

Marquette University Law School
1103 W. Wisconsin Ave.
P.O. Box 1881
Sensenbrenner Hall
Milwaukee, WI 53201-1881
(414) 288-7090
(Approved in 1925; Private)
Lib. (414) 288-7092
law.marquette.edu

University of Wisconsin Law School
975 Bascom Mall
Madison, WI 53706
(608) 262-2240
(Approved in 1923; Public)
Lib. (608) 262-1128
www.law.wisc.edu

## WYOMING

University of Wyoming
College of Law
1000 E. University Ave., Dept. 3035
Laramie, WY 82071
(307) 766-6416
(Approved in 1923; Public)
Lib. (307) 766-2210
www.uwyo.edu/law

# NON ABA-APPROVED LAW SCHOOLS

Abraham Lincoln Law School
American College of Law
Belmont University College of Law
Birmingham School of Law
Cal Northern School of Law
California Midland School of Law
California School of Law
California Southern Law School
California Southern University
Concord Law School of Kaplan University
Empire College School of Law
Eugenio Maria de Hostos School of Law
Glendale University College of Law
Humphreys College School of Law
Irvine University College of Law
John F. Kennedy University School of Law
Lincoln Law School of Sacramento
Lincoln Law School of San Jose
Lincoln Memorial University, Duncan School of Law
Massachusetts School of Law at Andover
Miles Law School
Monterey College of Law
Nashville School of Law
University of Northern California, Lorenzo Patino School of Law
Oak Brook College of Law
Pacific Coast University School of Law
Pacific West College of Law
Saint Francis School of Law
San Francisco Law School at Alliant International University
San Joaquin College of Law
Santa Barbara College of Law
Southern California Institute of Law
Taft Law School
Trinity Law School Trinity International University
Ventura College of Law
University of California, Irvine School of Law
University of Massachusetts School of Law - Dartmouth
University of West Los Angeles School of Law - West Los Angeles
Western Sierra Law School

# CANADIAN LAW SCHOOLS

University of Alberta
Faculty of Law
4th fl., Law Centre
111th St. & 89th Ave.
Edmonton, Alberta
CANADA T6G 2H5
(780) 492-3067
FAX (780) 492-5587
Lib. (780) 492-3371
www.law.ualberta.ca/

University of British Columbia
Faculty of Law
1822 East Mall
Vancouver, British Columbia
CANADA V6T 1Z1
(604) 822-6303
FAX (604) 822-9486
Lib. (604) 822-2275
www.law.ubc.ca/

The University of Calgary
Faculty of Law
2500 University Drive, NW
Calgary, Alberta
CANADA T2N 1N4
(403) 220-4155
FAX (403) 210-9662
Lib. (403) 220-6702
www.law.ucalgary.ca

Carleton University
Department of Law
C473 Loeb Building
1125 Colonel By Drive
Ottawa, Ontario
CANADA K1S 5B6
(613) 520-3690
FAX (613) 520-4467
Lib. (613) 520-2735
www2.carleton.ca/law

Dalhousie University
Dalhousie Law School
6061 University Ave.
Halifax, Nova Scotia
CANADA B3H 4H9
(902) 492-2068
FAX (902) 494-1316
Lib. (902) 494-2124
www.dal.ca/law

Laval University
Faculty of Law
Pavillon Charles-de-Koninck
Quebec, Quebec
CANADA G1V 0A6
(418) 656-2131
FAX (418) 656-7230
Lib. (418) 656-2317
www.fd.ulaval.ca

McGill University
Faculty of Law
3644 Peel St.
Montreal, Quebec
CANADA H3A 1W9
(514) 398-6602
FAX (514) 398-8453
Lib. (514) 398-4715
www.mcgill.ca/law

University of Manitoba
Faculty of Law
303 Robson Hall
Winnipeg, Manitoba
CANADA R3T 2N2
(204) 480-1485
Lib. (204) 474-6372
www.umanitoba.ca/law/

University of Moncton
Law School
Moncton, New Brunswick
CANADA E1A 3E9
(506) 858-4560
FAX (506) 858-4534
Lib. (506) 858-4547
www.umoncton.ca/umcm-droit/

University of Montreal
Faculty of Law
C.P. 6128
Succursale Centre-Ville
Montreal, Quebec
CANADA H3C 3J7
(514) 343-6124
FAX (514) 343-2199
Lib. (514) 343-7095
www.droit.umontreal.ca/

University of New Brunswick
Faculty of Law
P.O. Box 44271

Fredericton, New Brunswick
CANADA E3B 6C2
(506) 453-4693
FAX (506) 453-7722
Lib. (506) 453-4734
law.unb.ca

University of Ottawa
Faculty of Civil Law
57 Louis Pasteur
P.O. Box 450, Stn A
Ottawa, Ontario
CANADA K1N 6N5
(613) 562-5800
FAX (613) 562-5121
Lib. (613) 562-5812
www.droitcivil.uottawa.ca

University of Ottawa
Faculty of Law
Common Law Section
57 Louis Pasteur
P.O. Box 450, Stn A
Ottawa, Ontario
CANADA K1N 6N5
(613) 562-5800
FAX (613) 562-5124
Lib. (613) 562-5845
www.commonlaw.uottawa.ca/eng

University of Quebec at Montreal
455 boul. Rene-Levesque Est
Montreal, Quebec
CANADA H2L 4Y2
(514) 987-4133
FAX (514) 987-4784
Lib. (514) 987-6184
www.juris.uqam.ca/

Queen's University
Faculty of Law
Macdonald Hall
Kingston, Ontario
CANADA K7L 3N6
(613) 533-2220
FAX (613) 533-6509
Lib. (613) 533-6000 x32842
law.queensu.ca

University of Saskatchewan
College of Law

# CANADIAN LAW SCHOOLS

15 Campus Drive
Saskatoon, Saskatchewan
CANADA S7N 5A6
(306) 966-5045
FAX (306) 966-5900
Lib. (306) 966-6053
www.usask.ca/law/

University of Sherbrooke
Faculty of Law
2500 University Blvd.
Sherbrooke, Quebec
CANADA J1K 2R1
(819) 821-7500
FAX (819) 821-7578
Lib. (819) 821-7519
www.usherbrooke.ca/droit

University of Toronto
Faculty of Law
78 Queen's Park
Toronto, Ontario
CANADA M5S 2C5
(416) 978-3716
FAX (416) 978-0790
Lib. (416) 978-8580
www.law.utoronto.ca/

University of Victoria
Faculty of Law
P.O. Box 2400
Victoria, BC
CANADA V8W 3H7
(250) 721-8150
FAX (250) 721-6390
Lib. (250) 721-8565
www.law.uvic.ca/

University of Western Ontario
Faculty of Law
1151 Richmond Street
London, Ontario
CANADA N6A 3K7
(519) 661-3347
Lib. (519) 661-3171
www.law.uwo.ca

University of Windsor
Faculty of Law
401 Sunset Ave.
Windsor, Ontario
CANADA N9B 3P4
(519) 253-3000 x2925
FAX (519) 973-7064
Lib. (519) 253-3000 x2976
www.uwindsor.ca/law/

York University
Osgoode Hall Law School
4700 Keele St.
North York, Ontario
CANADA M3J 1P3
(416) 736-5030
FAX (416) 736-5736
Lib. (416) 736-5030
www.osgoode.yorku.ca

# BAR ADMISSIONS

## STATE BAR ADMINISTRATORS

### ALABAMA
**Dorothy D. Johnson**
Director of Admissions
Board of Bar Examiners
Alabama State Bar
P.O. Box 671
Montgomery, AL 36101
TEL: 334-269-1515
FAX: 334-261-6310
E-MAIL: adm@alabar.org
www.alabar.org

### ALASKA
**Deborah O'Regan**
Executive Director
Law Examiners Committee
Alaska Bar Association
P.O. Box 100279
Anchorage, AK 99510-0279
TEL: 907-272-7469
FAX: 907-272-2932
www.alaskabar.org

### ARIZONA
**Emily Holliday**
Attorney Admissions Manager
Arizona Supreme Court
Committee on Examinations
  and Character and Fitness
1501 W. Washington, #104
Phoenix, AZ 85007
TEL: 602-452-3963
FAX: 602-452-3958
E-MAIL: attorneyadmissions@
  courts.az.gov
www.supreme.state.az.us/admis

### ARKANSAS
**R. Christopher Thomas**
Executive Secretary
State Board of Law Examiners
Justice Building, Rm. 120
625 Marshall St.
Little Rock, AR 72201-0120
TEL: 501-374-1855
FAX: 501-374-1853
www.courts.arkansas.gov

### CALIFORNIA
**Gayle E. Murphy**
Senior Executive, Admissions
The State Bar of California
Office of Admissions
180 Howard St.
San Francisco, CA 94105-1639
TEL: 415-538-2300
FAX: 415-538-2304
www.calbar.ca.gov/admissions

### COLORADO
**Alan Ogden**
Executive Director
Colorado State Board
  of Law Examiners
1560 Broadway St., #1820
Denver, CO 80202
TEL: 303-866-6626
FAX: 303-893-0541
www.coloradosupremecourt.us

### CONNECTICUT
**Kathleen B. Wood**
Administrative Director
Connecticut Bar Examining
  Committee
100 Washington St., 1st Fl.
Hartford, CT 06106-4411
TEL: 860-706-5135
EMAIL: barexam@jud.ct.gov
www.jud.ct.gov/cbec

### DELAWARE
**Sarah Arnold**
Executive Director
Board of Bar Examiners
  of the Delaware Supreme Court
Carvel State Office Bldg.
820 N. French St., 11th Fl.
Wilmington, DE 19801-3545
TEL: 302-577-7038
FAX: 302-577-7037
www.courts.state.de.us/bbe/

### DIST. OF COLUMBIA
**Jacqueline M. Smith**
Director of Admissions
D.C. Court of Appeals
430 E St. NW, Rm. 123
Washington, DC 20001
TEL: 202-879-2710
FAX: 202-879-2794
E-MAIL: coa@dcappeals.gov
www.dccourts.gov

### FLORIDA
**Michele A. Gavagni**
Executive Director
Florida Board of Bar Examiners
Tippin-Moore Building
1891 Eider Ct.
Tallahassee, FL 32399-1750
TEL: 850-487-1292
FAX: 850-414-6822
www.floridabarexam.org

### GEORGIA
**Sally Evans Lockwood**
Director of Admissions
Supreme Court of Georgia
Office of Bar Admissions
244 Washington St. SW,
  Ste. 440
Atlanta, GA 30334
TEL: 404-656-3490
FAX: 404-657-9108
www.gabaradmissions.org

### HAWAII
**Naomi Komenaka**
Secretary
Board of Examiners
  of the Supreme Court of Hawaii
Ali`iolani Hale, #103
417 S. King St.
Honolulu, HI 96813-2912
TEL: 808-539-4919
FAX: 808-539-4978
www.courts.state.hi.us

### IDAHO
**M. Carol McDonald**
Admissions Director
Idaho State Bar
525 W. Jefferson
P.O. Box 895
Boise, ID 83701
TEL: 208-334-4500
FAX: 208-334-2764
www.isb.idaho.gov

### ILLINOIS
**Regina Kwan Peterson**
Director of Administration
Illinois Board of Admissions
  to the Bar
625 S. College St.
Springfield, IL 62704-2521
TEL: 217-522-5917
FAX: 217-522-3728
www.ilBarAdmissions.org

# STATE BAR ADMINISTRATORS

## INDIANA
**David J. Remondini**
Acting Executive Director
Indiana State Board
  of Law Examiners
30 S. Meridian St., #875
Indianapolis, IN 46204-3569
TEL: 317-232-2552
FAX: 317-233-3960
www.in.gov/judiciary/ble

## IOWA
**David M. Ewert**
Assistant Director for Admissions
Office of Professional Regulation
1111 East Court Ave.
Des Moines, IA 50319
TEL: 515-725-8029
FAX: 515-725-8032
www.iowacourts.gov

## KANSAS
**Francine D. Angell**
Administrator
Kansas Board of Law Examiners
Kansas Judicial Center
301 W. 10th St., Rm. 374
Topeka, KS 66612-1507
TEL: 785-296-8410
FAX: 785-296-1028
E-MAIL: admissions@kscourts.org
www.kscourts.org

## KENTUCKY
**Bonnie C. Kittinger**
Director & General Counsel
Kentucky Office of Bar Admissions
1510 Newton Pike, Ste. 156
Lexington, KY 40511-1255
TEL: 859-246-2381
FAX: 859-246-2385
www.kyoba.org

## LOUISIANA
**Denise S. Leeper**
Bar Admissions Administrator
Louisiana Committee
  on Bar Admissions
2800 Veterans Memorial Blvd.,
  #310
Metairie, LA 70002
TEL: 504-836-2420
FAX: 504-834-1449
www.lascba.org

## MAINE
**Deborah Firestone**
Executive Director
Maine Board of Bar Examiners
P.O. Box 140
Augusta, ME 04332-0140
TEL: 207-623-2464
FAX: 207-622-0059
www.mainebarexaminers.org

## MARYLAND
**Steven W. Boggs**
Secretary
State Board of Law Examiners
2011-F Commerce Park Dr.
Annapolis, MD 21401
TEL: 410-260-3640
FAX: Not published
www.mdcourts.gov

## MASSACHUSETTS
**Marilyn J. Wellington**
Executive Director
Massachusetts Board
  of Bar Examiners
Suffolk County Courthouse
3 Pemberton Square, Rm.114
Boston, MA 02108
TEL: 617-482-4466
FAX: 617-542-5943
www.mass.gov/bbe

## MICHIGAN
**Timothy J. Raubinger**
Assistant Secretary
Michigan Board of Law Examiners
P.O. Box 30052
Lansing, MI 48909-7552
TEL: 517-373-4453
FAX: 517-373-5038
E-MAIL: BLE-Info@courts.mi.gov
www.courts.mi.gov

## MINNESOTA
**Margaret Fuller Corneille**
Director
Minnesota State Board of Law
  Examiners
180 E. 5th St., #950
St. Paul, MN 55101
TEL: 651-297-1800
FAX: 651-297-1196
E-MAIL: ble.cle.blc@
  mbcle.state.mn.us
www.ble.state.mn.us

## MISSISSIPPI
**Linda B. Knight**
Bar Admissions Administrator
Mississippi Board of Bar Admissions
P.O. Box 1449
Jackson, MS 39215-1449
TEL: 601-576-4620
FAX: 601-576-4730
www.mssc.state.ms.us

## MISSOURI
**Colette Neuner**
Executive Director
State Board of Law Examiners
P.O. Box 104236
Jefferson City, MO 65110-4236
TEL: 573-751-9814
FAX: 573-751-5335
www.mble.org

## MONTANA
**Vanessa Sanddal**
Bar Admissions Administrator
State Bar of Montana
7 W. 6th Ave., #2B
P.O. Box 577
Helena, MT 59624
TEL: 406-442-7660
FAX: 406-442-7763
www.montanabar.org

## NEBRASKA
**Jane Schoenike**
Director of Admissions
Nebraska State Bar Commission
635 S. 14th St., #200
P.O. Box 81809
Lincoln, NE 68501-1809
TEL: 402-475-7091
FAX: 402-475-7098
www.nebar.com

## NEVADA
**Laura Meyers Gould**
Director of Admissions
State Bar of Nevada
600 E. Charleston Blvd.
Las Vegas, NV 89104
TEL: 702-382-2200 or
  800-254-2797
FAX: 702-382-6676
www.nvbar.org

# STATE BAR ADMINISTRATORS

## NEW HAMPSHIRE
**Eileen Fox**
Clerk of the Supreme Court
Supreme Court Building
1 Charles Doe Dr.
Concord, NH 03301
TEL: 603-271-2646
FAX: 603-513-5475
www.courts.state.nh.us

## NEW JERSEY
**Mark Neary**
Board of Bar Examiners Secretary
  and Clerk of the Supreme Court
New Jersey Board of Bar Examiners
P.O. Box 973
Trenton, NJ 08625-0973
TEL: 609-984-2111
FAX: 609-984-6859
www.njbarexams.org

## NEW MEXICO
**Carol Skiba**
Executive Director
New Mexico State Board of Bar
  Examiners
9420 Indian School Rd. N.E.
Albuquerque, NM 87112
TEL: 505-271-9706
FAX: 505-271-9768
www.nmexam.org

## NEW YORK
**John J. McAlary**
Executive Director
New York State Board
  of Law Examiners
Corporate Plaza, Bldg. #3
254 Washington Ave. Extension
Albany, NY 12203
TEL: 518-453-5990
FAX: 518-452-5729
www.nybarexam.org

## NORTH CAROLINA
**Fred P. Parker III**
Executive Director
Board of Law Examiners of the State
  of North Carolina
One Exchange Plaza, #700
P.O. Box 2946
Raleigh, NC 27602
TEL: 919-828-4886
FAX: 919-828-2251
www.ncble.org

## NORTH DAKOTA
**Penny Miller**
Secretary-Treasurer
  and Clerk of the Supreme Court
State Board of Law Examiners
Judicial Wing, 1st Fl.
600 E. Boulevard Ave.
Bismarck, ND 58505-0530
TEL: 701-328-4201
FAX: 701-328-4480
www.ndcourts.gov

## OHIO
**Lee Ann Ward**
Director of Bar Admissions
Supreme Court of Ohio
65 S. Front St., 5th Fl.
Columbus, OH 43215-3431
TEL: 614-387-9340
FAX: 614-387-9349
www.supremecourt.ohio.gov

## OKLAHOMA
**Cheryl Beatty**
Administrative Director
Oklahoma Board of Bar Examiners
1901 N. Lincoln Blvd.
P.O. Box 53036
Oklahoma City, OK 73152-3036
TEL: 405-416-7075
FAX: 405-528-4103
www.okbbe.com

## OREGON
**Jonathan P. Benson**
Executive Director
Oregon State Board of Bar Examiners
16037 S.W. Upper Boones Ferry Rd.
Tigard, OR 97224
TEL: 503-620-0222
FAX: 503-598-6990
www.osbar.org

## PENNSYLVANIA
**Gicine P. Brignola**
Executive Director
Pennsylvania Board
  of Law Examiners
601 Commonwealth Ave., Ste. 3600
P.O. Box 62535
Harrisburg, PA 17106-2535
TEL: 717-231-3350
FAX: 717-231-3351
www.pabarexam.org

## RHODE ISLAND
**Sherry L. D'Amico**
Administrator
Rhode Island Supreme Court
Frank Licht Judicial Complex
250 Benefit St.
Providence, RI 02903
TEL: 401-222-4233
FAX: 401-222-3599
www.courts.ri.gov

## SOUTH CAROLINA
**Gayle B. Watts**
Deputy Clerk for Bar Admissions
South Carolina Supreme Court
1231 Gervais St.
P.O. Box 11330
Columbia, SC 29211
TEL: 803-734-1080
FAX: 803-734-0394
www.sccourts.org

## SOUTH DAKOTA
**Sheridan Cash Anderson**
Secretary
South Dakota Board
  of Bar Examiners
500 E. Capitol Ave.
Pierre, SD 57501
TEL: 605-773-4898
FAX: 605-773-8479
www.sdjudicial.com

## TENNESSEE
**Adele Anderson**
Executive Director
Tennessee Board of Law Examiners
401 Church St., #2200
Nashville, TN 37243-0740
TEL: 615-741-3234
FAX: 615-741-5867
www.tennessee.gov/lawexaminers

## TEXAS
**Julia Vaughan**
Executive Director
Texas Board of Law Examiners
205 W. 14th St., #500
P.O. Box 13486
Austin, TX 78711-3486
TEL: 512-463-1621
FAX: 512-463-5300
www.ble.state.tx.us

# STATE BAR ADMINISTRATORS

## UTAH
**Joni Dickson Seko**
Deputy General Counsel,
  Admissions
Utah State Bar
645 South 200 East
Salt Lake City, UT 84111-3834
TEL: 801-531-9077
FAX: 801-531-0660
www.utahbar.org

## VERMONT
**Martha I. Hicks-Robinson**
Bar Admission Administrator
Board of Bar Examiners
2418 Airport Rd., #2
Barre, VT 05641
TEL: 802-828-3281
FAX: 802-828-1695
E-MAIL: jud-attylicensing@
  state.vt.us
www.vermontjudiciary.org

## VIRGINIA
**W. Scott Street III**
Secretary-Treasurer
Virginia Board of Bar Examiners
2201 W. Broad St., #101
Richmond, VA 23220-2022
TEL: 804-367-0412
FAX: 804-367-0416
www.vbbe.state.va.us

## WASHINGTON
**Mary B. Barnes**
Admissions Manager
Washington State Bar Association
1325 4th Ave., #600
Seattle, WA 98101-2539
TEL: 206-727-8229
FAX: 206-727-8313
E-MAIL: admissions@wsba.org
www.wsba.org

## WEST VIRGINIA
**Madeleine H. Johnson**
Bar Admissions Administrator
West Virginia Board of Law
  Examiners
City Center East, Ste. 1200 B
4700 MacCorkle Ave., SE
Charleston, WV 25304
TEL: 304-558-7815
FAX: 304-558-0831
www.state.wv.us/wvsca

## WISCONSIN
**Jacquelynn Rothstein**
Director
Board of Bar Examiners
P.O. Box 2748
Madison, WI 53701-2748
TEL: 608-266-9760
FAX: 608-266-1196
E-MAIL: bbe@wicourts.gov
www.wicourts.gov

## WYOMING
**Nancy A. Shore**
Admissions Director
Wyoming Board of Law Examiners
4124 Laramie St.
P.O. Box 109
Cheyenne, WY 82003-0109
TEL: 307-632-9061
FAX: 307-632-3737
www.wyomingbar.org

## GUAM
**Hannah Gutierrez-Arroyo**
Clerk of Court and Secretary
Supreme Court of Guam
Guam Judicial Center
120 W. O'Brien Dr., #300
Hagatna, Guam 96910-5154
TEL: 671-475-3120
FAX: 671-475-3140
www.guamsupremecourt.com

## NORTHERN MARIANA ISLANDS, COMMONWEALTH OF THE
**Nora V. Borja**
Bar Administrator
Commonwealth of the Northern
  Mariana Islands Supreme Court
P.O. Box 502165
Saipan, MP 96950
TEL: 670-236-9800
FAX: 670-236-9702
E-MAIL: supreme.court@
  justice.gov.mp
www.justice.gov.mp

## PALAU, REPUBLIC OF
**Rose Ongalibang**
Clerk of Court
Palau Supreme Court
P.O. Box 248
Koror, Palau 96940
TEL: 680-488-2607
FAX: 680-488-1597
E-MAIL: palaujudiciary@
  palaunet.com
www.palaubar.org

## PUERTO RICO
**Héctor Rodriguez Mulet**
Executive Director
Commonwealth of Puerto Rico
  Supreme Court
P.O. Box 9022392
San Juan, PR 00902-2392
TEL: 787-289-0170
FAX: 787-725-5030
www.ramajudicial.pr

## VIRGIN ISLANDS
**Hon. Geoffrey W. Barnard**
Chairman
Committee of Bar Examiners
Supreme Court of the Virgin Islands
Attention: Elsie-Mae King
Director of Bar Admissions
P.O. Box 590
St. Thomas, VI 00804
TEL: 340-774-2237
FAX: 340-774-2258
E-MAIL: bar.admissions@
  visupremecourt.org
www.visupremecourt.org

# MANDATORY CONTINUING LEGAL EDUCATION

| Jurisdiction | Yes | No | Description |
|---|---|---|---|
| | | | *Does your jurisdiction have a mandatory CLE requirement?* |
| Alabama | X | | 12 hours per year. |
| Alaska | X | | 3 hours of ethics per year; mandatory reporting of completion of ethics requirement and whether member has completed 9 or more additional CLE credits. |
| Arizona | X | | 15 hours per year, including 2 hours of professional responsibility including ethics, professionalism, malpractice prevention, substance abuse, attorney fees, client development, law office economics. |
| Arkansas | X | | 12 hours per year, which includes 1 hour of ethics. |
| California | X | | 25 hours per 3 years, including 4 hours in ethics, 1 hour in substance abuse prevention/detection and treatment, and 1 hour related to the elimination of bias in the legal profession. |
| Colorado | X | | 45 hours per 3 years, including 7 hours of ethics and professionalism. Newly admitted on motion must attend the Colorado Bar Association's Seminar on Professionalism in the first compliance period. |
| Connecticut | | X | |
| Delaware | X | | 24 credit hours per 2 years, including at least 4 credit hours in Enhanced Ethics. Requirements may differ for senior attorneys, newly admitted attorneys, and attorneys resuming active practice after a period of inactivity. |
| Dist. of Columbia | | X | |
| Florida | X | | 30 hours per 3 years, including 5 hours of ethics, professionalism, substance abuse, or mental illness awareness. |
| Georgia | X | | 12 hours per year, including 1 hour of ethics and 1 hour of professionalism. The mandatory Transition into Law Practice Program course required for initial admission is included in the 12-hour requirement in the year of admission or in the next calendar year. |
| Hawaii | | X | |
| Idaho | X | | 30 hours per 3 years, including 2 hours ethics. Practical skills seminar required within 6 months of admission for motion applicants. |
| Illinois | X | | 20 hours of CLE activity during initial 2-year reporting period, 24 hours of CLE during second 2-year reporting period, and 30 hours all subsequent reporting periods. A minimum of 4 of the total hours required for any 2-year period must be in the areas of professionalism, diversity issues, mental illness and addiction issues, civility, or legal ethics. |
| Indiana | X | | 36 hours per 3 years with a minimum of 6 hours per year; 3 hours of 36 shall be professional responsibility. |
| Iowa | X | | 15 hours per year; 2 hours of ethics per 2 years. Basic skills course for new lawyers applies to CLE requirement. |
| Kansas | X | | 12 hours per year, including 2 hours of ethics. |
| Kentucky | X | | 12.5 hours per year, including 2 hours of ethics. |
| Louisiana | X | | 12.5 hours per year, including 1 hour of ethics and 1 hour of professionalism. |
| Maine | X | | 11 hours per year with 1 hour covering ethics/professional responsibility. |
| Maryland | | X | |
| Massachusetts | | X | |
| Michigan | | X | |
| Minnesota | X | | 45 hours per 3 years, including 3 hours of ethics and 2 hours of elimination of bias in the legal profession. |
| Mississippi | X | | 12 hours per year. |
| Missouri | X | | 15 hours per year, including 2 hours of ethics, professionalism, or malpractice prevention every year. 2 hours of ethics required of all new admittees within 12 months of admission regardless of whether practicing in Missouri. |
| Montana | X | | A minimum of 15 hours per year; 5 hours of ethics per 3 years. |
| Nebraska | | X | |
| Nevada | X | | 10 hours per year; 2 hours of ethics. |
| New Hampshire | X | | 12 hours per year; 2 hours of ethics. |
| New Jersey | X | | 24 credit hours per 2 years, including at least 4 credits in ethics and/or professionalism. |
| New Mexico | X | | 12 hours per year, including 1 hour of ethics and 1 hour of professionalism. |
| New York | X | | 24 hours per 2 years. Newly admitted lawyers must complete 32 hours within the first 2 years of admission to the bar. |
| North Carolina | X | | 12 hours per year. At least 2 hours must be devoted to professional responsibility (ethics and professional liability); special 3-hour block ethics requirement per 3 years; 1 hour on substance abuse or mental disability per 3 years. |
| North Dakota | X | | 45 hours per 3 years, of which 3 hours must be ethics course work. |
| Ohio | X | | At least 2.5 of the 24 hours required per 2 years shall relate to professional conduct and include 30 minutes related to substance abuse, 60 minutes related to the Ohio Rules of Professional Conduct, and 60 minutes related to professionalism. |
| Oklahoma | X | | 12 hours per year, including 1 hour of ethics. |
| Oregon | X | | 45 hours per 3 years, 5 legal ethics, 1 child abuse reporting, and 3 elimination of bias credits. |

Credit: Comprehensive Guide to Bar Admission Requirements 2011. Copyright 2011 American Bar Association and the National Conference of Bar Examiners. Reprinted by permission.

# MANDATORY CONTINUING LEGAL EDUCATION

| Jurisdiction | Does your jurisdiction have a mandatory CLE requirement? | | |
| --- | --- | --- | --- |
| | Yes | No | Description |
| Pennsylvania | X | | 12 hours per year, including 1 hour of ethics. |
| Rhode Island | X | | 10 hours per year; 2 hours of ethics. |
| South Carolina | X | | 14 hours per year; at least 2 shall be devoted to ethics/professional responsibility. |
| South Dakota | | X | |
| Tennessee | X | | 12 hours per year plus 3 hours of ethics. |
| Texas | X | | 15 hours per year, including 3 hours of ethics. |
| Utah | X | | 24 hours per 2 years, including 2 hours of ethics and 1 hour of professionalism. |
| Vermont | X | | 20 hours per 2 years, including 2 hours of ethics and 2 hours of professionalism. |
| Virginia | X | | 12 hours per year, including 2 hours of ethics. |
| Washington | X | | 45 hours per 3 years, of which 6 hours must be devoted to ethics. New admittees are exempt during the year admitted and for the following calendar year. |
| West Virginia | X | | 24 hours per 2 years. At least 3 of these hours must be in ethics or law office management, substance abuse, or elimination of bias in the legal profession. |
| Wisconsin | X | | 30 hours per 2 years, including 3 hours of ethics. |
| Wyoming | X | | 15 hours per year, including 1 hour of ethics. |
| Guam | X | | 10 hours per year, including 2 hours of ethics. |
| Northern Mariana Islands | X | | 20 hours per year. |
| Palau | X | | 15 hours per 2 years. |
| Puerto Rico | X | | 24 hours per 2 years, including 4 hours of ethics. |
| Virgin Islands | X | | 12 hours per year, including 2 hours in legal ethics or professionalism. |

# LEGAL PERIODICALS

## LEGAL NEWSPAPERS IN THE UNITED STATES

**ALABAMA**

**Alabama Messenger**
706 Frank Nelson Bldg.
Birmingham, AL 35203
(205) 252-3672
FAX (205) 252-3679
www.alabamamessenger.com
weekly (Sat.)

**ALASKA**

**Alaska Journal of Commerce**
301 Arctic Slope Ave., Suite 350
Anchorage, AK 99518
(907) 561-4772
www.alaskajournal.com
weekly

**ARIZONA**

**Arizona Business Gazette**
P.O. Box 194
Phoenix, AZ 85001-0194
(602) 444-7300
FAX (602) 444-7363
www.azcentral.com/business/abg
weekly (Thurs.)

**Arizona Capitol Times**
1835 W. Adams Street
Phoenix, AZ 85007
(602) 258-7026
FAX (602) 253-7636
www.azcapitoltimes.com
weekly

**Daily Territorial**
3280 E. Hemisphere Loop,
 Suite 180
Tucson, AZ 85706
(520) 294-1200
FAX (520) 294-4076
insidetucsonbusiness.com
daily (M-F)

**The Record Reporter**
1505 N. Central Ave., Suite 200
Phoenix, AZ 85004
(602) 417-9900
FAX (602) 417-9910

www.recordreporter.com
(Mon., Wed., & Fri.)

**CALIFORNIA**

**Antelope Valley Journal**
3166 E. Palmdale Blvd., Suite 107
Palmdale, CA 93550
(661) 947-5009
FAX (661) 947-5208
weekly (Fri.)

**The Business Journal**
1315 Van Ness, Suite 200
Fresno, CA 93721
(559) 490-3400
FAX (559) 490-3526
www.thebusinessjournal.com
(Mon., Wed., Fri.)

**Daily Recorder**
901 H Street, Suite 312
Sacramento, CA 95814
(916) 444-2355
FAX (916) 444-0636
daily (M-F)

**Inter-City Express**
1109 Oak St., Suite 103
Oakland, CA 94607
(510) 272-4747
FAX (510) 465-1657
www.dailyjournal.com
(Wed. & Fri.)

**Los Angeles Daily Journal**
915 E. First St.
Los Angeles, CA 90012
(213) 229-5300
(800) 487-8262
FAX (213) 229-5481
www.dailyjournal.com
daily (M-F)

**Metropolitan News-Enterprise**
Metropolitan News Co.
210 South Spring Street
Los Angeles, CA 90012
(213) 346-0033
FAX (213) 687-3886
www.metnews.com

daily (M-F)

**Orange County Reporter**
600 W. Santa Ana Blvd. #205
Santa Ana, CA 92701
(714) 543-2027
FAX (714) 542-6841
www.dailyjournal.com
daily (M-F)

**Reporter**
3010 E. Anaheim St.
Long Beach, CA 90804
(562) 438-5641
FAX (562) 438-7086
(Tues. & Fri.)

**Riverside Business Journal**
4129 Main St., Suite 209
Riverside, CA 92501
(951) 784-0111
FAX (951) 784-6947
(Tues. & Thurs.)

**San Diego Commerce**
2652 4th Avenue, 2nd fl.
San Diego, CA 92103
(619) 232-3486
FAX (619) 232-1159
(Tues., Wed., & Fri.)

**San Diego Daily Transcript**
2131 Third Ave.
San Diego, CA 92101
(619) 232-4381
(800) 697-NEWS
FAX (619) 236-8126
www.sddt.com
daily (M-F)

**San Francisco Daily Journal**
44 Montgomery St., Suite 250
San Francisco, CA 94104
(415) 296-2400
FAX (415) 296-2440
www.dailyjournal.com
daily (M-F)

**San Francisco Recorder**
10 UN Plaza, 3rd fl.
San Francisco, CA 94102

# LEGAL NEWSPAPERS IN THE UNITED STATES

(415) 749-5400
www.law.com
 daily (M-F)

**San Jose Post-Record**
95 S. Market St., Suite 535
San Jose, CA 95113-1225
(408) 287-4866
FAX (408) 287-2544
 (Tues., Wed., & Fri.)

**Sonoma County Herald-
Recorder**
1818 4th Street
Santa Rosa, CA 95402
(707) 545-1166
FAX (707) 545-6310
www.dailyjournal.com
 (Mon., Wed., & Fri.)

## COLORADO

**Colorado Springs Business
Journal**
31 E. Platte Ave., Suite 300
Colorado Springs, CO 80903
(719) 634-5905
FAX (719) 227-5863
www.csbj.com
 weekly (Fri.)

**Colorado Tribune**
Colorado Printing of Pueblo
447 Park Dr.
Pueblo, CO 81005-1134
(719) 561-4008
FAX (719) 561-4007
 weekly

**Daily Transcript**
31 E. Platte Ave., Suite 300
Colorado Springs, CO 80903
(719) 634-1048
FAX (719) 634-0596
www.cstranscript.com
 daily (M-F)

## CONNECTICUT

**Connecticut Law Tribune**
201 Ann St.
Hartford, CT 06103
(860) 527-7900
 weekly

## DISTRICT OF COLUMBIA

**Daily Washington Law
Reporter**
100 E. Pratt St., Suite 2520
Baltimore, MD 21202
(202) 331-1700
FAX (202) 785-8476
www.dwlr.com
 daily (M-F)

## FLORIDA

**Broward Daily Business
Review**
633 S. Andrews Ave.
Ft. Lauderdale, FL 33301
(954) 468-2600
www.dailybusinessreview.com
 daily (M-F)

**The Daily Record**
10 N. Newnan St.
Jacksonville, FL 32202
(904) 356-2466
FAX (904) 353-2628
www.jaxdailyrecord.com
 daily (M-F)

**Miami Daily Business
Review**
1 SE 3rd Ave., Suite 900
Miami, FL 33131
(305) 347-6614
FAX (305) 347-6636
www.dailybusinessreview.com
 daily (M-F)

**Palm Beach Daily Business
Review**
324 Datura St., Suite 140
W. Palm Beach, FL 33401
(561) 820-2060
FAX (561) 820-2077
 daily (M-F)

**Gulf Coast Business Review**
412 E. Madison Street
Tampa, FL 33602-4607
(813) 221-9505
FAX (813) 221-9403
www.review.net/
 weekly (Fri.)

## GEORGIA

**Fulton County Daily Report**
190 Pryor Street, SW
Atlanta, GA 30303
(404) 521-1227
FAX (404) 525-1738
www.dailyreportonline.com
 daily (M-F)

## IDAHO

**The Idaho Business Review**
855 W. Broad St., Suite 103
Boise, ID 83702
(208) 336-3768
FAX (208) 336-5534
www.idahobusiness.net
 weekly

## ILLINOIS

**Chicago Daily Law Bulletin**
415 N. State Street
Chicago, IL 60610
(312) 644-7800
FAX (312) 644-4255
www.lawbulletin.com
 daily (M-F)

**Inside Counsel**
222 S. Riverside Plaza, Suite 620
Chicago, IL 60606
(312) 654-3500
www.insidecounsel.com
 monthly

**The Legal Reporter**
O'Fallon Progress
P.O. Box 427
Belville,, IL 62222
(618) 632-3643
FAX (618) 632-6438
 weekly (Wed.)

## INDIANA

**Court & Commercial Record**
41 E. Washington, #200
Indianapolis, IN 46204
(317) 636-0200
FAX (317) 263-5259
www.theindianalawyer.com
 daily (M-F)

# LEGAL NEWSPAPERS IN THE UNITED STATES

## KANSAS

**The Legal Record**
P.O. Box 273
Olathe, KS 66051-0273
(913) 780-5790
FAX (913) 780-5747
www.thelegalrecord.net
weekly (Tues.)

**Topeka Metro News**
P.O. Box 1794
Topeka, KS 66601
(785) 232-8600
FAX (785) 235-8707
www.topekametro.com
(Fri.)

**Wyandotte County Business News**
P.O. Box 13235
Kansas City, KS 66113
(913) 422-8232
FAX (913) 422-1359
www.wybiznews.com
weekly (Mon.)

## LOUISIANA

**Daily Legal News**
501 Texas St.
Shreveport, LA 71101-5413
(318) 222-0213
www.dailylegalnews.net
daily (M-F)

**New Orleans Citybusiness**
111 Veterans Blvd., Suite 1440
Metairie, LA 70005
(504) 834-9292
(800) 739-8836
FAX (504) 832-3550
www.neworleanscitybusiness.com
weekly (Mon.)

## MARYLAND

**The Daily Record**
11 East Saratoga Street
Baltimore, MD 21202-2199
(410) 752-1717
FAX (410) 752-2894
www.mddailyrecord.com
daily (Mon.-Fri.)

## MASSACHUSETTS

**Lawyers USA**
Dolan Media
10 Milk St., Suite 1000
Boston, MA 02108
(617) 218-8191
(800) 451-9998
FAX (617) 451-1466
lawyersusaonline.com
semimonthly (Mon.)

**Massachusetts Lawyers Weekly**
Dolan Media
10 Milk St., Suite 1000
Boston, MA 02108
(617) 451-7300
(800) 451-9998
FAX (617) 451-7324
www.masslawyersweekly.com
weekly (Mon.)

**New England In-House**
10 Milk St., Suite 1000
Boston, MA 02108
(800) 451-9998
FAX (617) 451-7324
www.newenglandinhouse.com
bimonthly

## MICHIGAN

**Detroit Legal News**
1409 Allen Rd., #B
Troy, MI 48083
(248) 577-6100
(800) 875-5275
FAX (248) 577-6111
www.legalnews.com
daily (M-F)

**Flint-Genesee County Legal News**
111 W. Young St.
Clio, MI 48420-1341
(810) 686-2080
FAX (810) 686-6850
www.legalnews.com/flint/
weekly (Fri.)

**Grand Rapids Legal News**
1430 Monroe Ave NW, Suite 140
Grand Rapids, MI 49505
(616) 454-9293
FAX (616) 454-9287
www.legalnews.com/grandrapids/
weekly (Wed.)

**Ingham County Legal News**
157 W. Maple St.
Mason, MI 48854
(517) 676-3395
FAX (517) 676-3495
www.legalnews.com/ingham/
weekly

**Jackson County Legal News**
304 Francis St.
P.O. Box 1090
Jackson, MI 49204-1090
(517) 782-0825
FAX (517) 782-4996
www.legalnews.com/jackson/
weekly (Mon.)

**Macomb County Legal News**
148 S. Main Street, Suite 100
Mt. Clemens, MI 48043
(586) 463-4300
FAX (586) 463-4554
www.legalnews.com/macomb/
weekly (Fri.)

**Michigan Lawyers Weekly**
7013 Orchard Lake Rd., Suite 110
West Bloomfield, MI 48322
(800) 678-5297
FAX (248) 865-3118
www.milawyersweekly.com
weekly (Mon.)

**Muskegon County Legal News**
950 W. Norton Ave., Suite 402
Muskegon, WI 49441
(231) 739-6397
FAX (231) 737-1520
www.legalnews.com/muskegon/
weekly

**The Oakland County Legal News**
1409 Allen Rd., #B
Troy, MI 48083-4003
(248) 577-6100
FAX (248) 577-6111
www.legalnews.com/oakland/
weekly (Fri.)

**Washtenaw County Legal News**
2301 Platt Road, Suite 300
Ann Arbor, MI 48104

# LEGAL NEWSPAPERS IN THE UNITED STATES

(734) 477-0201
FAX (734) 477-0345
www.legalnews.com/washtenaw/
weekly

## MINNESOTA

### Finance and Commerce
730 Second Ave. South
Minneapolis, MN 55402
(612) 333-4244
(800) 451-9998
www.finance-commerce.com
(Tues.-Sat.)

### St. Paul Legal Ledger
332 Minnesota St., #E1432
St. Paul, MN 55101-1309
(651) 222-0059
(800) 451-9998
FAX (651) 222-2640
www.legal-ledger.com
(Mon. & Thurs.)

## MISSOURI

### Daily Events
310 W. Walnut
Springfield, MO 65806
(417) 866-1401
FAX (417) 866-1491
www.thedailyevents.com
daily (M-F)

### Daily Record-Kansas City
Missouri Lawyers Media
319 N. Fourth St., 5th fl.
St. Louis,, MO 63102
(314) 421-1880
(800) 451-9998
FAX (314) 621-1913
molawyersmedia.com/
daily

### Missouri Lawyers Weekly
Missouri Lawyers Media
319 N. Fourth St., 5th fl.
St. Louis, MO 63102
(314) 421-1880
(800) 451-9998
FAX (314) 621-1913
molawyersmedia.com/
weekly (Mon.)

### St. Joseph Daily Courier
1020 S. 10th St.

St. Joseph, MO 64503
(816) 279-3441
FAX (816) 279-2091
daily (M-F)

### The Countian- St. Louis County
Missouri Lawyers Media
319 N. Fourth St., 5th fl.
St. Louis,, MO 63102
(314) 421-1880
(800) 451-9998
FAX (314) 621-1913
molawyersmedia.com/
daily

### The Countian- Franklin County
Missouri Lawyers Media
319 N. Fourth St., 5th fl.
St. Louis,, MO 63102
(314) 421-1880
(800) 451-9998
FAX (314) 621-1913
molawyersmedia.com/
weekly (Wed.)

### The Countian- Jefferson County
Missouri Lawyers Media
319 N. Fourth St., 5th fl.
St. Louis,, MO 63102
(314) 421-1880
(800) 451-9998
FAX (314) 621-1913
molawyersmedia.com/
weekly (Fri.)

### St. Charles County Business Record
Missouri Lawyers Media
319 N. Fourth St., 5th fl.
St. Louis,, MO 63102
(314) 421-1880
(800) 451-9998
FAX (314) 621-1913
molawyersmedia.com/
daily

### St. Louis Daily Record
Missouri Lawyers Media
319 N. Fourth St., 5th fl.
St. Louis, MO 63102
((314) 421-1880
(800) 451-9998
FAX (314) 621-1913
molawyersmedia.com/
daily

## NEBRASKA

### Daily Record
3323 Leavenworth St.
Omaha, NE 68105
(402) 345-1303
FAX (402) 345-2351
www.omahadailyrecord.com
daily (M-F)

### Daily Reporter
P.O. Box 5325
Lincoln, NE 68505
(402) 466-8521
FAX (402) 466-6272
daily (M-F)

## NEVADA

### Nevada Daily Legal News
930 S. Fourth Street
Las Vegas, NV 89101
(702) 382-2747
FAX (702) 598-0641
www.nevadalegalnews.com
daily (M-F)

## NEW JERSEY

### Metropolitan Corporate Counsel
1180 Wychwood Rd.
Mountainside, NJ 07092
(908) 654-4840
FAX (908) 654-4068
www.metrocorpcounsel.com
monthly

### New Jersey Law Journal
238 Mulberry Street
Newark, NJ 07101
(973) 642-0075
FAX (973) 642-0920
www.njlj.com
weekly (Mon.)

## NEW YORK

### The American Lawyer
120 Broadway, 5th fl.
New York, NY 10271
(800) 888-8300
FAX (646) 822-5146
www.law.com
monthly

# LEGAL NEWSPAPERS IN THE UNITED STATES

**The Brooklyn Daily Eagle and Daily Bulletin**
30 Henry Street
Brooklyn, NY 11201
(718) 422-7400
www.brooklyneagle.com
daily (M-F)

**Buffalo Law Journal**
465 Main Street
Buffalo, NY 14203-1793
(716) 854-2480
FAX (716) 854-3826
www.lawjournalbuffalo.com
(Mon. & Thurs.)

**The Daily Record**
16 W. Main St.
Rochester, NY 14614
(585) 232-6920
FAX (585) 232-2740
www.nydailyrecord.com
daily (M-F)

**Long Island Business News**
2150 Smithtown Avenue
Ronkonkoma, NY 11779
(631) 737-1700
FAX (631) 737-1890
www.libn.com
weekly (Fri.)

**The National Law Journal & Legal Times**
120 Broadway, 5th fl.
New York, NY 10271
(212) 457-9400
(877) 256-2472
www.nlj.com
weekly (Mon.)

**New York Law Journal**
120 Broadway, 5th fl.
New York, NY 10271
(212) 457-9545
www.nylj.com
daily (M-F)

## NORTH CAROLINA

**Mecklenburg Times**
1611 E. Seventh St.
Charlotte, NC 28204
(704) 377-6221
FAX (704) 377-4258
www.mecktimes.com

(Tues. & Fri.)

**North Carolina Lawyers Weekly**
107 Fayetteville St.Mall, Suite 300
Raleigh, NC 27601
(919) 829-9333
(800) 876-5297
FAX (919) 829-8088
www.nclawyersweekly.com
weekly (Mon.)

## OHIO

**The Akron Legal News**
60 S. Summit Street
Akron, OH 44308
(330) 376-0917
FAX (330) 376-7001
www.akronlegalnews.com
daily (M-F)

**Cincinnati Court Index**
119 W. Central Pkwy.
Cincinnati, OH 45202-1064
(513) 241-1450
FAX (513) 684-7821
www.courtindex.com
daily (M-F)

**Daily Court Reporter**
120 W. Second St.
Dayton, OH 45402
(937) 222-6000
FAX (937) 341-5020
www.dailycourt.com
daily (M-F)

**Daily Legal News**
2935 Prospect Avenue
Cleveland, OH 44115
(216) 696-3322
FAX (216) 696-6329
www.dln.com
(Tues.-Sat.)

**Daily Legal News**
100 Federal Plaza East, Suite 126
Youngstown, OH 44503
(330) 747-7777
FAX (330) 747-3977
www.dlnnews.com
daily (M-F)

**The Daily Reporter**

580 S. High Street, Suite 316
Columbus, OH 43215
(614) 224-4835
FAX (614) 224-8649
www.sourcenews.com
daily (M-F)

## OKLAHOMA

**The Journal Record**
101 N. Robinson Ave., Suite 101
Oklahoma City, OK 73102
(405) 235-3100
FAX (405) 278-2890
www.journalrecord.com
daily

**Tulsa Daily Commerce & Legal News**
20 E. Fifth St., Suite 105
Tulsa, OK 74103
(918) 259-7500
www.tulsabusiness.com
daily (M-F)

## OREGON

**Daily Journal of Commerce**
921 SW Washington St., Suite 210
Portland, OR 97205
(503) 226-1311
FAX (503) 226-1315
djcoregon.com
daily (M-F)

## PENNSYLVANIA

**The Legal Intelligencer**
1617 JFK Blvd., Suite 1750
Philadelphia, PA 19103
(215) 557-2300
FAX (215) 557-2301
www.thelegalintelligencer.com
daily (M-F)

**PaTLA News**
1617 JFK Blvd., Suite 1750
Philadelphia, PA 19103
(215) 557-2300
FAX (215) 557-2301
www.palegalpubs.com
monthly

**Pennsylvania Law Weekly**
1617 JFK Blvd., Suite 1750
Philadelphia, PA 19103

# LEGAL NEWSPAPERS IN THE UNITED STATES

(215) 557-2300
FAX (215) 557-2301
www.law.com/pa
weekly (Mon.)

## Pittsburgh Legal Journal
436 7th Avenue, Suite 400
Pittsburgh, PA 15219-2201
(412) 261-6255
FAX (412) 261-6438
www.pittsburghlegaljournal.org
daily (M-F)

## RHODE ISLAND

### Rhode Island Lawyers Weekly
10 Milk St., Suite 1000
Boston, MA 02108
(617) 451-7300
FAX (617) 451-7324
www.rilawyersweekly.com
weekly (Mon.)

## SOUTH CAROLINA

### South Carolina Lawyers Weekly
701 Gervais St., Suite 150-122
Columbia, SC 29201
(800) 876-5297
FAX (919) 829-8088
www.sclawyersweekly.com
weekly (Mon.)

## TENNESSEE

### The Daily News
193 Jefferson
Memphis, TN 38173
(901) 523-1561
FAX (901) 526-5813
www.memphisdailynews.com
daily (M-F)

### The Nashville Record
1100 Broadway
Nashville, TN 37203
(615) 259-8000
FAX (615) 726-5921
tennessean.com
weekly (Fri.)

## TEXAS

### Collin County Commercial Record
202 W. Louisiana, Suite 202

McKinney, TX 75069
(972) 562-0606
FAX (972) 562-2929
www.collincountycommercialrecord.com
daily (M-F)

### The Commercial Recorder
3032 South Jones Street
Fort Worth, TX 76104-6747
(817) 926-5351
FAX (817) 926-5377
www.commercialrecorder.com
daily (M-F)

### Daily Commercial Record
706 Main St.
Dallas, TX 75202
(214) 741-6366
FAX (214) 741-6373
www.dailycommercialrecord.com
daily (M-F)

### The Daily Commercial Recorder
P.O. Box 2171
San Antonio, TX 78297
(210) 250-2327
FAX (210) 453-3362
www.primetimenewspapers.com/dcr/
daily (M-F)

### Daily Court Review
6807 Wynnwood
Houston, TX 77008-5023
(713) 869-5434
FAX (713) 869-8887
www.dailycourtreview.com
daily (M-F)

### The Texas Lawyer
1412 Main St., Suite 1300
Dallas, TX 75202-4432
(214) 744-9300
FAX (214) 741-2325
www.texaslawyer.com
weekly (Mon.)

## UTAH

### Intermountain Commercial Record/Salt Lake Times
1950 West 1500 South
Salt Lake City, UT 84104-4122
(801) 972-5642

FAX (801) 972-4457
slcrecord.com
weekly (Fri.)

## VIRGINIA

### Virginia Lawyers Weekly
707 E. Main St., Suite 1750
Richmond, VA 23219
(804) 783-0770
(800) 456-5297
FAX (804) 783-8337
www.virginialaw.com
weekly (Mon.)

## WASHINGTON

### Daily Journal of Commerce
83 Columbia Street
Seattle, WA 98104
(206) 622-8272
FAX (206) 622-8416
www.djc.com
(Mon.-Sat.)

### Tacoma Daily Index
P.O. Box 1303
Tacoma, WA 98401
(253) 627-4853
FAX (253) 627-2253
www.tacomadailyindex.com
daily (M-F)

## WISCONSIN

### The Daily Reporter
225 E. Michigan St., Suite 540
Milwaukee, WI 53202
(414) 276-0273
FAX (414) 276-8057
dailyreporter.com
daily (M-F)

### Wisconsin Law Journal
225 E. Michigan St., Suite 540
Milwaukee, WI 53202
(414) 276-0273
FAX (414) 276-8057
www.wislawjournal.com
weekly

# LEGAL NEWSPAPERS ONLINE ON WESTLAW AND LEXISNEXIS

| WESTLAW | File Name | Coverage Dates |
|---|---|---|
| Daily Record (Baltimore) | DAILYREC | 8/91-4/99 |
| Daily Record (Rochester, NY) | DAILRECNY | |
| Daily Record (St. Louis) | DAILYRECMO | |
| Daily Reporter (Milwaukee) | DAIL-REPT | 8/88- |
| Inside Counsel | INCOUN | 1/06- |
| Journal Record (Oklahoma City) | JROKC | 1/85- |
| Kansas City Daily Record | DLYRECORDKC | |
| Mass. Lawyers Weekly | MASSLAWWKLY | |
| Merrill's Illinois Legal Times | ILLT | 1/90-8/99 |
| Metropolitan Corporate Counsel | METCC | 2/97- |
| Miami Daily Business Review | MIAMIDBR | 1/98- |
| Michigan Lawyers Weekly | MICHLAWWKLY | |
| Missouri Law Weekly | MOLAWWKLY | |
| New Jersey Lawyer | NJLNP | 11/96- |
| North Carolina Law Weekly | NCLAWWKLY | |
| Rhode Island Lawyers Weekly | RILAWWKLY | |
| South Carolina Lawyers  Weekly | SCLAWWKLY | |
| St. Paul Legal ledger | STPAULLEGLED | |
| Virginia Lawyers Weekly | VALAWWKLY | |
| Wisconsin Law Journal | WISCLAWJ | |

| LEXISNEXIS | | |
|---|---|---|
| Daily Record (Baltimore) | DLYREC | 3/95- |
| Daily Reporter (Milwaukee) | DLYREP | 3/01- |
| Illinois Legal Times | ILT | 1/90-8/99 |
| Indiana Lawyer | INLAWR | 11/94- |
| Inside Counsel | CORPLT | 12/91- |
| Kansas City Daily Record | KCDREC | 3/02-end |
| Lawyers USA | LWYWKU | 1/03- |
| The Legal Ledger | LEGLED | 3/01- |
| Massachusetts Lawyers Weekly | MALAWW | 1/04- |
| Metropolitan Corporate Counsel | MCC | 7/95-1/06 |
| Metropolitan News Enterprise | METNWS | 7/95-8/07 |
| Michigan Lawyers Weekly | MILAWW | 1/04- |
| Minnesota Lawyer | MINLAW | 3/01- |
| Missouri Lawyers Media | MOLAWW | 1/04- |
| North Carolina Lawyers Weekly | NCLAWW | 1/04- |
| Rhode Island Lawyers Weekly | RILAWW | 1/04- |
| South Carolina Lawyers Weekly | SCLAWW | 1/04- |
| St. Louis Daily Record / St. Louis Countian | SLDREC | 3/01-3/09 |
| Virginia Lawyers Weekly | VALAWW | 1/04- |

# FINANCIAL AND ECONOMIC INFORMATION

## STOCK AND COMMODITY EXCHANGES IN THE U.S. AND CANADA

### U.S. EXCHANGES

American Stock Exchange
see NYSE Euronext

Boston Stock Exchange
see NASDAQ

Chicago Board Options Exchange
400 S. LaSalle St.
Chicago, IL 60605
(312) 786-5600
(877) THE-CBOE
www.cboe.com

Chicago Stock Exchange
One Financial Place
440 South LaSalle St.
Chicago, IL 60605
(312) 663-2222
www.chx.com

CME Group
20 South Wacker Drive
Chicago, IL 60606
(312) 930-1000
or
World Financial Center
One North End Ave.
New York, NY 10282
(212) 299-2000
(800) 438-8616
www.cmegroup.com

Intercontinental Exchange (ICE)
World Financial Center
One North End Ave.
New York, NY 10282
(212) 748-4000
www.theice.com

Kansas City Board of Trade
4800 Main Street, Suite 303
Kansas City, MO 64112
(816) 753-7500
FAX (816) 753-3944
www.kcbt.com

Minneapolis Grain Exchange
400 South 4th Street
Minneapolis, MN 55415
(612) 321-7101
(800) 827-4746
www.mgex.com

NASDAQ Stock Market
165 Broadway
New York, NY 10006
(212) 401-8700
www.nasdaq.com

National Stock Exchange
440 S. LaSalle St., Suite 2600
Chicago, IL 60605
(312) 786-8803
FAX (312) 939-7239
www.nsx.com

New Orleans Board of Trade
316 Board of Trade Place
New Orleans, LA 70130
(504) 525-3271
FAX (504) 525-9039
www.nobot.org

New York Mercantile Exchange,
  Inc.
see CME Group

NFX Nasdaq Futures Exchange
1900 Market St.
Philadelphia, PA 19103
(215) 496-5000
www.nasdaqomxtrader.com

NYSE Euronext (NYX)
11 Wall Street
New York, NY 10005
(212) 656-3000
www.nyse.com

Philadelphia Board of Trade
see NFX NASDAQ Futures
Exchange

Philadelphia Stock Exchange
see NASDAQ

### CANADIAN EXCHANGES

ICE Futures Canada
850A Pembina Hwy.
Winnipeg, Manitoba R3M 2M7
(204) 925-5000
FAX (204) 943-5448
www.theice.com

Montreal Stock Exchange
800 Victoria Square
Montreal, Quebec H4Z 1A9
(514) 871-2424
(800) 361-5353
FAX (514) 871-3514
www.m-x.ca

Toronto Stock Exchange
130 King St. West, 3rd fl.
P.O. Box 450
Toronto, Ontario M5X 1J2
(416) 947-4670
(888) 873-8392
FAX (416) 947-4662
www.tmx.com

TSX Venture Exchange, Inc.
300 5th Avenue SW, 10th fl.
Calgary, Alberta T2P 3C4
(403) 218-2800
www.tsx.com

Winnipeg Commodity Exchange,
  Inc.
see ICE Futures Canada

# TABLE OF PRIME RATE CHANGES SINCE 1929

| | | | | | |
|---|---|---|---|---|---|
| 1929 | 5.50-6.00 | 11/04/71 | 5.50 | 02/18/75 | 8.75 |
| 1930 | 3.50-6.00 | 12/31/71 | 5.25 | 02/24/75 | 8.50 |
| 1931 | 2.25-5.00 | 01/24/72 | 5.00 | 03/05/75 | 8.25 |
| 1932 | 3.25-4.00 | 01/31/72 | 4.75 | 03/10/75 | 8.00 |
| 1933 | 1.50-4.00 | 04/05/72 | 5.00 | 03/18/75 | 7.75 |
| 1934-11/47 | 1.50 | 06/26/72 | 5.25 | 03/24/75 | 7.50 |
| 12/47 | 1.75 | 08/29/72 | 5.50 | 05/20/75 | 7.25 |
| 8/48 | 2.00 | 10/04/72 | 5.75 | 06/09/75 | 7.00 |
| 09/22/50 | 2.25 | 12/27/72 | 6.00 | 07/18/75 | 7.25 |
| 01/08/51 | 2.50 | 01/27/73 | 6.25 | 07/28/75 | 7.50 |
| 10/17/51 | 2.75 | 03/26/73 | 6.50 | 08/12/75 | 7.75 |
| 12/19/51 | 3.00 | 04/18/73 | 6.75 | 09/15/75 | 8.00 |
| 04/27/53 | 3.25 | 05/07/73 | 7.00 | 09/27/75 | 7.75 |
| 03/17/54 | 3.00 | 05/25/73 | 7.25 | 10/05/75 | 7.50 |
| 08/04/55 | 3.25 | 06/08/73 | 7.50 | 10/27/75 | 7.75 |
| 10/14/55 | 3.50 | 06/25/73 | 7.75 | 11/05/75 | 7.50 |
| 04/13/56 | 3.75 | 07/03/73 | 8.00 | 12/02/75 | 7.25 |
| 08/21/56 | 4.00 | 07/09/73 | 8.25 | 01/12/76 | 7.00 |
| 08/06/57 | 4.50 | 07/18/73 | 8.50 | 01/21/76 | 6.75 |
| 01/22/58 | 4.00 | 07/30/73 | 8.75 | 06/01/76 | 6.75 |
| 04/21/58 | 3.50 | 08/06/73 | 9.00 | 06/07/76 | 7.25 |
| 09/11/58 | 4.00 | 08/13/73 | 9.25 | 08/02/76 | 7.00 |
| 05/18/59 | 4.50 | 08/22/73 | 9.50 | 10/04/76 | 6.75 |
| 09/01/59 | 5.00 | 08/28/73 | 9.75 | 11/01/76 | 6.50 |
| 08/23/60 | 4.50 | 09/18/73 | 10.00 | 12/13/76 | 6.25 |
| 12/06/65 | 5.00 | 10/24/73 | 9.75 | 05/13/77 | 6.50 |
| 03/10/66 | 5.50 | 01/29/74 | 9.50 | 05/31/77 | 6.75 |
| 06/29/66 | 5.75 | 02/11/74 | 9.25 | 08/22/77 | 7.00 |
| 08/16/66 | 6.00 | 02/19/74 | 9.00 | 09/16/77 | 7.25 |
| 01/26/67 | 5.50-5.75 | 02/25/74 | 8.75 | 10/07/77 | 7.50 |
| 03/27/67 | 5.50 | 03/22/74 | 9.00 | 10/24/77 | 7.75 |
| 11/20/67 | 6.00 | 03/29/74 | 9.25 | 01/10/78 | 8.00 |
| 04/19/68 | 6.50 | 04/03/74 | 9.50 | 05/05/78 | 8.25 |
| 09/25/68 | 6.00-6.25 | 04/05/74 | 9.75 | 05/26/78 | 8.50 |
| 11/13/68 | 6.25 | 04/11/74 | 10.00 | 06/16/78 | 8.75 |
| 12/02/68 | 6.50 | 04/19/74 | 10.25 | 06/30/78 | 9.00 |
| 12/18/68 | 6.75 | 04/25/74 | 10.50 | 08/31/78 | 9.25 |
| 01/07/69 | 7.00 | 05/02/74 | 10.75 | 09/15/78 | 9.50 |
| 03/17/69 | 7.50 | 05/06/74 | 11.00 | 09/28/78 | 9.75 |
| 06/09/69 | 8.50 | 05/10/74 | 11.25 | 10/13/78 | 10.00 |
| 08/25/70 | 8.00 | 05/17/74 | 11.50 | 10/27/78 | 10.25 |
| 09/21/70 | 7.50 | 06/26/74 | 11.75 | 11/01/78 | 10.50 |
| 11/12/70 | 7.25 | 07/05/74 | 12.00 | 11/06/78 | 10.75 |
| 11/23/70 | 7.00 | 10/01/74 | 11.75 | 11/17/78 | 11.00 |
| 12/22/70 | 6.75 | 10/21/74 | 11.50 | 11/24/78 | 11.50 |
| 01/06/71 | 6.50 | 10/28/74 | 11.25 | 12/26/78 | 11.75 |
| 01/15/71 | 6.25 | 11/04/74 | 11.00 | 06/19/79 | 11.50 |
| 01/18/71 | 6.00 | 11/14/74 | 10.75 | 07/27/79 | 11.75 |
| 02/16/71 | 5.75 | 11/25/74 | 10.50 | 08/16/79 | 12.00 |
| 03/11/71 | 5.38 | 01/09/75 | 10.25 | 08/28/79 | 12.25 |
| 03/19/71 | 5.25 | 01/15/75 | 10.00 | 09/07/79 | 12.75 |
| 04/23/71 | 5.38 | 01/20/75 | 9.75 | 09/14/79 | 13.00 |
| 05/11/71 | 5.50 | 01/28/75 | 9.50 | 09/21/79 | 13.25 |
| 07/06/71 | 6.00 | 02/03/75 | 9.25 | 09/28/79 | 13.50 |
| 10/20/71 | 5.75 | 02/10/75 | 9.00 | 10/09/79 | 14.50 |

# TABLE OF PRIME RATE CHANGES SINCE 1929

| Date | Rate | Date | Rate | Date | Rate |
|---|---|---|---|---|---|
| 10/23/79 | 15.00 | 06/03/81 | 18.00 | 06/05/89 | 11.00 |
| 11/01/79 | 15.25 | 06/16/81 | 19.00 | 07/31/89 | 10.50 |
| 11/09/79 | 15.50 | 06/22/81 | 19.50 | 01/08/90 | 10.00 |
| 11/16/79 | 15.75 | 07/08/81 | 20.50 | 01/02/91 | 9.50 |
| 11/30/79 | 15.50 | 08/31/81 | 20.00 | 02/04/91 | 9.00 |
| 12/07/79 | 15.25 | 09/21/81 | 19.50 | 05/01/91 | 8.50 |
| 12/14/79 | 15.00 | 10/05/81 | 19.00 | 09/13/91 | 8.00 |
| 02/19/80 | 15.75 | 10/13/81 | 18.00 | 11/06/91 | 7.50 |
| 02/22/80 | 16.25 | 11/03/81 | 17.50 | 12/23/91 | 6.50 |
| 02/29/80 | 16.75 | 11/09/81 | 17.00 | 07/02/92 | 6.00 |
| 03/04/80 | 17.25 | 11/20/81 | 16.50 | 03/24/94 | 6.25 |
| 03/07/80 | 17.75 | 11/24/81 | 16.00 | 04/19/94 | 6.75 |
| 03/14/80 | 18.50 | 12/01/81 | 15.75 | 05/17/94 | 7.25 |
| 03/19/80 | 19.00 | 02/02/82 | 16.50 | 08/16/94 | 7.75 |
| 03/28/80 | 19.50 | 02/18/82 | 17.00 | 11/15/94 | 8.50 |
| 04/02/80 | 20.00 | 02/23/82 | 16.50 | 02/01/95 | 9.00 |
| 04/18/80 | 19.50 | 07/20/82 | 16.00 | 07/07/95 | 8.75 |
| 05/01/80 | 19.00 | 07/29/82 | 15.50 | 12/20/95 | 8.50 |
| 05/02/80 | 18.50 | 08/02/82 | 15.00 | 02/01/96 | 8.25 |
| 05/07/80 | 17.50 | 08/16/82 | 14.50 | 03/26/97 | 8.50 |
| 05/16/80 | 16.50 | 08/18/82 | 14.00 | 09/30/98 | 8.25 |
| 05/23/80 | 14.50 | 08/23/82 | 13.50 | 10/16/98 | 8.00 |
| 05/30/80 | 14.00 | 10/07/82 | 13.00 | 11/18/98 | 7.75 |
| 06/06/80 | 13.00 | 10/13/82 | 12.00 | 07/01/99 | 8.00 |
| 06/12/80 | 12.50 | 11/22/82 | 11.50 | 08/25/99 | 8.25 |
| 06/20/80 | 12.00 | 01/11/83 | 11.00 | 11/17/99 | 8.50 |
| 07/07/80 | 11.50 | 02/28/83 | 10.50 | 02/03/00 | 8.75 |
| 07/25/80 | 11.00 | 08/08/83 | 11.00 | 03/22/00 | 9.00 |
| 08/22/80 | 11.25 | 03/19/84 | 11.50 | 05/17/00 | 9.50 |
| 08/27/80 | 11.50 | 04/05/84 | 12.00 | 01/04/01 | 9.00 |
| 09/08/80 | 12.00 | 05/08/84 | 12.50 | 02/01/01 | 8.50 |
| 09/12/80 | 12.25 | 06/25/84 | 13.00 | 03/21/01 | 8.00 |
| 09/19/80 | 12.50 | 09/27/84 | 12.75 | 04/19/01 | 7.50 |
| 09/26/80 | 13.00 | 10/17/84 | 12.50 | 05/16/01 | 7.00 |
| 10/01/80 | 13.50 | 10/29/84 | 12.00 | 06/28/01 | 6.75 |
| 10/17/80 | 14.00 | 11/09/84 | 11.75 | 08/22/01 | 6.50 |
| 10/29/80 | 14.50 | 11/28/84 | 11.25 | 09/18/01 | 6.00 |
| 11/06/80 | 15.50 | 12/20/84 | 10.75 | 10/03/01 | 5.50 |
| 11/17/80 | 16.25 | 01/15/85 | 10.50 | 11/07/01 | 5.00 |
| 11/21/80 | 17.00 | 05/20/85 | 10.00 | 12/12/01 | 4.75 |
| 11/26/80 | 17.75 | 06/18/85 | 9.50 | 11/07/02 | 4.25 |
| 12/02/80 | 18.50 | 03/07/86 | 9.00 | 06/27/03 | 4.00 |
| 12/05/80 | 19.00 | 04/21/86 | 8.50 | 07/01/04 | 4.25 |
| 12/10/80 | 20.00 | 07/11/86 | 8.00 | 08/11/04 | 4.50 |
| 12/16/80 | 21.00 | 08/26/86 | 7.50 | 09/21/04 | 4.75 |
| 12/19/80 | 21.50 | 04/01/87 | 7.75 | 11/10/04 | 5.00 |
| 01/02/81 | 20.50 | 05/01/87 | 8.00 | 12/15/04 | 5.25 |
| 01/09/81 | 20.00 | 05/15/87 | 8.25 | 02/03/05 | 5.50 |
| 02/03/81 | 19.50 | 09/04/87 | 8.75 | 03/22/05 | 5.75 |
| 02/23/81 | 19.00 | 10/07/87 | 9.25 | 05/03/05 | 6.00 |
| 03/10/81 | 18.00 | 10/22/87 | 9.00 | 06/30/05 | 6.25 |
| 03/17/81 | 17.50 | 11/05/87 | 8.75 | 08/09/05 | 6.50 |
| 04/02/81 | 17.00 | 02/02/88 | 8.50 | 09/20/05 | 6.75 |
| 04/21/81 | 20.00 | 05/11/88 | 9.00 | 11/01/05 | 7.00 |
| 04/30/81 | 20.50 | 07/14/88 | 9.50 | 12/13/05 | 7.25 |
| 05/04/81 | 20.00 | 08/11/88 | 10.00 | 1/31/06 | 7.50 |
| 05/11/81 | 19.50 | 11/28/88 | 10.50 | 3/28/06 | 7.75 |
| 05/19/81 | 20.00 | 02/10/89 | 11.00 | 5/10/06 | 8.00 |
| 05/26/81 | 17.50 | 02/24/89 | 11.50 | 6/29/06 | 8.25 |

# TABLE OF PRIME RATE CHANGES SINCE 1929

| | |
|---|---|
| 06/29/06 | 8.25 |
| 09/18/07 | 7.75 |
| 10/31/07 | 7.50 |
| 12/11/07 | 7.25 |
| 01/22/08 | 6.50 |
| 01/30/08 | 6.00 |
| 03/18/08 | 5.25 |
| 04/30/08 | 5.00 |
| 10/08/08 | 4.50 |
| 10/29/08 | 4.00 |
| 12/16/08 | 3.25 |

# CONSUMER PRICE INDEX

U.S. Department of Labor
Bureau of Labor Statistics
Washington, D.C. 20212

Consumer Price Index

Urban Wage Earners and Clerical Workers - (CPI-W)

All items

U.S. city average

1982-84=100

| YEAR | JAN. | FEB. | MAR. | APR. | MAY | JUNE | JULY | AUG. | SEP. | OCT. | NOV. | DEC. | SEMIANNUAL 1ST HALF | SEMIANNUAL 2ND HALF | AVG. | PERCENT CHANGE DEC-DEC | PERCENT CHANGE AVG-AVG |
|---|---|---|---|---|---|---|---|---|---|---|---|---|---|---|---|---|---|
| 1970 | 38.0 | 38.2 | 38.4 | 38.7 | 38.8 | 39.0 | 39.2 | 39.2 | 39.4 | 39.6 | 39.8 | 40.0 | | | 39.0 | 5.5 | 5.7 |
| 1971 | 40.0 | 40.1 | 40.2 | 40.4 | 40.6 | 40.8 | 40.9 | 41.0 | 41.1 | 41.1 | 41.2 | 41.3 | | | 40.7 | 3.3 | 4.4 |
| 1972 | 41.4 | 41.6 | 41.6 | 41.7 | 41.9 | 42.0 | 42.1 | 42.2 | 42.5 | 42.5 | 42.6 | 42.7 | | | 42.1 | 3.4 | 3.3 |
| 1973 | 42.9 | 43.2 | 43.6 | 43.9 | 44.1 | 44.4 | 44.4 | 45.0 | 45.4 | 45.5 | 46.2 | 46.5 | | | 44.7 | 8.9 | 6.2 |
| 1974 | 46.9 | 47.5 | 48.0 | 48.3 | 48.8 | 49.3 | 49.7 | 50.3 | 50.9 | 51.4 | 51.8 | 52.2 | | | 49.6 | 12.3 | 11.0 |
| 1975 | 52.4 | 52.8 | 53.0 | 53.2 | 53.5 | 53.9 | 54.5 | 54.9 | 55.3 | 55.3 | 55.6 | 55.8 | | | 54.1 | 6.9 | 9.1 |
| 1976 | 56.0 | 56.1 | 56.2 | 56.5 | 56.8 | 57.1 | 57.4 | 57.7 | 57.9 | 58.2 | 58.3 | 58.5 | | | 57.2 | 4.8 | 5.7 |
| 1977 | 58.9 | 59.5 | 59.8 | 60.3 | 60.6 | 61.0 | 61.3 | 61.8 | 61.8 | 61.9 | 62.2 | 62.5 | | | 60.9 | 6.8 | 6.5 |
| 1978 | 62.8 | 63.2 | 63.7 | 64.3 | 64.9 | 65.6 | 66.0 | 66.4 | 66.8 | 67.4 | 67.7 | 68.1 | | | 65.6 | 9.0 | 7.7 |
| 1979 | 68.7 | 69.5 | 70.3 | 71.1 | 71.9 | 72.8 | 73.7 | 74.4 | 75.1 | 75.7 | 76.4 | 77.2 | | | 73.1 | 13.3 | 11.4 |
| 1980 | 78.3 | 79.4 | 80.5 | 81.4 | 82.3 | 83.2 | 83.3 | 83.8 | 84.6 | 85.3 | 86.1 | 86.9 | | | 82.9 | 12.6 | 13.4 |
| 1981 | 87.5 | 88.5 | 89.0 | 89.6 | 90.3 | 91.1 | 92.2 | 92.8 | 93.7 | 93.9 | 94.4 | 94.4 | | | 91.4 | 8.6 | 10.3 |
| 1982 | 94.7 | 95.1 | 94.8 | 95.2 | 96.2 | 97.4 | 98.0 | 98.3 | 98.3 | 98.6 | 98.0 | 98.0 | | | 96.9 | 3.8 | 6.0 |
| 1983 | 98.1 | 98.1 | 98.8 | 99.0 | 99.5 | 99.8 | 100.1 | 100.5 | 101.0 | 101.2 | 101.2 | 101.2 | | | 99.8 | 3.3 | 3.0 |
| 1984 | 101.6 | 101.8 | 101.8 | 102.1 | 102.5 | 102.8 | 103.2 | 104.2 | 104.8 | 104.8 | 104.7 | 104.8 | 102.1 | 104.4 | 103.3 | 3.6 | 3.5 |
| 1985 | 104.9 | 105.4 | 105.9 | 106.3 | 106.7 | 107.0 | 107.1 | 107.6 | 107.6 | 107.9 | 108.3 | 108.6 | 106.0 | 107.8 | 106.9 | 3.6 | 3.5 |
| 1986 | 108.9 | 108.5 | 107.9 | 107.6 | 107.9 | 108.4 | 108.4 | 108.6 | 109.1 | 109.1 | 109.2 | 109.3 | 108.2 | 109.0 | 108.6 | 0.6 | 1.6 |
| 1987 | 110.5 | 110.5 | 111.0 | 111.6 | 111.9 | 112.4 | 112.7 | 113.3 | 113.8 | 114.1 | 114.3 | 114.2 | 111.2 | 113.7 | 112.5 | 4.5 | 3.6 |
| 1988 | 114.5 | 114.7 | 115.1 | 115.7 | 116.2 | 116.7 | 117.2 | 117.5 | 118.5 | 118.9 | 119.0 | 119.2 | 115.5 | 118.4 | 117.0 | 4.4 | 4.0 |
| 1989 | 119.7 | 120.2 | 120.8 | 121.8 | 122.5 | 122.8 | 123.2 | 123.5 | 123.8 | 124.2 | 124.6 | 124.6 | 121.3 | 123.9 | 122.6 | 4.5 | 4.8 |
| 1990 | 125.9 | 126.4 | 127.0 | 127.3 | 127.5 | 128.3 | 128.7 | 129.9 | 131.1 | 131.9 | 132.2 | 132.2 | 127.1 | 131.0 | 129.0 | 6.1 | 5.2 |
| 1991 | 132.8 | 132.8 | 133.0 | 133.3 | 133.8 | 134.1 | 134.3 | 134.6 | 135.2 | 135.5 | 135.9 | 135.9 | 133.3 | 135.2 | 134.3 | 2.8 | 4.1 |
| 1992 | 136.0 | 136.4 | 137.0 | 137.3 | 137.6 | 138.1 | 138.4 | 139.1 | 139.1 | 139.6 | 139.8 | 139.8 | 137.1 | 139.3 | 138.2 | 2.9 | 2.9 |
| 1993 | 140.3 | 140.7 | 141.1 | 141.6 | 141.9 | 142.0 | 142.1 | 142.6 | 142.6 | 143.3 | 143.4 | 143.3 | 141.3 | 142.9 | 142.1 | 2.5 | 2.8 |
| 1994 | 143.6 | 144.0 | 144.4 | 144.7 | 144.9 | 145.4 | 145.8 | 146.5 | 146.9 | 147.0 | 147.3 | 147.2 | 144.3 | 146.8 | 145.6 | 2.7 | 2.5 |
| 1995 | 147.8 | 148.3 | 148.7 | 149.3 | 149.6 | 149.9 | 150.2 | 150.6 | 151.0 | 151.0 | 150.9 | 150.9 | 148.9 | 150.6 | 149.8 | 2.5 | 2.9 |
| 1996 | 151.7 | 152.2 | 152.9 | 153.6 | 154.0 | 154.1 | 154.3 | 154.5 | 155.1 | 155.5 | 155.9 | 155.9 | 153.1 | 155.3 | 154.1 | | |
| 1997 | 156.3 | 156.8 | 157.0 | 157.2 | 157.2 | 157.4 | 157.5 | 157.8 | 158.3 | 158.5 | 158.5 | 158.2 | | | 157.6 | | |
| 1998 | 158.4 | 158.5 | 158.7 | 159.1 | 159.5 | 159.7 | 159.8 | 160.0 | 160.2 | 160.6 | 160.7 | 160.7 | | | 159.7 | | |
| 1999 | 161.0 | 161.1 | 161.4 | 162.7 | 162.8 | 162.8 | 163.3 | 163.8 | 164.7 | 165.0 | 165.1 | 165.1 | | | 163.2 | | |
| 2000 | 165.6 | 166.5 | 167.9 | 168.0 | 168.2 | 169.2 | 169.4 | 169.3 | 170.8 | 170.8 | 170.9 | 170.7 | | | 168.9 | | |
| 2001 | 171.7 | 172.4 | 172.6 | 173.5 | 174.4 | 174.6 | 173.8 | 173.8 | 174.0 | 174.0 | 173.7 | 172.9 | | | 173.5 | | |
| 2002 | 173.2 | 173.7 | 174.7 | 175.8 | 175.8 | 175.9 | 176.1 | 176.6 | 177.0 | 177.3 | 177.4 | 177.0 | | | 175.9 | | |
| 2003 | 177.7 | 179.2 | 180.3 | 179.8 | 179.4 | 179.6 | 179.6 | 180.3 | 181.0 | 180.7 | 180.2 | 179.9 | | | 179.5 | | |
| 2004 | 180.9 | 181.9 | 182.9 | 183.5 | 184.7 | 185.3 | 184.9 | 185.0 | 185.4 | 186.5 | 186.8 | 186.0 | | | 184.5 | | |
| 2005 | 186.3 | 187.3 | 188.6 | 190.2 | 190.0 | 190.1 | 191.0 | 192.1 | 195.0 | 195.2 | 193.4 | 192.5 | | | 190.975 | | |
| 2006 | 194.2 | 194.2 | 195.3 | 197.2 | 198.2 | 198.6 | 199.2 | 199.6 | 198.4 | 197.0 | 196.8 | 197.2 | | | 197.142 | | |
| 2007 | 197.559 | 198.544 | 200.612 | 202.130 | 203.661 | 203.906 | 203.700 | 203.199 | 203.889 | 204.338 | 205.891 | 205.777 | | | 202.767 | | |
| 2008 | 206.744 | 207.254 | 209.147 | 210.698 | 212.788 | 215.223 | 216.304 | 215.247 | 214.935 | 212.182 | 207.296 | 204.813 | | | 211.053 | | |
| 2009 | 205.700 | 206.708 | 207.218 | 207.925 | 208.774 | 210.972 | 210.526 | 211.156 | 211.322 | 211.549 | 212.003 | 211.703 | | | 209.630 | | |
| 2010 | 212.568 | 212.544 | 213.525 | 213.958 | 214.124 | 213.839 | 213.898 | 214.205 | 214.306 | 214.623 | 214.750 | 215.262 | | | 213.967 | | |
| 2011 | 216.400 | 217.535 | 219.024 | 221.743 | | | | | | | | | | | | | |

# CONSUMER PRICE INDEX

Bureau of Labor Statistics
Washington, D.C. 20212

Consumer Price Index

All Urban Consumers - (CPI-U)

U.S. city average

All items

1982-84=100

| YEAR | JAN. | FEB. | MAR. | APR. | MAY | JUNE | JULY | AUG. | SEP. | OCT. | NOV. | DEC. | SEMIANNUAL 1ST HALF | SEMIANNUAL 2ND HALF | AVG. | PERCENT CHANGE DEC-DEC | PERCENT CHANGE AVG-AVG |
|---|---|---|---|---|---|---|---|---|---|---|---|---|---|---|---|---|---|
| 1970 | 37.8 | 38.0 | 38.2 | 38.5 | 38.6 | 38.8 | 39.0 | 39.0 | 39.2 | 39.4 | 39.6 | 39.8 | | | 38.8 | 5.6 | 5.7 |
| 1971 | 39.8 | 39.9 | 40.0 | 40.1 | 40.3 | 40.6 | 40.7 | 40.8 | 40.8 | 40.9 | 40.9 | 41.1 | | | 40.5 | 3.3 | 4.4 |
| 1972 | 41.1 | 41.3 | 41.4 | 41.5 | 41.6 | 41.7 | 41.9 | 42.0 | 42.1 | 42.3 | 42.4 | 42.5 | | | 41.8 | 3.4 | 3.2 |
| 1973 | 42.6 | 42.9 | 43.3 | 43.6 | 43.9 | 44.2 | 44.3 | 45.1 | 45.2 | 45.6 | 45.9 | 46.2 | | | 44.4 | 8.7 | 6.2 |
| 1974 | 46.6 | 47.2 | 47.8 | 48.0 | 48.6 | 49.0 | 49.4 | 50.0 | 50.6 | 51.1 | 51.5 | 51.9 | | | 49.3 | 12.3 | 11.0 |
| 1975 | 52.1 | 52.5 | 52.7 | 52.9 | 53.2 | 53.6 | 54.2 | 54.3 | 54.6 | 54.9 | 55.3 | 55.5 | | | 53.8 | 6.9 | 9.1 |
| 1976 | 55.6 | 55.8 | 55.9 | 56.1 | 56.5 | 56.8 | 57.1 | 57.4 | 57.6 | 57.9 | 58.0 | 58.2 | | | 56.9 | 4.9 | 5.8 |
| 1977 | 58.5 | 59.1 | 59.5 | 60.0 | 60.3 | 60.7 | 61.0 | 61.2 | 61.4 | 61.6 | 61.9 | 62.1 | | | 60.6 | 6.7 | 6.5 |
| 1978 | 62.5 | 62.9 | 63.4 | 63.9 | 64.5 | 65.2 | 65.7 | 66.0 | 66.5 | 67.1 | 67.4 | 67.7 | | | 65.2 | 9.0 | 7.6 |
| 1979 | 68.3 | 69.1 | 69.8 | 70.6 | 71.5 | 72.3 | 73.1 | 73.8 | 74.6 | 75.2 | 75.9 | 76.7 | | | 72.6 | 13.3 | 11.3 |
| 1980 | 77.8 | 78.9 | 80.1 | 81.0 | 81.8 | 82.7 | 82.7 | 83.3 | 84.0 | 84.8 | 85.5 | 86.3 | | | 82.4 | 12.5 | 13.5 |
| 1981 | 87.0 | 87.9 | 88.5 | 89.1 | 89.8 | 90.6 | 91.6 | 92.3 | 93.2 | 93.4 | 93.7 | 94.0 | | | 90.9 | 8.9 | 10.3 |
| 1982 | 94.3 | 94.6 | 94.5 | 94.9 | 95.8 | 97.0 | 97.5 | 97.7 | 97.9 | 98.2 | 98.0 | 97.6 | | | 96.5 | 3.8 | 6.2 |
| 1983 | 97.8 | 97.9 | 97.9 | 98.6 | 99.2 | 99.5 | 99.9 | 100.2 | 100.7 | 101.0 | 101.2 | 101.3 | | | 99.6 | 3.8 | 3.2 |
| 1984 | 101.9 | 102.4 | 102.6 | 103.1 | 103.4 | 103.7 | 104.1 | 104.5 | 105.0 | 105.3 | 105.3 | 105.3 | 102.9 | 104.9 | 103.9 | 3.9 | 4.3 |
| 1985 | 105.5 | 106.0 | 106.4 | 106.9 | 107.3 | 107.6 | 107.8 | 108.0 | 108.3 | 108.7 | 109.0 | 109.3 | 106.6 | 108.5 | 107.6 | 3.8 | 3.6 |
| 1986 | 109.6 | 109.3 | 108.8 | 108.6 | 108.9 | 109.5 | 109.5 | 109.7 | 110.2 | 110.3 | 110.4 | 110.5 | 109.1 | 110.1 | 109.6 | 1.1 | 1.9 |
| 1987 | 111.2 | 111.6 | 112.1 | 112.7 | 113.1 | 113.5 | 113.8 | 114.4 | 115.0 | 115.3 | 115.4 | 115.4 | 112.4 | 114.9 | 113.6 | 4.4 | 3.6 |
| 1988 | 115.7 | 116.0 | 116.5 | 117.1 | 117.5 | 118.0 | 118.5 | 119.0 | 119.8 | 120.2 | 120.3 | 120.5 | 116.8 | 119.3 | 118.3 | 4.4 | 4.1 |
| 1989 | 121.1 | 121.6 | 122.3 | 123.1 | 123.8 | 124.1 | 124.4 | 124.6 | 125.0 | 125.6 | 125.9 | 126.1 | 122.7 | 125.3 | 124.0 | 4.6 | 4.8 |
| 1990 | 127.4 | 128.0 | 128.7 | 128.9 | 129.2 | 129.9 | 130.4 | 131.6 | 132.7 | 133.5 | 133.8 | 133.8 | 128.7 | 132.6 | 130.7 | 6.1 | 5.4 |
| 1991 | 134.6 | 134.8 | 135.0 | 135.2 | 135.6 | 136.0 | 136.2 | 136.6 | 137.2 | 137.4 | 137.8 | 137.9 | 135.2 | 137.2 | 136.2 | 3.1 | 4.2 |
| 1992 | 138.1 | 138.6 | 139.3 | 139.5 | 139.7 | 140.2 | 140.5 | 140.9 | 141.3 | 141.8 | 142.0 | 141.9 | 139.2 | 141.4 | 140.3 | 2.9 | 3.0 |
| 1993 | 142.6 | 143.1 | 143.6 | 144.0 | 144.2 | 144.4 | 144.4 | 144.8 | 145.1 | 145.7 | 145.8 | 145.8 | 143.7 | 145.3 | 144.5 | 2.7 | 3.0 |
| 1994 | 146.2 | 146.7 | 147.2 | 147.4 | 147.5 | 148.0 | 148.4 | 149.0 | 149.4 | 149.5 | 149.7 | 149.7 | 147.2 | 149.3 | 148.2 | 2.7 | 2.6 |
| 1995 | 150.3 | 150.9 | 151.4 | 151.9 | 152.2 | 152.5 | 152.5 | 152.9 | 153.2 | 153.7 | 153.6 | 153.5 | 151.5 | 153.2 | 152.4 | 2.5 | 2.8 |
| 1996 | 154.4 | 154.9 | 155.7 | 156.3 | 156.6 | 156.7 | 157.0 | 157.3 | 157.8 | 158.3 | 158.6 | 158.6 | 155.8 | 157.9 | 156.9 | 3.3 | 3.0 |
| 1997 | 159.1 | 159.6 | 160.0 | 160.2 | 160.1 | 160.3 | 160.5 | 160.8 | 161.2 | 161.6 | 161.5 | 161.3 | 159.9 | 161.2 | 160.5 | | |
| 1998 | 161.6 | 161.9 | 162.2 | 162.5 | 162.8 | 163.0 | 163.2 | 163.4 | 163.6 | 164.0 | 164.0 | 163.9 | 162.3 | 163.7 | 163.0 | | |
| 1999 | 164.3 | 164.5 | 165.0 | 166.2 | 166.2 | 166.2 | 166.7 | 167.1 | 167.9 | 168.2 | 168.3 | 168.3 | 165.4 | 167.8 | 166.6 | | |
| 2000 | 168.8 | 169.8 | 171.2 | 171.3 | 171.5 | 172.4 | 172.8 | 172.8 | 173.7 | 174.0 | 174.1 | 174.0 | 170.8 | 173.6 | 172.2 | | |
| 2001 | 175.1 | 175.8 | 176.2 | 176.9 | 177.7 | 178.0 | 177.5 | 177.5 | 178.3 | 177.7 | 177.4 | 176.7 | 176.6 | 177.5 | 177.1 | | |
| 2002 | 177.1 | 177.8 | 178.8 | 179.8 | 179.8 | 179.9 | 180.1 | 180.7 | 181.0 | 181.3 | 181.3 | 180.9 | 178.9 | 179.9 | 179.9 | | |
| 2003 | 181.7 | 183.1 | 184.2 | 183.8 | 183.5 | 183.7 | 183.9 | 184.6 | 185.2 | 185.0 | 185.0 | 184.5 | 183.3 | 184.6 | 184.0 | | |
| 2004 | 185.2 | 186.2 | 187.4 | 188.0 | 189.1 | 189.7 | 189.4 | 189.5 | 189.9 | 190.9 | 191.0 | 190.3 | 187.6 | 190.2 | 188.9 | | |
| 2005 | 190.7 | 191.8 | 193.3 | 194.6 | 194.4 | 194.5 | 195.4 | 196.4 | 198.8 | 199.2 | 197.6 | 196.8 | | | 195.3 | | |
| 2006 | 198.3 | 198.7 | 199.8 | 201.5 | 202.5 | 202.9 | 203.5 | 203.9 | 202.9 | 201.8 | 201.5 | 201.8 | | | 201.6 | | |
| 2007 | 202.416 | 203.499 | 205.352 | 206.686 | 207.949 | 208.352 | 208.299 | 207.917 | 208.490 | 208.936 | 210.177 | 210.036 | | | 207.342 | | |
| 2008 | 211.080 | 211.693 | 213.528 | 214.823 | 216.632 | 218.815 | 219.964 | 219.086 | 218.783 | 216.573 | 212.425 | 210.228 | | | 215.303 | | |
| 2009 | 211.143 | 212.193 | 212.709 | 213.240 | 213.856 | 215.693 | 215.351 | 215.834 | 215.969 | 216.177 | 216.330 | 215.949 | | | 214.537 | | |
| 2010 | 216.687 | 216.741 | 217.631 | 218.009 | 218.178 | 217.965 | 218.011 | 218.312 | 218.439 | 218.711 | 218.803 | 219.179 | | | 218.056 | | |
| 2011 | 220.223 | 221.309 | 223.467 | 224.906 | 225.964 | 225.722 | 225.922 | 226.545 | 226.889 | | | | | | | | |

# NORTH AMERICAN INDUSTRY CLASSIFICATION SYSTEM

## 2007

| | | | |
|---|---|---|---|
| 111 | Crop Production | 485 | Transit and Ground Passenger Transportation |
| 112 | Animal Production | 486 | Pipeline Transportation |
| 113 | Forestry and Logging | 487 | Scenic and Sightseeing Transportation |
| 114 | Fishing, Hunting and Trapping | 488 | Support Activities for Transportation |
| 115 | Support Activities for Agriculture and Forestry | 491 | Postal Service |
| 211 | Oil and Gas Extraction | 492 | Couriers and Messengers |
| 212 | Mining (except Oil and Gas) | 493 | Warehousing and Storage |
| 213 | Support Activities for Mining | 511 | Publishing Industries |
| 221 | Utilities | 512 | Motion Picture and Sound Recording Industries |
| 236 | Construction of Buildings | 515 | Broadcasting (except Internet) |
| 237 | Heavy and Civil Engineering Construction | 516 | Internet Publishing and Broadcasting |
| 238 | Special Trade Contractors | 517 | Telecommunications |
| 311 | Food Manufacturing | 518 | Data Processing, Hosting and Related Services |
| 312 | Beverage and Tobacco Product Manufacturing | 519 | Other Information Services |
| 313 | Textile Mills | 521 | Monetary Authorities- Central Bank |
| 314 | Textile Product Mills | 522 | Credit Intermediation and Related Activities |
| 315 | Apparel Manufacturing | 523 | Securities, Commodity Contracts, and Other Financial Investments and Related Activities |
| 316 | Leather and Allied Product Manufacturing | | |
| 321 | Wood Product Manufacturing | | |
| 322 | Paper Manufacturing | 524 | Insurance Carriers and Related Activities |
| 323 | Printing and Related Support Activities | 525 | Funds, Trusts, and Other Financial Vehicles |
| 324 | Petroleum and Coal Products Manufacturing | 531 | Real Estate |
| 325 | Chemical Manufacturing | 532 | Rental and Leasing Services |
| 326 | Plastics and Rubber Products Manufacturing | 533 | Lessors of Nonfinancial Intangible Assets (except Copyrighted Works) |
| 327 | Nonmetallic Mineral Product Manufacturing | | |
| 331 | Primary Metal Manufacturing | 541 | Professional, Scientific, and Technical Services |
| 332 | Fabricated Metal Product Manufacturing | 551 | Management of Companies and Enterprises |
| 333 | Machinery Manufacturing | 561 | Administrative and Support Services |
| 334 | Computer and Electronic Product Manufacturing | 562 | Waste Management and Remediation Services |
| 335 | Electrical Equipment, Appliance, and Component Manufacturing | 611 | Educational Services |
| | | 621 | Ambulatory Health Care Services |
| 336 | Transportation Equipment Manufacturing | 622 | Hospitals |
| 337 | Furniture and Related Product Manufacturing | 623 | Nursing and Residential Care Facilities |
| 339 | Miscellaneous Manufacturing | 624 | Social Assistance |
| 423 | Merchant Wholesalers, Durable Goods | 711 | Performing Arts, Spectator Sports, and Related Industries |
| 424 | Merchant Wholesalers, Nondurable Goods | | |
| 425 | Wholesale Electronic Markets and Agents and Brokers | 712 | Museums, Historical Sites, and Similar Institutions |
| | | 713 | Amusement, Gambling, and Recreation Industries |
| 441 | Motor Vehicle and Parts Dealers | 721 | Accommodation |
| 442 | Furniture and Home Furnishings Stores | 722 | Food Services and Drinking Places |
| 443 | Electronics and Appliance Stores | 811 | Repair and Maintenance |
| 444 | Building Material and Garden Equipment and Supplies Dealers | 812 | Personal and Laundry Services |
| | | 813 | Religious, Grantmaking, Civic, Professional, and Similar Organizations |
| 445 | Food and Beverage Stores | | |
| 446 | Health and Personal Care Stores | 814 | Private Households |
| 447 | Gasoline Stations | 921 | Executive, Legislative, and Other General Government Support |
| 448 | Clothing and Clothing Accessories Stores | | |
| 451 | Sporting Goods, Hobby, Book, and Music Stores | 922 | Justice, Public Order, and Safety Activities |
| 452 | General Merchandise Stores | 923 | Administration of Human Resource Programs |
| 453 | Miscellaneous Store Retailers | 924 | Administration of Environmental Quality Programs |
| 454 | Nonstore Retailers | 925 | Administration of Housing Programs, Urban Planning, and Community Development |
| 481 | Air Transportation | | |
| 482 | Rail Transportation | 926 | Administration of Economic Programs |
| 483 | Water Transportation | 927 | Space Research and Technology |
| 484 | Truck Transportation | 928 | National Security and International Affairs |

# MISCELLANEOUS INFORMATION

## WEIGHTS AND MEASURES

### AMERICAN & BRITISH SYSTEMS

### CONVERSION TABLE

### METRIC SYSTEM

#### LINEAR MEASURE

12 inches=1 foot
3 feet=1 yard
5 1/2 yards=1 rod
220 yards=1 furlong
5,280 feet=1 mile
6 feet=1 fathom
6,080 feet=1 nautical mile

1 inch=2.54 centimeters
0.393700 inches=1 centimeter
1 mile=1.609344 kilometers0.62137 miles=1 kilometer

10 millimeters=1 centimeter
10 centimeters=1 decimeter
10 decimeters=1 meter
10 meters=1 dekameter
1,000 meters=1 kilometer

#### SQUARE MEASURE

144 square inches=1 square foot
9 square feet=1 square yard
30 1/4 square yards=1 square rod
160 square rods=1 acre
4,840 square yards=1 acre
640 acres=1 square mile

1 square inch=6.4516 square centimeters
0.15500 square inches=1 square centimeter
1 hectare=2.471 acres
1 square mile=2.58999 square kilometers
0.3861 square miles=1 square kilometer

100 square millimeters=1 square centimeter
100 square centimeters=1 square decimeter
10,000 square centimeters=1 square meter
100 square meter=1 are
100 ares=1 hectare
10,000 ares=1 square kilometer

#### CUBIC MEASURE

1,728 cubic inches=1 cubic foot
27 cubic feet=1 cubic yard

1 cubic inch=16.3871 cubic centimeters
0.061024 cubic inches=1 cubic centimeter
1 cubic yard=0.76455 cubic meters
1.30795 cubic yards=1 cubic meter

1,000 cubic millimeters=1 cubic centimeter
1,000 cubic centimeters=1 cubic decimeter
1,000 cubic decimeters=1 square meter

#### VOLUME MEASURE

16 ounces=1 (U.S.) pint
20 ounces=1 imperial (British) pint
2 cups=1 pint
2 pints=1 quart
4 quarts=1 gallon
1.2 U.S. gallons=1 imperial (British) gallon

1 ounce=0.46871 centiliters
0.33815 ounces=1 centiliter
1 (U.S.) liquid quart=0.9463 liters
1.0567 liters=1 (U.S.) liquid quart
1 (U.S.) gallon=.0037853 kiloliters
264.17 (U.S.) gallons=1 kiloliter

10 milliliters=1 centiliter
100 centiliters=1 liter
1,000 liters=1 kiloliter

#### WEIGHTS

Weights: Avoirdupois

Weights

Weights

16 drams=1 ounce
16 ounces=1 pound
112 pounds=1 long hundredweight
2,000 pounds=1 short ton
2,240 pounds=1 long ton

1 ounce (avoirdupois)=28.3495 grams
0.035274 ounces (avoirdupois)=1 gram
1 pound (avoirdupois)=0.453592 kilograms
2.20462 pounds (avoirdupois)=1 kilogram
1 (short) ton=0.90718 (metric) tons
1.10231 (short) tons=1 (metric) ton
1 pound (avoirdupois)=1.21528 pounds (troy)
0.82286 pounds (avoirdupois)=1 pound (troy)

10 milligrams=1 centigram
10 centigrams=1 decigram
10 decigrams=1 gram
100 centigrams=1 gram
10 grams=1 dekagram
10 dekagrams=1 hectogram
10 hectograms=1 kilogram
1,000 grams=1 kilogram
1,000 kilograms=1 ton

Weights: Troy and Apothecary

480 grains=1 ounce
12 ounces=1 pound

# PROOFREADERS' MARKS

| | | | |
|---|---|---|---|
| ⊙ | Insert period | *rom.* | Roman type |
| ⋀ | Insert comma | *caps.* | Caps—used in margin |
| : | Insert colon | ≡ | Caps—used in text |
| ; | Insert semicolon | *c+sc* | Caps & small caps—used in margin |
| ? | Insert question mark | ⩵ | Caps & small caps—used in text |
| ! | Insert exclamation mark | *l.c.* | Lowercase—used in margin |
| ⸗/ | Insert hyphen | / | Used in text to show deletion or substitution |
| ⩒ | Insert apostrophe | | |
| ⩔⩒ | Insert quotation marks | ⸗ | Delete |
| ⸝ | Insert 1-en dash | ⸝ | Delete and close up |
| ⸝ | Insert 1-em dash | *w.f.* | Wrong font |
| # | Insert space | ⌒ | Close up |
| *ld>* | Insert ( ) points of space | ⊐ | Move right |
| *shill* | Insert shilling | ⊏ | Move left |
| ⋁ | Superior | ⊓ | Move up |
| ⋀ | Inferior | ⊔ | Move down |
| (/) | Parentheses | ‖ | Align vertically |
| [/] | Brackets | = | Align horizontally |
| ☐ | Indent 1 em | ⊐⊏ | Center horizontally |
| ☐☐ | Indent 2 ems | ⊓⊔ | Center vertically |
| ⁋ | Paragraph | *eq.#* | Equalize space—used in margin |
| *no* ⁋ | No paragraph | ⋁⋁⋁ | Equalize space—used in text |
| *tr* | Transpose[1]—used in margin | ⋯⋯ | Let it stand—used in text |
| ∩ | Transpose[2]—used in text | *stet.* | Let it stand—used in margin |
| *sp* | Spell out | ⊗ | Letter(s) not clear |
| *ital* | Italic—used in margin | *run over* | Carry over to next line |
| —— | Italic—used in text | *run back* | Carry back to preceding line |
| *b.f.* | Boldface—used in margin | *out, see copy* | Something omitted—see copy |
| ∿∿∿ | Boldface—used in text | *⸮/?* | Question to author to delete[3] |
| *s.c.* | Small caps—used in margin | ⋀ | Caret—General indicator used to mark position of error. |
| ≡≡ | Small caps—used in text | | |

## DIRECTIONS FOR USE

Find the desired year in the index at left. The letter opposite each year is the letter of the calender to use for that year.

# 200 - YEAR CALENDAR

**A** **B**

**C** **D**

**E** **F**

## INDEX

| Year | | Year | | Year | | Year | | Year | | Year | | Year | |
|---|---|---|---|---|---|---|---|---|---|---|---|---|---|
| 1901 | C | 1930 | D | 1959 | E | 1988 | M | 2017 | A | 2046 | B | 2075 | C |
| 1902 | D | 1931 | E | 1960 | M | 1989 | A | 2018 | B | 2047 | C | 2076 | K |
| 1903 | M | 1932 | M | 1961 | A | 1990 | B | 2019 | C | 2048 | K | 2077 | F |
| 1904 | A | 1933 | A | 1962 | C | 1991 | C | 2020 | K | 2049 | F | 2078 | G |
| 1905 | B | 1934 | B | 1963 | D | 1992 | K | 2021 | F | 2050 | G | 2079 | A |
| 1906 | C | 1935 | C | 1964 | K | 1993 | F | 2022 | G | 2051 | A | 2080 | I |
| 1907 | K | 1936 | K | 1965 | F | 1994 | G | 2023 | A | 2052 | I | 2081 | D |
| 1908 | G | 1937 | G | 1966 | G | 1995 | A | 2024 | I | 2053 | D | 2082 | E |
| 1909 | A | 1938 | A | 1967 | A | 1996 | I | 2025 | D | 2054 | E | 2083 | F |
| 1910 | G | 1939 | A | 1968 | I | 1997 | D | 2026 | E | 2055 | F | 2084 | N |
| 1911 | A | 1940 | I | 1969 | D | 1998 | E | 2027 | F | 2056 | N | 2085 | B |
| 1912 | I | 1941 | D | 1970 | E | 1999 | F | 2028 | N | 2057 | B | 2086 | C |
| 1913 | D | 1942 | E | 1971 | F | 2000 | N | 2029 | B | 2058 | C | 2087 | D |
| 1914 | E | 1943 | F | 1972 | N | 2001 | B | 2030 | C | 2059 | D | 2088 | L |
| 1915 | F | 1944 | N | 1973 | B | 2002 | C | 2031 | D | 2060 | L | 2089 | G |
| 1916 | N | 1945 | B | 1974 | C | 2003 | D | 2032 | L | 2061 | G | 2090 | A |
| 1917 | B | 1946 | C | 1975 | D | 2004 | L | 2033 | G | 2062 | A | 2091 | B |
| 1918 | C | 1947 | D | 1976 | L | 2005 | G | 2034 | A | 2063 | B | 2092 | J |
| 1919 | D | 1948 | L | 1977 | G | 2006 | A | 2035 | B | 2064 | J | 2093 | E |
| 1920 | L | 1949 | G | 1978 | A | 2007 | B | 2036 | J | 2065 | E | 2094 | F |
| 1921 | G | 1950 | A | 1979 | B | 2008 | J | 2037 | E | 2066 | F | 2095 | G |
| 1922 | A | 1951 | B | 1980 | J | 2009 | E | 2038 | F | 2067 | G | 2096 | H |
| 1923 | B | 1952 | J | 1981 | E | 2010 | F | 2039 | G | 2068 | H | 2097 | C |
| 1924 | J | 1953 | E | 1982 | F | 2011 | G | 2040 | H | 2069 | C | 2098 | D |
| 1925 | E | 1954 | F | 1983 | G | 2012 | H | 2041 | C | 2070 | D | 2099 | E |
| 1926 | F | 1955 | G | 1984 | H | 2013 | C | 2042 | D | 2071 | E | 2100 | F |
| 1927 | G | 1956 | H | 1985 | C | 2014 | D | 2043 | E | 2072 | M | | |
| 1928 | H | 1957 | C | 1986 | D | 2015 | E | 2044 | M | 2073 | A | | |
| 1929 | C | 1958 | D | 1987 | E | 2016 | M | 2045 | A | 2074 | B | | |

# 200-YEAR CALENDAR

# FEDERAL LEGAL PUBLIC HOLIDAYS

New Year's Day—January 1

Martin Luther King's Birthday—the third Monday in January

Washington's Birthday—the third Monday in February

Memorial Day—the last Monday in May

Independence Day—July 4

Labor Day—the first Monday in September

Columbus Day—the second Monday in October

Veterans Day—November 11

Thanksgiving Day—the fourth Thursday in November

Christmas Day—December 25

# CALENDARS, 2012-14

| 2012 | Holiday | 2013 |
|---|---|---|
| Sun. Jan. 1 | New Year's Day | Tues. Jan. 1 |
| Mon. Jan. 16 | Martin Luther King, Jr. Day | Mon. Jan. 21 |
| Sun. Feb. 12 | Lincoln's Birthday | Tues. Feb. 12 |
| Tues. Feb. 14 | Valentine's Day | Thur. Feb. 14 |
| Mon. Feb. 20 | Presidents' Day, Observed | Mon. Feb. 18 |
| Wed. Feb. 22 | Ash Wednesday | Wed. Feb. 13 |
| Sun. Mar. 11 | Daylight Savings Time begins | Sun. Mar. 10 |
| Sat. Mar. 17 | St. Patrick's Day | Sun. Mar. 17 |
| Sun. Apr. 1 | Palm Sunday | Sun. Mar. 24 |
| Sat. Apr. 7 | Passover | Tues. Mar. 26 |
| Fri. Apr. 6 | Good Friday | Fri. Mar. 29 |
| Sun. Apr. 8 | Easter Sunday | Sun. Mar. 31 |
| Wed. Apr. 25 | Admin. Prof. Day | Wed. Apr. 24 |
| Sun. May 13 | Mother's Day | Sun. May 12 |
| Sat. May 19 | Armed Forces Day | Sat. May 18 |
| Mon. May 21 | Victoria Day (Canada) | Mon. May 20 |
| Mon. May 28 | Memorial Day , Observed | Mon. May 27 |
| Thurs. Jun. 14 | Flag Day | Fri. Jun. 14 |
| Sun. Jun. 17 | Father's Day | Sun. Jun. 16 |
| Sun. Jul. 1 | Canada Day (Canada) | Mon. Jul. 1 |
| Wed. Jul. 4 | Independence Day | Thur. Jul. 4 |
| Mon. Aug. 6 | Civic Holiday (Canada) | Mon. Aug. 5 |
| Mon. Sep. 3 | Labor Day | Mon. Sep. 2 |
| Mon. Sep. 17 | Rosh Hashanah | Thur. Sep. 5 |
| Wed. Sep. 26 | Yom Kippur | Sat. Sep. 14 |
| Mon. Oct. 8 | Columbus Day , Observed | Mon. Oct. 14 |
| Mon. Oct. 8 | Thanksgiving Day (Canada) | Mon. Oct. 14 |
| Wed. Oct. 31 | Halloween | Thur. Oct. 31 |
| Sun. Nov. 4 | Daylight Savings Time ends | Sun. Nov. 3 |
| Tues. Nov. 6 | Election Day | Tues. Nov. 5 |
| Sun. Nov. 11 | Veterans Day | Mon. Nov. 11 |
| Sun. Nov. 11 | Remembrance Day (Canada) | Mon. Nov. 11 |
| Thur. Nov. 22 | Thanksgiving Day | Thur. Nov. 28 |
| Sun. Dec. 9 | Hanukkah | Thur. Nov. 28 |
| Tues. Dec. 25 | Christmas Day | Wed. Dec. 25 |
| Wed. Dec. 26 | Boxing Day (Canada) | Thur. Dec. 26 |

## 2012

(Monthly calendar grids for January through December 2012)

## 2013

(Monthly calendar grids for January through December 2013)

## 2014

(Monthly calendar grids for January through December 2014)

# AREA CODES FOR STATES, CANADA AND THE CARIBBEAN

**200**

| | |
|---|---|
| 201 | New Jersey |
| 202 | Washington, D.C. |
| 203 | Connecticut |
| 204 | Manitoba (all) |
| 205 | Alabama |
| 206 | Washington |
| 207 | Maine (all) |
| 208 | Idaho (all) |
| 209 | California |
| 210 | Texas |
| 212 | New York |
| 213 | California |
| 214 | Texas |
| 215 | Pennsylvania |
| 216 | Ohio |
| 217 | Illinois |
| 218 | Minnesota |
| 219 | Indiana |
| 224 | Illinois |
| 225 | Louisiana |
| 226 | Ontario |
| 228 | Mississippi |
| 229 | Georgia |
| 231 | Michigan |
| 234 | Ohio |
| 236 | British Columbia |
| 239 | Florida |
| 240 | Maryland |
| 242 | Bahamas |
| 246 | Barbados |
| 248 | Michigan |
| 249 | Ontario |
| 250 | British Columbia |
| 251 | Alabama |
| 252 | North Carolina |
| 253 | Washington |
| 254 | Texas |
| 256 | Alabama |
| 260 | Indiana |
| 262 | Wisconsin |
| 264 | Anguilla |
| 267 | Pennsylvania |
| 268 | Antigua/Barbuda |
| 269 | Michigan |
| 270 | Kentucky |
| 274 | Wisconsin |
| 276 | Virginia |
| 281 | Texas |
| 284 | British Virgin Islands |
| 289 | Ontario |

**300**

| | |
|---|---|
| 301 | Maryland |
| 302 | Delaware (all) |
| 303 | Colorado |
| 304 | West Virginia (all) |
| 305 | Florida |
| 306 | Saskatchewan (all) |
| 307 | Wyoming (all) |
| 308 | Nebraska |
| 309 | Illinois |
| 310 | California |
| 312 | Illinois |
| 313 | Michigan |
| 314 | Missouri |
| 315 | New York |
| 316 | Kansas |

| | |
|---|---|
| 317 | Indiana |
| 318 | Louisiana |
| 319 | Iowa |
| 320 | Minnesota |
| 321 | Florida |
| 323 | California |
| 325 | Texas |
| 327 | Arizona |
| 330 | Ohio |
| 331 | Illinois |
| 334 | Alabama |
| 336 | North Carolina |
| 337 | Louisiana |
| 339 | Massachusetts |
| 340 | U.S. Virgin Islands |
| 343 | Ontario |
| 345 | Cayman Islands |
| 347 | New York |
| 351 | Massachusetts |
| 352 | Florida |
| 360 | Washington |
| 361 | Texas |
| 364 | Kentucky |
| 365 | Ontario |
| 385 | Utah |
| 386 | Florida |

**400**

| | |
|---|---|
| 401 | Rhode Island (all) |
| 402 | Nebraska |
| 403 | Alberta |
| 404 | Georgia |
| 405 | Oklahoma |
| 406 | Montana (all) |
| 407 | Florida |
| 408 | California |
| 409 | Texas |
| 410 | Maryland |
| 412 | Pennsylvania |
| 413 | Massachusetts |
| 414 | Wisconsin |
| 415 | California |
| 416 | Ontario |
| 417 | Missouri |
| 418 | Quebec |
| 419 | Ohio |
| 423 | Tennessee |
| 424 | California |
| 425 | Washington |
| 430 | Texas |
| 431 | Manitoba |
| 432 | Texas |
| 434 | Virginia |
| 435 | Utah |
| 437 | Ontario |
| 438 | Quebec |
| 440 | Ohio |
| 441 | Bermuda |
| 442 | California |
| 443 | Maryland |
| 450 | Quebec |
| 458 | Oregon |
| 469 | Texas |
| 470 | Georgia |
| 473 | Grenada |
| 475 | Connecticut |
| 478 | Georgia |
| 479 | Arkansas |

| | |
|---|---|
| 480 | Arizona |
| 484 | Pennsylvania |

**500**

| | |
|---|---|
| 501 | Arkansas (all) |
| 502 | Kentucky |
| 503 | Oregon |
| 504 | Louisiana |
| 505 | New Mexico (all) |
| 506 | New Brunswick (all) |
| 507 | Minnesota |
| 508 | Massachusetts |
| 509 | Washington |
| 510 | California |
| 512 | Texas |
| 513 | Ohio |
| 514 | Quebec |
| 515 | Iowa |
| 516 | New York |
| 517 | Michigan |
| 518 | New York |
| 519 | Ontario |
| 520 | Arizona |
| 530 | California |
| 534 | Wisconsin |
| 539 | Oklahoma |
| 540 | Virginia |
| 541 | Oregon |
| 551 | New Jersey |
| 559 | California |
| 561 | Florida |
| 562 | California |
| 563 | Iowa |
| 567 | Ohio |
| 570 | Pennsylvania |
| 571 | Virginia |
| 573 | Missouri |
| 574 | Indiana |
| 575 | New Mexico |
| 579 | Quebec |
| 580 | Oklahoma |
| 581 | Quebec |
| 585 | New York |
| 586 | Michigan |
| 587 | Alberta |

**600**

| | |
|---|---|
| 601 | Mississippi |
| 602 | Arizona |
| 603 | New Hampshire (all) |
| 604 | British Columbia(all) |
| 605 | South Dakota (all) |
| 606 | Kentucky |
| 607 | New York |
| 608 | Wisconsin |
| 609 | New Jersey |
| 610 | Pennsylvania |
| 612 | Minnesota |
| 613 | Ontario |
| 614 | Ohio |
| 615 | Tennessee |
| 616 | Michigan |
| 617 | Massachusetts |
| 618 | Illinois |
| 619 | California |
| 620 | Kansas |
| 623 | Arizona |
| 626 | California |

| | |
|---|---|
| 630 | Illinois |
| 631 | New York |
| 636 | Missouri |
| 641 | Iowa |
| 646 | New York |
| 647 | Ontario |
| 649 | Turks & Caicos Islands |
| 650 | California |
| 651 | Minnesota |
| 657 | California |
| 660 | Missouri |
| 661 | California |
| 662 | Mississippi |
| 664 | Montserrat |
| 670 | Commonwealth of the Northern Mariana Islands |
| 671 | Guam |
| 678 | Georgia |
| 681 | West Virginia |
| 682 | Texas |
| 684 | American Samoa |

**700**

| | |
|---|---|
| 701 | North Dakota (all) |
| 702 | Nevada (all) |
| 703 | Virginia |
| 704 | North Carolina |
| 705 | Ontario |
| 706 | Georgia |
| 707 | California |
| 708 | Illinois |
| 709 | Newfoundland (all) |
| 710 | US |
| 712 | Iowa |
| 713 | Texas |
| 714 | California |
| 715 | Wisconsin |
| 716 | New York |
| 717 | Pennsylvania |
| 718 | New York |
| 719 | Colorado |
| 720 | Colorado |
| 721 | St. Maarten |
| 724 | Pennsylvania |
| 727 | Florida |
| 731 | Tennessee |
| 732 | New Jersey |
| 734 | Michigan |
| 740 | Ohio |
| 747 | California |
| 754 | Florida |
| 757 | Virginia |
| 758 | St. Lucia |
| 760 | California |
| 762 | Georgia |
| 763 | Minnesota |
| 765 | Indiana |
| 767 | Dominica |
| 769 | Mississippi |
| 770 | Georgia |
| 772 | Florida |
| 773 | Illinois |
| 774 | Massachusetts |
| 775 | Nevada |
| 779 | Illinois |
| 780 | Alberta |
| 781 | Massachusetts |

# AREA CODES FOR STATES, CANADA AND THE CARIBBEAN

784 St. Vincent/
    Grenadines
785 Kansas
786 Florida
787 Puerto Rico

## 800

801 Utah (all)
802 Vermont (all)
803 South Carolina (all)
804 Virginia
805 California
806 Texas
807 Ontario
808 Hawaii (all)
809 Dominican Republic
810 Michigan
812 Indiana
813 Florida
814 Pennsylvania
815 Illinois
816 Missouri
817 Texas
818 California
819 Quebec
828 North Carolina
829 Dominican Republic
830 Texas
831 California
832 Texas
843 South Carolina
845 New York
847 Illinois
848 New Jersey
849 Dominican Republic
850 Florida
856 New Jersey
857 Massachusetts
858 California
859 Kentucky
860 Connecticut
862 New Jersey
863 Florida
864 South Carolina
865 Tennessee
867 Yukon/ NW Territories
868 Trinidad/ Tobago
869 St. Kitts & Nevis
870 Arkansas
872 Illinois
873 Quebec
876 Jamaica
878 Pennsylvania

## 900

901 Tennessee
902 Nova Scotia (all)
    Prince Edward Isl.
903 Texas
904 Florida
905 Ontario
906 Michigan
907 Alaska (all)
908 New Jersey
909 California
910 North Carolina
912 Georgia
913 Kansas
914 New York

915 Texas
916 California
917 New York
918 Oklahoma
919 North Carolina
920 Wisconsin
925 California
928 Arizona
929 New York
931 Tennessee
936 Texas
937 Ohio
938 Alabama
939 Puerto Rico
940 Texas
941 Florida
947 Michigan
949 California
951 California
952 Minnesota
954 Florida
956 Texas
970 Colorado
971 Oregon
972 Texas
973 New Jersey
978 Massachusetts
979 Texas
980 North Carolina
984 North Carolina
985 Louisiana
989 Michigan

# INDEX